"Who's in the Goose Tonight?"

"Who's in the Goose Tonight?"

An Anecdotal
History of
Canadian Theatre

VERNON CHAPMAN

ECW Press

NATIONAL LIBRARY OF CANADA CATALOGUING IN PUBLICATION DATA

Chapman, Vernon
Who's in the goose tonight?: an anecdotal history of Canadian theatre

ISBN 1-55022-482-4

1. Theatre — Canada — History — 20th century 1. Title.

PN2304.C46 2001   792'.0971   C2001-900804-X

Cover and text design by Tania Craan
Layout by Mary Bowness

Photos reprinted with the permission of the author.
Main cover photo: *Robin Hood, Wayne and Shuster Variety Show*:
Vernon Chapman (Sheriff of Nottingham), Johnny Wayne (Friar Tuck).

Printed by AGMV

Distributed in Canada by
General Distribution Services,
325 Humber College Blvd.,
Toronto, ON M9W 7C3

Published by ECW PRESS
2120 Queen Street East, Suite 200
Toronto, ON M4E 1E2
ecwpress.com

This book is set in Garamond and Mercurius.

PRINTED AND BOUND IN CANADA

The publication of *"Who's in the Goose Tonight?"* has been generously supported by the Canada Council, the Ontario Arts Council, and the Government of Canada through the Book Publishing Industry Development Program. Canadä

Table of Contents

For years, when I would relate to my friends some anecdote about myself or about the many fascinating people with whom I have been associated in a long career in the Canadian entertainment business, those friends would urge me to write a book about my experiences and the people with whom I have worked. My friends argued that a part of our history was going to be lost unless someone who had been actively involved in the development of the Canadian theatre wrote about that evolution. Having never written a book before, I found the prospect of writing a comprehensive history of the Canadian theatre too staggering. However, after frequent urging, I decided to use my career as a sort of hat rack on which to hang the hats of the founders of the theatres for which I have worked as actor and director, and of those performers with whom I have been privileged to associate.

At first I planned to cover the period from my amateur days in the 1930s and '40s to the time of writing in the late '80s and early '90s. But as the research led me deeper into the story of these various theatres and of the personalities involved, more and more details emerged that I felt were important and of interest. I concluded that if this book was to be even a cursory history of those selected theatres and a record of the contributions made by only some of the post World War II pioneers of the theatre in Canada, there would have to be an earlier cut-off date or I would never get it finished before time took its inevitable toll on me. Therefore, I have chosen to end this chronicle at about 1970, which was a transitional year for the Canadian theatre. Once this book is published, perhaps time will allow me to write a sequel covering the theatres and their founders that I worked for since 1970.

I have tried not only to write a combined history and biography, but also, by recording the triumphs, errors, misjudgements, and disasters of my career and of others, to help young artists who are beginning their careers to learn from our successes and failures. I have perforce had to rely heavily on the critical reviews as a gauge of the achievements of the various artists and of the productions mentioned. They are a very unreliable basis on which to judge because of the frequent diversity of opinion among the critics, but they do serve to reveal at least some reaction to the efforts of the theatre folk about which I write. Most artists look upon critics at best as a necessary evil, but it would be exceedingly hypocritical of me to deny that a favourable review is valuable on a curriculum vitae.

Since I began writing this book, other Canadian theatrical biographies have been published. I hope my contribution to this growing library will be worthy of their companionship.

ACKNOWLEDGEMENTS

This book could not have been written without the advice, assistance, and co-operation of dozens of people. I am particularly grateful to the following, who took the time to record their reminiscences by letter or on audio tape: Evelyne Anderson, Malcolm Black, Jack Blacklock, Peter Boretski, Patricia Carroll Brown, Paddy Browne, Harold Burke, Leo Burns, Anne Butler, Norma Clark, Mary Damer, Donald Davis, Jack Duffy, Donald Ewer, Timothy Findley, Ted Follows, Jill Foster, Colin Fox, David Gardner, Elspeth Gaylor, William Glassco, Joyce Gordon, Alexander Gray, Bruce Gray, Margaret (Nonnie) Griffin, Doreen Grinstead, Ivor Jackson, Robert Johnston, Tom Kneebone, Shirley Knight, Martin Lager, Ray Lawlor, Benjamin and Sylvia Lennick, E.M. (Moe) Margolese, Walter Massey, Irena Mayeska, Durward McGimsie, Jack Merigold, Patricia Moffatt, Gary Montgomery, Mavor Moore, Marylu Moyer, Sean Mulcahy, Louise Nicol, Jack Northmore, Sandra O'Neill, Gerard Parkes, Jenny Phipps, Sharon Pollock, Tedd Reed, Norma Renault, Milo Ringham, Allan Royal, Bernard Slade, Edwin Stephenson, Neil Vipond, Morna Wales, William Whitehead, and Chris Wiggins.

I am especially grateful to my editor, Richard Plant, who waded through the many pages making copious marginal recommendations as to how the book could be improved, while at the same time tactfully protecting my fragile ego. It is a much better book as a result of his association with it and I hope I am a more disciplined writer as a result of my association with him.

I must also thank those who had the patience to help me penetrate, as much as my brain will allow, the mysteries of the computer: Patricia Challen, Judy Chapman, Iain Deane, George Dick, Ron Hartmann, and Gary Montgomery. I am also indebted to Christopher Marston who was for many years the executive secretary of Canadian Actor's Equity Association, to the Thomas Fisher Rare Book Library of the University of Toronto, to the Theatre Department of the Toronto Reference Library, and to those friends and colleagues who encouraged me to write this book.

Above all I am especially grateful to Jack David of ECW Press, who had the courage to publish *"Who's in the Goose Tonight?,"* and to the associate editor, Tracey Millen, who unblooped my bloopers.

CHAPTER I

Actor Emergent

It is probably a cliché to say that every child is a natural actor. But it is none the less true. Most children bring to their play an imagination unfettered by self-consciousness. "Let's pretend" is one of their most common phrases. They can act out roles with a seriousness and intensity surpassing that of many an adult actor. This amazing ability of children lasts far too short a time. They become teenagers and this innate gift for losing oneself through acting becomes suppressed. External influences and a growing self-consciousness constrict and often smother it completely. But some people develop an ability to delve through the layers of inhibitions built up during this pubertal period. I think of this ability — to re-activate the imagination to the degree that one can become someone else — as "acting." Constantin Stanislavski in *An Actor Prepares* refers to the magical influence of the word "if" to start the imagination working: "There is no such thing as actuality on the stage. Art is the product of the imagination, as the work of the dramatist should be. The aim of the actor should be to use his technique to turn the play into a theatrical reality. In this process imagination plays by far the greatest part."[1] I consider myself lucky that my artistic imagination was rescued from extinction.

Most children growing up in Ontario during the '30s found very little to encourage them toward a career in the arts, which was fine as an avocation but not as a vocation. After World War II, the arts in Canada

■ *I*

flourished as never before, largely due to those artists who ignored the discouragement they received from a society just emerging from pioneer days when the hardships of opening up a country were not conducive to fostering the Fine Arts. Even now many professional actors are still asked, "But what do you do for a living?"

■

During the Depression years, for a boy in particular, it took fortitude to announce that he wanted to be an actor or a painter, or a concert pianist or a singer of classical music. To say that he wanted to be a ballet dancer was tantamount to admitting that he had developed bubonic plague. And yet there was ample precedent for choosing a life in the arts because even in Victorian Canada, painters, authors, actors, and musicians had become internationally renowned. I was to benefit from this legacy in the professional and amateur theatre. I was also fortunate in having my own personal Svengali.

However, if my parents had had their way, the last thing I would have been is an actor. My mother had dreams of my becoming a pianist and paid for lessons for five years until everyone, especially myself, concluded that I would never be another Paderewski. By the time I was 15, other interests had taken priority over learning how to massacre Beethoven sonatas. I am grateful to my mother for the lessons because they gave me an appreciation for music which, except for country and western, has been a joy all my life. Occasionally I still go to the piano and try to get right what I could not do 50 or more years ago. I am rarely successful but it is a worthy challenge.

One of my grade school teachers concluded that I had some artistic ability because I had managed to paint in water-colours a daffodil that was recognizable as a daffodil. As a penalty I was entrapped in an art class every Saturday morning at the Toronto Art Gallery. How I wished at the time that I had botched that daffodil. I had no real interest or talent for painting. However, I did absorb knowledge about European painting from the Renaissance to the Impressionists, and I was awed by the magnificent sweep of landscape in paintings by the Group of Seven, although I hadn't the slightest idea of their importance in Canadian art.

For some reason when I was about 10 years old, I was enrolled in the Fanny V. Birdsall Academy of Dance on Yonge Street just south of Bloor, where the Misses Fanny and her sister Helen Birdsall tried desperately to teach me the fundamentals of tap dancing. I derived two effects from this experiment — one physical and one emotional. The first was swollen glands caused by emerging hot and steamy from dance class into the cold winter's night. The swollen glands did not last but the second effect did. It was the ignominy in the class's annual spring recital at Massey Hall of being the only member of the chorus outside the curtain when it descended at the end of the routine, indicating that I had not been in line with the rest of the dancers during the number. I was later told that I had been out of step as well. The audience of doting parents had found that cute, but I found it an embarrassment. No amount of parental pressure could persuade me to "kick foot" again for the Birdsalls, pleasant though those two excellent teachers were.

My actual talent was discovered through no design of my well-meaning mother. The revelation took place at Essex Street Public School and it was there that I met my mentor. For the most part the teachers in the junior grades were a kindly, motherly lot (we had only one male teacher in the junior grades and he was a gentle giant). I liked school but academically I was just average. In the '30s in Toronto most public school classes were co-educational but boys and girls were segregated in the schoolyards, in gym classes, such as they were, and the girls took Domestic Science and the boys Manual Training. The girls learned sensible, practical matters such as how to cook and sew while the boys made wooden footstools and bookends. I managed to avoid carving myself up with a handsaw or lopping off a finger with a chisel, and I actually enjoyed Manual Training classes, largely because they were conducted by a genial, eccentric Englishman named Arthur J. Rostance.

What really interested me in the Manual Training room was a working model of a stage about four feet wide and four feet high that sat on a table in one corner. I always contrived to get a workbench beside this model. It had been built by Mr. Rostance and, I was later to discover, it was a scale model of the stage of Hart House Theatre. Small figures he had carved could be placed on the stage, and a variety of sets could be put into place. Strings at the side of the model raised or lowered different curtains or "drops." Mr. Rostance was very proud of his model, delighted in demonstrating how it worked, and appreciated any boy showing an interest in it.

Even before I was old enough to enter the Manual Training class, I knew that Mr. Rostance was not only a teacher, but also an actor. Just before Christmas each year, he and his wife would narrate Charles Dickens's *A Christmas Carol* accompanied by ancient lantern slides in the school auditorium. When I grew old enough to read Dickens I thought that both the Rostances themselves were straight out of the pages of those novels. Mrs. Rostance was a dead-ringer for how I imagined Aunt Betsy Trotwood to be in *David Copperfield*, and her husband for kindly old Mr. Fezziwig in *A Christmas Carol*.

One day when I was 11, I developed a toothache and was sent to the school dentist, whose office was next to the Manual Training room. In order to distract me as the freezing was taking place, he asked me to tell him a story. I immediately launched into *A Christmas Carol*. My reading up to that point had not included Dickens, but I remembered the details from the times I had heard the Rostances present it, and I mimicked their delivery of the dialogue. After about 10 minutes of my histrionics I became aware of a third person in the office. The dentist had quietly fetched Mr. Rostance from next door. How long he had been there before I was aware of him I never knew. But I was well into the story and was dramatizing it to a fare-thee-well. When I noticed him I immediately became self-conscious and stopped. The dentist then continued his nefarious work. But Mr. Rostance had heard enough to ask me a day or so later to help him realize something he had always wanted to do for the school's Spring Recital — the scene from Shakespeare's *King John* when the little Prince Arthur pleads with the jailer, Hubert, to disobey the wicked king's orders to put out the boy's eyes.

We rehearsed after school in the Manual Training room. Mr. Rostance loved Shakespeare. He was enthusiastic, encouraging, and patient. My initial reticence was gradually overcome and I began to enjoy "acting." I had a good ear and learned by example how to deliver the verse. While it was not the "method" but the "mimicry" approach, I was able to capture the emotion readily. Threatened with having Arthur's eyes burned out, I did not need much imagination to call up the panic the boy felt and the urgency in his frantic pleading with the jailer. As we rehearsed, I developed a deep affection for this remarkable teacher. Soon I was enjoying these afternoon rehearsals with Mr. Rostance more than anything I had in my young years. I began to look forward to playing the scene in front of an audience.

My parents were somewhat dismayed to find their son tackling Shakespeare, an author who had not figured much in their experience. They were, nevertheless, encouraging. My mother had her dressmaker create a blue velvet costume with lace collar and cuffs, more appropriate for Little Lord Fauntleroy than for a small medieval prince languishing in the dungeon of Northampton Castle. However, no one seemed to notice this discrepancy, least of all me, and, if Mr. Rostance realized that the costume was not right, he did not say. Before the night of the school recital, we had a tryout in a classroom in front of the students and the Toronto School Inspector. After it Mr. Rostance wrote me a note:

> My dear Vernon. I was delighted with your performance before room 12 and Dr. Doane yesterday. On Monday your work was rated at 60 per cent. Now I rate it at 80 per cent. You really brought tears to their eyes. Certainly their hearts were crying and that's what I want. Tears! Keep it up. Strive. It's a wonderful art. I am looking forward to still greater distress and clearer enunciation. AJR.

The big night occurred on March 14, 1935. The program consisted of a minuet danced by some students of the junior third grade, a recitation of Kipling's poem "Lead Kindly Light" by my friend William Freeman, dramatic readings from some of the teachers, Scottish dancing with pipes, and the scene from *King John*. Where students had been coached by a teacher, only the teacher's name got printed on the program, and I was chagrined that, after all my work, my school chum Bill Freeman's name appeared and mine did not. *Vanitas vanitatum* even in the young. But I was exhilarated and consoled by the satisfaction of performing before an audience. From then on I was a theatre addict. My child's vanity revelled in the recognition I received from the teachers and schoolmates. Some students tried to tease me by calling me "Little Prince" in derisive tones but that did not bother me because I ascribed their remarks to jealousy. They soon stopped when they saw that I liked the name and wallowed in the attention. I was probably quite insufferable. But the real reward for me was that in working with Mr. Rostance I learned how to analyse a line or a speech, how to interpret it vocally and physically, and how to interact with another performer.

As a result of this success, Mr. Rostance encouraged me to compete in that year's Elocution Contest at the Canadian National Exhibition. The competition piece was Whittier's poem "The Gift of Tritemius," which appealed to my sense of the dramatic, allowing me to be narrator, a frantic, elderly female supplicant, and the benign Abbot, Tritemius. For several hours each week that summer, A.J. patiently coached me. His efforts resulted in my winning the gold medal. I was disappointed to see that it was not really gold, but lead painted gold, and I would have preferred that the head embossed on one side of it was something more attractive than that of Mitch Hepburn, the publicity-seeking premier of Ontario. But the following winter I won a silver medal for Oratory at Essex School that was much more attractive.

By the time I left grade school, my parents realized that at last some sort of talent had been discovered in their son. But where did it come from? Was it inherited like haemophilia or picked up *en passant* like measles? My mother was born in Michigan of a Pennsylvania Dutch father and a Canadian mother whose derivation was Northern Irish Protestant. Mother evinced no interest in performing, except occasionally on the piano for which she had more talent than I and an ability I envy of playing by ear. But she did love going to the theatre and the movies. Moreover she had a great delight in vaudeville. Many a Saturday afternoon she would take me to see the latest acts at Shea's Hippodrome in Toronto. But I don't think my mother ever had any inclination to appear on the stage.

My amiable father, Charles, was born in Lowestoft, Suffolk, England, and immigrated to Canada in 1911. His first wife died in Hamilton in 1918 and he married my mother in 1922. During my childhood my father never showed much enthusiasm for things theatrical, but he was a member of the Fraternal Order Knights of Pythias and delighted in enacting the classical Greek story of Damon and Pythias which was part of the initiation ritual for that lodge. I would help him rehearse his lines and I was impressed with my father's over-ripe delivery. Years after his death, his sister in Yarmouth, England told me to my amazement that as a young man he had been a street-corner evangelist. He practised his harangue in front of the mirror, much to the disgust of my grandfather who was a part owner of a fishing fleet and staunchly Church of England. When the sect he preached for urged him to give up his girlfriend, Lily, because she worked in the box office of the local sin emporium, the Sparrows' Nest Theatre, he gave up the sect instead. Thereafter the only time he ever entered a church was for formal occasions such as weddings and funerals. But apparently there was a large slab of ham hidden in my father and likely it was handed down to me where it became unhidden.

THE VICTORIA CLUB

Presents

THE
THEATRE PLAYERS' GUILD
PRODUCTION

of

"IT TAKES ALL KINDS"

A Farce-Comedy in Two Acts
by
GEORGE L. WATSON

at

College Street Reference Library Theatre

on

November 7th, 1940

AT 8.20 P.M.

CHAPTER 2

Actor Pubescent

For two years in my early teens I was privileged to attend Harbord Collegiate located on the edge of "The Ward," that section of Toronto where most of the Jewish immigrants had settled during the early part of the 20th century. The majority of the students at Harbord were Jewish, which meant that on High Holidays there would be only a few gentiles left in the class. In those years Harbord Collegiate had one of the finest teaching faculties of any secondary school in the country and, because of the desire of most of the students to make good in the new land, the standard of scholarship was also one of the highest in the nation. My close friend from grade school, Bill Freeman, who despite his surname is not Jewish, and I determined to take as many subjects as we could handle — geography, history, English, German, French, Latin, physics, chemistry, and algebra. Although the atmosphere at Harbord was conducive to study, it was not all seriousness. The school had a good football team, and under the direction of Allister Haig, had a fine orchestra. Every year Mr. Haig and either Brian McCool or Charles Girdler staged a Gilbert and Sullivan operetta. Their high standard productions turned me into a G and S buff. At one of these, *The Mikado*, I first saw Frank Shuster perform in the role of Koko. Evelyn Gould began her singing career in these operettas and Victor Feldbrill played in the orchestra as Concert Master. Harbord also had an active drama club, but I did not join it because Mr. Rostance had persuaded me to perform with the Toronto Shakespeare Society and the Dickens Fellowship. I could not take on another extra-curricular activity.

I had enjoyed my first two years at Harbord, had fared moderately well academically, and was looking forward to three more years in that stimulating atmosphere when my parents decided to move from the semi-detached house on Shaw Street to a cosy bungalow in Mimico. On a pleasant tree-lined street within 15 minutes' walk to the country, it was an improvement in our living conditions and was a great convenience for my father, who could ride a commuter train for free to his office in Union Station where he was the Depot Ticket Agent for the Canadian National Railway. But this move to the suburbs proved to have a devastating effect on my academic achievements and, temporarily, on my social life. It is frequently traumatic for a child to be uprooted from a familiar environment and plunked down in a strange one. When one is at the awkward, self-conscious pubertal stage, it is particularly difficult.

I was 15 when I went to Mimico High from a Collegiate where I had been comfortable with my friends, some of whom had been my grade school pals. During the Depression there had been little new housing built in Mimico and for several years hardly any change-over of residents. Consequently, the students had grown to know each other through grade school. With adolescence I had become shy and I found the student body at Mimico was very closely knit. While not ostracizing newcomers intentionally, their cliquishness combined with my diffidence to have that initial effect.

The town of Mimico in 1938 was almost bankrupt so there were very few frills at Mimico High (it became a collegiate after the war). The auditorium was a flat-floored appendage on the back of the main building, with removable plywood seats, a small proscenium stage with tiny dressing rooms at either side but without wing space. This unimaginative room, called merely the "Study Hall," had desks at the entrance end of it where the library was located. Beneath the Study Hall was an extremely dank gymnasium. I know that frequently students have had to study under, and triumph over, much worse conditions, but, after Harbord Collegiate, I found Mimico High decidedly wanting, and, for the first few months, very depressing. As a result, my academic achievements suffered. Most of the Mimico teachers did not have either the ability or the inclination to stimulate a student's interest. The physics teacher mumbled, not caring whether he was understood, and the Latin teacher was a mercurial paranoid given to temper tantrums and tears. I failed Latin and dropped physics and chemistry. But, fortunately, there were three exceptional teachers: my German teacher, my English teacher, and particularly my history teacher, Miss Weir, who managed to make her classes so intriguing that when I attended university I majored in that subject.

It was through the Drama Club that I eventually entered into the social life of the school and of Mimico. The honorary president of that club was a handsome instructor of athletics, John Austen, who would later found John Austen Realty and Insurance. He had a disarmingly casual way with him that put everyone at ease, and also had that wonderful gift for a teacher of being able to keep control without being a strict disciplinarian. He immediately saw that I was not going to qualify for the football team, but realized that I might be of some use in the Drama Club. Thanks to him I was given the opportunity to try my wings as a director. The play was a one-act epic called *Bimbo the Pirate*, the title role of which was played by one of the school's star football players, from whom I managed, to my amazement, to extract a credible performance. I found that I could exert sufficient authority as a director without offending anyone, and that I had gained enough experience about blocking a play to keep the actors from colliding with the furniture or with each other.

■

As a result of my work at the Drama Club, John Austen introduced me to the Lakeshore Theatre Guild, where I met his pretty wife, Terry, for whom I immediately developed an adolescent and very private crush. The first program the Lakeshore Guild presented that involved me was an evening of one-act plays which included that favourite of amateur groups of the day, *Nellie McNab*, by Toronto's Lois Reynolds. I was given the juvenile role. The second play, in which I did not appear, was more serious:

Michael, adapted from Tolstoy's story *What Men Live By*. I turned up again in the last play of the evening, *Fame in the Family*, a comedy written by another Toronto playwright, George L. Watson. I played Marchmont Trevor, whose peculiar name was simply a surname and Christian name inverted. This performance began to teach me that all criticism is relative. One reviewer praised my performance, but another said, "Vernon Chapman was very good in an important part but was inclined to over-act slightly."[1] That reviewer was probably correct. Another wrote that my voice was too low for my age which was quite true because in my early teens my voice dropped an octave almost overnight.

My next role for the Guild was as the son, Willie, in Harry Delf's *The Family Upstairs*, one of those nauseatingly wholesome comedies of the *Andy Hardy* genre that extolled the imaginary virtues of middle class America. At the time I thought it was terrific and was looking forward to acting in it. But for some reason still unfathomable to me, though possibly due to a growing self-consciousness, I got such an attack of stage fright that on the first night I played the whole show like an automaton. I had never had such an attack of the jitters before, nor have I had one since. But evidently it was not noticeable to the audience, and apparently I had learned my lesson about overplaying, at least temporarily, because one of the reviewers wrote that I "showed restraint in a part that could easily be overplayed."[2] Following that I played a young English curate in a British farce called *Yes and No*, and revelled in it.

One of the great appeals of amateur theatre is the social activity. As a result of these rehearsals and the occasional Guild-sponsored party, I got to know many of the residents of Mimico, and within a year I knew many more than did my parents. The Lakeshore Theatre Guild gave me an *entrée* into the life of the community, and the loneliness I felt after arriving in Mimico was dispelled. Drama did it!

One night after a performance of *Fame in the Family*, a short man with a rather large head came backstage. He introduced himself as George Watson and offered me a role in *All the Vultures Were There*, another one-act play he had written which was to be performed in 12 days' time by his own group, "The Theatre Players Guild." He was the first real live play-wright I had ever met and, with my limited experience, his invitation seemed to me to be a passport to the big time. He certainly made it sound like that. By then I had become thoroughly addicted to acting, so I accepted. This city-based group ought to have been called the "George Watson Theatre Guild" because its sole *raison d'être* was to stage his plays. My first role with this group was a smart alec juvenile in *All the Vultures Were There*. It seemed like a good script at the time but Watson's plays are now so vague in my memory that I am unable to assess their merit. On late night TV I occasionally see movies of the '30s and '40s that impressed me then but now appear so inept and simplistic that I wonder if I had any critical judgement in those years at all. But I do recall that George's plays seemed to please the audiences and received favourable critical comment, particularly from Rose Macdonald, the drama critic of the *Toronto Evening Telegram.*

▪

During that period I acted not only with the Lakeshore Guild and the Players Guild, but with other amateur organizations. I was like an alcoholic. I could not get enough of acting. I had been introduced by Mr. Rostance to both the Dickens Fellowship and the Shakespeare Society of Toronto. In each case I was accepted as a juvenile, there being a dearth of young actors who could deliver lines, particularly in Shakespeare, with even a modicum of understanding and appreciation for their lyricism and rhythm. In these last two groups there were a handful of actors of Rostance's calibre, but for the most part the acting was mediocre. There were some who, lacking ability, made up for it in enthusiasm for the two great writers they championed. But there were also many who were members only for social reasons and who were under the delusion that they could act. I was accepted into a group of people who, on the whole, were many years my senior, who were primarily of British origin, and who accepted as normal the English accent I had acquired from Mr. Rostance and from contact with so many people of English birth.

By the time I was in my late teens and my voice had deepened, I was often cast in character roles that were much older than myself: Tullus Aufidius in *Coriolanus*, Philip, King of France, in *King John*, Proteous in *Two Gentlemen of Verona*, Salanio in *The Merchant of Venice*, and Puntarvolo in Ben Jonson's *Everyman Out of His Humour*. When I was 13 (too old) I had played young David Copperfield for the Dickens Fellowship, and at 19 (too young) I had the temerity to tackle Hamlet. Although in the late '30s Toronto was a numbingly dull town, The Dickens Fellowship and the Shakespeare Society were full of eccentric characters who made it fascinating for me to belong to the two organizations. One of these off-beat types had at least a temporary influence over me. Originally Australian, Elise Bernard had been an actress in England. She and her husband had become balletomanes during the heyday of the Ballet Russe de Monte Carlo. Her husband had died some years before the outbreak of World War II, and Elise had come to Canada where she remained during most of that conflict. When I first met her she was in her middle years with hair that at times bordered on auburn. She was an actress in the grand manner. Everything she did on or offstage was writ large. She was imperious, domineering, and critical of almost everything. She latched onto me probably because I was naïvely gullible and was easily impressed. I became her one-man fan club.

The Shakespeare Society staged *King John* in which I played Philip of France and Elise played Constance, mother to Prince Arthur. In a scene with Philip, Constance gives vent to her feelings about her son's imprisonment by King John. At rehearsals Elise had held back, but on the night of the performance, before the play began, she asked me if, after our scene together, I would be good enough to accompany her to the dressing room as she would be very overwrought. During our scene she let go with all stops out. I was awed and dismayed at such a display of raw emotion. Real tears streamed down her face and she sobbed her last lines in deep anguish. Then, crying copiously, she fled the stage. I quickly delivered my line "I fear some mischief and will follow her" and exited. She was waiting just offstage. I took her by the arm and led her, still sobbing, to the dressing room. There the emotion that had seemed so right on the stage now seemed a trifle forced. She gradually got control of herself while I patted her on the back to comfort her. I was really impressed and a bit alarmed. I had never before been involved in such an emotional storm onstage. Later I suspected that the continued crying offstage was for my benefit and anyone else who was watching. Nevertheless, such forceful acting only served to make me a greater fan. A few years later I had evidence that she could be not only an uninhibited actress but a very controlled one as well when she played The Marquise in Noel Coward's play of the same name in summer stock at the Royal Alexandra Theatre. There was a controlled grandeur in her performance that was most effective.

At the time of that performance I was a student at the University of Toronto and was earning some money from summer employment. I felt rather flush and just a bit grand and decided to take Elise to lunch. Aware that I was a student with limited resources she suggested that we lunch at a little restaurant just east of the Royal Alex on King Street West. This restaurant had recently been renamed "Winston's" by a Czech immigrant, Oscar Berceller, who had already begun his collection of autographed photographs from performers at the Royal Alex. I do not remember the details of what we ate, but I do recall that I was impressed with the huge salad he created for us and that the total cost for the lunch for two came to less than $2.

To repay me, Elise invited me to dinner one night in her bed-sitter on Charles Street East. There, while she prepared the food, she regaled me with anecdotes about the Ballet Russe, and told me the story of the ballet *Petroushka.* I had little knowledge of the story and even less about Stravinsky, but, by alternately relating the plot, humming the music, and demonstrating what the dancers were doing, she brought the ballet to life. Between stirring the soup or setting the table she would perform a *pirouette*, a *plié*, an *entrechat*, or a *jeté* (not a Grand one), as she vocalized Stravinsky's complicated score by a combination of singing, humming, trilling, and clucking. I was both amused and entranced. No cabaret has ever entertained me so effectively as this somewhat grotesque, middle-aged lady cavorting about her one-room theatre. The food was great too.

Eventually Elise escaped Toronto and found her way to New York where she obtained the major role of the old lady in a production of *Night*

Must Fall, which toured army camps in the United States and Europe. When that tour finished she became Beatrice Lillie's dresser and the model for one of Miss Lillie's funniest sketches in the revue *Inside USA.* It was a skit about a dresser who, with her disparagingly critical comments, reduces an actress, who had just scored a triumph, to a mass of insecure jelly. Elise dropped out of my sight toward the end of the war, but only temporarily, as we shall see.

The facilities the Shakespeare Society used for their monthly productions were pitifully inadequate but the annual major production usually took place on Hart House Theatre's proscenium stage with more elaborate scenery. Some of the monthly productions were presented at the old library theatre-cum-lecture hall, which in the '40s was a flat-floored auditorium with a small stage at one end but no wings and no backstage. Dressing rooms were the men's and women's washrooms down three flights of a staircase backstage. Often the Dickens Fellowship and the Shakespeare Society made use of such halls as the Arts and Letters Club and the Heliconian Club, neither of which was a proper theatre, although the Arts and Letters Club at least had a raised proscenium stage. The worst venue the Shakespeare Society used was the small auditorium of the Humane Society at 11 St. Albans Street. Formally Scholfield Hall, it was known to us as the "Dog House." It possessed a postage-stamp stage with two tiny cubicles right and left to be used as wings. There were no dressing rooms nor washrooms backstage. We dressed in the small washrooms the public also used.

One of the productions we staged at the Dog House was a shortened version of *Coriolanus* in which I played Tullus Aufidius. After the audience had been uncomfortably seated on hard wooden chairs, the cast, wrapped in white sheets representing togas, proceeded in as stately a fashion as possible down the central aisle trying desperately to look like Roman Senators entering the Senate Chamber. The procession ended up in the cubicles on either side of the stage where we had to remain for the rest of the evening except when we were onstage. One elderly cast member, who insisted on wearing his own high laced boots instead of slippers (we had no sandals), had a kidney problem. He was playing Menenius so, unfortunately for him, he was onstage for long periods. However, when he was not on, those of us who were onstage would be distracted by a white apparition passing between the edge of the stage and the front row of the audience and disappearing up the centre aisle toward the washroom until the squeak of his boots could be heard no longer. We worried if he would return in time for his next entrance. A few minutes later his squeaking boots heralded that he had relieved himself and the ghostly figure would re-emerge from the dark, once again pass in front of the audience, and disappear into the stage left cubicle. This happened several times during the evening, and, although the audience, consisting mostly of friends and members of the Society, seemed tolerant of the actor's bladder problem, his strolls up and down the aisle with his resonating boots proved disconcerting to some of the actors onstage and they became annoyed. I reacted differently. The absurdity of trying to perform Shakespeare under such circumstances struck me as so funny that this Volscian general had difficulty suppressing giggles during his scenes.

Although the production standard left a lot to be desired and the calibre of the acting varied greatly, these Shakespeare Society shows introduced the Bard of Avon to audiences and performers alike. The presentations were valuable to me in two ways: I was able to expand into verse drama, and I was gaining experience in my teens as a character actor.

■

In spite of my involvement in all these amateur theatricals I managed to graduate from Mimico High in the spring of 1941 dragging Latin behind me. But before I could enrol at the University of Toronto I needed fifth form Latin, which meant night school. Moreover, I needed to work for a year to earn money for my tuition. Immediately upon leaving high school I got a job as a stock boy for the National Drug and Chemical Company in a rat-infested warehouse on Front Street where the St. Lawrence Centre now stands, and that autumn I enrolled at the Dominion Business College on Bloor Street just east of Bathurst where I studied typing, shorthand, and the dreaded Latin. My salary at the National Drug Company was $10 a week which was not bad in 1941 for a young man starting out, when I could buy a lunch for 35 cents, obtain a haircut for 40 cents, and see a movie for 25 cents. But after working for two months I decided I deserved a raise to $11 a week, which the general manager refused, whereupon I quit on the spot. Jobs were easy to obtain during those early war years and the next day I took a job with the Heintzman Piano Company as a junior clerk. Despite the fact that my geometry teacher at Mimico High had told me never to take a job involving mathematics, I plunged with the enthusiasm of the innocent into bookkeeping and cost accounting.

The Heintzman Piano Factory was located appropriately enough on Heintzman Street in what used to be called the Junction area of Toronto. The factory was a smoke-blackened structure three storeys high adjacent to the railway tracks. The office was a large single room with a counter separating it from the main entrance to the building. It was furnished in the latest office style circa 1850, with two high slope-top desks. Bert Love, the bookkeeper, worked at one, and I at the other, both of us perched on tall stools. It was worthy of the Counting House of Scrooge and Marley except that it was brighter and warmer and the boss, Howard Heintzman, whose smaller office was just off ours, was much more amiable than old Ebenezer.

The Heintzman family divided the duties of operating the firm between Howard, who was in charge of the factory, and his brother, George, who was responsible for the downtown store on Yonge Street and other retail outlets. Howard was a genial man in his middle years who seemed to be much more interested in golf than running the factory. In fact, the employees, myself excluded, had been there so long and were so skilled at their jobs that the factory practically ran itself. Half the time Howard was absent, and when he did turn up he would often arrive late and leave early. He could not be called a hard taskmaster. The workers in the factory seemed to like him and, since they were a conscientious lot who took pride in their work, they turned out excellent pianos without any oppressive supervision. Bert Love, who was also the office manager (although the only person he had to manage was me), was very tolerant of my mathematical errors and ink-blots, although at first I must have tried his patience sorely. He was a quiet, timid man and both of us shared a fear of the auditor who seemed to delight in swooping down on us without warning. Our fear of him was not that the books had been cooked or that they were not up-to-date, but because he was completely humourless. He was a dour Scot with a cast in one eye and a face like a pig who flew into temper tantrums if he found an error. Naturally most of the errors were mine and I took the brunt of his fiscally righteous wrath. Despite this ogre, I rather enjoyed the time I spent at Heintzman's factory. The fact that I knew I would be leaving as soon as I had saved enough money for my college tuition made the dreary columns of figures tolerable.

Most of the factory workers were middle-aged or elderly and some were blind or partially blind. I enjoyed going out to the various departments to watch the precision with which a piano leg would be turned, the care taken in assembling the "action," or the diligence with which the polishers put a high gloss on the piano case. I learned how to tune a piano from watching the blind experts at work. Occasionally I would play some of my party pieces on a new piano just fresh from being fine tuned. It was a great satisfaction to pound away on a baby or concert grand even though the standard of playing was not worthy of the instrument. I got along very well with the workers and when I left they arranged a banquet for me in a local restaurant and presented me with a pair of beautifully turned walnut table lamps which I still cherish. But sometimes when I look at them I am saddened that those beautiful pianos are no longer made in this country, squeezed out by cheaper foreign competition.

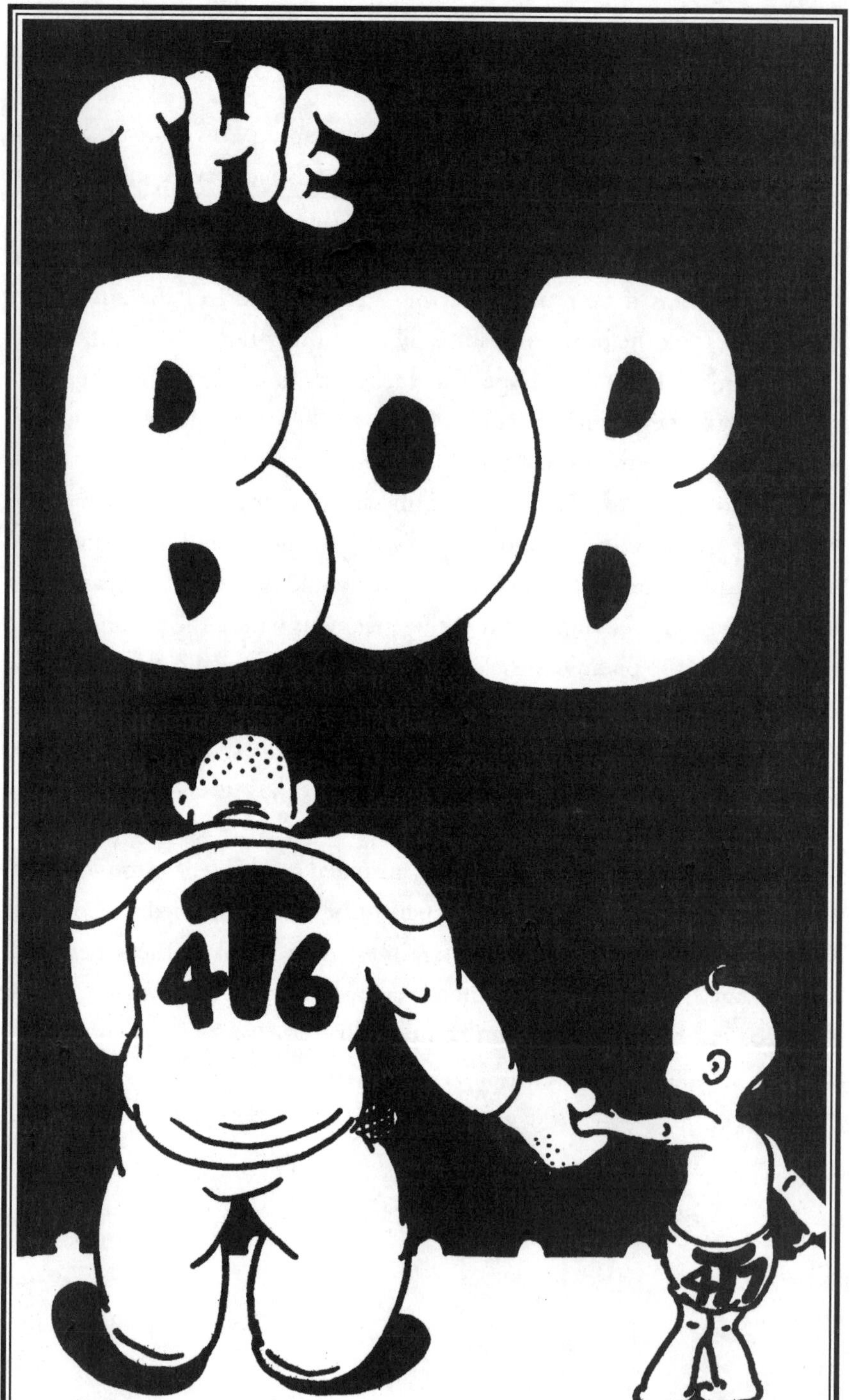
THE
BOB
4T6

CHAPTER 3

In Academe

During my 14 months of working I had saved more than the $223 tuition required at the University of Toronto. Because I lived at home I did not have to raise the extra money to live in residence, and my father gave me an allowance of $5 a week while I was attending classes (no allowance between May and September). Actually, although I was not so well off as some students, I had more spending money than many others who were there on scholarships or bursaries and whose parents, having suffered through the Depression, could not afford to give them even $5 a week. After a year or two of intensive study to obtain high marks so that they could keep their awards, many of these students felt that the pressure was too great, quit university, and thus relinquished their exemption from military service. When Canada eventually introduced conscription, university students were exempt but all male students had to maintain an average of 60 per cent to avoid active military service. I was exempt because of poor eyesight, so I did not feel the pressure that some scholarship students felt. Consequently I was able to relax and enjoy university life both intellectually and socially.

In 1942 I enrolled in Victoria College at the behest of my mother because it had been a Methodist college and was now the one to which United Church adherents gravitated. The fact that I practised no particular religion did not seem to matter. I immediately joined the Victoria College

Drama Club, but, to my chagrin, was not cast by the director, Earle Grey, in that year's major production, Shaw's *The Devil's Disciple*. However, in the autumn I was invited to meet a director who was planning a production of J.M. Barrie's *Quality Street* for the Pearson Players, the amateur drama club of the Pearson Institute for the Blind, then situated in a Victorian mansion on Beverley Street. We were to meet at an address on Cumberland Street. It was late one autumn afternoon when I knocked on the door of this old Victorian row house where a cockney landlady answered. I asked if the man I was to see, Mr. Joseph O'Sullivan, was in. "No, ducks," she replied, "but you go right up to his flat on the third floor." Wondering why she called me "ducks," an application of the word I had never heard before, I went up to the second floor and found a narrow, steep staircase at the top of which was a small Madonna, backed by a mirror tastefully framed in brass, with a votive candle flickering in front of it. To the right of this shrine was a kitchen-dining room, and to the left a combined living room and bedroom comfortably, if sybaritically, furnished including a daybed with a red and black velvet spread and matching cushions. The room had a cosy, lived-in feel but was overly plush and struck me as a bit decadent. I surmised that someone quite unconventional lived there. This was soon confirmed when a young man in his mid-to-late 20s entered. He was about 5´ 4´´, of slim build with wavy bleached blond hair. He had delicate features that on a girl would have been considered pretty. He wore his coat draped over his shoulders like a cape. He smiled radiantly and offered me an immaculately manicured hand. In an English accent he thanked me for coming, told me that he had seen me perform in one of George Watson's plays, that he had been impressed, and that he would like me to play the role of Captain Brown in *Quality Street*. He explained that the Pearson Players liked to mix sighted actors with the blind and semi-blind performers in case something went wrong and the sighted actor could, hopefully, save the situation.

While he was telling me this he proceeded to take off all his clothes, stripping to the buff. I became quite alarmed and prepared to make a dive for the door. Sensing my discomfort he explained that he had to go out again almost immediately and he had worn these clothes all day. I marvelled at his fastidiousness but thought that he could have changed in the other room. However, Joseph Royal O'Sullivan (his full name) had no false modesty. He was extremely effeminate with painted toenails. I have always wondered if his disrobing was a test to see if I would respond favourably to his nudity. Since I did not, our relationship developed on the basis of director and actor, and I grew to respect his talent and to like him as a person. He claimed to be of Irish birth but he did not speak with an Irish brogue, which might be explained by the fact that he had studied speech and become an actor in Britain. Why, when, and how he came to Canada I never did discover, but he seemed content to stay here during the war so long as he could support himself with theatre work. The only way he could do that in those days was by teaching acting and elocution, and by directing amateur groups for a fee. Joseph was paid for directing the Pearson Players. But in the Toronto of the early '40s, there were not many places a young man of Joseph's type could find employment so he had to use his wits and charm to help him get by. People found him to be a curio, and women especially liked having him around as a breath of fresh air without his being a threat to them on a sexual level. For my mind he was the epitome of Marchbanks in Shaw's *Candida*. In fact he played that role in summer stock at the Royal Alex, and, although I have seen several Marchbanks since then, no one seemed to fit that role more perfectly or play it more expertly than Joseph O'Sullivan.

Quality Street was to be presented at Eaton Auditorium for one performance on December 4, 1942. The two female leads, Miss Susan Throstle and Miss Phoebe Throstle, were played by two blind actresses, Gabrielle Allan and Pauline Butler, respectively. Gabrielle was the switchboard operator at the Pearson Institute and her father was the lighthouse keeper on Hanlan's Point, Toronto's most westerly island. Gabrielle had a contagious sense of humour and spread cheer all around her. Once when escorting these two ladies home after rehearsal I slipped on a car ramp and fell into the gutter. This caused great hilarity at the thought that it was the sighted one who was such a stumble bum as to fall off the sidewalk.

Joseph directed the actors with care and consideration but he did not mollycoddle them. The aim was to give the blind actors enough confidence that they could move around Miss Phoebe's "blue and white" room as though they had vision. Every piece of furniture, every object that was handled had to be in exactly the same position for each rehearsal. There was a ticking clock on the mantle. Runners on the floor led from one piece of furniture to another. Joseph demonstrated great patience. When the night of the performance came the only mishap was that Miss Susan dropped her ball of knitting wool and it rolled about 10 feet away from her. I was onstage and was able to retrieve it for her. Although I suppose I was too young and too lightweight (not in size but in character) to do justice to Captain Valentine Brown, I delighted immensely in playing him and I delighted in the company of these remarkably cheerful people who rose above adversity to entertain others. I was later privileged to direct a one-act play for the Pearson Players, *The Twelve Pound Look*, also by James Barrie, and I borrowed heavily on Joseph's techniques for getting it staged. After that I never worked with the Pearson Players again, but often, while I was going to college I visited Gabrielle for lunch at Baker Hall. Once, I was delighted to be invited to dine at her parents' home beside the lighthouse on Hanlan's Point. After the Pearson Institute was moved to more remote headquarters on Bayview Avenue I saw less and less of the friends I had made on Beverley Street, and I wondered if they still had a drama club, and if so, whether they had a director as sympathetic and as inventive as Joseph Royal O'Sullivan.

■

During my second year I was cast as Algernon Moncrieff in the Victoria College Dramatic Society's production of *The Importance of Being Earnest*, directed by Dora Mavor Moore — who was to have a profound influence on me. Because there was no money for elaborate costumes, *Earnest* was presented in modern dress, and the director opted for an all black and white production even to the tea service and the roses on the wall. Algernon wore a black and white tweed suit (my own) when he went Bunburying. My previous stage experience gave me some sense of the style required and Mrs. Moore and I were immediately on the same wave length.

For a student production it succeeded remarkably well. Hart House

Theatre being closed for the duration of the war, it was presented in the auditorium of the University of Toronto Schools. The Vic Dramatic Society shared the bill with the Vic Music Society, which staged Gilbert and Sullivan's *Trial by Jury* with Jack McAllister as the Council for the Plaintiff. Jack was eventually to be one of the founders of the Theatre Arts Course at Ryerson Technical Institute in Toronto. Dennis Wrong, the drama critic for the student newspaper *The Varsity*, gave me a glowing review: "His performance was professional in its smoothness and deftness of execution. . . . He played his role to such perfection throughout the play that we began to wonder who he was, where he came from, and whether he was Noel Coward in disguise."[1] What an intelligent young man was Dennis Wrong! One gets such a rave review so rarely in one's career that I hope the reader will forgive my crowing a bit. As a result of this performance I gained a certain recognition on the campus, and was asked to become a drama critic for *The Varsity* and to join the prestigious Historical Club. Both invitations I accepted.

More important for me, my performance as Algernon got me invited to join the Village Players, one of the best amateur groups in the city. The Players operated out of Dora Mavor Moore's house on north Bathurst Street. *The Importance of Being Earnest* began a close association with Mrs. Moore that lasted for at least 10 years. It also cemented my friendship with Ralph Hicklin, whom I had met in my first year at Vic and who played Canon Chasuble. Ralph had been raised in Chatham, Ontario, the son of a photographer, and he was one of the wittiest people I have ever met. If he liked you he was capable of deep affection, but, he could be quite intolerant and would often utter the most acid remarks about someone he disliked. Ralph had quickly established his territory at Vic. He became a member of the Wymilwood Concert Committee, a member of the Vic Dramatic Society, and stood first in most of his subjects. He formed a coterie of friends drawn mostly from among the male students in his residence but which occasionally admitted an outsider like myself. Over the years, during his roller-coaster career, we were to become the closest of friends. In later years I was to discover that Ralph was subject to periods of depression, but in those university days that was never evident. We found we had much in common. We both had a love of the stage, and appreciated classical music and good jazz. I soon learned that he also had an interest in ballet, an art form which, through Ralph's influence, became a continuing source of delight for me over the years.

One day in 1943 Ralph told me that the Ballet Russe de Monte Carlo was coming to the Royal Alex and he asked me if I would accompany him to see it. Except for my introduction to *Petrouschka* by Elise Bernard, I knew little about ballet and cared less, so I balked at going. "For a dollar a piece," he urged, "we can get seats in the top balcony." Reluctantly I agreed, largely because Ralph was always so much fun to be with.

The Ballet Russe was at that time on its last legs and so was its prima ballerina, Danilova. The company had recruited some youthful American dancers such as Frederic Franklyn, Maria Tallchief, and Leon Danielian, but the sets and costumes were far from young. The evening we attended, the company performed *The Snow Maiden*, choreographed by Bronislava Najinska to Alexander Glazounov's music; *Scheherazade* to the music of Rimsky-Korsakov, choreographed by Michel Fokine with sets and costumes by Leon Bakst; and *Le Beau Danube*, a ballet danced to a pastiche of Johann Strauss tunes. The story of *Scheherazade* deals with an episode from *The Arabian Nights* when the Shah takes his palace guard on a hunting trip. During his absence the Shah's wives release the male slaves and an orgy ensues. The Shah and his soldiers unexpectedly return, catch the harem girls and the slaves in flagrante delicto, and make shish kebabs of them with their scimitars. The harem ladies were all dressed in filmy costumes with flowing veils. The paramount hoorie, Zobeide, wore peek-a-boo pantaloons which seemed to be held together with strings of pearls. The male slaves, who were supposed to be black, were scantily clad in pantaloons, ballet slippers, bands around their heads that Ralph dubbed "headache bands," and acres of dark brown body paint. As the ballet progressed, Ralph and I became intrigued with the eroticism of the dancing which was *risqué* for staid old Toronto of 1943. At one point Frederic Franklyn had to mime caressing Zobeide's body. One of his fingernails caught a string of pearls on the ancient costume. The strand broke and it seemed as though the whole costume was disintegrating as dozens of beads rolled across the stage floor. Much to my disappointment the basic costume remained intact, but I wanted to know how the dancers would cope with those little oval hazards under foot. With only a flicker of hesitation they pressed on and the ballet progressed to its ultimate tragic conclusion. "Well," I thought, "if this is ballet I can do with some more of it. It's sexier than the Casino Burlesque and more dangerous." That evening I failed to appreciate the fine points of *The Snow Maiden* or *Le Beau Danube*, but the sheer colour of the sets and costumes, the athleticism, grace, and delight in dance displayed by the dancers won me over completely. I became a ballet fan for life. Since that evening I have seen many ballets by many companies but none has left such an indelible impression on me as *Scheherazade* danced on beads.

Up to then Ralph had never seen a ballet, but he had read about the Ballet Russe and studied photographs of their performances under Diaghilev. He knew the company's history, the ballets they had staged, the composers they had used, the designs of the sets, and the dancers who had been involved. When I learned of his erudition, I was astonished that this Ontario boy from small town Chatham would know and care that much about ballet. Ralph was so thrilled by the performances that he insisted we go backstage to meet the dancers. With some reluctance I tagged along. Ralph's brashness got us past the stage doorman and we met Danilova and Franklyn. Most of the company were staying at the King Edward Hotel, and Ralph was so excited about being able to talk to real live dancers that we accompanied some of them on the streetcar to the hotel. If he had not been one before, after that encounter Ralph became an avid balletomane. He saw every ballet available to him, he read extensively, and went on to become one of the most knowledgeable and respected ballet critics in North America.

■

Yet another result of my appearing in *The Importance of Being Earnest* was an invitation to perform with the University College Players Guild in *Candle in the Wind*, a play adapted by Maxwell Anderson from the novel *Flight to Arras*. I could not resist the romantic role of a French airman killed in the defence of his country during the German invasion. Hart House Theatre being closed, the young director, John Peck, somehow raised enough money to rent the Victoria Theatre, a large vaudeville house built at the corner of Victoria and Richmond streets in 1910 by the Shea Amusement Corporation, but which had been dark for several years. It was a 1940-seat house with two balconies, a vast orchestra pit, a huge stage with a fly gallery, two tiers of boxes, and faded gilt paint. Even though I was involved in only an amateur college production, the opportunity to play on such a stage in such an impressive theatre gave me a feeling of exhilaration. I thought that this was what the "big time" must be like. Unfortunately the production was not very "big time" because the University College Players Guild and the college hierarchy disapproved of the ambitious project and refused to put any money behind it. Because there were no funds for adequate lighting, the royal garden seemed to be enveloped in the gloom of an impending storm. For a scene that took place in the formal gardens of Versailles, John Peck covered the expanse of stage with pine trees left over from Christmas — hardly the foliage that Louis XIV would have planted.

The play was presented for only one performance, but, because it was in the Victoria, it attracted attention, particularly from the critics. Rose Macdonald in the *Toronto Telegram* wrote, "Vernon Chapman, most experienced of all the players, appears only three times as the Frenchman, St. Cloud, but the serious quiet of his work on these occasions fulfilled its purpose."[2] However, she also wrote, "The settings were admirable, the Versailles garden being achieved with considerable ingenuity,"[3] a statement that made me query the soundness of her judgement about my performance. One of the most difficult roles in the play was that of Lieutenant Schöen, a disillusioned German officer torn between his sense of duty to the Fatherland and his conscience. This was played with understanding and sensitivity by Mel Breen who later became one of Canada's most brilliant television directors until his untimely death in his middle years. My experience with *Candle in the Wind*, working with people like Mel Breen, and in particular with John Peck, opened a new vista for me into the art of acting. Mr. Peck was a pleasant young director with some knowledge about and much enthusiasm for the "method," the Stanislavski approach to acting as preached by the Group Theatre in New York. Except for the brief coaching I had received from Mr. Rostance, my acting had been intuitive and imitative of others. Under Peck's direction I was encouraged to think about the character in more detail and analyse it in greater depth than had been my practice hitherto.

But it was Mrs. Moore, whom I always addressed in that fashion out of respect, who had the most profound influence over me at this point in my life. Although she had invited me to join the Village Players, in order to become a member one had to be sponsored by two existing members and then approved by a majority vote of all the members. The VPs, as they were more commonly known, had been formed in the late '30s and by the time I joined them in 1944 had established quite a reputation in Toronto's amateur theatre world. The members were dedicated to the arts of the theatre, and were, for the most part, concerned much more about doing the best job of acting than in self-display. During the winter season the VPs gave their performances in the Forest Hill Village High School auditorium — not a bad theatre for its day — and at other halls around town, most frequently the Heliconian Club on Hazelton Avenue. But their most active season was the summer when they operated as a non-professional stock company in a small barn adjacent to Mrs. Moore's backyard at 2600 Bathurst Street (now 8 Ridelle Avenue). Mrs. Moore paid a dollar a year rent for the barn that the Village Players had converted into a tiny theatre accommodating 80 spectators on hard, backless, wooden benches. The stage was at the west end of the structure and was no more than 18 feet across and about eight or nine feet deep. When an actor stepped offstage into the wings he would be in either Mrs. Moore's yard or in an empty field. A lean-to at the back of the barn served as miniature dressing rooms and sometimes as storage space, but most often actors dressed in the kitchen of Mrs. Moore's house. Lights and sound were controlled from a loft over two small storage rooms, one of which also served as the box office. Seats were not reserved. The first to arrive on the night of a performance had the choice of the bottom-numbing benches. Performances were given on Thursday, Friday, and Saturday nights during the summer months. Almost every member had to earn a living at daytime jobs, and those of us who were students had to work at day jobs during the summer to earn our tuition. As a result rehearsals were in the evenings or during the day on Saturdays and Sundays.

Mrs. Moore offered to coach me in speech craft for no fee because she felt that I warranted supervised training and because she knew that I could not afford to pay for lessons. I adored having these lessons in the living room of her unique house, a charming relic of Canada's pioneer days. Originally a log cabin built in 1815, it had since been enlarged and stuccoed so that from the side it resembled a Pennsylvania salt-box house. A porch had been added to the front overlooking a small lawn and a grove of trees, which in the summer obscured the house from Bathurst Street to the east. In winter there was always a warming fire in the deep fireplace. Through the casement windows set in two-foot thick walls, you could look out on the snow-covered fields and see no other house in the immediate vicinity. In his autobiography, *Reinventing Myself*, Mavor Moore relates how the house was acquired in 1938 and how for four years Mrs. Moore and her three sons lived there with no electricity or running water.[4] By the time I was taking my speech lessons these amenities had been installed. Nevertheless, every time I stepped into that house I felt as though I had been transported back to Upper Canada in the middle of the 19th century.

With the exception of my own mother, no woman has so commanded my respect and devotion as Dora Mavor Moore. She wove a spell over me that lasted for over a decade. Having raised three sons of her own she seemed to have more empathy for young men than for young women. But not exclusively. During the 11 years of our relationship, many young men and women came under her influence, and she inspired and encouraged them to express themselves in the theatre. At first our relationship was all give on her part — the teacher giving and the student absorbing sponge-like. Later, after the New Play Society had been formed and I was a few years more mature, I sometimes felt that I was being used, but I continued our association through a sense of obligation for the time and effort she had spent training me.

Much has now been written about Dora Mavor Moore. For the

fascinating story of her early years, Mavor Moore's autobiography makes for engrossing reading, as does Paula Sperdakos's biography of her.[5] But if the reader of this book is to appreciate fully her influence on me and what I consider her contributions to the Canadian theatre, some background information is necessary. She was born in Glasgow, Scotland, in 1888, the middle child of three. Her mother was a music teacher and her father, James Mavor, a political economist. In 1892 Professor Mavor accepted the chair of Political Economy at the University of Toronto and transported his wife, daughter, and two sons to that bastion of colonial propriety, "Toronto the Good." Mrs. Moore rarely told me about her early life, but when she did reminisce she spoke of her father with respect. She admired his intellect, his academic stature, and his acquaintance with some of the great writers of the day such as Count Leo Tolstoy and George Bernard Shaw. Apparently the Reverend Mavor Morell in Shaw's *Candida* is partially modelled on Professor Mavor. From those brief glimpses of Dora Mavor Moore's childhood and adolescence, I concluded that her relationship with her father had not been altogether benign. In a rare moment of personal revelation she told me that because she was the one daughter with two brothers, she was not given the same amount of paternal encouragement as they received. I do not recall her ever mentioning her mother.

Self expression can often be very difficult for children with a brilliant, dynamic, celebrated parent. It was doubly difficult for a daughter in an age when opportunities for females were restricted by traditional concepts of their role in society. At the University of Toronto, D.M.M. did not stand out academically, but her interest in the theatre was stimulated by being cast as Rosalind in *As You Like It* for the University College Women's Dramatic Society. She enrolled in the Margaret Eaton School of Literature and Expression in 1911. Mrs. Moore always gave the impression that in 1912 she was the first Canadian to win a scholarship to and graduate from the Royal Academy of Dramatic Art in London, England, then known simply as the Academy of Dramatic Art. But the Sperdakos biography reveals that her scholarship was for $50, won at the Margaret Eaton School, and that Mrs. Moore studied at the Academy for only one month before she returned home to join the Colonial Stock Company in Ottawa.[6]

After a stint with the Colonial Stock Company, she tried her luck in New York. She eventually joined the Ben Greet Players on tour in the United States and later in Great Britain. After several seasons she returned to Toronto, married an Anglican Clergyman, Francis John Moore. They had three sons, Francis, Mavor, and Peter. When I first met Mrs. Moore in the early 1940s, her eldest son, Francis, who had graduated as an engineer from McGill University, was in the United States acting as a liaison for the Canadian government with the American aircraft industry, Mavor was a captain in the Canadian Army Intelligence Corps, the youngest son, Peter, was a captain in the army serving in Italy where he was wounded in action, and the Reverend Moore was conspicuous by his complete absence. I never asked Mrs. Moore about her husband and she never volunteered any information about him. For a long time I assumed she was a widow until a mutual friend informed me that she was separated from her husband. For those curious about the matter consult Mavor Moore's autobiography where he gives a detailed blow by blow account of that stormy marriage.

■

During those war years many amateur groups undertook to entertain the troops in camps, service canteens, and hospitals. As the Village Players' contribution, two companies were organized to take Brandon Thomas's *Charley's Aunt* to the soldiers. The talent was substantial. In both companies the gifted young Jack Medhurst played Lord Fancourt Babberly, who masquerades as Charley's aunt. In one company Don Harron and Geoffrey Waite, both from Victoria College, played the other Oxford undergraduates, Jack Chesney and Charley Wickham. Phillip Tyas played Spettigue and his new wife Billi Tyas alternated with Jane Mallett and Barbara Kelly (Mrs. Bernie Braden) as the real aunt, Donna Lucia D'Alvadorez. In the second company, Jack Anderson, yet another Victoria College student, who later built a career as a stage manager on Broadway, played Jack Chesney, and I Charley Wickham. In this company Guy Purser was Spettigue and Duncan Chisholm was Sir Francis Chesney. In her biography of her father, Martha

Harron quotes her father Don about my performance as Charley: "Vern adopted a comic walk which Don believes is a foolproof way to get laughs. 'Short, very rapid steps with absolutely no movement of the arms'."[7] True, it is an easy way to get laughs. But how appalling! Here was a young actor, too sure of himself, saying, "Look at me. I'm being funny." Although to modern audiences Jack and Charley might look effete, a bit unreal in their Victorian reserve toward the opposite sex, the actors playing those roles must play them as perfectly normal, upper crust Victorian males trying to make out with two lovely young Victorian ladies. They should not be turned into gormless English twits. I have directed *Charley's Aunt* twice since then and have not permitted the actors playing those roles to be guilty of my error of turning Charley into a silly ass. Farce must have a basis in reality.

As a *quid pro quo* for my free lessons, I persuaded the Victoria College Dramatic Society to hire Mrs. Moore to direct the major production for 1944, Oliver Goldsmith's *She Stoops to Conquer*, which she did with profound understanding. I was cast as Marlow and strove not to overplay. Ralph Hicklin portrayed Mr. Hardcastle, and a remarkable young character actress, Pegi Brown, played Mrs. Hardcastle as though she was not only born to the role but also into that country society of 18th-century England. It was a happy production and personally one of the most satisfying experiences of my amateur days.

Because I had a voracious appetite for acting, I did not limit my performing only to university or Village Players' productions, but continued to tackle roles for the Shakespeare Society and The Dickens Fellowship. I even had the temerity to take on the role of the portly Lord Burleigh for the Welsh Dramatic Society in a hodge-podge of scenes from British history grandiosely entitled *Victory Review: A Pageant of the British Empire*. For the Toronto Conservatory I played a role more my age, Mr. Bingley in *Pride and Prejudice*. But the most fun of all was to portray Professor Havelock of Victoria College in a skit written by Don Harron in the Vic "Bob" for the class of '46. In those days "The Bob" was Victoria College's annual, exclusively male students' satirical revue. Ralph Hicklin was chairman of the Bob Committee and had a large hand in the writing of the sketches. The third act was a parody of both ballet and academia with the title *Le Fils Prodique,* danced by the Ballet Russe de Longbranch, with choreography by Sonya Machine and music by Repyakosetzov "et oh just oodles of al." Some of the dancers were Yura Schlemiel, Yanka Stedyum, and Sonia Mondialwez. The humour of the pun was rampant in the comic writing of both Hicklin and Harron, and certainly continued in the latter's contributions to *Spring Thaw* and his Charlie Farquharson character. For me the names given to the dancers by the Harron-Hicklin team are just as inventive and funny as the names of the ballerinas in the all-male, satirical Ballet de Trocadero.

In my final year at the University of Toronto I was elected president of the Victoria College Dramatic Society. We chose as our major production an extremely ambitious play that seemed somewhat avant-garde for its day, Thornton Wilder's *The Skin of Our Teeth.* If not the first, it was certainly one of the first productions of this exceedingly theatrical work after its successful Broadway run. It had a large cast and three sets with a host of costumes, including one for a baby dinosaur and another for a baby mammoth. The sheer logistics of such a production were staggering for the Society. Murie Kelly, later a professor of Fine Art at Queen's University, designed not only the sets and costumes, but also the cover of the program. In the style of William Blake, it was a work of art in itself. Rather than offer myself as an actor to the director, Dora Mavor Moore, I became producer and supervised the organizing of the production. Royce Frith, with his rich booming voice, doubled as an announcer and a broadcast official. Don Harron was Henry (Cain), son of the Antrobus family, who is the enemy that Mr. Antrobus has perpetually to combat. Don's performance was frightening in its somewhat uncontrolled intensity and was only equalled in the production by Pegi Brown who played the Cassandra figure of the Fortune Teller in the second act, and completely dominated the scene.

Prior to the war an Inter-College Drama Festival existed at the University of Toronto, and an Inter-Varsity one in Ontario. In January 1946 some of us decided to revive these competitions. A student representative from each of the campus drama clubs was appointed to a *pro temps* committee until a permanent committee could be elected the following September. Joy

Sanderson of University College and I became the prime organizers for a one-act drama festival to be held in the auditorium of University of Toronto Schools. We decided to have three adjudicators so that there would be less likelihood of one adjudicator favouring one group over another; Dora Mavor Moore, E.G. Sterndale Bennett, and Professor John Robbins of Victoria College were selected.

Three colleges chose to compete. Trinity College presented Noel Coward's study of the hypocrisy of mourners, *Family Album*; University College staged *Hands across the Sea*, also by Noel Coward; and Victoria College entered *Riders to the Sea*, by Ireland's John Millington Synge. In the Trinity production I was impressed by a tall young actor named Drew Thompson, who a few years later was to be producer of the International Players in Kingston, Ontario. The University College entry had two fine performances: one by Arthur Hiller who later became a TV director for the CBC and eventually moved to Hollywood to become a successful film director and president of the Academy of Motion Picture Arts and Sciences, and the other by Murray Davis who, along with his brother Donald, would found the Straw Hat Players in Port Carling and the Crest Theatre in Toronto. Henry Kaplan, who also became a CBC–TV director and later directed soap operas in New York, directed the U.C. production. I directed the Vic entry and was fortunate in having Pegi Brown in my cast, as the matriarch of this Aaron Islands family. Don Harron played the vitally important role of the son, Bartley, who gets drowned at sea and is brought home as a corpse on a plank covered in a white sail. The only sail we could find was a bed sheet that was too short to cover the whole length of the corpse. Knowing Mr. Harron's propensity for comedy, I debated whether to cover his face or his boots. I opted for the face but I sat in great apprehension during the performance that the big sea boots he was wearing would suddenly become puppets and do an act of their own. Fortunately they remained inactive, but, when the grieving mother raised the sheet to have a look at her dead son's face, she was greeted by a leering, winking corpse.

Designer Murie Kelly and I had taken great pains to research the play. I had read all I could get my hands on about Synge, the Irish Renaissance, and the Aaron Islands. I had brightly coloured skirts made as authentic reproductions of the kind worn by the women of those islands, and Murie tried to create onstage a typical western Irish cottage. To establish a proper mood before the curtain opened I played several minutes of Debussy's "La Mer." The adjudicators, through their spokesperson Sterndale Bennett, severely criticized me because "the costumes and some of the props were out of tune with the spirit of the play." They said that the music at the opening and close was "unnecessary and theatrical in the worst sense and the keening was pitifully ineffective."[8] Despite the criticisms, Victoria College won the Cody Award. Naturally I was delighted, but I learned from the written judgements that the three directors received that we had won by only about three points based primarily on the choice of play. *Riders to the Sea* was more within the scope of university students than the sophisticated Noel Coward entries. This began to make me think that competitive drama festivals do not really prove anything, an opinion that was to become more solidified years later. However, that thought did not prevent me from helping re-activate the Inter-Varsity Drama Festival. I attended an organizational meeting at the University of Western Ontario and plans were drawn up for the first post-war competition the following year — in which I would not be involved, having graduated.

All this time I continued with the Village Players. Mrs. Moore had recruited Pegi Brown, Don Harron, Mel Breen, Charles Brown, and Ralph Hicklin from the U of T, and Gwendolyn Dainty, the daughter of the pianist/composer, Ernest Dainty. Gwen had just returned in 1946 from overseas where she had been performing in *The Army Show*. John Hayes, who later became one of the linchpins of the Stratford Festival, also joined us. With these additions, the VPs presented scenes from Shakespeare for four performances at The Heliconian Club: the casket scene from *The Merchant of Venice*, the murder of Duncan from *Macbeth*, the closet scene from *Hamlet* with John Hayes as the moody Dane and Vincent Tovell as the ghost, and the letter scene, or "The Tricking of Malvolio," from *Twelfth Night*. I played Malvolio and Patricia Arthur (Mrs. Bud Knapp) was Olivia. I was excited by the challenge and rehearsals went along smoothly, but on opening night things changed. The small, low platform stage under the Gothic arch of the Heliconian Club could be crossed in about five or six paces. The scene was set with a small bench stage left for Malvolio and a cardboard cut-out of a bush stage right behind which were hidden the three tricksters, Fabian, Sir Toby Belch, and Sir Andrew Aguecheek. They were to pop their heads out only when Shakespeare gave them something to say as Malvolio read the phony letter. On the first night I quickly became aware of sniggers coming from the audience at wrong moments. I looked over to the bush to catch one of the actors poking his head out and grimacing at the audience. After the performance I went to Mrs. Moore and asked her to speak to the actor about it. She astonished me by saying she thought it was quite funny but placated me by promising to do so. The next night the same thing happened and I suspected that she had not spoken to him at all. At the third performance, I determined to retaliate. When the actor stuck his head out I walked across the platform, stood in front of the bush and put the letter in front of his face every time it appeared. If the audience found this very peculiar staging, I did not care. For the fourth performance the head only appeared when Shakespeare gave it something to say. But I was so apprehensive that I was ill at ease during the whole scene. At the time I was exceedingly angry with both the actor and Mrs. Moore. I felt that my carefully prepared portrayal had been diminished and I resented it deeply. But, when I look back on it, I realize how young and inexperienced we all were. Performing by instinct, learning via the trial and error method, many of us lacked sufficient self-discipline to suppress our egotistical desire to keep the audience's attention on ourselves, as my own scene-stealing in *Charley's Aunt* had already shown. Some of us even thought that a performer's obligation in a comedy was to make the audience laugh at all costs.

During my college years the Village Players' summer stock brought several new plays to Toronto audiences. One was John Van Druten's period drawing room comedy *The Damask Cheek*, which included Vincent Tovell as the male lead, Dora McMillan and her daughter Beryl, Jack Medhurst, Patricia Arthur, and myself as Neil Harding, a sophisticated young man-about-town. Rose Macdonald in the *Toronto Telegram* kindly wrote that my performance was "eminently satisfactory,"[9] but I am not so sure. It was a type alien to me and I probably modelled my playing on some romantic movie hero. Also in *The Damask Cheek* was a lovely young actress named Frances Goffman from Dauphin, Manitoba, who was breaking into radio at the time. After the war she dropped out of my ken. But in November of 1999, while in Victoria, British Columbia filming a charming script called *A Day in a Life*, about a group of senior citizens who go off on a toot on the town and the mischief they get into, I worked with a diminutive elderly actress named Frances Bay who had spent many decades making movies in Hollywood. She seemed very familiar to me. When I asked her what her maiden name was she told me Frances Goffman. I was delighted. Here we were 55 years later working together again. It is a crazy, wonderful business.

If, back in 1943, I was not overjoyed with my performance as Neil Harding, I was happier with my portrayal of Don Blackbird in Federico Garcia Lorca's *The Shoemaker's Prodigious Wife*, directed by Francess Halpenny and featuring Gwendolyn Dainty in the title role. I played a character in a black straw hat who only appeared at the cottage window but who spoke and moved in a bird-like fashion. This was the play's Canadian premiere and there had been only one previous showing of it in North America. On the same bill the VPS also presented two scenes from Bertholt Brecht's study of Nazi psychology, *The Private Life of the Master Race*, also a Canadian premiere, intelligently directed by Vincent Tovell who used as theme music some of Kurt Weill's "The Threepenny Opera." It was my introduction to Weill, and I became an instant enthusiast. Yet another premiere for the Village Players was J.B. Priestley's *They Came to a City*, the cast of which included among others Don Harron, Pegi Brown, and myself. As I recall it was a valiant effort but I think most of us were out of our depths with Priestley's fantasy.

Some people who were introduced to the Village Players were not compatible with the group. My friend Ralph Hicklin did not stay with them for long because he was involved with too many other activities and because he and D.M.M. were not exactly sympatico. Another such person was James Reaney. I had met James during one of my summer jobs. We were co-workers filing away examination papers for the Ontario Department of Education then housed in the back wing of the Legislative Building. James was at University College and I had greatly admired a poem he had written that appeared in *The Varsity* entitled "Abortion," in which he described a puddle after a rain storm as "bits of sky standing in the street." This poem caused quite a sensation. In those days James Reaney was a slightly built, diffident, self-effacing individual given to nervous giggles. I liked him very much and Vincent Tovell and I arranged for him to read some of his work at a gathering of VPS in Mrs. Moore's living room. In the '40s abortion was a taboo subject and his avant-garde poetry did not sit well with the more staid members of the VPS. Mrs. Moore herself was not amused.

With a lot of men and women starting to return from the war and picking up their education under the Federal Department of Veteran Affairs program (DVA), some of us in the various campus drama groups thought that they should be given the option of choosing courses that included Theatre Arts. In 1946 there was no bona fide theatre course at any university in Canada, except for brief summer sessions at Queen's University in Kingston. Although I do not believe it is essential to have a university education to become a good actor or director, a grounding in the humanities certainly helps in understanding the historical and social background of a play and the characters in it. We could see no reason why a young person with aspirations to the theatre should either have to forgo university and enrol in a drama school in England or the United States, or take three or four years of university courses followed by several more years at a drama school. Why could a student not train for the theatre and get a university education at the same time in Canada as was possible in the United States? I began to write articles and agitate for a Theatre Arts Course at the University of Toronto. I met a stone wall from the colleges, Victoria in particular. The old Methodist attitude toward the theatre as iniquitous still prevailed. Even Professor Moffat St. Andrew Woodside, who had been the patron of the Vic Dramatic Society, told me that he did not think Theatre Arts was a suitable subject for an Arts College but belonged in a trade school. "Then," I replied, "it should be called 'Theatre Trade'." In an article on the year's drama activity for the

University of Toronto Monthly, I wrote, "University drama is hampered in its development because it is solely dependent on the students for finance. In order to remove these fetters the University must assume its cultural responsibility to the younger generation and inaugurate a course in Drama as it has a course in Fine Art."[10] A bit presumptuous perhaps telling the almighties at the University of Toronto that they "must" do something but I felt very strongly about the matter. Of course they did not "must" do it at all, and they didn't for many years.

Our voices were not completely ignored. The University coughed up some money to channel the demand for a Theatre Arts course into extracurricular activity. An American, Robert Gill, was hired as the resident director of Hart House Theatre where he was to produce a series of plays each year and train those students who had the talent and the desire to act. Because this training did not lead to a degree in Theatre Arts, students who appeared in the productions still had to make their grades in traditional courses. Many students were not able to afford the time to be involved in Mr. Gill's productions. He found that he could stage only four plays per year, with precious little time for teaching. The students learned largely from acting in the plays he presented. Despite these limitations, Robert Gill managed to foster some of the finest acting and directing talents in the country. But that was after I graduated.

■

How I managed all my extra-curricular activities, passed my grades, and took compulsory military training amazes me. All physically able male students had to take this latter training on the assumption that when we did join the regular forces, we would be officer material, a very false assumption in my opinion. We learned the rudiments of soldiering: how to march in step, how to order arms (outdated Lee-Enfield rifles), and how to disassemble and reassemble a Bren gun in less than a minute — a mechanical challenge I found most daunting. There was always a part left over. For three late afternoons a week we would drill on the back campus or in the Armoury on St. George Street. Before the war ended in Europe, we spent two weeks "roughing it" in tents at Camp Niagara where we learned about bayonet charging with appropriate blood-curdling screams, how to aim at a target and hopefully hit it with bullets from our ancient rifles, and how to negotiate obstacle courses. I do not know whether our platoon was typical of others in the Canadian Officers Training Corps, but, I am convinced Hitler would have rejoiced if he could have seen our motley group of sad-sacks, including myself. Fortunately for the Allied cause, the war ended before any of us were involved or victory might have been set back several years.

In addition to all this activity during my college years, I continued to attend movies and the legitimate theatre. Not only did I see many of the local amateur performances, but I was a regular patron of the professional shows that toured to or were produced at the Royal Alexandra. From 1940 to 1946 I saw 72 plays at that venerable theatre including two *Private Lives, Pygmalions, Blithe Spirits,* and *Candidas.* During the years when Frank McCoy and later, Robert Henderson, produced summer stock there, I was in attendance every week, studying the acting avidly from the rarefied atmosphere of "the gods." Although the nucleus of the summer stock company was primarily American with visiting stars mostly from Hollywood, the casts were fleshed out with Canadians such as Lloyd Bochner, Jack Medhurst, Cosette Lee, Norman Roland, Elise Bernard, Mackenzie (Mack) Inglis, Earle Grey in Shakespearian roles, and Barbara Davis (Chilcott) who made one of her earliest stage appearances as Snow Bird, an Eskimo, in *Petticoat Fever.* Even though I had this insatiable desire to act, at the time I was not sufficiently confident to approach the producer, Robert Henderson, or Ernest Rawley, the general manager of the Royal Alex. I was content to be a student spectator. Those years of observing the varied theatrical fare that the Royal Alex offered were an invaluable adjunct to my active participation in Toronto's amateur theatre.

But in 1945, the amateur group with which I was most heavily involved, the Village Players, faced a crisis that split the membership. In his column for the *Globe and Mail,* critic Roly Young suggested that a civic theatre be started by amalgamating all the major Toronto amateur groups into one body. He argued that individually each group's chance of forming a professional theatre and obtaining proper performance space was slim, but, "if gathered together into a federation for co-operative effort [they] might be able to achieve a much greater degree of success."[11] He visualized that this umbrella organization would include not only drama societies but musical and dance organizations as well. To this end he invited interested groups to send in their respective names, the names of the officers, a brief history, and a record of audience attendance. The VPs held a discussion of the matter in Mrs. Moore's living room with those present equally divided for and against joining the Civic Theatre, as it was now called. Some of us, who had ambitions to become professional actors, were quite excited by the proposal. Others were seriously concerned that joining such an all-embracing organization could spell doom for the VPs. The supporters of the Civic Theatre argued that it seemed the best hope at the time for establishing a professional theatre and that an organization which purported to be so devoted to the arts of the theatre as the Village Players should give its full support. To the amazement of the supporters Mrs. Moore came out against it. We were surprised because Mrs. Moore had often spoken of the need to re-establish a professional theatre in this country. Ostensibly her reason was that an organization such as the proposed Civic Theatre would be too unwieldy and could not work. But some of us suspected an underlying reason sprang from the fact that she was too individualistic and egocentric to play second fiddle in anyone else's orchestra.

In his autobiography, Mavor Moore lends some credence, unintentionally I am sure, to our suspicions of Mrs. Moore's motives. He quotes from a note she wrote him after she had attended a meeting with Roly Young in which she was "impressed with his sincerity," but "cannot get connection with Royal [Alexandra Theatre] and Young straight. Suspect something behind venture. No need for anxiety — feel this will not receive sufficient backing to put it through."[12] He then writes, "The reason for this last re-assurance was that she had embarked on a similar adventure of her own."[13] However, in 1945 that adventure was still only a dream in Mrs. Moore's mind which she did not communicate to us. We renegades from the VPs wanted some action then.

At that meeting in Mrs. Moore's house, tempers flared and the pro-joiners were threatened with excommunication from the VPS. In spite of this, four of us, Billi and Phil Tyas, Beryl McMillan, and I, attended an organizational meeting of interested groups and individuals arranged by Roly Young. There the various amateur groups decided to band together in the Civic Theatre Association. Young subsequently published an article, "Toward a Civic Theatre," in which he listed the Village Players as one of the groups at that inaugural meeting, but it was only the four dissidents. The Village Players as a group were never part of the CTA, although Young's article has probably led Paula Sperdakos and others to believe that the VPS joined and later withdrew.[14] We four rebellious VPS were allowed to join as individual members and were not expelled from the Players, although Billi and Phil Tyas and Beryl McMillan gave up their membership in the group. I continued as a member of both organizations.

The goals of the Civic Theatre as set down by Roly Young were idealistic indeed and reveal what was lacking in the Canadian theatrical scene at the end of the war — which was almost everything. The immediate aims were

> (a) to provide a self-sustaining cultural outlet for Canadian talent in the various arts,
> (b) to keep talented young Canadians in their own country,
> (c) to provide them with an understanding and appreciative audience,
> (d) to present them under the most auspicious circumstances,
> (e) to publicize them before the Canadian public and build a reputation for them here so that they will not have to go abroad to gain recognition,
> (f) to educate the Canadian public to appreciate Canadian talent.[15]

The long-range objectives included acquiring a suitable theatre that would be a permanent home for the organization and establishing a professional (but not commercial) company that would provide an opportunity for our most talented artists to make a living here in their native land. This would apply not only to actors but also to designers, playwrights, singers, dancers, and others. Mr. Young went on to write in his manifesto that the Civic Theatre "should be divorced from 'artiness' and from all the usual implications involved in the term 'Little Theatre'." He added that there would be no money "to squander on highbrow experiments or 'arty' presentations" and that after initial goals had been won "there will be ample time to consider educating the public and raising their standards of taste . . . by presenting first-class entertainment on a consistent basis."[16]

Now that we have legitimate professional theatre companies in all the major centres from coast to coast, now that it is possible for performers, designers, and directors to eke out a living, albeit a small one, working in the various entertainment media within Canada, it must be a source of amazement to young theatre artists these days to realize that only 50 years ago the only opportunity to earn money performing was in radio and that was rarely enough to live on. Although I managed to earn some pocket money while at college by acting on radio, I could not have sustained myself on that pittance. Several more meetings were held and by July 26, 1945, the Civic Theatre Association had been formed with Roly Young as general manager, Dorothy-Jane Goulding as secretary, and Kenneth Collen as treasurer. The *Civic Theatre Magazine* was published, and during the autumn of that year an ambitious series of productions was scheduled for one performance each at the Eaton Auditorium. These included *Aladdin* by the Toronto Children's Players, a new Canadian comedy, *The Lady Intervenes*, and Robert E. Sherwood's romantic Viennese marzipan, *Reunion in Vienna*, the latter to be staged by E.G. Sterndale Bennett. The series would end with Boris Volkoff's Canadian Ballet Company. There was also to be a production of Gounod's opera *Faust* on November 19 of that year. Tickets for all events were 50 cents, $1, and $1.50. One of the reasons ticket prices were so low even for 1945 was because these shows were all to be presented

by amateur companies in which no one was paid, with the possible exception of the directors and choreographers.

Despite the resolution to present first-class entertainment, the initial
show produced by the Civic Theatre Association itself, *The Lady Intervenes,*
was considerably less. Authored by Arthur Stringer, a prolific Canadian
writer then living in the United States whose stories and poems seem to
have been almost forgotten in recent years, it starred Anna Russell who had
just begun to develop as a comedienne and musical satirist. In spite of her
talent and Sterndale Bennett's direction, the play was not well received by
the audience or the critics. Even the usually benign Rose Macdonald called
it a fiasco. The second offering, *Reunion in Vienna* fared better. Not only a
well-written play, it had the benefit of Pegi Brown as the female lead, and
a very large but reliable supporting cast including Ben Lennick, Douglas
Rideout, Dora McMillan, Jan Chamberlain, W.S Milne, A. Campbell
Munroe, E.M. Margolese, Jack Medhurst, and me. The audience was put
off by a half-hour delay at curtain time because Eaton Auditorium had
been rented to another organization that afternoon preventing our crew
from beginning to set up before 6:30 p.m. However, the critics were more
favourably disposed than they had been to the previous play.

During its brief life, the Civic Theatre managed to publish four editions
(October, November 1945 and January, February 1946) of a pocket-sized
magazine containing articles about Gilbert and Sullivan, Children's Theatre,
a brief history of the theatre in Canada and of theatre buildings in Toronto,
articles on dance and ballet with a glossary of ballet terms, recent record
listings, brief biographies of some of the people involved in the artistic side
of the Civic Theatre, articles about Canadian performers who had emigrated, and several more features about theatres past and present. Indeed,
they were very informative booklets. The subscription fee of $2 was also
supposed to give the subscriber a reduction on the already low prices for
tickets to the CTA shows. After the brief flurry of activity in fall 1945, the
Civic Theatre began to fade. It sponsored a drama festival held at Northern
Vocational School in April 1946 with various member groups participating,
the winner being the Belmont Group for their production of Saroyan's

Hello Out There. Then in January 1947, Noel Coward's *Tonight at 8:30* was presented at Hart House Theatre, followed in February by a comedy about Little Theatre, *The Torchbearers*, in March by a thriller, *Blind Alley*, and in April by the religious play, *Family Portrait*. After that the Civic Theatre petered out without achieving much of its promise, the victim of its own cumbersomeness and of the arrival on the scene of a more tightly organized company led by a strong-willed, determined lady. Mrs. Moore had been proven correct. Each amateur group was too involved with its own programs. Most groups had a large dilettante core with no personal interest in creating a professional theatre. The birth and almost instant infanticide of the Civic Theatre convinced me that if Canada were to have an indigenous professional theatre, it could not be achieved via the amateur theatre. It would be up to us who wanted careers as performers to see that it came about. And that is what happened.

CHAPTER 4

Among
the Mummies

There were three events that greatly affected my life in the spring and summer of 1946. First I graduated with a Bachelor of Arts degree in history. I had decided on a career as an actor, a seemingly foolhardy decision because the only source of income for an actor in Canada was radio. To support myself, I had to find employment in some other field. On the bulletin board of the Students' Administrative Council office, I noticed an advertisement for a statistician in the Department of Biology at the University of Toronto. Not quite sure what a statistician was, and mindful of my less than brilliant showing in mathematics at Mimico High School, I decided to apply. This led to the second important event in my life that year, my obtaining a full-time job that gave me financial support while I became involved in the third important event, the founding of the New Play Society.

With a "what have I got to lose?" attitude, I went to the Department of Biology where I was interviewed by a Doctor Frye, an amiable man in his late 20s or early 30s who had recently been demobilized from the Royal Canadian Air Force. The Biology Department, in conjunction with the Ontario Department of Lands and Forests, wanted a person to correlate information on thousands of creel census cards that had been accumulating during the war. These cards recorded data on the lake trout and bass caught in Algonquin Park. I told Dr. Frye that I knew nothing about fish and that my maths left a lot to be desired. "Good!" he exclaimed, "You're virgin territory. I can teach you." Prior to the war he had done research on the lake trout of Algonquin Park and in 1939 had published a booklet promulgating his theories. Now he wanted to find out if the information on the cards would substantiate those theories. When the data had all been correlated, another pamphlet on the subject would be published. Not only did he teach biology, he had several research projects going and did not have the time to devote himself to the new publication. Moreover he disliked writing. He would show me how to use a slide rule, guide me in the drawing of the graphs and charts, and correct any errors I might make. It sounded like a fascinating challenge so I accepted and plunged immediately into a sea of statistics. With his help I soon learned to swim. When work on the pamphlet was finished by the end of August 1946, and published under the title "Cristivomer Namaycush Walbaum," by Dr. Frye M.S., Ph.D. Sc., and Vernon Chapman, B.A., I thought the job would end. But the Department of Lands and Forests planned an expanded research program for the following year and needed someone to purchase supplies. I was switched from the Biology Department payroll to that of the Department of Lands and Forests at a considerable increase in salary. I had become a civil servant!

A detailed narration of my involvement with fish and the Fisheries Laboratory is not germane to this book, but some of it is necessary. That winter of 1946–47 I purchased the necessary supplies and equipment for the expanded program, including many items the purpose of which was a mystery to me. By March 1947 once again I thought the job would end, but Dr. Langford, in charge of the Fish Lab at Lake Opeongo, hired me as its business manager, responsible for the purchase of equipment, supplies, and food to keep the 30 students (to be hired) working and eating. Because Dr. Langford would be busy with his own research, I was also to see to it that the students were carrying out their assignments, although, for the most part, I hadn't the slightest clue what they were doing. As a result, from the beginning of May to the end of September of 1947 I found myself second in command of a fish lab. As a consequence of my wandering into the Student Administrative Council office in the spring of 1946, a series of beneficial results followed: through a regular day job I was able to sustain myself while helping the New Play Society in my spare time; I was forced to take on responsibility and discovered I could handle it; I had developed an appreciation of the wondrous beauty of the wilderness of this country; and I managed to save a nest egg to support myself for a while when I decided to pursue my ambitions as an actor. I had also enjoyed every moment of my involvement with fish.

The third important event for me in 1946 was the post-war beginning of a professional theatre in English Canada. That summer the Ontario Government obliged the Royal Ontario Museum to make the lecture hall in its basement available for public use. Mrs. Moore saw her chance and approached the Village Players to help her establish a professional theatre there. Some of the vps were reluctant because it meant the demise of their amateur group, but a handful of us were wildly enthusiastic and pledged all the help we could give her. Don Harron, Pegi Brown, Jean Cruchet (Keller), Vincent Tovell, Glenn Burns, and myself were among the small group of supporters. Mrs. Jean Atkinson became the honorary secretary and The Right Honorable Arthur Meighen lent the prestige of his name as honorary treasurer. Barbara Allen became the acting secretary and Victor Barnett the acting treasurer. When D.M.M. saw a desirable objective on the horizon, she steamed toward it like a dreadnought and we formed the crew. No one can argue that the New Play Society could have been born without Dora Mavor Moore, but she could not have tackled the monumental challenge of establishing, against staggering odds, a professional theatre company where none had existed for years, without our willing help.

Plans were hurriedly made for a season from September through December of 1946 and specific dates were booked for the Museum Theatre. We would wait to see how well we did with our opening shows before committing ourselves to a season in the new year. Nor were we sure at first what plays we would present that autumn. Initially each show would be presented on Friday and Saturday nights on a fortnightly basis. This would give us four performances of each production. In addition to acting we were all supposed to help in various other capacities, but, in actuality, it worked out that some had more "capacity" than others. Among us we decided to name the organization "The New Play Society" because it was a new theatrical venture which planned to present some plays that would be new to Toronto audiences, and some that would be newly written by Canadian playwrights and premiered by us.

From the first I found myself willingly spending all of my spare time working for the NPS, as it came to be known. I was wildly enthusiastic not only because I was contributing toward what we considered to be an important objective but also because I was being given an opportunity to learn by trial and error how to run a theatre company. We were all learning, including Dora Mavor Moore. To establish the NPS as professional we were paid a monstrous $15 every two weeks (about $100 in current money). I resolved that after I received my first salary payment as an employee of a professional theatre company I would never again perform as an amateur. I believed that if we were to survive as professionals, the public had to recognize that we were not dilettantes, and, that if they wanted to have professional actors in this country, they would have to support them with their patronage. Therefore, it was important that the public not be confused as to the performer's status. Since 1946 I have kept to that resolve although I have directed amateur groups for a fee.

The Village Players' 1946 summer season in the barn had to be concluded, and, until that happened, we held the NPS planning meetings in Mrs. Moore's living room. But by September a small office was acquired on the second floor of 21 Prince Arthur Avenue next to the Women's Art Association. I remember how thrilled I was that we were a professional company with an office of its own, albeit a small one. I was even more thrilled that we now had a home, although inadequate, in the heart of Toronto in which to perform. The elongated lecture hall-cum-movie theatre in the basement of the Royal Ontario Museum was hardly an appropriate venue for a legitimate theatre. The so-called stage was a space 18 feet by 18 feet surrounded by solid concrete walls with a door on either side in the upstage corners. The wings were small rooms on either side of the concrete box. In the west wing there was a stairwell that led up to the cafeteria, through which one had to pass in order to get backstage. The only other access was through the auditorium. Behind the stage were two small dressing rooms. Needless to say this telephone booth of a stage left much to be desired. Nevertheless, its very smallness was a boon when there was no money for elaborate stage sets. Murie Kelly, who had designed the sets for the plays Mrs. Moore had directed for the Victoria College Dramatic Society, was hired as the designer, and Bob Simkins, also from Vic, and Jacqueline Keens constructed Murie's sets. Neither of these assignments was too challenging because economy and the space dictated the simplest of staging. A set of neutral grey drapes were purchased to cover the stage walls as the basic set for several of the first plays we presented. Against them pieces such as doors, windows, and fireplaces would be inserted. Such items, plus appropriate furniture, we hoped would be acceptable to our audience. We would have to rely on the quality of the acting to win our public.

The plan for the first season was to present plays of international renown that had rarely, if ever, been seen in Toronto. The first salvo fired in this ambitious campaign was John Millington Synge's Irish masterpiece, *The Playboy of the Western World.* For this Murie Kelly turned the limitations of the stage into assets. Michael James's County Mayo pub was a simple place so a simple set was placed on this simple stage. The neutral grey drapes were the walls into which were inserted a cottage door, divided into upper and lower halves, and a small window. Against the drapes were a fireplace over which was a plain pendulum clock, a rustic sideboard with open shelves, a rough table, some benches, a three-legged milking stool, and a wooden bar with shelves behind it for mugs and glasses. In front of the bar was a small barrel as a bar stool and beside it a large barrel for beer. Et voila! Michael James's pub. Or at least enough to stimulate the audience's imagination and give the actors a helpfully appropriate background. The Museum Theatre stage was devoid of any proper theatrical lighting so a suitable system had to be installed. Some of this equipment was brought from the barn at 2600 Bathurst Street. Ancient dimmers were wired into floods and spots attached to batons just behind the proscenium and above the front row of seats. A grid was added to the stage ceiling from which to hang batons for more curtains. Much of the credit for the conversion of this austere lecture hall into a workable theatre must go to the ingenious John Richardson who had been brought in as stage technician.

The Playboy was directed by Dora Mavor Moore with some advice from the Irish-Canadian playwright, John Coulter. Mrs. Moore had a deep understanding of the play and an appreciation for its lyric quality. A young Irish visitor to Canada, Timothy Curran, who had performed with the Abbey Players of Dublin, was recruited to coach us into capturing the melodic lilt of Synge's colourful speeches without sounding like phony, vaudeville Irishmen. The whole cast delved into the project with intense enthusiasm because we were determined that this first English-Canadian post-war production by a "professional" theatre company would be a whopping success. And it was!

But it nearly wasn't. Permission to produce *The Playboy* had been granted to us by the copyright owners, Samuel French Theatrical Publishers of New York, through its Canadian branch in Toronto. Halfway through the rehearsals the tough manager of their Toronto office, Mona Coxwell, notified us that the rights had been withdrawn because there was a New York production pending that might tour to Toronto. Mrs. Moore decided to press on regardless of the threat of a court injunction. She argued that permission had already been granted and therefore could not be rescinded. Fortunately she did so because the New York production was postponed and we were allowed to continue with no more threats from Ms. Coxwell. Paula Sperdakos writes in her biography of Mrs. Moore that Andrew Allan, the internationally known CBC radio producer, flew to New York and intervened with the producers of the Broadway production.[1] I knew nothing of that at the time and wonder at Allan flying to New York specifically to save our show. However, if he had gone to that city on other business, he might have pleaded our case with the Broadway producers. And to think I have had the impression all these years that it was Mrs. Moore's sheer stubbornness that saved the production. This incident made me aware just how much the theatre life in Canada could be controlled from New York.

Mrs. Moore had assembled a group of exceedingly talented and enthusiastic actors for the show. Don Harron filled the role of Christy Mahon, the playboy, as though born to it. His uncanny ear for dialects allowed him to capture easily the lilt and melody of the dialogue, and his natural ebullience allowed him to portray the braggadocio of the character. Jean Cruchet was a beautiful and fiery Pegeen Mike. Pegi Brown created a characterization of the blowsy, sexually predatory Widow Quin that, several Widow Quins later, I have never seen equalled. Bill Needles and John Conway made a bucolically convincing pair of local yokels as Philly Cullen and Jimmy Farrell, and the village girls were played with infectious exuberance by Isa Dale, Sandra Scott, Charmion King, and Barbara Allen. George Gibson brought a scruffy, unwashed quality to Old Mahon, and Peter Mews, although still a young man, demonstrated his ability to characterize in his bibulous portrayal of Michael James. I delighted in playing the role of the gormless Sean Keogh who fancies Pegeen Mike but can't compete with the dashing Christy Mahon. Although Sean is described as being chubby, and I was bone lean at the time, I tried to capture his cringing wimpishness by bringing a touch of Uriah Heep to him and by playing him stoop-shouldered, with my hair parted in the middle and a wispy moustache — and although I cannot claim to have been the definitive Sean Keogh, it worked. There was not a weak performance in the show, and Mrs. Moore's direction was strong and certain. Later that winter I saw the Broadway production of *The Playboy* starring Burgess Meredith. I was disappointed with Meredith because I was always conscious of a clever actor "acting," whereas Don Harron *was* Christy Mahon. Of course the set for the New York production put our meagre efforts into the shade, but, so far as the acting was concerned, the Toronto cast compared more than favourably with the Broadway one. Am I prejudiced? Why, of course! But we were all proud of our efforts with this, the New Play Society's first show. It had to be a success artistically or there might not be a second one. This production was a milestone, one might almost say a cornerstone, of the development of professional theatre in English Canada, so I consider it necessary to emphasize its importance.

The comments of the critics are testimonials to its success. Colin

Sabiston of the *Globe and Mail* wrote, "A capacity audience greeted Dora Mavor Moore's first play of the season . . . and was rewarded with an excellent production." He went on to say, "Not the least remarkable feature of the performance was the convincing delivery of the lines with the true lilt and cadence of the Irish countryside."[2] Augustus Bridle in the *Toronto Star* wrote that the company had achieved such authenticity of speech that "the whole troupe seemed to be Irish Players from Dublin."[3] Rose Macdonald in the *Telegram* wrote that this opening show "might well be a contribution of durable value to the establishment of an essentially Canadian theatre on a professional non-profit basis."[4] All three critics plus the one for the *Varsity* praised the acting, particularly that of Don Harron and Pegi Brown. The New Play Society was off to a good start.

The Playboy was followed by August Strindberg's *The Father* directed with great sensitivity by Karen Glahn who had played the female lead in this play for the Strindberg Theatre in Denmark. Glenn Burns was powerful in the title role. Rose Macdonald wrote, "This was one of the most striking theatre performances seen here in some time."[5] As part of the Society's policy of presenting international plays for the enlightenment and edification of the Toronto public, the next offering was *Lady Precious Stream* brought from the Chinese Theatre on Elizabeth Street in Toronto. It was part of the repertoire of the Gin Hong Sing Dramatic Society of the Chinese Masonic Order, which had been performing at that Elizabeth Street theatre for years. Many of the actors in the company had been stranded in Canada during the war. On two occasions during my university days some friends and I dropped into that theatre to observe Chinese drama in action. In the smoke-filled theatre I admired the ability of the actors to perform while members of the audience wandered in an out of the theatre at will. But Chinese theatre was virtually unknown to non-Chinese Canadians. It proved to be quite an experience for our audience.

Although originally we had planned to present each show for four nights on the Fridays and Saturdays of consecutive weeks, we decided, for the first season at least, to concentrate them into two performances. Because *Lady Precious Stream* was such a long play it was divided into two halves, the first to be performed on the Friday night and the second on the Saturday. To accommodate our occidental audiences who are not accustomed to wandering in and out of the theatre during a show, a further division was made of each performance into two acts with an intermission. Mrs. Moore had a knack of persuading important dignitaries to attend the opening nights. For *The Playboy*, the premier of Ontario, George Drew, and his wife had been in attendance. For *Lady Precious Stream,* the Chinese consul general and his wife, the mayor of Toronto and his wife, and other honoured guests were present in the front row. The Chinese orchestra had been placed between them and the apron of the stage. The cacophony from the orchestra was so great that in the interval the whole of the front row, including the consul general fled to the empty back row of the theatre for the second half. I expect that our occidental audiences, like myself, did not understand the conventions of Chinese theatre such as the actors walking in a circle to indicate a change of scene or the significance of different sizes and shapes of beards, but extensive program notes told the story line and the brilliance of the costumes, the visible activity of the stage managers, and the beauty of the stylized make-up and movement of the actors kept the spectators attentive.

The NPS had presented an Irish play, a Swedish play, and a Chinese play. The fourth of its first season was a British play, Somerset Maugham's comedy *The Circle*, in which I had the opportunity to display my wares as the pompous Arnold Champion-Chesney, a starring role for John Gielgud in a recent London revival. Arnold is much more interested in his furniture and his *objects d'art* than in his wife who, at the end, decamps with an ardent young lover, urged on by Arnold's mother, Lady Kitty, who had previously departed from Arnold's equally stuffy father — hence the "circle." One of the reviewers with the initials J.A.M. found my performance "overly studied and stiff" so I must have succeeded in my objective of making Arnold intolerably fastidious and reserved, ensuring the audience's sympathy for his wife, Elizabeth. I was fortunate in sharing the stage with such splendid Canadian actors as Jane Mallett as Lady Kitty, Jean Cruchet as Mrs. Shenstone, Bernard Braden as Lord Porteous, Barbara Kelly (Mrs.

Braden) as Elizabeth, and Glenn Burns as Clive Champion-Chesney. In the small part of Teddy Luton, with whom Elizabeth elopes, was the dashingly handsome Lloyd Bochner. Once again the acting was successfully thrown into relief by the same minimalist set of grey drapes and once again the audience and the critics, with the exception of the adverse comment by J.A.M on my performance, were appreciative.

Because our duties were manifold, definitive titles were difficult to apply to our functions. For some unknown reason, unless I was performing, my name was not included in the first programs of the NPS even though one of my duties was to compile these programs, which in the beginning were simple two page affairs. Why I did not insist on program recognition is a mystery to me. Could it have been from a misguided sense of false modesty? In my early years I was very self-effacing, a weakness, which in my middle years, I overcame with a vengeance. Another of my jobs was to arrange for newspaper advertising. The experienced newspaper woman, Marjorie Chadwick, was nominally in charge of publicity but she did not concern herself with the newspaper advertising. My responsibility was to draw up ads, larger ones to be used to promote advance sales for a new production and smaller, less expensive ones as reminders to the public once the show had opened. Because we presented a new show every fortnight and because we could not afford to be wasteful of money, this kept me hopping. No advertising campaign could be planned in advance and left in the hands of the newspapers' advertising departments. If sales were going well I had to be prepared to curtail the size of the ads and their frequency on 24 hours' notice. I also had to be persuasive with advertising managers to put our ads in the most favourable position on the entertainment page, and not where they would be swamped by the much larger motion picture ads. The result was that I spent hours each week in newspaper offices, an experience that taught me how to use newspaper advertising effectively and economically. All of this for the salary of $15 every two weeks. But then, Mrs. Moore, who had put up $2,000 to get it all started, was receiving no salary at all in those early days, and had to exist on the small support payments her estranged husband sent her, which no doubt accounted for her thriftiness in running the NPS. At least I had a well-paid daytime job, and an understanding boss, Dr. Frye, who was tolerant about my taking time off on NPS business.

By the time *The Circle* was staged, Mavor Moore had joined us as production manager, which also entailed much of the business side of the operation. After being demobilized from the army, Mavor had worked for the CBC in Vancouver while we were organizing the New Play Society. In her biography of D.M.M., Ms. Sperdakos implies that Mavor was involved in the planning from the beginning,[6] although Mavor makes no such claim in his autobiography. No doubt Mrs. Moore had consulted Mavor over the telephone, but she drew up the plans in consultation with the Village Players and in particular with those of us who formed the original nucleus of the NPS. Her son Francis was involved from the beginning in helping to convert the Museum hall into a theatre. I felt more confident about the New Play Society's chance of success once Mavor had joined the team, if only — like the rest of us — on a part-time basis, because he also had to earn a living, which he did acting on the radio, writing for it, and teaching at Lorne Greene's newly founded Academy of Radio Arts.

Mavor helped organize the business side of the venture as much as he could with his other commitments and with his mother in charge. It gradually began to dawn on me that although Dora was very shrewd and tight-fisted with a buck, she really knew very little about the business of "show business." But then, neither did any of us. She worked on instinct rather than on business acumen. She was wise to be parsimonious with the finances because the original money was very soon gone. Later in the history of the NPS during one of many financial crises, she mortgaged her house to pay the bills. Her experience over the years of trying to raise her family on very little money and her Scots instinct for thrift were vital safeguards in the early days of the NPS. But this essential frugality annoyed some talented performers and alienated others.

The first two plays in which I had performed that autumn of 1946 had been challenging and rewarding showcases for me. However, the next role I tackled had an adverse effect on my career and began the slow erosion of my relationship with Mrs. Moore. The early December production was Eugene O'Neill's *Ah, Wilderness!* for which the guest director was the great god of CBC radio drama, Andrew Allan. During the war years Mr. Allan had begun the Stage Series, which had gained recognition by 1946 as the finest series of radio dramas in North America, challenged only by Orson Welles's Mercury Theatre. The Stage Series had won many awards and Allan had established himself as a top-notch radio director. He had assembled a radio stock company of remarkably fine performers including some that became Canadian household names. Deservedly the most celebrated was John Drainie, but equally skilled were such actors as Tommy Tweed, Frank Peddie, Ruth Springford, Bud and Patricia Knapp, John Bethune, Al Pearce, and Larry McCance, most of whom were not originally from Toronto but had followed Allan from Vancouver. By 1946 Don Harron had been admitted into that closely knit circle after being recommended to Allan by the radio writer, Fletcher Markle, who had seen Don in the Village Players' production of *Hello Out There*. Almost all of the cast of *Ah, Wilderness!* were drawn from this stable of radio actors: Bud Knapp, John Drainie, Tommy Tweed, Don Harron, Claire Murray, and Ruth Springford.

When the cast list for the production was announced, Mrs. Moore came to me in an agitated state. She felt that control of the New Play Society was being taken away from those who had initiated it, and that, to use her phraseology, "The radio crowd are moving in." This notion was compounded by the fact that rehearsals were to be held at John Drainie's house, which she interpreted as an indication that they wanted to exclude her from the rehearsals, leading her to suspect that there was a plot to take over the NPS. "We have to have some representation of the NPS in this show," she said. "So I want you to play Wint Selby. I shall insist on it." Selby was a role that had not been cast from among the radio group. A Yale University student, he is described by O'Neill as "nineteen, a hell-raising sport type." Wint introduces the teenage son of the family to the wild college life of the early part of the 20th century including wine and (horrors!) women. I was torn between a desire to be directed by Andrew Allan, which might let me into the radio clique, and the realization that the role was not really my cup of tea. The extroverted college rake was alien to my own personality. However, I had given a competent performance in a similar role for the Village Players, that of Neil Harding in *The Damask Cheek*, and I hoped that with work I might be able to get away with it. With some apprehension, I agreed. That proved to be a serious mistake.

From the very first rehearsal I detected in Allan a resentment at my being forced on him. With my glasses and slight frame I am sure I did not look like his idea of a "hell-raising sport type." Nor did I look like the character in my own mind's eye. I began to lose any confidence I had in my own ability to overcome my deficiencies. I was over-awed by being directed by the great man himself and from rehearsing with such a talented cast. Possibly if Allan had not shown an antipathy toward me and had encouraged me with helpful words and direction I might have overcome my lack of self-confidence and found a way to "lose myself" in the role, which in turn might have led to a creditable performance. As the first week of rehearsals wore on, as much as I liked Claire and John Drainie, I dreaded going to their house. Moreover, I began to suspect that although Allan knew how to extract vocal performances from his actors on radio, he did not know how to help them physicalize a performance on stage. This suspicion was confirmed for me years later by other actors who had been directed by him in the theatre.

On the Sunday after a week of rehearsal I received a phone call from Mavor in which he said that Andrew had asked him to tell me he wanted me to give up the part. I was somewhat relieved, but I was also resentful and angry — resentful of Andrew Allan who did not have the courage or decency to ask me in person to leave the show but got Mavor to do the dirty work, and angry at Mrs. Moore for pushing me into the role, and at myself for having allowed myself to be talked into attempting a role for which I was not psychologically suited. My anger led me to make my second mistake. I went to my typewriter and in white heat dashed off a letter to Allan in which

I was rudely critical of him as a stage director. Although it made me feel better at the time, it was a stupid, tactless thing to do if ever I wanted to break into radio's inner sanctum. But that afternoon I had thrown my common sense out the window. Since then I have learned not to act before thinking carefully about the consequences. This hot-headed palliative to my injured pride marked *finis* to any hope I had of becoming one of Allan's radio actors. It is small consolation to think that during those years of his heyday when he was receiving well-deserved praise for his radio dramas and when people often made obsequious obeisance in his direction, I was probably the only actor who dared to write him a critical letter.

However, for me the story has a semi-happy ending. Some years later when TV had supplanted radio drama as the public's darling, and after I had directed many plays myself, I met Andrew Allan on Jarvis Street. By then he had descended from the Olympian heights. Sadly he had not succeeded as a TV director and was on the skids into alcoholism. I decided to apologize for my rudeness of a decade before. I stopped him and told him that I was sorry for sending him that letter and that since then I myself had been obliged to ask an actor to give up a role and I knew how hard it was to do so. He stared at me in astonishment and was quite speechless, a rare condition for him. Having delivered my apology I walked away. Andrew may have been baffled by my words but it eased my conscience. A few years later when he and Sean Mulcahy were co-directors at the Shaw Festival, over a drink at the Oban Inn, I realized that all was forgiven, or possibly forgotten, when he asked me to play General Burgoyne in the Festival's production of *The Devil's Disciple* the following year. I was delighted. Unfortunately for me, neither he nor Sean Mulcahy returned to direct the Festival the next year, and the new artistic director, Barry Morse, cancelled *The Devil's Disciple*. But the fact that Andrew Allan had invited me to perform for him after the debacle of 1946 was immensely satisfying.

Despite my foolishly antagonizing the top banana of CBC radio back in 1946, I managed to break into that medium via such producers as Alan Savage, Esse Ljungh, and J. Frank Willis, all of whom accepted me as a competent radio actor. And Andrew Allan and I eventually became quite good friends. I joined "The Celebrity Club," that comfortable oasis on Jarvis Street ostensibly founded to offer a place of refuge to performers and employees of the CBC. This club had a very fine dining room and on occasion I would have dinner there. Often Andrew Allan would be dining there alone and he would invite me to join him, or vice versa. It was during these dinners that I got to know him better. By then he was recovering from several bouts of alcoholism, and, to quote from his autobiography, he had "come through a dark time, living on the edge of despair."[7] He had reconciled himself to his much less important position in the world, and was obtaining an income from radio with his brilliance as a conversationalist and raconteur. During these dinners he would enthral me with his wit, his erudition, his command of the language, his astuteness as an observer of life, and his fundamental humanity. No mention was ever made of the contretemps over *Ah, Wilderness!* He was not the same man in the '60s that he had been in the '40s. Adversity had mellowed him.

▪

The production of *Ah, Wilderness!* was one of the best the New Play Society ever presented due largely to the abilities of the actors involved. The grey drapes had given way to a box set which did a lot to establish the atmosphere of the Miller's home. Bud Knapp was in top form as the father of the family. Tommy Tweed gave a brilliantly funny performance as Uncle Sid, and Don Harron once again revealed his instinctive talent and increasing technique in the role of the youthful Richard. Lloyd Bochner took over the role of Wint Selby for which he was much more suited than I. *Ah, Wilderness!* revealed that Andrew Allan's coterie of radio actors were splendid stage actors as well.

Reasonably so or not, I blamed Mrs. Moore for having forced me on Andrew Allan. I felt that, in her attempt to retain some control over the production, I had been exploited for her own purpose. The result was that we had unpleasant words about it. Now that I had been disgraced, as I then thought, before a group of the finest actors in Canada, perhaps my future did not lie with the New Play Society, and perhaps not even in Canada. I began planning a sojourn in Britain to seek experience in repertory theatres, to check out my English roots, and to see firsthand some of the sites I had learned about through my studies of British history. I set as my objective a passage to that country in the autumn of 1947. Gwen Dainty had returned to London and with her knowledge of the British theatre scene she would be at least one valuable contact for me there.

However, by the final performance of *Ah, Wilderness!* we had not yet concluded the first season. I set aside my annoyance over the Wint Selby affair and continued to work assiduously for the NPS because I strongly believed in our objectives. I was involved in two more NPS productions, which helped restore faith in myself. For the Christmas 1946 show, control of the NPS was reclaimed by Mrs. Moore. It was a double bill from the Medieval Cycle plays: the *Coventry Nativity Play* and the *Wakefield Second Shepherd's Play*, one of the oldest comedies in the English language. They required extremely large casts with many of the old Village Players included along with students from the University of Toronto. I was cast as the First Shepherd, Stafford Lawrence as the Second Shepherd, and Melwyn Breen as the Third Shepherd. Mavor played the role of a Herald, and Vincent Tovell was Joseph, Pegi Brown the Angel Gabriel, and Charmion King a Third Woman. Peter Mews and Jean Cruchet used their flair for comedy to good effect in the Wakefield Play. Dr. Healey Willan arranged the music and conducted the superb choir of the Church of St. Mary Magdalene, which contributed much to the beauty of this Yuletide offering.

We took a brief break between Christmas and New Year's, as did the Department of Biology. I had saved a little money so I decided to use that week to get an injection of theatre by visiting New York. My parents had taken me to the World's Fair there in 1939 and I had found the city's entertainment stimulating. I told Ralph Hicklin of my plan and he decided to go with me, a decision that I welcomed. He had to spend Christmas with his parents in Chatham, but we agreed to meet at Union Station in Toronto the day after Boxing Day. When he arrived carrying two suitcases he announced that he could not go because his father had not given him the money and he had none of his own. Travelling in 1946 was still under wartime controls and a Canadian visiting the United States was allowed only $100 to take out of the country. I had my $100 and a bit more. Ralph had none. There he was standing beside me looking forlorn. It crossed my mind that he could have phoned me to tell me he could not come, and it did occur to me that he had arrived at the station hoping to hear me say what I had now no choice but to say, "Very well. We'll go on my money, stay as long as it lasts, and then come home." He promised to repay me as soon as he could. I used my small emergency reserve supply of cash to purchase his return ticket to New York.

We stayed at the moderately priced Piccadilly Hotel and the first morning there we rushed out and bought tickets for all the shows we wanted to see over the next five days. This left us short of money for food, so we ate sparingly, mostly hot dogs and English muffins, known to New Yorkers as "British Bagels." With the money disappearing fast I worried that I would not be able to pay the hotel bill. One of the four renegades from the Village Players who joined the Civic Theatre, Beryl McMillan, was living in New York attempting to break into radio "soaps." I contacted her and borrowed $100, which I paid back via her father when I returned to Toronto. Fed up to our follicles with hot dogs, that evening Ralph and I dined in the hotel dining room listening to the "Three Sons" musical group. We thought this the height of sophistication.

But the food Ralph and I found most nutritious was the theatrical repast of the fare of Broadway and the embryonic "Off-Broadway" theatres, and we gorged ourselves on jazz in the clubs of 52nd Street. Those six days went all too quickly, but Manhattan's cornucopia of theatrical delights with superb acting, sets, and costuming made me dream of what our indigenous theatre in Canada should be and, I hoped, would be soon. I returned to Toronto with renewed enthusiasm for theatre itself and with increased zeal to do what I could to create a viable professional theatre at home.

Immediately after New Year's Day of 1947, I plunged back into acting for the NPS in James Bridie's comic allegory *Mr. Bolfry*, my last performance for the Society in its first year of existence. It had been a great success in London and our production was its North American premiere. The cast included Mavor Moore in the title role, and Frank Peddie, Pegi Brown, Babs Hitchman, Ruth Springford, myself as the intellectual soldier, and Michael Ney as his earthy sidekick. The ubiquitous grey drapes were once more used as the walls and it is to the credit of the designer, Murie Kelly, that the stage was a convincing room in a remote Highland Scots manse. The production proved to be a hit with both audience and critics. Frank Chamberlain wrote in *Radio World*, "Mr. Bolfry was the third production of the NPS that I have seen. Each one of them was better than 75 per cent of the plays produced at the Royal Alexandra."[8] Nat Cohen, a recent arrival from the Maritimes, raved in the *Canadian Jewish Weekly*, "If any doubts lingered about the important contribution which the New Play Society is making to the Canadian Theatre, they can now be dismissed. The Society's productions are of remarkably high standard, showing imagination, intelligence, and good taste."[9] And Rose Macdonald added her praise: "Another of the surprisingly polished performances which in the New Play Society's to date short existence have given it a remarkable prestige."[10]

By January, despite our artistic success, consistently favourable reviews, and a growing audience, Mrs. Moore's original investment of $2,000 had been used up, and a $1,448.30 deficit existed, of which $750 was owed to the Museum.[11] Nevertheless, she and Mavor decided to press on with a show a month into the spring of that year. In March, Fletcher Markle directed William Saroyan's *The Time of Your Life*. There were 22 characters but doubling was not required of any of the cast, which included John Drainie, Frank Willis, Alfie Scopp, Don Harron, Lorne Greene, Jane Mallett, Sandra Scott, and in the tiny role of a newsboy, George Luscombe, who some years later made his own unique contribution to Canadian theatre. The "radio crowd" were back with a vengeance, but Mrs. Moore, probably influenced by Mavor, realized that the NPS could not present quality shows without them. *The Time of Your Life* proved popular with the audience, but the next play received a mixed reaction. Ronald Duncan's masque, *This Way to the Tomb*, written in verse with musical accompaniment was somewhat too highbrow for the Toronto theatre public at that time.

Mavor Moore's rather free adaptation of Gogol's *The Government*

Inspector was the foreign entry. Because of the broadness with which it was played, I enjoyed it immensely but some purists of the Russian stage found it disturbing. Then came the Canadian offering for that season, *The Man in the Blue Moon* by Lister Sinclair. This play had even a larger cast than *The Time of Your Life*, with 36 named characters plus 11 crowd members. In a small role was an emerging young talent, Jerry Sarracini, who, amid a meteoric career, was murdered in New York. With the economic pressure on the theatre in the latter part of the 20th century, except for opera, ballet, and the mega-musicals, plays with such gargantuan casts have, unfortunately, become a rarity. The only way the NPS could stage such shows was to pay the actors nothing, or, at best, a small honorarium to make them feel that they were being recognized as professionals. Unfortunately, that led to resentment against the NPS and even against Dora Mavor Moore among some of the cast members who were not paid.

The season concluded in May 1947 with a visit by Les Compagnons de Saint-Laurent, an amateur company with professional standards from Montreal who brought two Molière plays, *Le Médecin Malgré Lui* and *Les Précieux Ridicules*. This was the first time a French-Canadian company of such stature had played in Toronto and they were invited because Mrs. Moore believed that there should be more links between our two major cultures.[12] Alas, I did not see this production because by then my regular job, which would be paying for my planned trip to Britain, demanded that I be in Algonquin Park.

But before I stopped working for the NPS, I had a chance to meet one of my theatre heroes. It was an event that bolstered my respect for the profession I had entered and gave me further incentive to travel to England. John Gielgud brought his superb company to North America with *The Importance of Being Earnest* and Congreve's *Love for Love*, both of which had been staged in London, England. The schedule was to have brush-up rehearsals for *The Importance* at the Grand Theatre, London, Ontario, perform it for a week there and then for a limited engagement at Toronto's Royal Alex before going to New York where *Love for Love* would be added for a brief season. The company would then play Boston and return with

Love for Love to the Royal Alex and the London Grand. The Canadian visit was backed by the Canadian lawyer and theatre buff, Brian Doherty, author of an internationally acclaimed play, *Father Malachy's Miracle*, which had been a success in both London and New York.

I do not recall how I met Brian, but by this time I knew him sufficiently well to ask his permission to watch the rehearsals in London, Ontario. He readily arranged it with the London Little Theatre, the amateur group that owned the Grand. I had been a fan of Gielgud's even before I saw him onstage. I had admired his performance in the film *Disraeli*, had read his autobiography, *Early Stages*, and every article about him in magazines and newspapers that I could obtain. For a decade or more he had been hailed as the Dean of Britain's classical actors. I was thrilled and considered myself privileged to be allowed to watch him onstage. In the Grand Theatre I sat with a friend from the Village Players, Eric Atkinson, who had become a lecturer at the University of Western Ontario. *The Importance* had a stellar cast: Gielgud as John Worthing, Robert Flemynge as Algernon, Margaret Rutherford as Lady Bracknell, Pamela Brown as Gwendolyn, Jean Cadell as Miss Prism, and Jane Baxter as Cecily. Mindful of the Victoria College rendition, I was eager to see how some of the cream of Britain's actors performed this classic. It proved to be a profound education.

The first thing that impressed me was the consistent style these actors brought to the play. All carried themselves as though they were stiffly corseted, including the men. All moved as though they were accustomed all their lives to wearing such clothing. All spoke the language beautifully, except for Robert Flemynge, who was inclined to a monotone and to throw his lines away. No one really touched each other physically until the end. Handshakes consisted merely of a touching of fingertips. During one interval in the first rehearsal, some ladies of the London Little Theatre asked Eric and me if we would get coffee for the cast from the adjacent ptomaine pit. We did so, and I was over-awed to be in the presence of these theatrical greats in the theatre's Green Room. I presented a paper cup of coffee to Pamela Brown who had fascinated me in the film *I Know Where I'm Going*, and to Margaret Rutherford who had killed me with laughter as

Madame Arcati in the film version of *Blithe Spirit*, and one to John Gielgud who politely said in his mellifluous tones, "No thank you." Also trying to be polite I meant to say something in reply like, "It is here for you if you want it." But what came blurting out was, "Well, I've got it for you so you might as well take it." Surprised and somewhat cowed, Mr. Gielgud replied graciously, "Oh, very well." I must have blushed 10 shades of scarlet. I could have cut out my tongue. What a dumb thing to say! And it was poisonous coffee to boot. Apparently he did not hold my social gaff against me because at the next interval he sat in the row of seats ahead of Eric and me and asked us about ourselves. This time I thought carefully before opening my mouth and asked him if he had liked the coffee "I forced on you?" He laughed and said, "Not really. I only took a sip, and that was enough." I felt greatly relieved.

Gielgud had played Worthing for innumerable performances in the '30s and '40s, yet he was still creating, still seeking ways to improve. For example, towards the end of the play when John Worthing has to look up the Christian names of his father, General Moncrieff, in the Army Lists, Gielgud eagerly mounted the ladder to the upper bookshelves, had a little difficulty in finding the book in which he searched frantically for the Ms, hurriedly read the names under M until he found Moncrieff, then with building vocal tension he read the ranks and dates of promotion, and finally came to the words "Christian names . . . ." Next, to add a little more suspense, he had difficulty turning the page and in irritation could only do so by wetting his fingers on his tongue. Then, when he succeeded, he read with a great sigh of relief "Ernest John!" Although Gielgud was the actual director of the play, he had an assistant to whom he then turned and asked, "Do you think that is too much?" Clearly, the difficulty in turning the page was a new bit of business he had just added. The assistant director replied, "No. It was just right." And, of course, it was. Gielgud's inspiration of the moment was apt, was introduced during a rehearsal, and affected no one but himself. The lesson for me was never let yourself grow stale in a role. Keep creating. But make sure that you have a sufficiently developed critical eye to tell you whether or not what you innovate fits and what effect it will have on the other actors. Innovation for the sake of innovation is pointless.

When the rehearsal was over, Eric and I left by the stage door. We found Gielgud, still in his white suit as John Worthing, pacing all alone behind the set. When he saw us he dashed over eagerly and asked us what we thought of the show. Eric managed to say something intelligent but I could only stammer, "Oh, Mr. Gielgud, it was just great." He thanked us for staying to watch and said that it helped them having someone to play to. If I had been a fan of his before that, I became an absolute devotee thereafter. I walked out of the theatre more convinced than ever that this was the profession I wanted to be in for the rest of my life. Some years later, when Gielgud was in Toronto performing his one man *tour de force, The Seven Ages of Man*, I met him by chance outside the Park Plaza Hotel where he was staying. By that time I had been to England and we had a mutual acquaintance we talked about. Later still, when he was playing in *Tiny Alice* on Broadway with Bill Hutt, I went backstage to see them both. When I went to Gielgud's dressing room I said to him, "I enjoyed your performance very much Mr. Gielgud, but I really don't understand what the play is all about." "Oh my dear fellow," he replied, "Neither do I." Such frankness is all too rare among actors. A remarkable actor! A remarkable man!

CHAPTER 5

Abroad

After 16 months of gainful employment I had had enough of working nine to five. I had saved approximately $1,000 and in the autumn of 1947 I decided to leave drearily conservative "Toronto the Good" and hie me to the art galleries, museums, theatres, and pubs in the city with almost 2,000 years of history: London, England. When I was a child I had seen pictures and brochures of the Canadian Pacific's gleaming fleet of white Empress liners. I decided to book passage on the Empress of Canada sailing from Montreal, which I soon learned was not the original — it had been sunk during the war — but one of CPR's three "Duchess" ships repainted and renamed. The "three drunken Duchesses," as they were nicknamed, had been built with U-shaped hulls which caused them to pitch and roll. Soon after leaving the Gulf of St. Lawrence we ran into a storm and I was so violently sea-sick I took to my bed for two of the seven days at sea.

We docked in Liverpool and following an uncomfortable train ride to London, I arrived at 5 a.m. at Euston Station lugging two heavy suitcases and groggy from lack of sleep. I staggered to a line of taxis and told a driver that I wanted to go to the Charing Cross Hotel. He refused to take me, and every other driver also refused. I wondered if I showed signs of some horribly infectious disease. Because of the fuel shortage they all wanted to take passengers in the direction of their own homes, which were mostly in London's east end. I then had my first experience of the English class system at work. One cab was already occupied by a well-dressed, mustachioed, middle-aged Englishman. When he saw my plight he ordered me to get in. Then in the imperious tone of at least a brigadier-general he commanded the cab driver, "You will drop me off first, then you will take this gentleman to his hotel." Confronted with such authority the cabby grumblingly complied. But once he had taken my benefactor to his home and received payment for that portion of the trip, he gave me a wild, high-speed ride along Bond Street, bounced over the curb at Piccadilly Circus and hurtled down the Haymarket to Charing Cross. After I paid him for the whole ride from Euston station, I barely got my bags out of the luggage space beside him when he took off a mile-a-minute. "Welcome to London," I thought.

Exhausted, I got to my mausoleum of a room and fell asleep immediately. Four hours later I awoke to the door handle rattling and the maid's voice saying: " 'Ere, this bloke's still asleep." Thinking I had broken some house rule by sleeping until all of 10 a.m., I got up, put a shilling in the heater to warm up the damp, frigid room and gave myself a sponge bath from the wash basin, there being no bath or shower. I then went downstairs for my first meal in Britain. At the entrance to the dining room there was a long buffet arrayed to entice any gourmand. But it was all artificial. My breakfast, served with great style, consisted of a piece of cold, unbuttered toast, a greasy sausage, and café-au-lait. I was quickly being introduced to austerity Britain. I was already homesick and depressed.

After breakfast I wandered onto the Strand and looked at the Victorian Gothic horror in which I was staying. The Charing Cross is a railway hotel built over the station during the hey-day of railway expansion in mid-19th century Britain. In its day it was probably the latest in comfortable convenience for travellers. When I first saw it, the building had been blackened from the soot of countless trains and the coal fires of London, and possibly even from the fire bombings of the war years. At first I thought, "How grim. What a sad sight." But as I studied its ornate facade and the cairn marking Charing Cross, I began to realize that this building revealed the enterprise and confidence of a by-gone era, and my interest in the past began to take over. As I walked toward Trafalgar Square my spirits lifted, and the sense of history overwhelmed me. There was Nelson's Column, the Admiralty Arch, and to the left Whitehall with its impressively solid government buildings. All around me was the visual representation of Imperial Britain. Beyond Nelson's Column was the National Gallery with its ridiculous pimple of a dome. Over there was Canada House and I felt not quite so alone. As I soaked in the atmosphere of old London, my morning's depression completely vanished. That day I wandered through the heart of the great metropolis discovering something new and intriguing at every turn. In the evening I returned to my hotel in far different spirits than when I had left in the morning. London had worked its magic on me.

Even the news from the desk clerk that I would have to vacate the room in three days did not dampen my elation, at least not at first. He informed me that there was to be a convention of dairymen in London and another of brewers at the same time and that the room was booked. I was under the impression that it had been reserved for me for two weeks allowing me time to find other accommodation. I showed the desk clerk the communication from the CPR stating that the room had been booked for two weeks. With great hauteur the clerk said that the agent must have been mistaken and that he regretted that I would have to leave in three days. That evening I began to phone other hotels. With growing concern I contacted 20 hotels including the Dorchester, the Savoy, and Grosvenor House — all beyond my purse, but I was desperate. All were booked solid. "Well," I thought, "I have relatives in West Ewell. I can contact them." I searched my luggage for my small address book. It was missing. I began to panic. I imagined myself having to sleep in the park, being arrested for vagrancy, and spending days, possibly weeks, in some dark Dickensian prison — Newgate or Wormwood Scrubs. The only person I knew in London was Gwen Dainty but her number was in my missing book.

The next morning I was about to take my problem to Canada House when I thought of one other person I knew, whose address, fortunately, was on a small piece of paper in my wallet. Clifford Baburam, a West Indian of Asiatic-Indian antecedents, had been one of the students at Algonquin Park that previous summer and had come to England to enrol in the London

School of Economics. I had no telephone number so I decided to travel out to his address in the suburb of West Acton with the hope that he might have a sofa I could doss on. I found my way on the tube to Princes' Gardens, a neatly boulevarded street with rows of Tudor-style houses, three to a semi-detached group. They were called "picture front houses" because they offered a charming facade that was quaintly Elizabethan with tidy front gardens surrounded by a low brick wall or a hedge, each with a wooden gate, and each with a leaded paned bay window at the front. But the sides and backs of the houses were plain stucco with ugly water and drain pipes running up the outside of the rear wall. I walked the quarter of a mile from the tube station and knocked at number 97. A short lady with a big smile and a cockney dialect opened the door. "Does Clifford Baburam live here?" I asked. "Well 'ee did until last Saturday when 'ee returned to Canada," she replied. Without showing any regrets at not seeing Clifford I asked eagerly, "Is his room available?" "Yes it is," she replied, "Two guineas a week including breakfast." I was shown into a moderately spacious downstairs front room which boasted the bay window, a table with two chairs in the bay, a large wardrobe, and two easy chairs by a fireplace containing a small electric heater. Against the wall opposite the fireplace was a single cot with cushions which served as both a sofa and a bed. The room was not luxuriously furnished but it was clean, had a pleasant view of the street and front garden, and looked comfortable. I took it immediately and moved in the next day. I have never seen nor heard of Clifford Baburam since, but I am very grateful to him for returning to Canada.

■

My landlord's name was Marlow, but as they were very open people, I soon learned that his real family name was Moskva and that they were both of Polish-Jewish extraction and were born in that section of east London known as Mile End. They were also active, enthusiastic, card-carrying members of the Communist Party. As a result of the war-time alliance with the Soviet Union, being a Communist did not have quite the same stigma it had prior to the war or was to have again after the Cold War began.

Although I had socialist leanings in common with most students of my generation, I had never read the writings of Marx or Engels and I had no strong opinion either for or against Communism. I had learned enough about the Soviet Union to know that Communism as practised there was repressive and imperialistic. I thought the Marlows were politically misguided, but I had no reservations about living with charming people who had a social conscience that they were expressing through the Communist Party. In 1947 that party had two Communist members of Parliament, Harry Horner from the Mid-lands and my landlady's brother-in-law, Phil Piratin, from Mile End.

Mr. Marlow was a barber and an erstwhile "bookie" who had been squeezed out, he claimed, "by the big boys." Possibly his failure as a capitalist entrepreneur in that highly risky business turned him toward Communism. But the Marlows' conversion was primarily due to another event. While the blitz was on in 1940–41, the children from the poorer sections of London were evacuated to country towns and villages. The Marlows' young son was chosen by a family that kept a loaded pistol in the house. The boy found it, played with it, and shot himself fatally. People are often driven to embrace extremism to alleviate grievances. The Marlows looked to Communism to eliminate "the exploitation of the masses by capitalist bosses" and "to eradicate the class structure in Britain." These were some of the catch phrases Mr. Marlow occasionally spouted at me. However, there seemed to be very little rabid fanaticism in his brand of Communism and a lot of inconsistency. Once I asked him what would happen to the Royal Family if the Communists took over. "Oh well," he replied, "We'd keep them. They're nice people." Hardly a Bolshevik approach. When the wedding of Princess Elizabeth to Prince Philip occurred, the Marlows were rivetted to their radio and were as enthusiastically royalist as any monarchistic Tory.

One evening when I was engaged in a chess game with my landlord in front of a warm coal fire in the grate of their dining-living room, Phil Piratin came to visit while his wife was in hospital having a baby. He was a short, stocky man with a massive round head like a pumpkin in which were set small round eyes that closed up when he laughed. With the brashness of a recent, know-it-all college graduate, I questioned him on the aims of the British Communist Party. He outlined an idealistic political and social philosophy that had a lot to do with the equality and brotherhood of man. With a cynicism not usually associated with the young, I stated that these goals were impossible of achievement because they overlooked a certain basic flaw in man's nature, namely greed. I then used a catch phrase I had heard somewhere. I said that the Communists were "rank idealists." His face went scarlet. If I had insulted his mother he could not have been more apoplectic. I thought the pumpkin head was about to explode. "Not so! Not so!" he shouted, "We are pragmatists! Out and out pragmatists! We believe these things can be achieved. Man will use his common sense and see the injustice of the present system." I was then subjected to a polemic on the evils of the capitalist system, with much of which I had to agree. After a few minutes he calmed down and gave me a smug, condescending smile that indicated that he was tolerant of the ill-informed opinions of the young. I decided not to pursue the subject any further. Soon his good humour returned and we chatted about other matters such as his concern about his wife and anxiety about himself as an expectant father. As he left he gave me a signed pass into the visitors' gallery of the House of Commons, which I was thrilled to have. But when I used it, to my horror, it was taken by a policeman. I have often wondered since then if I am on file with Scotland Yard, MI5, the RCMP, the FBI, and the CIA as being a friend of a British Communist MP.

Periodically the local Party Cell of the British Communist Party would meet in the Marlows' living room. The walls were paper thin and I could hear everything that transpired. There were only a handful of members, yet the meetings never ran smoothly. At least one person per meeting would storm out and swear never to play again. Individualism kept rearing its non-egalitarian head. I concluded that Communism did not have a hope with the British.

As part of Mr. Marlow's campaign to convert me to "the cause," I was taken several times to see performances at the Unity Theatre in the

St. Pancras area of London. This theatre had originally been established as a socialist, Labour Party theatre, but in the immediate post-war years had been taken over by the Communists. The first play I saw there was a translation of a contemporary Soviet original. It took place on a collective farm where the smooth running of this Kolkhoz was disturbed by the desire of two young lovers to leave to try a more independent life in the city. But a kindly, old, white-bearded professor persuades them to sacrifice their dreams for the greater good of the community. They are made to realize their selfishness and decide to remain. The plot was extremely simplistic and the characters were one dimensional, like the figures on a Soviet propaganda poster. Another presentation of the Unity Theatre was a staging of Constantin Simonov's *The Russian Question*. The setting was the editorial office of a Chicago newspaper. The plot, which has some basis in reality, dealt with the efforts of a reporter on that newspaper to report honestly about the Soviet Union. His stories were continuously suppressed or re-written by his boss. This play, if somewhat heavy-handed, was better written than the previous one, but the characterization of "the Boss" was portrayed in such an exaggerated manner that it ceased to be real and resembled a Crocodil cartoon version of an American tycoon. It was blatant propaganda, but, because it was what they wanted to hear, the audience lapped it up.

However, the Unity Theatre did not present only translations of Soviet propaganda plays. I saw a most moving production of a play by Miles Malleson and H. Brooks entitled *Six Men of Dorset* about the Tolpuddle martyrs — six farm labourers who were transported to Australia in 1834 for trying to form a trade union. There was such a hue and cry against this decision that two years later they were pardoned. Needless to say this play, powerfully acted, had an enthusiastic response from its pro-labour audience, including me. Not all serious, the Unity Theatre also staged a clever revue called *What's Left*. Several of the sets for the sketches were designed by John Osborne who shook the theatre world in 1956 with *Look Back in Anger*. Despite my reservations about the Unity Theatre's left wing message plays, I had to recognize that they performed an important function in post-war Britain. They presented another, balancing point of view — a democratic privilege that, ironically, they probably would not have enjoyed under the Communism they espoused. I had never been particularly politically conscious until I met the Marlows. While at university my only socio-political act had been to sign a petition organized by students nationally to free the Japanese-Canadians from internment camps. But the influence of the Marlows and the Unity Theatre created in me a new awareness even though I did not subscribe to their political philosophy. Later during the Cold War and the American paranoia about Communism, I knew from the example of the Marlows that, contrary to the general opinion, one could be a Communist and still be a good person.

Although the Marlows and I agreed to differ about Communism we remained good friends and they were very kind to me. The winter of 1947–48 was a severe one for Britain, which was suffering an acute food and fuel shortage. The American war-time lend lease policy had ended, and the Marshall Plan to rescue Europe from starvation, anarchy, and a possible Communist takeover had not yet begun. Rationing in Britain was in full force. Because I ate only breakfast at home, my ration coupons added to the Marlow's meagre food allotment. They would share their late night snack with me if I was visiting them in their living room, or Mrs. Marlow would bring a piece of cake or a pastry into my room for me. If I had been out of an evening, I would arrive home to find some goodie Mrs. Marlow had left on my table. The Marlows practised nothing of the Jewish faith or culture, and being Communists, were presumably atheist. They had two sons living, one of pre-school age and one in his early 20s who was in the Royal Air Force. The Marlows were British to the core, even royalist. They were proud of their own and their country's role in the war, and were hopeful for a happier, more prosperous future for themselves, their children, and their country — a country which they believed could be reformed through Communism. They made me feel that with them I had a home away from home.

■

As soon as I had settled in I began to pursue my real reason for being in England. Brian Doherty had given me five letters of introduction, one of which was to Virginia Vernon, then in charge of foreign correspondents for the *London Daily Mirror*. Born in New York, she was the daughter of theatre manager Joseph Brooks. She had studied singing in Europe and made her debut in London in 1912 with her godmother, the brilliant French chanteuse, Yvette Guilbert. After a career in opera and operetta, and as a non-singing actress, she married Frank Vernon, an English stage director. Virginia's career had faded by the time he died in 1933, so she took to writing novels of the Harlequin type for a living. During the war she became secretary to Basil Dean, the producer-director in charge of ENSA (Entertainments National Service Association), which organized entertainment for the armed forces. Brian had told me that she had many theatre contacts and could be very helpful.

I went to the *Daily Mirror* and sent in Brian's letter. The reply told me to come to her house at 1 Barton Street that evening. I turned up at the appointed hour in my best bib and tucker. Barton Street is a short S-shaped road just south of Westminster Abbey, lined with row houses, two rooms deep, three storeys high with the "buttery" (kitchen) in the basement. Built in 1722 for civil servants, these houses were not large but had become fashionable. John Gielgud lived just down the street. A rather demur, middle-aged female housekeeper ushered me into a small vestibule where I was warmly greeted by another lady of middle years, with iron grey hair done in mannish style, wearing a skirt suit with sensible shoes. When we entered the living room I was astonished to see that the walls and the ceiling were painted solid black. Seeing my wonderment Virginia explained that the house had once belonged to the Marchioness of Queensbury who was a spiritualist and held séances. In this depressingly sombre room, I momentarily expected some ectoplasmic manifestation or a horn to materialize. Instead, an elderly gentleman with a bristling moustache arose from a corner armchair. Brigadier Morgan, apparently a recent acquaintance of Virginia's, was visiting her to reminisce about a mutual friend who had died that year, Marie Belloc Lowndes, author of *The Lodger*. I had seen the movie starring Laird Cregar and was fascinated by the old gentleman's opinion about who Jack the Ripper really was. It was a great surprise to hear him expound the theory that Jack might have been the Duke of Clarence "who was quite mad, you know."

Apparently tiring of this conversation, Virginia switched the subject from Jack the Ripper to me, a much less fascinating topic but one which seemed to pique her curiosity more. She asked me several questions about myself, particularly about my theatrical experience. Then she abruptly dismissed the Brigadier by announcing that she was taking me to meet Claire Wallace who at the time had a gossip program on the CBC. We met her at the BBC Oxford Street studios where she had just finished a broadcast to Canada. Ms. Wallace advised me to contact Al Pearce who had left Andrew Allan's radio company and was performing in *Carissima* in the West End. Virginia promised to give me letters to various producers, including Basil Dean. Virginia exuded confidence and optimism from every pore and I left feeling distinctly more cheerful about my own chances of breaking into what had seemed to be a formidable theatrical fortress. My diary entry for that day, November 20, 1947, concludes with the statement that I felt so happy about meeting Virginia "that I treated myself to dinner at the Brasserie Universelle on Piccadilly Circus and left a whole shilling tip. Ghastly extravagance!"

After that I visited Virginia quite frequently, and often she would take me to see theatrical productions. On my second visit we went to the Arts Theatre Club for the opening of a revival of *The Moon on the Yellow River*, which boasted a strong performance from a young actor named Jack Hawkins. On several occasions I visited Virginia to find that she had distinguished guests. Once I found her comforting a very beautiful lady dressed in black, the widow of the late Air-Vice Marshall Cunningham, one of the architects of the Allied air-war over Germany, and who had been lost earlier that year in a plane crash off Bermuda. I felt privileged to be sent by Virginia the two blocks to Whitehall to fetch a taxi for Lady Cunningham. Of the many visits, two others stand out in my memory. She and I had planned to go to the Embassy Theatre in Swiss Cottage to see the Dublin Gate Theatre's production of Shaw's *John Bull's Other Island*. When I arrived at 1 Barton Street, Virginia and a friend were in great consternation over the genteel little housekeeper who was sprawled in an armchair, giggling merrily and obviously stewed to the gills. It seemed that she was periodically given to bouts of hysterical dipsomania. That day, while Virginia was at work, she had consumed a whole bottle of Virginia's best French brandy, and had started on a second. Eventually, with Virginia and her friend pulling and me pushing from behind we managed to get the housekeeper up the narrow stairs and placed her on her bed to sleep it off. When we returned downstairs Virginia introduced me to her helpful friend, Rebecca West. Virginia was furious because she had been completely taken in by her housekeeper. What annoyed her most was the loss of her best brandy. She vituperated with awesome alliteration: "I can't be bothered buggering about the bloody bitch if she is going to drink herself into a stupor on my best brandy!" Rebecca West departed and Virginia and I went to the theatre. When we returned we found that the sweet little housekeeper had come downstairs and had purloined a bottle of sherry, which Virginia found half empty beside her bed. "She goes straight to her mother's tomorrow," Virginia decided. While we were consuming the rest of the sherry, the housekeeper appeared on the staircase like Lady Macbeth in her white nightgown and asked Virginia if she had some luminal tablets, revealing her taste for variety. The next time I visited Virginia the tipsy housekeeper had been packed off and Virginia had hired a part-time cleaning woman. And she had locked up her liquor just in case.

Every month my mother would send me a food parcel. Most frequently I would share a portion of it with the Marlows, but several times I took half of it to Virginia. Although I knew that she had a very educated palate, so starved were they for meat in Britain in 1948 that even the tinned meatballs and ham I brought her were welcome. To reciprocate Virginia often invited me to tea and once invited me to dinner to meet her nephew Bobby. Bobby worked in an antique store (he might have owned it) and was house-sitting for John Gielgud who was in New York directing Judith Anderson in *Medea*. Because I told Bobby what a fan I was of Mr. Gielgud he asked if I would like to see inside his house. I jumped at the opportunity. When we entered the house, I learned that the plainness of the exterior belied the sumptuousness of the ground floor which was obviously a showroom like those in a furniture store or museum, meant to be looked at but not used. The decor was a work of art in itself. Everything harmonized. The chairs belonged to the period of one of the Louis and were upholstered in pink brocade with the wood painted white or cream with lots of gilt. Above the mantle was the first Dufy painting I had ever seen, which made me want to see more work by that cheerful artist. We passed through this room and mounted the stairs to the real living quarters on the second floor. Here was a comfortable lived-in room with a baby grand piano that occupied almost half of it. The walls were lined with bookshelves that reversed in sections to reveal Gielgud's extensive record collection. It was a cosy room that reflected a surprisingly modest lifestyle for such a successful actor and I was thrilled to be in the living room of one of my theatrical idols.

Another of the social contacts I made, but I cannot remember how, was with Mr. Barry Jones. He and Maurice Colbourne had brought their productions of the latter's play *Charles the King* and Shaw's *Geneva* to Canada in 1939. I had seen both at the Royal Alex and remembered them vividly. Mr. Jones was one of the aristocrats of the English theatre with a long and distinguished career onstage in England and North America and in films. Anyone who saw the Hollywood version of *War and Peace* will remember Barry Jones as the head of the Muscovite family. He invited me to tea in his charmingly modest house on Campden Hill Square where a rather gushy, vapid female who had something to do with writing for films was also in attendance. Barry Jones made me feel like an old friend. He served buckets of tea in cups the size of soup bowls, and while I listened fascinated, he held forth on a variety of topics. He told about the exciting trip to Canada in the autumn of 1939 when their ship was chased half-way across the Atlantic by the German warship Tirpitz, the predecessor of the Tirpitz that was sunk by British bombers in Tramso Harbour, Norway, later in the war. Once they had outrun their pursuer, they stopped to pick up survivors from the torpedoed liner Athenia. They had planned to leave Britain three weeks earlier but were not allowed to because of wartime travel restrictions. The company reached Toronto just in time for the opening at the Royal

Alexandra but with no time to rehearse the local supers recruited to play soldiers in this epic about Charles I and Cromwell. Nor was there time to fit them properly into costumes, which had been packed away in crates for over three weeks. It was after this first performance in Toronto that B.K. Sandwell, who used the pseudonym Lucy Van Gogh, published in *Saturday Night* his succinct criticism that "the play stank." Possibly the shambles of opening night warranted such a comment, but I saw the play later in the run, and it impressed me as being a well-acted historical drama. But then I was only 16 years old and easily impressed. According to Jones, this review had an adverse influence on the box office all across Canada. When the tour was over, once again because of wartime priorities, they had to abandon most of their scenery and technical equipment. He told me that much of the lighting on the stage of the Royal Alex really belonged to his and Maurice Colbourne's production company. When I suggested that now with the war over he should try to get the equipment back, he exclaimed, "What? And pay all that storage?"

After two huge cups of tea, Mr. Jones served rum cocktails. I imbibed two while I continued to be absorbed in his observations on such subjects as the bombing scare in San Francisco after the Japanese attack on Pearl Harbor; New York's single air-raid siren in December of 1941; mixed comments on Kit Cornell; the frivolous, expensive parties the Labour Party, which he detested, held at Claridge's; and the sad state of the country. Said Barry Jones, "What we need in this country is an inspired leader. We have him, poor old dear. He's 73 now and we can't expect much more of him. Even Lord Woolton might do. Anything would be better than these amateurs." He probably split himself in ecstacy when Churchill and the Tories were returned to power a few years later. After I left Barry Jones, I walked about among the common folk in Piccadilly Circus and Leicester Square to wear off some of the faded aristocratic purple and gold before I donned my red cockade to return to the proletarian haven of the Marlows.

People who move to another country have a natural tendency to seek the companionship of friends from the homeland. I sought out Gwendolyn Dainty and we renewed our acquaintance as soon as she returned from performing on a tour of the north country. During her brief sojourn in Canada after the war, she realized that there was a lamentable lack of professional opportunity there, so she returned to the theatrical excitement of London. Gwen proved a most entertaining, if sometimes overwhelming, companion. She was a buxom, happy, ebullient young lady who was prone to doing things on the spur of the moment. This unpredictable behaviour gave a certain suspense to any date with her. Underneath the arches of Charing Cross Station near the Thames embankment was The Players' Club. This was a type of cabaret where performers went to sing and dance as a showcase for themselves between engagements. Often the club was patronized by very distinguished actors, producers, and celebrities from other walks of life. One who visited on occasion was Princess Margaret who would drop in with friends to spend some diverting and relaxing hours, quite often a-glow with high spirits. Gwen Dainty decided to perform at the club and I was invited to attend. For the occasion she changed her name to Dante, donned her version of a French-Canadian Habitant costume, and impressively sang "Alouette" in bare feet.

Gwen was a friend of that splendid actress, Barbara Davis, later known as Barbara Chilcott. One day I was suddenly surprised to find myself invited to a roast beef dinner at the apartment in Hammersmith that she shared with an opera singer, Laura "Cookie" Hamilton, a female ballet dancer from Winnipeg, Lillian Lewis, a male dancer also from Winnipeg, Paddy Stone, and another male dancer, Irving Davies, from Wales. Mr. Stone was dancing the role of the Indian Chief in *Annie Get Your Gun* at the time. Later he would divide his life between dancing and choreographing in London and for the Royal Winnipeg Ballet. It was very generous of them to share their treasure of a roast of beef with me. How they managed to acquire it I never asked. I assumed they had saved their ration coupons for months. I was made most welcome and for the first time I began to feel part of a community of London performers. I was bowled over with Barbara's sultry beauty. But there were not many plays being produced in London that could use her particular quality. However, she did obtain a job as understudy to Polly Rowles and Eugenie Delarova in *Dark*

Eyes, and got the opportunity to perform impressively at a matinee that I attended. Fortunately for Canadian theatre she eventually returned home where she has been a power on the stage ever since. It is delicious irony that a few years later J.B. Priestley wrote *The Glass Cage* especially for Barbara and her brothers, Murray and Donald Davis, in which Barbara returned to the West End as a star.

I became friends with two other Canadians, Shirley Kerr and Kay Hawtrey, while I was in England. Kay had been fortunate in landing a job at her cousin's theatre, The Embassy, in the Swiss Cottage area of North London. Kay eventually returned to Canada where she built a successful career as a character actress in film, television, and on the stage. Television viewers will know her from the *Road to Avonlea* series. Shirley Kerr was a pert, diminutive, cheerful but reserved young lady whom I thought was too self-effacing for the cut and thrust of theatrical competition. She found her niche back in Vancouver where she married a Mr. Hunter and had an important career as a wife and mother. Other expatriate Canadians whom I met in London who were helpful to me with advice were George Patton, erstwhile with the Earle Grey Players, and Al Pearce who gave me some insight into the way the West End theatre operated, and how the producers regarded all Canadians as Americans.

■

While actively seeking work, I was also being a tourist. Sometimes both interests could be indulged simultaneously as when I travelled as far north as Dundee, Scotland, to meet A.R. Whatmore of the Dundee Repertory Theatre. On that trip I spent a week in Edinburgh taking in its impressive history. I combined my visit to relatives in Lowestoft with inquiries about my chances of acting at the Sparrow's Nest Theatre where my father's first wife had worked in the box office. I wrote to 40 repertory theatres throughout the United Kingdom and received replies from most of them, all of which were negative. Some held out hope for the future, but most replied that they seldom staged American plays, despite the fact that I wrote in all my letters of application that I had played English roles in Canada, had been trained by English people, and did not sound North American when I spoke.

The most encouraging reply was from Peter Potter, the "producer," to use the English term, of the Guildford Rep. In November of 1947 I travelled down to Guildford to meet him. Mr. Potter was a handsome, youngish man who had been wounded in the war and walked with a limp. He was most gracious and gave me a complimentary ticket to see his production of *The Rivals*, which he said was not very good, but which impressed me favourably. He told me that there might be some hope of my joining the company after Christmas. To survive in the entertainment world one must condition oneself against perpetual disappointments. I returned in January to see a production of a new play, *The House Is Dark*, and Peter Potter and his wife took me to dinner where he told me that he had resigned from the Guildford Rep. Some years later he was brought to Canada to direct a play for the Crest Theatre and we renewed our acquaintance briefly. I was able to repay his generosity by taking him to dinner. I regret that I never got the opportunity to work with a director who had shown more consideration than most. Soon after returning to England, he died.

One of my letters of recommendation from Brian Doherty was to Martin Browne, producer of the Mercury Theatre in the Notting Hill Gate area of London. Mr. Browne was renowned for producing T. S. Eliot's *Murder in the Cathedral*, and I had heard that he was planning a revival of it. I contacted him and he agreed to audition me. As an audition piece from Eliot's play I had learned Becket's speech that begins, "Now is my way clear, now is the meaning plain." When I delivered it Mr. Browne was impressed with the interpretation but said, "As for the accent, you have all the vowel sounds correctly, but you do not stress the line as my English actors do. I suggest you take some speech lessons." Whereupon he gave me the name of a speech teacher. I was not sure what the difference would be between my way and the English-bred actors' way of saying Mr. Eliot's lines, but I had noticed that many English actors had the annoying pattern of stressing the early part of a sentence and letting the end trail off into inaudibility. Or was it the kind of delivery of other English actors who spoke everything in a monotonous monotone? If it was either of these lazy types of speech, I figured I could achieve that without taking lessons. I suspected that he really wanted to help his friend the teacher earn some money. Nevertheless I decided to follow his suggestion and contacted Norma Davis, an actress and speech teacher sometimes employed by J. Arthur Rank to teach his film starlets how to speak their own language. She charged me a guinea a lesson, and I learned very little from her, but she was a delightful person, had a charming little flat — always with a cosy fire in the grate — and always served me tea and crumpets. It was an expensive afternoon tea. I took one lesson a week from her for four weeks, at the end of which she told me that to take any more money from me would be unfair because I would pass for an Englishman any day. However, I continued working with her for another month because I figured I needed the vocal exercises. Besides, the tea was awfully good and she was generous with the crumpets.

The letter on my behalf from Brian to Kitty Black, casting director of H.M. Tennent Ltd., magically opened the door to that theatrical sanctum. She interviewed me but someone more important came into her office and I was asked to leave with the promise that I would hear from her. Shortly thereafter I received a call to meet Kitty Black's assistant, Daphne Rye, at the Globe Theatre on Shaftesbury Avenue. When I arrived Ms. Rye was on the stage with about 20 people. When it came my turn she was surprised that I sounded so English and asked me if I could be more American. I immediately tried to find my way back to a more Canadian dialect. I must have succeeded because she told me that they were planning a London production of John Van Druten's *I Remember Mama* early in 1948 and she promised to notify me when they would be auditioning for that show.

In the meantime Virginia Vernon had contacted Kay Bradley, manager of the tiny New Lindsay Theatre at 4 Notting Hill Gate, on my behalf. Robert Henderson, who had directed many of the shows I had seen in summer stock at the Royal Alexandra, was now producing at the New Lindsay and Kay Bradley said that she would speak to him about me. Despite her encouraging words, nothing came of that. But Ms. Bradley did arrange an interview for me with the producer-manager Henry Sherek for a part in a Swedish play called *Frenzy*. There were three people in Sherek's office when I arrived: Sherek himself, the director of the play, and a portly, youngish man with a clammy handshake who turned out to be Peter Ustinov. Although for the previous 10 years he had been making his mark in the theatre, at the time Mr. Ustinov's name meant very little to me. Since then I have become a great fan. Who hasn't? I was asked if I would be interested in a small part as a Swedish student in the play, which was to tour for six weeks before opening at the Lyric Theatre. I said, "Yes," and was told to go for a further interview to a theatre on Shaftesbury Avenue a few days later. When I turned up for that interview I went onto the stage to find that the stage lights prevented me from seeing who was in the audience. But the director, Mr. Macdonald, came down to the footlights and chatted privately with me. When I told him I was Canadian he was very surprised and said, "You have very little accent." Apparently my speech classes with Norma Davis were having some result. He then asked me why I had come to England? "To obtain experience in repertory companies," I replied. "Well," he said, "We could use you as a student. We need blondes. But is that what you want? Do you realize that you could be sitting in the classroom scene for months, possibly a year, without a line to say. Is that what you want? If you have come all this way to get rep experience, don't be sidetracked. Go after it." Because I had been in Britain only about two months, was still financially solvent, and because I had not yet contacted all the repertory companies, I felt independent enough to accept Mr. Macdonald's advice. Faced with the depressing prospect he had outlined, I said, "Thank you, Mr. Macdonald, I think you're right." I bent down, shook his hand over the footlights, and departed. When I got out onto the street I was immediately overwhelmed with doubt.

"You fool," I thought. "It would mean at least a couple of months' work with a regular weekly salary." I also thought that during the time I would meet more people who might be helpful and I would have more time to find out how the system worked. Repertory experience could be picked up later. But it was too late. I had cooked my goose so far as being in *Frenzy* was concerned. Had I known then what a brilliant actor Peter

Ustinov is, I probably would have jumped at the chance of being in the same show with him, if only in a silent capacity. But was it poor judgement? In the long-run I really don't think so.

Before I left Canada, Brian Doherty had told me he was going to sponsor the Canadian portion of the Dublin Gate Theatre tour planned for North America in 1948. He asked me to see their productions at the Embassy Theatre in London and write reviews that I would send to him to be published in the Toronto weekly *Saturday Night*. Virginia Vernon and I attended the Gate's presentation of *John Bull's Other Island* and neither of us thought highly of the production. Nor was I thrilled with *The Old Lady Says No*, although I was impressed with the lighting and with Michael MacLiammoir, who, despite laryngitis gave a brilliant performance as the Irish patriot, Robert Emmet. The London critics thought even less of these productions than I did. I decided I could not in all honesty write reports of these two plays that would be helpful to Brian at the box office. Instead I decided to interview Hilton Edwards and Michael MacLiammoir, the co-founders of the Gate Theatre, and send the interview to Brian to be published or not as he saw fit. After several phone calls a meeting was arranged in the lounge of the Embassy Theatre. Hilton Edwards did most of the talking in his plummy voice. Both were very co-operative and I made copious notes. On a borrowed portable typewriter I hammered out a history of the Gate Theatre and sent it off to Brian. I heard nothing from him as to whether or not the article was acceptable, or even an acknowledgement that he had received it. But a friend in Toronto wrote me that an article had appeared in *Saturday Night* about the history of the Dublin Gate Theatre under Brian Doherty's name. Naturally I wondered if it was my article. I decided not to confront him about it and shrugged it off as repayment for the letters of introduction he had given me. Nor did I ask him about it on the many occasions I met him in subsequent years.

At the end of January of 1948, Daphne Rye made good her promise and a notice was sent to me from the office of H.M. Tennent to appear for an audition the following day at the Globe Theatre for *I Remember Mama*. I was extremely excited about this audition because I greatly admired the play. I had seen it either on Broadway or on tour at the Royal Alex and I had read it in John Gassner's anthology, *Best Plays of the Modern American Theatre*. Mady Christians, who had made a tremendous success of the role of Mama in New York, was to star in and direct the London production. I knew the major roles had been cast by Van Druten the previous summer, but there were a few minor roles still open. I arrived at the theatre at my appointed time of 11 a.m. to find about 40 actors waiting in the wings, among whom was Norma Davis. These people were of a wide age range and were all blondes. My heart sank, but I waited. I had decided that if anything came of this audition, my quest for repertory experience would have to be postponed. There was a procession of actors onto the dazzlingly lit stage. Not one auditionee spoke, and the only voice, which I presumed was Mady Christians's, came from the dark depths of the auditorium. All it said was "Thank you" if the person onstage was male, or "Thank you, darling" if female. Nobody read from the play nor dared suggest doing an audition piece for her. Nothing but a silent parade of male and female blondes. "This is like a flesh market," I thought.

An hour and a half later, when it came my turn, I walked onto the stage clutching my copy of Gassner's anthology and said "I would like to read for the part of the doctor." A deadly hush descended on the actors waiting in the wings, and there was a beat before a rather surprised voice from the abyss of the theatre replied, "You are a little young." "Yes," I replied, "but I have often played character parts as old as 60." (When I was 25, 60 seemed to me to be very old.) "Oh, very well," the disembodied voice said. "Stage Manager, would you read with this gentleman?" The stage manager emerged from the wing in considerable dismay. "I just have to get a copy of the play," he stammered and disappeared back into the stage left area where I could hear him asking if he could borrow a copy from one of the auditionees. When he re-appeared he was quite flustered. I read the role of Dr. Johnson while the stage manager stumbled through the speeches of the other characters in the scene. I lowered my voice to get more maturity, and switched to my Canadian dialect. When the scene was finished to my great surprise and delight, the voice said, "Thank you. Come Monday." The stage manager told me to be at the Piccadilly Theatre the following Monday at 2:15 p.m. for a reading of the play. Norma Davis congratulated me. "You're in," she said, "Good for you." I walked out of the theatre dazed but feeling 10 feet tall. I was tempted to wire home that I was in a West End show, but decided to wait until I could find out what part I would be playing. I could hardly wait until Monday rolled around.

When I arrived at the Piccadilly Theatre, Mady Christians welcomed me and made me feel accepted. I was introduced to the general manager of H.M. Tennent, Hugh Beaumont, known in show business as "Binkie." I was thrilled to meet that powerful actor with the rumbling voice, Frederick Valk, who was to play Uncle Chris. I was told that I would not be playing Dr. Johnson, but would be an orderly who crossed the stage carrying a tray of dressings. However, I was also told that I would be understudying other characters. Naturally I was disappointed, but I consoled myself with the thought that I might occasionally get a chance to play one of the major roles. With the exception of Ms. Christians and Mr. Valk, the rest of the company were unfamiliar to me. Some of the smaller supporting roles had not yet been cast, which stirred hope in me that I might corral one of those. With this bait dangling in front of me, when I was asked at the reading to substitute for Gerard Heinz who had been cast as Papa but who was absent because he was filming, I readily agreed. I tried for a lower vocal characterization to impress everyone that I could sound more mature than I looked. I listened carefully to Ms. Christians's accent and tried to imitate it. After the first read through Ms. Christians seemed satisfied. Mr. Beaumont left without any comment, and I left the theatre still uncertain as to what I would be playing and understudying, but happy that I had been accepted by Mady Christians and the other actors as one of them.

The next day I continued to read the role of Papa. That day I had lunch with Frederick Valk, Adrienne Gessner (Aunt Trina), and Lilly Kann (Aunt Jenny). I was startled to hear Valk compliment me on my voice and my reading. The ladies agreed and my ego received a much needed boost. That afternoon and the next morning I read with increased confidence. When we broke for lunch on the third day I asked the stage manager if he knew yet what I would be understudying. He said that he would find out and let me know that afternoon. At the conclusion of that day's rehearsal, the stage manager came to me in great embarrassment. "I have a sad task to perform," he said. "The front office has decided that all the walk-ons should be older men to understudy the older men. I am sorry to have to tell you that there is nothing for you in this show after all."

Stunned, I looked at Mady Christians who was picking up her script from the table. She had heard what the stage manager had said and she blushed scarlet. The other actors had left the stage and she quickly followed them without a word. Now it all became clear. Gerard Heinz was to be present the next day. I no longer would be needed to stand in for him. I was not a member of British Actors' Equity and consequently had no protection from this kind of exploitation. There would be no payment for the time I had spent substituting for Mr. Heinz. When I realized how I had been used, I began to fume inside. I told the stage manager that I was going to see Mr. Beaumont. He replied that Mr. Beaumont was expected backstage at any moment. I waited in the stage left wing, pacing furiously. After a few minutes "Binkie" appeared stage right, saw me, turned on his heel and disappeared into the darkness. By the time I had crossed the stage he had vanished completely. His avoiding me confirmed that I had been used deliberately, and this made me even more angry. I started to follow him up the aisle of the theatre when a cautionary thought intervened. I remembered the *Ah, Wilderness!* incident and my angry, impetuous letter to Andrew Allan. I thought, "Should I storm into H.M. Tennents' office and tell them what I think of them?" Then I also thought, "If I do so it is more than likely that I will never work for Tennents either in London or the 14 repertory theatres they control throughout the country. Better think carefully." I left the theatre in an emotional fog, seething with anger, disappointment, and chagrin. I did not snap out of my daze until I realized that I had walked, oblivious of my surroundings, all the way from Shaftesbury Avenue to the Victoria and Albert Memorial in Knightsbridge. There was only one thought that slightly cheered me. I thanked my unlucky star that I had not wired home that I was in a London show.

This incident determined me to seek some protection against exploitation by obtaining an agent. Norma Davis went to bat for me and persuaded Miriam Warner to take me on. Ms. Warner had a small office several flights up in a dingy Victorian building on Cambridge Circus. My inexperience of the London entertainment world prevented my judging whether or not she would be a useful agent, but I was in no position to choose. She was encouraging and we worked out a fair agreement that obligated me to pay commission only on those engagements for which she had submitted me. If I found employment on my own no payment to her would be required. However I soon found that her theatrical contacts were not exactly top drawer. She arranged an audition for *No Orchids for Miss Blandish* that was to tour the country. After I left her office I discovered in a bookstore a pocket edition of the novel from which the play had been adapted. I bought it and read it that night. My agent had told me that it had been very popular with the troops during the war, which did not say much for the literary taste of the average soldier. It was an Englishman's fictionalized interpretation of a sexually sadistic shocker based on the American Ma Barker and her sons who went on a criminal rampage terrorizing Appalachia and the south-eastern United States in the 1930s. For me it had no redeeming features whatever. I decided that it would do me no good to have this play on my credits, so I missed the audition. I did not see the stage version at that time, but a third-rate movie was made of it in England starring the American "B" movie actor, Jack La Rue, and, although it had been considerably toned down from the novel, it was still an abomination.

One day Ms. Warner sent me to audition for a production of *Diamond Lil* that Mae West was going to stage in London. With some misgivings I wandered into the backstage of the theatre where the auditions were being held and found myself surrounded by a dozen or so muscle men all flexing and pumping. Feeling like Casper Milquetoast about to have sand kicked in his face I realized that this was no place for me. Apparently the director felt the same way because he took one look at me and said, "Don't waste my time." I slunk away feeling very insignificant with growing doubts about my agent. During the rest of my stay in Britain she never sent me for any more auditions. I suppose she gave up on me as a bad investment. I was beginning to feel that way about myself.

■

The optimism that had sustained me during my first two months in London had faded by the end of January 1948. As the grey sunless days stretched on week after week, and as the atmosphere both inside and outside my room became more and more damp, I became more and more depressed. I found escape from my doldrum by attending the theatre and concerts and in the companionship of those few friends I had made in London, particularly that of Gwen Dainty, whose incurable optimism was like a tonic to me. But all of a sudden two people re-entered my life who lightened the gloom.

One mid-winter afternoon, as I was entering the then grimy Westminster Abbey, whom should I meet but Elise Bernard, the actress-balletomane from Toronto. She let out a whoop of recognition that threatened to shatter the stained glass: "My dear boy, what the hell are you doing here?" We embraced affectionately and I explained that I had come to England to seek my fame and fortune in the theatre. When I in turn asked her what she was doing in London she explained, "Oh my dear boy, I'm married again. To the most marvellous piece of English mutton. I met him coming out of a crypt. We are an idyllic twosome in a flat in Ealing Broadway." When I told her that I lived in the next borough, West Acton, she insisted that I visit them. Curious to meet this piece of English mutton, I did so. It was a snug, cosy flat if unimaginatively furnished, but a great improvement for Elise over her one room bed-sitter on Charles Street in Toronto. It boasted a television set, the first one I had seen in a private home. As I observed the room I noticed that part of the furnishings was a roly-poly elderly gentleman watching the "tely." He was amiable enough but I got the impression that he did not care if I was there or not just so long as his TV viewing was not interrupted. He had retired and, much to Elise's annoyance, his only activities seemed to be eating, sleeping, and TV watching. He tolerated me and I became a frequent visitor. It was a novelty for me to watch television and

I particularly enjoyed BBC specials such as a memorable *King Lear* starring the up-and-coming Harry Andrews.

The other person who had a cheering effect on me was Joseph Royal O'Sullivan, the clever director of *Quality Street*. He was on a London holiday and was a guest of Elise and her tubby hubby. Because of my conservative nature, in Toronto Joseph's flamboyance was something I could tolerate only in small doses. But in London he was less conspicuous and was certainly more accepted. Variety among friends makes life more intriguing and we met quite frequently during his stay. The last I had seen of him was in Toronto towards the end of the war just before he departed for Hollywood. There he had run afoul of American Immigration and had undergone the trauma of being shipped back to Canada in a trainload of prisoners being moved from Alcatraz to penitentiaries in the eastern United States. During part of the journey he had been chained to a hatchet murderer. It had been a journey of terror and when he eventually got to Canada he had to go to a friend's cottage in Muskoka to recover. His story received wide newspaper coverage in Toronto at the time. I was very happy to see him in London with his irrepressible I-am-what-I-am defiance restored. On the day we met we decided to have high tea at the Piccadilly Hotel. In those days of rationing, each customer was restricted to one plate of four tiny sandwiches, but by smiling oh so demurely and fluttering his eyelashes at the waiter, Joseph managed to obtain a second plate for both of us. For a few weeks Joseph was a welcome breeze blowing away some of my mid-winter blues.

When Joseph had been at Elise's flat for three weeks, the piece of English mutton showed that he could be a ram and turfed Joseph out. Elise took to her bed in a dramatic swoon for three days, while the ram returned to docility, soothed by his TV. Joseph shortly returned to Toronto. The last time I saw him was several years later in the CBC canteen on Jarvis Street but after that I regret I completely lost track of him. This Ariel had cheered me during some of my more depressed moments in that dreary London winter.

▪

By late February I had not yet obtained employment with a repertory company and my financial reserves were dwindling. The thought of returning to Canada without at least one British stage performance was too defeatist to contemplate. I decided to take advantage of an offer by Billi and Philip Tyas, two supportive friends the reader will remember from the Village Players and Civic Theatre days. They had told me that if I needed any financial assistance in England to call on them. Much of the original $1,000 I had saved had been consumed by the boat fare and by the necessity of eating my evening meal in restaurants. I had also left a portion of that money with my father to pay for my return passage if that became necessary. I sent the Tyas's an SOS. The response was immediate. Phil would send me $200 a month up to $1,000. Although Billi and Phil said this money was a gift, I looked upon it as a loan and determined to repay them. It was many years before I could afford to do so.

With the financial worry temporarily removed, I decided to change my story in my letters of application. As a result of my sessions with Norma Davis, I knew that I sounded as British as the Brits, so I wrote that I was an Englishman who had been in Canada through the war years, had only recently returned to England, and was seeking a career in the theatre of my motherland. I worked out a false biography for myself and wandered through a private boys school in Ealing Broadway so that I could describe the school I had attended before being sent to Canada as a war refugee. I had some new photographs made by the famous theatre photographer, Landseer of London, and revamped my audition material to be more suitably English.

Shortly after I had begun to pass myself off as a Britisher, Billi and Phil arrived in London with a huge trunk load of food. They saw the hilarious comedy *The Happiest Days of Your Life*, starring Margaret Rutherford, and wishing to share their culinary largesse with actors, they invited the cast to their suite at the Mount Royal Hotel for a feast. On the appointed night I was the only guest present. None of the cast showed up. The Tyas's were greatly disappointed. Not wanting to see the food wasted, I telephoned Gwen Dainty about the situation. Within half an hour at least 10 starving actors had arrived, including Gwen, and were busy tucking away ham, breast of turkey, and assorted other delicacies. It developed into a wonderful party and Billi and Phil were delighted. The Tyas's planned to spend some time in Paris and generously offered to take me with them. I refused, in part because I did not want to be further indebted to them, and also because I wanted to see if the new "English" me would bring results. It did. While they were in Paris, I received an invitation for an interview with the Amersham Rep. Masquerading as an Englishman had paid off!

Amersham is a charming community in the Chiltern Hills north-west of London. It exemplified my romantic concept of an English country town: Miss Marple country — beautiful, traditional, quaint, sedate. It boasted a small repertory company run by Sally Latimer and Caryl Jenner. They were a "pair" or, as people now say euphemistically, "an item." Sally was very pretty and very feminine. Caryl was very plain and very masculine. Sally was spotlessly clean; Caryl had dirty fingernails, dirty clothes, and her teeth looked as though she had never heard of a toothbrush. She was lean, with a cadaverous face and dressed in men's clothes. I was interviewed by both, but Caryl was obviously the boss. She did most of the directing while Sally confined herself to acting, at which she was very good.

The Amersham Repertory Theatre operated all the year round, and I was offered the job of replacing some of their actors who would be taking summer holidays. Amersham worked an exchange feature with the Guildford Rep., so shows would run for two weeks instead of one, more like North American stock than true repertory fashion. The offer from Caryl meant that I would have a summer's work in circumstances that would allow me to test myself against experienced English actors in the pressure-cooker of stock with only two weeks to rehearse. I readily agreed even though I would have to join British Equity and earn only the Equity minimum, the equivalent of $18 Canadian a week.

When Billi and Phil returned from Paris they attended the annual Royal Garden Party given in the grounds of Buckingham Palace for visitors from the Colonies and Dominions. Although they already had a small daughter in Canada, they had applied to adopt a British war orphan, and had just received word the day of the garden party that they had permission to adopt a boy. To celebrate these twin events, they invited me to dinner and arrived at my humble abode in a Bentley limousine with liveried chauffeur. Mrs. Marlow and the neighbours, who had peeked out from behind their lace curtains, were all agog. As soon as I entered the car I told the Tyas's my good news about Amersham. I felt that their financial assistance to me was now going to be justified. We three had a lot to celebrate that day and we enjoyed a jolly evening at a restaurant in Soho where we sat at a table next to that massive British character actor, Francis L. Sullivan, and derived as much pleasure watching him tuck away his food as we did from our own. The Tyas's visit to England, my good fortune in obtaining work, the arrival of spring, the return of the sun, and the blossoming of the cherry trees down the boulevard of Prince's Gardens all contributed to transforming gloomy, grimy London into a city of beauty for me.

The Amersham Repertory Players had been founded on a shoestring in 1936 by Sally Latimer and had endured several financial crises. But by 1948 they were well supported by the townspeople and firmly established as a non-profit venture in The Playhouse, a tiny theatre in the heart of town. Attached to it was a small tea room operated by a very butch, middle-aged lady with iron grey hair cut in a Buster Brown style who owned a smelly, bad-tempered Bedlington terrier. She was a very brusque individual to be serving the public. Fortunately I had little to do with her except to order an occasional cup of tea or coffee and a fly-blown gateau. The dog hated everyone except its mistress, and I hated it back. However, the actors in the company were not hateful and made me feel welcome. Caryl Jenner proved to be as beautiful a person on the inside as she was unprepossessing on the outside. She was a very sensitive director, treated me kindly, and was a great help to me in my roles that summer.

I approached my first part with some trepidation. It was the major role of the Nobleman in Ashley Dukes's comedy-melodrama, *A Man with a Load of Mischief*. The Nobleman does not appear for the first seven pages, but once in he launches into lengthy speeches, one of which is a page and a half, interrupted only briefly by his manservant. After his first entrance, he leaves the stage only for short periods. It was a role I relished, requiring hauteur, panache, and variety to prevent the character from becoming a crashing bore. The play is set in Regency England, an age of elegance before the clammy hand of Victorian Puritanism. My costume was particularly elaborate, with a high stand-up collar that tended to keep one's head upright. I also had a quizzing glass, which I tried to use sparingly. A lot was riding on this role. If I faltered, the rest of the summer's work could disappear and I would be unable to claim Amersham as a credit in seeking other employment. I had notified my parents and friends in Canada that at last, after eight months, I had a job, and they would want to hear how it all turned out. I had to succeed.

Just prior to the first performance I had a severe attack of nerves, but once onstage I relaxed, and after I had finished the opening soliloquy I began to enjoy myself as the conniving villain of the piece. After the final curtain on opening night, I was moved that the rest of the cast made a point of congratulating me and that Carol and Sally were pleased, and I was delightfully surprised that Barbara Davis, Shirley Kerr, and Gwen Dainty had travelled all the way from London for my first performance in England. I will never forget the effect the three of them, gorgeously dressed in Dior's "New Look" gowns, had on me and the other men in my dressing room when they appeared at the door. My stock went up several notches. That night, all the way back to London on the train with these three charming ladies, I was on cloud nine.

At last my career as a British actor had been launched. I had held my own with experienced actors in a British repertory company. When I joined British Equity I had decided to change my name. I had never liked Vernon as a Christian name. It was too easily corrupted in the school yard to "Vermin." Parents should think of these things when they name children. But I thought it made a good surname, so I took my father's first name, Charles, to become Charles Vernon. I concluded that my new name along with my newly acquired English background had brought a change in my luck.

I had determined to be word perfect as the Nobleman, with no paraphrasing whatever. I went through the heavy schedule of performances flawlessly until the final moments of the final show in Amersham. The performance week ran from Tuesday through Saturday with two performances on Wednesday and Friday and three on Saturday. As the last performance drew to a close and I was just congratulating myself on this marathon achievement, I blew my fourth to last line. It was spoken to the maid and should have been, "It shall be made worth your while. Here is my purse, girl. Can I depend on you?" The maid replies, "No, my Lord, you cannot!" and slaps my face. But I blurted out, "Here is my girl, purse." After that I had difficulty getting through the rest of the speech. The actress playing the Maid choked back a laugh on her line and fled the stage without giving me the slap. Although later I too laughed about my blooper, at the time I was furious with myself for relaxing my concentration a moment too soon.

That valuable lesson was joined by another in my second Amersham Repertory show, *Little Women*. I was playing old Mr. Laurence, a benign fuddy-duddy, which depended on my ability to characterize. At one performance I was enjoying a dressing-room conversation with a fellow actor when I heard a line over the Tannoy only three short speeches from my entrance cue. I raced out of the room, bounded up the stairs three at a time and entered on cue, but moving like a young sprinter. The audience was then treated to 50 years of ageing in a few seconds as I slumped into the posture and gait I used to convey my concept of a septuagenarian. The salutary lesson: when offstage, pay attention to what is happening onstage.

In my third play, *Payment Deferred*, I had the small part of a doctor who appears in the third act. During the scene, the doctor leaves the leading male character, Will, in the living room, to examine Will's wife who is ill in bed upstairs. He returns almost immediately, holding a glass from which the wife has drunk poison. The direction was to enter the room, slowly approach the husband who was seated by the fireplace, and say "She's dead." One matinee in this intimate theatre, as I entered the room an elderly lady in the front row said to her equally elderly companion, "She's dead." The companion asked loudly, "What?" "I said she's dead," the first lady replied. Trying to be sufficiently serious as befits a doctor who has just discovered a corpse and a glass of poison, I then had to say my line,

"She's dead." "I told you so" came immediately back from the front row. Fortunately I did not have the next line, but the fine actor, Robert Jarvis, did, except that he could not speak it for laughing. His laughter broke me, and then the audience picked it up. The thriller's climactic moment was completely shattered. I managed to get control of myself and sternly repeated the line from the lady in the front row: "I said she's dead." Robert pulled himself together and falteringly picked it up from there.

When *Payment Deferred* closed, my job as a summer replacement came to an end. For 10 weeks I had acted in a convivial company playing roles that stretched me as a performer. I had been accepted as an Englishman and nobody questioned my credentials. Caryl Jenner said she regretted having to let me go and gave me a glowing letter of recommendation. I left the Amersham Playhouse optimistic about my career and confident that I could hold my own in any company of English actors. But I was beginning to worry again about my financial situation. The Amersham-Guildford exchange made it sensible for me to continue living in London and commute rather than pay for dubious accommodation in those towns. But travelling back and forth resulted in my spending an average of $25 Canadian a week when I was being paid only $18. The monthly subsidy from the Tyas's would soon run out, and I could see penury looming in about two months. I decided on the 1st of September of 1948 that I would find a job outside theatre while still seeking work inside. In Ealing Broadway there was a cinema I frequented that had an "ushers wanted" sign from the time I arrived in England. I went around to the theatre and sought out the manager who informed me that he could not hire me directly. I would have to go through the local Labour Exchange. Thus began a frustrating encounter with socialism and bureaucracy.

The next day I went to the local Labour Exchange where a young clerk gave me an application form on which were spaces for one's previous work experience and level of education. That is when I made a serious mistake. I was honest and recorded my work for the University of Toronto Department of Biology and the Ontario Fisheries Laboratory, and that I had a Bachelor of Arts degree in History with an English option. I took the completed application to the counter where the clerk glanced it over and said, "Oh, I'm sorry, but we can't place you 'ere. You are over-qualified. You'll 'ave to go to our Special Placements Branch."

"But," I protested, "all I want is to get a job as an usher or a waiter."

"Sorry. Can't 'andle you 'ere, he replied, "Regulations. Government 'as to control the work force. Reconstruction purposes."

"But I am not going to harm the reconstruction effort by taking a job as an usher," I argued.

"Sorry," he said, "but there is nothing I can do. You'll 'ave to go to our Special Placements Branch and take it up with them."

He then gave me the address of the Branch in central London. The next day I paid those offices a visit where in a cavernous foyer I was greeted by a lone receptionist who served as a sort of guard dog to prevent undesirables from accosting the mandarins on the upper floors. She gave me an application that was the exact replica of the one I had filled out at the local Labour Exchange. I was to take it home, fill it out, and return it. I filled it out on the spot and handed it to her.

Two weeks later I was summoned for an audience with my Interviewing Officer, a man in his late 30s or early 40s who exuded self-importance. He began by saying that he could not get me any work as an actor. I told him that I did not expect him to and that all I wanted was to get a job as an usher or a waiter so that I could sustain myself until I got work in the theatre. "Ah, but you see," he replied, "that poses a problem. The government wants to utilize people to the best of their ability and you would be wasted as an usher. They want to get people into work that will help with the reconstruction." Yes, I thought, the Labour Government's argument for regimenting the work force, but I said only, "Well I appreciate the need for reconstruction so what can you do for me?"

"First of all we have to have a chat," he said and after perusing my application he asked me about my work at the Ontario Fisheries Laboratory. I explained that I was not a trained biologist, botanist, or physicist but had only co-authored a pamphlet on the lake trout and had been business manager of the Fisheries Research Station in Algonquin Park. He was amazed at the salary I had received ($175 a month) and stated that very few positions paid that much in Britain. He then began to question me about Canada, Toronto in particular. He wanted to know what work opportunities there were and what living conditions were like. It occurred to me that he might be considering emigrating to Canada and I remember telling him that Canada was about to enter a period of expansion and that I was sure the Federal and Provincial Governments would need experienced civil servants. Most of the hour-long interview was taken up with a discussion about Canada. I began to feel that I was interviewing him and I wondered if he was really interested in carrying out the Labour Government's socialist program. He had probably been appointed by the Conservatives and was not enthusiastic about his present bosses. At the end of the interview he surprised me by saying:

"Your placement officer will be a Mr. Nuttall. You will hear from him presently."

"But," I replied, "I thought you recommended me for a job."

"No. I speak to your placement officer who then deals with it."

"Then why have I been talking with you? It is Mr. Nuttall who has to know me in order to recommend me for work."

"Yes, well," he said very haughtily, "You'll find we do things differently over here."

"You certainly do," I replied angrily and stomped out, annoyed with the casualness with which he treated my pressing need for employment.

Two weeks went by. It was now the end of September. I received a card in the mail from the Special Placements Branch stating that my name had been submitted to Lever Brothers as a lab technician. A footnote read, "Do not do anything until you hear from them." Naturally I heard nothing. A quick glance at my application would tell him how little I qualified. Two more weeks went by. My finances were dwindling fast. I received notification that my name had been submitted to Woolwich Arsenal as a lab technician. Obviously Mr. Nuttall had only noticed that I had worked for an organization that had "laboratory" in its title. Ergo I must be a chemist. Then I received a notice that my name had been submitted as a teacher of history and English to the Government of Kenya.

Well, I thought, Mr. Nuttall is at last reading my application more thoroughly. But how I could help with the reconstruction in Britain by teaching in Kenya eluded me. I began to wonder if the authorities wanted me out of the country. As much as I would have liked to have seen Kenya, I had not come to Britain to be shunted off to Africa. Despairing of any employment through the Labour Exchange, I returned to the manager of the theatre. No dice. I sought employment as a waiter in several restaurants in Ealing Broadway and Notting Hill Gate. They would not even interview me unless I was sent from the Labour Exchange. There was probably a heavy fine if they broke the regulations. In desperation I phoned Virginia Vernon to see if she knew of any jobs going. She asked me if I knew anything about Guarneri violins because her nephew Bobby needed someone with specialized knowledge in his antique shop. I admitted that I knew nothing about violins. Virginia had been my last hope. So with poverty only a few weeks away I went to the Cunard office (no CPR tubs this time), arranged to have my passage home paid for with the money I had left in my father's care in case of just such an emergency, and was booked on the Aquitania to sail from Southampton in 12 days' time. My two-month long entanglement with British socialism was at an end.

■

The next 12 days were filled with mixed thoughts and emotions. I was relieved to be out of a deteriorating financial situation but I regretted that circumstances had blocked any further repertory experience. I was sad at saying goodbye to London friends, particularly Virginia Vernon, who thought that I was doing the wisest thing. She advised me to return to Britain when labour restrictions had become less severe. The thought occurred that I was chickening out, taking the line of least resistance. Perhaps I should stick it out, borrow the money to continue. Theatre work was bound to turn up now that I had the Amersham credit. But borrow the money from whom? My parents would not give me any because they wanted me to come home, and they would have been furious if I had put the touch on any of my English relatives. The best thing for me was to return to Canada, recoup my finances and return to the assault on the English theatre at a later day. I could derive satisfaction from the fact that I had accomplished what I originally came to the United Kingdom for — experience in repertory theatres, although it was not as much as I would have liked. With that achieved there would be no shame in returning to Toronto.

But that was not the only satisfaction I received from the English adventure. During my 12 months in Britain I attended one ballet, three operas, two revues, 19 concerts, and 54 plays, some as far afield as Dundee and Edinburgh. I had seen great performances and not so great, wonderful productions and not so wonderful. I had acquired many theatre books that were not readily available in Toronto at the time. I had read copiously during the long winter nights. I had voraciously indulged myself in the cornucopia of art and sculpture at London's many galleries, and steeped myself in antiquities at the British, and Victoria and Albert Museums. No one could have done that in Toronto. The one year in London had been a period of tremendous intellectual stimulation. It was worth 10 courses in art and history at a university. It had expanded enormously my appreciation for classical music, opera, ballet, and above all the legitimate theatre. I had seen what had been achieved by a nation with centuries of tradition in the development and appreciation of the arts of the theatre, and I wondered if we in Canada could ever hope to achieve the quantity and, above all, quality I had enjoyed in Britain. Of equal importance to me were the fascinating people I had met. Being Canadian I had no class consciousness, so I "did not know my place." I felt quite at home in the different strata of English society. Although I could not take British Communism seriously, my association with the Marlows made me more politically aware than I had been, and since then my political leanings have always been slightly left of centre. Although I was not conscious of it at the time, that one year in Britain accelerated the maturing experience and boosted my self-confidence immeasurably. But all this devouring of culture also devoured my finances, although for me attendance at plays, operas, and concerts was worth every penny. By October when I booked my passage home I was down to only a few pounds of the Tyas's money, my own savings had gone long before.

CHAPTER 6

Return to the Mummies

It had been a fabulous year in Britain and I hated to leave. When the time came, I sadly said goodbye to the Marlows, and took the boat train to Southampton where I boarded the 49,000 ton, 4 stacker, Aquitania. To my horror I found myself assigned an upper bunk in a dormitory of 30 on F deck just above the giant twin propellers. Well, what could I expect for $164 economy class? The Aquitania had been a troop ship during the war and had not been reconverted. I learned she was due to be scrapped shortly. I shared this dorm with a forlorn little Englishman and 28 Irishmen who seemed to possess only one adjective in their vocabulary — the "f" one. I decided to spend as little time as possible there and found my way through the bowels of the ship to an elevator up to the first-class lounge, which seemed to be as large as the lobby of Toronto's Royal York Hotel. A long table laden with hors-d'oeuvres, snacks, and pastries ran down the middle of it. A half dozen stewards stood around with no one to serve. I ensconced myself in a comfortable armchair, ordered a scotch and soda, and tipped the waiter an extravagant 10 shillings. I later learned that there were only 250 first-class passengers in two-thirds of the ship, and 1,100 in the remaining third. It looked to be a lean voyage in tips for the first-class stewards, so I became their very welcome visitor. I strolled the first-class promenade deck, saw the first-class movies, and even read in the first-class library. I had to eat in the E deck dining room and sleep in the F deck dorm, but otherwise

I escaped the congestion and the *mal de mer* that prevailed in the third-class areas of the ship. The Aquitania was quite a fast ship, but we had just sailed past Land's End when the Captain received instructions that he was to slow down. A dockers' strike had erupted in New York City and Cunard was rerouting its liners to Halifax. As a result what was normally a five-day crossing took eight. I was very happy to arrive in Halifax and even happier to see my parents who had travelled to Halifax to meet me with a welcoming gift of spending money and a pullman ticket to Toronto.

But I had been home less than two weeks when the euphoria of the journey and settling into familiar surroundings wore off. The doubts about whether or not I had made a wise decision in returning home began to recur. The immediate necessity was to earn some money. I got a job as Christmas help in the Robert Simpson store as a sales clerk in men's underwear, which helped make Christmas of 1948 back home a joyful one. But when the job at Simpsons ended, I fell into a blue funk. I was broke, in debt, and without work. The lack of theatre in Toronto made me wish I had found some way to remain in England. So far as professional theatre was concerned, the only game in town was the New Play Society and, after my falling out with Mrs. Moore over *Ah, Wilderness!* two years before, I was averse to getting involved with that organization again. Consequently, all through January of 1949 I sat at home and moped until once again Billi and Phil Tyas came to the rescue.

They were members of the North Toronto Theatre Guild, an amateur group planning a production of *Quiet Wedding* by Esther McCracken. They persuaded the Guild to hire me as director. Most of the cast I already knew and I delighted in working with them. It was an enthusiastic group with some very competent actors, particularly among the women, who outnumbered the males of the group three to one. Of professional calibre in the show were Doris Gill, Muriel Cuttell, Billi Tyas, and Frances Tobias. As with most amateur groups rehearsals were held in the evenings at members' homes, and these sessions usually turned into social affairs after the rehearsal. We had fun preparing this pleasant romp about the tribulations in getting ready for an English wedding. My return to activity snapped me out of my doldrums and for that I have ever been grateful to Billi and Phil and the North Toronto Theatre Guild.

Just after *Quiet Wedding*, I was asked by the Canadian Committee on Civil Defence to stage a demonstration of *Casualty Care in a Mass Disaster*, a manifestation of the hotting up of the Cold War between the Soviet Union and the western powers. While I was in Britain the Berlin blockade and the Allied airlift had raised the spectre of war once again. In Canada the threat of atomic bombing was taken seriously by the authorities although the general public did not seem alarmed. This assignment was a massive challenge for me. It took considerable time, effort, and organization to co-ordinate the parts to be played by nurses, doctors, stretcher bearers, auxiliary workers, and victims in a disaster. There was very little dialogue or acting in the theatrically accepted sense, but the people involved acted out their assignments for the public as they had rehearsed them many times. The story line, such as it was, had been prepared by the Civil Defence Planning Group and dealt with a situation when casualties would be brought from a nearby community on which the atomic bomb had been dropped. Elaborate make-up was required for the victims: profile burns of face and neck, flash burns of face and eyes, severe multiple glass cuts, fractured femur, head wound and spinal injury, dazed woman, simple fracture of the right forearm, abdominal wound and eye injury, sucking chest wound, third-degree burn on back, radiation sickness, and, one which required some real acting, an hysterical mother. The make-up for these injuries was vividly realistic, so much so that looking at them made me feel sick and I could not go into the backstage area of Harbord Collegiate Auditorium where these "victims" were waiting to make their dramatic entrances. The set represented a kindergarten room of a public school that had been converted into an emergency casualty ward. I managed to marshall the entrances of the wounded to give variety in horror to the spectators, leaving the most horrendous cases to the end. The organizers and the cast were delighted that the demonstration had been a gruesome success, but I came away from the presentation convinced that in the event of a real atomic attack all this could be useless.

These two directing assignments had put me back on course. I decided to seek non-theatrical work in order to recoup my finances and return to Britain. By rising above my inferiority complex about mathematics I once again was employed doing costing, only this time costing cigars for the Wilson Tobacco Company, a subsidiary of Imperial Tobacco. These offices were on Front Street just east of Bay and it was a pleasant enough place to work, the maths involved not being too taxing for my brain. I decided to augment my Tobacco Company income by taking on an evening job. I had met the manager of the restaurants and bars of the Park Plaza Hotel and through him I got a Thursday, Friday, and Saturday night job as host of the Roof Lounge, one of the earliest and most tastefully decorated of the growing number of cocktail bars in the city, which resulted from the Ontario Government's lifting of the ban on such watering holes in 1946. But just as I was beginning to put a few shekels into the bank, Imperial Tobacco decided to close their cigar manufacturing branch. My job with Wilson Tobacco would terminate at the end of August. Hurriedly I applied to the Canadian National Exhibition and was hired to sell tickets at the Dufferin Gate.

One morning when I was very busy, to my great surprise, who should appear before my window but Dora Mavor Moore. She had heard that I was back, had phoned my mother who told her where I was working, and had come to talk to me about returning to the NPS. My first concern was that her ample girth was blocking the line. With several dozen people wanting to get into the "Ex" this was not the time to discuss business with D.M.M. But she wouldn't budge. She wanted to know why I had not let her know that I had returned from England. She said that because I was one of the original members of the NPS, she wanted me to come back and help, and she offered me the position of business manager. She added smilingly that she wouldn't take no for an answer and that she would not go away until I said yes. As the line of people grew more and more agitated, I capitulated. We agreed to meet the following day to discuss the matter further. She left without buying a ticket for the Ex.

In spite of my holding her largely responsible for my humiliation in the *Ah, Wilderness!* incident, I was delighted and flattered that this lady whom

I still admired so much had come to me. I thought I could now return to the NPS in a position with some influence on its future development. However, the next day I discovered that she did not have in mind a position as specific as business manager. I would be given the title of production assistant with a variety of responsibilities — a sort of general dogsbody. These duties would involve arranging for props, some publicity and promotion, acting, and, as an added inducement, perhaps some directing. I was also to fill in when needed in the office. It was much the same work as I had been doing for the Society before I went to England. In exchange for all this I was to receive the sum of $35 a week. Well, I thought, it is an improvement over the $15 I received every two weeks for working my buns off three years before. But it was not for the money that I returned to the NPS fold. It was Mrs. Moore's persuasiveness, my affection for her, my respect for what she was trying to accomplish, and the thought that I would once again be involved in helping to develop professional theatre in my own country. I agreed and was back in the theatre world. When the Ex closed, I took up a position at a desk in the New Play Society studio, which was then at 53 Avenue Road, a portion of the book storage warehouse of McClelland & Stewart publishers, now the address of the fashionable Hazelton Lanes. On that day in September of 1949 I began what I had never dreamed would be possible in Canada — continuous employment in the theatre for three years, during which time I lost any desire to seek a career in Britain.

■

The New Play Society had expanded its activity and staff since I left it in 1947. Dora Mavor Moore was still the vortex around which everything circled, but she had able assistance. Mavor was dividing his time between the NPS and New York where he was busy helping to establish United Nations Radio. Mrs. Ernest Dainty, widow of the pianist-composer and mother of my friend Gwen, had become a sort of semi-business manager responsible for the box office and the accounts, but only peripherally involved in policy decisions and program planning. Those matters were handled almost exclusively by D.M.M. and Mavor. Mrs. Dainty's major task was to supervise ticket sales. In addition to her salary, which was also $35 per week, she was paid 10 per cent commission on all sales to organizations that booked large blocks of tickets. Because in 1949 social and recreational groups were not accustomed to having "theatre nights," Mrs. Dainty did not get rich through this policy, but it was an incentive to her to try to persuade these organizations to do so. Pegi Brown was in charge of publicity, which she handled in her spare time between figure skating at the Granite Club and acting. She had such charm she could wheedle concessions out of any hard-headed advertising manager, and sell advertising in the NPS program to the most reluctant of purchasers. Isabelle Dunlop had become the conscientious secretary who had to type all the letters to be sent out. Ben Gans took over the responsibilities of stage manager from Larry McCance who had held that position in the 1947–48 season. In those penurious, pre-Actors' Equity days the duties of that position were ill-defined. The stage manager not only ran the show during performances but also functioned as a production manager and stage carpenter, as well as co-ordinated the acquisition of props, furniture, and costumes, worked out a lighting plot with the director and designer (if there was one), arranged for the sound and any special effects, and most importantly, dealt with temperamental actors. All this Ben carried off with cheerfulness and efficiency in the face of considerable difficulties.

During my absence, a season of 12 shows had been mounted with subscriptions available for six or for all of the shows. They exemplified Mrs. Moore's desire to bring some of the world's greatest plays to Toronto: in the autumn *What Every Woman Knows, Macbeth, Charley's Aunt, Juno and the Paycock, Amphitryon '38*, and a revival of the 1946 production of the *Coventry Nativity Play*; the new year saw *Candida, The Little Foxes, The Tempest, Uncle Harry, Spring Thaw '48*, and ended with *The School for Scandal. Spring Thaw* had not been planned as part of the season, but when a proposed dramatization by Hugh Kemp of Hugh McLennan's novel *Two Solitudes* failed to materialize, a quickly whomped-up revue was substituted. The writers decided to satirize events that had occurred in Canada during the previous year, so they concluded that it should be a "review" rather than a "revue." Andrew Allan suggested the title of *Spring Thaw*. The original cast included: Don Harron, Alfie Scopp, Eric Christmas (a recent immigrant from England), Peter Mews, Mavor Moore, Tommy Tweed, and Jane Mallett and Connie Vernon, two experienced revue artists. The music was by Mavor Moore and Lucio Agostini, and Lister Sinclair contributed the lyrics for the opening song, "We All Hate Toronto." During one of the performances, Connie Vernon, dressed in a skimpy, sparkling, follies girl costume, danced a routine with Peter Mews. While attempting a lift of her, he lost his grip and Connie crashed to the concrete floor of the Museum Theatre stage, causing her nose to bleed profusely over herself, her costume, and Peter. Mrs. Moore rushed her in a taxi to the emergency ward of the nearest hospital where it took a lot of persuasion to convince the staff that Connie was not a beat-up hooker and Mrs. Moore was not the madam. Despite this incident, *Spring Thaw* '48 was an unqualified success and ran for an unprecedented 34 performances. Thus out of necessity was born a show that became an institution over almost a quarter century and that helped keep the NPS afloat when waves of debt threatened to drown it.

But public apathy was proving to be a hard nut to crack. Indicative of D.M.M. and Mavor's pioneering spirit was their plan to bring a production by the Ottawa Stage Society, predecessor of the Canadian Repertory Theatre, to Toronto during the '47–48 season. However, the public's failure to support their importing of the Montreal Repertory Theatre's *Amphitryon* '38 in November of 1947 left the NPS in a financial bind and it could not afford to sponsor the Stage Society's visit. Amelia Hall, who was to be one of the guiding spirits behind the CRT, wrote to Mavor deploring the lack of public support "when people talk so much about building up a pro theatre in Canada."[1]

With its minuscule financial resources the NPS could not afford the luxury of more than one dress rehearsal on the Museum Theatre stage. This led to an opening night for *Macbeth* that lived up to the play's unlucky reputation. Apparently the smoke solution used by the witches in their cauldron was not available for the dress rehearsal. On opening night, not knowing the potency of their capsules, they tossed a whole week's supply into the pot. Instantly clouds of smoke began to fill the small stage and drift out over the audience. Very soon the stage was completely enveloped and when Banquo's ghost entered down a stairway, he became disoriented, wandered forward, and fell off the apron landing at the feet of the choking front row of the audience. Fortunately the drop was only a few feet and the ghost was unhurt, but the rest of the cast were almost asphyxiated along with several members of the audience. At least that is the story as told to me by the late Drew Thompson who was no stranger to hyperbole.

For a more detailed history, including the financial crisis the New Play Society faced during my two year absence, I refer the reader to Paula Sperdakos's biography of Dora Mavor Moore. She reports:

> A large meeting was held in the fall of 1947 with the company members of the Society, during which an agreement was reached to carry on and try to make up the deficit, until which time no one would receive payment. Participation in NPS shows would be on an 'all for fun' basis. At this point, as well as at several later points, the New Play Society was partly subsidized by personal loans from both Dora and Mavor.[2]

But by September of 1949 the finances were on a more solid foundation largely due to the box-office success of the 1948 and 1949 *Spring Thaws*. Now the permanent employees received $35 a week, which was at least a bare living wage for a single person like myself.

The opening play of the '49–50 season was *Who's Who*, a clever comment by Mavor Moore on Canadians, their attitudes, and customs. This was followed by *She Stoops to Conquer*, which had a shaky first performance. Nathan Cohen writing in the *Canadian Jewish Weekly* referred to ". . . opening night when indecisive lighting, bad make-up, disorganized exits and entrances, and faulty cues had the audience in some confusion."[3] His justified criticism reflected the lack of money for adequate rehearsal time on the stage. But *She Stoops* had a remarkable cast whose work drew general favour. Robert Christie played Marlow and I his sidekick, Hastings. Pegi Brown was cast as Kate Hardcastle, Toby Robins as Constance Neville, Colin Eaton as Mr. Hardcastle, Margot Christie as Mrs. Hardcastle, and Don Harron as an irrepressibly oafish Tony Lumpkin. Gwen Dainty was the buxom maid, Pimple, Peter Legge was the landlord of the Three Pigeons Inn, and Ted Follows stood out as one of the doltish servants. Even Cohen, after noting the opening night bloopers, went on to praise members of the cast, especially Robert Christie who, he wrote, played "Marlow with an ingratiating union of shyness and swagger, investing his scenes with a premeditated elegance almost as good as the real thing."[4] I am not quite sure what he meant by that, but I think it was intended as a compliment.

It was during the troubled opening night that Don Harron and I got into "the battle of the grape pulp." As Lumpkin, Don sat sprawled in a chair eating grapes while as Hastings, I questioned him about the young ladies. When he spoke, grape pulp spewed onto my elaborately brocaded costume. As each bit of grape landed I quickly flicked it back with my finger in a contest that went on through the lengthy scene much to the audience's delight. I could not be annoyed with him because it was a very Tony Lumpkin thing to do. He was so right for the role, bringing to it a bumptiousness and a braying laugh that were precursors of Charley Farquharson's trumpeting. But the next night I stood five feet from him. Deprived of a close target, he stopped spitting grapes. And his acting in the next production once again revealed his amazing versatility. As Oswald in Ibsen's *Ghosts*, Don had no opportunity for comic mugging. He proved he had the discipline to give a controlled yet emotionally disturbing performance.

Ghosts was followed by *The Inheritance*, adapted by Harry Boyle from the novel *The Macdonalds of Oak Valley* and directed by Robert Christie. Included in the cast were Frank Peddie, Don Harron, and John Drainie. The play was set in the kitchen of the Macdonald's farm house in Nova Scotia, and I was in charge of obtaining the furniture and supplying the props. The only time this large family ever got together was around the dining table at mealtime. There were to be two meals eaten onstage, breakfast and a full-course turkey dinner, but without water backstage at the

Museum Theatre keeping hot food even lukewarm was difficult. I decided that the easiest and quickest porridge I could prepare was instant mashed potatoes mixed with warm water. The budget was so tight that when Mrs. Moore heard there was to be a roasted turkey that had to be carved, served, and eaten, she refused to let me buy one and undertook to supply the turkey herself. For some reason that escapes my memory, there seems to have been no dress rehearsal when the food was tried out. The first time the cast tasted my culinary delights was opening night.

I had set up my prop table below the stairs that led to the museum cafeteria so that, while the play was in progress, I could dash through the darkened restaurant to the men's washroom in the lobby to replenish my warm water supply. The porridge served to the unwary actors had the consistency of paste and tasted much the same, but they gummed their way through the breakfast scene. Because we could not afford a second set of dinnerware, the breakfast plates were merely scraped off into a garbage bucket and sent right back onstage. I felt like a busboy in a busy restaurant. The secretary, Isabelle Dunlop, arrived with the turkey half way through the first act. She had helped Mrs. Moore concoct it. To my horror it was also made of solid mashed potatoes, burnished with brown gravy and baked in Mrs. Moore's oven. From the audience this perfectly sculpted turkey looked delicious, but when Frank Peddie started carving, it began to crumble into a disgusting mass of brown and white goop. To serve it he had to spoon it onto the plates. Anyone who has tried to speak with a mouthful of mashed potatoes knows that one's articulation suffers, and that there is a tendency to shower the person opposite with white flecks of masticated mush. It was a credit to the actors that they managed their way through the scene, but it must have appeared to the audience that Mrs. Macdonald was a lousy cook because the farmhands ate little of what she had prepared. After the performance the cast berated me for trying to sabotage the show. I in turn accosted Mrs. Moore in the lobby and threatened to resign unless I was allowed to buy a bona-fide turkey and prepare proper food for the cast. She had seen the results of her handiwork and agreed. For the rest of the run the cast was served more palatable fare, but

Frank Peddie and John Drainie likely went to their graves convinced that I had tried to ruin the show.

■

In the spring of 1949, Mrs. Moore had entered into negotiations with the Riverdale Kiwanis Club about their sponsoring a Christmas pantomime at the Royal Alex. Toronto had seen English pantos years before when Vaughan Glaser and Frank Ennery had produced them in the 1920s, but this would be the first at the Royal Alex in 15 years, and the first all-Canadian one ever to play there. Eventually Mavor, with the co-operation of Ernest Rawley, the general manager of the Royal Alex, worked out an arrangement whereby if the Kiwanis would sponsor the production up to a ceiling of $26,000, the Club would get 75 per cent of the box office, and the New Play Society the remaining 25 per cent. With ticket prices ranging from $1 to an exorbitant $2.50, the potential gross revenue for two weeks of performances would be $52,140, the second week being mostly matinees with prices ranging from 50 cents to $1.50. Rawley advised us to budget for only 60 per cent of the potential gross, $31,284, of which the Kiwanis would get $19,500 and the NPS $6,500. This looked like a practical arrangement for all concerned so we decided to plunge ahead with *Mother Goose*. In those days the Ontario Hospital Tax was levied on all entertainment, but the NPS went to the Ontario government on behalf of the Riverdale Kiwanis and itself as non-profit organizations and succeeded in having the tax removed. Although this was only for *Mother Goose*, it was a break-through. The law was later changed to exempt all Canadian productions from the tax, at least until recently.

Since 1957 I have been a staunch supporter of Actors' Equity. I have been involved in negotiations for improved fees and working conditions, and I look back in dismay at the arrangements between the NPS and the Kiwanis about the priorities of payment in the case of a deficit. The first were to be the orchestra because no one dared cross the powerful Toronto Branch of the American Federation of Musicians under the implacable Walter Murdoch, then all advertising bills, the rent to the theatre, and then the union crew who ran the show and built the scenery. Then, and only then, "if funds are available the payment to the cast."[5] Typical of the time, the actors were to be the last considered. Is it any wonder that stage performers very soon in the 1950s sought protection through Actors' Equity?

The performers in *Mother Goose* were paid a lump sum covering the rehearsal period and the two weeks of performances. Their fees ranged from $25 to $140 for a lead dancer. A specialty act of Highland dancers was allotted "expense money of $30 plus $4 each for 'shoe allowance'."[6] Most of the leading actors were paid a bit more, and the "star," the director, the choreographer, and the musical director naturally received the highest fee. Of course the musicians and the stage crew, who were members of the International Alliance of Theatrical Stage Employees (IATSE), received much higher payment than most of the cast, a source of irritation to many of the performers who were making personal sacrifices to help create a Canadian professional theatre that would employ IATSE members in the future. The Royal Alex rented for $3,500 a week including box-office staff, but not the stage lighting equipment, which was rented from an IATSE member, and which, you will recall, Barry Jones had told me actually belonged to him.

The musical arranger and conductor was Samuel Hersenhoren, later musical director of the *Wayne and Shuster* television show. The scenery was built by John Kastner and designed by Peter Mews, who with a decent budget could reveal his real talent. Costumes came from the Malabar and Keay companies, except for the goose costume, which was specially constructed by a seamstress. The director of the show was Eric Christmas who had had experience in pantomimes in Britain. Diminutive, full of energy, and a clever comic performer, Eric also played the vital role of the "Dame," in this case Mother Goose. The rest of the cast consisted of some NPS favourites such as Pegi Brown as the principal boy, and Jack Medhurst whose brilliance as a mime artist created an endearing Priscilla, the goose that laid the golden eggs. E.M. ("Moe") Margolese was Squire Longacre and Peter Mews and Al Pearce, back from England, were the Broker's Men. Al also got to cavort about as the King of Gooseland. Beth Corrigan was

Jill, Al Harvey played Jack, and Gladys Forrester, one of Toronto's foremost
dancers of the day and known from the film *The Red Shoes*, was the lead
dancer as the Fairy Queen. Edmund Hockridge as a singing Crofter
stopped the show with his beautiful voice.

During rehearsals there was a deterioration in Dora Mavor Moore's relationship with Eric Christmas and his assistant, the show's choreographer,
Betty Oliphant. The space the NPS rented for $100 a month at 53 Avenue
Road was a large room at one end of which were various staff members'
desks and at the other the passageway allowing McClelland & Stewart access
to its book storage. The space between was the large rehearsal area. None of
this was even curtained off, so that anyone working at the desks could be distracted by rehearsals and rehearsals distracted by office activity. But with this
open space arrangement Mavor (when he was present), D.M.M., Isabelle
Dunlop, and I could observe the rehearsals. Everything worked smoothly
enough until Mrs. Moore began to be "helpful" by advising Mr. Christmas
on how to direct the show. This naturally led to resentment from Eric and
eventually words were exchanged. The situation grew worse. Mrs. Moore
would watch rehearsals with such a grim expression on her face that the performers' enthusiasm was greatly dampened. After tolerating this situation for
several rehearsals, Eric contacted Mavor and insisted that Mrs. Moore absent
herself from the studio. Realizing that drastic steps had to be taken, Mavor
had a rousing contretemps with his mother and barred her from the office-
cum-studio. During the remaining weeks of rehearsals, the founder and
director of the NPS had to stay home in deepest dudgeon.

I was responsible once again for obtaining the furniture and properties,
but when rehearsals moved to the Royal Alex, and for the run of the show,
I was not allowed to touch any of the items I had borrowed, bought, or
made. The IATSE property man assigned to the Royal Alex took over. His
age mitigated against any rapid movement, and he was not well organized,
but fortunately he was assisted voluntarily by other crew members. Some
of the props taxed my ingenuity: a long whip made of bolognas was fine
but a trick chair that tipped back to allow Eric to roll from beneath the banquet table had to be cut when we discovered that despite the castors I had

put on its back, the chair would not roll across the Alex's rough stage. The most important prop, of course, was the huge golden egg that Priscilla laid. I had arranged weeks in advance for the egg but there was a delay in its manufacture. Minutes before curtain time of the opening on Boxing Day, I arrived with the monster plaster oval, disengaged it from the taxi, and staggered through bemused customers up the side alley to the stage door. I was terrified that I would drop it and smash the climax of the show, but I managed to get it to the ancient prop man who stared at it in dismay.

Considering that the public was not accustomed to British pantomime, *Mother Goose* did well financially, but not as well as had been hoped. After ticket sales had been totalled and expenses deducted, the NPS had a modest profit of $1,343.48,[7] and a huge *succès d'estime*. Not within living memory had there been a Canadian stage production on such a scale with actors, singers, dancers, and musicians. It put the NPS in the forefront of Canadian producing companies. The profit the Riverdale Kiwanis received was sufficient to encourage them to sponsor a Christmas show for the following year. Everyone got paid and the cast had a good time on the Royal Alex stage spreading joy to adult and child alike. All the *Mother Goose* characters lived happily ever after, and Mrs. Moore was allowed to return to the NPS studio.

■

The first play of the new year was *Narrow Passage*, written and directed by Andrew Allan. Although I was listed on the program as production assistant, I had nothing to do with it. Before rehearsals began Mavor asked me, "Whatever did you do to Andrew Allan? He won't have anything to do with you." "The feeling is mutual," I replied and told him about the *Ah, Wilderness!* incident. I was shifted to publicity. But I was sorry for the New Play Society's sake that it turned out to be a mediocre production that met with unfriendly reviews. Perhaps that is the reason why Allan, in his autobiography, devotes only five lines to this episode in his life.[8]

The British entry for the '49–50 season was G.B. Shaw's attempt to write a Chekhovian play. In my opinion, *Heartbreak House* resembles a Chekhovian play only because it has very little action. Shaw's characters are much more one dimensional and there is scarcely any subtext. Yet the critics were enthusiastic largely because of the outstanding cast director Mavor Moore had assembled. Toby Robins was Ellie Dunn and Colin Eaton her father, Mazzini. As Captain Shotover, W. H. Brodie displayed a standard of speaking that he exercised also as the arbiter of speech for CBC announcers. Marjorie Leete was Nurse Guiness, and Pegi Brown, Lady Utterword. Margot Christie played Hesione Hushabye and her husband in real life, Robert Christie, played her stage husband, Hector. Lorne Greene was a powerful Boss Mangan, Garth Magwood was a burglar, and I had great fun playing Randall (the Rotter) Utterword, in addition to resuming my duties as production assistant. Herbert Whittaker wrote that Eaton was a "remarkably good Mazzini Dunn. . . . Lorne Greene walked off with the show at times with his powerful, imposing, and collapsing Mangan" and "Vernon Chapman and Garth Magwood, respectively, upheld the standard of the brilliant company they kept."[9] However, he did not like Peter Mews's set, stating that "Captain Shotover's strange, ship-like Heartbreak House had dwindled to Humdrum Cottage."[10] I thought it was a credit to Peter's ingenuity that he had managed to create anything at all of Shotover's stern gallery of "an old-fashioned high-pooped ship" on that impossible, square concrete box of a stage.

Only two weeks after *Heartbreak House* we opened another difficult, large cast, multi-scene show, John Coulter's historical drama *Riel.* A cast of 24 actors was assembled under Don Harron's direction with Robert Christie supervising the technical side. Among the actors were Mavor Moore as Louis Riel, Sandy Webster doubling as a settler and Dr. Jukes, Leslie Rubie as both Archbishop Taché and Dr. Roy, Margot Christie as Riel's mother, and Pegi Brown his wife. I doubled as the surveyor, Colonel Stoughton Dennis, and as Mr. Justice Richardson who presided at the trial after the second rebellion. As production assistant I had to do some heavy scrounging and persuading to obtain authentic articles or realistic reproductions. I consulted advisors from the Royal Ontario Museum, the Archivist of the Provincial Library in Winnipeg, the Librarian of the Military Institute, and assorted military authorities about the costumes and properties. Genuine period firearms were obtained from the Military Institute, and period furniture was borrowed or made by our own technical crew.

The script calls for 15 different locations connected with Riel in the first rebellion (1869) and the second (1885). Obviously 15 locales could only be suggested on that inadequate stage and essential items of furniture and scenery were brought on and removed by the actors themselves. The Regina Court Room scene was the most difficult because it required a prisoner's dock, a witness box, the judge's stand, and a place for barristers to sit. The stage became so crammed with chairs, set pieces, and actors that it reminded me of the Marx Brothers' shipboard cabin in *A Night at the Opera*. Backstage, every inch of space was utilized. In addition to the actors and the crew, there were members of the Schola Cantorum of St. Michael's Cathedral led by Monsignor Ronan who were brought in for each performance to sing a Requiem chant. The spaces below the stairwells on either side of the stage were chock-a-block with furniture and props. In the tiny dressing rooms 20 men making quick changes led to such chaos that there was a danger of putting your leg into another fellow's trousers. Where the women changed, I have no recollection — probably in the women's washroom off the lobby.

Because Mavor was balancing his commitment to the NPS with his commitment to United Nations Radio, we often had to rehearse without him. Such was the case for the dress rehearsal when Mavor's train from New York was delayed. We wondered if Louis Riel would make it for his trial. I felt sorry for Don Harron whose best efforts in his first venture into directing were being frustrated. As Mavor suggests in his autobiography, *Reinventing Myself,* he always had too many irons in the fire.

The first night was not without untoward incident. First the curtain had to be delayed because Mavor had got a fish bone lodged in his throat and was rushed to hospital to have it removed. Thereafter I resolved never to eat fish before a performance. Then, early in the first act, Don Harron as the bigoted Orangeman, Thomas Scott, had to pluck Riel's crucifix from his neck, spit on it, and hurl it to the ground. I, as Colonel Dennis, was to pick it up and politely give it back to Riel. But Don hurled the crucifix to the concrete floor with such force that it bounced and nobody could see where it went. Devoid of our glasses, Mavor and I stared myopically at the floor. Even Don with better vision could not find it. We looked around for what seemed like an eternity before Don moved his foot and we discovered that he had been standing on it.

Mavor's responsibilities elsewhere had not let him gain absolute security of his lines. During the complicated interrogation in the trial scene, he needed his script in the witness box where a concealed shelf had been constructed to hold it. The focal point in that scene is the witness box and not the judge's stand, so the former was centre stage and I, playing the judge, was on a slightly raised position down left just inside the stage curtain. At one performance just after the scene had begun, I felt a hand groping up the backside of my black gown, followed by a thick sheaf of rolled paper. Simultaneously the stage manager, hiding behind the curtain, whispered, "Get this to Mavor. It's his script." Mavor was at least eight feet away in the box. I could see that he was beginning to look more agitated than was normal even for Riel. I could not leave the judge's bench and approach him with the script so there was nothing but to goose the adjacent solicitor. I reached over, shoved the script up his gown and whispered, "Pass it on." After the script had travelled under the gowns of several court officials, it eventually reached Riel who sighed with relief as though he had been found not guilty.

As the reader can judge, *Riel* was not an unqualified success. Critical comment was lukewarm at best, but the NPS and everyone involved deserved an A for tackling this demanding historical drama. Because Riel was one of the most colourful characters in our history, the cast felt that they were accomplishing something important in bringing his story and that of the Métis people to an English-Canadian public. Moreover, our production led to radio and TV versions of Coulter's *Riel* and was a significant step in the repatriation of a national hero.

Undaunted by the problems of staging a multiple-scene play on the small box-like stage, we plunged into preparations for *King Lear* as soon as *Riel* had opened. Again we had a strong cast. Toby Robins made a beautiful

Cordelia while Margot Christie's Goneril vied in malevolence with Pegi Brown's Regan. Robert Christie was Kent, and Colin Eaton, Gloucester. Frank Perry's Edgar proved that he was not only a fine radio actor but splendid on stage as well, and Jack Medhurst was brilliant as the Fool. John Howe played Albany and I, Cornwall. Don Harron added another triumph in a chilling performance as Edmund, played as a young man who delights in evil. While performing the exhausting Riel at night, Mavor tackled the even more daunting role of Lear. Still young, Mavor nonetheless had an ability to characterize, the intellect, the technique, and talent to present an outstanding Lear. But, in my opinion, although a creditable performance, it never realized its full potential. Mavor did not give himself half a chance. Dividing himself between New York and Toronto was taking its toll. Again we often rehearsed without the lead, which was unfair to himself and the cast. At the dress rehearsal we had a Lear with laryngitis because he had temporarily damaged his vocal chords with brandy on the train from New York.[11] On opening night the audience was treated to a very quiet Lear because Mavor had not yet fully recovered.

Dora Mavor Moore had staged the play quite simply, which Mavor justified in a program note referring not only to the limitations of the stage, but also to the writing: "While *King Lear* is grand, it is in fact the grandeur of simplicity. At its most tremendous heights, the language is either elemental or elementary; where the former, no stage effects can hope to match its power; where the latter, stage effects are often an embarrassing sophistication, like artificial grass at a burial."[12] Mavor also "arranged" the production, which meant that the simple design was his, and a practical one it was. Halfway upstage from the permanent curtain was a false proscenium that framed another stage opening. Behind this was a platform about a foot above the stage floor. On either side of the centre opening were two smaller curtained archways for entering and exiting the lower downstage area. While action was happening on the lower stage, this upstage area could be closed off with two burlap curtains that could be drawn from off-stage. This allowed the action to flow from one area to the other with a minimum of delay. The costumes from Malabar were intended to give an impression of the Anglo-Saxon period, long dresses for the women and tunics and heavy capes for the men. Once again lack of funds prevented our renting the theatre for sufficient rehearsal on the stage. We met the completed set only on opening night. At the conclusion of one of the scenes on the downstage area, a group of us, capes flowing grandly, swept toward the up-left exit through the false proscenium. We had taken only about two steps when we collided line astern as the first actor tried to fight his way through not only the exit curtain but also the heavy curtain of the centre opening, which had been quickly pulled back to reveal the scene upstage. In panic he struggled with the two seemingly impenetrable layers of sacking while the rest of us waited in a queue blocking the audience's view of the actors on the riser already into the next scene. The remaining performances progressed without incident, except that one night we were amazed to hear Mavor ad lib in perfect iambic pentameter about a stool that was missing from the stage.

One of the memorable moments for me occurred when, as the wicked Cornwall, I got to put out Gloucester's eyes. Concealed in a pouch hanging from my belt were two pieces of sponge rubber soaked in a blood solution. When the moment came to gouge out his eyes with my thumbs, I turned upstage to the Earl, who was tied to a chair, pressed these bloody pieces of rubber to his eye lids, then turned, walked downstage and flicked the gory pulp of his eyes to the ground. It gave me great satisfaction every night to hear a gasp of horror from the audience.

■

The previous season the NPS had enjoyed success with Morley Callaghan's *To Tell the Truth*, which opened at the museum but was transferred at the invitation of Ernest Rawley to the Royal Alex. In an attempt to duplicate that success the NPS next staged Callaghan's new opus *Going Home*, which was fortunate to have in its cast Robert Christie, Toby Robins, and that very macho young leading man (an uncommon type in the Toronto theatre of those days), Gerry (now not spelled with "J") Sarracini. Herbert Whittaker's considerable design talent was put to good use as he learned the difficulties of putting a multi-set show on that awkward stage. But *Going*

Home did not repeat the success of Callaghan's previous play. The critics received it coolly and audiences were small. As a result of this and the costs of the large cast shows, the NPS again found itself almost broke and looking to *Spring Thaw '50* to bail it out. During the preparations for that revue I got sucked into arbitrating between Mrs. Moore and Don Harron, who had decided that he deserved a royalty fee for the sketches he had written. The NPS had never paid any royalty to any of its *Spring Thaw* writers. Mrs. Moore's attitude was that such contributions were freebies to help establish a professional theatre, similar to actors performing for free duties other than acting. She was doubly resistant to royalties if the writer was also being paid as a performer in the show, which was Don's case. Having contributed some of the funniest sketches to previous *Thaws*, he was beginning to appreciate his worth. When he confronted D.M.M. in her office, a decided row ensued. To my embarrassment she called me in for support. I resented being put in the position of arguing against a friend whom I thought was justified in his request. I sided with Don, much to Mrs. Moore's annoyance. In her biography of her father, Martha Harron states that "Don and Dora settled on $2 per major sketch per performance plus 50 cents for blackouts."[13] It wasn't much, but at least I helped get him some monetary recognition for his clever writing.

For this *Spring Thaw*, Margaret Ness and Mavor contributed sketches and lyrics for which, so far as I can recall, they did not get paid. Lucio Agostini once again joined Mavor in composing the music. How Mavor found time is a mystery to me. Charles Tisdall did the arranging, particularly for the "opera" that closed the first half. Don Harron's hand can be seen in its plot and words. "La Traviesti — a near myth in Two Acts for the Symbol Minded" was a lyrical satire on the proposed amalgamation of Toronto and its suburbs into Metro. Its chief characters were Taranna (a bandit), Zcarborro (leader of the Villagers), Mimi-Co (beloved of Zcar-borro), Teetisi (enamoured of Zcar-borro) and other villagers, Longebranchi, Yetobico, Leah Side, and Swansi. My favourite names among the opera singers were Grease Stevens, Curson Flagstaff, "a second mezzanine," and Sub Rosa Ponselle, an understudy. Once again the cast included some of Toronto's best comedy performers: Jane Mallett, Jack Medhurst, Connie Vernon, Pegi Brown, and Lou Jacobi. Lou, a stand-up comedian, had honed his skills in the Jewish banquet and Bar Mitzvah circuits. He was a tremendous asset not only as a performer but as a writer of a couple of the sketches, one of which, *One for the Birds*, revealed him as an inept Scout Master trying to cope with the wilds of Canada's bush. In 1951 Lou left for London where Garson Kanin cast him in *Into Thin Air*, which was a flop, but Kanin remembered Lou and in 1956 cast him as Mr. Van Daan in *The Diary of Anne Frank*. I saw him in that role on Broadway and found his performance proof that he is a fine serious actor as well as a clever comic.

Again I was production assistant and I had a ball performing in *Spring Thaw '50*, mostly as a straight man setting up the comedy, an experience valuable some time later when I joined the *Wayne and Shuster* television show. This *Thaw* ran for four weeks to capacity houses and pulled the NPS out of its deficit situation. For the fiscal year ending June 30, 1950, the revenue for the Society had been $37,240 and the expenditure $36,927.70, leaving an awesome profit of $317.30. In 1948–49 the profit had been $860.24.[14] Obviously nobody was getting rich working for the NPS. But it was a triumph that there was any profit at all those two seasons.

September 1949 to the end of May 1950 had been the busiest time of my life. For most shows I was the production assistant, but I did much more than that. Mavor was nominally managing director, but he was absent so often that I had to fill in. Mrs. Moore and I consulted regularly about the day-to-day operation of the Society and discussed future plans. I wrote letters of thanks for loaned props and furniture, or letters of apology for items lost or damaged. I dunned actors who had not paid for their photographs of the shows they were in. I drew up letters of agreement for the rentals of our scenery or studio space. I addressed community theatre groups about the NPS in particular and the professional theatre in general. I helped Mrs. Moore draft letters and filled in at the box office if necessary. In short, I was general factotum. When acting in a show I would often be working from 10 o'clock in the morning until midnight. No union hours then. But I was enthusiastic and believed deeply in what we were trying to achieve, and with D.M.M. there was never a dull moment. For me that '49–50 season was the happiest of my tenure with the NPS. I was glad that Mrs. Moore had blocked the CNE ticket window.

But the pressure of the past nine months persuaded me to take a busman's holiday part of that summer to visit theatres in New York. Then as now, every time I visit New York, I return to Canada with renewed enthusiasm for the theatre. The productions I have seen there have been for me a touchstone against which to compare our achievements at home. Although in 1950 we could not come close to Broadway's production standards, the acting in Toronto was comparable to anything I saw in New York that summer. I returned to the Little Apple to help prepare for the 1950–51 season, which I hoped would surpass the previous season's achievements. My expectations were soon dashed.

Mavor was now deeply involved in the United Nations and could not spare much time for the NPS. I could see that after four years of almost steady activity Mrs. Moore's energy was flagging, and without Mavor to organize the season she seemed momentarily lost. I could not pin her down to planning a season. In Mavor's autobiography and in Ms. Sperdakos's biography of D.M.M. we learn that Mrs. Moore tried to set an alliance with the Straw Hat Players, which had been founded by Murray and Donald Davis and which performed during the summer at Port Carling. I was under the impression that it was Mavor's idea to bring in the Davis brothers to assist Dora and to fill the NPS season with the Strawhatters. The arrangement suddenly gave the Davises influence on NPS policy. For this to be Mrs. Moore's decision seems contrary to her reluctance to share control with anyone except Mavor, and especially with people who had nothing to do with the NPS in the past. But whoever made the decision, no one consulted Isabelle Dunlop or me, the two permanent NPS employees. Because I knew how strong-willed Mrs. Moore could be, a trait in her that I admired, I had profound misgivings.

The museum raised our rent. Mrs. Moore thought that if the theatre was left empty for a while, the museum authorities would relent, but the fact was they were indifferent to our performing there. Moreover, because the steady flow of McClelland & Stewart employees in the passageway to their warehouse had become a disruption to our rehearsals, we decided in late August to move to the second floor of 782 Yonge Street, above a Honey Dew restaurant and below Boris Volkoff's School of Ballet. It was the very studio where Fanny V. Birdsall had vainly tried to teach me to tap dance. All this resulted in no NPS productions in the autumn of 1950. I tried to persuade Mrs. Moore to plan for a post-Christmas season, and was encouraged when Mavor came up with a proposal to rent the Arts and Letters Club auditorium in the heart of downtown Toronto. At first I had been opposed to the idea because the much smaller capacity of the Arts auditorium would mean less revenue. As well, it had a flat floor and hard wooden seats not nearly so comfortable as the Museum Theatre, which in itself was no theatrical paradise. But when I gave the idea more consideration, I changed my mind. We would become a "Theatre Club," and the existing members of the Arts and Letters would form the nucleus of our audience. We would sell memberships to the general public as well, and all members would be given a reduction on the price of tickets offered to the public at large. Although smaller, the auditorium was more intimate than the long funnel of the Museum Theatre. The more Mrs. Moore and I considered Mavor's idea, the more enthusiastic we became. I hoped that the Arts and Letters Club could become our home for a series of productions in winter 1951 because I did not want a whole year to pass without a regular season for fear we would lose our supporters gathered over the previous years.

However, when the Davis brothers were approached with the idea, they turned it down. I could not fully understand their reluctance because the proposal meant that their company would have been employed at least for several months in early 1951 and possibly even for a show or two in the late fall of 1950. In all fairness they did argue that the capacity of the Arts and Letters Club was not sufficient to make the venture financially viable. I realized it would be a gamble, but what theatrical venture is not? The New Play Society itself had been, and still was, a huge gamble. But the Davises persuaded D.M.M. not to risk it, and the proposal was killed. When they left the meeting I said to Mrs. Moore, "You watch. Pretty soon they will have their own company here in Toronto." When they opened the Crest

Theatre a few years later, she reminded me of my prediction. For a long time she was very bitter about the Crest, and considered that Donald and Murray had deliberately blocked the Arts proposal, but personally, I feel they were not that premeditated. I believe that they based their objections on practical business reasons.

By September it was too late to plan a fall season. We decided that if a space became available after Christmas, we might stage some productions in January and February, but otherwise, we would concentrate on only two productions that year: the Christmas show at the Royal Alex, and *Spring Thaw* for which the Museum Theatre had already been booked. That autumn some of the acting community got the impression that the New Play Society had expired. In *Living the Part*, Bronwyn Drainie writes, "The actors and writers felt great frustration at the folding of the New Play Society, which had been their only outlet for legitimate stage works."[15] She uses that argument to explain the need for the founding of the Jupiter Theatre the following year by a group of radio actors and writers. But the New Play Society had not died. It was enjoying a breather out of which I hoped a regular production season would emerge.

Our new quarters on Yonge Street were reached by a long flight of stairs from the street to a small anteroom, on the left of which were a cluster of small offices we sublet to the Keay Costume Company. Beyond the anteroom was a large studio at the end of which was an office enclosed by a wooden partition not quite ceiling high, and an open space separated from the large rehearsal area by a counter. Mrs. Moore took the office, which gave her a semblance of privacy, because it had a door she could close. The half partitions proved an advantage because we could not afford the luxury of dictaphones or intercoms, so if Mrs. Moore wanted Isabelle or me she simply shouted for us. Isabelle and I shared the open office space. Grimy windows at the back of both offices offered a depressing view of a sordid alley and the dirty brick building opposite. The disadvantage with the half partition was that every conversation could be heard in the next office. As a result, there was very little about Mrs. Moore's personal life of that time that Isabelle and I did not learn. But we kept it private.

There was always a paucity of office furniture. Mrs. Moore had an old desk that was vintage Salvation Army. Isabelle, needing something solid on which to type, had a used stenographer's desk. I worked from an old kitchen table with a central drawer that I had purchased for $5 from a second-hand furniture store. Cardboard filing cabinets were sufficient for our purposes and I bought a small portable typewriter for my own use. That autumn the NPS was so poor that carbon copies of letters were made on the backs of old press releases and other discarded printed material. When I compare those conditions with the huge administrative bureaucracies many of our large arts organizations have built up over the years, I am amazed at how much we achieved with so little.

■

After the Arts and Letters plan was cancelled and the Davis brothers bowed out of the picture, Mrs. Moore, Isabelle, and I, the only staff left, began to work together more closely than ever. With no box-office money coming in, we sought other ways to raise revenue. We rented the studio space to various groups for rehearsals. We even rented copies of *Heartbreak House* to the Canadian Repertory Theatre in Ottawa for $1 a piece for three weeks. Through such efforts we survived until we could organize the Riverdale Kiwanis Christmas show. But before that Mrs. Moore and I became involved in two ventures, one directly under the aegis of the New Play Society, and the other under the auspices of the Presbyterian Church of Canada.

As another source of revenue, that autumn of 1950 we started the New Play Society School amid a dearth of good theatre schools in Toronto. Whoever wrote the brief history of the NPS, published for an exhibition (20 June–3 August, 1979) at the Thomas Fisher Rare Book Library of the University of Toronto, was misinformed when recording, "She [D.M.M.] decided to create the New Play Society School with herself as the only teacher and only five students."[16] Copies of our press releases, such as the one sent to Jack Karr of the *Toronto Star* come closer to the truth:

The course will be under my personal supervision and

> we are fortunate in having on our teaching staff one
> Dr. Diana Ewing who studied at the Comédie
> Française and the Royal Academy of Dramatic Art,
> and has played leading roles in both French and Eng-
> lish repertory companies; and Mr. Vernon Chapman
> who, after graduating from Victoria College, spent
> some years in England studying with Lorna Davis, one
> of England's foremost speech teachers, and subse-
> quently has had extensive experience as an actor and
> teacher in both England and Canada.[17]

Even this press release is free with the truth because I had not done any teaching, and the typist misread Norma Davis's first name for "Lorna." The facts are that, although the school was Mrs. Moore's idea, I did the actual organizing and, with Diana Ewing, did the teaching. Mrs. Moore did not teach anything that first year. Originally there were to be two courses: Acting, conducted by Diana Ewing, and Speech, which I taught. But before the school opened, at my urging, we added a course in the history of the theatre, which I also taught.

The classes were held in the NPS studio on two evenings each of 10 weeks. We wanted students of high calibre, those with a love of acting and the theatre, although a planned career as a professional actor was not a requirement. We auditioned applicants and screened out those we thought were lacking in talent because we did not want them to waste their money, and those who had a frivolous reason for enrolling. The result was a class of about five or six students in the beginning, one of whom, Claude Rae, went on to become a professional actor. Another, Larry Stone, was studying law, and eventually, under Herbert Whittaker's encouragement, dabbled as a drama critic. He was much more at home with law, and is now my lawyer. Our objective was to give students acting and voice fundamentals that they could apply to any endeavour they pursued. Though few in number, our first class proved to be enthusiastic and responsive. The New Play Society School had got off to an encouraging start.

Because Mrs. Moore paid herself a salary only when the NPS had a financial cushion, which was seldom, she felt it necessary to take on outside work when the Society was not producing. As well as a fee for herself, these assignments often brought the NPS revenue from the rental of rehearsal space and the use of NPS equipment and office services by the group for whom she was working. In the autumn of 1950 she undertook a mammoth celebration for the 75th Anniversary of the Presbyterian Church in Canada, and I was hired to be her assistant director. In consultation with a covey of Presbyterian ministers, we decided to create an historical pageant depicting the origins and development of the Canadian branch of the Church. *The Burning Bush* would be presented for four performances at Eaton Auditorium in December 1950 for the "praise and glory of the King and Head of the Church and the Saviour of the World, Jesus Christ." Mrs. Moore had been greatly impressed with a fashion show she had seen in Eaton Auditorium during which the action moved from live models onstage to filmed models on the screen. She thought that this technique would be ideally suited to depicting the growth of the Church, only we would reverse the process and go from filmed action to live stage tableaux. Mrs. Moore had discovered Alan Fairlie, a budding young film director from, I believe, Trinity College, who was to film the scenes I was to direct. We were fortunate to have him because, at the time, neither Dora nor I knew anything about the technical side of movie making.

The various scenes were to tell the story from John Knox's confrontation with Queen Mary Stuart in Holyrood Palace in Edinburgh, through the Westminster Assembly of 1643 when a group of divines drew up the Confession of Faith and Catechism in the Jerusalem Chamber of Westminster Abbey, and the arrival of the first Scots settlers to Nova Scotia in 1760. There were to follow scenes of the building of the first Presbyterian Kirk in Canada, the first Ordination, a baptism in Quebec of a child of a soldier in General Wolfe's army, an early wedding, an open-air service in Manitoba, missionaries to the savages of the New Hebrides and the savages of Canadian saloons, the "Trail of '98," and finally, the Church Union of 1925 at Knox Church in Toronto. There were to be 16 scenes onstage, plus four on film, two narrators at lecterns on either side of the stage, Dr. David Ouchterlony at the organ, an actor playing Moses, and a choir. Parishioners from churches throughout the city made up the rest of the large cast. The logistics of such a spectacle were staggering to contemplate. Mrs. Moore and I could not have pulled it off without the assistance of some very dedicated people: Reverend Stuart Parker who wrote the initial script; James Scott, book review editor of the *Toronto Telegram*, who completed the script after the Reverend Parker's untimely death; David Ouchterlony who composed the music; the T. Eaton Company; the Eaton Auditorium staff; the IATSE stage crew; and the students of the Royal Conservatory Drama Department who applied theatrical make-up to all those inexperienced actors/parishioners. Period costumes were organized by Dorothy Cleveland. Peter Mews designed the sets, which were built in their spare time by Presbyterian Church members in the NPS studio, IATSE for once waiving its rules about union-made scenery in a union house.

Rehearsals were at the NPS studio, and some of the parishioners, particularly some dour, middle-aged women, at first appeared distinctly uncomfortable about being involved in "the theatre" — a notorious hotbed of rogues, vagabonds, and loose women. However, Mrs. Moore put on her most respectable mask, soon put them at ease, and they entered into the spirit of the event with vigour. Staging the tableaux was no great problem, but the creation of the film sequences was another matter. The lack of funds meant that the shore of Lake Ontario had to serve as the original site of the first Scots settlers' landing in Nova Scotia, and the vacant lot north of Mrs. Moore's house substituted as the location for the building of the first log church. I had been delegated to direct the film sequences, which consisted mostly of herding the actors into filmable groups and improvising the action with the helpful advice of young Mr. Fairlie. On the level of home movies, the filmed sequences turned out to be quite effective and added needed variety to the pageant. As we approached the opening performance, everything was going quite smoothly. Too smoothly.

Mrs. Moore's propensity for getting something for nothing, or the lowest possible price, often essential for the survival of the NPS, now almost doused the fire of *The Burning Bush*. Rather than hire a stage manager whose credentials could be checked but who might demand an appropriate fee for energy, skill, and experience, she discovered a middle-aged man who claimed to have had a wealth of stage-managing some decades before. He asked a very low fee because he wanted to get back into the business. I urged her to employ one of the reliable stage managers who had worked for the NPS, but she was convinced this man would be ideal. There had been no indication of it in advance, but at the dress rehearsal, with the assembled multitude, it became apparent that we had given the responsibility of running this complicated show to a dipsomaniac. He kept nipping during the rehearsal until he became befuddled. Chaos reigned. I had to take over because I was the only one who knew the sequence of the show, having done most of the planning for it. It was obvious that he would not be able to cope with opening night, so, with some trepidation, I became the stage manager for that and the three subsequent performances.

In those days the stage manager was almost always in one of the stage wings close to the front curtain. Now, in the well-equipped theatres, the stage manager is in a booth at the back of the house communicating with the various technicians via microphone and earphones. At Eaton Auditorium in 1950 I had to use a series of buttons with lights to cue the various participants: the projectionist in the booth, the organist, the choirmaster, the two lectors, Moses, the stage-hand raising and lowering the movie screen, the one opening and closing the curtain on the stage scenes, and the assistant stage manager organizing the change of scenery. The two Presbyterian ministers who acted as monitors marshalling the cast on and offstage also had to be cued verbally when to go into action. Considering that I had never stage-managed anything before, opening night went off smoothly except for one miscue from me that the projectionist caught and corrected. But there was a moment of panic when I saw to my horror that the scene on the film was coming to an end and my two clerical monitors were so busy enjoying it from behind the screen that they had failed to marshal the actors for the next scene. With only seconds to go I ordered them, "For Christ's sake! Move it! Get those actors onto the set!" Shocked, they moved as though jet propelled, and, for Christ's sake, the actors were there just in the nick of time.

The remaining performances went like clockwork. The combination of organ, choir, narrators, and actors onstage and on film made for a most impressive and moving experience. The Presbyterian organizing committee was delighted and I was given a bonus, in addition to my assistant director's fee, for jumping in to stage manage the whole event. But the bonus did not add up to the fee a regular stage manager would have received, so Mrs. Moore saved money at the expense of my nervous system.

■

Once the Presbyterians had been disposed of, D.M.M. and I turned our attention to organizing the 1950 Christmas pantomime whose combined title *Babes in the Wood or Bold Robin Hood* indicated that great liberties were going to be taken with both stories. Sponsored again by Riverdale Kiwanis, the NPS mounted an even more extravagant show than our *Mother Goose.* Mavor had somehow found time to write the book and compose the music. Samuel Hersenhoren was again the musical director, and the musical arrangements were by Phil Nimmons. The rest of our production team matched their skill and experience. Larry McCance was stage manager and Eric House his assistant, Gertrude Dainty resumed her title of business manager especially looking after ticket sales, Ted Follows arranged the props, and I was administrative assistant, a mantle which covered a multitude of duties. We had also recruited a remarkable "old stager," George Keppie, from the halcyon days before the advent of talkies when he had been a producer and business manager for the Vaughan Glaser Stock Company.

Our director was Don Hudson, who had staged the brilliantly successful *Army Show* starring Wayne and Shuster. He was able to draw his cast from a very talented pool including Peter Sturgess who was loaned to us from the Canadian Repertory Theatre in Ottawa to play the role of the "Dame," the Baroness de Gisbourne. He was surrounded by performers with great comic flare: Lou Jacobi as Sir Guy of Gisbourne, Ron Leonard as Whittaker, and that superb vaudevillian with the clown face, Doug Romaine, as Humphrey.

Peter Mews, the show's designer, was also a leading actor in the roles of The Aunt and the dog, Towser. Ted Follows was one of the nasty nephews and the singer, Andrew MacMillan, played a villager and King Richard. I tripled as a Knight, Will Scarlet, and a Messenger. Carolynne Allen and a young Donald Saunders, who built a career in musical theatre when he grew up, were the "babes." Pretty Patsy O'Day was in the soubrette role of Maid Marion, and the star of the show — as Robin Hood — was Gisèle LaFlèche, that terrific vocal stylist from Manitoba whom later radio and television audiences came to know on her own show and many others as Gisèle Mackenzie. She was a favourite performer of Jack Benny and often appeared on his show. Not only was she a great pop singer and a charming personality, but she filled the Lincoln-green tunic and tights to perfection.

The lion's share of credit for the panto's success must be Don Hudson's, but kudos must also go to Boris Volkoff who choreographed the dances using students from his ballet school. During the production I got to know and respect this temperamental little Russian-Canadian. Boris had danced with the Imperial Russian Ballet before the revolution. A White Russian sympathizer, he managed to escape from the Soviet Union in 1929 via China. That same year he settled in Toronto where he lost no time in setting up a ballet school in a city where most people looked upon the form at best as an exotic dance practised by weird foreigners, some of whom were mad, like Nijinsky. Volkoff must have been a bit mad himself to persevere in establishing classical dance in a country not long out of its pioneer period and in the throes of a major economic depression. But persevere he did. It took him nine years but eventually he created a company of dancers trained in the best Russian tradition. Melissa Hayden, who became one of Balanchine's early Prima Ballerinas, was a product of the Volkoff School, as was Janet Baldwin who became Mrs. Volkoff. By 1939 his company began doing one-night stands, all a limited public could support. At rehearsals for *Babes* I realized that he was a bit of a martinet, but he soon had his student dancers performing like seasoned pros. Celia Franca and Betty Oliphant would have had a more difficult time of it when they established the National Ballet if Boris had not developed a nucleus of dancers, and, most important, an appreciative if small public on which the National Ballet could build. I am told that he died a somewhat embittered man, but that is an attitude he shares with many of Canada's pioneers in the arts who have not received the credit they deserve.

Boris had an earthy sense of humour. After the closing-night party in the NPS studio, there were four of us left having a final drink: George Keppie, Boris Volkoff, Mrs. Moore's youngest son Peter, in the uniform of his Highland Regiment, and myself. As Peter was leaving, Boris hollered after him, "And what *does* a Scotchman wear under his kilt?" Peter immediately showed us, to Boris's delight and my astonishment.

Earlier that same closing night, I had received a lesson in theatrical etiquette. Some members of the cast were indulging in a bit of last-performance kibitzing. I decided to participate. My third role was as a messenger impressively dressed in chain-mail with a heraldic cuirass over it. Heralded by a trumpet fanfare, I would step onstage and make an announcement in a booming baritone. But on the final night I delivered my message in a wimpish whine. The audience laughed at the let down after the trumpet build up, but I noticed Sammy Hersenhoren in the orchestra pit put his baton down on the music rack and shake his head in disgust. When I asked him about it later he said, "I give you a big fanfare and you spoil it by changing your delivery. The final night audience deserves as good a performance as you gave on other nights." He was right and I have never indulged in final night shenanigans since then.

Babes was a success on all fronts. It delighted the capacity audience at the Royal Alex and made money for the Riverdale Kiwanis. It also made enough money to tide the NPS over for a few weeks. But its most important result was to show that Canadians could mount a spectacular production that equalled the best Christmas pantomimes one could find in Britain, and were even superior to most of them.

A week after *Babes* closed, Fridolin (Gratien Gélinas) brought his production of *Tit-Coq* from Montreal to the Royal Alex prior to its engagements in Chicago and New York. Mrs. Moore thought we should try in our small way to bridge the gap between the two solitudes by inviting the cast to an after-opening night reception at the NPS studio. We agreed that it was a splendid idea, and the staff (all three of us) eagerly organized it. I think it was a success and I hope Mr. Gélinas and his company felt welcome in Toronto. But I regretted personally that our Ontario educational system had stressed the ability to read French rather than converse in it.

Because there were no government subsidies and because Canadian corporations and philanthropists, unlike their American counterparts, were notoriously niggardly in funding the arts, we were almost completely dependent on earned revenue. At one point the City of Toronto, after much protest from some councillors, did cough up $500, and one man, rather than underwrite a bank loan, donated another $500. There were some loyal friends who sent in donations, but not nearly enough to keep three or four people on the payroll despite our modest salaries. Even with our penny-pinching, there was not enough money in the treasury to sustain the NPS through the four lean months from the close of *Babes* to the opening of *Spring Thaw* in May, so we decided to mount a production of Shaw's *Arms and the Man*. Don Harron was originally to play the down-to-earth soldier, Bluntschli, and Robert Christie the flamboyant poseur officer, Sergius Saranoff. Apparently at Don's request, the roles were switched, which I thought was wise. Don's own temperament was more suited to the dashing cavalry officer. But he overplayed it. I quote from his daughter's biography of him, "The combination of rampant insecurity and self-miscasting made Harron go overboard in *Arms and the Man*."[18] Nevertheless, the production pulled in the audience and revenue enough to sustain us.

▪

Spring Thaw once again saved our bacon. I had now been given the title of business manager, a function I had been performing for some time and I drew up a budget for *Thaw '51*. This time Robert Christie directed and the sketches were written by newspaper columnist Ted Reive, Mavor Moore, Lou Jacobi, and Sammy Sales. The song lyrics were by Mavor, Reive, and Charles Tisdall, the pianist. Don Harron, who had gone with his wife and daughter to seek fame and fortune in England, was not available, but many familiar performers were back along with a newcomer to *Spring Thaw*, David Gardner. Again I did triple duty on stage as a Villager, a Friar, and an Animal Trainer for the same basic salary that I received as business manager. The show was a great audience tickler, ran to full houses for five weeks, and gave the Society sufficient profit to tide it over the summer. *Thaw* also re-affirmed what had been established by previous *Spring Thaws*, that Canadians could present a very difficult theatrical form, the satirical revue, as competently as anyone. It also settled *Spring Thaw* deeper into the hearts of the Toronto public so that it became an annual event for over two decades.

One of the steps that made its long history possible was that we had the *Spring Thaw* name copyrighted. During the negotiations with the performers prior to rehearsals in 1951, Jane Mallett held out for more money. When Mrs. Moore balked at an increase, Jane threatened to withdraw from the show and revive *Town Tonics*, a revue that she and her husband, Frederic Manning, had started and performed in for many years until 1945. A compromise was reached and Jane stayed in the show, but I became concerned that any number of performers and writers could create a rival *Spring Thaw* and plagiarize the title. I persuaded Mrs. Moore to get the name copyrighted and our lawyer, Stuart Parker, arranged it. This eventually enabled Mrs. Moore to sell the name to Mavor, who in turn made money from leasing the name to Robert Johnston who took the revue on several successful national tours until he met with financial disaster in 1969.

Copyrighting was only one new aspect in the professionalising of postwar Canadian theatre. An occurrence during the run of *Spring Thaw '51* reveals a dilemma faced by performers caught in the transition from the amateur to professional worlds. The sketch "Babes in the Subway" parodied the *Babes in the Woods* and *Mother Goose* pantomimes as well as the building of Toronto's first subway. Performing as the Goose in that skit was Ted Follows. Prior to the opening of *Spring Thaw '51* he had played Isaac Newton in the University Alumnae Dramatic Club's production of Shaw's *In Good King Charles' Golden Days*, directed by Herbert Whittaker. Ted did not know when he signed for *Spring Thaw* that the Alumnae production would win the Ontario Regional Drama Festival and go on to compete in the

Dominion Festival to be held in London, Ontario. Because the London performance was scheduled during the run of *Spring Thaw '51*, Ted found himself on the horns of a dilemma. He approached Mrs. Moore requesting that he be replaced for one night. Mrs. Moore gave him a definite "No." She argued that he had a professional contract that must take precedence. She did not approve of aspiring professional actors taking roles with amateur groups. It confused the public. I agreed with her. Moreover, he would be difficult to replace temporarily because he played several other roles in the show. He pleaded that the cast of the amateur production were depending on him and he could not let them nor the University Alumnae down. I suspect that antagonizing the director, a powerful critic at the *Globe and Mail*, bothered Mr. Follows as well. But nothing he said could persuade Mrs. Moore. Ted decided he had an ethical obligation to the University Alumnae and gave Mrs. Moore a week's notice. Privately I tried to persuade D.M.M. to accede to Ted's request, pointing out that, although difficult, with some adjustments in the cast his roles could be covered. However, my intercession was unsuccessful and she replaced him for the run with Jack Merigold.

Because I did not appear in that *Spring Thaw* until the final sketch of the first half, I served as house manager until it was time for me to go backstage and get into costume for the subway sketch. Immediately after my part early in that scene, I would change back into my civilian clothes and resume my duties as house manager during the interval. One night, after he had been absent from the show for over a week, Ted turned up backstage and persuaded the stage manager and Jack Merigold to let him get into the goose costume but not to tell Peter Mews who was playing Mother Goose. I told them I thought it was not a wise idea, but the stage manager thought it would be a good joke on Peter. Jack Merigold, who was new to the company and did not want to offend the stage manager, reluctantly acquiesced. After I had performed my bit onstage, I hurried into my street clothes and dashed out to sit beside Mrs. Moore in the back row. For a while the sketch progressed normally until the Goose suddenly whispered something into Peter's ear, which caused him to react with a laugh. Mrs. Moore shot forward in her seat like a bird dog pointing, jumped up, almost knocking me out of my seat, and to my horror, started down the aisle as though she was going to accost the actors on the stage in front of the audience. But she thought better of it, turned, charged back up the aisle and through the front doors of the theatre with me travelling along behind. You may remember that in order to get backstage at the museum one had to go through the cafeteria. She sailed through that darkened restaurant like a dreadnought, all battle flags flying. When she got to the stairwell leading down to the dressing rooms, she rested her ample bosom on the railing and hollered, "Who's in the Goose tonight?" This rendered me powerless with laughter and I retired to the cafeteria. But her question caused pandemonium backstage. Ted had fled to hide under the stairwell on the opposite side of the stage where he was scrambling to get out of the goose costume and avoid this bundle of wrath descending the stairs to the dressing rooms. According to Jack Merigold, when she got there she was so angry she was speechless and could only hoot like an owl, "Who's . . . who's . . . who's. . . ."[19] When she found the words, the stage manager took the full blast of her wrath and was fired on the spot, although I believe necessity dictated that he finish that performance and he was rehired the next day. Ted never worked for the NPS again and for years after that, whenever Ted and I would meet, we would greet each other with "Who's in the Goose tonight?"

■

After *Spring Thaw '51*, I went off the NPS payroll in order to develop my career as a director by staging a long season of plays from May through November for the International Players in Kingston. However, each week I took a few hours to deal with some of the routine business of the NPS. With Mavor and me both busy elsewhere, Mrs. Moore and Isabelle Gale (Dunlop) were left to hold the fort in the Yonge Street studio. During that autumn Mrs. Moore, now 63 years old, was feeling very tired, very much alone, and, after five years struggling to establish a permanent professional company, very discouraged because, despite previous achievements, without a season of plays that goal seemed as remote as ever. There was no one to tackle the detailed work of organizing a new season for 1951–52.

A planned September production at the museum was cancelled, and no plans were made to produce a Christmas pantomime.

Without box-office revenue coming in, the NPS School took on more importance. When I returned from Kingston in November, classes were again organized. When we screened the applicants for their talent and interest, there were several whom I thought should be rejected, but Mrs. Moore, eager for the fees, vetoed my recommendation. The result was a different course from what it might have been. I have always felt that the dictum "physician heal thyself" should be applied to all psychiatrists. We had a pair of them who tried to sidetrack the classes with behavioral theories of their own. Another student, we later discovered, had just been released from a mental institution and made the women in the class uncomfortable with his excessive attention to them. I wanted to drop him from the course, but D.M.M. thought it would be good therapy for him. Besides, it would have meant refunding his money. Overall, we had a course that some members did use as a kind of therapy, giving it less of an orientation toward a career in theatre than in 1950. No one from the 1951 class became a professional actor.

While we were free of production, Mrs. Moore and I decided to investigate possible sites for a permanent home. The Royal Ontario Museum authorities had made us feel that we were allowed to use their theatre on sufferance. From July 1, 1947, to June 30, 1952, the NPS paid $20,969.28 in rent for this most inadequate theatre. We figured that if we were to make a down payment on a building we could convert into a theatre, we could gradually pay off the mortgage and be further ahead in the long run. To this end Mrs. Moore used her ability in playing the role of a helpless female to persuade such firms as Morani and Morris Architects, Gibson Brothers Real Estate, and others to search for suitable locations for us. Among the places we considered were Trinity Anglican Church Parish Hall on Trinity Square, which had previously been used by CKEY as a radio studio, and an ice rink on north Yonge Street that seemed a likely bet to me. I even designed moveable bleachers to allow us to stage shows in arena, semi-arena, or proscenium style. Another location we looked at was the Crest Theatre, which we could have obtained for a low down payment. Eventually this was the theatre that Murray and Donald Davis acquired. For each of these locations Mrs. Moore would wax enthusiastic for a week or two and be diverted by some other scheme or activity such as the Heliconian Club, the Zonta Club for career women, the worthy cause of the Mental Health Association for which Mrs. Moore staged a series of playlets, and the occasional amateur theatre group that she directed for a much-needed fee.

During the winter of 1951–52, a side-tracking of her interests began that was eventually to consume all her enthusiasm and much of her energy for several years. I had heard on CBC radio an interview with a young man from Stratford about his desire to establish a Shakespeare Festival there. I told Mrs. Moore the following morning about this "nut" and his plan. She agreed the idea was daft. When we were having so much trouble establishing a theatre in a metropolis like Toronto, what hope was there in a small community like Stratford? Months went by and we did not give it another thought until one day, Mavor, who was busy organizing CBC television, phoned his mother to tell her that he was sending over a young man who needed her advice about a plan for a Shakespeare Festival in Stratford. When she told me about our imminent visitor, I expected to see either an unkempt Bohemian, or an arty-farty dilettante. Instead in walked a slim, neatly dressed man in his mid-to-late 20s with glasses, a balding head, a shy manner, and a winning smile. I showed Tom Patterson into Mrs. Moore's office and soon she made use of our intercom by shouting over the partition for me to join them. When I did so she explained Patterson's idea for Stratford, but added, "He has a problem. The Dominion Drama Festival people have invited him to a party at which Michel St. Denis [the adjudicator] will be present. They want him to bring the mayor of Stratford with him. He's worried that his idea may be stolen from him." "That's simple," I replied. "You should go to the party, be polite and listen to what they have in mind, but leave the mayor, who controls the purse strings, at home." Which is what he did.

In *First Stage*, Tom Patterson recalls his first visit with Dora Mavor Moore differently. He writes that he arrived with a friend and relates a different conversation with Mrs. Moore that does not include what I have described.[20] I have checked my version with Isabelle and with Gary Montgomery who had recently been hired. They were present at the time and both agree that he arrived alone.[21] When I wrote Tom about this confusion, he telephoned me and said, "Vern, that was many years and many drinks ago. You could be right." I believe he has confused the first visit with Mrs. Moore with a second when he did arrive with a friend. Subsequently he was a frequent visitor to the NPS office.

The more often he talked with D.M.M. the more she became caught up with his idea. On several occasions after a visit with her, Tom and I would repair to the Honey Dew downstairs for cups of their appalling coffee, over which we would chat about his dream for the Shakespeare Festival and mine for the New Play Society. Although my knowledge and experience of theatre were limited, they were voluminous compared with his. But his disarming manner and infectious enthusiasm made a person want to help him. I found myself falling under his spell, and for a while I too became a seeker after his dream until I realized that because the Stratford Festival was becoming Mrs. Moore's main fixation, our plans for the NPS were being shoved aside. I began to suspect that in following Mrs. Moore's footsteps I was walking toward a dead end. In February 1952, the Society could no longer afford to keep me on the payroll. I wanted more experience as a director, so I returned to the International Players in an assignment that was interrupted by an SOS from Mrs. Moore. I took a leave of absence from the Players to resume the position of NPS business manager during the rehearsals and run of *Spring Thaw '52.*

Mavor had collected another cast of performers who were becoming more and more expert at revue: Don Harron, home from abroad, Andrew MacMillan, Peter Mews, Jane Mallett, Connie Vernon, and Patsy O'Day were the alumni of previous *Thaws,* to whom were added Sheila Craig and the freshmen William Copeland and Norman Jewison. Mews and Rudolf Dorn, who later designed for CBC–TV, designed the sets. Mavor, Keith Macmillan, Cliff Braggins, and Ron Bryden, later theatre critic for London's *Observer,* wrote the songs, and the sketches were by Don Harron, Norman

Jewison, and Margaret Ness. Braggins wrote a show-stopping number entitled "We're from the R.M.C.," which for me was just as clever as my
favourite song from the *Army Show*, "On Behalf of the General Staff."
"We're from the R.M.C." was performed by MacMillan, Mews, Copeland,
and Vernon. There was another clever parody by Harron called "Guys and
Squaws," a take-off on *Guys and Dolls* but including Canadian references
and typical Harron pseudonyms for the characters: Alf de Rake, Ethyl
Mermer, Moira Merrier, and my favourite, Eazion Pinbois. Harron also
created a skit called "Torontovideo" in which a TV host (Don) tries to
interview a hockey player called Teeter Totter (Norman Jewison), who
became so mesmerized by the TV camera that he could only grin in frozen
inanity at it. As house manager, I watched fascinated every night as Harron
struggled to win the scene back from Jewison but to no avail. He had
loaded it too much in favour of the hockey player and Jewison's idiotic grin
was so infectious he kept the audience rolling about with laughter. I was so
impressed with Norman's flare for comedy that one night I asked him what
he wanted to be. He replied in his diffident way that he really did not know.
I suggested that he become a comedian. That idea did not seem to appeal
to him, fortunately, because very soon he found his *métier* in television and
films and we know how the world has benefitted from that.

    Spring Thaw '52 was another hit but it nearly did not open. Approxi-
mately a week before opening night we received an ultimatum from the
International Alliance of Theatrical Stage Employees to include a member
of their union in our backstage crew. In view of the sacrifices we had made
to start the NPS and keep it going, we could not see why we should be
forced to hire an outsider who had made no contribution whatever to the
establishment of an indigenous Canadian theatre and on top of that, who
would take home a weekly pay cheque larger than any of ours. Hitherto
IATSE had been content with crewing the Royal Alex and Eaton Auditorium
and had left the smaller venues alone. Mrs. Moore and I decided to reject
their demand, but IATSE quickly found our Achilles heel. Mavor had hired
union musicians, Marion Grudeff and Charles Tisdall, as our pianists. IATSE
enlisted the help of the dreaded Walter Murdoch, uncompromising head of

the Toronto branch of the A.F. of M. who threatened to withdraw the pianists unless we accepted the IATSE stage-hand. As a result of my association with ACTRA and Equity years later I learned that the tactic was legally questionable but at the time we did not know our legal rights. I considered this threat blackmail and urged Mavor to fire the two union musicians and hire the non-union pianists from *Spring Thaw* '50 while there was still time to rehearse them into the show. I advised this in the presence of the local IATSE head who threatened to blacklist me in every theatre across the country. This was a hollow threat because the only productions in the IATSE houses were foreign touring shows. My performing there seemed less likely than the melting of Antarctica. But hoping that Murdoch would not carry out his threat, Mavor balked at my suggestion. It was a vain hope. Murdoch waited until three days before opening when it was too late to rehearse new pianists, and instructed Ms. Grudeff and Mr. Tisdall to withdraw from the show. We had to capitulate. And that is how Victor Egglestone got his first job as a stage-hand. He proved to be a very amiable, capable, hard worker, one of the new, young breed of IATSE members. He eventually rose to be head of the Toronto locale of IATSE. However, in 1952 his being forced on us was deeply resented. Financially speaking, although his salary threw my budget for *Spring Thaw* '52 out of kilter, we still made a sizeable profit.

After *Spring Thaw* '52 I resumed directing for the International Players, but in September I returned to the NPS as business and house manager. For several years the incomparable Anna Russell had been performing her unique musical satires and had twice already rendered audiences at New York's Town Hall incapable of taking the art song or *Der Ring Des Nibelungen* seriously ever again. She very generously offered to give a week of performances gratis to raise money for the NPS. It proved to be a very rewarding week at the box office, which now boasted as one of its ticket sellers Gary Montgomery, the nephew of the Field Marshall, Sir Bernard Montgomery of Alamein. Mrs. Moore had hired Gary to sweep floors and empty waste paper baskets but he had begun his career in Britain acting in Howard Hanson's Court Players. After his required 18-month stint in the British Army, he got a job with the Yarmouth Rep. where a reporter from the *London Evening Standard* asked him what his uncle thought of his leaving the army and what he himself had to say about it. Gary replied that he was happy to be a civilian again and that it was really none of his uncle's business. The next day the *Standard* had a large heading: "Uncle can lump it. I hate the army."[22] The Field Marshall was not amused. Gary decided to put the Atlantic between his uncle's wrath and him, took his savings, and flew to Vancouver to visit relatives, where he ran out of money. He had heard there were some tender shoots of theatre growing in Toronto so he hitch-hiked across the country in the dead of winter and arrived at the doorstep of the NPS in February 1952. At the time, John Conway shared the studio and hired Gary to manipulate some of his hand puppets, which added to Gary's meagre earnings from the NPS. When Stratford began in 1953, he was hired as a spear carrier for $35 a week, but the International Players offered him $37.50 a week. In his naïveté, he went to Tyrone Guthrie and said, "Mr. Guthrie, sir, I cannot afford to work for you this summer. I have been offered $2.50 more." Guthrie put his hand on Gary's shoulder and said, "That's right, my boy, always go for the bucks."[23] Gary acted with the International Players for one summer and worked for the NPS for a year or so. When his uncle came through as the commander in chief of NATO on an inspection tour of Canadian bases, Gary made his peace with him. He persuaded his uncle to use his influence to get him into the United States. A phone call from Monty to President Eisenhower did the trick, and Gary received a letter signed by Eisenhower giving him entry into the U.S. He bought a car but at the border he was promptly arrested and jailed, the Buffalo immigration authorities concluding that the letter was a forgery. A lawyer-uncle from Toronto arrived to vouch for him, and a phone call to the President's office in Washington clarified the matter. Gary then continued on his way to Hollywood. After a brief movie career and a variety of other jobs he moved to Denver, eventually creating a one-man show about his uncle, which he has performed in the United States and Britain.

Just as it offered Gary a port in his travels, the NPS provided a home for John Conway and his puppets who performed on Saturday mornings in the studio. John had played small roles for the Society including Jimmy Farrell in *The Playboy of the Western World*. He had become a clever puppeteer and when television started in Canada he had his own puppet show, one of whose most endearing characters was Uncle Chichemus, closely resembling Mavor Moore in appearance. In a symbiotic relationship, John paid rent for studio space and Mrs. Moore and the NPS helped sustain him until the opportunity arose to make good on television.

These were changing times for Canadian theatre. In 1951, the Royal Commission on National Development in the Arts, Letters, and Sciences, chaired by Vincent Massey, submitted its now-famous report that led to the creation of the Canada Council and the subsequent provincial arts councils within a few years. I like to think that perhaps our efforts at the NPS might have had something to do with the establishment of the Commission in the first place. Certainly Mavor's writing on the theatre in Canada had considerable influence on the Commission. People not involved in the arts cannot realize the psychological effect the Massey report had on us. For the first time in Canada's history, there was a recommendation that the arts should be subsidized from public funds. It was as though the sun was beginning to break through the clouds and send its life-giving rays down on our tender plant. There was hope for the theatre after all.

■

That winter of 1952, following my advice as well as our lawyer's, Mrs. Moore reluctantly allowed the NPS to have a board of directors. It was a bit of a wrench for her to surrender any of her autocratic authority, but she had come to realize that we needed financial help and sound business advice. As I argued, we would stand a better chance of obtaining public and private support if we could show that we had a group of reliable citizens behind us. I considered her acceptance of this a step in the right direction, even though she immediately packed the board with her friends and fellow members of the Zonta Club.

Our Christmas show followed the sold-out Anna Russell concerts, but this time the Society planned to stage it without the support of the Riverdale Kiwanis Club. Instead of a pantomime, Mrs. Moore and I liked the challenge of producing J.M. Barrie's *Peter Pan*. It had been revived successfully in New York the previous year (the musical version was still a distance down the road) but was so difficult to stage that no professional production had been seen in Eastern Canada for 25 years. In retrospect the idea seems insane because we had only our own small bank account and a limited line of credit at the bank as our backing. But at the time it seemed propitious because by the autumn of 1952, as a result of revenue from leasing the studio space, from the school, from *Spring Thaw '52*, and from the Anna Russell performances, all the New Play Society debts had been paid off. As the business manager I drew up a detailed budget for *Peter Pan* that Mrs. Moore agreed to stick to rigidly. We hoped to make a healthy profit on the show in order to sustain us until *Spring Thaw '53* opened, and to become the basis for a building fund we planned to inaugurate. The Royal Alex was either not available or too expensive, so we reserved Eaton Auditorium, although its concert platform framed by a proscenium was hardly ideal for the complicated *Peter Pan*.

D.M.M. wanted to obtain director Laurier Lister, the Englishman who had staged the Broadway revival. He was not available, but recommended an expatriate Englishman, Basil Langton, then living in New York and teaching at a girls' school on Long Island. I had counted on having a Canadian director, although I had to recognize that there were not many of them around with the experience to handle productions as complicated as *Peter Pan*. I reluctantly agreed with Mrs. Moore to pay the cost of flying Mr. Langton from New York for a consultation. This was the first inroad on my budget that had to cover the cost out of its contingency fund. I was soon to learn that it was but the first of several contingencies.

When Mr. Langton arrived I settled him in a comfortable room at the University Club, which cost much less than a room at a decent hotel. That evening, he, Dora, and I had dinner at her house. During dinner I explained to Langton our limited resources and Langton seemed to understand. I became slightly concerned when he told Mrs. Moore that she reminded him of Lilian Bayliss, the founder of the Old Vic Company. Ms. Bayliss had been an idol of Mrs. Moore's and she saw herself playing a similar role in

Toronto. If Basil Langton had offered her the Order of Canada, she could not have been more delighted. Little discussion ensued about the financing of the show, and I sensed, rightly or wrongly, that Mr. Langton was waiting for me to leave before discussing his fee with D.M.M. He did insist in my presence that he would direct *Peter Pan* only if we could obtain the Kirby Flying Ballet. Because *Peter Pan* cannot be staged without such equipment, I had allowed for that in the budget.

I had allocated $1,500 plus expenses for a director, recognizing that it was not a princely sum even in 1952 for a director accustomed to the fees paid outside Canada. But in Toronto where actors rarely got more than $50 a week, it was considered generous. My own salary as business manager was $45 a week and when I directed for the International Players I received $50 a week which, because it was weekly stock, was $50 per show. However, *Peter Pan* would require the services of a director for several weeks. Mrs. Moore and I had figured that $1,500 would be adequate if we also paid expenses. I had also planned that the assistant director, who was to be me, would receive half the director's fee. Although I would continue as business manager, I would not receive two salaries. I would officially go off the payroll as business manager and collect only my assistant director's fee.

The next morning Mrs. Moore came into the office: "Vernon, I want you to sit down because what I am going to say will shock you." Sensing what was coming, I sat down. "He wants $3,000 plus expenses." After I gasped I said, "Well, its obvious we can't afford him. We'll have to get someone else." Mrs. Moore replied, "I think he will be worth it." "But it throws my budgeting all off," I countered. "I think he will save us money in the long run," she said. As I continued to object the smile she had worn to win me over disappeared and I saw the jaw set and the mouth purse, which I knew to be signs of her determination. She abruptly went into her office indicating that all was settled, leaving Isabelle Gale and me to stare at each other in dismay. After a moment I followed Mrs. Moore into her office and said, "Well since I have budgeted a fee for the assistant director at half what the director will get, I assume I shall get $1,500 instead of $750." This did not sit well with her at all and she became just as determined that I would not be paid $1,500 as she was that Basil Langton would be paid $3,000. I was tempted to quit on the spot, but I thought if I do there will be no spending restraints and the NPS could sink into a morass of debt. Besides, I needed the money. I did not resent Mr. Langton trying to get as much money as he could, but I did resent Mrs. Moore arbitrarily making a decision contrary to her business manager's advice.

Another decision she made put the whole production in jeopardy. She had discovered a man with a carpentry shop who undertook to design and build the sets. I was appalled and argued that not only was he untried but he was not a member of IATSE, and Eaton Auditorium was an IATSE house. She maintained that there would be great savings in the set construction and that she could "get around" the union. I reminded her that a dispute with IATSE could prevent us from taking a show into the Royal Alex ever again and that *Spring Thaw* could also be jeopardized because of its union stage-hand. Once again I was overruled. I began to realize that Mrs. Moore would never be capable of running a fully professional company because she would never be guided by anyone on financial matters. Moreover, she had allowed her attention to be spread among so many different projects and organizations that she could no longer concentrate her great energy on what I had been led to believe was her main objective: the establishment of a permanent stock or repertory company. In spite of all my hopes and all our planning, the NPS could never become a viable theatrical company producing on a regular basis.

I determined to see *Peter Pan* through and then decide what to do. I hoped I could be a restraint on over-spending. We were lucky and obtained Kirby's Flying Ballet because the ice show they were working with closed down over Christmas. We negotiated a reasonable fee for the rental of the flying apparatus for our two-week run and we obtained their representative Mr. Foy's services at no extra cost to train our crew. The fee was much less than I had budgeted, so what we lost in the director's salary we partially made up on the "flying."

But that was the only savings. The carpenter's design used a six-foot-high bridge half-way up the stage, which stretched from one wing to the other. The top of this doubled as the ground above the boys' subterranean home and as the poop deck of the ship. Large panels swung open to reveal the boys' home, and closed up to become the exterior wall of the ship's cabin below deck. Visible onstage were to be two ladder-like stairways on either end of the bridge that would allow actors to go from the lower to the upper deck. I pointed out to the designer and director that these two stairways would not be seen by the audience because, as indicated on the plans, they would be out in the wings. Obviously the designer had the wrong measurements for the Eaton Auditorium stage. Basil Langton dismissed this point with a "nonsense" and dismissed me with a wave of his hand. When the set was mounted on the stage those stairs were in the wings and the audience was baffled by actors going into the wings and suddenly appearing on the bridge or below on the stage. I determined to have nothing whatever to do with the production side of the show. But I broke this vow when I expressed my disapproval of his casting two different actors as the father, Mr. Darling, and as Captain Hook, when traditionally, and for very good plot reasons, both roles have been played by the same actor. Besides, it added another salary to the payroll.

We got hoist with Mrs. Moore's own petard when, a few days before opening, IATSE objected to putting up a non-union set. Mrs. Moore's attempts to cajole them into taking pity on the financially strapped NPS were to no avail. IATSE insisted that the sets have the union stamp or there would be no *Peter Pan*. Mrs. Moore had put herself over the proverbial barrel and IATSE took advantage of her. They estimated how much the existing sets would have cost if they had been constructed by union carpenters and charged the NPS accordingly. As a result, we paid for the scenery twice, once to the carpentry firm that built it and once to the union.

Another problem neither of us had bargained for came from the demand by the Musicians' Union that we hire a small group of musicians to play before the show began and during the intervals, similar to the practice at the Royal Alex. This was a surprise to me because I did not recall any musicians when the Civic Theatre had produced straight plays at Eaton Auditorium, and there certainly were none when I played there in *Quality*

Street. Paula Sperdakos writes in *Dora Mavor Moore* that "because the New York production of *Peter Pan*, with Mary Martin, had been classed as a musical, the union insisted that Dora hire no fewer than 15 musicians."[24] That was not the reason, because the musical version did not open on Broadway until 1954. It was simply the Musicians' Union finding work for some of its members. IATSE threatened to withdraw its stage crew unless we agreed to the musicians' terms. Consequently we were forced to hire, to the best of my recollection, four or five musicians and not the 15 according to Ms. Sperdakos. However, she is correct when she states that rather than have them sit around doing nothing, Mrs. Moore had them play in the lobby during the intermissions, a less than ideal atmosphere for the musicians with a chattering audience milling about.

These added expenses shot my budget all to hell even before we opened. I had sleepless nights worrying over the mounting costs but I left the NPS before the accounts were totalled. Mavor writes in his autobiography that the profit was $5,000.[25] If so it must have been the result of a miracle or weird accounting. The miracle could have been that, in spite of its shortcomings, the show was a genuine audience pleaser by a company very skilled right down to the "lost boys"— who for some reason seem to have got lost from the program because they are not listed in it. Jan Campbell was a charming Wendy and the beautiful Toby Robins lowered her voice and swashed and buckled with great delight as Peter. Jack Medhurst gave a sensitive performance as the dog, Nana, and Hugh Webster was a wonderfully comic Smee. Neil Vipond, with whom I had worked in the International Players, was Mullins and Peter Scott used his aristocratic profile to great advantage as Gentleman Starkey. The flying worked moderately well although it was somewhat restricted by the limitations of the stage. When the children "flew" we had to take great care that they did not soar into the wall in the wings.

But the run of *Peter Pan* did not progress without untoward incident. In addition to his duties as janitor and as a teacher in the children's class that had been inaugurated that year as part of the NPS School, Gary Montgomery was cast as the understudy for the male characters. It was never made clear to him that he was expected to learn *all* the male roles — a marathon challenge. At one matinee he learned that he would have to go on as Captain Hook in place of Bruce Belfrage who was *hors de combat.* Undoubtedly Drew Thompson, who played Mr. Darling, would have been a better Hook than the ex-BBC announcer, Belfrage, who was addicted to the grape. With the first act to learn the lines before Hook appeared, Gary sat in the dressing room he shared with Drew Thompson suffering the actor's worst nightmare. Not sure of Captain Hook's movements, he was shunted around the stage by the other actors. He also had to substitute for Belfrage for the evening performance. According to Gary, he felt very proud when I told him the next day that during the matinee he was "like a sleep-walker," but that for the evening performance "it was beginning to work."[26] I rather hoped that Mr. Belfrage would continue to be unavailable because I thought Gary would have developed into a better Hook. With that exception, *Peter Pan* went smoothly, and children and adults alike were delighted with the show. It is to the credit of the cast, Peter Foy, and the crew that the show worked as well as it did, and it is to the credit of Dora Mavor Moore and the NPS that *Peter Pan* was brought to the Toronto public at all with most of its charm intact.

However, the accumulative disillusionment and frustration I was feeling culminated in an incident that was the last straw. The children rehearsed in the evenings and during the mid-rehearsal break would go to the Honey Dew below our studio. Some of them would be short of cash and would borrow from the costume mistress who served as the boys' supervisor. One boy accumulated a debt to her of $5. They were not paid for rehearsals but received $10 for the week they performed both matinees and evenings. Mrs. Moore cut their stipend to $5 for the second week when they performed only matinees. A few days before the show was to close, Mrs. Moore asked me when making up the payroll to stop the money of the boy in debt to the costume mistress, which meant that he would receive no pay for that second week. I refused because the money was not owed to the NPS. I argued that it was up to the costume lady to collect her own debts and that we had no right to give the boy's meagre stipend to anyone but him or his parents. Mrs. Moore insisted and I adamantly refused. I even offered to pay the $5 myself because I suspected that the child came from a family not well off. Mrs. Moore would not hear of it. Nor would she countenance the NPS paying the debt even though that very day she spent $75 on linoleum for the studio so the space could be rented to CBC-TV for dance rehearsals. We came to an impasse. I decided that I could no longer function as business manager and I resigned. I finished the two-week run of *Peter Pan* and saw to it that the payroll was met including the $5 to the boy who had caused the clash between D.M.M. and me.

I deeply regretted that we had had another falling out. I am sure Mrs. Moore never understood that the $5 incident was the last straw on a large pile. In previous disagreements I had always been at great pains to control my temper, which has a quick flash point. Once I was so exasperated with her that I hurled a folded newspaper across the office at her. It unfolded in mid-flight and showered her in sheets of paper, which struck us both as funny and we burst into laughter. But by 1953 working for the NPS had become too aggravating and too disappointing.

■

During the preparation of *Peter Pan*, like the camel in the tent, the Stratford Festival grew to occupy more of our time and working space. Mrs. Moore had become an avid supporter of Patterson's dream and to save it money during its formative stage she had invited the Festival to share our offices. At the time, its staff consisted of only Mary Joliffe in Public Relations and Patterson, but two more desks in our small space made it very congested and impossible to conduct business privately. When I realized that the Festival had become a fixation with Mrs. Moore, I asked her, "Are you working for the New Play Society or the Stratford Festival?" She replied, "The Festival must be pushed through. It can't be allowed to fail." "Well," I said, "They won't thank you, you know." Two decades later as chairman of the Canadian Actors' Equity, I had the honour of presenting Mrs. Moore with Equity's first Life Membership Award. I drove her home after the party and she invited me into her small apartment. After reminiscing about old times over a glass of wine, she made a remark that caused me to choke up: "I always remember that you said, 'They won't thank you, you know'." To that time, she had been given only slight recognition for her contribution to Canadian theatre and she had not received proper credit for giving Patterson and the Festival a leg up. After all, she was the one who wrote to John Coulter in England at the time asking him to introduce Patterson's idea to Tyrone Guthrie. Hers was the place Guthrie stayed the first night he came out to meet the Stratford organizing committee. She used her contacts with influential people such as Leonard Brockington, president of Odeon Theatres of Canada, whom she urged to bring pressure on his boss J. Arthur Rank to persuade some of his "stars" to perform at Stratford. Her assistance to the Festival was extensive but often well in the background.

But, I outrun my tale. By late autumn of 1952, the Stratford Festival was a going concern, largely due to Tyrone Guthrie's enthusiasm and his charismatic personality. Just before Christmas, he returned from Britain to interview applicants for the Festival company. The interviews were to be in the NPS studio. I had not met Guthrie but I had been made aware by Mrs. Moore and Tom Patterson of the honour being bestowed on the NPS by having this distinguished British director in our midst. Therefore, as business manager, I wanted everything to run smoothly. In honour of the occasion but not knowing anything about his personality or taste, I decided to put on my only suit. Mrs. Moore, who seldom arrived anywhere on time, was not at the office that morning so Tom, who already knew Guthrie, and I were the welcoming party. I was not prepared for the towering, casually dressed, hawk-like figure who climbed the long flight of stairs to our office.

To allow for privacy I had placed chairs in the vestibule for waiting actors and a table and two chairs for the interviews at the far end of the studio beside a window. After the first interview, Guthrie came to me and requested that he be moved into the anteroom at the front of the building. The view he had out of the dirty studio window overlooking the sordid lane had been too depressing. Tom and I moved the table and chairs to the equally dirty window overlooking busy Yonge Street. The view was more interesting, but privacy was sacrificed. With no doors on Mrs. Moore's office or on the one shared by Isabelle Gale, Mary Joliffe, Patterson, and myself, everything said in the outer office could be heard by all of us. I knew most of the actors and had worked with many of them. Those interviews proved quite revealing about a number of the applicants — some of whom were too modest, others prone to gross exaggeration — and about Tyrone Guthrie.

I was an applicant as well. No sooner had we got Guthrie re-established than Tom came to me and said, "There has been a cancellation. Would you like to be interviewed by Mr. Guthrie now?" A trifle nonplussed, I had to shift from being the welcoming manager of the NPS to being a supplicant. However, I said yes and sat down in front of the great man. During the interview I became conscious of my clothes. In my dark suit and conservative tie I looked more like a bank manager than a starving actor. He asked me about my career, which by then included several seasons as a director. Smiling, he suddenly asked me, "What in Shakespeare would you ultimately like to play?" "Ultimately?" I asked. "Yes," he replied. With no hesitation I blurted out, "Hotspur, Hamlet, and Richard the Second." The smile vanished from his face, "Yes. I can see why you would." "Oh, oh," I thought, "He did not like that reply. But he did say 'ultimately'." The interview came to an abrupt conclusion after that.

As I listened all that day to the interviews, I detected that Guthrie was friendlier and responded more positively to those who took a humble approach than to those who appeared confident and tried to impress. At the end of the day he asked me about an actor I had directed in the International Players. Edward Holmes had been an accountant in Calgary and an amateur actor. In his middle years he had decided to turn pro and come to Toronto to build a career. He was handsome, distinguished-looking, prematurely grey, with a classic actor's profile and a resonant, rich voice. He had only one problem — difficulty memorizing. He had never developed the technique of learning lines quickly for weekly stock. In several plays for the International Players, he had been shaky on lines. But I liked him very much as a person and we had become good friends. When Guthrie asked me what I thought of him, he really put me on the spot. Ed and I were actors suitable for similar roles and as such were rivals for a berth at Stratford. If I gave Guthrie an untruthful answer, and Ed were hired and came a cropper, Guthrie might hold it against me. I decided to give him my honest opinion. I told him that Ed was a splendid character actor, but that he had not yet developed the ability to learn quickly enough for weekly stock. "But," I hastily added, "if he has several weeks to learn a role, he should be alright." "Well," said Guthrie, "I liked his attitude. He came hat in hand." I was shocked. So humility is the requirement for getting into Stratford, I thought. I also wondered if this was Guthrie's way of telling me that I did not qualify because I did not come "hat in hand." Some years later when I told Eric House this story, Eric, who had worked with Guthrie and had a high regard for him, reacted with disbelief. He maintained that Guthrie must have meant something else. But that conversation is seared in my memory and I cannot think that it meant anything but what he said. I was happy that Ed Holmes was hired for that first Stratford season. I have been told by several Stratford actors that even with many weeks of rehearsal, he was often uncertain with his lines. But Guthrie liked him and was loyal. After Ed moved to New York, Guthrie hired him for several of his Broadway productions. For this I admire Guthrie as well as for his brilliance as a director and his immeasurable contribution to the Stratford Festival. Ed and I remained good friends even after he left Canada. When he died some years later of a brain tumour, I began to wonder if the early roots of that tumour might have affected his ability to memorize.

■

The existence of Jupiter Theatre, founded in 1951 by a small group of radio actors and writers including John Drainie and Lorne Greene, spurred Mrs. Moore to produce another full season in 1953–54. Its line-up consisted of a stage adaptation of *Mistress of Jalna*, Christopher Fry's *Venus Observed*, *Duet for Two Hands*, the pantomime *Cinderella*, *The Play's the Thing*, *The Silver Tassie*, *The Miser*, and *Spring Thaw '54* — an impressive list. I saw several of these productions and they continued the high standard of acting previously established by the NPS. During March 15 to 27, 1954, the NPS participated in the International Theatre Month. But that winter marked the last full season for the Society. After that it produced only spasmodically: the annual *Spring Thaws* at the Avenue Theatre, a converted movie house on Eglinton Avenue, *Sunshine Town* in 1955, and *The Optimist*, Mavor Moore's musical adaptation of Voltaire's *Candide*, the charmingly *déja vu* music for which suffered in comparison with the dynamic originality of Leonard Bernstein's score for his version of *Candide* that was produced at about the same time. A show called *Holiday Party* was staged from December 26 to January 5 of 1957, and in January a Canadian play about World War II, *Turvey*, adapted by Don Harron from Earle Birney's novel. But following that success, the NPS had to vacate the Avenue Theatre and future productions were limited to those produced in conjunction with the NPS School at the old Moulton College coach house on Asquith Avenue and finally in a studio at 88 Bloor St. East, and to those produced for the Canadian Mental Health Association.

After I quit the NPS, I performed for them only once. I was cast in Mavor's version of Stephen Leacock's *Sunshine Sketches of a Little Town*. Mrs. Moore and I continued to be friends and I often visited her in her office where we would chat about theatre in general. The NPS went on through the '50s, '60s, and into the '70s, its entropy often imminent. But somehow Mrs. Moore would revive it. The last days of that organization are poignantly described in Mavor's biography.[27] Eventually D.M.M. began to get the recognition she so richly deserved, when she was honoured with the Centennial Medal, Actors' Equity Life Membership, a Doctorate of Fine Arts, an Honourary L.L.D., the Order of Canada, and other tributes. However, I am sure she would be the first to concede that all those other hard working and talented people, without whom the New Play Society could not have existed, were also being honoured.

In this account of my on-again, off-again association with Dora Mavor Moore over a 10-year period, I have tried to reveal her not as the legend posterity is beginning to make of her, but as a remarkable human being with all her virtues and foibles. I once told Mavor that I had had a kind of love-hate relationship with his mother, and he replied, "You were not alone."

She had a disarming way of using people. You knew you were being used, but you somehow felt privileged to be used by Mrs. Moore. Even though we had our rows and I eventually concluded that a thoroughly professional theatre company on a sound business basis was not possible under her guidance, I admired her drive, her determination, her sense of humour, particularly about herself, her lack of affectation in her clothes, her acceptance of everyone no matter what social status, race, or religion, her encouragement of young people, her self-sacrifice, her dreams. She once said to me, "Other people have their religion. Some are Catholics, Anglicans, Jews, whatever. But my religion is the theatre." And it was. There never was a more devoted worshipper.

Third Annual
Open Air
TORONTO

𝔖𝔥𝔞𝔨𝔢𝔰𝔭𝔢𝔞𝔯𝔢 𝔉𝔢𝔰𝔱𝔦𝔳𝔞𝔩

Under the Distinguished Patronage of

HIS HONOUR THE LIEUT. GOVERNOR OF ONTARIO AND MRS. RAY LAWSON

HIS WORSHIP THE MAYOR OF TORONTO AND MRS. H. C. MCCALLUM

RT. HON. VINCENT MASSEY, C.H., CHANCELLOR OF THE UNIVERSITY OF TORONTO

THE HON. LESLIE M. FROST, K.C., PREMIER OF ONTARIO, AND MRS. FROST

DR. SIDNEY E. SMITH, PRESIDENT OF THE UNIVERSITY OF TORONTO AND MRS. SMITH

DR. R. S. K. SEELEY, D.D., LL.D., D.C.L., PROVOST OF TRINITY COLLEGE

DR. J. G. ALTHOUSE, DIRECTOR, DEPT. OF EDUCATION, AND MRS. ALTHOUSE

by

𝔗𝔥𝔢 𝔈𝔞𝔯𝔩𝔢 𝔊𝔯𝔢𝔶 𝔓𝔩𝔞𝔶𝔢𝔯𝔰
July 2 to July 28, 1951

in

Trinity College Quadrangle

COVER PHOTO: By Nelson Smith

CHAPTER 7

In a Quad

The New Play Society is generally accepted as the first English-Canadian theatre company after World War II to pay its actors and thus win the label of "professional." But pre-dating the September 1946 advent of the NPS by several months was a production that used actors who had already built careers as professionals. I was involved, although unpaid, and I assume that most of my fellow supporting actors performed as amateurs, but I expect that the leads were paid. The production was Shakespeare's *Twelfth Night* staged in the open air in the incomplete quadrangle of Trinity College at the University of Toronto. The producer and director was the expatriate Anglo-Irishman, Earle Grey. When the visiting Barry Jones/Maurice Colbourne company of *Charles the King* disbanded in autumn of 1939, some of the cast remained in Canada. Among them were Grey and his wife, Guinevere. Mr. Grey was born in Dublin where during his formative years he acted with the Abbey Players. At the age of 20 he went to England where he performed at Stratford-on-Avon and at the Oxford Playhouse when Tyrone Guthrie was a budding stage manager there. In 1930 he was one of the actors in the first play ever televised, Pirandello's *The Man with the Flower in His Mouth* presented by the BBC. He toured South Africa with Sir Frank Benson's Shakespeare Company, and appeared on Broadway in *The Matriarch* with Constance Collier. Back in London he played in the first production of *Richard of Bordeaux* with John Gielgud and Irene Vanbrugh.

Guinevere, whose stage name was Mary Godwin, was born in London, England, where through amateur productions she worked her way into the professional West End theatre. She eventually toured in *St. Joan* with Sybil Thorndike and Lewis Casson, and *Measure for Measure* with Flora Robson and Robert Donat. She met Earle Grey when they were both playing at the Old Vic and they soon married.

In Canada, Grey supported himself and his wife by writing, directing amateur groups, and performing on radio. In collaboration with Canon Ward of the Anglican Church, he wrote, acted in, and directed many religious plays for radio. He was instrumental in the founding of RATS (Radio Actors' Toronto Society), the first association of professional actors in the country, formed to protect the radio artists from exploitation by public and private broadcasters. Eventually RATS became ACRA (Association of Canadian Radio Artists) and then ACTRA (Association of Canadian Television and Radio Artists). Mr. Grey was president of that organization for seven years.

During an evening stroll around their newly adopted city, they discovered the beautiful Tudor-Gothic structure of Trinity College with its incomplete quadrangle, the north terrace of which backed onto a playing field. A perfect location for open-air Shakespeare, they agreed. With the support of Trinity's Provost, R.S.K. Seeley, they planted the roots of Canada's first Shakespeare festival, recruiting some of the best actors in Toronto for "The Earle Grey Players." In their first show, *Twelfth Night,* Grey himself played Malvolio, Vincent Tovell played Duke Orsino, Robert Christie, who had just returned to Canada from the Old Vic, was Antonio, George Patton was Sir Toby Belch, Dorothy Jane Goulding was Maria, and the profoundly talented but perpetual amateur Norman Green played Sir Andrew Aguecheek. Mary Godwin appeared as Olivia, and their son, Anthony Grey, was a courtier, as was Walter Plinge, whose singularly fascinating name appeared in many of Grey's productions. He had already played two roles in *Charles the King.* Mr. Plinge was the British equivalent of George Spelvin, a name covering the identity of an actor doubling a role and who had been listed earlier on the program. Among the highlights was music composed by Godfrey Ridout — especially his treatment of "Come

Away Death" — played by a six-piece orchestra of strings and woodwinds. A lesser highlight was the appearance of a Russian wolfhound, Michaelhoff, who succeeded in stealing every scene he was in, which was quite an accomplishment when Mary Godwin was onstage. I played Valentine but I certainly did not electrify the Toronto theatre world.

Grey was very much a Shakespearian purist, as he explained in a progam note:

> Of late there has been a tendency to present Shakespeare in a mannered style — either acting, mounting, or costuming. But most playgoers do not relish these attempts to bolster the playwright's work, nor are they pleased when self-conscious directors interpose themselves between author and audience. It is in this connection that the director of these performances offers them in plainness and simplicity.[1]

The only editing he did was to shorten the play slightly, recognizing that an untrained Toronto audience of 1946, no matter how "cultured" it considered itself and no matter how gripping the drama, could not be expected to tolerate a production longer than two-and-a-half to three hours.

The two performances of *Twelfth Night* in June 1946 were successful enough that the next year in May the Greys staged *The Quality of Mercy* written by Grey himself, and in July, *A Midsummer Night's Dream*. In October 1948 they took Sophocles' *Antigone* to McMaster University, and in February 1949, with great fortitude, they tackled Toronto secondary school audiences at Oakwood Collegiate and Danforth Tech with *Twelfth Night*. But the major development, for which all this had been a preparation, came in June 1949 with the establishment of the Earle Grey Shakespeare Festival in the Trinity College quad. The opening play was *As You Like It* with John Drainie in the role of Touchstone, and Margot Christie as Rosalind. In smaller parts were two actors who were to build successful careers, Louis Negin as the First Lord and a young Timothy

Findley as both Second Lord and Dennis. For the first production there had been enough money to build a set as background for the action, but, apparently not enough to build a wall to conceal the actors in the wings as Rose Macdonald noted in the *Toronto Telegram*, a comment that says a lot about people's expectations at the time: "It is a bit disconcerting to have stage folk in their off moments strolling about in full view of the audience."[2] *As You Like It* was followed by *A Midsummer Night's Dream* in which a young William Hutt made an appearance as Duke Theseus. They followed the latter play with a revival of *Twelfth Night.*

The next spring they presented *Measure for Measure* in Hart House Theatre, and that summer back in the quadrangle added a fourth play, extending the season to four weeks. *A Midsummer Night's Dream* was repeated followed by *The Taming of the Shrew* with Lorne Greene as Petruchio and Mary Godwin as Kate, *The Tempest* in which Earle Grey played Prospero and John Drainie was Caliban, and yet another revival of *Twelfth Night*. In subsequent years the Festival staged *Much Ado About Nothing, Julius Caesar,* and *The Winter's Tale.* Ernst Wanger wrote in the *Globe and Mail* about that production: "In tackling this difficult piece the Earle Grey Players gave proof of their growing faith in themselves and their public."[3] Later years saw them staging still another *Twelfth Night* in which Daniel Hyatt took on the role of Valentine. Mr. Hyatt was to become an ambassador from the Canadian theatre to the Soviet Union when years later he gave one-man readings of Shakespeare in that country.

For many years concerts of "The Music of Shakespeare's Day" were arranged as an adjunct to the Festival. Renowned singers such as contralto Portia White and mezzo-soprano Joan Hall, supported by the Klemi Hambourg String Ensemble or the Marcus Adeney String Quartet, presented songs and music appropriate to the period in which each play was staged, under the stars surrounded by the suitably Elizabethan architecture of Trinity College. From 1954 through 1958 there were revivals of *A Midsummer Night's Dream, The Merchant, The Winter's Tale, The Tempest,* and new productions of *Hamlet, King Lear, Two Gentlemen of Verona, The Comedy of Errors,* and *As You Like It.* During those years the Players expanded their touring throughout Ontario and even as far afield as Halifax, braving the unpredictable monsters known as secondary school audiences. Before the Canada Council Touring Office, they were dependent on the small fees paid by the schools and on the sponsorship of such organizations as the Halifax Kiwanis Club and the Prince Edward Island Shrine Club. The Earle Grey Players were one of the first companies to tour after the war and the conditions they met were most frequently primitive. Dressing rooms were often classrooms with no proper lighting for putting on make-up. Facilities for washing were inadequate and often downright sordid. Hotel accommodation had to be inexpensive and therefore often dirty, dreary, and depressing. It was truly pioneering work, introducing Shakespeare to audiences who might never have seen a play before. Altogether these intrepid players clocked over 21,000 miles around the roads of Ontario. On one trip in 1954 Hurricane Hazel had created so much havoc that the main road between Walkerton and Thornbury was blocked. But after some detouring they found a road that took them to Thornbury, much to the pleasant surprise of the patient audience.[4] During one high school performance when Mary Godwin as Portia in *The Merchant of Venice* opened the curtain to reveal the three caskets by which she plans to test her suitors, she was dismayed to discover the actor playing Tubal perched like a leprechaun on top of the golden casket. He was simply resting there having forgotten that this crucial scene was next. Startled and flustered he scuttled off. The audience roared with laughter.[5] What Ms. Godwin roared at him later has not been recorded.

In 1959 the Festival was denied use of Trinity College because a new addition was to be built on its north side, thus completing the quadrangle. The Greys investigated other venues but nothing was either suitable or available. The result was no Shakespeare Festival in Toronto that year. Nor was there ever another by the Earle Grey Players. Mr. Grey had directed other organizations during his years in Canada, such as the Victoria College Dramatic Society, and a private presentation for the Arts and Letters Club of John Coulter's stage adaptation of *Oblomoff*, a novel by the early 19th-century Russian novelist, Ivan Gontcharoff. But when he could no longer produce his beloved Shakespeare Festival, I believe the heart went out of him. In 1960 he and his wife returned to England, where they tried to pick up careers after a 21-year absence.

As everyone knows, the advent of the Stratford Shakespeare Festival in 1953 was tremendously beneficial to the young Canadian theatre and to the culture of this country. But it had a negative effect on the Earle Grey Festival. Stratford, with its million dollar budgets, its new, innovative theatre, its famed directors and its international stars, put the Toronto Festival into the shade. Inevitably the shoe-string productions of the Earle Grey company seemed tacky in comparison. They received no support from any government body until 1958 when Metropolitan Toronto granted them $5,000, the Atkinson Foundation $5,000, and the Ontario Department of Education, which benefitted most from the company's school tours, a measly $2,000. That year the Canada Council added a matching grant of $12,000. But from its inception, the company had always had to operate on a small budget. Naturally, this was reflected in the quality of the productions. But it must be admitted that part of the problem was the tendency of Earle Grey, a benign man, to permit his wife to perform roles for which she was too old and physically too matronly. It sometimes sorely tried one's willingness to believe.

After my one appearance in 1946 I did not perform with the Earle Grey Players again, largely due to my commitments with the NPS. But after I returned from England I tried to see as many of their shows as possible because, until the Stratford Festival, they were the best Shakespeare available. Even so I find it difficult to assess the overall effect these more than 10 years of Shakespearian productions had on the theatrical community. Certainly they introduced more Ontario residents to Shakespeare than ever before. Certainly they upped the standard of production several notches above Toronto's Shakespeare Society. Certainly there were many fine individual performances seen in the Trinity quad. In general the productions were beautifully spoken because Mr. Grey instilled in his actors a deep appreciation for Shakespeare's poetic line. But the treatments were pedantic and often unexciting. His commendable approach to Shakespeare's plays, "to offer them in plainness and simplicity," led him to eschew any innovation whatever. Nothing was done to make the presentations visually arresting or to find in the text new and revelatory interpretations for a modern audience. Nevertheless, the Earle Grey Shakespeare Festival filled a gap in the Toronto theatre scene and brought live portrayals of Shakespeare's plays to young audiences who otherwise would have known his works only from the dreary approach taken by most Ontario teachers of English literature. In an interview with Mr. Grey shortly before he returned to England, Herbert Whittaker commented on the demise of the Festival: "Mr. Grey is speaking more in sorrow than in anger."[6] But that very observation indicated Grey's disappointment and disillusionment. To create an audience for his beloved Bard and to bring these great plays to Ontario's theatrical heathen, he spent 21 years in Canada, which, if they had been spent elsewhere, would probably have been more rewarding. He and his wife contributed enough to Canada that they deserved better from their adopted country. At least ACTRA recognized his contribution and in 1972 created the Earle Grey Award, and further to ACTRA's credit, brought Mr. Grey back from England to present it.

Fourth Annual Season
Seventh Week
HOTEL LA SALLE
KINGSTON, - ONTARIO

ARTHUR SUTHERLAND and DREW THOMPSON
— PRESENT —
THE INTERNATIONAL PLAYERS
IN
The World Famous Melodrama
"East Lynne"
BY MRS. HENRY WOOD
STAGED BY VERNON CHAPMAN
SCENERY BY WARREN COLLINS
Furniture courtesy of Cramer's Antique Shop
Stage properties courtesy of Spearn's Gift Shop

OUR NEXT ATTRACTION
Week Beginning Monday, July 16th, 8:45 Nightly
COSY LEE
With MARY DRAMER and KATHLEEN ROBERTS
In the laugh-a-minute Broadway comedy riot
"CRADLE SNATCHERS"
Twice as funny as last season's "Stepping Sisters"

CHAPTER 8

In Limestone City

In February of 1950 I had found time, between NPS shows, to direct *Mrs. Moonlight* by Benn Levy for the International Players' winter season at the Leaside high school auditorium in Toronto. When the scheduled director, Ted Follows, had to bow out, I was asked to take over, the first of three occasions when I would benefit by Ted's giving up one job for another. It also marked the first time I had directed a professional company. Rose Macdonald wrote that I brought this play "of fancy and representational theatre" to the stage with "felicity,"[1] whatever she meant by that. It was a schmaltzy play from 1930 that is seldom performed now, but I was fortunate in having an actress who brought great warmth to the role of Mrs. Moonlight in the person of Mona O'Hearne who was by then well established as a radio artist. That very handsome, suave leading man, Douglas Ney, was Tom Moonlight and quite up to the challenge of ageing 50 years during the course of the play. It was the success of this production that convinced Drew Thompson and Arthur Sutherland to employ me later as the permanent director for their summer season in Kingston.

These two producers were a combination of opposites. Drew Thompson was the scion of a prominent Ottawa family who had been involved in that city's social and political life. I always thought that Drew was born in the wrong century because his manner, poise, and good taste reflected that of an 18th-century aristocrat. He had a wicked sense of humour and a profound sense of the ridiculous. He was neat and fastidious, with an appreciation of life's finer things. When he was pleased, his face would light up with an impish grin, and when displeased it could twist in a second into a vision of apoplectic rage. However, his bark was always worse than his bite. He was a dream to work with because his intelligence and talent were such that he responded immediately, and usually positively, to a director's suggestions. Although the International Players presented comedies more frequently than dramas, Drew was expert in both. I do not believe he had any formal training but like so many other great actors he was a "natural" who performed instinctively and perfected his craft through the school of experience. When I first saw him as a student actor in the Trinity College production of *Chicken Every Sunday*, he already seemed an experienced performer. He was a brilliant *farceur*. I thought of him as the rich man's Clifton Webb, whom he resembled facially. But he was much more versatile than Webb. Not only could Drew play with the arch style that epitomized Webb's performances, but he could also perform with a common, earthy quality, and he was meticulous in his preparation for every role even in the limited time afforded by weekly stock.

Arthur Sutherland, on the other hand, was the personification of casual. Although quite handsome, he did not concern himself about his appearance, had little or no interest in the finer things of life, and was a mediocre actor at best, but he had a deep love for the theatre. He was imperturbable, invariably courteous, never got angry, had an unsophisticated sense of humour, and seemed perpetually disorganized. Although I suspect there were some accounts for the International Players that were kept by Arthur's father in his home, the company never seemed to have an office. So far as I could judge, the office was Arthur's pockets, or the glove compartment of his car. He was an incurable optimist, and it was this optimism that founded the International Players and kept it going through great difficulties until his untimely death in 1953. Born in Kingston in 1910 of moderately well-off parents, Arthur developed an interest in theatre, as did many Canadian performers, from seeing amateur productions. His enthusiasm was stimulated by the Queen's University Drama Guild, where he met fellow students Robertson Davies and Lorne Greene and where he received the nickname "Suds," possibly as a diminutive of Sutherland, but more probably because he drank a lot of foaming beer. He won a Dominion Drama Festival award that "hooked" him into the theatre and he cajoled his parents into sending him to one of North America's few theatre schools, the American Academy of Dramatic Art in New York. When he graduated, he and a group of fellow students formed the Imperial Players who toured the greater New York area until the United States was sucked into World War II. Arthur joined the Special Services branch of General Patton's Third Army, and with a bevy of Hollywood and Broadway stars toured the United States and Europe entertaining the troops. After the war he toured in Maurice Evans's *Hamlet*, appeared on Broadway in *Brother Rat*, and played in a stage version of the comic strip, *Blondie*. In 1948, when visiting his parents in Kingston, he went to see Charles Orenstein, owner of the La Salle Hotel, and persuaded him to rent the ballroom where Arthur established the International Players. It is to Charles Orenstein's credit that he took a tack at variance with other businessmen of the day, and gave an artist the opportunity he was seeking. Arthur then contacted Dora Mavor Moore who put him in touch with Glenn Burns, who in turn introduced him to Drew Thompson who joined the company as an actor before becoming Arthur's co-producer.

The name International Players was chosen partly because Arthur thought he might bring some of his actor friends from the United States, which rarely happened. Arthur hoped also that with Kingston's closeness to the border, the name might attract American tourists. At first the money backing the venture was Arthur's savings, but Drew brought additional funds when he became a partner. Over time I believe Drew used most of an inheritance in supporting the Players. The first acting company included such fine performers as Josephine Barrington (at one time drama teacher to Lloyd Bochner and many others), Jean Cruchet of the NPS, Marion Jones, the expatriate English character actor Frank Wade, Glenn Burns, Drew, and Arthur. They began with *Apron Strings*, which established a pattern of light comedy for them, although occasionally they threw in heavier drama for variety. Their purpose was primarily escapist summer entertainment designed to entice an audience into the La Salle Ballroom and keep it returning for more. However, during that first season they also were willing to gamble on a new Canadian play, Robertson Davies's *Fortune My Foe*. The celebrated Canadian artist Grant Macdonald was recruited to do the sets and he was to design many more for them in the years to come.

The first season, which ended on a two-week run of *Fortune My Foe*, had been encouragingly successful, but the opening weeks of summer 1949 had seen a drop in attendance. The problem was suspected to lie in the admission price, a whopping $1.20 with back row seats at 60 cents,[2] more than most movies. Arthur and Drew decided to undercut them with a "pay-as-you-like" policy. Arthur also introduced a "spiel" to the audience before the final act of each play. After Arthur's speech in which he plugged next week's play and urged the audience to be generous to this week's effort, baskets were passed around. Just as the collection in church increases if the choir has been singing well or the minister has given a rousing sermon, when I was directing I often doctored the end of the act to give a stronger final moment before the curtain closed in order to stimulate the audience toward greater generosity. Comedies usually elicited a larger take, and the International Players became expert at comedy and farce. Some people would contribute as much as $5, and some as little as five cents, but there was never any evidence that La Salle audiences contributed nothing. This policy allowed Arthur to advertise the company as "The World's Only Pay-What-You-Like Theatre." Audiences increased, revenue grew, and they extended their 1949 season to 16 weeks, the longest of any summer stock company in Canada at that time.[3] Their 1950 season continued in the same vein and included the expansion into Toronto in which I directed *Mrs. Moonlight*.

When I joined as their director for the 1951 Kingston season, Drew and Arthur had hired a nucleus of tried-and-true performers from Toronto to be fleshed out with local talent and the occasional visiting performer for a special role. Billing was not a common practice in the Canadian theatre in the '40s and '50s, but with the International Players — reflecting Arthur's American conditioning — visiting performers would often be given top billing over the title, and with unprecedented generosity, even over the names of the two producers. The acting company that year consisted of Drew Thompson, Cosette Lee, Ron Poffenroth (later Hartmann), Sandy Webster, Christine Thomas, Neil Vipond, Timothy Findley, and Mary Damer (an Eve Arden type), with local talent such as the strong character actress Kathy Roberts, the charming, beautiful Margaret Shortliffe, and Letitia Edinborough, who seemed delighted to play bit parts — a rare attitude indeed. Among the actors brought in from Toronto to play in one or two shows were Sandra Scott, who had built a reputation for herself as one of Andrew Allan's radio stock company, Pegi Brown, Deborah Turnbull, and Barbara Davis, who had by then become Barbara Chilcott. Later on Norma Renault joined the company. She was not only a fine character actress and comedienne, but had been a vocalist with the Leslie Bell Singers. Occasionally when a character actor was needed in a supporting role, I would step in to save the management money. Sometimes Arthur would appear in a small role. Obviously this was no union company. If there was any "star" in the company, it was Drew Thompson who proved his wonderful flexibility in a variety of roles. Cosette Lee was much loved by the Kingston public and deservedly so. She was not only clever at comedy but also a solid character actress. She too was an instinctive performer who worked from gut feeling rather than from intellect. During the course of that long season, which ran from May 15 to November 24, with a change-over almost every week, each actor in the permanent company was given a chance to play several leading roles. Timothy (Tiff) Findley and Neil Vipond shared the juvenile roles. Both were very sensitive young actors, and, although Tiff gave up performing to become one of Canada's most popular and prolific authors, Neil became an established character actor in both Canada and America.

Because we could not afford them and the stage space did not allow for lavish sets, the scripts and the performances were the criteria on which audiences based their opinions of the shows. Therefore the acting had to be very good. I cast as aptly as possible with the actors available, most of whom were talented enough to make each role distinct from previous ones, but they had to prove their versatility over and over again by stretching into a range of parts. Many of the scripts were forgettable but there were several highlights that compared favourably with what was then being presented elsewhere in Ontario. In my opinion the best production of that summer was *Yes, M'Lord*, which I had seen in London as *The Chiltern Hundreds* starring A.E. Matthews as the vague, dithering Earl of Lister. Drew played the Earl, revealing an ability to throw away lines so that they became even funnier. Notable in one of his few romantic roles, Sandy Webster played Lord Pym and then moved on to the unkempt father in Noel Coward's *Hay Fever*, which starred Sandra Scott as the scatter-brained Judith Bliss. Drew, far from ideally cast, was successful in the challenging role of the boxer, Sandy Tyrell. Later in the season he wore the role of Gary Essendine in Coward's *Present Laughter* as though it was tailor made for him, and Timothy Findley shone as the obnoxious Roland Maule. Hugh Webster joined the company as Henry Lippiatt for that show.

In the autumn I was privileged to direct Barbara Chilcott as Regina Giddens in *The Little Foxes* and she remains in my mind the best Regina I have seen on any stage since. She is a powerful actress who has too seldom been given the opportunity to reveal her range. It was exciting to be onstage experiencing the vibrations she radiated as that monstrous woman. I played Horace Giddens, Ron Hartmann a weak-willed, bullying Oscar, and Tiff Findley a suitably smarmy Leo. Drew Thompson oozed malevolence as Benjamin Hubbard. To get this production mounted at all was something of a triumph because it was performed in the untheatrical ambience of Memorial Hall of which I shall tell you more shortly.

That autumn we also essayed J.B. Priestley's *Dangerous Corner*, an extremely subtle work requiring controlled playing, which was a welcome change from the light comedy usually offered. Despite intelligent performances by Drew, Barbara Chilcott, Norma Renault, Ron Hartmann, and Timothy Findley, I do not think we quite pulled it off, although the very discerning Grant Macdonald wrote a letter to the *Whig-Standard* in which he said, "The International Players meet the demands of the play, in production and performance, affording Kingston an opportunity that cannot be called less than special."⁴ The set for that production was not designed by Mr. Macdonald, but by Neil Vipond.

We closed the season with *The Late Christopher Bean*, a study of how a kindly country doctor, when faced with the possibility of wealth derived from a dead artist's paintings stored in his attic, becomes a grasping, conniving trickster. Ron Hartmann played this role with insight and intelligence. According to Helen Milton reviewing for the *Whig-Standard*, "He makes it one of the finest things he has done."⁵ Norma Renault, who portrayed the doctor's wife, remembers an incident that reveals the somewhat cavalier attitude of one of our crew. In all fairness, I should point out that there were only two crew members, the stage manager and his assistant, who were often overworked. In those pre-Actors' Equity days, if a show was really complicated sometimes the younger actors would be drafted to help. The script calls for a glass of milk for the doctor, which he never drinks. I suppose for economy the property person decided that the milk did not have to be replenished for each performance. Why the glass was not simply painted white, I do not know. As the week of performances wore on this milk became cottage cheese. During one show Ron accidentally knocked the glass over, spilling the white, lumpy goop down the front of his suit. Almost immediately Norma entered, walked up to Ron and, overcome with the stench, retreated to the far side of the stage. Thereafter each actor on entering recoiled to the remote corners of the set, until most of the cast formed a ring around the wall, leaving a forlorn Ron Hartmann isolated in the middle.⁶

For me another of that season's most satisfying productions was one of my favourite American plays, *Life with Father*. For this we augmented the company with local performers, including Margaret Shortliffe's son Gary as Harlan. It was perfect casting for Drew to play father Day and for Margaret to be his wife. Timothy Findley and Neil Vipond shed a few years to be the teenage sons and Hugh Webster became deliciously unctuous for the Reverend Doctor Lloyd. Father and the boys had to have their hair coloured a light auburn. When none of them wanted actual dye, a combination of auburn rinse and coloured powder was used, effective under lights but garish otherwise. Normally, the pressure of preparing a show in a week made rehearsals on Sunday afternoon necessary, although the Lord's Day Alliance Act forbade Sunday performances in Ontario. *Life with Father* was popular enough to be held over, so we had the luxury of a whole free day. Naturally we decided to take a busman's holiday and visit Clayton, New York where a theatre company performed on Sunday and there were no antediluvian blue laws. To get there we had to take the Thousand Island Bridge across the St. Lawrence River at Gananoque. Halfway across on one of the islands stands the Thousand Island Club, once the preserve of American millionaires, but by 1951, deigning to accept even vagabond actors. Because the sale of liquor on Sunday was still taboo in puritan Ontario, we decided to partake of the cocktails at the Club. It was a motley crew that entered the bar of that staid establishment with three men whose hair under the light of day took on hues never found in nature. As a result of American gin being more powerful than the Canadian variety, the drinks being much cheaper, and the cocktail glasses much larger, we quickly began to glow. After several martinis each, we staggered out, much to the relief of the management, and found our way to a riverside restaurant in Clayton where I could apply my formula for quickly sobering up: a half dozen raw oysters followed by a half dozen clams on the half shell. All those uncooked shellfish absorb the alcohol. *Et voilà!* Instant sobriety! Arthur, who was driving, drank hardly anything, but Drew kept indulging. On the way home, just as the Canadian Customs officer was asking us if we had anything to declare, Drew opened the opposite car door and threw up. In disgust, the officer quickly waved us on.

We did not have many such incidents, but we were a convivial company and our need for a respite from our vigorous schedule occasionally put us in conflict with the puritan restrictions on pleasure in Ontario. On another occasion, we decided to have a Sunday morning rehearsal and a picnic in the afternoon. We all contributed food and Arthur bought several cases of beer. We drove to a lovely parkette nestled between the Macdonald-Cartier Highway (401) and the St. Lawrence River where we enjoyed a delicious lunch with beer to wash it down. No one got drunk, and Cosette

Lee, who was naturally abstemious and suffering from a cold, drank nothing at all. Suddenly, as I was relaxing on the front seat of Arthur's car, listening to the radio, Arthur opened the door, thrust a beer bottle under my feet and told me to hide the one I was drinking. "There's a cop on the highway at the top of the road." As Arthur said that, Tiff, anxious to get rid of incriminating evidence, threw the bottle he was drinking into the river. Until then it had never occurred to us that we were doing anything illegal. The cruiser came down the road into the park. A young policeman got out and spoke to us in a lilting Irish dialect: "Did I see somebody throw a bottle into the river?" Drew became quite indignant, but Arthur succeeded in shutting him up. The policeman opened the front door and discovered the two beer bottles. Then he opened the back door where Cosette Lee was sound asleep. Startled awake, she became alarmed on seeing the officer and asked groggily in a wheezy voice, "Whazza matter?," giving the impression that she was absolutely stoned. "Let me look in your trunk," the policeman ordered. Arthur obliged and revealed the remaining beer. The young officer turned to us and smilingly said, "I wouldn't have believed it. I wouldn't have suspected anything had I not seen that bottle thrown into the river." He continued in a crescendo of mock horror: "I can't believe that you would be drinking beer, in a public park, on the King's Highway, on a Sunday, IN ONTARIO!" We had broken the liquor and Lord's Day laws on five counts. Being Irish he was sympathetic, but he had to confiscate the beer "as evidence," and he laid a charge against Arthur in whose car he had discovered the booze. The next day Arthur paid a fine of $60 to which we all contributed, even Cosy Lee who had not drunk a drop. We tried to get the beer back but to no avail. I suspect "the evidence" had been consumed. After that, any picnics we had were held indoors where only one of the blue laws was broken — drinking alcohol on Sunday.

That same season I gained great satisfaction, as did our audiences, from our revival of *East Lynne*, the famous melodrama adapted from Mrs. Henry Wood's novel. Although a favourite with our Victorian ancestors, it had not been performed locally for decades. Drew wanted to send it up, but I persuaded Arthur that it would be more interesting for the audience, more challenging and rewarding for the actors, to do it "straight," in the style and manner of its 19th-century origins. Drew disagreed vehemently, and was furious with us both. What bothered Drew, who had a deserved popularity for his comic ability, was that Arthur and I wanted him to play Archibald Carlyle, the kindly husband who was without a comic line in the whole play. As director, I was fortunate to have some of the best actors available at the time who for weeks had been involved in comedies and farces: Cosette Lee as Archibald's sister, Cornelia; Timothy Findley as Richard Hare, the much wronged brother of Barbara Hare, portrayed by Mary Damer; Gary Shortliffe was cast as Little Willie; and Pegi Brown was imported all the way from Toronto to play the dual role of Madame Vine and Lady Isabelle, the bride of Archibald. The remaining cast consisted of Hugh Webster, Deborah Turnbull, Ron Poffenroth (Hartmann), Neil Vipond, and Cathy Patterson. All welcomed the change to serious, if melodramatic, drama. All except Drew. To everyone's concern but mine, Drew absented himself from the first morning's rehearsal. We rehearsed anyway. He did not show for the afternoon either. I continued to block the play, unperturbed, because I knew that if Drew boycotted this production, I could step in and play the role myself and Arthur would support me. The following morning he still did not appear. Cosette Lee said that she thought she knew where he was. I asked her to find him and tell him that if he did not attend rehearsal that afternoon, he was out of the show and I would play the role. She found him seated by one of the redoubts at Fort Frontenac, assiduously studying his lines. He returned that afternoon, dark as a thundercloud, but after a few rehearsals he began to warm to the task. Throughout the entire run he gave a well-controlled performance without even a smidgen of a comic inflexion.

The initial challenge for the actors was to throw off our own prosaic idiom and embrace the grandiloquent speech familiar to actors and audiences before naturalism became pervasive on our stages. Ben Travers, author of those famous Aldwych farces, referring to the plays he saw in his youth, wrote in his autobiography *A-sitting on a Gate*, "The stage play was not, as it has now become, a representation of life; it was a dramatization of life. Nobody would have paid sixpence to see a mere representation of life. People wanted to be elevated from the humdrum daily routine by the colourful excitements of exaggeration."[7] Although unaware of Mr. Travers' sentiments at the time, I knew that the seemingly stilted language should not be suppressed but should be spoken as though it were the most natural speech in the world. The result was a triumph with our audience, and on the final night over 300 people were turned away. It was nostalgia time for many of the older members of the audience who had seen *East Lynne* some-time in their past, and it was a curio for the younger audience, many of whom came to scoff but stayed to cry along with the rest of the audience at the deaths of Little Willie and Lady Isabelle. Rose Macdonald travelled from Toronto and wrote a glowing report in the *Telegram*. She was partic-ularly impressed with the restraint Drew Thompson demonstrated, with the "sweet seriousness" of Pegi Brown's Lady Isabelle, with Hugh Webster's "waspishness" and with seven-year-old Gary Shortliffe for "a remarkably intelligent deathbed scene."[8] As I have said, children are natural actors, and I had no trouble getting a heart-rending performance from that bright boy.

We were fortunate in having an inventive young designer, Warren Collins, for *East Lynne* who surmounted the ballroom's limited stage by designing flats with changeable panels to indicate the different rooms. To create a proper mood, I had recordings of old favourites played over the speakers: "Just A'wearying for You," "Love's Old Sweet Song," "Come Where My Love Lies Dreaming," "When You and I Were Young, Maggie," and other such treacle. It all had a cumulative effect, breaking down the audience's resistance to the melodrama, and preparing them for the emo-tional bath of the twin deaths of Little Willie and Lady Isabelle, at which, as the saying goes, "there wasn't a dry eye in the house." Some decades later, in a thesis by Florence McHugh, Timothy Findley was quoted as saying, "I have since played *East Lynne* twice in other productions and on both occa-sions we played it for laughs, and it was not nearly as exciting a theatre experience as when we played it straight."[9]

Many actors in Canada now, particularly younger ones, have never known the exigencies of weekly stock. They have no conception of the pressures involved, especially if the company is poor, as most of them were in the '50s. The actors in the International Players had to be versatile and possess celerity at memorizing. They had no time to sit around exploring the character's "id." Swift analysis of the role and equally swift conversion into its physical and psychological persona were required. When later in my career I acted with companies able to afford lengthy rehearsal periods, I often thought that the time was being wasted because I would have discovered the essence of my character early in rehearsal, and I found endlessly chatting about it frustrating. However, this is not to decry the slower, more careful method of preparation. No actor in his right mind would prefer only one week's rehearsal to a longer period so long as the time spent did not become tedious and atrophy invention. On the other hand, the pressure-cooker of weekly stock can cause the actor to become a trickster relying on gimmicks easily adapted from one characterization to another. Truthfulness in portraying a role is essential in all circumstances, but the stock actor has to discover it quickly. Quite often I would first "externalize" a character, finding in the reaches of my memory how a person resembling the character I was portraying moved and sounded, or acted and reacted under similar circumstances to a scene in the play — what Stanislavski calls "emotional memory." Often my portrayal would be modeled on a performance I had seen on the stage or screen. Sometimes the characterization would not jell completely until my experimentation with make-up in front of the mirror created a look that said, "Ah yes! That's it. That's what this guy looks like." Sometimes, but not often, the characterization did not jell at all. Character and situation analyses were always present, but these "externalizations" accelerated the process to meet the needs of weekly stock.

Because the International Players could not afford the luxury of a complete stage crew separate from the actors, after the Saturday night performance the younger actors, some of whom were hired as apprentices, would become the crew, strike the old set, and construct the new one. "Construct" here is a euphemism for "re-arrange." There was only one complete box set with a few additional pieces. With a case of beer supplied by Arthur, we would remove the furniture, move the flats to their new position as indicated by the designer's floor plan, and then help paint them the basic colour. When we had finished this in the small hours of Sunday morning, we would stagger home exhausted, having rehearsed the new show all Saturday and performed the old one on Saturday night. The designer would remain and paint any details wanted on the flats. The striking and setting up were not too difficult at the La Salle Hotel because the storage space for flats and props, though small, was near the stage. But when we moved to the Memorial Hall in October, the change-over became much more strenuous and exhausting. Because there was no backstage space everything had to be stored in the dank basement making for many treks up and down two flights of stairs carrying flats, furniture, and other set "dressing." Most of us would help the stage manager and his assistant. Certainly I never excluded myself from these activities, and quite often Drew and Arthur would participate, although when it came to working with his hands, Arthur was quite hopeless, and likely to get more paint on himself than on the flats.

Every strike night the bats living in Memorial Hall would swoop down to see what was going on and give us encouragement. However, they were less welcome when one or two would fly down to watch the show, as their ancestors no doubt had done at council meetings in the past century. The occasional pigeon also left its calling card. Memorial Hall, an institutional opulence built in the mid-1800s as part of a municipal building suitable for the capital of the Province of Canada, had originally been intended only as a concert hall and council room. It now had portraits of Kingston's ex-mayors glowering down disapprovingly from the rounded wall that half surrounded the platform. There were large Windsor windows in both side walls, which had to be heavily draped to black out daylight for matinees and early evening performances, and the street lights at night. It had a flat floor and fold-down wooden seats that came in groups of three. The one dressing room was a converted storage space and, of necessity, was co-educational. From this bleak room we had to pass through a corner of the Council Chamber, even when council was in session, to the stairs that led up to the stage. The justification for the title "Memorial" was found inside the entrance where, just to put the audience in a receptive mood, was a memorial "to our glorious dead." It was hardly an atmosphere conducive to theatre, particularly to comedy. But theatres as well designed and equipped as we have now either did not exist or were inaccessible to Canadian producers, so companies such as ours were forced to play in generally inadequate conditions.

When the International Players moved into the Memorial Hall, the platform was completely bare. There were no curtains or battens on which to hang anything. Although it was permissable to screw things into the floor of the platform, it was understandably forbidden to attach anything to the walls. The dour portraits were inviolate and could not be removed even for safe-keeping. These restrictions, and the limitations of the hall, posed severe obstacles. Thanks to actor Hugh Webster's ingenuity, some of the problems were solved sufficiently to allow staging in some cases better than we had at the La Salle Ballroom. He devised a scaffolding of three pipe frames crossing the platform, which were braced together and screwed into the floor. Although the pipes were only the size of your average household plumbing, they proved strong enough and rigid enough to hold a travelling curtain and light battens. The framework was also used to anchor our sets and supported the flats and masking curtains. I doubt if there would have been an autumn season in 1951 had it not been for Hugh's inventiveness.

The capacity of the Hall at 650 was twice that of the La Salle Ballroom. Arthur decided to reserve a block of 100 in the first few rows of the centre for those who were willing to pay $1 for a guaranteed seat. This proved unwise because those who arrived early to secure good unreserved seats resented that a section was roped off for those who had the privilege of arriving just before curtain. This block of seats was usually half empty so people moved into them without paying the dollar price. Because the policy at the Memorial Hall was still pay-as-you-like, when the basket was passed at intermission, many who had paid their dollar for a reserved seat considered that to be the full price of admission and contributed no more. As an attempt to wean the Kingston audience away from the pay-as-you-like policy, this was a failure.

Another problem the company faced was the need to alter Kingston's social pattern. Our audiences had become accustomed to attending plays in the summer, but their autumn social commitments did not include a weekly theatre trip. There had to be some heavy persuasion to entice people away from other activities and into the gloomy Memorial Hall, which was not as easily accessible as the La Salle Hotel. Our first show starred one of Kingston's favourites, Cosette Lee, in a perfect role for her talent, the lead in *The Mollusc*, a fascinating study of a woman whose inactivity and lack of ambition harm everyone around her. The other characters were ably performed by Alice Atak, Ron Hartmann, and Timothy Findley, and the workable set was designed by Neil Vipond. But the conditions of opening night, October 1, 1951, did not encourage repeat attendance. The lights we had ordered from Toronto had not arrived. A quickly improvised lighting system left the actors enveloped in mirk. In addition, the weather turned cold and damp and the Hall's maintenance staff had not turned on the heat for the winter, so the audience and performers glaciated. Attendance remained low for the next play, *Dangerous Corner*, but picked up for *The Little Foxes*. The quality of acting was having an impact, and attendance grew again for *Private Lives* with Drew Thompson as Elyot, matched by Barbara Chilcott as Amanda. Norma Renault gave an admirably understated performance as the meek Sybil. But still, the revenue was not sufficient to prevent Arthur and Drew from having to draw on their own funds to keep the company going. They tried two more shows that fall before calling a temporary quits. The first was *Clutterbuck*, in which Ron Hartmann and I played the Basil Radford and Naughnton Wayne-like parts, and Tiff Findley had a rollicking good time in the title role. The understated, throw-away type of humour of the talkie play was probably too English even for Kingston. Helen Milton in the *Whig-Standard* wrote, "Unfortunately, the producers are making the success of this week's production a test. It is unfortunate because *Clutterbuck* is not one of the company's best efforts. Benn Levy's play is mostly talk, talk, talk."[10] But she did go on to praise the performances. I have to agree with her that it was a bad choice if the producers wanted to stimulate the box office. The last play of the season was the aforementioned *The Late Christopher Bean* which had more appeal for the Kingston theatregoer. Attendance picked up again but not enough to save the producers from taking a loss, so Drew and Arthur closed the 1951 season after that audience pleaser and retired to lick their wounds.

During the Christmas break they decided to open again in the same bleak hall on February 4, 1952 with *The Bees and the Flowers*, a frothy comedy that Arthur directed and performed in with, according to Helen Milton, not much success. But the second offering was critically acceptable. I played in and directed *Out of the Frying Pan*. Norma Renault walked away with the show, but also appearing in it were two newcomers, Jill Foster and Audrey Monture, who became great assets to the IPS. The box office for these first two offerings was still not at a break-even point, so Drew and Arthur continued to subsidize the operation. Determined to swell the attendance and gain respect from the culture vultures of Queen's University, they mounted Shaw's *Arms and the Man* in which Jill Foster's fiancé, Bernard Slade (their romance had begun in a summer company several seasons earlier) joined us in the role of Bluntschli. Jill, a fine all-round actress, an attractive blonde, and one of the most level-headed people I have ever known, played Raina Petkoff. I had a great time as Major Sergius Saranoff, the arrogant and absurdly foolish war-lover. Bernie proved to be an effective counter balance as the down-to-earth soldier. None of us had the slightest inkling that Bernie, a rather quiet, somewhat diffident actor with an off-beat sense of humour would become the Bernard Slade of the immensely successful plays *Same Time Next Year* and *Tribute*. When he joined the IPS he actually struck me as a bit helpless. He was not very dextrous with his hands, and was perpetually getting Jill to do things for him. His slight build and thin vocal quality limited his acting range, but as I directed him in more roles, I developed a respect for his ability, particularly in comedy.

Arms and the Man was followed by the recent Broadway hit *Goodbye, My Fancy*, which was followed in turn by Robertson Davies's *At My Heart's Core*. This was not the play's premiere but it was sufficiently new that I got a charge out of staging a script lacking any previous director's instructions

— and I was grateful to Mr. Davies for writing me a letter explaining how his work should be presented. But, the limitations of one week's rehearsal did not allow for sufficient investigation of the play's potential. The speeches were overly long, reflecting more the approach of a novelist than a playwright, and the cast found them difficult to memorize in a week. It was not fair to the author, the cast, to me, nor to the audience to stage a new play in so short a time. The production became one about which I was not at all happy. Nor was Helen Milton, who wrote in the *Whig-Standard*, "The production lacked the polish and assurance necessary to bring the play to life except in occasional moments."[11] I later became an avid fan of Robertson Davies as a novelist, but not as a dramatist. With this experience in mind, decades later, when I was the artistic director of the Gryphon Theatre in Barrie, I refused to produce new plays with only a short rehearsal period. It seemed fairer to stage new Canadian works after they had been broken in elsewhere.

The Philadelphia Story proved to be a more successful venture, and that splendid, versatile, powerful actress, Betty Leighton, came to us from a season in Bermuda to play Tracey Lord. This production included me as Seth Lord, the wayward father of the family. In the early '50s there were very few middle-aged or elderly actors available for the professional stage in Ontario, so youngish performers like myself attempted these older roles with the aid of hair whitener, a voice usually altered to a thinner timbre, and a changed walk. The older the character, the easier the transformation. It is very difficult for a young actor to achieve the subtle differences of middle age, but old age gives scope for broader physical, vocal, and ambulatory changes. Often these are overdone and the elderly character becomes a caricature of old age. Painting with a subtle brush is better, and for the most part it worked for me. The audiences accepted that they were witnessing a studied attempt by a young actor to portray an older man. Now there is a stable of reliable, experienced elderly actors who can take on these vintage roles, although there are not many plays being produced to utilize them. The right actor in the right role is a consummation devoutly to be wished, but I find it regrettable that young actors are now rarely given the opportunity to stretch their talent by essaying these character roles.

Betty Leighton also starred in the next play and it led to a severe test of me as a director. *The Silver Cord* is an ideal vehicle for an actress of Ms. Leighton's talent and intelligence. It is the story of a strong-willed woman who dominates her children, particularly the younger of her two sons, played in our production with great sensitivity by Timothy Findley. At one point during rehearsals I gave Betty a direction, the specifics of which escape my memory, but which had to do with her interpretation of the role. She disagreed and said so bluntly. I have noticed that many actors, including myself, take on some of the temperament of the character they are portraying and I think that is what happened because in the previous production Betty had not questioned my suggestions so brusquely. I dared not let her challenge go by or my control over the company would have been undermined. Theatrical production is of necessity a director's dictatorship, preferably a benevolent one. Co-operative art, or art by a committee, never works. Even when a group of actors voluntarily band together for a show, one guiding individual always dominates. Since the director's responsibility is to pull together the diverse elements of a production, directors must be the final arbiters. They must also be willing and able to guide the actors in interpreting their roles. Yet they must be understanding of the problems actors face and have an open mind to their suggestions when compatible with the director's over-all view of the play. It was not the fact that Ms. Leighton questioned my opinion, it was the manner in which she did it that threatened to undercut my authority.

A fierce argument ensued. I told the other actors to wait in the dressing room while Betty and I battled. Although I secretly admitted to myself that she could be right, I dared not give in to her prematurely. Eventually I reluctantly had to pull rank and told her that she must try it my way or she would not play the role at all. This threat put an end to the argument. The cast was then summoned back to rehearsal where Ms. Leighton reluctantly played the scene my way. I then asked her to play the scene her way, and I conceded, that for her, her idea was better. It was now my decision that her interpretation was preferable. I had managed to keep control. I had no more challenges of that nature from any of the company, and Betty and I became very good friends. I have always been grateful to her because as a result of our contretemps, I gained confidence in myself as a director. Helen Milton, who had become a more astute critic as the shows rolled past, wrote, "Much of the success of the production is due to Betty Leighton, the accomplished actress who appeared with the company last week." She then went on to say, "Some of the main kudos, however, must be kept for Vernon Chapman, who staged this demanding play."[12] In the next production, Terence Rattigan's *O Mistress Mine*, I not only had the pleasure of directing Betty, but I also had the privilege of acting with her again. *O Mistress Mine* was a play I had greatly admired when I saw the Lunts perform it on Broadway, and I had longed to play the role of Sir John Fletcher, the British cabinet minister. Once again Betty Leighton challenged me, but it was the kind of challenge I appreciated — to try to live up to her high standard of acting. She brought great dignity to the role of Fletcher's long-time mistress, Olivia Brown. Once again to quote Helen Milton, "The casting of the three main characters is excellent. Miss Leighton is an enchanting Olivia, playing the role with warmth, vivacity, and tenderness. Mr. Chapman is at his best as the clever, urbane Cabinet Minister lover. Mr. Findley is equally good as the priggish, leftist young son."[13] The Kingston audiences were beginning to find Memorial Hall and found our production a delight but I expect this charming, romantic play has dated badly and would not be accepted by today's audiences.

Nor would *Kiss and Tell*, our next offering. But *Light Up the Sky*, Moss Hart's brilliant comedy about Broadway, would stand the test of time and deserves to be presented more frequently. Edward Holmes, who had joined the company for *Kiss and Tell*, stole every scene of *Light Up the Sky* he was in as an old-school ham actor, despite the fact that he was shaky on his lines. Norma Renault showed her versatility by playing the very cynical Jewish wife of a typical New York theatrical producer. Helen Milton was unenthusiastic about other characterizations in this show, accusing them of overplaying, but as director I was really responsible. Hart's comedy requires an extravagant approach to live up to the extravagant characters he has created, which Milton did not seem to appreciate.

The financial situation dictated that I not only direct but act in the following show, *Harvey*, and I had a delightful time as Dr. Chumley. As director I received the handsome fee of $50 a week, but if I acted in the same show, a small honorarium was added — large enough for the management to feel they were acknowledging the extra work but small enough to save on an actor's full salary (usually $35 or $40 a week). Regrettably in those days before subsidies and Actors' Equity, with producers operating on minuscule budgets, the practice of directors and even stage managers acting was commonplace. A drawback to both acting and directing a show is that the director cannot be out front each night watching to see if the actors are changing their performances. Because Drew was usually in the play as well, the task of monitoring the production fell on Arthur and he was not conscientious about it. Fortunately, adversely altered performances rarely occurred because with only a week's rehearsal and during only six or seven performances, an actor was rarely sufficiently confident about a role to start experimenting.

Hoping to duplicate the phenomenal success we had enjoyed the previous year with *Life with Father*, Drew and Arthur decided to present the sequel, *Life with Mother*. Sequels rarely live up to the original and this was no exception, but it still presented the same loveable, audience-pleasing characters. Once again Margaret Shortliffe displayed her charm and warmth as Vinnie, Drew was sufficiently blustering as Father, and Gary Shortliffe again stole the show as Harlan. Our production was a Canadian premiere and it received a rave notice from the *Whig-Standard's* new critic, Val Lewis.[14] After *Life with Mother* I returned to Toronto to become business manager for *Spring Thaw '52* but I resumed my directing duties at Kingston in June.

During my absence, the International Players had extended their bailiwick to Gananoque, that picturesque town on the St. Lawrence River. Each show opened in the high school auditorium there, played for two nights, then moved to the Memorial Hall in Kingston for the rest of the week. It was a sort of out of town try-out. The Gananoque audience proved very receptive and that scheduling continued throughout the summer. Although Drew and Arthur had managed to rent high school auditoriums in Gananoque and Toronto, they always got nowhere with the Kingston School Board who resolutely refused to let them use any auditoriums. Had the school board been more amenable neither the actors nor the audience would have been obliged to suffer the inconvenience of Memorial Hall. Difficult to heat during the winter, it became a sweat box during the summer. Members of the audience were bathed in perspiration and would put their programs behind their backs to prevent their shirts and dresses from sticking to the hard, varnished wooden seats. Many got into the habit of bringing cushions to sit on. As the summer wore on, more and more of the seat backs and some of the bottoms grew mottled with a plethora of old programs that had become stuck to the wood. Sometimes the print from the programs came off on the backs of ladies' dresses and men's shirts, and one might find members of the audience walking out with the cast list or an advertisement for next week's show imprinted on their backs. Kudos should go not only to the actors and crew who worked under these primitive conditions, but also to the loyal Kingstonians who suffered the discomfort of hot summer nights in this sombre room in order to escape into the magic world of theatre.

But there was little magic in the first play I was asked to direct on my return. *Petticoat Fever* is one of the most inane comedies ever written. Drew, Arthur, Margaret Shortliffe, Neil Vipond, Jill Foster, and myself were the unfortunate performers. We found it so impossibly silly that we decided to have a romp, feeling that our regular audience would understand if we tried to enjoy ourselves in this turkey and entertain them in the process. To compensate for the triteness of the lines and the absurdity of the plot we overplayed shamelessly. That season no reviewers from Toronto had been to any of our more successful efforts, but with a perversity known only to critics, one of them decided to visit Kingston that week and subject himself to our on-stage fun. A few days later a scathing review of our efforts, of Memorial Hall, and of Kingston in general appeared in a Toronto paper. All were found wanting. I have cherished this review ever since because it honestly reveals how a critic can be affected not only by the show but by extraneous events and conditions.

The critic had not checked ahead to ascertain what play we were doing, and on his arrival had discovered to his horror it was *Petticoat Fever*. He wrote, "Last year it so happened that we turned up in Kingston unexpectedly and they were doing *Petticoat Fever* that week too."[15] I suspect he confused us with some other summer theatre because I have no record or memory of our having presented *Petticoat Fever* in 1951. He went on to say, "But it is hard to understand why constant repetitions of *Petticoat Fever* wouldn't help to improve the production. . . . The two producers and the director, Vernon Chapman, were all equally to blame."[16] He lambasted the set and the other actors and concluded, "But why go on? I'm probably prejudiced because the outside of the Municipal Building proved so unrewarding." In a previous paragraph he had written, "Particularly admirable is the Municipal Building, a spacious design topped by a fine dome."[17] I think he meant that the *inside* of the Municipal Building proved unrewarding. He continued to justify his prejudice with, ". . . because the room I got in the charming guest house opened onto a shed rather than directly outside, because the International Players weren't five times better than when they started five years ago. Probably I caught them on an off night, probably they were as bored with the play as I was."[18] There this critic was dead right. His review taught me another lesson. Theatre artists can never afford to let their standards down, not only because it is unfair to the public, but because one never knows who is out there forming judgements. Fortunately, a much better comedy, *Lo and Behold*, followed *Petticoat Fever*. It tapped Drew Thompson's talent more suitably and it marked the debut of the beautiful, talented, and sexy Carol Starkman to the company. Ironically, two shows later Carol had to make herself unattractive and unkempt in *The Curious Savage*, a challenge for someone so naturally pretty.

One of the highlights for me that summer was directing *Born Yesterday* with Drew as Harry Brock and Jill Foster in the Judy Holiday role of Billie Dawn. I also played the corrupt lawyer, Ed Devery, on the first of three occasions I have acted in *Born Yesterday*. Drew once again demonstrated his range, triumphing over his own refined sensibilities by playing Harry as a redneck slob and bully. Jill really shone as Billie Dawn revealing her ear for dialects and her ability to play a brash dumb blonde, the exact opposite of her own nature.

That spring and summer season had been a directing *tour de force* for me. Except for the interlude to manage *Spring Thaw '52*, I had directed a play a week from February to the end of August. Added to the previous year's directing, it was a marathon that left me somewhat punchy. I had become stale and had run dry of invention. By August I felt that the IPS needed a director with fresh ideas, so I quit and rejoined the New Play Society in Toronto.

■

In the first week of 1953 I renewed my involvement with the International Players in Toronto and directed *Lo and Behold*, which opened on January 23 at the Western Technical School and then moved to Leaside High School for two more performances. Ernst Wanger said in the *Globe and Mail*, "By virtue of flawless casting, the accurate and spirited staging by Vernon Chapman, and a few inspired individual performances, they have achieved a show that keeps the audiences laughing to the point at which they frequently drown out the lines."[19] If that was the case we were not doing our job. A stage actor should always wait until the laughter has half-way decreased in volume before cutting in loud and clear with the next line — a technique I have too often found lacking in contemporary actors. I then directed *Yes, M'Lord* in which I played the dotty old Earl of Lister. Hugh Webster designed the set and the cast included Peter Scott, Norma Renault in a very funny performance as a cockney maid, Christine Thomas as Lady Lister, and Sheila Craig as the Listers' American guest. Wanger wrote that she gave "a brisk and winning performance."[20] He subsequently married her.

My third show that winter, *Oh, Mr. Meadowbrook* with Drew Thompson, Cosy Lee, and Norma Renault, was my last directing assignment for the International Players. Drew and Arthur planned to return to Memorial Hall for the summer of 1953 and wanted me back. But again I felt they needed a fresh director with fresh ideas. I had staged 45 of their productions and acted in many of them. The three plays I had directed for them in Toronto that winter had been well received by audiences and critics, so I decided to quit on an upbeat. Drew, Arthur, and I had been a mutually understanding trio. I knew I had to operate on a shoe-string budget. I did not demand extravagances of them and they did not expect me magically to create elaborate productions with almost no money. Our sets were often quite shoddy. When Murie Kelly, Grant Macdonald, or Warren Collins designed them they reasonably resembled what the script called for. But Murie, who had graduated from Victoria College and married John Meisel, was a busy professor of Fine Art at Queen's University. Warren Collins was in demand by other companies, and Grant Macdonald had his career as one of Canada's foremost artists. When these three or Neil Vipond were not available, the only people Arthur could get to design were well-meaning amateurs. One of our "designers" was a local window dresser who persistently over-decorated his sets with cheap gilt paint whether it was appropriate or not. Often there were no designs or floor plans in advance of rehearsal for me to approve. I had to content myself with discussion of the play with the designer and hope that at the rehearsal on Sunday, the day before opening, there would be a set that reasonably resembled the playwright's intention.

The flats were canvas because wood was too expensive, and although stiffened with glue sizing and layers of paint, they trembled when doors were closed too violently. The doors had solid wooden frames, but warping led to improper fitting, and often when shut, or even "locked" by an actor, they could mysteriously open. We were also limited to the props and furniture we could scrounge from merchants and private individuals. Renting was out of the question. Arthur would exercise his great charm to persuade various shopkeepers or householders to part with items we needed for a week or two. The actual furniture we were to use never arrived before the Sunday or even the Monday afternoon dress rehearsal. Kingston was not overly stocked with furniture stores and often we had to settle for a piece that was not quite right. Every time Drew, Arthur, or I were invited into a

Kingston home, we would make a mental note of anything we could use in a future production. We were actually more fortunate with antique than modern furniture. The local antique dealers were often sweetened by Drew, who had an unerring eye for valuable antiques and often bought a piece for his own collection. Breakages were paid for out of the producers' pockets, but, I am happy to say that there was not much of that because we were all conscious of the importance of returning a borrowed object undamaged.

The lack of money to create impressive sets was a chronic ailment with most of the summer stock companies of the early '50s. Therefore to win the audiences the acting had to compensate. To Drew and Arthur's credit, they created an amiable atmosphere where actors wanted to work despite the small salary. They attracted some of the finest Canadian performers then available. I am forever grateful that they gave me the opportunity to work with such splendid performers in such a variety of plays where I was able to hone my skills and develop confidence as both actor and director.

In 1953 they planned another spring-to-autumn season, but expanded it to include performances in Napanee and Prescott, as well as Gananoque and Kingston. This necessitated having two acting companies with alternating plays. One company would play two nights in each of the smaller St. Lawrence River towns and then a week in Kingston while the company that had played a week in Kingston took its production to the other three towns. The logistics of this schedule were very daunting because when on the road an enlarged crew had to strike a set every two nights and erect it in a different site the next day. Sometimes the scheduling got confusing. Gary Montgomery remembers that once when they were doing *Ladies in Retirement* in Prescott, the leading lady failed to turn up. The character she played had to wear a red wig, so, undaunted, Arthur Sutherland read the role with the script in one hand and, to indicate what character he was representing, the red wig perched on the index finger of the other.[21]

That summer season the shows were presented in Kingston back at the La Salle Ballroom rather than in the sweltering Memorial Hall, but Drew and Arthur planned to return to that location in the fall. However, that was not to be. The Parks and Property Commission, responding to the protests of some narrow-minded councillors, suddenly refused to rent the Hall on the grounds that to stage plays there was a fire hazard. If it was a fire hazard in September of 1953, it had been a fire hazard in 1951 and 1952 when the commission had been quite willing to overlook the risk in order to collect $5,000 in rent for a room that only a few people had previously entered. Drew and Arthur protested the commission's decision and held a press conference. Citizens objected and wrote letters to the editor and to the Parks and Property Commission, but it was all to no avail. The 1953 season closed in September and one week later Arthur Sutherland died of heart failure. He was worn out at 43.

Until recently this country has not been generous in recognizing its arts pioneers. On Arthur's death, a concerned citizen of Kingston wrote a letter to the newspaper eulogizing him, the last paragraph of which reads, "And I hope too, that in the not too distant future some organized plan will be set up to build, buy, erect, or rent an Arthur Sutherland Memorial Theatre. Surely no one has done, or could have done, so much in and around Kingston to foster the legitimate theatre here, or given young up-and-coming enthusiasts that all-important encouragement and chance at actual participation in drama."[22] So far as I know at the time of writing this, Arthur Sutherland's name does not honour any building or memorial anywhere, let alone in Kingston. He is just another of those who dedicated themselves to fostering the arts and thereby improving the quality of life in this country. He loved the theatre, he loved this country, but all memory of him is fading into the mists of time.

His partner, Drew Thompson, tried to carry on the following year, but without Arthur it proved too daunting. The International Players closed at the end of the summer of 1954 after six years as the world's only "Pay-As-You-Like" company, which could also claim at the time to be Canada's only "Theatre of the Four Seasons." After that, Drew was greatly in demand as a stage and TV actor, and became a favourite with the children for his portrayal of Clarabelle the cow on the Canadian version of *Howdy-Doody*. I remember one day when I was directing the International Players, Drew asked my advice about the future of his career. At the time I had few clear ideas about my own career, but I was quite definite about his. His talent was so towering that it belonged to the world, like Christopher Plummer's, and not just to Canada. I told him that he must go to New York where he would get a better chance of being recognized internationally. Eventually he did so and he soon clicked. Shortly after arriving in Manhattan he went on tour with Fay Emerson and Gig Young. By the late 1950s he was happily ensconced in a charming little bachelor pad on Beekman Place, a not unfashionable address. But Drew always had a hankering to be "landed gentry." He always knew that after his grandfather's second wife died, he would inherit one of Ontario's oldest estates with one of the most beautiful period houses in the country, "Ruthven," on the Grand River near Simcoe. Every time he visited there after his grandfather's death, he would return livid that his step-grandmamma had sold off another *objet d'art* that Drew had cherished. When he did inherit this estate about 1960, he abandoned his burgeoning career in New York and began to live the life of the country squire. When in New York in 1962, I had a chat with the casting director of the Theatre Guild who asked me anxiously, "What ever happened to Drew Thompson?" When I told her that he had given up the profession, she said sorrowfully, "What a shame. He was just on the verge of making it down here. People were beginning to think of him as the next Clifton Webb. Too bad. He had a brilliant career ahead of him."

When Drew retired to Ruthven, he cut himself off from most of his friends, although he did keep in touch with Cosette Lee. He chose the reclusive life over the public life of the theatre. I trust he was happy with that decision. But what a loss we had! A brilliant, natural actor who could play comedy or tragedy in all the media chose to play the solitary role as Lord of the Manor for only his gardener and his dogs to see. Over the years I would occasionally phone him, hoping he would be willing to see me. He always refused until Christmas 1992. Our mutual friend Gary Montgomery was on his annual pilgrimage to Toronto and I invited him to lunch. I decided, with little hope, to invite Drew as well. To my astonishment he accepted. When he walked in the door of my apartment the first thing he said to me was, "Of course, you know that I am riddled with cancer."

When I rallied from that shocker, I made him laugh by saying I hoped it would not spoil his lunch. He refused the Bloody Caesars I had prepared but smoked continuously and kept Gary and me in paroxysms of laughter with stories about himself, and other denizens of the Canadian entertainment world, none of which he would let me tape. Eight months later he died and the only mention of his passing was a tiny death notice in the newspaper. Not one columnist commented on the life of one of the most uniquely remarkable actors of the Canadian theatre and television. He was unknown to them.

CHAPTER 9

In Jalna Country

The spring of 1953 brought the most momentous event before or since in the growth of the English-Canadian Theatre — the opening of the Stratford Festival. But another company opened that summer and its brief story has been completely forgotten except by me and a dwindling handful of those involved. By 1953, summer theatres had sprung up in various parts of the province, including Port Carling, Allanburg, and Jackson's Point. In 1952, Hugh Webster and a group of performers had established a co-operative company in the Pine Room Ballroom of the recently constructed Oakville Arena. I was too busy to see any of their productions, but I understand that while the box-office receipts were low, their standard of performance was high and the "co-operation" of the temperamental actors did not last the season. In 1953 I decided to try my own hand at producing, and looked about for a likely location. I learned that Hugh and his group did not plan to return to Oakville and that the ballroom was available. I took a deep breath and plunged in with my magnificent savings of $500, although I knew it was insufficient.

Fortunately, after I had asked Carol Starkman to join the company, she approached her husband, Mort Rapp, and persuaded him to add another $500. Mort and I went into partnership to establish the Oakville Summer Theatre. I had met him several times when he visited Carol, then his fiancée, in Kingston the previous summer. I knew he was the owner of the

Smith Belting Company and, by my standards, was rich, but I did not know how rich and I had never thought of him as a potential backer. It was Carol's idea. I was grateful at the time, but had even more reason to be grateful later on.

There was not much time to get the season organised, so I quickly selected the plays — 100 per cent shows the public had likely heard about, and 90 per cent comedy — and scurried around to line up my casts and crew. I knew I dared not produce, direct, and act at the same time, so I hired John Hardinge, a recent emigrant from England, to direct some of the plays. His credentials included Manchester Rep., Leeds Rep., and the Theatre Royal, Windsor. He in turn recommended a designer who was living in Ed Mirvish's new artist's colony on Markham Avenue, later known as Mirvish Village. I obtained a stage-hand from the newly formed CBC-TV as our carpenter. Lillian Grudeff, the sister of the pianist Marian Grudeff, became an apprentice actress in charge of props.

Before opening I did a lot of lobbying in the Oakville area. The American-born editor of the *Oakville-Trafalgar Journal* was most supportive and remained so throughout the season, as did many of the merchants. Mrs. Hindmarsh gave a garden party for the Independent Order Daughters of the Empire and invited me to speak. All the ladies present were enthusiastic, particularly about my selection of plays. I felt highly encouraged and expected that the local response would be positive. I hoped Oakvillians would come out in sufficient number to provide enough revenue to meet the expenses, and that people from Toronto and Hamilton would provide the profit. I was soon disillusioned on that score. Oakville was a small community in 1953, and when we opened I discovered that most of the wealthy decamped to their summer cottages after the July 1st weekend and did not return until Labour Day. Only about 50 per cent of the audience ultimately came from the local area. However, I was pleasantly surprised at the number of people who were willing to travel all the way from Toronto and Hamilton.

I retained the name "Oakville Summer Theatre" to profit from the groundwork Hugh and his colleagues had done the previous year. But my venture was far from a co-operative. Although the program read

"V. Chapman and M. Rapp present," Mort was a silent partner, and even though I did hire a director, I kept a supervisory eye on everything that occurred. I carefully planned the advertising campaign based on the knowledge and experience I had received at the New Play Society. I had a happy clown's face designed as a trademark to be printed on all advertisements and programs, and advertised a "10-week season of gay hit comedies" (in the days before "gay" took on its current meaning). I made contacts with local merchants in advance of the season to condition them to be generous when I sent my people around to borrow furniture or properties. I did everything I could think of within the limitations of time and money to make sure that the people from Port Credit to Burlington knew of the proposed season. I also advertised in the Toronto papers.

The manager of the Oakville Arena was most co-operative and rented the Pine Room and a dressing room on the lower level at a reasonable rate. We were also permitted the free use of the box office. Everything augured well for a reasonably safe gamble. I tried to lure the promising young Kate Reid to play Sadie Thompson in *Rain*. At first she agreed and I sent out a press release announcing that, but she changed her mind and went elsewhere. I cancelled *Rain* and opened with *Harvey*, sure-fire box-office hit in that decade. As Elwood P. Dowd I was lucky to get Joe Austen who was appearing regularly as the flying postman on the Ed McCurdy television show. Joe admirably captured the fey quality required in the role. Christine Thomas, whom I had directed in the International Players and who had come into the profession via the London Little Theatre, was Vita Louise. I believe I gave Margaret "Nonnie" Griffin her first Toronto area stage appearance in the role of the very plain Myrtle May, which belied her own natural attractiveness. I had decided not to be involved with the first production except in a supervisory capacity so John Hardinge directed and played Dr. Chumley. A very appealing young actress, Aylene Kamins, was introduced in the role of Ruth Kelly, and Tommy Paton, an alumnus of the New Play Society, played Judge Gaffney.

Although the local paper, the *Hamilton Spectator*, and the *Toronto Telegram* gave us good notices, the attendance that first week was disappointingly small. The *Spectator* critic conjectured that the heat (the ballroom was not air-conditioned) and the Royal Coronation film, which opened in Oakville that very week, were to blame, and went on to say, "It is to be hoped that the talented company of the lakeshore's only summer theatre were in no way discouraged for a fine company they are."[1] I had arranged with the Hamilton Players Guild to have a display of their costumes in the lobby and this brought some of the Guild members to swell the audience. Business began to increase the second week when we presented *O Mistress Mine.* This time Christine Thomas warmly played Olivia and I repeated my performance as Sir John Fletcher. The show was well received by the audience, the local papers, and the *Hamilton Spectator.* We followed it with *Hay Fever* starring Sandra Scott as Judith Bliss. Sandy Webster, then working for a Hamilton radio station, played her dishevelled husband, Jean Caine, a delightful local actress was cast as Myra Arundel, and I played the stuffy diplomat, Richard Greatham. John Hardinge directed.

The *Oakville-Trafalgar Journal* applauded Monday's opening night: "*Hay Fever* just for once is funny."[2] But on Tuesday a Toronto critic paid us a visit. Tuesday was wrestling night in the arena and the critic spent part of his column, which did not appear until three days later, describing the wrestling. Then he went on to say, "Should I wait until the Oakville Summer Theatre has staggered to its feet or should I hit them while they are still shaky?" Continuing his wrestling metaphor he wrote, "There was no doubt in my mind . . . that the Oakville Players deserved the body blow. Here they were before me making less fun out of Noel Coward's old workhorse, *Hay Fever,* than any of the millions of amateurs who have played it since it first appeared in the last 25 years."[3] He found nothing good to say about the production whatsoever, and made some suggestions as to how to play it. He concluded, "If such body punches are of no avail, future visits to the Oakville Arena will find me spending all of my time at the wrestling."[4] I do not challenge that reviewer's opinion of our production, but I resented his writing a review of it having spent half the evening watching wrestling on our complimentary tickets. I instructed the person in charge of press tickets that in the future that critic was to come on

Monday night or not at all, and I persuaded the arena manager that if he showed up on Tuesday he was not to be let in unless he purchased a ticket either to the play or to the wrestling. To the best of my knowledge he never returned. However, Rose Macdonald of the *Telegram* attended regularly and Hugh Thomson of the *Toronto Star* was an occasional visitor.

I am not sure what the critic would have written on one other wrestling night. The dressing room allotted to us in the Oakville Arena was on a level below the ballroom off a long corridor that surrounded the bleachers area. On Tuesday nights adjacent dressing rooms were allotted to the wrestlers. In that corridor we would hear and often meet these sweaty behemoths, who, after having thumped and banged each other about in the ring, would be chatting together as they entered the dressing rooms. Arch enemies in the ring, they would often arrive and leave together in the same limousine. One of the most popular wrestlers of the day was Yukon Eric, a mountain of a man who wrestled in overalls and bare feet. The manager of the arena had a little dog that was not completely house broken and would some-times escape the manager's office and leave its deposit in inappropriate places. One night those of us in the dressing room heard a rafter-shaking bellow. We dashed out to learn that Yukon Eric's huge right bare foot had found one of the dog's calling cards — and we quickly fled back into the dressing room so that the furious wrestler would not hear our laughter.

Casting Carol Starkman as the seductive mermaid in *Miranda*, a role originally played in London by Glynis Johns, was a happy choice. She was ideally suited to it. Carol had been a cheerleader, a runner up in a Miss CNE beauty contest, and a model, and was a talented actress with a distinct flair for comedy. Hugh Thomson in the *Toronto Star* wrote, "She took to the role like a duck to water."[5] The growing audience loved both her and Sandy Webster, the doctor who brings the mermaid home to London. Although at the time still in her teens, Margaret Griffin displayed the maturity nec-essary for the doctor's wife. The next show, *Claudia*, gave Nonnie her chance to show what a splendid actress she is. I did not include that play in my summer schedule until I could find an actress suitable for the title role, and I had found her in Margaret. In *The Chiltern Hundreds* I appeared for the second time that season and had fun playing the vague, dithering Earl of Lister. Next I directed *Lo and Behold* but I do not think it was as successful as the production I had staged for the International Players with Drew Thompson in the lead.

To vary the fare for the by-now well increased number of regulars, I scheduled Christopher Fry's *A Phoenix Too Frequent*, a gem of blank verse comedy, on a double bill with Terence Rattigan's *The Browning Version*. Nonnie Griffin as Dynamene, Dorothy Foster — whom I borrowed from the Hamilton Players' Guild — as Doto, and John Hardinge as Tegeus-Chromis were sound in the Fry play but as its director, I did not quite succeed in getting the style I wanted. It remained too off-beat for the audience who were barely tolerant of it. I longed to direct it again with time to develop it properly. *The Browning Version* was an audience pleaser. I played Crocker-Harris and had a genuine empathy for this supposedly reserved British professor. Aylene Kamins skillfully revealed the sexual frustration of his wife, and a newcomer, David Major, played the very difficult role of the wife's lover in such a way that he was not a cad. Taplow was a talented youth named Nestor Mitto, who had Hollywood ambitions and eventually moved there. Jack Northmore, who had been part of the successful singing group The Billy Van Four, was now trying his wings as an actor in the role of the new school master, Peter Gilbert. His performance passed muster, but, as he later reminded me, his English accent "fell just east of Nova Scotia." For a cast made up exclusively of Canadians, none of whom, except myself, had been to England, the "cultured" Ox-Cam English was there to a sufficient degree to be acceptable to a Canadian ear.

For me the really high point of the season was the final show, *Life with Father*, which I directed and for which Drew Thompson took a leave of absence from the International Players to return to the role he had so successfully performed in Kingston. I was also fortunate in getting Christine Thomas who gave us a superb Vinnie. Fortune smiled on me again when I recruited three members of an Oakville area family, the Washbrooks. The mother, Joyce, played Maggie the cook, her son Donald played Whitney, and her younger son John played Harlan. Both sons went on to careers in

TV — John becoming the lead in that charming series, *My Friend Flicka*. Beth Amos appeared as Cousin Cora and Nonnie Griffin was an effervescent Mary Skinner. By the time *Life with Father* opened it was clear that my first venture into production would meet with financial failure, but I was happy that the play ended the summer on a triumphant note.

One of our staunchest supporters was Jane Grey who had a large following on a Hamilton radio station, and I think that it was due to her plugging the Oakville Summer Theatre that as many people travelled from Hamilton as came from Oakville. Originally from England, Jane had been a Canadian radio pioneer and had become famous as Princess Musk-kee-kee, the name of a patent medicine she had been hustling for years. One day I was invited to be the guest on her breakfast show, which was broadcast from her apartment on Aberdeen Avenue in Hamilton. As required I arrived 15 minutes early and was greeted by the announcer. Jane was just getting up. She bustled into her dining room where the program originated, wrapped in a dressing gown looking as though she had just tumbled out of bed, which she had. If she had been the model for the Indian Princess on the Musk-kee-kee posters, she had long since outgrown that svelte figure. She sat down opposite me, welcomed me heartily, poured us warmed-over, stale coffee, and instructed me to stir mine occasionally letting the spoon tinkle against the saucer to give "breakfast atmosphere noises." At the proper moment the announcer introduced the program and Jane and I began to chat into the microphone, which was between us on the table. My purpose in being there so early in the morning was to promote my theatre, but I had difficulty keeping her to that subject. When she learned that I had been to England she started talking about her home town, which was on the English south coast. Suddenly she said, "I want to show you something," and completely forgetting that she was on the air, jumped up from the table and disappeared down the corridor leaving me to stare all alone into a live microphone. The announcer who was as startled by this as I, was slow to react, so I explained to the listeners that Jane had just left the room and I went on to describe haltingly this "beautifully decorated dining room," which was actually a mishmash of bad taste. As I chuntered on we could hear Jane banging about in the next room. Seeing that I was running out of things to describe, the announcer mercifully jumped in and returned me to the subject of the Oakville Summer Theatre. No sooner had I started to talk about that than Jane abruptly returned, thrust a medium-sized oil painting before me and announced that it was a view of the harbour of her home town. She then started pointing out various things of interest in the painting. I thought it incumbent on me to tell the listener, "Jane has just pointed to a cream-coloured house by the wharf," or "What a lovely blue sky," and other inanities. Before I knew it the broadcast was over and I had not said half of what I had planned about the Oakville Summer Theatre. After the broadcast we spent half an hour reminiscing about England. She was a very dear lady, if somewhat eccentric, and I wished that I could have spent more time with her. But theatre business called and I had to leave, although I immediately went to a restaurant for a decent cup of coffee.

I had planned an autumn season, but sober second thoughts prevailed. I had been involved as an actor, director, business manager, publicity manager, and even props and furniture collector. I had arranged for radio interviews for cast members, my director, and myself. Aylene Kamins had given me much appreciated assistance with publicity and bookkeeping, and the Misses Fairbairn of Clarkson Market Antiques were proven godsends because they were so enthusiastic about our venture that we were allowed to borrow virtually everything from their huge stock of valuable antique furniture and *objets d'art*. But when the season ended I was exhausted. I spent the first week of September totalling the bills. Although I had carefully husbanded our resources, the season lost money. I had paid an average of $40 a week to the performers, which was far below what they were worth or deserved, but it was all we could afford, and was comparable to what other companies were paying. By careful timing of advertisements of varying sizes, I had managed to get maximum newspaper coverage at a minimum cost. Despite the penny-pinching, we concluded the 10-week season having spent the original investment of $1,000 plus the box-office revenue, and we owed approximately another $1,000. I was broke and, although I knew that the season had been moderately successful artistically, I felt that I had failed. I also felt the shame of owing money, a notion inherited from my parents who grew up in an era when people paid cash for something or they did without. I did not want to postpone to the following year payment of bills owing to Oakville merchants or for the ads in the newspapers because it would be difficult, if not impossible, to recapitalize for the following summer with debts hanging over our heads. I thought that I would have been personally liable for the debts because I, of necessity, had been the signing officer of the company. I swallowed my pride and went to Mort Rapp. He had agreed to be a partner only up to his original contribution, and he had every right to refuse. But he didn't. When I told him we had outstanding bills amounting to about a $1,000, he said simply, "Oh well. We can't go on owing money. I will give you a cheque. It is the rent from one of my buildings for this month."

I could have kissed him, but I doubted that he would have appreciated it. Later on that autumn he and I discussed the possibility of an Oakville season in 1954, but, quite understandably, he did not appear enthusiastic. Nor was I eager to take on the financial headache of another season. It looked unlikely that I would be able to save enough money by the following summer from my own unpredictable earnings. Thanks to Mort my first fling at producing came to a relatively happy end so far as my owing money was concerned, but I was disappointed that I had not been able to build a company in Oakville, in my view an ideal location for a theatre. But, only since the opening there of the Oakville Centre for the Performing Arts in 1982 has a summer theatre operated in what is now a city.

Some of the employees of the Oakville Summer Theatre were strangers to me when I hired them, and, due to the hurly-burly of producing a play a week, I did not get to know them well. I had had a nodding acquaintance with the stage carpenter at the CBC and he proved to be very conscientious and proficient. My associate director, John Hardinge, I only met in the spring of 1953 and, on the whole, I was satisfied with his work as director and actor. The designer and scene painter was a talented artist friend of John's who willingly co-operated with the directors and whose designs were ideally suited to our operation. To me they all seemed reasonably well-adjusted. Therefore I was shocked to learn that shortly after the season closed, the carpenter was arrested after going berserk and slashing a movie screen; the designer, hallucinating that he was Vincent van Gogh, cut off one of his own ears; and John Hardinge committed suicide in Ottawa. I hesitate to think that these sad events were the result of working for me in Oakville, but, one never knows.

CHAPTER 10

In the Fruit Belt

After four years of almost steady work, the autumn of 1953 found me without job prospects following my abrupt descent from the lofty station of a theatrical producer from whom other actors sought employment. Moreover, I was stone broke again. I began to make inroads into TV and renewed my acquaintance with CBC radio. Soon I was earning enough to get by. But I had to look to the future. As winter wore on I began to worry that I would have no summer employment. That eventuality was avoided by the intercession of the man who seemed so impractical when he was with the International Players, and his very practical wife. During my Oakville season, Jill Foster and Bernard Slade had continued with the IPS. In the autumn they married and moved to a little basement apartment on the Lakeshore Road in Mimico, just three blocks from me. That winter we all began to work in television, and I was frequently a guest in their apartment. Bernie took various jobs to make ends meet. For a while he was a shoe salesman, and that winter he briefly became a Trans-Canada Airlines steward. In the spring of 1954 he joined with Warren Hart, an actor friend from New York, to become producers at the newly built Garden Centre Theatre in Vineland, Ontario. They invited me to become their resident director.

The first Garden Centre Theatre had been built in 1952 by John and George Prudhomme as an attraction at their expanding motel complex on the Queen Elizabeth Highway just west of Jordan Harbour. The motel was on the family farm where the Prudhommes had amassed a fortune from supplying nursery stock and flowers to the Niagara Peninsula and Hamilton. John and George were not theatre enthusiasts, but shrewd businessmen wanting to lure people to their motel, its restaurant, and bar. As an occupant for their new theatre, they enticed Jack Blacklock's company away from Allanburg, just south of St. Catharines. The Prudhommes' "Barn" — it had been built on a barn foundation — had a capacity of 450 divided between an orchestra and a small balcony. Oddly the theatre was wider than it was deep. The stage was a slit in one wall with a proscenium opening that was long and not very high. It reminded one of Cinerama. The building was in a hollow and the basement formed a coffee shop in rustic style with Grandma Moses wallpaper. All very quaint. As usual with people who build theatres whose sole purpose is making a buck, the stage and backstage areas were given only cursory consideration. There was very little depth, not much wing space, and no apron. A sloping roof over the stage allowed only modest flying of scenery in the downstage area. The dressing rooms were ridiculously small. Nevertheless, for Blacklock's company it was a vast improvement over the ancient barn they had been performing in near Allanburg.

Although I never worked for Jack Blacklock, he figured very largely in the embryonic theatre of the late '40s and early '50s, and his career is worthy of some attention here. Hailing from Woodstock, he became interested in the theatre in his youth, obtained a teacher's certificate in Fine Art, and he directed school plays at the various high schools where he taught. During the war years, when on leave from the Canadian army, he travelled to New York to see Broadway shows, which thrilled him so much that he determined to do what he could to develop professional theatre in Canada. In 1946 he established The Vagabond Players, an amateur group, in Toronto. He booked the Museum Theatre in October and applied to the New Play Society to rent the lighting equipment the NPS had installed there. When he came to see Mrs. Moore, she gave him a blast, demanding to know why he was renting "her theatre." He pointed out that it belonged to the Royal Ontario Museum and not to her and that he had every right to rent it.¹ She was concerned that her efforts to educate the public that she was operating a professional company would be undermined by an amateur group operating in her bailiwick. Despite her disapproval, she wasn't above renting him the lights.

In 1948 on $400 of his savings, he founded the Midland Players, a professional summer stock in the curling rink where a portable stage from the Midland Chamber of Commerce was placed halfway along one wall. Jack and the actors built the sets, hung the lights and curtains. There were five summer stock companies founded in Ontario that spring: a company started by Henry Kaplan in Bracebridge, the Straw Hat Players in Port Carling, the International Players in Kingston, the Holloway Bay Players near Sherkston in the Niagara Peninsula, and Blacklock's company in Midland. After two summers there he found an abandoned barn that had been used as a country music dance hall near Allanburg where he could run a longer season. It was an ideal location amidst the larger population centres of St. Catharines, Welland, and Niagara Falls where Maude Franchot, the aunt of the Hollywood actor Franchot Tone, had started a "star" system summer stock company in the high school auditorium.

In Allanburg, Blacklock founded the Niagara Barn Theatre and built up a large following with tried-and-true plays such as *Born Yesterday* (its first production in Canada), *The Moon Is Blue, Separate Rooms,* and *The Family Upstairs.* He also presented *Tobacco Road* without the vulgarities that had crept into the Broadway run. Bernard Slade, Jill Foster, Elwy Yost, and Cecil Linder, who called himself Paul Linder then, were his nucleus company. Linder will be remembered for his film performances, particularly as the FBI agent in *Goldfinger,* and, of course, Mr. Yost as the celebrated host of *Saturday Night at the Movies* on TV Ontario. A sensitive young actress, Shirley Knight, was an apprentice in charge of properties with that company. Bernie Slade and Jill have a fund of anecdotes about their experiences at the Niagara Barn Theatre. Once when they were presenting *Uncle Tom's Cabin,* complete with cardboard ice flows and an old fashioned roll-down curtain, the stage manager accidentally rolled it down on Simon Legree's head in his solo curtain call, whereupon Jack as Legree went after him with his bull whip. On another occasion as the cast was taking a company call, the whole curtain fell in a heap before them. The audiences loved these little extras thrown in at no added charge, and gradually attendance swelled to such a degree that they added a second performance on Saturday nights.[2] After two years at Allanburg, John Prudhomme offered Jack the prospect of a better theatre right on the Queen Elizabeth Highway, and with his new partner, Mark Saunders, Jack opened in Vineland on April 4, 1953. They ran for 34 weeks. While I was losing my shirt in Oakville, Blacklock and Saunders proved themselves the most financially successful of all the summer theatre managers by clearing $55,000 profit that year. But all was not smooth sailing. John Prudhomme was the kind of man with whom you shook hands and then counted your fingers to see if you still had all five. Jack and Mark had difficulty persuading him to heat the theatre for the cool nights of early spring and late fall. Disagreement followed disagreement. They decided not to return to the Prudhommes' the next year, and with the profit from their previous seasons they built themselves a theatre on the Queen Elizabeth Highway closer to Hamilton at Fruitland.

The first year in their bright new frame theatre, which boasted a proper fly gallery, was fairly successful, but the following year, 1955, was a financial disaster. Sadly, they had to declare bankruptcy, and Jack Blacklock found himself on the verge of a nervous breakdown. The worries of seven years of production had taken their toll. He blamed the demise of his theatre on the increase in the number of television sets. CBC-TV had opened in Toronto in 1952, Buffalo TV had been operating for several years, and a new station opened in Hamilton. But I think the growth of other summer companies in the area, all of whom suffered that year, and the draw of the Stratford Festival added to the effects of television. Blacklock maintains that if they had been able to obtain sponsorship, almost non-existent in those days, or subsidies, which were completely non-existent, they could have continued. He turned his attention to teaching Theatre Arts at Ryerson Institute of Technology for one year and then began writing TV commercials and plays for radio, particularly for Rupert Kaplan in Montreal. But this was too uncertain an existence and he eventually returned to teaching English in secondary schools in 1960. His interest in theatre continued, and in 1962 he was on a committee to establish Theatre Arts courses in Ontario schools. Some of the people in his companies say that he was not always an easy man to work for, but he was the only one who had made summer stock pay for at least two years and the only one who managed to build his own theatre — an impressive achievement in those theatrically lean days.

When Blacklock and John Prudhomme had their falling out in 1953, Bernie, Jill, and Warren saw their opportunity. They had very little money but decided to risk their savings anyway. One has to have a gambler's instincts to promote theatre anywhere but particularly so in this country. They were encouraged to open with the advent of spring because Blacklock and Saunders had started early the previous year and by the ready-made audience built up in Allanburg and Vineland. But Blacklock's and Saunders's departure from the Garden Centre Theatre posed a few problems for the new producers and for me, their director. The lighting equipment used the year before belonged to them and, naturally, they took it with them. There were no costumes and, of course, no stock of flats or properties. We had to start from scratch as I had done the year before in Oakville. We could not afford proper stage lighting, so I had to cope with mushroom floods and spots designed primarily for window displays. By opening night, April 5, 1954, there were no dimmers and an insufficient number of colour frames. This resulted in a production bathed in white light about which the critic for the *St. Catharines Standard*, E.H. (Betty) Lampard, complained, although she found the comedy *Dear Barbarians* quite enjoyable. She concluded, ". . . the Niagara district is fortunate to have the Garden Centre acting company playing in its midst"[3] and remained a staunch, if critical, supporter of the Garden Centre Theatre during the 13 years of its life.

As Drew and Arthur had been obliged to do in Kingston, and I in Oakville, with little money for elaborate settings Bernie and Warren placed emphasis on the acting and assembled a strong company of performers. I was fortunate to have in the first show Jill Foster, Diane Vickers, Bernard Slade, Warren Hart, and a splendid, sensitive young actress, Olga Winters, who was studying with Uta Hagen at the Herbert Berghoff Studio in New York. Originally from Wisconsin, her real name was Olga Bielinska, a beautiful name worthy of a ballerina but one which Olga thought would be too restricting in Manhattan theatre agents' offices. Here was an actress who knew how to act in depth without sitting around for weeks analyzing the character and all its relatives for generations back. Even in the lightest of comedy, Olga managed to imbue rather surface characters, as written, with a depth that made them more believable. I was also lucky in having Mark Furness, an expatriate Englishman, as stage manager.

I had feared that Warren Hart, whom I did not know, might use his position as producer to force me to cast him in roles for which I might not think him suited. But he had a clear sense of judgement about himself, and if he wanted to play a role it was always one that fit him. Such was the case with Bernie as well. Diane Vickers, also new to me, proved versatile and a great asset to the company. Jill was her usual reliable self. After our fluffy opening show, the producers hit the audience with one of the great postwar American plays, *The Hasty Heart*. Any doubts I had about Warren's ability were completely dispelled by his strong performance as the dour Scots soldier who rejects the sympathy of his hospital ward-mates upon learning that he is terminally ill. Economics at the Garden Centre Theatre, as was the case in Kingston and Oakville, dictated that I had to act for my bread and butter as well as direct. In *The Hasty Heart* I played the Colonel, known as "Old Cobwebs." Type casting. In the next one, *Hay Fever*, I again played the diplomat, Richard Greatham, a younger "Old Cobwebs." Indicative of how some actors had to double in brass, Diane Vickers played Myra Arundel and also arranged for the furniture and props, and the far-from-shy box-office manager, Patricia Moffatt, played the extremely shy Jackie Coryton. An "anyone for tennis?" type of British actor, Roland Bull, who had acted with the Earle Grey Players, joined the company for this production. I got a chance to play Sir John Fletcher again in *O Mistress Mine*, hoping that with repetition I might get it right. Olga Winters, who was younger than I, nevertheless managed to obtain the dignified maturity of Sir John's mistress.

As the season wore on we staged such eclectic choices as *The Patsy*, *Candle Light* adapted by P.G. Wodehouse from a play by Siegfried Geyer, and Emlyn Williams's *Night Must Fall* with Warren as a blood-chilling Danny and Sandy Webster as a rumpled Inspector. Mr. Webster was rapidly becoming an extremely reliable character actor. For me as the director there were three highlights that season. The first was a new Canadian play by Leo Orenstein, *The Big Leap*. Although it had premiered the year before at the Royal Alex in Toronto, and despite the limitations of our one-week preparation schedule, Leo wanted an opportunity to try it out again and was understanding about our shortcomings. Fortunately, *The Big Leap* is a very stage-worthy play full of interesting characters and situations, and the cast were gung-ho to do it. The story is about an off-beat character named "Lucky" Keeler, modelled on Red Hill, who plans to go over Niagara Falls in a barrel. The plot thickens when the racketeers move in to get a piece of the betting action. We were fortunate in having Sean Sullivan in the lead and Bernie as the high pressure promoter. Sandy Webster changed his style to play a broadly comic Toronto taxi driver, and garnered most of the laughs, and in the small but effective part of the hotel bell-boy was Howard Engel who went on to become an author and creator of the unique fictional detective, Benny Cooperman. In Betty Lampard's opinion, *The Big Leap* was a success. She began her review with, "It's a winner at the Garden Centre Theatre this week."[4]

Another of the peaks for me that summer was Jan de Hartog's charming *The Fourposter*, starring Jill and Bernie, whose deep rapport as a loving couple in real life enhanced their portrayal of a loving couple on the stage. Bernie brought to the role of the husband the same seemingly helpless quality he displayed in real life, which made his understated performance very funny and very endearing. Jill balanced him with warmth and understanding as the wife-mother. One particular scene is vivid in my memory. On the couple's wedding night in 1890, the husband has to enter the bedroom in his night-shirt, nightcap, and bare feet. At the dress rehearsal I was convulsed when I saw that Bernie's toes curled downward. They were the funniest feet I had ever seen. Accidentally Bernie's right foot found the lidded chamberpot I had placed under the fourposter and it gave a hollow clunk. I kept that action in, a bit cheap perhaps, but the audience loved it.

However, a much greater challenge for me was *A Streetcar Named Desire*. The movie had been released in 1951 and was still fresh in people's minds. I knew that I could not afford to take liberties in order to adapt the production to actors who might not conform to the roles as delineated by Marlon Brando and Vivien Leigh in the film. Nor did I have time in one week of rehearsal to experiment with the staging originally worked out for the Broadway production by Elia Kazan and that brilliant designer, Jo Mielziner, which served Tennessee Williams's remarkable play so well. I had in Olga Winters an actress with the right acting approach, technique, and emotional power for Blanche. Jill Foster was perfect for the more extroverted Stella. Warren Hart was ideal for Mitch. In Shirley Knight, Diane Vickers, Sandy Webster, and Ron Weston I had actors who could easily portray the neighbours and Stanley Kowalski's poker-playing buddies. But where to find a Stanley? In those days the Toronto acting pool was short on husky male animals with sex appeal who could also act. There were a couple of actors who could have performed it, but when they removed their shirts their torsos turned to flab. I thought I might have to use one of them when fate intervened. The producers had received a letter that amazed and amused them from a brash young actor in New York who wrote that he had heard of our planned *Streetcar*, and that, next to Marlon Brando, he was "the only actor in America capable of playing Stanley." This egotistical approach somewhat alienated Bernie and Warren, but I persuaded them to take a chance. I asked them to contact him and tell him that if he could get up to Vineland, I would audition him, with no commitment to use him. Warren did so and in a few days a ruggedly handsome man in his mid-to-late 20s in a black leather jacket, blue jeans, and heavy black boots walked into our theatre. He had driven all the way from New York City on his motorcycle. His name was Jay Warren and when I spoke to him he sounded exactly like Brando as Kowalski. He so idolized Brando that he had changed his own pattern of speech to imitate Brando in *Streetcar* and *On the Waterfront*. When he removed his leather jacket revealing a black T-shirt and a well muscled torso I thought, "if only he can act, I'm all set." He had memorized some of Stanley's speeches and gave a remarkable imitation of Brando in the role. For my purpose he was ideal. Belying the menacing motor-biker facade, he was actually a very sweet man and very easy to direct. He had studied for the priesthood and had been an amateur middle-weight boxer. He was not stage-wise, having had very little acting experience and no formal training, but he was eager to learn and the rest of the company, realizing that he was a perfect type for the role, did all they could to help and put him at his ease. Olga, as Blanche, had the crucial scenes with him and showed great patience as we worked at breakneck speed to get this most difficult play ready in seven days. How I wished I had weeks to prepare it.

The mushroom floods and spots and the beat up old crank dimmer we had were inadequate to get the necessary lighting effects. The New Orleans neighbourhood outside the Kowalski's flat must be revealed from time to time to crowd in on Blanche. Mielziner in his original design made a transparency of the back wall of Kowalski's flat so that the audience could see a street scene in the Latin Quarter beyond. How could our limited lights and tiny budget accomplish this? We obtained another ancient dimmer and a few more store window lights. We stretched double layers of cheesecloth on frames and sized them to make a scrim, which became the back walls of the two-room, dingy apartment. I did not allow our designer, Robert Byrnes, to deviate much from the Mielziner design except to adapt it to the size of our "cinerama" stage. Byrnes skillfully painted the sordid street scene in perspective on our old, beat up sky cloth. (I am reluctant to give this cracked stretch of canvas its proper title of "cyclorama.") We made floods out of tin cans to light this street scene. Miracle of miracles it all worked, not the way I would have preferred had there been proper equipment, but, within the limitations, the lighting and set served the play quite well.

But it was the acting that impressed most. The whole cast rose to the occasion to demonstrate that fine acting, even great acting, can be found in the most unexpected places — even in weekly stock. The reviews give testimony to that. Herbert Whittaker in the *Globe and Mail* wrote, ". . . we can report that the Garden Centre Theatre is doing this play this week and doing it well. . . . Miss Winters gives a most sympathetic interpretation of Tennessee Williams's haunted heroine. . . . She is an actress well worth the watching."[5] He criticized Jay Warren for over-emphasizing Stanley's inarticulateness, for which I, as director, take responsibility since it is what I wanted from the character. He was also critical of the lack of atmosphere, "largely due to the lack of lighting equipment."[6] In a conversation after opening night, Herbert helpfully suggested that the windows in the apartment be outlined with tape on the scrim. We did so and it made a great improvement. Betty Lampard in the St. Catharines paper raved about the show as did another reviewer with the improbable name of Peter Pylypiw. Nat Cohen told me before he saw the production that he hated the play, but wrote a begrudgingly favourable review, although he did not care for Jay Warren's Stanley. But then he had not liked Brando's either. On the whole, the show was a success and I derived great satisfaction from it. I am forever grateful to Messrs Hart and Slade for giving me the opportunity to direct it.

There were three other productions that summer that also gave me satisfaction: *Light Up the Sky* for which Deborah Cass joined the company as Stella Livingstone and delivered her comedy with great effect, *Lo and Behold* in which Shirley Knight won the hearts of the audience as the demure Honey Wainwright, and *Nina* in which Diane Vickers shone in the title role with Sandy Webster as her husband.

Bernie and Warren decided not to extend the season into the autumn and abruptly announced that they would close at the end of August. Warren wanted to return to New York. Jill now had a contract to appear on the new Peppiat and Aylesworth comedy series on CBC-TV and had persuaded them to hire Bernie as a continuity writer. They had presented a five-month season of entertaining and often exciting theatre. Despite the occasional frustration due to financial restrictions and inadequate technical equipment, I had enjoyed a very stimulating and satisfying five months with a group of extremely talented and intelligent actors.

For those readers who have not had the joy of reading Bernard Slades's informative and amusing autobiography, *Shared Laughter*, here is a thumbnail sketch of his life after Vineland. Shortly after being employed by Peppiat and Aylesworth he found his *métier* when he began writing TV drama in the style of Paddy Chayefsky, the guru of TV drama in the '50s and '60s. He soon developed a style of his own and wrote plays that were sold to CBC-TV and to the United States Steel Hour. He then turned to writing situation comedy for TV and he and Jill moved to Hollywood in 1964 where he became rich and famous writing several series for Columbia Studios, including *Bridget Loves Bernie*, *The Flying Nun*, *Love on a Rooftop*, and *The Partridge Family*. He had tried his hand at writing for the stage in 1960 with a play called *Simon Says Get Married*, which was produced at the Crest Theatre for a six-week run and which the audiences loved but the critics lambasted. After his success writing for television he turned to the theatre once again and wrote three hit plays: *Same Time Next Year*, *Tribute*, and *Fatal Attraction*. It had been a relatively rapid climb from the parsimonious existence they had in their basement apartment in Mimico to the Spanish-style mansion in Brentwood, California where I visited them in 1966. Bernie, who at first gave me the impression of being a bit unfocussed, had become a millionaire and had out-shone us all.

Olga Winters, who also acted under the name of Olga Bellin, continued to study with Uta Hagen and Herbert Berghoff. She married an attractive young actor, Paul Roebling, who was the grandson of the designer of the Brooklyn Bridge, and who eventually appeared in the film *Prince of the City*. Olga's career expanded and during one of my many visits to New York I saw her perform in Turgenev's *A Month in the Country* starring Uta Hagen and directed by Sir Michael Redgrave. In January 1958, Olga turned up at the Royal Alex in Toronto in a touring production of *Cat on a Hot Tin Roof* with that powerful Hollywood film actor, Victor Jory, as Big Daddy. Sadly, in the late '80s, Olga lost a two-year struggle with cancer.

Warren Hart, whose real name was Warren Erhardt, gave up his acting career to build a successful one publishing magazines in New Jersey. He married happily, had several children, and expressed himself as an actor in amateur theatricals. Jay Warren, my Stanley, also returned to New York. Against my advice, Bernie and Warren kept him on after *Streetcar* to perform in another show, but without the versatility required for summer stock he was out of his depth. I believe with training something could have been done with him. He had a bravado that put some people off, but beneath this macho surface was vast insecurity. I knew that when we started to rehearse *Streetcar* I had to win his confidence quickly so that I could channel his ability to imitate Brando into a more than adequate performance in the one role with which he identified. A few years later, a friend of mine in New York, who also knew Jay, wrote me that he had become an alcoholic and had died on skid row. A tragic waste! Had a good teacher taken him in hand he might have made his mark. His one great moment of triumph had come in a small, rustic theatre at a roadside motel in rural Ontario far from the "big time" he dreamed about. But at least he had that moment.

CHAPTER 11

In a Hurricane

When Bernie and Warren announced that they would not operate in the autumn of 1954, the dormant producer virus in me awakened. Since in the previous year Jack Blacklock had run until December with reasonably good houses, why couldn't I? Moreover, I would put a clause in the contract with John Prudhomme guaranteeing me the theatre for the summer of 1955. It was worth a gamble. But, as usual, I lacked sufficient capital. I had to move quickly because I did not want to start too late in the fall. I began a search for a backer. Coincidentally at a show in Toronto, there was a man I had seen at numerous theatrical presentations over the years. He was usually alone, and we had frequently chatted. He was a real theatre buff. That particular night I told him my dilemma, and he said that he might be interested and that we should talk. His name was William Watkins and he was a bachelor living with his mother in a large house in Rosedale. The family money had come from the Wright House Department Store in Hamilton. He told me that his occupation was Investment Broker. A few days later we met and he agreed to put up $2,000 for a four- to six-week season to begin as soon as I could get it organized. Two thousand dollars was not much, but it was better than I had had in Oakville. Before I agreed I stipulated that it must be his own money and not money entrusted to him to invest. He assured me it was his own and he travelled down to St. Catharines to open a bank account over which I would have power of attorney. With the money secured I set about hiring my company.

I had already selected my season of five plays: Oscar Wilde's *The Importance of Being Earnest*, Christopher Fry's *A Phoenix Too Frequent* and Wilde's *Salomé* on the same bill, Shaw's *Heartbreak House*, and *The Holly and the Ivy* to put people in a Christmas mood. It was rather more highbrow than hitherto offered to the Niagara peninsula public, but I hoped that there was an audience for more intellectually stimulating fare than on the usual summer stock menu. For some time I had desperately wanted to direct these plays, particularly *Salomé* and *Heartbreak House*, and I wanted another shot at *A Phoenix Too Frequent*. I lined up a group of reliable and versatile actors. Sandy Webster rejoined me to act and to alternate with me as director. Ron Hartmann and Barbara Field from my International Players days, the character actor Harold Burke with whom I had worked as an amateur at the Toronto Conservatory under the direction of Clara Salisbury Baker and who now was turning professional, and a sexy *ingénue*-cum-leading lady, Audrey Kniveton, formed the nucleus of the company. James Pearce became my stage manager and an amiable young Graham Parker persuaded me to gamble on him as assistant stage manager because he was working as an undertaker's assistant and was anxious to escape the world of cadavers. Both the stage manager and his assistant would be occasionally required to play small parts. Actors' Equity had started organizing in Canada that year, but this was no Equity company, although I paid the going rate of between $40 and $50 a week.

I drew up a contract for Bill Watkins and John Prudhomme to sign that would give me the use of the theatre on a weekly rental basis for that autumn with an option to renew for the following summer, said option to be picked up by March 1, 1955. Bernie and Warren had left owing Prudhomme $1,000 in rent. They were both insolvent so I persuaded Prudhomme to accept their scenery, properties, and meagre lighting equipment in lieu of payment. This bailed them out of debt. I then wrote a clause with Prudhomme that Watkins would purchase the scenery and equipment for $500. I thought this quite shrewd of me and I was amazed that Prudhomme agreed. Later I was to learn that he agreed because he wanted a theatre tenant to bring him revenue that fall. I also arranged that an old farm house on the property that had been the residence for some of the actors during the summer, be allotted to us as accommodation for the actors that fall. It was a bright, Victorian-Gothic style house near the shore of Lake Ontario with four bedrooms, a bathroom upstairs, another room downstairs that could also be used as a bedroom, and a spacious dining room. I hired James Pearce's wife as cook-housekeeper and den mother. She was a large, jolly lady who persisted in corrupting the name of the ballet *Les Sylphides* to *Les Syphildes*.

Because it took me longer to organize than I had expected, I was unable to start rehearsals until the first week of October with an opening date for *The Importance of Being Earnest* planned for Monday, October 18. No sooner had I assembled the company at Vineland when the weather, which had been pleasant through September, turned sour. Hurricane Hazel was rolling up the east coast, and, instead of moving out to sea as most Atlantic hurricanes do, with a perversity directed specifically at me, it decided to come inland. The rain poured down for a whole week before the hurricane's full force struck. The winds built up and two days before Hazel arrived officially, I opened the stage door and had it ripped off its hinges. Bone chilling damp permeated the theatre, which Prudhomme refused to heat until the first audience arrived. On October 15 when Hurricane Hazel in all its fury finally struck, I collected cast and crew in the old farmhouse where that night we had a "Hurricane Party," drinking, playing cards, and watching the rustic lawn furniture from the motel blow away toward Lake Ontario. While the storm raged outside, Graham Parker kept us in paroxysms of laughter with his experiences as an undertaker's assistant. He related how startled he was when the first cadaver he ever worked on broke wind. Wondering if there might still be some semblance of life, he was reluctant to approach it again until obliged to do so by his boss. That fateful October night, although there were 81 people killed in Toronto, we were safe, snug, and glowing with alcohol in our sturdy farmhouse by the lake.

The next morning the wind had abated but the rain continued. There had been so much in the weeks before Hurricane Hazel that the ground was saturated and the torrential rain of October 15 caused considerable flooding. The following morning we found John and George Prudhomme in hip waders in the Grandma Moses coffee shop below the theatre pumping out the mud that was up to their thighs. It continued to rain for a week after the hurricane. This was definitely not the kind of weather to entice people away from the dry warmth of their homes and from their TV sets to drive through incessant downpour and sit in a cold, damp theatre to watch a group of actors, no matter how talented, perform comedy, no matter how classic. It was not surprising then that the opening night audience was small.

However, the production pleased those who did show up. Once again I had great fun playing Algernon, and Ron Hartmann was a perfect balance as the more reserved John Worthing. Betty Lampard in the *St. Catharines Standard* wrote, "He [Hartmann] has mastered to perfection the light art of playing Oscar Wilde well. . . . Cosette Lee [as Lady Bracknell] is priceless and perfect in the role."[1] Harold Burke was right at home as Canon Chasuble, and Shirley Knight as Cecily and Barbara Field as Gwendolyn were ideal in their roles. Sandy Webster proved himself a top-notch director with this production. The only criticism levelled at the show was that the sets did not quite capture the proper atmosphere for the play, especially Algernon's flat in the Albany. Clearly we had to improve in that department. Nevertheless, it was a strong, slick opening production and I hoped favourable word-of-mouth would stimulate the box office.

With the monsoons still drowning us we felt as though we were operating in the heart of Burma, except that it was much colder. We pressed on. The second week saw the twin bill of Oscar Wilde's erotic and erstwhile controversial *Salomé* and Christopher Fry's *A Phoenix Too Frequent*. The critics from the Welland and St. Catharines papers were very supportive of our venturing to offer these two plays to a public unaccustomed to this type of theatre, and I think, as a result, they were too kind. Certainly the acting was of a high calibre with Harold Burke as Herod in *Salomé* and Tegeus in *Phoenix*. Barbara Field was a very commanding Herodias and Audrey Kniveton made the transition from a prissy Miss Prism in *The Importance* the week before to a voluptuous Salomé. Ron Hartmann used his rich, powerful voice to great advantage as Jokanaan. There was a misprint in the program, which gave credit to Sandy Webster for directing both plays, but I directed *Salomé* and he *A Phoenix Too Frequent*. The dance of the seven veils was by ballerina Patricia MacLean wearing a wig that made her look very like Audrey Kniveton. I rented the costumes from Sterndale Bennett who had staged the play in his small studio theatre the previous season. With some adjustments they fit our actors well enough, but at a dress rehearsal, when the First Centurion, Sandy Webster, turned his head suddenly, his helmet stayed put — an intriguing effect that I was tempted to leave in, but thought better of it.

To attempt Shaw's great allegorical *Heartbreak House* in a week of rehearsals while performing another play at night was insane. I came to that conclusion after two days of rehearsal. It was particularly daft of me to direct it, play Hector Hushabye, and business manage the whole enterprise at the same time. In order to keep this fascinating work to a length tolerable to a theatrically unsophisticated audience seated in a damp theatre, and in order to help the cast learn this long, wordy play in so short a time, I did some judicial cutting, which I feared might cause old G.B.S. to rise from his grave and haunt me. We approached our opening night in a very shaky state. We were so insecure that whenever there was a pause, I thought someone had dried and to fill the gap would jump in with one of Hector's lines, "Is this England or is it a madhouse?" There were so many pauses on opening night as the cast felt its way through the script that that line became a recurring refrain. On the second night the rest of the cast were so afraid that I would utter that line whenever there was dead air that they went at a breakneck pace and often jumped each other's cues. However, by the third performance we had control of it and began to enjoy playing those clever Shavian lines. By the end of the week's run we felt that we had mastered the play and were ready to open.

During the week's run of *Heartbreak House* the rain continued. Most of October in 1954 was devoid of sun. On opening night of *Heartbreak House* the cast outnumbered the audience of five. Nevertheless, because we needed the run through, we played for them and they seemed appreciative. The human audience was small in number, but the audience of field mice that invaded the theatre to escape the cold and damp outside was extremely large. They seemed unperturbed by human presence. They would run along the edge of the stage between the footlights and the auditorium, suddenly stop, sit up, and peer out at the darkened theatre or up at the actors. Then, curiosity satisfied, they would scurry on. To the actors they were a damned nuisance, not just as an audience distraction but in other ways too: when making up you could hear them behind the mirror or you might find one in your costume or shoe. They had a nasty habit of skittering among the audience's feet. A lady became hysterical at seeing one and had to be taken out of the theatre. But most of the few people who ventured out to see our show found them a cute added attraction.

Immediately after opening *Heartbreak House*, we started on our last play of the by-now financially disastrous season, *The Holly and the Ivy*. I had taken on the role of the Reverend Gregory, which I had longed to play ever since seeing Ralph Richardson in the film version. The weather forecasts were promising improved conditions. We hoped that the next week would bring out the sun and we would perform this warm-hearted play to larger houses. But that was not to be. Prior to our opening the season I had had a visit from a Charles Michael Turner who had produced a season of summer theatre that year in Maude Franchot's old stamping ground, the Niagara Falls High School. Instead of organizing his own troupe, he had hired Leslie Yeo's London Theatre Company, which originally consisted of actors recruited in Britain and brought over to play in St. John's, Newfoundland. It had subsequently moved to London and was then enticed to Niagara Falls in 1954 by Mr. Turner. It was a top-notch company whose fascinating history is revealed in Mr. Yeo's book *A Thousand and One First Nights*. During that previous summer I had seen them in a gripping production of *Johnny Belinda*, and a frothy comedy, *The Perfect Woman*, starring Mr. Yeo's lovely wife, Hilary Vernon. Despite the high quality of their productions, Turner had lost money and ended his season in debt to Yeo's company.

Mr. Turner came to see me ostensibly to offer his assistance with my imminent autumn season. He was a very smooth talker. He proposed that he handle special promotion for theatre parties and bus tours. I was sceptical that such parties and bus loads could be organized on that short notice. I refused to put him on the payroll, but he made an end run. He went to my backer, Bill Watkins, in Toronto and talked him into putting up an additional $500 on the vague promise of persuading people by the bus load to attend. I was appalled Bill would be so gullible. Mr. Turner may have tried hard but no theatre parties or bus loads of customers ever turned up, although he would come by occasionally and tell me of his great plans to fill the house. On the Friday of the run of *Heartbreak House* I received a telephone call from Turner in Rochester, the reason for which was so unimportant that I have forgotten why he called. But his final remark just before he hung up I shall never forget. He said:

"Anyway it doesn't matter now that you have closed."

"What do you mean?" I asked.

"I was just talking to Bill on the phone and he told me that he has decided to close tomorrow night."

"Well he hasn't told me," I said in shock.

"You'd better call him to see if he means it," Turner said, "but he seemed quite decided."

He then offered to give a closing night party for the cast and crew after the show Saturday night at his home in Niagara Falls. Determined to retrieve something for Watkins' $500, I accepted his invitation. I phoned Watkins immediately and he confirmed what Turner had told me. "But we have the next play almost ready," I argued. "The weather looks as though it will break and next week might be good for business." He refused to alter his decision. "But," I went on, "if you close now you will have to pay the cast and crew one week's salary in lieu of notice because I had that clause written into their contracts that you signed." He replied that he wouldn't pay it. I was flabbergasted and very angry. I did not care for myself, but I knew that the other actors were counting on another week's salary. The bank account, over which I still had power of attorney, had $900 left in it, but there were also outstanding bills.

After the show Friday night I called the company together and told them the sad news. I cancelled next day's rehearsal and drove to Toronto to confront Watkins at home. He invited me in and I was aware of his mother glowering at me from the living room. Bill took me into a side room and explained that he had used his mother's money, and she had found out about it. He was very upset and regretful, but he could not continue. I reminded him that he had assured me that he would use only his own funds. He had no reply but simply looked ashamed and on the verge of tears. He was like a boy who had been caught with his hand in the cookie jar. I suddenly felt sorry for him. He was a loner who loved the theatre, but, until I came along, had always been on the fringe of it. When I approached him for backing, he at last saw a chance to be part of something he adored. For a brief time he had become an "impresario," and was welcomed into the exciting world of the theatre. For a few weeks he was no longer a loner. Under the circumstances I did not feel that I should pressure him further, and returned to Vineland.

That night after the final performance we all repaired to Charles Michael Turner's house in Niagara Falls. It was a good party because everyone was in a party mood. I think the cast was relieved that the season had closed. At least they would get away from the dreary greyness of soggy Vineland. I had done some quick calculations and discovered that the $900 remaining in the bank account would cover the outstanding bills owing to merchants in the area and the amount owing to the federal government for unemployment insurance and income tax deducted from the artists' pay. But if these sums were paid there would be too little left for the week's salary owed to the actors. Turner's lawyer was at the party, after winning an acquittal for an accused hatchet-murderer in St. Catharines, and I told him about the financial situation. He said to pay off the actors first. He alarmed me by saying that Watkins could rescind the power of attorney over the bank account at any moment, and that it would be advisable for me to get into the bank the first thing the following Monday. I took his advice and withdrew $900, leaving only a few dollars in the account to keep it active. I took the money back to the farmhouse where I was now the only resident.

I sat at the kitchen table with more cash than I had ever seen at one time piled in front of me.

"You stupid fool," I thought, as it dawned on me that although Watkins was the official producer of the company, I was in association with him, and as business manager was a signing officer and probably also personally liable for debts. I took the money back and re-deposited it. I then wrote certified cheques to the creditors and to the Department of National Revenue and the Unemployment Insurance Commission. I then wrote letters to all the actors giving them Bill Watkins's address and telling them that they should collect their week's-notice payment from him as the producer. Some of them tried, but did not succeed. At least they had been paid up to the final performance. The week's-notice clause that I had included in the contract was not customary nor expected by Canadian performers in 1954. But this incident converted me to supporting the Actors' Equity Association currently getting organized in Canada. Later that autumn I read in a newspaper that Mr. Turner had been charged by the Department of National Revenue for not remitting the income tax and unemployment insurance he had deducted from the actors that previous summer. I believe there was a settlement out of court and the charges were dropped. Had I heeded his lawyer, Bill Watkins and I could also have been hauled into court by the DNR. So much for the advice of lawyers.

Considering that the weather had conspired to turn what could have been a successful financial season into a disastrous one, I felt convinced that if I held onto the theatre I could recoup the loss the following summer. Without his mother's approval, Bill could not put any more money into the venture, so that winter I set about to find another backer. However, I stopped when I heard that John Prudhomme, ignoring the terms of our contract, had signed an agreement with the radio producer, Alan Savage, to take over the Garden Centre Theatre for 1955. I protested to Prudhomme but to no avail. A written agreement was to be honoured only when it was of value to him. I could not afford to take him to court and I was reluctant to antagonize Alan for whom I had appeared in several programs on the CBC radio. When I learned that Alan and his partner, John Yorke, were planning to put $20,000 into the venture, I decided not to contest the matter. As a result, Savage and Yorke obtained the GCT for 1955, and got to use the equipment for which Bill Watkins had paid Prudhomme $500. Prudhomme got the scenery, props, and lights, the rent paid on the theatre for four weeks, and $500 to boot. In the next decade I was to get to know and dislike John Prudhomme even more.

CHAPTER 12

In Mariposa,
a Chicken Coop,
and a Phone Booth

After my mad adventure in Vineland, I once again found myself a supplicant performer with very little cash. Fortunately, since my return from
England in 1948 I had managed to break into CBC radio drama without
belonging to Andrew Allan's charmed circle. If God himself wouldn't use
me, some of his Archangels would. Esse Ljungh, Alan Savage, and J. Frank
Willis employed me quite frequently, and I found the Ford Radio Theatre,
which broadcast first from McGill Street and then from the Parliament
Street studio, a very exciting experience.

Television drama was also beginning to offer exciting possibilities.
During the summer of 1952 while I was directing for the International
Players, I applied to be trained as a director for the newly opened CBC-TV.
The winter before I had learned something about TV production by
attending a series of lectures in which Mavor Moore had been one of the
guest speakers. I was invited to an interview with Stuart Griffiths, the newly
appointed program director for CBC's English TV network. It meant taking
time off from my busy directing schedule in Kingston but fortunately not
in a week when I was also performing. I drove to Toronto eager for the
meeting because there was the likelihood that, with my experience as a
stage director, I might eventually be accepted as a television producer. A lot
was at stake for me. I arrived at the CBC only to be told that Mr. Griffiths,
who had complete say over who would enter the training course, had gone

to a wedding in Ottawa. His secretary assured me that it was not her fault and that Griffiths knew of the appointment. I had a letter that confirmed the appointment so there was no error about dates on my part. Naturally I was furious and went immediately to Mavor who was then chief producer for television. Much embarrassed, Mavor could only advise me to arrange another appointment. With my hectic schedule that was impossible in the short time before the training courses were to begin. My chances of getting in on TV's ground floor were sabotaged by wedding bells. When I next had time to travel to Toronto it was too late. The CBC had its complement of aspiring television directors. But if I could not get into TV as a director (producer), I could as an actor, which I managed to do through Drew Crossan who had succeeded in becoming a producer in the CBC Variety Department. As a result I was able to sustain myself that winter chiefly with radio and the new medium of television, about which I shall soon say more.

My financial situation was also improved that winter by an assist from the New Play Society and Mavor's musical adaptation of Stephen Leacock's *Sunshine Sketches of a Little Town*. Called, appropriately enough, *Sunshine Town*, it is very pleasant family entertainment, with some charming songs and amusing characters and situations. It offers a lovingly satirical glimpse into the life of a small Ontario town and lampoons Canadian politics of the John A. MacDonald and Wilfrid Laurier era. It is not difficult to stage and has ample opportunity for good musical comedy singers and dancers to display their talents, as we discovered. Everyone in the cast had a ball with it, as did the audience, and it should be revived periodically as a Canadian folk musical.

· I was cast as Doc Gallagher, described as a "medico-political expert." Among his cronies were John Henry Bagshaw M.P. (Robert Christie), Dean Drone, C. of E. (Drew Thompson), Golgotha Gingham, the Undertaker (Ed Holmes), and Henry Mullins, manager of the Exchange Bank (Norman Roland). Mavor had written the book, lyrics, and music, and raised the production money. He also directed and had obtained a talented team of assistants: Howard Cable as arranger and musical director, Set Designer Jack McCullough, Choreographers Alan and Blanche Lund, and as company general manager, John Hayes, who was beginning to evince an ability for the production and business side of theatre. To complement this outstanding production team, Mavor had assembled a cast of some of the best variety performers in Toronto, a city which was seeing an influx of talent from across the country and even from Britain, hoping for careers in Canadian television. Joe Runner played the juvenile lead, Peter Pupkin; Jacqueline Smith was the *ingénue*, Zena Pepperleigh, the daughter of Judge Pepperleigh, played by that reliable character actor, Alex McKee; Sandy Webster doubled as George Duff and the Presbyterian Minister; and Louis Negin as Billy, the hotel clerk, made one of his earliest appearances. Appearing before professional theatre audiences for the first time was that handsome, dashing Robert Goulet as Mal Tompkins, reporter for the Newspacket.

A tour had been arranged that was extensive for the time — all of three cities — opening in London's Grand Theatre for a week, then two weeks at the Royal Alex in Toronto, followed by a week at Her Majesty's in Montreal. Four whole weeks of performing! And no government subsidies! But the show nearly did not leave London. Despite Mavor's valiant fundraising, there was insufficient capital up front with the result that a few days after opening in London the cast heard rumours of a financial crisis and we wondered if we would make it to Toronto, let alone Montreal. But Mavor is very persuasive. He has an essential attribute of a good commander and can give the impression that all is just hunky-dory while the walls are falling in around you. He scurried around London and raised enough money to get us to Toronto. Not until four decades later, when I read his autobiography, did I realize the size of the financial burden he had shouldered.

This was a thoroughly delightful company to be with. The effervescence of the young dancers affected the whole company, and Robert Goulet, exuding confidence, *joie de vivre*, vast amiability, and great talent was the life of the party. One day as I entered the stage door for a matinee performance, I walked straight into a scene from a Hollywood musical of the '30s or early '40s. The stage doorman was standing enraptured listening to a rich baritone voice singing a new hit song from *Paint Your Wagon*. I walked onto the stage and discovered Robert in the orchestra pit playing the piano and singing his heart out with "I Call the Wind Maria." To complete the movie scene, a charlady in the balcony was nodding her head sagely as if to say, "Yes. This boy will go far." As we know, he did, from his own television show on CBC, through the original stage version of *Camelot* to New York, and thence to Hollywood where he fell victim to what I call the "Mario Lanza syndrome," when an initially controlled, mellifluous voice is ruined by persistent show-stopping bellowing.

After the Friday night performance in London, a party was given for the company in one of the mansions along the Thames River. In attendance were a number of Londoners, one of whom, in his inebriate state, showed a deep interest in young Mr. Goulet. When the party broke up at about 3 a.m., Bob and I decided to go to an all-night eatery for sobering coffee. To our dismay this little man tagged along. At the restaurant he became embarrassing with his overtures to Bob. Plainly uncomfortable, but not wishing to hurt this man's feelings, Bob suddenly exclaimed, "Oh gosh! I just remembered I ate meat on Friday before midnight. I must go to mass right now." At that he jumped up from the table to leave. Not wishing to be left alone with this man I declared, "Good Lord! I ate meat too. I'll go with you." Eating meat on Friday had never previously been one of my concerns. Bob and I hurried off to St. Mary's Cathedral for 5 a.m. mass leaving the little man surprised and obviously disappointed.

Including the priest there were only five other people in the vast church. Not being a Roman Catholic I was unfamiliar with the procedure. However, I did whatever Bob did and managed to look reasonably devout despite my alcoholic buzz. I even contributed handsomely to the collection plate — a whole 50 cents. I was just congratulating myself on being a generous Christian when the collection plate returned. "Not again!" I loudly blurted out, and my Christian charity vanished. "It's alright. It's alright," an embarrassed Goulet said, "I'll pay." And he did. Robert Goulet was so jovial and generous that I expect he was exonerated for eating meat on Friday. I am not so sure about myself.

By the mid-'50s Toronto had not completely emerged from its cocoon of Victorian respectability. In those days, Buffalo or even Niagara Falls,

New York, were more swinging towns than Toronto, and for those of us who relished a little night life, Montreal was Mecca. So, with great expectations, we closed our two weeks at the Royal Alex and headed for that wicked city (Montreal not Mecca). Her Majesty's Theatre was ornate, old, and past its heyday but contained echoes of former glories. That the lovely old showplace was eventually torn down is a blot on the City of Montreal, and particularly its Anglo community. No Ed Mirvish emerged from the wealthy of Montreal to save it from the wreckers. Nor did the English-speaking public of Montreal give our show the support expected. Our sojourn at Her Majesty's lost money. With hopes of recuperating some of the loss, Mavor tried a return engagement in London, but that city's audiences had been exhausted in the tour's first week. Mavor sank deeper into debt. In his autobiography he reveals that at the end of the second London week he personally owed $30,000[1] — information which, to his credit, he did not allow to worry the cast.

■

When *Sunshine Town* closed in spring 1955, the summer loomed ahead with no promise of work. As well as the Garden Centre Theatre, now under Alan Savage's control, I also contacted another company I had vaguely heard about. Once upon a time in the city where Lake Erie flows into the Niagara River and that the early French explorers called "Belle Fleuve," and which Americans later corrupted to "Bellflow" and thence to "Buffalo," there grew a young girl named Gloria Tripi, who in her early years developed an enthusiasm for acting. At a young age she helped organize the Lakeshore Playhouse in Derby, New York. By the spring of 1948 she concluded that residents of the southern part of the Niagara Peninsula, many of whom were Americans, could benefit from a summer theatre. She and her friend, Virginia Murphy, began looking for a location. This they found in the barn, dating from 1866, of the Michener Dairy Farm near Crystal Beach that was then owned by some of Gloria's friends who agreed to rent it to her with the hope that its conversion into a theatre would bring electricity not only to the barn but also to their house.

A formidable task faced the two young ladies. Tons of hay had to be removed along with considerable animal residue. The floor had to be sloped, the stalls torn out, a stage, proscenium arch, and dressing rooms built. A heavy steel beam had to be installed and the red silo converted into a refreshment stand. They obtained seats from the Oddfellows Hall in Ridgeway, and they begged, borrowed, or scrounged all the accoutrements necessary. Gloria and Virginia did most of the interior renovation themselves wielding crowbars, axes, saws, and hammers with the zeal of the dedicated. Caught up by their enthusiasm, friends joined in to get the barn ready for summer 1948. And ready it was in five weeks except for one essential item — electric power. All the wiring had been installed, but Ontario Hydro, despite many visits from Ms. Tripi, would not promise power by their opening date. Undaunted, she and a contractor friend of her father's scoured southern Ontario for a gasoline-powered generator, but to no avail. In desperation they corralled a batch of kerosene lamps to light the stage. Fortunately these were unnecessary because just two hours before curtain on opening night, Ontario Hydro stirred itself and turned on the power. However, they faced their first opening night with no rehearsal under the proper lighting.

Lacking funds, Gloria had found two investors to subsidize the actors' salaries and the royalties on the plays. But there was soon a falling out over her business partners' desire to cut corners, so she departed the scene in August of 1948. Her inexperienced ex-partners tried to operate in 1949 with disastrous results. Gloria bought them out for a mere $2,000, took back her dream and produced summer stock in Crystal Beach under the banner of the Holloway Bay Players every summer thereafter through 1955. Her acting company over the years was recruited mostly from the increasing community of professional actors in Toronto, with a sprinkling from Buffalo, and included such performers as Mary Damer, Cosette Lee, Hugh Watson, Mack Inglis, and in 1955 for one show only, myself.

I was to play Chauffourier Dubieff, a French government official, in *Tovarich*. Because I was unfamiliar with this theatre, two weeks before the season was scheduled to open, I drove down to Sherkston to see where I would be performing. To my dismay I found the barn choc-a-bloc with free running chickens and their residue. But two weeks later when the season opened not so much as a feather could be found. *Tovarich* was directed by Stuart Beebe who was related to the famous Boston Beebes. A charming, elderly gentleman of the old school of manners, he wore a white shirt, jacket, and tie even on the hottest day. We would begin rehearsals at 10 a.m. At 1 p.m. we would return for lunch to the farm house where we all lived. In me Mr. Beebe had found a kindred appreciator of a shot of whisky, and he and I would repair before lunch to his room for a mid-day pick-me-up. Because Dubieff appeared only in the first act, I was usually excused from rehearsal for the afternoon, so I would take my beach blanket to a nearby private beach, which its wealthy owners opened to members of the acting company. My brief sojourn with the Holloway Bay Playhouse was more of a summer vacation with pay.

I suppose *Tovarich* was as good as could be expected with a week of rehearsal. Hugh Watson from Toronto was cast as the Soviet Commissar, Gorotchenko, but could not be present for the first few days of rehearsal. At the dress rehearsal Hugh was secure with his lines for the second act, but was shaky on the third. During the opening performance, between acts two and three, he suddenly doubled over in pain with what appeared to be appendicitis. Naturally he could not continue. I was drafted to read the role of the Commissar for the third act. Realizing that the company was too poor to employ understudies, the audience, sitting in the informal atmosphere of a barn, was inclined to be very understanding about such incidents and accepted my reading the role with great tolerance. The critic for the *Buffalo Evening News* wrote, "Chapman was so successful a substitute that the audience probably forgot that he was getting it all out of a book."[2] The doctor who examined Hugh the next day gave him a clean bill of health and he played the role very capably for the rest of the week.

Mary Damer, who joined the Holloway Bay Players in their first season, recalls the traumatic experience of taking over the marathon role of Tracey in *The Philadelphia Story*. When the actress cast as Tracey fell from a tree and broke her ankle — a peculiar accident for an actress — Mary was asked to fill in. It was Saturday night; her opening was Monday. The director, the former female lead, and the two leading male actors stayed up all night teaching Mary the moves and helping her learn the lines. The director, Dennis Murphy, gave her instructions that any actress essaying the role might do well to know. "We don't have time to go through the Stanislavski bit," he said. "All you need to know about the character is that she [Tracey Lord] is a classy woman and you should move like a thorough-bred racehorse with your red hair flying like a mane in the breeze." Mary says that his advice worked, but opening night was a horror for a young actress with relatively limited experience. She had slept little over the weekend and had to have costume fittings and her hair dyed auburn while she studied the lines. She even lost weight. As curtain time approached, her nervousness affected her kidneys. In those early Holloway days, there were no washrooms backstage for the actors. Performers had to cross a neigh-bouring farmer's field to his privy. During the opening performance, Mary had to make several trips. It must have been a bit disillusioning for the audience during the interval to see Tracey Lord, daughter of a wealthy and distinguished Philadelphia family, making a beeline for an outhouse, her hair "flying like a mane in the breeze." The last act of that opening night Mary performed in a daze. When it was over, she came offstage and burst into hysterical tears in the producer's arms.[3] Mary was involved in another incident revealing the rigours of summer stock. During a performance of *Springtime for Henry*, she was playing a scene when the character played by Charlie McBride entered, exclaimed "Hello Julia darling," and promptly collapsed. The curtain was lowered and he was rushed to the hospital. Ner-vous exhaustion had taken its toll. The doctor prescribed a week's rest, but Charlie, being an actor, was onstage the next night.[4]

The summer of 1955 was Holloway's final season. I don't think the com-pany's closing resulted from my having played there. It really had more to do with the barn's being sold and the new owner raising the rent. Moreover, Gloria's reliable business manager of several years had succumbed to a summer romance, and with his new bride had decamped to teach in Greece. Unable to cope with both the business and artistic aspects of the company, and with expenses sky-rocketing, she decided not to re-open in 1956. From then on Gloria devoted herself to her husband, her family, and her other vocation, painting. During its seven summers, the Holloway Bay company had staged 39 plays as diverse as J.M. Barrie's *Alice Sit by the Fire*, the thriller *Night Must Fall*, the farcical *Out of the Frying Pan*, the romantic comedies *Meet the Wife*, *Craig's Wife*, and *The Constant Wife*, dramas such as *The Heiress* and *Anna Christie*, and Molière's satirical *School for Husbands*, a theatrical diet that revealed more variety than some other summer theatres. In 1993 I visited the area again but the barn had vanished along with the memory of the Holloway Bay Players.

In August of 1955 I returned to the Garden Centre Theatre to play Doctor Bradman in *Blithe Spirit*, directed by the young Arthur Hiller. Katherine Tremblay was Mrs. Bradman. Arthur Hiller and Alan Savage had corralled four of the finest comic actors in Toronto: Cosette Lee as Madam Arcati, Jacqueline Barnett as Ruth, Corinne Conley as Elvira, and Jack Creley, one of Canada's most suitable performers for the sophistication of Noel Coward. Jack is a master of what I call the "laugh now" technique, which, when done subtly, signals the audience that a laugh is required without their realizing that they have been signalled. Fleshing out this excellent cast was Sylvia Gillespie as the maid. Because the producers, Alan Savage and John Yorke, had more to spend than I, Blacklock, or Messrs Slade and Hart had possessed, the Garden Centre sets improved over previous years. They were also able to pay higher fees to the performers, which enabled them to hire some Canadians with star appeal: Austen Willis and Kate Reid in *The Fourposter*, Wayne and Shuster in *Room Service*, Anna Cameron (Blanche), Charmion King (Stella), and Larry Solway (Stanley) in *A Streetcar Named Desire*. What I specifically remember about this *Streetcar* — directed by Herbert Whittaker — was the phallic Greek column dominating the centre of the stage and that several people sat about eating bananas.

Despite having more gelt to spend and despite the presence of "name" performers, Alan and his partner had to call a halt after two summers. The years of 1957–58 saw an American producer, Nat Godwin, at the Garden

Centre Theatre, whose director was Robert Herrman. Godwin lasted two seasons but decamped after the theatre burned down ironically during a run of *Cat on a Hot Tin Roof.* This fire broke out when nobody was in the theatre and consumed everything, including, mercifully, the Grandma Moses wallpaper. This catastrophe was suspiciously fortunate for the Prudhommes who had grand plans for expanding their complex. They soon built a much larger theatre with which I was to become deeply involved in the future.

■

Long since replaced by an office building, the Toronto residence of Ernest Sterndale Bennett and his wife Hilda stood on the south side of College Street just west of Bay. Ernest, who has already appeared in this chronicle as a director for the Civic Theatre, boasted a famous relative, Sir William Sterndale Bennett, a distinguished Victorian composer who had founded the Bach Society in London, England, and become the conductor of the Philharmonic Society in 1849. Ernest also had a famous niece, Joan Sterndale Bennett, who carved a niche for herself in the British theatre, particularly in musical comedy. In 1954 he launched one of the most daring theatrical ventures in Toronto to that time.

The Bennetts immigrated to Canada early in the 20th century and settled in Moose Jaw where Ernest quickly involved himself in theatrical activities and became a director of the Green Room Club, an organization of ex-professional theatre types. He moved to Lethbridge and organized the Players' Club and an Alberta Drama Festival first held in Calgary in 1930. When the governor general, Lord Bessborough, summoned theatre enthusiasts to Ottawa to discuss the possibilities of a nation-wide festival, Sterndale Bennett was one of those who nurtured it into fruition. He continued to be a strong supporter of the Dominion Drama Festival and encouraged the development of regional festivals throughout the provinces. Having moved to Toronto in the 1930s, he directed the Toronto Masquers, and several times led them to success in the Ontario region and the DDF finals. Sent to the United States on government service during the war, he returned imbued with enthusiasm for a Canadian professional theatre. This led him to throw his whole-hearted support behind Roly Young's Civic Theatre in 1945. Along with Clara Salisbury Baker and Frances Tolhurst, he taught acting and "dramatic presentation" at the Toronto Conservatory until Ettore Mazzoleni became principal and brought in Mavor Moore to organize and teach courses in Theatre Arts. Bennett then left the Conservatory and, with Hilda, established their Canadian Theatre School above a store on lower Church Street.

Among their earliest students were Hugh Webster, Jan Campbell, Lew Davidson, Peter Cherrie (who later changed his name to Peter Wilde), John Douglas, and Timothy Findley. With parental encouragement Tiff enrolled in the Bennetts' school in autumn of 1950. He had not yet passed through the maelstrom of summer stock, but he had performed with other groups including the Earle Grey Players. Tiff has told me that it was one of the wisest decisions he ever made.[5] He admired the way Ernest accepted a student's approach to a role, even though he might have disagreed, and through a Socratic method of questioning and discussion urged the student to justify the approach. Ernest insisted on "consistent integrity" in the actor's interpretation. The handful of students learned not only acting technique, but were required to build sets, make properties, and create costumes. In a comprehensive theatrical training, they were urged to read criticism in books, magazines, and the daily press. They were encouraged to see as many plays as possible and, as Tiff explained, "[you] never failed to debate what you had seen. . . . It was a terrific experience for me because it brought a sense of discipline which I lacked. . . . You don't do everything just by instinct if you are an instinctual performer. You also must bring it under control. Everything is done with great purpose."[6] Directly from that school, Findley went to the International Players where he became a valuable asset due in good part to the Bennetts' training.

Occasionally the Canadian Theatre School would display their achievements to the public. One such occasion was a bill of Sean O'Casey's *The End of the Beginning*, a three hander with Hugh Webster, Lew Davidson, and Joan Miller, and Oscar Wilde's *Salomé* with John Douglas as Herod Antipas, Jane Acker as Herodias, Jan Campbell as Salomé, Hugh Webster as Jokanaan, and Timothy Findley as a Nazarene. It was the impact of this production that encouraged me to stage *Salomé* during my hurricane season at the Garden Centre Theatre.

After a few years the Bennetts moved the school to their home where they converted the living and dining rooms into a tiny theatre, with a small stage and a seating capacity of 35. In 1954 Ernest invited some of his graduates to help him form "The Proscenium Club" to offer the Toronto public plays that would be too much of a financial gamble for the emerging professional theatre. The Bennetts mixed gifted amateurs with some professionals, who performed for a nominal fee. Actors' Equity had begun organizing that year, but most performers had not yet joined. Ernest rehearsed his actors five nights a week for five weeks, and on the weekends had them build sets, make props, and sew costumes, which were usually designed by Hilda. In a staggering schedule, the Bennetts were immersed in their school from 10 a.m. to 5 p.m. on weekdays and otherwise in these productions. Six performances of each play were given to an elite audience of invited theatrical enthusiasts.

The opening production, Plautus's *Casina*, set the policy for their ambitious program of plays that might not otherwise have been seen in Toronto. *Casina* was followed in order by Maeterlink's *Pelleas and Melisande*, an original revue called *Skits 'n Phrenia*, and *Flamacue Serenade* by Canadian playwright Donald Jack. *Happy As Larry* by the Irish Donagh McDonagh was staged for one performance in Hart House. It had been given a lavish production on Broadway in 1950 by Burgess Meredith, but had closed within three days. The second season consisted of Ibsen's *The Lady from the Sea*, *The Marriage* by Nicolai Gogol, *Trifle Not with Love* by Alfred de Musset, and John Millington Synge's *Deirdre of the Sorrows*, which was presented at Hart House. I was invited to be in *The Marriage* in January 1956, portraying with sheer pleasure, as Ernest Wanger wrote, "a stiffly idiotic officer,"[7] with the euphonious name of Nikanor Ivanovich Anuchkin. Nathan Cohen on CBC radio said that, "Robert Peace, David Bedard, Ivor Jackson, Eleanor Beecroft, Vernon Chapman, and especially

Rex Sevenoakes interpreted the antics with vitality and a thin line of pathos that made the evening a delight."[8] Although not uncritical, Cohen was very supportive of what Sterndale Bennett was trying to do and added that "wonderful things go on in this enlarged telephone booth."[9]

Ernest managed to interest talented performers in his adventure. In addition to those already mentioned were Charles Hayter, who later toured Canada and the United States enlightening school children and adults alike about the life and poetry of Robert W. Service; Robert Huber who gave up a promising acting career to take over the Revue Cinema on Roncesvalles Avenue in Toronto and successfully operated it as an independent avant-garde movie house; and Pamela Terry, who continued as an amateur, directing shows of professional calibre, particularly for the University Alumnae Drama Club.

The Proscenium Players had only a two-year existence. The Bennetts, who were getting on in years, decided that producing these plays and operating the school were too much. However, Ernest continued to direct on occasion. In 1961 he staged John Coulter's *Sleep My Pretty One*. They moved to an apartment in Rosedale when their rented house was sold and torn down. Hilda worked for some years for the National Ballet and then they both retired to Vancouver where they died with hardly anyone in the Toronto theatre taking note. Ivor Jackson, who performed frequently for the Proscenium Players, has this to say about them, "They were truly lovers of the theatre, scraping along on very little money, and working 16 to 20 hours a day until age forced them to stop."[10] Ernest was a rather shy, self-effacing man, with a gentle sense of humour. One could not conceive of him losing his temper or raising his voice. In his later years he felt that he had been born a trifle too early. By the time the Canadian professional theatre came into life, he was approaching the final years of his. He was rather shunted to one side as others came along to occupy the spotlight. The NPS, Jupiter Theatre, the Crest Theatre, and the Stratford Festival left him standing in the wings. Timothy Findley aptly comments, "They gave themselves to the theatre in the very best sense and received nothing material back from it, but did receive the thing they basically wanted, which was the flowering of the talent they encouraged. I think they gave their lives to the theatre in the most literal sense, and in some ways they were the casualties of their own devotion to the theatre because they were always in the front rank of those who got mowed down."[11]

CHAPTER 13

The Devil,
a Diseuse,
and a Follies Girl

Most everyone has heard of Rosencrantz and Guildenstern, but I doubt if many have heard of Rosenzweig and Jacobson, although the latter pair were the more successful in their careers. In 1956 Mervyn Rosenzweig and Stan Jacobson were budding television producers who had already tried producing for the stage at the Red Barn Theatre in Jackson's Point. Unfazed by that experience, they decided to tackle Toronto. They formed a company, the Premiere Theatre, and rented the Avenue Theatre on Eglinton near Avenue Road. Originally designed for movies, the Avenue possessed a small stage that the New Play Society had used for some plays and several *Spring Thaws*. Premiere Theatre's first production there was *The Fifth Season*, directed by Ben Lennick, which paid off at the box office largely due to the drawing power of that gentle comedian Sammy Sales, the television personality Bill Walker, and experienced stagers such as Sylvia Paige, Johnny Shapiro, Muriel Ontkean, and Stan Francis. They then approached George Axelrod, the author, and Julie Styne, the Broadway producer, to let them stage *Will Success Spoil Rock Hunter?* while it was still packing them in in New York. They must have been remarkably persuasive, because rarely was a show released, to be produced in Toronto, until the New York producers had decided whether or not there would be a tour. But these two Canadian theatrical novices obtained the rights for Toronto and planned a production for March 1956. They brought a young director from New York, William S. Taylor, who was familiar with the show.

I do not recall auditioning but I must have been interviewed because I was cast as Irving LaSalle, an unscrupulous New York theatrical agent, played by Martin Gable on Broadway. With my hair dyed black, I enjoyed myself immensely as I oiled my way through the role of the devil incarnate. Ron Hartmann took the male lead. For the female lead, a role originated on Broadway by Jayne Mansfield, the producers were fortunate in finding the ideal person, as Herbert Whittaker said in his review, "The play's most celebrated role and its hardest to cast is that of a reasonable facsimile of Marilyn Monroe. She must be incredibly blond, wonderfully shaped, and giddily extravagant. Sandu Scott is, I am happy to report, admirably cast."[1] Sandu had come to Toronto via Montreal. She was no slouch as a performer of comedy and was a chanteuse of no mean ability. She eventually won a spot as a singer on the Ed Sullivan Show. She was also an intimate friend of Solly Silver, a powerful figure in the Montreal underworld. The reviews by Whittaker, Rose Macdonald, and Jack Karr were favourable on the whole, but Karr, having extolled most of the performances and credited Mr. Axelrod for some funny lines, aptly summed up the evening: "It is a play that will be remembered — almost as far as the exit door."[2]

Because of the lack of dressing room space at the Avenue, we dressed in two trailers parked behind the theatre. The two women were fine in one trailer but the seven men made our trailer very crowded. Fortunately, we were a genial company. Sandu herself proved to be very pleasant to work with. But one night when Ron Hartmann and she were scheduled to appear after the performance on a late night radio talk show, to the amazement of all of us in the men's trailer and to Ron's consternation, a huge hulk of a man in black overcoat and fedora suddenly filled the trailer doorway. He announced that he had come to get Ron and that Mr. Silver was waiting in the car to escort him and Sandu to the radio station. None of us envied Ron his golden opportunity to ride in a black limousine with a mobster and his moll. He told us afterwards that Solly Silver came right into the broadcast studio with them, presumably to make sure that his gal got treated right by the interviewer. Ron wisely resolved to let Sandu do most of the talking.

Will Success Spoil Rock Hunter? had a very happy three-week run. Shortly after it closed, Stan Jacobson invited some of us to drive down to New York with him to see the Broadway production and to meet the cast. Sandu had already gone to New York. We set out late one afternoon and drove all night. Stan had booked us into the Claridge on Times Square, a fascinating old hotel built in 1911, which, with 14 floors, was the first sky-scraper hotel in Manhattan. He had arranged for a large corner room in which the management had put extra cots. In spite of the long drive, none of us was in the mood to sleep. Partying was more in order. We caught the matinee the following day and afterwards went to the theatre's green room to meet the cast. I was disappointed that Martin Gable did not appear, but the rest of the cast did including Walter Mathau and Jayne Mansfield. She was dressed very simply, and, although naturally sexy, did not flaunt her charms. Miss Mansfield had no sooner entered the green room when in burst Sandu, flamboyantly over-dressed. Her eruption into the room com-pletely killed Mansfield's entrance. It was as though her timing was deliberate. I was impressed with the amused aplomb with which Miss Mans-field dealt with Sandu. As is often the case with two women who have an instant aversion to each other, they were overly sweet in their conversation. Walter Mathau, who in a conversation with me had evinced an interest in our production, decided to leave. What had begun as a friendly meeting between actors now turned decidedly chilly, and the reception soon broke up. We were all a little embarrassed, but it did not faze Sandu, who com-pensated by giving us a party in her apartment. She was a very ambitious lady whom I lost track of after her spot on the Ed Sullivan Show. Some years later I heard a rumour from Montreal that Solly Silver was sent to the mob-sters' Valhalla in a gang war. I hope Sandu was not also a victim.

■

The day after my return from New York I travelled to Chatham to direct for a company recently founded by a charmingly eccentric lady. Paddy (not Patricia) Browne was born in 1908 in London, England. When she was 14, with her father too ill to work, Paddy gave up school and sought employment. At school she had revealed a talent for writing, but young Miss Browne had another interest. At the age of three she had seen a production of *Salomé.* Since then she had secretly nursed a desire to be a performer. Her father urged her to apply for a job as a reporter at the *London Times,* but on the way she noticed a sign in the window of an exclusive ladies shop advertising for models. She applied and was hired to start the next day. To the conservative English middle class, modelling was not quite so unsavoury as acting, but it came close. So, she led her parents to believe that she had been hired by the respectable *London Times.* The next day when she went to work she was handed a pair of overalls. When she asked why, she was told that a junior stock girl needed to protect her own clothes. "Junior stock girl!" Paddy exclaimed. "But I was hired as a model." "A model!" the manageress replied. "You were hired as a junior stock girl at 10 shillings a week."

Crestfallen but in need of the money, Paddy did her work conscientiously and won the respect of her superior. She soon felt confident enough to ask to try out as a model. It was the beginning of the "flapper era," and Paddy's prettiness and bubbling enthusiasm convinced her manager to give her a trial. She was a great success, soon became much in demand as a professional model, and was employed by Harrods department store. But her dream of becoming an actress was still with her, and she managed to obtain small parts in British movies. Her first film role was in a musical called *Splinters for the Navy.* With her face appearing on movie screens, she had at last to confess to her parents that she was not a reporter for the *Times.* After their initial shock and disappointment at her dissembling for so long wore off, they reluctantly accepted her new career.

Paddy considered that she had a moderately good singing voice so she went to a singing coach, Madame Arcano, who advised that she would be right for musical comedy — and promptly became Paddy's agent at 15 per cent.[3] As well as doing shows for the BBC, she began to work up original comedy material for a solo night club act. She soon became a hit and appeared at the exclusive Grosvenor House and Dorchester Hotels. She discovered an ability to improvise quickly and often incorporated members of the audience into her routines. When I interviewed her at the age of 80, she asked me to give her a word. I looked around her apartment. "Clocks," I said. Without a second's hesitation she improvised:

> Once upon a time before I was wearing socks,
> I had a fascination for old, old clocks
> And now I'm one of the old, old crocks
> I have to face it this time.

When C.B. Cochran sent a tour of his revue Big Top to the major British cities, Paddy took over the routines that Bea Lillie had played in London, including the ever popular "Wind Around My Heart." She was involved in three tours after that, playing major roles in *The Dominant Sex* and *The Count of Luxembourg*. By World War II she was recognized as a star of the British musical stage. But cupid put an end to all that. She met a dashing young doctor with the Canadian army in Britain and fell deeply in love. He was about to be posted to France, but had two weeks' leave. They had a quick, quiet wedding and two glorious weeks of honeymoon. Then his posting was postponed and they decided to have a proper wedding in a London church. It became a gala affair with a mixture of show business greats and officers of the Canadian army. There was no time for a second honeymoon because her doctor husband was sent to France and she went back to playing Juliet in *The Count of Luxembourg*. When that closed, she joined a revue playing Winnie the Wopper, sidekick to Michael Moore's imitation of Lord Haw Haw, the Englishman broadcasting Hitler's propaganda from Berlin.

When the war ended, as Mrs. Patrick Robertson she came to Sarnia where her husband established a practice. A few years later he transferred to Chatham where he became chief surgeon for the Hotel Dieu Hospital. After a life in one of the great entertainment capitals of the world, Paddy felt a profound shock to find herself in an apparent cultural backwater. She began to have regrets. Giving up the theatre had been like "cutting off a limb."[4] War brides were treated with hostility by some Canadian women.

Because she thought that people might consider it pretentious and probably would not have believed her anyway, Paddy did not speak about her past career. Frustration soon set in. She could not leave Pat and her daughter and return to England, and when two other children were born a return to London became totally impossible. Resolved to make the best of her new life in Canada, she joined the Sarnia Drama Club, and soon details of her career leaked out from other British immigrants who knew of her. She was asked to direct children's plays. Her acting with the Sarnia Drama Club, and later with the Chatham Little Theatre, led to the Dominion Drama Festival. She made trips to Toronto to see what professional theatre was being offered there, and one such visit proved momentous for her.

As Paddy left an NPS show, she saw a dignified, smiling lady talking to patrons. She decided that the lady must be the producer, and introduced herself. It was instant admiration. Paddy and Dora Mavor Moore's mutual love of the theatre led to a deep friendship. They eventually spent so much time together that Mavor considered her one of the family.[5] Whenever she came to Toronto she visited D.M.M., who lent a sympathetic ear to her frustrations and became her mentor. Paddy decided to try in Chatham what Dora had in Toronto. Dora encouraged her but advised her not to act as well as produce if the project were to succeed. Determined to go ahead, Paddy combined her life savings with some money from her husband Pat to found the Globe Theatre, Chatham, in a former dance hall on the third floor of a building opposite the William Pitt Hotel. The conversion to a theatre was designed to give the space utmost flexibility. There was a medium-sized stage at one end, but the seats could be re-arranged to accommodate arena or thrust staging in a cosy 200-seat auditorium. My friend Ralph Hicklin, a man of many talents and at the time a reporter for the *Chatham Daily News*, was hired to design the sets. Because Paddy's friends had told her that they would subscribe only if they could see her act, she let the frustrated actress in her triumph over Dora's advice. However, she did acquire a business manager, a wise decision because business acumen was not one of her many attributes.

The plan was to open *Private Lives* in autumn of 1955 with Barry Morse as Elyot and Paddy as Amanda. But three weeks before rehearsals Barry changed his mind. He subsequently explained to me that he had played Elyot several times and wanted a new challenge. He suggested Coward's *Present Laughter* with himself in the lead role, which did not sit well with Paddy because in *Private Lives* the male and female roles are equal in size and importance, whereas in *Present Laughter* the other characters revolve around the male lead. Paddy consulted her friends again. Not surprisingly, they had never heard of Barry Morse. The TV series *The Fugitive* had not yet made him an international star. Paddy's friends reiterated that they wanted to see her perform. *Present Laughter* and Barry Morse were replaced by Shaw's *Pygmalion*.

At 47, Paddy was a bit old for Eliza Doolittle, but her growing deafness made her realize that this might be the last chance to tackle a role for which she was otherwise ideally suited. There was ample precedent for the role being played by an older actress. Mrs. Patrick Campbell was 49 when she introduced Eliza in 1914. I had seen an ageing Ruth Chatterton successful as Eliza at the Royal Alex, admittedly a large theatre where make-up can conceal the mountains and valleys. But Paddy was a well-preserved 47 and was hopeful that the audience would accept her. Years later she admitted to me that it had been foolhardy.[6] She asked Mavor to direct. By 1955 the two-year-old CBC Drama Department was toddling along on its own and Mavor was looking for new worlds to conquer. Perhaps a new theatre in a medium-sized Ontario town was that challenge. His mother was encouraging its development and his name would add a certain cachet. Moreover, he was bearing the burden of a heavy debt from *Sunshine Town*. Chatham money was as good as any other. He accepted Paddy's offer and lined up a stellar cast.

A too young, but handsome and capable David Gardner was hired as the egocentric Professor Higgins. Kathleen Kidd, of radio fame, was brought in as Mrs. Higgins, Geoffrey Alexander as Colonel Pickering, and a real coup, Tony Van Bridge as Doolittle. As Mrs. Pearce, Mavor hired my old friend Elise Bernard, who had recently returned from England, her "piece of English mutton" having gone the way of all flesh. Ralph Hicklin was designer and actor in the role of Nepommuck, the phoney phoneticist from Hungary. The Eynsford Hills and other characters were cast locally. As a further coup Mavor decided to use the film version of the story with comments by G.B. Shaw himself personified by Sandy Webster. Rehearsals were held in the New Play Society studios. On weekends the cast travelled to Chatham to work with the local actors. The schedule was daunting for David Gardner and Tony Van Bridge who were both at Toronto's Crest Theatre in *Othello* starring Frederick Valk. Gardner was playing Montano and understudying Valk. One Saturday matinee, Valk developed laryngitis and Gardner had to replace him after the first act. There was no wig for him so he had to wear the cap he wore as Montano, even in the bedroom scene or the audience would have seen a very blond Othello. He had played the role in college days at Hart House, but on this occasion, as he told a reporter, he "re-arranged the lines somewhat." David was more confident in the evening performance, which Nat Cohen called "a moving one."[7] After that draining experience, David rehearsed in Chatham the next day and returned to Toronto the following Monday not knowing whether he would have to play Othello again that night.

The opening of *Pygmalion* was a gala affair for Chatham. Guests came from far afield including Herbert Whittaker to review it for the *Globe and Mail*. He praised Paddy for realizing her dream of establishing a theatre in Chatham but he had reservations about her performance. "Paddy Robertson," he said, "is a former professional admittedly too long away from the acting end of the theatre. There is energy and raucous humour here and a kind of impudent charm, but in the moments when Eliza has to be still, she seemed to be absent. Only in attack did she seem to exist."[8] He commended David Gardner's Higgins and wrote, "One could hardly imagine a better Doolittle than that of Tony Van Bridge."[9] The *London Free Press* joined in the general praise, but Fraser Kent in the *Windsor Star* wrote a review that belied its heading, "Fine Performance Given Shaw Play," and was monumental in its petty meanness.

Other plays were scheduled to follow *Pygmalion* that season but it appears none ever materialized. Instead, early in 1956, Paddy decided to open a spring season with Coward's *Hay Fever* and invited me to direct it. When I arrived in Chatham, Ralph Hicklin, who would be designing the production, invited me to stay with him. By the time the Globe Theatre reached its spring season, its treasury (Paddy's pocket book) had been somewhat depleted, which resulted in my director's fee being sufficiently small that I welcomed any chance to economize. I took advantage of Ralph's invitation.

Because much of Coward's early work seems dated if staged as contemporary pieces, I decided to set *Hay Fever* in the period of its writing, the '20s. I was successful in finding a cast that not only could play the necessary style but also understood the period. However, there was one problem that none of us knew about in advance. It was Paddy in the lead role. She had an endearing, but ultimately frustrating tendency to stop rehearsal to reminisce about her theatrical past. Also she was not a quick study. As producer she had a lot on her plate, but she allowed distractions, often of her own making, to prevent her from concentrating on the tedious business of learning lines. She was Judith Bliss in real life. Her ofttimes exasperating but always disarming vagueness ideally suited the role. But she shortchanged herself of the optimum chance to portray Judith properly onstage. Nonetheless, the production was well received by its audiences and by the two newspapers that reviewed it. We were spared a visit from Fraser Kent of the *Windsor Star,* and his replacement remained anonymous. The generally favourable review in the Chatham newspaper was by Ralph Hicklin. Talk about conflict of interest. But, in spite of his involvement he was critical of his employer's staccato delivery and her tendency "to fall out of period."[10] He faulted me for letting the young local actor playing Simon do the same occasionally. But he also wrote, "Brilliant is the best word for Christopher Wiggins's playing of Richard Greatham, the diplomat. . . . A thousand times in the three acts he proved what a consummate player of comedy he is."[11] He had kind words for the remaining cast members as well, especially for Margaret Griffin as the frizzy-haired daughter Sorel. About June Lehman's Myra Arundel he said, "Here was the '20s. Miss Lehman moved as though she were doing a perpetual camel walk. . . . Add to that a deep voiced drawling of lines and you have a high comedy performance."[12] *Hay Fever* proved to be an artistic achievement for

Paddy Robertson's Globe Theatre. My casting had paid off.

During the rehearsal period there were several parties hosted by Paddy and Patrick in their beautiful, spacious Victorian house. As one such party faded into the wee hours of the morning, Paddy regaled a group of us with some of her own and Bea Lillie's comedy routines from her days as a diseuse in England. We all were amazed at the talent and skill this lady demonstrated as she kept us in laughter for hours. It was then I began to realize that the Globe Theatre had been created to ease the frustration this bright entertainer felt in the sedentary atmosphere of an Ontario town.

Another play was to follow *Hay Fever* in a proposed "Spring Festival of Plays." Brendan (Barney) Dillon was to direct it with some of the cast from *Hay Fever*. Rehearsals were to start the day after *Hay Fever* opened. But Paddy would not make up her mind what it was to be. After the final performance of *Hay Fever*, Nonnie Griffin, Chris Wiggins, and Barney Dillon cornered Paddy in her kitchen and told her that she had to make a decision. Despite their efforts she refused to be serious and would not keep to the subject. Eventually Barney, desperately trying to control his impatience said to her:

"Paddy, do you know about alligators?"

"No. What about them?" she asked.

"Do you know that the female alligator lays 1,000 eggs and the male alligator comes along and eats 999, and if he didn't we would soon be up to our ass in alligators?"

"What has that got to do with the subject?" Paddy asked indignantly. "We're here to decide what the next show will be."

"Precisely," said Barney, pleased that he had at last got her to admit it.

"Well," she went on, "I've decided to continue *Hay Fever*."

"But Paddy, nobody knows that you are going to hold it over," Chris argued.

"Oh, that's alright. I'll get on the radio tomorrow and announce it, and I'll get on the telephone. Word will soon get around."[13]

On opening night of the extended run they played to three stalwarts. Because this was a pre-Equity company, no advance notice of closing was required. The prospect of playing a comedy for another week to a handful of self-conscious patrons afraid to laugh was not the cast's idea of a jolly time. They were quite willing to close the show. Thus ended the Chatham Globe Theatre, not with a bang but a whimper. It had not really been a serious effort to establish a professional theatre in Chatham but born from the desire of a frustrated actress to tread the boards once again. It died primarily because of her waning enthusiasm for the project. She was a talented, charming, loveable, disarmingly ingenuous, delightfully wacky, highly disorganized, fiscally naïve, and managerially inept lady who ought to have followed Dora's advice and not tried to be leading actress and producer together. She had undertaken more responsibility than she was capable of handling. She had lost her savings and some of her husband's money as well. But she had enjoyed the satisfaction of playing two roles dear to her heart with top-notch casts around her.

She and Pat eventually separated and she moved to Toronto where she set about to fulfil her father's ambitions for her to become a writer. She travelled extensively and sent back articles for various publications and the CBC. For years she suffered the slow degeneration of osteoporosis and her death was barely noticed in the Canadian theatre world, hardly a suitable end for a lady who had once been a rising star in the British theatrical firmament.

▪

Shortly after I returned from Chatham, Donald Ewer asked me to play the Chairman of the Board, T. John Blessington, in *The Solid Gold Cadillac* at the Princess Theatre in Niagara Falls, Ontario. It was to star one of my favourite movie comediennes, Miss Billie Burke. I had adored her, as had millions, in the *Topper* series, in *Dinner at Eight*, and of course, as the good witch, Glenda, in *The Wizard of Oz*. I had read her autobiography and knew about her life on the stage and about her marriage to Flo Ziegfeld. Fortunately, the producer, Eric Greenwood, did not realize it, but I would have paid him for the privilege of appearing with this lovely lady. Eric was a newcomer to the Ontario theatre scene but, perhaps with the blissfulness of ignorance, had launched an ambitious season based on the "star" system.

Cadillac was to open on May 28, 1956 in a converted movie house at Main and Ferry Streets.

Miss Burke had been touring the American stock circuits with this Broadway hit and would not be present for early rehearsals. An advance director was sent from New York to prepare the large cast drawn from Toronto, Hamilton, and the Niagara Falls–St. Catharines area. It was predominantly an Equity company, with Iggie Wolfington as Clifford Snell and Milo Bolton as Edward L. McKeever, both from New York. The advance director's primary function was to block the play so that on arrival Miss Burke could fit in without being confused by actors turning up in positions on the stage to which she was not accustomed. It was my first experience with this rigid approach, which completely suppresses the actor's inclination to move as the emotion of the scene leads him. The actor is restricted to the decisions made for the first production of the tour. I was to meet this frustrating condition many times in the future. The young "advance man" (I hesitate to call him a director) performed his task with such affability that no one wanted to make his work more difficult, so no one challenged what little direction he gave us, including Sheila Haney, who has been known to be outspoken when dissatisfied with the proceedings. In 1956 Sheila was living in Hamilton, performing with the Hamilton Players Guild, and making the transition to professional theatre. After the death of her husband she managed to eke out a living and raise a family never dreaming that her daughter, Mary, would become one of Canada's stellar performers, and that her sons would make her wealthy by inventing that internationally successful game, "Trivial Pursuit." Also in the cast was a shapely model named Nancy West who later spent many years in Hollywood as the wife of John Vernon, who became a motion picture star.

Eventually Billie Burke arrived for an afternoon rehearsal. When I returned from lunch I found most of the cast clustered in one corner of the room. As I broke through the circle to meet her all my vision of the beautiful, gleaming Glenda vanished. Seated there was a little old lady of 76 with a wrinkled, freckled face. However, there was still auburn in her hair, and she gleamed from an inner beauty and sweetness. Blessington is an unscrupulous tycoon who becomes irritated and frustrated with the obstructionism of a lady shareholder who throws a monkey-wrench into the plans of the crooked board of directors. At first I found it difficult to speak harshly to her, she was so sweet. But I overcame my heroine worship and we had some rewarding moments together. During one performance she spied a dime on the carpet. Forgetting she was onstage she said, "Oh look. A dime," and she stooped to pick it up. "Oh good," I said. "We'll put it in the treasury," and I snatched it out of her hand, which made her laugh and the audience along with her.

Miss Burke had been booked into the General Brock Hotel, reputedly the best in Niagara Falls at the time. However, the noise of a partying convention kept her awake, so the theatre management found her a quiet motel on the scenic highway to Fort Erie, and the proprietor gave her the use of the kitchen where she could prepare her vegetarian meals. This made her perfectly happy. A local car dealer had laid on a white Cadillac convertible for her (a golden one was not available) with Iggie Wolfington the designated driver. After each day's rehearsal he would drive Miss Burke to her motel, and then he would pick me up and we would drive off to exotic places such as Niagara Falls, New York, or Buffalo. Once we even ventured to Toronto where we had dinner at Winston's, which had by the mid-'50s metamorphosed from a lunch counter to a fashionably chic gourmet dining room.

The story of how Billie Burke married Flo Ziegfeld and ultimately made Hollywood films in the '30s and '40s is well known. A great beauty and a talented actress, during her stage career she was in demand on both sides of the Atlantic. She specialized in light comedy but was not limited to that. When Flo Ziegfeld died in 1932, his lifestyle, which was just as lavish as the 24 *Follies* he produced, left a mountain of debts that Billie Burke determined to pay off. In 1934 she produced *The Follies* and from then on she devoted most of her income from stage and films to honouring her commitment. In 1956 she told me that only a few years before she had attained that objective. I was amazed that this elderly lady, who had led such a wondrous, glamorous, sparkling life, had remained unspoiled by it.

I recalled that stage door Johnnies, Caruso among them, used to bring her American Beauty roses. On opening night we Canadians in the cast bought her a dozen such roses. She had announced that she would close her dressing room door to all except her dresser at 7 p.m. and would not open it again until 8 p.m. When she did, the magical transformation had occurred. Gone was the little old lady, and before us stood the Billie Burke of *Topper*. Tape had pulled the skin of the face back and firmly anchored it under her hairline. Her eyes sparkled and her body was erect and youthful. When we presented her with the dozen roses, she wept. They evoked so many memories.

The Solid Gold Cadillac was very well received by the public who could not help loving Miss Burke. The cast and I enjoyed ourselves and I am forever grateful to Don Ewer for asking me to perform with one of my idols. That summer the Princess Theatre continued its series of weekly stock with stars such as Red Buttons and Lilian and Dorothy Gish (how I would have loved to perform with those two). Many of these were "package shows" from the U.S., which brought most of the cast with them. They were costly with expensive stars who were cashing in on their film or television success while they were still popular. Producer Eric Greenwood, a jovial fellow, struck me as commendably enthusiastic but surprisingly casual in operating a "star" system company. None of us in *The Solid Gold Cadillac* could discover where the backing came from. We were all paid but I suspect that Eric had bitten off more than he could digest financially. The result was that the Princess operated for only one season. However, in 1960 he produced a modern dress *'Tis Pity She's a Whore* at the Lansdowne Theatre in Toronto, during which he got into trouble with Actors' Equity.[14] After that he disappeared from the Ontario scene. For one brief summer he had given the Niagara Falls area a dynamic season of entertainment, and, if *The Solid Gold Cadillac* is an example, top quality entertainment at that.

Yes and No, Lakeshore Theatre Guild, February 1942: Vernon Chapman (Reverend Bagshott).

The Importance of Being Earnest, Victoria College Dramatic Society, December 1943: Vernon Chapman (Algernon), Mary Ellen Fenwick (Cecily).

She Stoops to Conquer, Victoria College Dramatic Society, 1944: Ralph Hicklin (Squire Hardcastle), Rosalind Falk (Kate Hardcastle), Vernon Chapman (Marlow).

The Playboy of the Western World, New Play Society, October 11 & 12, 1946: Donald Harron (Christopher Mahon), Jean Cruchet (Margaret [Pegeen] Flaherty), Vernon Chapman (Shawn Keogh), Peter Mews (Michael Flaherty), Bill Needles (Philly Cullen), John Conway (Jimmy Farrell).

She Stoops to Conquer, NPS, October 1949: Vernon Chapman, Toby Robins.

She Stoops to Conquer, NPS: Vernon Chapman, Don Harron, Bob Christie.

Spring Thaw, NPS, 1951: Andrew McMillan, Vernon Chapman, Connie Vernon, Lou Jacobi, Jane Mallett, Patsy O'Day, Pegi Brown, Peter Mews, David Gardner.

Waiting for our scene, backstage at Memorial Hall, 1952:
Vernon Chapman, Boyd Adams, Carol Starkman.

Dressing room at Memorial Hall: Cathy Roberts, Neil Vipond,
Carol Starkman, Jill Foster.

Sunshine Town, NPS at the Royal Alexandra, January 10-22, 1955: Norman Roland (Henry Mullins), Robert Christie (John Henry Bagshaw), Vernon Chapman ("Doc" Gallagher), Ed Holmes (Golgotha Gingham).

Will Success Spoil Rock Hunter?, Premiere Theatre, March 5, 1956: Ron Hartmann (George MacCauley), Alex de Naszody (Harry Kaye), Sandu Scott (Rita Marlow), Brian Davidson (the Masseur), Vernon Chapman (Irving LaSalle), Larry Solway (Michael Freeman).

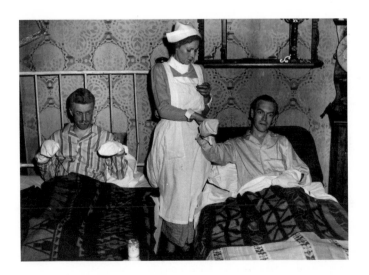

All for Mary, Maple Leaf Theatre Company (Grand Theatre, London, Ontario), July 15-20, 1957: Eric Donkin (Humphrey Millar), Jacqueline Barnett (Nannie Cartwright), Vernon Chapman (Clive Norton).

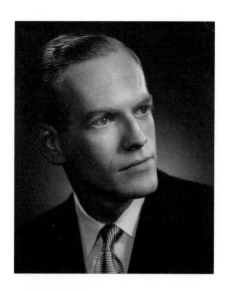

Vernon Chapman, 1957.

Witness for the Prosecution, Crest Theatre, September 1957 and January 1958.
Back row: Vernon Chapman, Raymond Carl, Robert Levine, Mavor Moore.
Front row: John Sullivan, Leo Leyden, Ronald Hartmann.

Arms and the Man, Crest Theatre, January 1963: Gerry Parkes (Nicola), Joyce Gordon (Louka).

The Diary of Anne Frank, London Little Theatre, November 1964: Eleanor Ender (Mrs. Frank), Victor Garber (Peter Van Daan), Sheila White (Miep), Gordon Askwith (Mr. Dussell), Vernon Chapman (Otto Frank), Kenneth Mesbur (Mr. Van Daan), (seated with back to audience) Caroline Donly (Anne Frank), Joy Richmond (Mrs. Van Daan).

Kiss Mama Goodbye, Red Barn Theatre publicity photo, 1964: Sylvia Lennick, Paul Soles, Irene Balzer (Byatt), Roger Dauphin.

The White Sheep of the Family (rehearsal photo, no make-up), Garden Centre Theatre, 1964: Michael Snow (Sam Jackson), Vernon Chapman (The Vicar), Moya Fenwick (Alice Winter), Edward Everett Horton (James Winter).

Champagne Complex, GCT, 1964: Greta Thyssen (Allyn Macy), Vernon Chapman (Dr. Carter Bowen).

Good Night Ladies or Ladies' Night in a Turkish Bath, GCT, 1964: Larry Beattie, Vernon Chapman, and Tom Kneebone.

Witness for the Prosecution, Rainbow Stage (The Playhouse, Winnipeg), 1965: Franchot Tone (Sir Wilfrid Robarts), Vernon Chapman (Mayhew).

Tartuffe, Crest Theatre, 1966.
Standing: Montgomery David, Joyce Gordon.
Seated: Anna Cameron, Douglas Marland, Joyce Campion.
Seated front: Shirley Knight.

The Rehearsal, Aries Production at the Poor Alex Theatre, 1965: Bruce Gray, Paisley Maxwell.

Barefoot in the Park, Red Barn Theatre (Jackson's Point, Lake Simcoe), 1968: Jack Duffy, Marilyn Stuart, unknown.

Filumena Marturano (Marriage, Italian Style), Belmont Theatre, 1969: Jane Mallett (Rosalind), Lawrence Elion (Alfredo Amoroso), Ben Lennick (Domenico Soriano), Sylvia Lennick (Filumena Marturano).

CHAPTER 14

At the Grand

In February of 1956 a pint-sized dynamo, familiar to British audiences as "Junior Miss," arrived in Canada. Joan White began her professional career under Tyrone Guthrie's directing at the Festival Theatre in Cambridge. Her first leading role was written for her by the Scots playwright, James Bridie, and she subsequently performed in several of his plays. She married, and during the war gave up acting to raise two daughters. After the war, because of her short height and little girl looks, she was cast in *ingénue* and children's roles, which culminated with her starring in the West End production of *Junior Miss*, and performing opposite Robert Donat in *The Cure for Love*. During a live radio performance of this play, she made one of the most horrendous gaffs on British airwaves. Supposed to say to Mr. Donat, "Oh, it is so wonderful having you here beside me again," she blurted out, "Oh, it is so wonderful having you here inside me again."

However, her blooper was not why she came to Canada. Joan had branched out into directing when the director of a play in which she was acting suddenly took ill and she stepped in to give the show its final touches. After directing a number of shows, she realized that the profession was very crowded in Britain. She consulted her friend and mentor Tyrone Guthrie, who told her that although Canada had some very fine actors, directing was a wide open field. No sooner had she arrived than she was invited to direct for the Davis brothers at the Crest Theatre in Toronto. I met her when she and Ken Baskette, general manager of London's Grand Theatre, were interviewing actors for a season of summer stock in 1956.

London's beautiful theatre had been built in 1901 as the Grand Opera House. Although by 1924 it had become primarily a movie palace, it was still available for touring companies and local productions. In 1934 Famous Players put it up for sale, and London's amateur theatre groups, with great perspicacity, united to purchase it for what seems now a ridiculously low sum of $35,000 with only $5,000 as a down payment. Based in this well-equipped space, the London Little Theatre became one of the most successful and prestigious amateur groups in the country. Although they jealously guarded their valuable theatre, the members of the LLT were practically minded enough to rent it to other organizations and visiting companies: John Gielgud's in 1946 and *Sunshine Town* in 1953, for example. For 12 summers, the Grand had been leased by an American husband and wife team who produced stock there as the "Shelton-Amos Players." But in 1956 they bowed out. With a lot of courage, foresight, and persuasiveness, members of the LLT took the unprecedented step of sponsoring a professional company. One of the prime movers was Ken Baskette, a theatre buff who had friends and acquaintances not only throughout the Canadian amateur and professional theatres, but in New York.

As I was to discover, Joan was not only a go-getter, but a marathon dreamer. I suspect her influence named the new venture the "Trans-Canada Theatre Company" because part of the mandate was to take plays from the summer season on a cross-country tour in the fashion of the Canadian Players, established two years earlier by Tom Patterson and Douglas Campbell. I also have a sneaking suspicion that there might have been a soupçon of jealousy in the LLT and in London's artistic community over the success of the Shakespeare Festival in neighbouring Stratford. To the artistic movers and shakers in London, the creation of an all-Canadian professional company to replace an American one was likely quite timely and prudent.

Of the 180 performers that Joan and Ken interviewed, 14 were hired for the permanent company. Others were to be jobbed in as the season progressed. But the core consisted of some of the top performers in the country, particularly for comedy: Cosette Lee, Charmion King, Deborah Cass, James Edmond, and Eric Donkin, who was just beginning to reveal his comic brilliance. Another reliable performer, Muriel Ontkean, provided beauty and sex appeal, and a matinee idol type was present in the singer/actor Juan Root, who came to Canada from Philadelphia in the late '30s to perform with the John Holden Players at Bala. He liked Canada so much he became a Canadian citizen. Joan White's exuberant teenage daughter, Susannah Scott, the versatile Patricia Moffat, the juveniles Gary Gray and William McNeill, the *ingénues* Nancy Lou Gill and Doris Peroff, and I filled out the acting complement. The juveniles and *ingénues* also doubled as production assistants under the stage management of Graham Parker (of my hurricane season). He was also required to perform occasionally. The set designer, Robert Grose from New York, had designed for the Shelton-Amos Players for three seasons and was a great asset because he knew the Grand's stage and had made valuable contacts in the city.

But oh, it was a mad, mad company! From the outset, a collection of characters. Later in the season Drew Thompson joined us to add to the zaniness of one of the most convivial groups with whom I have ever worked. The attitude was reflected in the performances. I can recall no instances of temper or temperament. However, Ken Baskette, a bit old school, saw us as ambassadors representing the profession and the particular theatre where we were performing. He did not want in London the resentment that had developed in some of the more staid citizens of Stratford as a result of the public shenanigans of some Shakespeare Festival performers during that company's early years. We were advised against any drunkenness and immorality, and the actresses were ordered to wear skirts and not slacks in public. This last ukase seems absurd now, and was the most irksome, but the actresses went along with it. Although Ken's rules were strict, he laid them down with such affability and reasonableness that no one objected.

It seems a tradition for all old theatres to have ghosts. The Grand boasts the ghost of the fabled theatre owner Ambrose Small. On the night of his disappearance in 1919, he was reported to have last been seen at the Grand. Some claim it was Toronto's Grand Opera House, but Londoners dispute that. Ken, with ghoulish delight, had told us of a mysterious light that sometimes appeared in different places at the top of the fly gallery, and that inexplicable noises could often be heard. Most of us could not take any of this seriously, but Charmion King seemed to attract peculiar phenomena. She had been assigned dressing room "A" up several flights of stairs at the side of the stage where she reported strange happenings. In a *London Free Press* interview she claimed that "an unearthly presence" had made itself known to her on several occasions up near her dressing room. "I don't know whether it is because I am particularly susceptible to this kind of thing," she was quoted as saying, "but the place (dressing room 'A') scares me silly. Last week a magazine I was reading was hurled down the stairs that lead to the dressing room by someone — or something."[1] Subsequently, Charmion asked to have her dressing room changed. On her birthday, as a joke, Eric Donkin presented her with a tiny doll wrapped in a ghostly white handkerchief with a card that read "From Ambrose." She thought of exorcising the ghost by sticking pins in the doll voodoo fashion, but worried that it might agitate the "whatever" even more. Although Ken pooh-poohed Charmion's fears, he was partially responsible for the company's interest in the supernatural, and, according to the *Free Press* article, "wondered what the reaction would be if we learned that the Grand Theatre was built on the unconsecrated portion of a pioneer cemetery [of] more than a hundred years ago."[2] In the concrete floor of my dressing room, which was underneath the stage, there was a neat indentation about half-an-inch deep, seven feet long, and two-and-a-half feet wide. No one connected with the theatre could explain it, but I have conjectured ever since that if people really wanted to find Ambrose J. Small, that is where they should dig.

■

That season marked the first time I had worked in summer stock on a proper size, well-equipped proscenium stage and in front of sets that were top quality in design and execution. Doors did not stick, furniture was appropriate to the scene, lighting was used effectively to create the required atmosphere as well as to illuminate the set. This professional slickness in staging was due to Joan's accustomed standard of production in Britain, and because Robert Grose possessed an ability to analyse a play. Moreover, unlike some designers on whose sets I have worked, he understood the problems actors face and did not create obstacles for us. Taken all together it was the most thoroughly professional stock company I had yet worked for, including my own. Of course, the fundamental reason for this was that the London Little Theatre funded the operation adequately — not princely, but enough to give the shows a high lustre of commercial theatre. By 1956 the standard of production was on the increase all over the country. In Ontario the Crest Theatre had set an example for improved staging and the lavishness of the Stratford Festival productions had given audiences otherwise tolerant of shoe-string approaches a taste of what theatre could be. As public attendance at professional theatre grew, audiences became more educated, more sophisticated, and consequently, more critical.

With the support of the LLT the season was not hard to sell. For subscribers, the 10 plays cost $8, the regular price of eight. In a very safe program of escapist entertainment, the opener on June 25th was *Dear Charles* starring Cosette Lee. I had seen Yvonne Arnaud perform this in England. Tallulah Bankhead played it in New York. Cosette, with her husky voice, was ideally suited to the female lead.

For me one of the high points of the season was Charmion King as Sabrina in *Sabrina Fair* whom the *Free Press* critic, J. Burke Martin, said gave "a sparkling, thoroughly delightful performance."[3] Norman Welsh proved himself a splendid character actor as Linus Larrabee. I played the austere son, Linus Larrabee Jr. and apparently got away with it. But the opening night of *Lucky Strike* proved to be a bit of a hazard. This was the North American premiere of this English play about organized labour and it marked Drew Thompson's guest appearance as Tom Spragge, the shop steward. Two hours before curtain, Cosette Lee's laryngitis was so severe that she could not perform. Rather than cancel and refund the money, Joan White went on holding the script. She "read" a wonderful performance in the female lead and received a standing ovation. But the really outstanding performance was Jimmy Edmond as the frustrated political candidate, Hugh Wallis.

We played *The Happiest Days of Your Life* at breakneck speed from beginning to end, an approach to farce with which I do not agree. In any play it is important to establish the characters and the situation but it is essential in farce. If the pace is too fast in the early moments, the audience is frequently baffled as they try to deal with, as the master farceur Feydeau says, real people in absurd situations. As the plot becomes more frantically complicated the pace needs to accelerate but even then the actors need to wait for the laughs. The hectic speed with which we played left the audience afraid to laugh for fear of missing the next line. And surely laughter is the purpose of comedy and farce. In my view, it was not one of our successful productions.

Until the appearance of Miss Marple and Hercule Poirot on television, the appeal of Agatha Christie's mysteries baffled me. They seemed so unreal. But I have concluded that their appeal is their very unreality. Poirot, Miss Marple, and Father Brown are "never-never-land" creatures. Along with Sherlock Holmes they could never exist in the real world. They are creations that are truly fictional entertainment. I have turned against most other detective and police series because they are dramatizations of the horrors I see on the nightly news. But now I can read about or watch Miss Christie's detectives and be fascinated with the uncommon characters involved, the intrigue, the suspense, and the deductive game we are called upon to play, knowing that it is very unlikely that I shall meet these people or be involved in a similar plot in real life. I feel the same when I see Agatha Christie's plays in the theatre. But they are very difficult to act because their fantasy world characters, the locales, and the plot situation challenge the actor to make it all appear natural and believable. Never-never-land must seem real. Moreover, Miss Christie does not help the actor with her dialogue, which seems quite stilted, particularly to North American actors, and most of the characters speak in a like manner. She is not adept at writing English dialects or using the vernacular, and has a propensity for writing lines that become hazards for actors with minds less naïve than hers. The actors in the Trans-Canada Theatre's production of *Ten Little Indians* (originally in England, *Ten Little Niggers,* and now for ethnic propriety,

And Then There Were None) had difficulty suppressing the smirks and giggles when a character named Blore had to report the death of Rogers by saying, "With an axe. Somebody caught him bending over the wood box." Later, when the murderer was about to hang the *ingénue*, he had to deliver a long explanation of his motives in the middle of which Christie has him say, "Besides, it's always more exciting to have a girl at the end." In spite of all this, her plays are so very rewarding when done with conviction. Our cast achieved this largely due to James Edmond, who, with his cherubic face, gave the judge a misleading benignity that enhanced the surprise ending. As Dr. Armstrong I got the chance to break down hysterically.

Because of previous television commitments I left the Trans-Canada Theatre Company after *Ten Little Indians,* but, for the last three shows (*The Tender Trap, The White Sheep of the Family,* and *I Found April*), the company seemed to get along quite well without me. Having reliably played supporting characters all season, Eric Donkin had an opportunity in the last play to demonstrate his comic ability in a leading role. Apparently this show was also directed to be played at high speed because the *London Free Press,* although commenting favourably on the whole, wrote, "Rapid fire delivery left the audience restraining guffaws in fear of missing the next delicate phrase."[4]

The final night of *I Found April* was also the final night of the Trans-Canada Theatre Company. The possibility of a tour of Canada was never seriously pursued. None of the shows was designed with touring in mind. Moreover, very few people outside of south-western Ontario had heard of that one season wonder, the Trans-Canada Theatre Company. It is probable that if a tour had been arranged of only one of the shows it would have been a financial disaster. As it was, although the summer season of 1956 had not been a financial failure, with large cast shows, elaborate settings, and a ticket price of only 75 cents and $1 for evenings, and 50 cents for matinees, it had not been an overwhelming financial success either. The LLT did not lose money but was sufficiently chastened to discourage backing professional theatre again.

The T-CTC was just one of 16 summer theatres, including Stratford, which operated in Ontario during 1956. Actors were treading the boards of the Red Barn in Jackson's Point; the Garden Centre Theatre in Vineland was now operated by American Nat Godwin II, with a company mostly from Buffalo; the Princess Theatre housed a company in Niagara Falls, as did the La Salle Ballroom in Kingston where Barbara Field, formerly of the International Players, tried to carry on after Drew Thompson and Arthur Sutherland. Other companies operated in Peterborough at Queen Mary Auditorium, at the Sun Parlour Playhouse in Leamington where George C. Scott was gaining stage experience, at Port Carling and Gravenhurst where the Straw Hat Players continued, and yet another company operated in the Town Hall at Southampton. Araby Lockhart took her revue to Windermere and Bala, and the Earle Grey Players continued their Shakespeare Festival at Trinity College. There was also an attempt, in which Andrew Allan and many of his radio players were involved, to run summer stock in a movie theatre on the main street of Toronto's Centre Island. In those days before the cottages and permanent residences had cleared from Hanlan's Point and Centre Island, there was a street of shops, restaurants, and hotels leading from the bridge over the lagoon on Centre Island to the lake front. During the summer it was a vibrant place.

If one excludes Araby Lockhart's home-made brew, of all the plays presented by all these summer theatres, not one was by a Canadian. There are two very good reasons for this. First, there were not many good Canadian plays available at that time, and secondly, the box-office imperative. With the exception of the Stratford Festival, financial backing for these smaller companies was inadequate, and box-office revenue marked the difference between success and closing. Tried and true plays and musicals that had saleable qualities had to be the policy. Only after the system of government subsidy had been inaugurated could producers afford to take a gamble on untried Canadian plays. This should be kept in mind by those who would cut back public funding for our so-called "not-for-profit theatres." Should they have to bow to the mercenary god of private enterprise, and become totally reliant on box-office revenue, the country can say goodbye to Canadian plays and Canadian playwrights.

▪

The 1956 season at the Grand in London has given me many pleasant memories, but the following summer season gave me very few. It was a venture Eric Donkin and I became gradually drawn into where we both discovered that Joan White could be a very persistent and determined lady. When it became apparent to her that there was no likelihood of any of the Trans-Canada Theatre productions touring, she began to plan for the following year. She discovered that I had at one time been business manager for the NPS, and had twice produced a season of shows (if one can call my four-week debacle at the Garden Centre Theatre a season). In the autumn of 1956, she approached me with a scheme to take over the Grand Theatre the following summer. She had rented a cosy basement apartment on Isabella Street between Jarvis and Huntley. She invited me to dinner, and after wining and dining me broached the subject of our forming a producing partnership. With my own recent experience as a producer still causing me nightmares, I wanted no part of the idea and told her so. Moreover, I had no money to put into so much as a paper route let alone a theatrical company. She also tried to persuade Eric Donkin to come into the plan. He too refused. We both held out for months, but we both liked her and often went to her flat for tea or dinner. I found her delightful company and we attended various theatrical events together. It soon became apparent that Joan was determined to take the Grand Theatre the following summer even if she had to go it alone. In view of such resolution, Eric and I decided to help, although Eric, wisely, bowed out as a producer. She had contacted Robert Grose in New York who agreed to join us in a producing triumvirate. In order to raise the necessary funding we decided to become a private company in which we would sell shares. After some rough budgeting I concluded that we would need $10,000 to launch the project. The previous season had been so well attended that we were optimistic that we could reach our revenue goals. Hopefully we would make running costs and also recoup the launch money from box-office receipts. I was being converted by Joan's euphoria and dynamism but I made her agree that if we failed to raise the $10,000 we would cancel and buy back the shares we had already sold.

The theatre was reserved and Ken Baskette, who had resigned as the manager of the Grand, agreed to become our business manager. He too admired Joan and had been impressed with the quality of the shows the previous year. Joan was also quite popular with the influential people in the LLT. One of our staunchest supporters was Libby Murray who was highly respected and wielded considerable influence in the community. On the strength of this we incorporated under the name of the Maple Leaf Theatre Company and launched a campaign to sell shares in and around London. We retained $700 worth of shares for ourselves as a reward for all the preliminary work we had done, hoping that they might eventually pay dividends. Such optimism! We quickly sold approximately $5,000 worth of shares to well-wishers, but then sales levelled off, and I began to worry. But not Joan. She sailed on with great confidence disregarding the fact that our craft was not sea-worthy.

She got the idea that she might entice her old friend Hermione Gingold, then residing in New York, to play Mrs. Hardcastle in *She Stoops to Conquer*. I agreed that it would be a real coup. Her name would not only stimulate subscription sales but also of our by now sluggish shares. Accordingly, Joan and I flew to Manhattan at our own expense. Joan bubbled with enthusiasm upon seeing her "old friend," but, old friend did not seem to reciprocate to the same degree. She also showed little enthusiasm when Joan informed her that Hermione Baddely had just arrived in New York. Gingold said acidly, "Oh. Did she come over on a tramp steamer?" When Joan presented our proposition to have her star in *She Stoops to Conquer* she replied icily, "I know what you're up to. You want to use my name to raise backing for your company." Deciding to fight candour with candour I jumped in: "Yes, of course. Isn't that common practice? If you agree to come to us for our opening show, I'm sure we could raise more than enough money to get us through the whole season and pay you a reasonable fee as well." At this direct, honest reply, she thawed a bit, but regretted that she could not help us out because of a previous commitment. With the business out of the way, she became almost friendly. While she and Joan chatted about mutual acquaintances, I sat back and vicariously enjoyed their reminiscences and Gingold's acerbic tongue.

Despite Gingold's refusal, I thought *She Stoops* would be a prestigious opener and wanted to approach Anna Russell to play Mrs. Hardcastle. But Anna's name did not seem to impress Joan and she cooled on the whole idea. Instead she wanted to open with the *Reluctant Debutante* with herself as the mother and her daughter, Susannah, as the debutante. She would approach another old friend, the English director Laurier Lister, then in New York, to direct it. She thought his name would be exploitable for publicity purposes. Mr. Lister might have been well known in Britain, but his name meant nothing in Canada even among the acting community. However I had to recognize that Susannah and Joan would be good casting. I would play the much-put-upon husband who has to foot the bill for his daughter's coming-out party and follow along in the wake of his wife and her social ambitions. I began to feel that the real life business relationship of Joan and myself was following a similar course.

We planned to follow *Debutante* with *Bus Stop*, *Tea and Sympathy*, *Picnic*, *The Spider's Web*, *Gigi*, *The Circle*, *Janus*, *King of Hearts*, and finally *The Deep Blue Sea*. It was a line-up of plays similar to that of the previous year. We recruited a versatile company of performers, which, after Joan White, her daughter Susannah, Eric Donkin, and myself, consisted of Anna Cameron, Jacqueline Barnett, Deborah Cass, Norman Welsh, Norman Stewart, Anne Derflinger, Roland Bull, Elizabeth Beattie, Larry Reynolds, Gary Gray, Martin Lager, Steven Lord, Barbara Works, and Nancy Haskell. Not all would be on the payroll the whole season. Some like Anna Cameron would guest star for us in one or two plays.

When we had not raised the $10,000 from sale of shares by June 1st, I reminded Joan that we had agreed to cancel the season and refund the money in that case. But by now she was waxing more optimistic every day, and refused to turn back. She made the point that there had been expenses — the legal fee for incorporating, the printing of the shares, the unfruitful trip to New York. She argued that there would be no way to reimburse her, myself, and, to a lesser degree, Eric Donkin if we refunded the money raised so far. I was willing to cut my losses. However, I had to agree with her that it would be bad press if we ran a season and failed, but it would be worse if we folded before we opened without even trying. Joan plunged on with Eric and I swimming in her wake. I determined to work hard to make the season a success.

Like the shares, subscriptions had sold quickly for the first two weeks but they too levelled off after the core London theatregoers had committed themselves to us for the summer. In 1956 the members of the LLT were not involved in selling the season as had been the case with the Trans-Canada Theatre Company the year before. Nevertheless there was every indication that they were very supportive and wanted us to succeed. However, this support was not to last. In order to promote the season Joan was interviewed on television. During the program she said that if the summer season was a success she hoped to produce in the Grand Theatre the following winter. When I heard that my heart sank. She could not have been aware how protective the LLT was about its theatrical bailiwick. It would be many years before the amateur actors of London would be willing to release their control over the Grand Theatre and surrender their monopoly on winter productions to a fully professional company. I can only ascribe this unfortunate statement by Joan to an assumption on her part that most people would prefer regular professional theatre productions to regular amateur ones. Perhaps that could be so in Britain, but not necessarily so in parochial Canada, where, in some communities amateur companies have been known to stubbornly oppose the advent of a professional theatre. From that moment support from the LLT fell away except for a handful of members who did not see the Maple Leaf Theatre Company as a threat. Subscription sales dwindled to a trickle. Our only hope was that the shows would be so good and appealing that box-office sales would sky-rocket and save us from what I felt in my bones was going to be an economic disaster.

As opening night approached even the persistently optimistic Joan began to show signs of anxiety. As producers we had many other responsibilities in addition to acting in the first show. Robert Grose was not only one of the three producers but also the designer, and production manager, although he did not have that title. Consequently he was responsible for the creation of the set, the lighting of it, the stage dressing, the costumes, and all the myriad problems that arise during the physical preparation of a show. Ken Baskette was officially our business manager, and a very capable one he was. But I made it my concern as a third of the producing triumvirate to keep a watchful eye on the revenue and expenditure. Another responsibility of mine was to arrange lobby exhibitions of works by local artists on a weekly rotating basis. I felt a great satisfaction in being able to arrange a showplace for a few of London's finest aspiring artists.

If there was a lack of support at the box office it was not because the productions were shoddy. Robert Grose's Mayfair apartment set for *The Reluctant Debutante* was worthy of any stage anywhere. Tyrone Guthrie, who had directed *Twelfth Night* at Stratford that spring, attended the opening night performance and saw fit to congratulate the company. Laurier Lister, who had built a reputation directing Joyce Grenfell's revues, had been an admirable director for such a fluffy drawing-room comedy, and an altogether pleasant person to work with. Joan and her daughter were dead right for their roles. Roland Bull stole every scene he was in as the vapid Guardsman, and, although I had not had the pleasure of seeing Wilfrid Hyde White's clever performance as the husband in the West End production, Laurier Lister directed me in such a way that I managed a reasonable facsimile. Norman Stewart was a little too cool as the Duke of Positano, but Deborah Cass made the most of the role of Mabel Crossthwaite, another mother of a debutante played by Elizabeth Beattie. Writing in the *London Free Press*, J. Burke Martin concluded his review with, "This is an excellent start for the summer theatre season, and last night's enthusiastic reception must have been gratifying to the trio who have labored so hard to get this company underway. If last night's standard can be maintained, it should be a pleasant summer at the Grand."[5]

Well, the standard was maintained. But for the trio of producers it did not become a pleasant summer at the Grand, although I received a great deal of satisfaction from directing Robert Anderson's *Tea and Sympathy*. I had in Norman Stewart an actor ideally suited to the introverted Tom Lee, who is labelled a queer by his insensitive school mates and his misunderstanding housemaster. Jacqueline Barnett brought great warmth and sensitivity to the role of the wife, and Kenneth Le Maire, recruited from the London Little Theatre, proved himself of high professional calibre as the intolerant, but sexually insecure husband. Larry Reynolds was added to the company as Tom's father, and Martin Lager brought a solid but sympathetic masculinity to the character of Al, Tom's only friend. There is a challenge to prevent *Tea and Sympathy* from becoming maudlin, and with the help of this intelligent cast I succeeded. Herbert Whittaker travelled to London to see it and wrote, "Mr. Chapman, who has directed this particular production, has obviously understood what Robert Anderson is saying in his play. He has brought the two principal characters together in just the right relationship and kept the sensitivity of that relationship the dominating element of the play." He concluded, "It is on the whole a most meritorious production and one of which any summer theatre can be proud."[6] Indeed I did feel very proud of this production put together with only a week's rehearsal. It proved that intelligent, experienced actors can deliver the goods even under such pressure.

Robert Grose not only designed the set for our next show, *Bus Stop*, but also directed it. Anna Cameron played Cherie. In 1957 she was host of the CBC talk show *Open House*, but had a varied background as a performer. She began acting as a teenager in Quebec, then attended the University of Toronto where she performed at Hart House before joining the Mountain Playhouse in Montreal. Summer stock in Connecticut was followed by acting classes in New York, touring with Katherine Cornell in *The Constant Nymph* (she impressed me at the Royal Alex), and modelling in New York, as well as Herbert Whittaker's production of *A Streetcar Named Desire* at the Garden Centre Theatre. The role of the unsophisticated, effervescent Cherie was a stretch for Anna, an extremely sophisticated person in real life, but she pulled it off. She was fortunate in having as the equally ebullient young cowboy "Bo," Martin Lager, a sturdy and intelligent young actor-cum-playwright. Eric Donkin showed his versatility by becoming suitably western as Bo's sidekick, Virgil. Jacqueline Barnett switched from the quiet wife of *Tea and Sympathy* to the outgoing, brash Grace, proprietress of the bus stop, and I got to sink my teeth into the coveted role of the dissolute Dr. Gerald Lyman. Marilyn Monroe had so indelibly left her stamp on the role of Cherie in the film of *Bus Stop* that for years no actress could play that part without inviting invidious comparison. Anna Cameron was her own woman in the role and sensibly did not try to imitate Monroe. She was not quite so wide-eyed and dumb as Monroe portrayed her. Yet it worked. In the *London Free Press*, J. Burke Martin succinctly said, "Miss Monroe has more curvature, but Miss Cameron can act."[7]

Attendance had been depressing for our first three shows so Joan wanted to substitute a broad English farce in the place of *Picnic*. I wanted to stick to our season as published because that was the program our subscribers had purchased. She and Robert Grose voted against me and *All for Mary* was substituted with Joan directing. By now Joan and I were at loggerheads on a number of matters. Bob Grose tried to be neutral, but succumbed more and more to Joan's influence. Joan had become somewhat cavalier about expenditures and had a tendency to rehearse overtime. I was worried that the Equity Deputy would report this to Equity and we would be penalized with overtime payments. Joan and I had a row over this, but overtime rehearsals were stopped after that because as an actor I refused to rehearse overtime. This could have cost me my job had I also not been one of the producers. Joan also interfered with reponsibilities others had assumed. It was my job to line up artists whose works we would display in the lobby. We had agreed that we would give relatively unknown local artists a helpful showcase. But when a London businessman persuaded Joan that the work of more prestigious artists should be displayed, Joan and I had another disagreement, and I turned over to her the responsibility of obtaining a "prestigious" artist for the fifth show. However, it was too late. There was no fifth show.

All for Mary was a passable production, but it did not stimulate the box office. On the weekend of the opening of *All for Mary*, Joan took ill, partially from exhaustion, and was rushed to the hospital. Faced with this disaster, the bickering between Joan and me, the public apathy, and a growing debt, we decided that discretion was the better part of foolhardiness, and cancelled the remainder of the season. No new show went into rehearsal and the actors were given their week's notice. Ken had very wisely paid out money only on a per show basis, and, despite Joan's urging, had adamantly refused to turn over all the subscription money to us. I supported his fiscally-responsible attitude. I was chagrined that we could not give a dividend to that handful of people who had shown enough faith in us to buy shares, but we were able to refund to each subscriber an amount covering the six shows that never materialized. Otherwise I would have felt that I could never show my face in London again. Joan, Bob, and I agreed not to dissolve the Maple Leaf Theatre Company for the time being. I hoped that by retaining the corporation I might be able to use it to raise money for future productions, if not in London, possibly elsewhere, and eventually pay a dividend on the shares or buy out the existing shareholders.

It is easy to blame the apathetic public for our debacle, and, of course, that was a factor. J. Burke Martin wrote an "obituary" about the company in which he said that he had enjoyed our four productions and that he was saddened because our closing was symptomatic of public indifference toward legitimate theatre. He pointed out that London Little Theatre productions had suffered a diminution in attendance in recent years and conjectured that the advent of television could be responsible. He finished his article by writing, "Incidentally, if only one quarter of you LLT members had gone to the Grand once a week — and not one outsider — the Maple Leaf troupe would still be doing business. But you didn't, and they're not."[8]

I have to admit that we jumped into the season without sufficient funding. My previous ventures into production had operated with less money than we had raised, but the performing venues and stages were smaller, and they were non-Equity and non-IATSE companies, making production costs much lower than at the Grand, a union house. The London public had become accustomed over the years to a high production standard commensurate with the atmosphere of the Grand Theatre. We knew that we had to offer shows every bit as polished as those of the year before, when the LLT had put the support of its membership and its treasury, albeit limited, behind them. To a degree I blame myself for ceasing to listen, under pressure of our enthusiasm, to my better judgement that we should not open unless we raised $10,000. Nevertheless we gave it a good shot. We maintained a high standard of production. Looking back, although it seems a callous thing to say, I feel it was perhaps fortunate that Joan took ill, otherwise we might have persisted with the season. We would likely have had to declare the corporation bankrupt, and perhaps even declare personal bankruptcy because the mounting deficit on the full season would have been too large for Joan, Bob, and myself to deal with even collectively. As it was to turn out, I managed to get the company out of debt in a rather unorthodox manner.

After a period of rest, Joan soon bounced back, but now our attitudes were reversed. I wanted to re-capitalize and plan for a 1958 season, but Joan's enthusiasm for the project had waned. She was also ready to give up on Canada, and was looking for a future south of the border. She needed money so she performed in a Toronto production of *The Drunkard* and saved enough to visit Robert that winter in Florida. Although of British parentage, because she was born in Alexandria she was on the Egyptian quota so far as American immigration was concerned, which meant that it could be about the year 3000 before her number came up. But Joan was a very resourceful lady and found a way around that. In spring of 1958, she married Robert, an American citizen, and as his wife became a resident alien. They lived together for a number of years, and worked together operating the Berkshire Playhouse in Stockbridge, Massachusetts from 1960 to 1964, but they divorced in 1970.

Joan's departure rather left me holding the baby. I was the only person on the spot to deal with the Theatre Company and its unpaid bills. There had been enough money to pay off the actors and the small creditors but we owed about $500 to the printer of our programs and about $1,000 to the *Free Press* for our newspaper advertising. The best I could do was hold out hope that they might get their money eventually and offer them shares in the company as payment. They agreed with a generosity and understanding that encouraged me to try to sell more shares that winter to back a future season. I approached two potential backers, but both argued that they would prefer to put money into a brand new company. My lawyer advised me to dissolve the company and start afresh. But with scruples that revealed my naïveté about business practice, I was reluctant to abandon the share-holders, and for a time I ignored his advice. With Joan and Robert's consent, I decided to keep the company in existence in case an opportunity arose to make use of the legal, if inactive, corporation. To keep the company registered all we had to do was pay $30 a year to the Provincial Secretary and have an annual shareholders meeting. The first requirement was easy. Once a year Bob and Joan would send me $10 each from New York and I would add my $10 to make up the fee. But the prospect of a shareholders meeting filled me with consternation. What could I say to them? Most of the shareholders were fairly wealthy and I assumed had written off the money as a donation to a worthy cause. Since I had nothing to offer them I did not see the point of calling the shareholders together. But each year I would receive a letter from Mr. Ozolins of the Provincial Secretary's office reminding me that by law I was to have a shareholders annual meeting. I would reply that if he could suggest anything for me to meet them about, I would call such a meeting. He never did suggest anything. After this had been going on for several years, I told my lawyer of this state of affairs. He was appalled and urged me once again to close the company. It had cost $700 in legal fees to incorporate, but I could not afford $700 to dis-incorporate. I sought advice from my annual pen pal, Mr. Ozolins, who informed me that if we did not pay the annual registration fee for three years, the government would close the company for me. Joan and Bob agreed on this course of inaction, and after three years, Mr. Ozolins informed me that the Maple Leaf Theatre Company was defunct. I have kept the stock certificates I had in the company as a memento of dabbling my toe in the murky waters of corporate finance. For the third time I emerged from a season as a theatrical producer financially free of personal debt. But it was more good luck than good judgement. Thereafter, every time I saw Eric Donkin, I would make him wince by offering to sell him my shares in the Maple Leaf Theatre Company to add to his own.

No longer business partners, Joan and I renewed our relationship on an amicable basis. I would always see her when I visited New York, where she had very quickly established herself in the resident colony of British actors. She played in many Broadway shows and on TV, and toured as Mrs. Higgins in a road company of *My Fair Lady.* Eventually she obtained a position teaching Theatre Arts at the University of Washington in Seattle. After she retired from university teaching, Joan and I trod the boards again in 1981 at the Gryphon Theatre in Barrie. Back in New York she continued with the "Joan White Theatre School" that she had organized some years before. In the mid-1980s she returned to London where in 1985, in collaboration with Alan Sleath, a BBC producer and director, she formed the Next Stage Company to give aspiring young actors the benefit of their knowledge and experience. She also renewed her career on British television. Those viewers who saw the mini-series *The Singing Detective* will remember her as the old cockney lady, Mrs. Adams, who visits her ailing husband in the hospital, and Ruth Rendell Mystery enthusiasts saw her as old Grandma Pinkham in *Some Lie and Some Die.* But, regrettably, despite an indomitable determination to "carry on," in 1994 at the age of 86, she vacated her Chelsea pad and entered Denville Hall, a senior citizens' home for retired actors, because she had developed a tendency to topple over, which she said became most disconcerting to her friends and neighbours. She died there in June 1999 at the age of 90.

Even though we had our differences over the Maple Leaf Theatre Company, and I often found her headstrong approach frustrating, I have always admired her drive and fortitude. She had an optimistic, "never-say-die" attitude. Actually, had she been more prone to accept advice, we would have made a great team as theatre producers. All my life I have been quite laid back about adversity. While it has saved me from ulcers, I recognize that it is too often an easy way out. I could have done with some of Joan's determination and perseverance. I have often conjectured what a beneficial contribution she might have made to the development of the Canadian theatre had our adventure in London been a success and she remained here. But after several years in Canada, when her efforts did not pay off, she went where the opportunities were greater — south of the border. Who can blame her?

CHAPTER 15

In a Peterborough Theatre Scandal

With the sudden demise of the MLT Company, I was sorely in need of employment when Henry Comor asked me to play the police inspector in *The Peterborough Theatre Scandal*. Professional summer theatre had existed in Peterborough for eight years by 1957, operating in one of the best summer venues at the time, the air-conditioned Queen Mary School auditorium. Producer Michael Sadlier assembled strong resident companies, augmented occasionally by guest performers, such as myself. Part of the inducement for actors to work at a reasonably low salary in Peterborough during the summer was the lure of acting in Bermuda's lush warmth where Sadlier ran a company in the winter. High-powered talent appeared in Peterborough over the years. In July of 1950, Bill Hutt appeared as the young psychopath in *Night Must Fall* with the notable Catherine Proctor as his would-be victim and Henry Kaplan directing. For the 100th anniversary of the founding of Peterborough (1850), Sadlier premiered *At My Heart's Core* by Robertson Davies, who was then editor of the *Peterborough Examiner*. It starred Kate Reid as Catherine Parr Traill, Clarene Jackman as Susanna Moodie, Brenda Davies as Frances Stewart, and Donald Glen as the Honourable Thomas Stewart. Robert Gill directed the 1953 season highlighted by *The Winslow Boy* with Harry Geldart as Sir Robert, Brenda Davies as Mrs. Winslow, and David Powell as Mr. Winslow. Gill also took on the thankless role of the Winslow daughter's rejected suitor. That same season Edward Everett Horton appeared in the French comedy, *Nina*, and the Peterborough Summer Theatre staged the first Canadian production of *Bell, Book and Candle*. In 1954, *Come Back Little Sheba* starring Lorne Greene broke PST attendance records. That play's leading female character has lost her dog and keeps calling at the back door, "Little Sheba. Come back, little Sheba." At one performance a dog wandered onto the set and for a long time eluded all efforts at capture, which left the perplexed audience wondering why the mistress of the house was still calling for Sheba.

In 1957 Sadlier had hired as director Henry Comor, a recent immigrant who had an extensive background with English repertory companies. Sadlier had chosen plays that should have been box-office bonanzas: *Teahouse of the August Moon*, *The Patsy*, *The Deep Blue Sea*, *Tons of Money*, *Witness for the Prosecution*, *The Solid Gold Cadillac*, *Wishing Well*, *Murder without Cause*, and *The Peterborough Theatre Scandal*. Despite my appearance in *The Scandal*, it was not the high point of the season. That honour went to *Teahouse of the August Moon* about which Herbert Whittaker wrote that Henry Comor as Sakini, "overshadows the other actors," quite an achievement with Tom Kneebone and Ed MacNamara in the cast. The final show was to be the premiere of *A Leacock Holiday*, starring and compiled by John Drainie from the works of Stephen Leacock, but when that fell through, a British comedy, *Husbands Aren't Angels* was substituted.

Despite the choice of popular shows and ticket prices still at 1949 levels, the box office was not as enthusiastic as hoped. When salary cuts became necessary, the non-Equity people suffered, and some assistant stage manager salaries, small as they were, were eliminated altogether. William Whitehead, who had quickly been promoted to stage manager after being hired as an apprentice assistant stage manager, fed one of the ASMs out of his own salary of $25 a week. He remembers it as a "gruelling summer" but still feels the experience was rewarding, in spite of an almost steady diet of hamburgers, hard work, and very little sleep, because of the friends he made and the calibre of the acting company. He also recalls that designer Bill Lord lived in the production workshops, an old barn close to town. Here the apprentices built, painted, and cleaned flats, and inadvertently, while burning refuse, set fire to the dry grass in an adjacent field. Great panic ensued, but they managed to extinguish the fire before it spread to other fields or buildings.[1]

Over the years, there had been fires of other kinds to put out. One occurred in 1952 when a taxpayer living near Queen Mary School complained that patrons had been parking their cars on his street, and, apparently still under the clammy hand of Victorian puritanism, also complained that the cast and crew had been working on Sundays. The Board of Education, fearing an injunction for infringement of the zoning by-laws, refused to rent the air-conditioned auditorium to the PST for that summer. They offered another location far less convenient, less suitable for staging plays, and less comfortable for the public. There is every likelihood that the fledgling PST would not have survived that transfer. A great hue and cry arose to get the decision reversed. Petitions signed by members of the public were circulated, people spoke against the board's decision at public meetings, and lawyers were consulted. Under mounting public pressure the board reversed its decision. Michael Sadlier was allowed to produce his summer season at the Queen Mary School, the patrons continued to park on the irate taxpayer's street, and apparently the Lord was not offended at the actors and crew working on Sundays. A minor triumph of reasonableness over outmoded attitudes, it also exemplifies the support for the arts that was blossoming throughout the country after World War II. In 1952, people in Peterborough realized that they had something worth saving in their summer theatre and rallied around to save it.

Michael Sadlier had sustained personal financial losses of $400 in 1955 and $1,000 in 1956, so when he lost a further $1,500 in 1957, he called it quits. The PST closed and the Peterborough area had no professional theatre until 1974 when an enterprising Joseph McLeod dared to present a festival of Canadian plays. He budgeted his six-week season at $30,000 and financed it himself. He revived *At My Heart's Core*, and staged Morley Callaghan's *Season of the Watch*, *Charbonneau et le Chef* by John Thomas McDonough, *Yesterday the Children Were Dancing* by Gratien Gélinas, and *The Black Bonspiel of Willie MacCrimmon* by W.O. Mitchell. His productions received mixed reviews, and amassed a $43,000 deficit. Not surprisingly, the experiment was not repeated. Peterborough saw no more professional summer theatre on a permanent basis until the Arbor Theatre in the 1980s with John Plank as the artistic director. But it faded away in the early 1990s. At the time of writing, Peterborough has no professional theatre company, which is sad when one remembers those enthusiastic citizens who once collectively rose up to save the Peterborough Summer Theatre, and the efforts of Michael Sadlier and all those talented people who worked so hard to establish a theatre there.

CHAPTER 16

Things Pleasant and Unpleasant on Mount Pleasant

A few weeks after my detective work in that Peterborough scandal, I was asked to prosecute in Toronto. Murray and Donald Davis at the Crest Theatre had scheduled Agatha Christie's *Witness for the Prosecution* as the 1957–58 season opener and asked me to play Myers, the Crown Attorney. When I began to write about the Crest I thought that the chapter would be brief considering that I performed for them only twice. But as I researched further and recalled incidents to memory, the saga of the Crest Theatre became for me a Canadian lesson in how an enterprise founded on the best of intentions, with high theatrical ideals and what seemed at the time a sound business approach, was gradually eroded by controversy, attacks by a mercurial press, insufficient public or private funding, possibly political intrigue, and above all, by public apathy. My reflections are those of someone who lived through the Crest years, always aware of its presence, but when I performed in *Witness for the Prosecution*, I was only vaguely aware of the crises surrounding the Crest at the time.

The role of Myers is a gem. He does not appear until the second act when he conducts the prosecution against the accused Leonard Vole. At the end of the act he shares the climactic moment with Vole whom he bullies into a breakdown. Except for that moment, Myers lacks the sustained theatrics of the lead role, Sir Wilfrid Robarts, but he achieves maximum effect with much less effort. Although a bit young for Sir Wilfrid, Mavor Moore has always been a splendid character actor, and was an excellent choice. Jonathan White, who died young before fully realizing his potential as an actor, was the accused murderer, and Patricia Moffatt was his lover. Ronald Hartmann was cast as the solicitor, Mayhew, Leo Leyden as Inspector Hearne, John (Sean) Sullivan as Doctor Wyatt, Edwin Stephenson, who eventually became artistic director of the Bastion Theatre in Victoria, B.C., was Mr. Clegg, and that reliable character actress, Maude Whitmore, was Janet Mackenzie. Even in supporting roles the show had performers who went on to make their mark. As a policeman in the courtroom scene there was Orest Ulan who later became a radio announcer and found his niche in Newfoundland. Graham Spicer played a warden. After many years as a stage manager, Graham joined the staff of Canadian Actors' Equity and in time assumed the heavy responsibility of Equity's executive director. A cast of 22 was to be directed by John Holden, who had his own company in Bala in the 1930s but in 1957 was working out of New York as a director and stage manager. The set designer was Murray Laufer and the production manager was Malcolm Black, who went on to build a successful career as a director in both Canada and the United States. It was a cast crammed with talent.

Witness was the Crest's 56th production, and, after three years of its existence, I was ecstatic to be asked to perform for what I then considered the most prestigious stock company developed by Canadians after the war. From its beginning I had expected the Crest to be a success because the Davis brothers seemed to be going about things the right way with more financial backing than had been available to the Crest's predecessors. However, by 1957 Murray and Donald Davis Productions Inc. was in the midst of a monetary crisis, the first of several the Crest was to face in its 13-year history. Agatha Christie's play marked an effort by the Crest management to attract a broader cross-section of the Toronto public.

■

What induced these two brothers into the theatre? During their last years at the University of Toronto, they came under the influence of that mentor of many of our finest actors, Robert Gill, who during his first year at Hart

House Theatre, 1947, was still the resident director of the Woodstock Play-house in New York State. That summer he took some of his U of T students as apprentices to Woodstock, including Araby Lockhart, Charmion King, Bea Lennard, Henry Kaplan, and the Davis brothers. The following summer with the assistance of some of their university colleagues, Donald and Murray decided to establish their own summer stock theatre. Their mother had died when they were quite young, and their father enlisted the help of an aunt to raise them. She operated on the principle that children must be kept occupied. The result was that much of the children's leisure time, both winter and summer, was taken up with singing, dancing, art, and acting classes. For several weeks each summer Josephine Barrington was trans-ported to the Davis family cottage in Muskoka to give acting training to the Davis children and the children of neighbours and friends. Naturally when the Davis boys looked for a location for their new summer theatre they decided on familiar childhood haunts: Port Carling, Gravenhurst, Muskoka.

In the beginning they were sponsored by the Gravenhurst Rotary Club. In the summer of '47 they gave three performances a week for four weeks for a fee of $100 per performance. A year later in Port Carling they were not blessed with a sponsor, but before opening their first show, *Blithe Spirit*, they had an opportunity to "take it on the road in order to shake it down."[1] They played one-night stands in Camp Borden and Beaverton before opening in "the big time" at Port Carling. They followed *Blithe Spirit* with such typical summer stock fare as *Papa Is All, Dear Ruth*, and *The Drunkard*, which they adapted, with the aid of Robert Gill, from a long running San Francisco pro-duction that had been well larded with songs, dances, and vaudeville sketches. This show was such a hit that, in conjunction with Brian Doherty, they toured it across Canada and into the U.S. The following summer they launched another hit, a revue called *There Goes Yesterday*, which also toured. But the brothers found little work in Canada during the long months between summer seasons, so they spent winters in England.

Touring *The Drunkard* and *There Goes Yesterday* was extremely taxing. The long distances and the lack of audiences conditioned to attending the theatre persuaded them that theatre could be established more effectively by producing in one location. When the plan to amalgamate with the New Play Society did not work out, the brothers decided to go it on their own and apply their experience as producers to another location they knew well: Toronto.

With the advent of television, business at neighbourhood movie houses had begun to fall off and in 1953 a number of Toronto's motion picture theatres were for sale or lease. One such theatre was the Crest, formerly the Belsize, built in 1927 on Mount Pleasant Avenue. You'll remember that Dora Mavor Moore and I had looked at it a few years before but concluded that with 835 seats in the orchestra and balcony, it was too large for our purpose. Yet it had some advantages. Even though remote from downtown, it was on a streetcar route, was in the middle of a residential area, and it had a large enough capacity that if the box office thrived, there could be a handsome profit. The drawbacks included poor parking facilities in the area, a long transportation ride from most of the city, and in 1953 no reputable restaurants or bars within miles. Recognizing that it was not ideal and that a lot of work would be required to make it useable, the Davises took a lease on the Crest. They never intended that it would become a permanent home.

Without government funded arts councils at the time, there was very little precedent for a non-profit theatre company. The New Play Society had tried and had yet to prove that approach financially sound. To the Davises it seemed that the only course was a private enterprise company with shareholders, who would be induced to purchase shares with the promise of an eventual profit. I suspect that most of those who did buy shares were motivated by a desire to see a viable theatre established in Toronto on a thoroughly professional basis. If a dividend should ever be paid on their investment, so much the better. The Davis brothers sought a capitalization of $75,000. They themselves, with the help of a few other members of the family, purchased $25,000 worth of shares. The remainder were sold to the public through a series of meetings and parties organized by supporters and friends. That they succeeded in obtaining the necessary money indicates that they went about their fund-raising campaign with a know-how not previously demonstrated by Toronto theatre pioneers, and that the public, possibly conditioned by the success of the Stratford fund-raising campaign of the previous year, was gradually becoming more willing to give financial backing to theatrical ventures. The success of their campaign left Murray and Donald confident about proceeding.

To get full use of the 25-feet-wide and 18-feet-deep stage, the massive air-conditioning unit that was sitting just behind the movie screen had to be moved above the stage house, and the stage had to be extended forward. Dressing rooms had to be built, a pin rail for lights installed in the auditorium and a proper grid constructed on which to attach curtains, light battens, and other stage paraphernalia. Box-office, management, and technical staff had to be hired, the season planned, directors hired, and the plays cast. Clearly they could not be ready for an autumn season, so they wisely planned to open in the new year. Much of this organization fell on Murray's shoulders because, when the decision was made to proceed, both of the brothers were in Britain. Donald was playing at the Glasgow Citizens' Theatre and could not get out of his commitment there for several months. Some years later, when the love affair between the press and the Crest Theatre had somewhat cooled, the *Toronto Star* published a story that in 1953 Donald and Murray had tossed a coin to see who would return to Canada to promote their project and Murray lost. The reality was that Murray was free to take on the challenge and Donald was not.[2]

They set themselves four lofty objectives: to attain a high standard of artistry and entertainment, to develop Canadian theatrical talent, to present widely diversified plays, and to operate on a sound commercial basis. They planned on having a Canadian company with "perhaps an occasional star brought in from England or the U.S."[3] They also planned to import a director, production manager, business manager, and designer. Because they feared that they could not afford the luxury of dark weeks, they decided to run each show for two weeks and immediately after its closing open the next one. Murray is quoted in Jack Karr's column in the *Toronto Star* saying that they wanted "to present popular plays at popular prices on a fortnight basis. We are not attempting to set up an art theatre."[4] Two-week stock was slightly less strenuous than weekly, to which most of the professional stage actors in Canada had become accustomed, nevertheless it proved a hectic schedule for 40 weeks of the year, and was not always conducive to achieving their first objective, a high standard of production.

They determined to open with Gordon Daviot's *Richard of Bordeaux,* an historical vehicle that had made John Gielgud into a star back in 1933. They imported John Blatchley, a young director from England. Murray, in true actor/manager tradition, cast himself as King Richard. Backing him was a solid cast consisting of his sister Barbara Chilcott, Patrick McNee, Irving Lerner, Earle Grey, Max Helpman, Ian Fellows, George McCowan, and David Gardner. Hutcheson Scott had the challenge of delivering a set that captured the period in nine scenes. I wangled my way in to watch one of the final rehearsals and I came away thrilled that at last in Toronto was a well organized, adequately funded company, employing a skilled director and designer, extremely competent performers, in a proper theatre with comfortable seating, and with producers who had the courage to open their theatre with a play that challenged the actors, displayed them to advantage, and said to the public that the Crest aspired to a high standard of theatre. I left that rehearsal green with envy that I was not part of this venture.

The opening night was momentous for Toronto theatre because it was done with style and with sufficient brouhaha to notify the whole country that a significant theatre had been born in Toronto. The press responded favourably. Herbert Whittaker wrote that, "The company lived up to its claim of professionalism. The production was of a standard with which one cannot quarrel. John Blatchley's staging of the play and Hutcheson Scott's settings carried theatrical effectiveness often to a point of brilliance, while the acting hit, time and time again, the proud peaks of fine performance."[5] But he does mention that the play was "a curious choice in some ways being overlong and episodic and lacking the high flights of Shakespeare's chronicle of the same subject."[6] By all standards it was a triumph but one used years later by some members of the press to belabour the Crest management. There was at least one problem on opening night. The pleasure of some of the audience was marred when the police ticketed many cars parked illegally because there was a dearth of public parking lots and too few parking meters in the area. The following night, Brian Maller, the administrator the Davises had brought in from England, announced from the stage that the management would pay for the parking fines incurred by their patrons. Only one person ever took up the offer. Eventually the management got the fines cancelled by special action of City Council, and thereafter, except on matinees, the Toronto police were less zealous in ticketing Crest patrons.

The Davises had wisely chosen an American comedy, *The Philadelphia Story*, to follow the English historical drama and followed that with an English comedy-drama, *The Light of Heart*, by Emlyn Williams. These choices served as a signal to the Toronto public that their eclectic approach would not be too highbrow but would present quality plays. That winter and spring revealed the wide variety of their choices. Following *The Light of Heart* they staged *Lord Arthur Saville's Crime*, then *Sorry, Wrong Number* and Strindberg's *Miss Julie* on the same bill. This last proved to be a worthy vehicle for Barbara Chilcott. *Escapade* by Roger MacDougall came next, starring Max Helpman and Betty Leighton with Eric House, John Clark, and John Washbrook (between his performing for me in Oakville and his *My Friend Flicka* days on TV). *Murder in the Cathedral* was the Easter offering in which Drew Thompson and Bruce Swerdfager joined the company and Donald Davis played Becket. Next Toby Robins appeared in *Dream Girl* and the season concluded with a world premiere of Tyrone Guthrie's play *Haste to the Wedding*, in which Joy LaFleur was added to the company. All in all a selective season with something for everyone, but an exceedingly taxing one for a fortnightly stock company. They had budgeted for attendance at 50 per cent of the theatre's capacity. That goal was not reached leaving the Crest management worried over finances, but not discouraged.

In April of 1954, IATSE tried to muscle in and demanded three backstage personnel as department heads: electrician, properties, and carpenter. When the Davises rejected them IATSE picketed the theatre. The brothers worried, as all managements do with IATSE, that once one IATSE person is in the door, their numbers tend to proliferate. Moreover, since the Musicians' Union and IATSE were both affiliates of the American Federation of Labor, a demand from the musicians could follow. As theatrical parents they were in no position to cope with these added expenses when the baby was only three months old, but they won that first skirmish with IATSE.

▪

During the next three years Crest productions dominated the Toronto theatrical scene, and in that time the producers attempted to bolster attendance and support by establishing the Crest Theatre Club for subscribers. In the summer of 1955 they founded the Crest Summer School of Theatre. Basil Coleman lectured on directing, Anne Casson taught speechcraft, John Wilson, the Crest's designer (originally from the Glasgow Citizens' Theatre), lectured on staging and on theatre design, Jonathan White instructed in sword fighting, and Jack McAllister from the Ryerson School of Technology conducted a "survey of dramatic literature and its relationship to the contemporary stage."[7] Included in the training experience was a trip to a production at the Stratford Festival and to the Davises' Straw Hat Players, which they still operated in Muskoka. Unfortunately, this school lasted no more than two seasons because by 1956 the producers realized that they were spreading themselves too thin and needed the summer to catch their breaths after the hectic winter season.

The 1956–57 season was notable for two events: first a production of *Come Back Little Sheba* with the refined Amelia Hall stretching herself into a slatternly Lola, and Donald Davis coarsening himself as her husband. Among an outstanding supporting cast was John Vernon from the Prairies beginning his career in the east. Then a second high point came when the Davises won kudos for *The Glass Cage*, a play written especially for them by J.B. Priestley, which had their best box office to date and ran for four weeks. After that, under the auspices of a limited company they formed separate from the Crest, the play was transferred to London, England, where the Davis brothers and sister appeared in it. I was delighted that Barbara, who had difficulty getting work in England in 1948, returned there in 1957 to play a leading role in London's West End. While the Davises were in London and the business manager, Malcolm Black, was left in charge, the Crest's first economic crisis arose.

Despite a generally higher standard of production than its predecessors, and despite offering a variety of plays, the Crest did not draw the number of patrons hoped for. From 1954 to 1957 the company had averaged an annual gross revenue of approximately $170,000, against operating costs averaging $200,000. By late summer of 1957 they faced a grim economic reality. To solve the problem they decided to convert Murray and Donald Davis Productions from a private enterprise to a non-profit company. But money was urgently needed: $9,000 was required to renew the theatre lease and $15,000 to launch the new season. Pearl McCarthy wrote in her *Toronto Star* column, "Toronto's Royal Family of the Theatre are in a strange position of hoping to see an arrangement by which they will sacrifice control of an institution they have built up not only by work and talent but by putting in more than $70,000 of their family money. What the Club is trying to do is bring about a re-organization of the theatre as a non-profit organization eligible for grants."[8] The Canada Council had just been established by the federal government with money derived from the death duties on two large estates, and Metro Toronto had set up its own funding agency. The Crest management looked forward with renewed optimism, hoping for assistance from the new granting bodies and for increased attendance. The business manager stated that a mere seven per cent increase in attendance would handle the running losses. A vigorous subscription campaign raised the Crest Theatre Club to 1,500 members. In September of 1957 the future of the Crest looked a bit brighter.

That's when I joined it. *Witness* was both a box-office and critical success. Mavor was in his element as the wily defence attorney, and although at times a bit shaky on lines, he gave a wondrously theatrical performance that I admired greatly. I received profound enjoyment from playing Myers, much of which was derived from the unpredictability of Jonathan White as Leonard Vole. My approach to acting is to develop a role until I feel satisfied that it is as right as I can get it, then freeze it, varying from performance to performance only if change becomes necessary as a result of a deeper understanding of the character and the situation, or as a reaction to an altered performance by a fellow actor. Jonathan White was an actor whose intensity of emotion depended on the mood he was in at the moment. This varied from one performance to another, and, although I would have preferred that he settle on one approach and keep it, his fluctuations kept me on my toes. I had to gauge the intensity of my attack on the intensity of his response. For some performances something electric sparked between us and it was vastly exciting. On those nights the audience was held tightly in our grasp. This "act-as-you-feel" approach is unfair to one's fellow actors, yet, I got a thrill out of playing the scene with him. It was gratifying, if only occasionally, to set off theatrical fireworks. *Witness* was so successful that it was revived for a limited engagement in January 1958.

With the company on a non-profit basis and a hit show to start the 1957–58 season, the Crest had weathered its first financial storm. That autumn the Crest succumbed to the wooing of IATSE and became a union house. This necessitated altering each show's opening night from Tuesday to Wednesday because to strike one show and set up another between late Saturday night and Tuesday ran the risk of hours of overtime at union rates that the treasury could ill afford. Opening one day later avoided this unnecessary expense. That season the Crest obtained support from the newly created government funding agencies. A request had been made to the Metropolitan Special Grants Committee for $5,000, but Controller Brand thought the amount was extreme so it was whittled down to $3,500. When that $3,500, which was to help with the Crest's proposed staging of 14 productions at a budgeted cost of $229,592, is compared with what Metro Toronto and its municipalities have been doling out in recent years to the arts, it looks miserly indeed. But it was a considerable achievement to pry even that amount for the theatre from politicians who as yet did not understand that the arts are as essential to the quality of life as schools, libraries, food inspection, and sanitation.

Another Agatha Christie, *The Mousetrap*, which was held over for a sixth week, ended the 1957–58 season. The two Christie mysteries had enticed people into the Crest who had never attended before. Hope was that some of them would return. But this policy of kowtowing to popular taste was attacked by Antony Ferry in the *Globe and Mail*.[9] His view was a manifestation of a growing dichotomy among Toronto critics, some urging a less highbrow approach to entice a larger public, and others who deplored the Crest's catering to a more general public taste. As the years wore on the Crest management found itself in a no-win situation about their policy so far as the press was concerned.

My second and last appearance at the Crest was in the 1958–59 season, this time as Dr. Vince in Denis Canaan's insipid comedy *Misery Me*, an unfortunate title that invited the critics to compare the misery onstage with the misery in the audience. To put it mildly, it was not a success even though it had in its cast that splendid émigré Welsh actor, Powys Thomas, who made a very substantial contribution to the Canadian stage and television before death cut him off in his prime. The season is noteworthy in part because of its opening show, a revival of a production of *Salad Days* produced by Barry Morse and Bill Freedman, which had played five weeks at Hart House Theatre and two weeks at the Royal Alex. A delicately charming, tiny British musical with a clever Canadian cast of Richard Easton, Barbara Franklyn, Jack Creley, Eric Christmas, Betty Leighton, Norma Renault, and Walter Burgess, it re-opened at the Crest prior to travelling to the Barbizon Plaza Hotel in New York. Another highlight was the first revue the Crest produced, *This Is Our First Affair*, starring Jane Mallett and directed by Donald Davis. That season the Crest also staged one of the first Canadian plays to receive a grant of $5,000 from the Canada Council. Originally titled *The Centaur*, Jack Gray and Lou Applebaum's musical *Ride a Pink Horse* gained at best mixed reviews. Nathan Cohen's typically acerbic comments included "This Crest entry should have been scratched."[10]

By 1959 the Crest had clearly established itself as the paramount company in Toronto and one of the most prestigious in the country. The 1959–60 season continued the policy of a permanent company and included such varied plays as *The Matchmaker, Under Milk Wood*, Pinero's *The School Mistress, A Moon for the Misbegotten* by O'Neill, Eliot's *Murder in the Cathedral*, and *Mrs. Gibbon's Boys*, with Eric House repeating the role in which he had distinguished himself in London, England. In January a popular production of *You Can't Take It with You* marked the Crest's 82nd production. Two new Canadian plays — an untitled one by Michael Jacot, and *Out of Dry Ground* by Howard Adelson — were also scheduled with Canada Council subsidy, but as the season progressed changes were made, and, for economic reasons, Agatha Christie's *The Uninvited Guest* was slipped in, starring Dawn Greenhalgh and Geoffrey Alexander, and did the best box office in years.

Despite this kaleidoscope of plays, another financial crisis loomed. In 1957 Donald and Murray had arranged to alternate each year as artistic director. Donald took over first and attendance rose, but it declined the following year under Murray. In spring 1960, while Donald was wowing New York with his brilliant performance in *Krapp's Last Tape*, Murray was holding the fort in Toronto bemoaning that the average attendance had been only 35 per cent and that the operating deficit would be approximately $35,000. Box-office revenue was short of their target. Production costs, an average $4,000 per show in 1954, were now $6,500 per show. Murray expressed his opinion to Ron Evans of the *Toronto Telegram* as to why the public was not responding to the Crest. "The city lacks a geographical centre," he said. "There is no one area you can go to for good food, good theatre, or anything else," he continued. "Toronto is too close to New York. . . . Toronto has grown used to the Crest."[11] Morris Duff in the *Toronto Star* quoted Donald from New York saying that the Crest should be closed. Donald was "convinced that Toronto people don't particularly want the Crest. . . . [Even] the artistic successes have not been good box office."[12] Several performers jumped to the defence of the Toronto public. Hugh Webster "disagreed categorically with Donald Davis. I don't think the people should lead the theatre. The theatre must lead the public, because while the public may realize it likes something it's seen, it does not know what it likes before it is produced. I think if a theatre has gotten to the point where this is not the case, there is something wrong with the theatre — not the public."[13] "I don't feel the public is indifferent to the Crest," said Norma Renault. "It might be indifferent to the plays produced there, although I am not even sure of that. The Crest has made every effort to produce plays the public wants to see, yet hasn't been supported. Of course if you could predict what the public wants to see, you'd be God."[14]

As a member of the board of directors, Bill Freedman urged that a means be found to keep the Crest alive. Kate Reid agreed, but added, "If the disinterest of the public is this great, perhaps it hasn't been made interested in what's being presented. I don't think you should blame the public this way."[15] Herbert Whittaker got into the act by comparing the previous season with the one just ended, which he referred to as "a rather typical Crest season. Up to now the plays have varied sharply. Its more serious and distinguished offerings have been *The Seagull, Under Milk Wood, Heartbreak House, Macbeth,* and an original play, *Honour Thy Father.*"[16] The other plays in the season he described as "in a lighter vein" and added:

> If the public may have been degraded by Tennessee Williams, the Crest had no part of it. No blood and guts for Crest audiences. The *Macbeth* was much muted. *Mrs. Gibbon's Boys* did not frighten and even Agatha Christie committed her latest murder before the curtain rose. We stress this delicacy because last year under Donald Davis's regime, the Crest attempted three more forceful works in *Inherit the Wind, The Summer of the Seventeenth Doll,* and *The Entertainer.* At the end of the season it had increased its audience by 25 per cent.[17]

Mavor Moore came to the Crest's defence in the *Toronto Telegram:* "It is the only continuing native theatre we have, and the leading one in English-speaking Canada."[18]

According to Maurice Hecht in *Executive Magazine,* the '59–60 season was the Crest's worst year yet financially and things were getting worse rather than better. Needing 50 per cent attendance to break even, they got only 37 per cent, which he compared with the Stratford Festival's 90 per cent attendance and 80 per cent break even point. The Crest's income of $211,000 for '59–60 was roughly $20,000 less than the previous season, and actual ticket sales were $35,000 less. To balance that, expenditures were $20,000 under the previous year at $245,000. There had been $38,000 in subsidies, half of which came from the Canada Council, $5,000 from the City of Toronto, $5,000 from the T. Eaton Company, and $5,000 from the McLean Foundation. The Crest Club members raised $4,000.[19] These increases in government and private funding indicate how attitudes toward supporting the arts had begun to change since Dora Mavor Moore's struggles to squeeze $500 out of the city and scarcely anything out of private companies. Although the cost to produce a show had gradually increased over the years, the artists involved were not being overpaid. During the '50s and early '60s, stage directors in Canada were not represented by any union or professional association. Only the rare one had an agent. The minimum paid to a director was $300 per show for several weeks' work; the minimum for an Equity actor in a stock operation was $65 per week but Actors' Equity permitted a lower fee for rehearsal than for performance weeks, a practice borrowed from the United States. It saved management money but was unfair to the artists because the harder work and longer hours are put in during the rehearsal period. With such fees the Crest management was not squandering money on the artists and when compared with earnings in other fields of endeavour, the artists were heavily subsidizing the theatre.

That autumn, Norma Renault, who had appeared at the Crest in several shows, and who had married Avram Isaacs, a prominent Toronto art gallery proprietor, offered to co-produce John Osborne's and Anthony Creighton's success, *Epitaph for George Dillon*. She wanted to do something to help the Crest and to prove to herself that, although inexperienced, she could be a producer. The Crest contributed seed money to launch the project. Norma undertook to indemnify the Crest against any loss, which meant that she had to canvass dozens of people to obtain the promise of money, if needed. She had great difficulty in raising the guarantee, even though the people she approached were all citizens of substantial means. Signe Eaton was very generous, but a prominent writer, whose books sold like hot cakes, made the excuse that he could not contribute because he might be called upon to review the show, although he did not review shows in the press or on radio. In spite of many rebuffs indicative of the stinginess of individual Torontonians in donating to the arts, Ms. Renault managed to raise enough to warrant her proceeding with the project. She hired George McCowan to direct a cast that included such experienced per-formers as Betty Leighton as the mother, Donald Ewer as the father, Jeremy Wilkin in the title role of George Dillon, Charmion King, and a newcomer, Martha Buhs, who changed her name to Martha Henry. In a cameo role, making one of his rare appearances as a stage actor, was Andrew Allan, who, according to Norma, did a splendid job. Four days before opening Norma saw a car accident, and, upon arriving at the theatre began to tell the cast all about it only to learn that they already knew. The driver was Don Ewer who had been rushed to the hospital where his injuries kept him for several weeks. Frantically Norma and George McCowan searched for a replace-ment. They found him in Henry Comor who, with the assistance of a willing and dedicated cast, managed to master the role in the four days.

Epitaph for George Dillon was the first show of the Crest's 1960–61 season. It corresponded with the grand opening of the O'Keefe Centre, that theatrical cavern whose prestigious world premiere of *Camelot* overshad-owed all around. Consequently, Norma's adventure into production did not meet expenses, and she next faced the embarrassing task of collecting on the guarantees. Fortunately she did not have to collect the entire amount promised by each donor, and she was able to pay the creditors and the initial money the Crest had loaned her to launch the production. In the end, the Crest gained a free production, and Norma gained a nervous breakdown, with ensuing visits to a psychiatrist, and an aversion to any-thing theatrical that lasted for several years. She also developed a horror of producing that has lasted a lifetime.[20]

The 1960–61 season went ahead as scheduled. But by now the love affair between the press and the Crest had decidedly cooled. As well as dis-enchantment by some columnists over the Crest's play selection, Murray's style of management was perceived by some as aloof and autocratic. Increasing criticism brought a somewhat paranoid public response from Murray, who claimed that he stayed on as producer because "not so many people are willing to stick themselves up so that they can be shot at from every angle and still think the job worth doing."[21] He suggested that a proper public subsidy for the Crest should be $100,000 a year, far more than had hitherto been granted. If the quantity of plays was any criterion — 100 by the 1960–61 season — then the Crest deserved such financial support. The new season progressed and on the anniversary of its founding, Ron Evans spun the following doggerel in his column:

> The fates be blessed,
> And for providence cheers,
> The redoubtable Crest
> Has survived seven years.[22]

The most popular play of the season was *The Long and the Short and the Tall,* followed in second place by *The Marriage Go Round,* starring Barbara Chilcott. Attendance increased that autumn and by February 1961 things were looking so much brighter that Murray told the *Globe and Mail* that they had enjoyed an infinitely better year than last. When asked why, he replied, "Well, I suppose because we have presented more contemporary plays. I have decided that satirical or high comedy — or the way we do them — does not suit the kind of audience that comes to the Crest."[23] This statement would indicate that, some opinions to the contrary, Murray was willing to adapt his policy when he thought he had a clear indication of public preferences. However, as anyone knows who has tried to please that hydra-headed monster, public taste is fickle and it is impossible to ascertain what the public will buy 100 per cent of the time. Murray's own words best describe the difficulties any producer of a stock company, or any theatrical venture, faces. In *Mayfair Magazine,* Murray is quoted as saying:

> The first season we scheduled two sure-fire perennial hits: *Charley's Aunt* and *The Man Who Came to Dinner.* The public, much to our surprise, stayed away in droves. We then switched to two highbrow, off-beat plays: Graham Greene's *The Living Room* and

T.S. Eliot's *The Confidential Clerk*. They were immediate successes. "Aha!" we said to ourselves, "The
Toronto public wants serious plays they can't see elsewhere." So we proceeded to give them a few more
plays of the same calibre. We might just as well have
hung a quarantine sign on the box office. Even the
people with season tickets avoided us. Yet when we
decided to cast experience to the wind and wind up
our season with *Hay Fever*, we had to hold it over an
extra week.[24]

But in 1960–61 it seemed as though Murray and the Crest were on the right
track at last. *Long Day's Journey into Night*, *The Long and the Short and the
Tall*, and a revue the Crest staged made a profit. *The Marriage Go Round*,
despite its popularity, suffered a minor loss. The musical, *The Gay Chap-
eron*, based on Sheridan's play *The Duenna*, took a heavy loss, and both *The
Heiress* and *King Lear* also lost money because they were presented before
high school audiences for several performances at $1 per person, far below
cost. But for the first time they ended the season without a deficit on the
year's operation, even though the funding from the Canada Council, the
city, and corporate and private donors had not increased substantially.

Canada Council funding did increase for the 1961–62 season. Still in its
infancy and without the massive public sums it has come to possess, the
Council had $166,000 for theatres that year. The awards are revealing. The
Crest got $25,000 (an increase of $5,000), and the touring Canadian Players
$32,900, $7,500 of which was to pay the salary of an executive producer.
The Montreal International Theatre (La Poudrière), then in its fifth season
performing in an abandoned gunpowder magazine on St. Helen's Island,
got $2,500. The newly formed Manitoba Theatre Centre received $30,000,
and George Luscombe's Toronto Workshop Productions was given a special
grant of $4,000. The largest grant, $35,000, went to Montreal's Théatre du
Nouveau Monde to offset the costs of a 30-week season, and the Théatre
du Rideau Vert received $15,000 for a 9-play season. A total of $47,500 was

granted to theatres in Montreal, and, if one omits the grant to the Canadian Players touring company, only $29,000 was granted to exclusively Toronto theatres, almost all to the Crest.

This money and the comparative success of 1960–61 behind him, Murray offered a widely varied season of contemporary plays mixed with some classics for 1961–62. It included a comic Christmas show, *Simon Says Get Married*, written by Bernard Slade and starring Austin Willis; the Broadway hit *Big Fish, Little Fish* with Larry Mann in the lead; and a double bill of *Krapp's Last Tape*, starring Donald Davis, and Albee's *The Zoo Story*. Two Arnold Wesker plays, *Roots* and *Roar Like a Dove*, joined *The Mad Woman of Chaillot*, Shaw's *Caesar and Cleopatra* with Toby Robins as the Egyptian queen, and an Australian play, *The Shifting Heart*, to round out the schedule. The Crest was also used for the annual *Spring Thaw* and sponsored a studio production of *The American Dream* and *The Zoo Story* (its second that year) directed by Fred Euringer. In my view it was a balanced season, with something for everybody.

Perhaps that was the trouble. A *Toronto Star* article (21 April 1962) stated, "A lack of daring characterizes the Davis trio. A conspicuous failure has been Murray Davis's inability to provide the Crest with an identity." It was a comment revealing the ignorance of its author about repertory and stock theatre. Experienced producers know that it is exceedingly difficult to provide a specific identity for a theatre whose mandate is to put a varied menu before the public. Even the Stratford Shakespearean Festival and the Shaw Festival over the years have relegated Shakespeare and Shaw to less paramount positions in the respective repertoires. In fact, Stratford has dropped the name of Shakespeare from its title altogether. But grossly unfair or not, that article marked the return of critical sniping at the Crest. Even Herbert Whittaker, who had been less severe than other columnists, attacked the new season in November 1962: "One has only to look at the banal parade of shows done so far this year to recognize that Murray Davis . . . has no practical idea how to shape a program and to select the talent (for he chooses the players and directors and designers as well as the plays) to bring it to vital life."[25]

■

Quite a lot was changing in Toronto in those years. Down on King Street West, Ed Mirvish had purchased the Royal Alexandra and was sprucing it up to the tune of a quarter of a million dollars. The Crest considered moving to the theatre in the new Inn-on-the-Park, but its north-east Toronto location seemed even more inaccessible than Mount Pleasant. Then another possibility developed. The City Planning Board had drawn up a proposal for a theatre either east of the O'Keefe Centre or in the O'Keefe Centre parking lot. Since it was to be a centennial project and not open until 1967, the Crest management contented itself with making alterations to the Mount Pleasant stage. These were complemented by the hiring of a permanent company for 1963–64 and several directors: John Hirsch, co-founder of the Manitoba Theatre Centre; Kurt Reis, who in the seven years since he played Foreman of the Jury in the Crest's *Witness for the Prosecution* had made a mark for himself as an exciting young director; and an American, Rocco Rufman, of whom no one had ever heard. That innovative season also saw the establishment of the Crest Hour Company under Barbara Chilcott's guidance, to take hour-long shows to the schools. It had the additional purpose of breaking in new talent.

At the same time, Canadian nationalism began to have an adverse effect on the Crest. True Davidson, the Reeve of East York, suggested that Metro Toronto cut its grant to the Crest unless it produced more Canadian plays. Assuming the mantle of a critic she referred to the previous season as "conventional and second rate." At this point Metro's grants to the Crest had reached $10,000 and grants from all sources were $50,000, but that was still far short of what was needed to fill the gap between operating costs and box-office returns. The frank reply to Ms. Davidson from John C. Lockwood, chairman of the Crest Board, though undiplomatic, nevertheless reveals the dilemma then faced by any major theatre company largely dependent on gate receipts when contemplating the staging of new Canadian plays: "The Crest would be better off to lose the Metro grant than to take a chance on Canadian plays. We could lose that amount in one week.

It's the Crest's task to produce first-class plays, and so far there are relatively few Canadian plays that fall into that class."[26]

Pro-Canadian play enthusiasts could have challenged that statement with the argument that there were few quality Canadian plays in existence because no one would produce them. How could we develop an indigenous Canadian theatre unless someone took a chance on our playwrights? A publicly subsidized theatre ought to take that chance. Yet Lockwood's comments were realistic. The Crest's government grants were less than a quarter of its revenue. With the public attitude of the time and the danger of escalating the debt to the degree that could close the theatre, they dared not risk experimenting on a new product by an unknown author. This declared policy, now in the open, further alienated the columnists, some of the performing community, and even some of the public. Ironically, such policies were an incentive in the creation of an alternate theatre, which, within a decade, specialized in new plays particularly by Canadian playwrights.

■

In late August of 1964 a life-threatening crisis arose. Just as the first production of the season was in rehearsal, the Canada Council suddenly refused the $20,000 grant the Crest had sought for its season. Panic ensued. The recently created Ontario Arts Council refused to increase its grant from $10,000 to $20,000 to help offset the loss. The cast of the opening show, *Brecht on Brecht*, was paid a week's notice, and the production postponed. The appearance of Irene Worth to play in *The Glass Menagerie* later that season was cancelled. It looked as though the Crest would have a dark year. At first no explanation was forthcoming from the Canada Council. A hue and cry arose from some of Toronto's acting community. Some, such as Charmion King, implied that there was a conspiracy afoot. On September 4, 1964, Herbert Whittaker quoted her in his column: "It was Miss King who hinted darkly at politics connected with the St. Lawrence Theatre Centre which has been mentioned as a future home for the Crest. 'Who are the Canada Council's advisors?' she asked pointedly."[27] Toronto Mayor Philip Givens deplored the loss of the Council grant, but held out no hope of aid from the city or Metro because their cultural funds for the year were all used up. Murray Davis expressed his fear that not only actors, but also the theatre's permanent personnel would be laid off: "The number of people it will effect is legion."[28] His hyperbole may have been referring to the public, but actually 41 staff members were eventually let go.

The Council's action prompted an outburst from Larry McCance, the Canadian representative of Actors' Equity, who reflected the reaction of many in the performing community. He declared it to be "a serious threat to the life of the performing arts in Canada," and added:

> To have given the Crest as an institution its support over several years can only be considered as an indication that the Council, in its wisdom, has decided that the Crest was worthy of their support. To suddenly withdraw that support can only mean one of two things. Either the judgement was faulty in the first place or their sudden withdrawal of support is an irresponsible act. If there is some valid reason for withdrawal then the Council owes an explanation to the many prominent, wise citizens who have supported the Crest for many years with their time, energy, and money. Not to do so is to indicate to all such public spirited citizens across the country that the Canada Council cares not a whit for their judgement, their public minded sense of responsibility, or indeed, their money.[29]

Shocked by the vehemence of the attack, the Council broke its rule against making public its reasons for refusing or giving grants. By keeping its reasons privy to itself and the organization involved, the Council tries to avoid any embarrassment for that organization. I believe that the Council's reluctant reply had a further damaging effect. In a lengthy letter sent to the Crest and to the press, Dr. A.W. Trueman of the Canada Council explained that in the past two seasons the Crest's accumulated deficit had grown to $127,000, that the average attendance the previous season had been 44 per cent and that "the last two productions of the Crest played to an average of only 19 theatregoers in every 100 of its seats." He wrote, "Critical reviews in the press and reports we have from advisors suggest that many of the Crest's productions are considered to be indifferent and have not recently provided the standard of theatre Toronto might now expect."[30] His letter went on to say that the Council saw no change in policy from the Crest for the next season. Dr. Trueman pointed out that the Crest's "budget for the coming years was up to $309,000. Last year the theatre only raised $16,000 from donations apart from foundation money. (Winnipeg, with less than one third of Toronto's population, last year raised for its theatre from similar sources over $26,000.) With an apparently accumulated deficit of $127,000, the Crest hoped to raise its regular donations in Toronto only to $25,000, a sum which, in relation to the financial situation, is clearly inadequate."[31]

Andrew Kershaw, a vice-president of the Crest, replied publicly that the Crest's deficit was not so large as those of other arts organizations supported by the Canada Council, that the private donor support, excluding foundations, had increased over the years by 90 per cent, that attendance had increased over the previous four years by 20 per cent, and that it was precisely because of the $127,000 deficit that the grant from the Canada Council was necessary. He went on to point out that "an assessment of the standard of production is, of necessity, a very subjective matter."[32] Although it was not his purpose, he then demonstrated the real importance the theatre community gave to the critics by saying that the first three productions of the previous season had a batting average of seven favourable reviews out of nine. Even two members of the opposition in the House of Commons took up the cudgels on behalf of the Crest forcing State Secretary Maurice Lamontagne to point out that the Canada Council was not a crown agency and therefore not answerable to Parliament. In addition the managers of the rival Royal Alex, Yale Simpson, and the O'Keefe Centre, Hugh Walker, criticized the Council for not giving more warning before lowering the boom. At no time during the controversy was it published that the subsidy from the Canada Council was needed to keep theatre prices low so that the performances could be within the financial reach of the majority of the citizenry. To me that was a major reason for the founding of the various arts councils in the first place. In the '80s and '90s, with funding from both the public and private sector lagging far behind the costs of maintaining these arts institutions, the cost of tickets has sky-rocketed, making opera, ballet, and many major theatres and symphony orchestras across the country once again the elitist preserve of the rich.

As a result of all this *Sturm und Drang*, the Canada Council agreed to meet with the Ontario Arts Council and the Crest management to re-examine the matter. But without the grant the Crest was unable to operate that autumn and opened its new season only in December. That it opened at all was something of a miracle. Many of its supporters rallied around to help raise its new objective of $75,000 from private donors. Benefits were given by the casts of shows performing at the O'Keefe Centre, the Poor Alex, and the Central Library Theatre. Even a nearby pancake restaurant donated part of its nightly take from the sale of flap-jacks. But the biggest rally, "Light Up the Crest," was organized at the Royal Alex. Some of Canada's foremost performers participated. Barry Morse flew in from Hollywood to be the *compère*. Anna Russell came from New York to demonstrate the care and manipulation of the bagpipe. Rich Little also came from Manhattan where he was appearing at Basin Street East. Kate Reid performed a scene from *Who's Afraid of Virginia Woolf?*, in which she was performing on Broadway and in which Donald Davis had taken over the male lead. William Hutt and Frances Hyland acted a scene from Congreve's *The Way of the World*, directed by Robert Gill. Also on the bill were Joan Van Ark and Richard Benjamin, currently at the Royal Alex in *Barefoot in the Park*, as well as Tom Kneebone, Barbara Hamilton, Anna Cameron, Charmion King, Corinne Conley, and Phyllis Marshall. Gratien Gélinas spoke movingly of theatre as a necessity, not a luxury. The show was a gala affair produced by CBC-TV's Bob Jarvis but the mediocre attendance with tickets at $12.50 demonstrated Toronto's apathy toward the Crest. Only about $7,000 was raised.

This whole brouhaha turned the spotlight not only on the Crest but on the funding bodies. The newspapers published a series of revelatory articles about them. Nat Cohen pointed out that the Metropolitan Council, feeling themselves incompetent to judge who should get money they had allocated to the arts, and wishing to avoid any wrangling over the matter, established the Provincial Metropolitan Council of the Arts, and appointed eight people to serve on it. Cohen felt that it was "a strange system because the eight men who have the effective control over the spending of $171,000 of tax money are themselves leading officers of the best known groups making applications for this money."[33] He named Arthur Gelber, chairman of the Council and also chairman of the National Ballet Guild, "which got $25,000. Other members include R.W. Finlayson, president of the Toronto Symphony Orchestra ($37,500), George R. Harris, vice-president of the Crest Theatre Foundation ($10,000), Frank F. McEachren, executive member of the Canadian Players ($1,500), Lieutenant General Guy Simonds, president of the National Ballet Guild, and J.W. Westaway, president of the Toronto Mendelssohn Choir ($6,000)."[34] Cohen went on to point out that, according to Dr. Trueman, the Canada Council in a private interview with the Crest management in April (1964) had expressed its concern over the way the Crest was being operated. The Crest had said nothing about this meeting and Cohen conjectured that it was a secret meeting held by the Crest vice-president, George R. Harris, in May when the Toronto Arts Council, of which Mr. Harris was a member, granted $10,000 to the Crest. He went on to wonder whether Metro politicians might have been more cautious had they known the truth.

In September 1964, Herbert Whittaker came out with at least a half-hearted defence of the Crest. He challenged the Canada Council's criticism of the standard of production and listed the many Crest shows that he considered to be triumphs, from *The Cherry Orchard*, *The Three Sisters*, and *The Seagull*, through the *Othello* of Frederick Valk, to modern plays by Tennessee Williams and Edward Albee. He also noted that the Crest had produced 12 Canadian plays, mentioned the new talent it had introduced, as well as the international stars it had brought to Toronto, and the aspiring young directors as well as the experienced ones it had employed. He then argued that the Council's action was justified: "The revelation that the Crest proposed a budget of $300,000 for the current season, notwithstanding a deficit of $127,000, and lacking credit, throws serious doubts on the management of the theatre." He concluded, "The Crest . . . will either die from self-pity and inadequacy or defiantly demonstrate by efficient management and attractive productions that it is worthy of public support."[35]

The *Toronto Telegram* joined the controversy in an article without a by-line that began, "Just what is it we want of the Crest Theatre?" Implying that the Canada Council "wants the theatre to diminish its deficit and while it is about it develop a radical new theatre policy," the author crystallized the dilemma:

> Well, that's an exciting challenge, but how do you go about it? You can probably achieve financial success with a large popular theatre offering only safe, familiar fare. Or you may have artistic success with a small, experimental theatre presenting only unknown, untried plays. But I don't know how you can have both in the same place. . . . If you're wise you decide to be one or the other — popular or pioneering. . . . But the Crest hasn't been wise, it has tried to march down the middle. It has attempted to coax customers in from both sides, the casual, easily diverted on one hand, the devoted and demanding from the other. And it hasn't worked. The Crest has ended up with neither popularity nor prestige, neither money nor praise.[36]

Having succinctly stated the problem, the author of this article then argued that it was not fair to compare the Crest with the Manitoba Theatre Centre, which did not have such formidable competition as the Crest had with the Royal Alexandra, the O'Keefe Centre, and six television channels "competing for patrons, nor the National Ballet, the Canadian Opera, the Toronto Symphony, or Canadian Players for donor dollars. Things are much less complicated in Winnipeg, Halifax, and Vancouver."[37]

In an interview with the *Telegram's* Ron Evans, Murray responded and seems to have joined those wanting the Crest to be more daring when he announced that if the renewed financial campaign was successful, the Crest would present Hochhuth's controversial *The Deputy*: "Probably not everyone will like it, but they can't ignore it, and I think this is perhaps the function of a theatre such as the Crest in a community such as Toronto."[38] Mr. Evans then reminded him of the meeting of experts under the aegis of the Ontario Arts Council where it was stressed "that a theatre, to be successful, must provide entertainment of a type that the audience cannot find anywhere else . . . or cannot find better done anywhere else."[39] Davis agreed but pointed to the crux of the dilemma facing any repertory theatre producer: "This becomes an economic problem, of course, because in order to get new exciting works one has to pay for them. Then to have them 'better done' is an ideal phrase, which, I suppose, every producer strives for. No producer attempts to do a play badly." He then noted that the Crest had operated for 11 years as a fully professional theatre with a present staff of 50: "You have to . . . meet the payroll. This means that you curb your imagination in terms of an exciting work that might stimulate a small percentage of theatregoers, but would have no interest to the general public." They did not want to become a purely "entertainment" theatre, he said and continued, "We now must become more controversial, more stimulating — I don't want to use the word "intellectual" — but a more provocative kind of theatre."[40]

Following this approach, the Crest scheduled six plays, the first to open December 31, 1964 after the objective of $75,000 from private donors had been reached. This abbreviated season was a mixed success artistically and financially. *The Deputy* was reported to be the biggest hit in the Crest's history, but *Oh Dad, Poor Dad* did not fare as well at the box office, although in my view it should have. I had seen the New York production and thought the Crest's equally good. The critics continued to snipe. Ron Evans wrote, "Sometimes I think the Crest theatre wants to die,"[41] and went on to criticize the Crest's choice of *The Provoked Wife*. Jeremy Brown in the *Telegram* attacked the choice of Herbert Whittaker as a director for Jack Gray's satirical *Emmanuel Xoc,* and wondered why a critic was functioning also as a stage director. He then commented on the play itself: "Those who have seen *Emmanuel Xoc* can testify to the fact that it is indeed a terrible play. The selection of *Xoc,* coupled with the other plays the Crest has put on this season, and the theatre's enormous inability to keep some actors more than 10 minutes, has resulted in the same mishmash-trash we have been fed for a portion of the last 10 years."[42] Murray Davis countered with, "Some savants in the theatre seem to think that to attempt a new play is some kind of venial sin. But we believe that this is part of our role."[43] The apparent change of heart since Mr. Lockwood's comment two years before simply exemplified confusion in the ranks of the Crest's policy makers. In 1964, Murray had asked the board to relieve him of his producer's responsibilities but they urged him to continue as both artistic director and producer, which prompted Nat Cohen to write, "Murray Davis is doing the best he can and it's not good enough, and after all these years we know it will never be. The board continues to indulge him and hope for a miracle. In that sense they are even more responsible for the Crest's woes than he could ever be."[44]

The Crest's deficit in 1964 had tripled from $48,528 to $131,289, as Ron Evans reported in his column of March 9, 1965. But *The Deputy* had been successful and the fund-raising campaign had reached its goal. A hard push by the Crest management to sell subscriptions — they increased to 3,000 by October — encouraged the Canada Council, possibly chastened by the furore caused when it refused the $20,000 grant in 1964, to promise $25,000 for the '65–66 season. The result was the scheduling of an ambitious season that might have appealed to the theatrically converted but not to John and Jane Doe: *The Private Ear and the Public Eye* by Peter Shaffer, *The Physicists* by Frederich Durrenmatt, once again the musical *Mr. Scrooge,* Brecht-Weill's *Threepenny Opera, Man and Superman* by Shaw, Ibsen's *Hedda Gabler, The Ballad of the Sad Café* by Edward Albee, Chekhov's *Uncle Vanya,* and Thornton Wilder's *Our Town.*

In February 1966, Murray resigned. The following day Nat Cohen outlined his views on the 12-year history of the Crest, and why it had not been a success. He referred back to the opening play of the first season, *Richard of Bordeaux*, which he called a "British historical pot-boiler." "There are some people," he wrote, "who feel that the Crest never recovered from the shock and dismay that first attraction caused."[45] When I read those words I found them astonishing and irresponsible. My good wishes had not been diminished because, although it might not be the best historical drama ever written, it was highly theatrical, well-acted, and it held my interest. I thought it one of the most professional productions staged by Torontonians since the war. Cohen criticized the Crest for having a permanent staff of 50 that "was simply too large for a theatre of this size running shows on stock company lines, two or three weeks or in repertory."[46] Perhaps so, but compare that with the Canadian Stage in 1994 operating two companies in the St. Lawrence Centre and the Berkeley Street Theatre that listed in their program for *Hay Fever* a staff, exclusive of performers, of 76 plus 3 co-op students and a playwright in residence subsidized by the Ontario Arts Council. To mitigate his criticism he added, "One thing must be made immediately clear, of the man's [Murray Davis] devotion to the Crest, no doubt is possible. . . . Check his statements over the years and his sincerity, his eagerness to make the Crest meaningful is blinding. So is his capacity for self-criticism." After several more paragraphs relating the history of Murray's statements and decisions about the Crest, he wrote:

> Everything Murray Davis has ever said privately, or for the record, about the Crest, the nature of his contribution, and the course it should follow, has been marked by good sense and an apparent grasp of the artistic, economic, educational, and promotional necessities. But, somehow, when it came to putting his views into practice, things always went wrong. . . . Uncoordinated, his actions were in devastating contradiction to his intentions. The realities of the Toronto theatre scene constantly eluded his vision and his grasp.[47]

After Murray departed, there was renewed speculation about the Crest moving into the proposed St. Lawrence Centre, and overtures were made by the Crest Board of Directors to the Canadian Players for a merger. The latter had been sustained over the years largely by Arts Council subsidy and the generous donations of private citizens such as Lady Eaton and Samuel Zacks. For the previous two years the Players had presented a Toronto season at the 209-seat Central Library Theatre under the guidance of Marigold Charlesworth as artistic director and Jean Roberts as administrator. They were asked to take over the operation of the combined companies. The two boards of directors decided to vacate both the Crest and the Central Library and contemplated using the 500-seat Playhouse on Bayview Avenue recently converted from a movie house by David Mann of Mann and Martell Real Estate. But the Canadian Players Board balked at assuming the Crest's debt on top of their own (approximately $100,000) because the new organization would have to assume a seemingly monstrous liability for the time of over $200,000. This created a schism on the Canadian Players Board, and Samuel Zacks resigned. Charlesworth and Roberts had submitted a report estimating the cost of operating at the Bayview Playhouse, but, when the combined boards could not get their financial house in order, they informed the board that unless this matter was settled by July 15, they would not have time to organize a season for that autumn. The board waffled on a solution but cancelled all negotiations with the Playhouse, whereupon Charlesworth and Roberts resigned. The result of all this turmoil was aptly put by Nat Cohen: "Theoretically merger talks are still going on, but the way things look now, the Crest and the Canadian Players, which entered the Canadian theatre scene the same year, will also be leaving it the same year."[48] And that is what happened. The Crest Theatre was converted by Famous Players back to a movie house and opened with *The Great St. Trinian's Train Robbery*. Trash had returned to the Crest.

■

I have dealt at length with the rise and fall of the Crest because it is an object lesson for all those who would wish to run a stock or repertory company in Toronto. No doubt all the reasons the columnists and critics listed contributed to the Crest's ultimate demise. In a postmortem written three years later, Nat Cohen presented a theory of his own:

> From the time the Crest opened it was evident that the Davises were out of touch with Toronto. They had not grasped the degree to which even by *1954*, the city had lost its identity as a white, Anglo-Saxon, Protestant conclave with pronounced British accent and a predilection for empire and attitudes imperial. They assumed that the organization of the Crest after the model of a British provincial repertory company was just what the theatre public wanted. They didn't realize that public had perished during World War II and they had no idea of the nature or taste of the emerging new public."[49]

It would be to assume the omnipotence of God to know what the general public of such a rapidly changing community wanted in the way of legitimate theatre. Never in any of the articles criticizing Murray Davis and the Crest's policy was it even suggested that the writers knew with certainty what the public would support. When one looks at the list of plays the Crest presented it becomes apparent that Murray was not narrow in his approach to play selection. There was a wide variety offered, and the plays were, on the whole, of considerable merit. Secondly, some of the productions were of a very high calibre, but under the pressure of a stock company operation high standards of staging could not always be maintained. Cohen, the Crest's most severe and persistent critic, faulted the Davis brothers for establishing a British style repertory or stock company. But what other choices were open to them? The Royal Alexandra was the city's touring house bringing in road shows, often second rate ones, from New York, and in 1960 it was joined by the O'Keefe Centre, which housed big budget, imported musicals, and opera and ballet. In spite of the efforts of the New Play Society and Jupiter Theatre, the theatre-going public was still small and still lacking a tradition of attending professional legitimate theatre on a regular basis. Only a stock company approach could give the variety of choice that would stimulate the habit of regular attendance at the theatre. If the Crest seemed too highbrow initially, soon economic necessity forced it into middle-of-the-road programming, which brought criticism that it had no definite policy.

Although the Canada Council's cancellation of its 1964 grant was ostensibly based on an analysis of the Crest's operation, some people believe that influential anti-Crest citizens influenced that decision. The question of who was to occupy the proposed St. Lawrence Centre divided many in the arts community and some politicians into pro- and anti-Crest camps. Donald Davis expressed his personal opinion that, "It was essentially a political argument that was taking place very much behind the scenes, which really had very little to do with what was going on on the stage of the Crest theatre."[50] He believed that the Canada Council was supplied by the anti-Crest group with negative criticism that persuaded the Council to withdraw its support, which in turn gave impetus to those against the Crest to intensify their criticism. This combination of factors made it extremely difficult to operate the Crest in its later years.

To fill the vacuum left by the demise of the Crest and the Canadian Players a new company was organized, called Theatre Toronto. Two shows were presented at the Royal Alex, after which it became clear that, whereas the Crest had been castigated for its annual operating deficit of about $30,000, a more tolerant attitude by the politicians and theatre power-brokers was applied to the newly formed company. The English director, Clifford Williams, was brought in to direct these two shows and was reportedly paid $40,000 for four months' work — an astronomical sum for a director in the Canadian theatre in the mid-'60s. Donald Davis indignantly points out that, "They [Theatre Toronto] were represented to the public and government agencies as being a wonderful, responsible, reasonable, non-extravagant unit, when barely moments before we had been raked over the coals for being in the red to the extent of $20,000 or $30,000 for an entire season. It seemed a curiously unbalanced attitude toward the spending of money."[51]

There were two positive results from the disappearance of the Crest, and soon after Theatre Toronto. Their demise left a theatrical void that was soon filled by those enterprising young entrepreneurs who created the so-called "Alternate Theatre." As well, the Crest's financial headaches taught some of the politicians in charge of the purse strings to take a more tolerant attitude toward deficits in arts organizations. It is essential that public and private funding organizations understand the financial difficulties of theatrical companies who create a cultural and entertainment product that they feel they must sell at below cost to keep the public attending and thereby justify the company's existence. But unfortunately, in my view, since then those responsible for doling out public funds have become too prone to look the other way and have permitted unnecessary extravagances and the growth of enormous bureaucracies, which in turn have made too many arts organizations overly dependent on the public purse. The result has been that when cut-backs began in the 1980s, many managements were unaccustomed to economizing and deficits soared.

When the Crest and the Canadian Players disappeared in the morass of Theatre Toronto, there was one vestige of the Crest that continued for many years to fulfil an important mandate. The Crest Hour Company had been founded by Barbara Chilcott and Professor John Dodd of the Ontario College of Education, with the blessing of Barbara's brother, Murray, who saw in it the opportunity to accustom young audiences to the personal contact of live actors performing for them, and to create an experienced theatre public for the future as well as to bring the magic of theatre to Ontario's schools. It received an annual Ontario Arts Council grant that sustained it and sent the company of mostly young actors back and forth across the province by bus. In its repertoire was the play being studied that year in the province's high school graduating classes. The troupe continued under the aegis of the St. Lawrence Centre as the St. Lawrence Centre Hour Company and had an influence on several generations of potential theatre patrons — probably the most important of the Crest Theatre's bequests to Toronto and to Ontario.

In my opinion, one of the most regrettable results of the death of the Crest was the loss of Murray Davis as an actor. Embattled, embittered, and disillusioned, he retired to his country house near Glen Huron, Ontario, to raise livestock, which I presume he found less frustrating and more rewarding than dealing with critics, politicians, bureaucrats, boards of directors, and the unpredictable denizens of the theatre world. On January 22, 1997, Murray Davis died, and I hope that, despite his wounds from the theatrical wars, he had derived satisfaction from a theatre that staged 149 productions, and from the knowledge that he and his brother Donald were instrumental in presenting the Toronto public with many of the world's greatest plays.

After the closing of the Crest, Donald continued his brilliant career on the stage and in television. He performed at the Stratford Festival and on Broadway and appeared with many international stars, but was most celebrated for his interpretation of the plays of Samuel Beckett for which he had a deep empathy and understanding. In 1960 he won an Obie Award for his performance in *Krapp's Last Tape*.[52] When in 1954 American Equity established a Canadian branch, he was one of the earliest members of the Canadian Executive Committee and had a profound influence on the early policy of that Association. For many years he skillfully championed Canadian performers' interests as a member of the Council of American Equity in New York. For him the art of the theatre transcended international boundaries. Regrettably, on January 23, 1998, a year and a day after his brother's death, Donald followed Murray to the actors' Valhalla — another of our artists who never received the recognition from his fellow Canadians that he deserved.

The Red Barn Theatre

presents

"ALL FOR MARY"

by K. Bannerman & H. Brooke

CAST

Alphonse	JERRY ROSEN
Humphrey Millar	NORMAN ETTLINGER
Mary Millar	PADDY CROFT
Victor Montenay	HUGH ALEXANDER
Clive Norton	NICHOLAS SIMONS
Nannie Cartwright	JOYCE GORDON

Directed and Designed by KEITH GREEN

CHAPTER 17

In a Peacock House

About an hour by car from Toronto is one of the most beautiful scenic drives in Ontario. It extends along the south shore of Lake Simcoe from Keswick through Jackson's Point and ends at an Anglican church that might have been lifted from the Victorian English countryside. In one corner of the churchyard is the family plot of the Sibbalds, among the first families to settle in the area. Also at rest there under the protective branches of an umbrella tree is Canada's most celebrated humorist, Stephen Leacock, and lying not far from him is one of our greatest novelists, Mazo de la Roche. This enchanting drive often hugs the shoreline, or is lined on both sides with summer homes of varying size and luxury until it arrives at the outskirts of Jackson's Point where De La Salle School and the Canadian National Institute for the Blind have their summer camps. Jackson's Point itself is a community of cottages haphazardly crammed into street after street. Just beyond this jumbled area, on the south side of the road, is an old red barn, east of which the road narrows into an English country lane lined with hedges and some of the most attractive homes in the area.

Although the Sibbalds have donated much of the original family property to the province as a park and museum, in 1949 they still owned large amounts of land including the acreage on which the old barn is located. Precisely when this structure was built is unknown, but it is believed to have been 1876. A short distance to the east of the barn is the Briars Hotel and Country Club, operated by a scion of the Sibbald family, John Sibbald. Behind the main building of this fashionable resort is a brick building that once served as a stable and a summer house for peacocks. In the winter they lived in the old barn and were often seen roosting on the roof.

In 1949, with an optimism born of innocent enthusiasm, a young impresario, Alfred Mulock, took a 10-year lease on the barn. The 23-year-old Mulock was the grandson of Sir William Mulock and a descendent of the family that built the Royal Alexandra Theatre. Although Toronto-born, he had spent some time in New York City where he graduated from the Dramatic Workshop of the New School of Social Research, where one of his teachers was Stella Adler. Smitten by the love of the theatre, he dreamed of operating a barn theatre like Judy Garland and Mickey Rooney in the film *Summer Stock*. He remembered the old barn from his childhood visits to Jackson's Point, so he brought some of his friends up from New York to case the location. Legend has it that one of those friends was the then-unknown Harry Belafonte who, it is said, was the first person to perform in that barn by singing a song while perched on a beam. Mulock named it the Red Barn Theatre even though at the time it was still a weather-beaten dull grey. He christened it by breaking a bottle of beer against the silo.

Mulock raised his initial capital by borrowing from his inheritance, by a $2,500 donation from his Uncle Cawthra, and from contributions of $500 and $1,500 from two friends.[1] The conversion to a theatre was carefully done, preserving the barn's rustic character. The old cow stalls in the stone and concrete lower floor became dressing rooms. Washrooms, which were to be shared by audiences and performers, were installed just off the lobby, in itself almost as spacious as the auditorium. The workshop and storage space were in the south wing of the barn. E.M. (Moe) Margolese, the Toronto actor hired by Mulock as business manager, had contacts with various merchants and suppliers in the Toronto area and obtained 120 seats from a defunct movie house in Guelph. Reportedly, additional seats were obtained from Lloyd Bochner's father to increase the capacity to 290. The stage was, and still is, extremely large for a barn theatre. Mulock rightly claimed that it was the biggest stage of any summer theatre in Canada —

not much of a claim because the number of summer theatres in the whole country in 1949 would not have exceeded the number of fingers on one hand. A small glass lean-to that had been a chicken coop at the side of the barn was converted into office space. When completed, the rustic charm and pastoral setting of the Red Barn created an enticing ambience for summer theatre.

Mulock's plan was to bring experienced, union actors from New York for a company he erroneously boasted was the only one in Canada franchised by American Actors' Equity Association. The caption on a newspaper photograph of American actors Stuart Nedd, Steffi Lock and her dog, Mr. Snow, stated, "Nedd is a United States actor hired by Mr. Mulock for the first season, so less experienced Canadians can work in a professional group."[2] Presumably too a Canadian dog could learn a few things from the American Mr. Snow. This attitude towards Canadian actors seems condescending now, but in 1949 there were not many skilled Canadian performers available for professional theatre, a state of affairs that altered quickly in the next few years. Steffi Lock, who was to play female leads, was Mrs. Alfred Mulock. She also has the dubious distinction of introducing to Toronto the pyramid club craze that soon was made illegal. Sydney Banks, the assistant director of the Canadian film *Whispering City*, was hired as the first stage manager, and Mulock brought a complement of experienced people from Manhattan, including Isobel Bonner and the director, Joseph Kramm.[3] He already had several Broadway credits and soon after was to win a Pulitzer Prize and a Tony award for his production of *The Shrike*. Among the Canadians in the company were Beverley Milne, the novice Gerry Sarracini, and Larry Henderson, who later became a CBC-TV announcer.

Mulock contemplated featuring guest stars for each show. The first was to be Larry Parks in *The Voice of the Turtle*, but this fell through. Wayne and Shuster also declined his offer, so Mulock elected the reliability of a group of resident actors. *The Little Foxes* was substituted as the first production. But 10 days before the opening an event occurred that did not augur well for this pioneering venture. The business manager resigned. Margolese had been given $8,000, which he was told was to furbish the theatre and purchase supplies. He was to have approval of all purchases but he was receiving bills for items he had not authorized. Young Mr. Mulock was running up expenses in excess of the $8,000. According to Margolese the bills soon exceeded $15,000.[4] His protests to Mulock fell on deaf ears. He was assured that the bond covering the actors' salaries had been posted, but to his dismay a communication arrived from American Equity in New York saying that the necessary security had not been received and demanding a bond in the amount of $2,500. In the face of this Mr. Margolese felt he could not continue. He left without receiving any salary and without being reimbursed for any out-of-pocket expenses.[5]

After a further alteration in the program the season was duly launched. *The Little Foxes* was to be followed by *Room Service, The Voice of the Turtle, The Glass Menagerie, Night Must Fall, The Late Christopher Bean, Call Me Mister,* and *My Sister Eileen,* but the final three were never produced. Moe Margolese speculates that when the original group of actors discovered that they were not protected by a bond, they either withdrew or were recalled by Equity at the end of July. Mulock likely settled with American Equity because he replaced the first actors with equally experienced ones from New York, including Florence Beresford, who had appeared on Broadway in *The House at Sly Corner* and had toured with Elizabeth Bergner in *Escape Me Never.* He found a director in Will Davis, who had directed in Pittsburgh and who had acted in the Eva Le Gallienne Civic Repertory Company. Apparently there was also a change-over of Canadian apprentices in mid-season because Jack Karr published in his column that the Red Barn was looking for "neophyte actors and actresses."[6]

Mr. Mulock appears not to have been the wisest nor most scrupulous of producers. But, in all fairness, when one considers the small capacity of the theatre, the necessity of keeping prices low to woo audiences unaccustomed to live theatre, and the responsibility of meeting American Equity rates and bonding requirements, the dice were loaded against him. The season progressed but despite the pedigree of the performers it was not a financial success. He was unable to recoup the initial investment and called a halt after one summer, suffering a reported loss of $23,000. But thanks to him the most charming and long-lived of the burgeoning number of summer theatres was founded, and in 1998 celebrated its 50th anniversary.

▪

In 1950 the old barn marked the emergence onto the summer theatre scene of Brian Doherty. I have already mentioned him in connection with his sponsorship of the Canadian appearance of the John Gielgud Company and the Dublin Gate Theatre, and the letters of introduction he gave me to contacts in England. In the 1960s he culminated his many theatrical achievements by founding the Shaw Festival in Niagara-on-the-Lake. But in 1950 he was a lawyer yearning to be a producer again. When he learned that Al Mulock would not be returning to the Red Barn, he teamed up with the son of a wealthy Montreal family, Roy Wolvin. Their decision to stage revues was largely because Wolvin had written a lot of sketches and songs for the "Red and White" revues at McGill University and had this material available. They planned to operate on a fortnightly basis, presenting four different shows over the two summer months, after which they would compile the best sketches and songs from those shows into a final revue that they would take on tour. They appropriately called their company "The Barnstormers."

From the still small pool of musical theatre talent in the Toronto and Montreal areas, they obtained some of the tops. John Pratt, who had made a name for himself in *The Navy Show* where he popularized the comic lament "You'll Get Used to It," led the company with support from Sheila Craig, Barbara Field, and Anne Wickham. In addition there were Terry Johnson, Garth Magwood, Dick Nelson, who had been heard on Wayne and Shuster's radio show, John Moreland, and Jack Northmore, fresh out of the University of Toronto where he had performed and written skits and songs for the "All Varsity Revue," and who, three summers later, was to try his wings as an actor for me in Oakville. For that 1950 summer season, Gladys Forrester was to share choreography with Sydney Vousden, a protégé of the Boris Volkoff Dance Studio. Henry Kaplan was hired to direct.

Mr. Northmore was surprised to discover that, although it was ostensibly promoted as a professional company, he was expected to perform that summer for no pay. The more senior members of the company were paid, but the young members were expected to give of their time, energy, and talent for the sheer joy of performing and the reward of experience. Northmore told Doherty and Wolvin that he could not join the company because he had no money of his own and had to earn some. They made an exception and paid him the handsome sum of $25 a week.[7] Even though these were perilous times for Canadian theatrical ventures, such extreme penny-pinching is hard to fathom particularly when both men were not wanting for ready cash and the season was sponsored by the Sutton Kinsmen's Club.[8]

Dominion Day of 1950 saw the Red Barn season begin with the new producers' first revue, *Crazy with the Heat*, starring John Pratt. Hugh Thomson, writing in the *Toronto Star*, opined that the show was unbalanced, with most of the best sketches in the first half. From the interval on, he wrote, "a strange form of rigor mortis set in which may be checked the next two weeks by pruning and shifting to tip the balance more equitably."[9] Knowledgeable producers of revue try to place most of the best material in the second half. But what the writers and producers may think is hilarious does not always get a similar response from an audience. The creation of a revue is an unpredictable business.

After the next show, *Fair and Warmer*, they abandoned the weather report titles for the double-entendre, *Rollin'-the-Hay*, with the then embryonic comedienne, Barbara Hamilton. From these and the next two revues, *One for the Road* and *Here and There*, they assembled their touring show, which they also called "One for the Road," and played Ottawa, His Majesty's in Montreal, and the Royal Alexandra in Toronto. Business at the Red Barn all summer had been encouraging. A lot of enthusiasts from Toronto had made the pleasant drive to Jackson's Point. But that rather depleted the audience for the subsequent appearance at the Royal Alex, with the result that box-office receipts were not as rewarding as they had been in Ottawa and Montreal, John Pratt's hometown.

These five revues consisted mostly of Roy Wolvin's material but some of Jack Northmore's sketches were also included, and John Pratt's celebrated "You'll Get Used to It" was inserted into *One for the Road*. Jack

Northmore recalls that he had to practise looking happy because his heavy eyebrows gave him a sullen look. During one rehearsal he was made to cross the stage from one side to the other and back, smiling idiotically. If he stopped smiling, the pianist was instructed to stop playing and they would begin the song over again. This continued for most of the afternoon until it was ingrained into Jack that for a musical comedy performer the smile is *de rigueur.*[10] He developed a smile that, like a sunbeam, illuminated the whole theatre. Most of the company shared accommodation in a converted two-car garage, three guys in one room, two in another, and two girls in the combination dining/living room. They existed primarily on peanut butter sandwiches and beer, and pigged out when invited to parties at the homes of local supporters. They were a young, wildly enthusiastic group, with a determination to create a show business in a country where hardly any had existed for many years. They were willing to work hard and play hard both on and offstage.

Although Doherty and Wolvin had enjoyed more success with their season than had Al Mulock the previous year, they also decided against a second summer. Brian Doherty had picked up Al Mulock's long lease on the theatre, so he sublet it for the 1951 season to another group of young enthusiasts. Amelia Hall, Bruce Raymond, and Silvio Narizzano, who had been working together at the Canadian Repertory Theatre in Ottawa, took over on short notice in June of that year. In her autobiography, *Life Before Stratford,* Millie Hall narrates in great detail their Red Barn story, but I cannot pass by without some reference to their trials and tribulations. Each of the three put up $500. Silvio's family was the wealthiest of the three and he was able, according to Ms. Hall, to borrow the money from his father, a Montreal businessman. Amelia was given the money by her mother, who had recently had an insurance policy mature. Armed with $1,500 they agreed to $100 a week sublet. In addition to the theatre, they would receive from Doherty his rather dubious "extreme know-how in public relations and [he would] introduce [them] to people around the lake and in Toronto."[11] They had only four weeks to plan their season, audition actors, hire crew, arrange for publicity, find accommodation not only for themselves but also for the actors and techies, and see to the myriad other details involved in launching a theatrical company. It was a daunting task. Millie wrote in her autobiography, "I suppose we would all three have liked to pull out before the first play got under way, but we were bound and committed."[12] They planned on staging only seven shows instead of the usual eight, which most weekly summer stocks attempted in those days, but the plays chosen were audience pleasers: *Life with Father* as an opener, *Charley's Aunt*, *Elizabeth Sleeps Out*, *Born Yesterday*, *Arsenic and Old Lace*, *Harvey*, and *The Man Who Came to Dinner*.

Unfamiliar with most of the actors in the Toronto area, they held several days of auditions in Doherty's Toronto office and obtained a group who were making the transition from amateur to professional theatre, not many of whom had met the frantic experience of weekly stock. Some of these were Guy Purser, a founder of one of Toronto's best amateur groups, Muriel Cuttle whom I had directed in the North Toronto Theatre Guild, Carol Starkman with whom I was to work in Kingston and Oakville, and Daphne Goldrick, who would later build a career on Canada's West Coast and become a champion of performers' rights through her voluntary work with Canadian Actors' Equity Association. Also in this company of enthusiasts were Phyllis Malcolm Stewart and Norma Renault. John Frid, from the prominent Hamilton construction family and who later disappeared into the jungles of American television and films, and Timothy Moxon, a young actor from England passing through on his way to oblivion in Hollywood, also joined the company. Warren Wilson was an apprentice who later became a CBC announcer and writer. Not all performers were enlisted for the whole season. Some were "jobbed in." For the role of Billie Dawn in *Born Yesterday* they imported Dolores Dawson, not because a Billie Dawn could not be found in Toronto or Montreal, but because, as Ms. Hall reports in her autobiography, "Silvio wanted somebody new and sensational, some sexy piece from New York who would turn them on. . . . Silvio had his way."[13] The "sexy piece" from Gotham was, apparently, a happy choice. That season Millie took ill in the last week and there were disagreements among the trio, particularly between her and Narizzano, although they remained close friends. Public apathy worked against the shows and at the season's end the trio limped back to Ottawa and Montreal having lost their original investment, sadder and wiser, but with the satisfaction of knowing that they had produced a season of quality performances.

■

There was a dearth of gamblers willing to tackle the Red Barn in summer 1952, so Brian Doherty tried variety shows on Saturday nights with square dancing on Wednesdays and Fridays. To manage these programs he hired Walter (Muzzi) Muzylo, who is reported to have taken the delights of square dancing to Liverpudlians when he had managed the Marionette Club in Liverpool, England, in 1946. For the opening show Doherty presented the English Music Hall comedian Eddie Bankey, whose credits included the London Palladium and night clubs in Montreal. The next show featured comedian Billy Meek, recently a headliner sandwiched between stripteasers at Toronto's Casino Burlesque. The Master of Ceremonies was Harold Barry, MC of the *Bonnie Maids* TV show from New York and another Canadian making a reputation south of the border. To add a soupçon of culture, the lyric soprano Hilda Veenstra was hired. Meek returned for an engagement in the last week of the season with Hamilton-born Gordie Tapp, who became one of our most popular entertainers on Canadian TV and on *The Grand Old Opera*. The vocalist for that evening was Howard Manning.

The most popular show that summer was the appearance of John Pratt and Murray Matheson in comedy routines and song and dance numbers from the Victorian and Edwardian eras, including such gems as "Pretty Little Pansy Faces" and "Tessie Stop Teasing Me." Originally from Australia, Matheson appeared on many shows during the halcyon days of live CBC-TV and onstage in Canada before he built a successful career in Hollywood films. For me, his versatile performing style, akin to that of one of my favourite comic actors, the late Cyril Ritchard, has always been a pleasure to watch. Also on this program was the accordionist, Len Moss. Brian Doherty even made one of his own rare stage appearances in a sketch satirically dedicated to

"Mother" in which he entered as the impersonation of a mother worthy, according to one reviewer, of the Abbey Theatre. But trying to produce theatre in Jackson's Point proved to be too discouraging even for Doherty and he gave up on the Red Barn.

For the next two years it reverted to a home for pigeons, bats, and field mice before it was sold along with 18 surrounding acres to James Farrell, who was anxious that the Red Barn continue as a theatre. In 1955 Stanley Jacobson and Mervyn Rosenzweig, those two ambitious young impresarios whom you have already met in connection with their subsequent production of *Will Success Spoil Rock Hunter?*, tried their luck. Although inexperienced recent graduates from college, they had the good sense to hire a promising young director, Leon Major, also a recent graduate. At the University of Toronto he too had come under the influence of Robert Gill. Major brought with him Wally Russell from Hart House as technical director and Les Lawrence as the designer and sometime actor. They planned eight typically varied shows on a weekly basis. The opener was to be *Nothing but the Truth*, and the rest of the season was to consist of such potential box-office drawing cards as: *The Moon Is Blue, A Streetcar Named Desire, The Fifth Season, Pure As the Driven Snow, Sabrina Fair, My Three Angels*, and a musical revue. They recruited Diana Laumer, Patricia Moffatt, Aylene Kamins, who had been a great help to me in Oakville, June Lehman from the Canadian Repertory Theatre in Ottawa, Harold Burke, my King Herod from the Garden Centre Theatre, Sandy Webster, and Cecil Linder. To pay for this talent they charged an across-the-board ticket price of $1.50. Accommodation for members of the company was no better than it had been in previous years. Stan Jacobson lived and worked in the glass lean-to at the side of the barn. Harold Burke describes the shack he shared with Les Lawrence as "only slightly larger than a two-hole outhouse."[14]

The advent of television in Canada had created TV personalities who had become household names. Percy Saltzman had become famous as the happy weatherman whose cachet was to toss his chalk in the air and catch it when he had finished. No slouch on the subject of science, he interviewed scientists on the TV program *Tabloid* and was MC of his own show,

How About That? He also appeared with Uncle Chichimus on the puppet show of that name. Because he had managed to make the dull weather report entertaining, it was a natural assumption that he could apply his "Happy Harry" persona to the leading role in *Nothing but the Truth*. To his credit he succeeded.

Leon Major had been persuaded to join the company with the inducement of directing *A Streetcar Named Desire*. As I have mentioned, Elia Kazan and Marlon Brando had so recently left their stamp on *Streetcar* that to differ from their interpretation was venturesome indeed, but Major did so. In his review Herbert Whittaker wrote:

> Leon Major has staged a production . . . which is fresh and original. . . . Cutting through the southern decadence, the symbolism, and most of the trappings, he gives us a *Streetcar* which pits a pathetic, weak woman against a man who enjoys with deliberate cruelty bringing her to her destruction. It is probably in the characterization of Stanley Kowalski that Mr. Major's production establishes its claim to originality, departing from the traditional portrayal of Stanley as pure animal, big and brutal. Neil McCallum who plays it here, makes him more faun than bull. He is vicious not brutal, and his attack on Blanche seems personal rather than defensive. To balance the portrait Mr. McCallum gives Stanley a great deal of charm and a kind of elfin humour which is as effective as it is surprising in a Kowalski.[15]

Whittaker does express a reservation that "this performance takes from Blanche Dubois much of the sympathy which is properly hers. Susanne Finlay's portrayal of the fallen southern belle is a pathetic rather than a tragic figure." Nevertheless, he considered it to be a performance "with many moments of fine sustained playing."[16]

Neil McCallum was an intelligent actor who eventually returned to England and had a career onstage and in films. A slightly built man, he could not have portrayed Stanley as a brute. One wonders if he was cast deliberately to fit Major's different concept of the play, or whether the different approach was dictated by the lack of a brutish actor in the Toronto acting pool. In either case the result considerably alters the play and raises inexplicable questions. For example, how does the actress playing Stella justify her sexual animalistic attraction to a Stanley who does not have animal appeal? Directors and actors are essentially interpretive artists. Liberties can be taken with a text but only so far as they will enhance the creator's intentions, not pervert them. Despite McCallum's and the other actors' skill, I think I would have been annoyed with this production because, as Whittaker pointed out, it throws the play out of balance.

At mid-point in the season came *Belly Acres*, a revue for which Jack Medhurst joined the company and shared honours with Diana Laumer. Marion Grudeff supplied the music at the piano. Much of the material was written by George McCowan but the high point was "I'm in Love with the Village Idiot," a song written by Stan Daniels. Following this excursion into variety was *The Fifth Season*, a successful Broadway play about the New York garment industry. The production was enhanced by a set by Errol Preston and costumes by Web Catherwood. It starred that gentle comedian Sammy Sales in the role of Mr. Pincus. "It is no great shakes as a play by any standards," wrote Jack Karr, "but it has been made amply amusing in its present production through a sly and cunning performance by Sammy Sales as one of the partners in a faltering dress business."[17] He also praises the rest of the cast, which included E.M. Margolese as the partner who acted "with relish and some gusto," and Pat Moffat who "is perhaps the most successful in a quiet and appealing performance as a refugee girl."[18] Whittaker had a few more reservations but echoed Karr's praise of Sammy Sales: "The simplicity of the man, the world weary shrug, the high-flying excursions into fantasy when he is covering up for his partner — Mr. Sales does all the things delightfully. . . . He is an extremely loveable actor."[19]

Through my involvement with the Wayne and Shuster TV shows I got to know Sammy quite well and I can vouch for the fact that he was not only an "extremely loveable actor" but an extremely loveable human being. Tragically, in his later years when he was acting as a comic Master of Ceremonies at a downtown Toronto tavern, he was set upon by a drunken customer and badly beaten. This attack not only weakened his health but also his faith in humankind and probably hastened his death soon after. At his funeral the Rabbi displayed our common Canadian distorted sense of values by implying that because Sammy had not been famous in New York or Hollywood, he had not "made it." But Sammy had made it where it really matters — in the hearts of his friends and fellow performers, and in the hearts of the thousands of people who had seen him perform over the years onstage and on Canadian television.

Shortly after the success of *The Fifth Season* a crisis arose. One of the promises the producers had made to Leon Major was that they would schedule a Restoration comedy. But in that slot they substituted *Blithe Spirit*. According to Harold Burke who was to play Charles Condomine, the dispute between Major and Jacobson was aired in the theatre before the whole company, much to their embarrassment. Not satisfied with the outcome, Mr. Major refused to direct *Blithe Spirit* and walked out. Jacobson then asked Harold Burke to direct it as well as play Condomine. One can admire Leon Major for defending his rights, but in view of a mounting deficit the producers needed to substitute a play that could be mounted at less cost and had a track record for being rewarding at the box office. As the season wore on, the receipts, in spite of some well-attended performances, did not keep up with the expenses, which led to a further re-arrangement of the program. This in turn resulted in some contracts being terminated a show earlier than originally promised, a further indication that it is most frequently the performer who suffers because of circumstances beyond his or her control.[20] At the summer's end, Jacobson and Rosenzweig were battered but not sufficiently bowed to prevent them from staging *The Fifth Season* and *Will Success Spoil Rock Hunter?* in Toronto.

They were followed at the Barn in 1956 by another young producer, Douglas Henderson, a native of Niagara Falls who began acting in amateur theatre, worked for a period in British television, and switched to stage management and design back at Hart House Theatre in Toronto. He had designed what Herbert Whittaker called "the bleak, prison-like, and rather expressionist"[21] set for Major's *Streetcar* the year before, and was familiar with the territory. Apparently undismayed, he plunged ahead, hiring a group of actors — some of whom were to use the season to gain experience as directors. He planned to direct one show himself, with Lew Davidson and Sean Sullivan sharing other directing chores. To direct the first show, *The Tender Trap*, he hired Joe Austen, who had been Elwood P. Dowd in my Oakville production of *Harvey*. By 1956, Mr. Austen had made inroads into television and was branching out as a director. All the shows that followed — *Rain, Dream Girl, Laura, I Am a Camera* — had marvellous leading roles for women, an emphasis continued when Araby Lockhart presented her one-woman revue. These were followed by *Nina* with June Lehman and Harold Burke, who had returned from the previous year. Alas, at the end of the summer Mr. Henderson joined the ranks of wounded producers of the Red Barn, which lay fallow in 1957.

■

No one had yet found the formula to balance the ticket prices against the small capacity of the auditorium. But Norman Stewart, who had acted with the Maple Leaf Theatre Company in London the previous season, and his mother, Nan, decided to try in 1958. Nan, then in her late middle years, was one of Toronto's most reliable character actresses. Although I had misgivings about their ability to overcome the Red Barn's financial obstacles, I had high regard for them as people and performers, so I was pleased to be asked to direct their season. As usual there was not much money to play with. One of the reasons I was hired was that they knew I had been through the shoestring-theatre mill before, and that I was accustomed to staging plays on small budgets.

We hired people accustomed to working in weekly stock. Wilf Pegg, one of the best available, was persuaded to design the shows with Hal Travis as his assistant. Joan Westlake, who had experience at Hart House, became the property mistress, and Godfrey Jackman was our business manager and general factotum. Martin Lager, also an alumnus of the Maple Leaf Theatre Company, was hired as an actor and stage manager. (Equity had not yet introduced the days of restricted activity for stage managers.) Norman and Nan could not afford the luxury of a resident stock company so actors were jobbed in for each show. I had staged Jan de Hartog's brilliant, warm comedy *The Fourposter* for the old Garden Centre Theatre, so Norman and Nan decided to open with it. In Ron Hartmann and his wife, Edna Pozer, I had two actors for whom this two-hander might have been written. Herbert Whittaker travelled up from Toronto and next day had a glowing review faulting me only on the music bridging the scenes — and that resulted when the person charged with obtaining the music failed by opening night to have all I had requested. During the play the two actors must show the changes that occur both physically and in their marital relationship over a period of 30 years. Of Ron and Edna, Whittaker wrote, "They measure up to the demands in a remarkably satisfying fashion. There is variety and colour here and humour found in every situation."[22] Both these actors were so easy to work with and so intelligently inventive, and Wilf Pegg's set was so right and helpful that this production proved to be one of my most rewarding directorial assignments. It had a favourable response from the audience, and got the new season off to a happy start.

Tea and Sympathy followed in which Norman Stewart repeated the role he had played so effectively the year before in London. Martin Lager played his friend, Al. I had cast Daryl Masters, a very handsome, middle-aged actor whom I had first met in amateur days as Bill Reynolds, the professor and house master of the residence of a boys' school in New England. Although helped greatly by Wilf Pegg's splendid set, the first scene on opening night did not play as it should have. When Daryl entered, his fly was wide open and a patch of white shirt shone through. Horrified, I dashed backstage hoping to get a message to Daryl to zip up. I arrived in the left stage wing beside the young assistant stage manager, who because she was prompter had her eyes glued to the script and had noticed nothing amiss onstage. Frantically I waved my arm at Daryl and pointed to my crotch several times. He ignored me. Meanwhile the audience had developed a large case of the titters. So concerned was he about remembering his lines that he seemed oblivious of the audience and of me. In desperation I began to unzip and zip up my own fly in the hope that he would look into the wings and get my message. After I had done that several times I became aware of the young promptress looking up at me with apprehension on her face. Covered with embarrassment I returned to the back of the theatre. Only when Daryl sat down facing the audience and his crotch gap became cavernous did the audience laughter make him realize that something was wrong. Embarrassed, he rose, turned upstage and zipped up, which earned him a round of applause. A very proper man, Daryl was mortified, and the young apprentice eyed me suspiciously for the rest of the summer.

Another production from that summer stands out in my memory. I staged *Bus Stop* with Martin Lager again as the cowboy Bo Decker, Nonnie Griffin in the role of Cherie, Billi Tyas as Grace, Grant Reddick as the Bus Driver, Peter Peers as Virgil, and Godfrey Jackman as the Sheriff. Whittaker was justifiably lukewarm in his review gently rapping my knuckles for indulging my desire to play Professor Lyman while also shouldering the responsibilities as the director. But the role is one that might have been tailor-made for me; I could not resist the temptation. However, I agree the show did suffer somewhat as a result. Whittaker had reservations about almost everyone's performance except Mary Barton as Elma about whom he wrote, "But the surprise of the evening was Mary Barton's performance of the young girl — which was sensitive and intelligent throughout. Miss Barton's showpiece, the balcony scene from *Romeo and Juliet*, was an integral part of an excellent and revealing performance."[23] He seemed to search for a quibble about Nonnie: "Miss Griffin makes an amusing Cherie with a baby southern accent and a mop of blond hair. Her singing of 'Old Black Magic' provided the climax to the first half of her performance which satisfied itself with caricature. Then she deepened noticeably to turn Cherie into a real person. Perhaps Mr. Inge wrote it that way but it is still up to the actress to dig a little deeper a little earlier."[24] He was right. Mr. Inge has written it that way. That is the pitfall for the actress playing Cherie. If she reveals too soon that she is more than just a scatter-brained "chanteuse," the comedy is diminished. She could be turned into the desperate victim of a man who, instead of appearing as a naïve, bumptious cowboy smitten with his first love for a sexy young woman, could be made to appear as a bullying ruthless male bent on sexual conquest. Miss Griffin wisely let her portrayal alter as she came to sympathize with Bo when his anguish became clear to her and she saw how her refusals humiliated him. It is love that changes them both. The whole play is an analysis of various types of love, from the professor's perverted affection for young girls to the idealized romantic love of Elma and the innocent love of Bo for Cherie. Although my production this time was moderately successful, decades later I was to direct the play again, and, on the whole was much more pleased with the results.

Also included in that season was *The Little Hut* by André Roussin in the first of several productions of this charming but limited sex comedy I was involved with over the years. It deals with a stuffy Englishman, his wife, and her almost as stuffy lover, who are shipwrecked on a desert island. There is a fourth character, the Danish cook from the ship, who masquerades as a savage resident of the island and appears halfway through the play clad only in a feathered head dress and a loin cloth. In contrast with the effete Englishmen, he must be a reasonably attractive physical specimen. Martin Lager was cast as the savage. A body make-up was concocted for him that he claims left him with a rash for years. The things we will endure for our art! Nonnie Griffin was appropriately cast as the bone of contention among the three men. Relying less on comedy of dialogue than of situation and character, this play requires style and a light touch, which we gave it. We also staged *Janus* that season and concluded the summer with *The Voice of the Turtle*. So far as my memory serves, neither of these productions was particularly outstanding, although the actors gave competent performances. My direction was merely adequate.

The problem with chronicling that particular season at the Red Barn is the paucity of information on it in public sources and even in my own files. But one fond memory I have is of the Sunday morning when we attended the charming St. George's Anglican Church. A fellow graduate from Victoria

College, John Speers, who officiated there and in Sutton, asked Grant Reddick to read the lesson. Most of the company turned out to give Grant our moral support and we were all pleased that Grant read the lesson with all the polish and panache of the accomplished actor. It was one of those magic moments. With the light streaming through the stained glass windows of this tiny Gothic church, I felt that I had been transported from Canada to St. Mary Meade and I looked around the congregation expecting to see Miss Marple sitting in a pew.

Nan and Norman fortunately ended the season without a great financial loss, and aware that, inexperienced as producers though they were, they had presented a season comparable in quality to any that had preceded theirs. Judging from the comments I heard, the public certainly thought so. However, the pressure of summer stock with little or no financial reward did not entice them back for a second year, and the Red Barn Theatre once more came up for grabs. Shortly after the 1958 season concluded, Norman went to England where he became involved with television and dropped out of my ken, but Nan and I were to work together again several times and she remained a good friend of mine through the rest of her days.

■

In 1959 the Red Barn was taken over by Marigold Charlesworth and Jean Roberts who had come to see one of our productions. Their tenure lasted four years and they became the most celebrated of all the Red Barn producers before or since. Both originally hailed from the United Kingdom and brought with them theatrical experience gleaned from that theatrically prolific land. No slouches in business, they knew the value of publicity. Their first summer consisted of *The Skin of Our Teeth, Night Must Fall, Tunnel of Love, Bell, Book and Candle, Champagne Complex, Love from a Stranger*, and, appropriately, *Maria Martin, or Murder at the Red Barn*. Obviously their play choices were no more highbrow than in previous years, but they were fastidious about their productions and their shows were presented with a consistent slickness that had been seen only occasionally in earlier seasons. The following year they opened with *Teahouse of the August Moon,* followed by *Will Success Spoil Rock Hunter?* with James Douglas and Carol Starkman, who graduated to the female lead from the role of a secretary in the Premiere Theatre production. Then came *Murder without Crime, Dial M for Murder, Private Lives,* and *Springtime for Henry.* The real hit of that season was the Australian play, *Summer of the Seventeenth Doll,* with the women of the company predominant. Kenneth Johnson wrote in the *Globe and Mail,* "Mary Savidge carries the brunt of the drama as Olive, and brings a fine talent to that moment when she breaks down and we see through her childish dreams. Joyce Gordon is stolid and wary as Pearl, and both manage to give the impression that they really are barmaids."[25] He went on to praise Paddy Croft and Martha Buhs, "pretty and enticing as the girl next door."

By 1960 working conditions in summer stock had altered from the time when an actor could be called upon to rehearse and perform in 12- or 13-hour stretches seven days a week. Actors' Equity restricted rehearsal hours to eight in one day, five on a one-performance day, and none on a two-performance day, unless the producer was willing to pay double for overtime. The purpose was not to obtain more money for the actors and stage managers, but to discourage the excessive work days. Under these rules, management can save money by operating a permanent company. Actors can be rehearsed and perform on the same day with no extra pay, although restricted in the number of rehearsal hours. Having separate casts or "jobbing in" actors for each show is more costly because there are duplicate casts on the payroll. But performers have more rehearsal time and, in theory anyway, the results are more accurate casting and a better production. Marigold and Jean opted for the latter approach in 1961. By 1962, as we'll see, it was causing problems.

Life with Father opened the 1961 season with Norman Ettlinger as Father Day, and Peter Tully, aged 9, and Michael Tully, aged 7, as Harlan and Whitney respectively. Both these boys were to appear in the very successful Canadian children's television series, *Forest Rangers.* The *Seven Year Itch* followed and then *The Rainmaker* in which Marigold took on the role of Lizzie, and turned her directorial duties over to her partner. The next production was *Arms and the Man* with Ettlinger as Bluntschli, followed by yet another staging of *Blithe Spirit*. That they presented this play only three summers after the Stewarts had indicates that either they were receiving sufficient public response to risk it, or they had thrown caution to the wind. *Nina* succeeded *Blithe Spirit* and they closed the season with that melodramatic ode to temperance, *Ten Nights in a Bar Room*.

According to my ex-pupil from the New Play Society School, Lawrence Stone, the critic the *Globe and Mail* sent to review *Nina*, "It was hard to determine which was enjoying itself more, the audience or the cast. Naughty, and yet restrained, the production sparkled like a glass of seltzer and the Red Barn audience chug-a-lugged liberal drafts with enjoyment."[26] Jean Roberts directed this brittle comedy and Helene Winston played the title role. David Renton was the hypochondriacal husband, and Henry Hovenkamp played Gerard. Mr. Stone wrote about Mr. Hovenkamp that he "was the only member of the trio who underplayed, and the contrast proved successful."[27] The production of *Ten Nights in a Bar Room* is noteworthy because it had in the cast Joseph Maher, Paddy Croft, and Terry Tweed, who was to become one of our most vital performers and directors, as well as president of Canadian Equity. The night Larry Stone saw the show there were only two rows of patrons, which he described as "the pitiful remnants left after the annual Canadian National Exhibition barrage."[28] This was a chronic problem at the Red Barn. The week of the opening of the CNE saw a mass migration of cottagers back to the city. However, I suspect that the dwindling of patrons had less to do with the CNE than with preparing of the children for school. Incidentally, the reviewer was E. Lawrence Stone when he reviewed *Nina* but became Lawrence E. Stone when he reviewed *Ten Nights in a Bar Room*. Such indecision as to one's identity does not augur well for a critic. But he was also a lawyer, which may account for the confusion.

Not content with staging 10 shows during the summer, the intrepid duo joined forces with Michael Tabbit to take over the newly renovated Central Library Theatre in Toronto for the winter of 1961–62. This theatre, though small, was one of the most charming and intimate in the province.

There, under the banner of the Red Barn Theatre, they staged a first-rate production of *The Fantasticks* with a stellar company. Ben McPeek was the musical director and Mark Negin the set and costume designer. The choreographer was Partick Hurd; the stage manager was Andis Celms. The whole production was directed brilliantly by Marigold Charlesworth — and no wonder. Its cast was Bruno Gerussi as El Gallo (eventually Don Franks took over the role), Jake Dengel as the Mute, Diane Stapley as Luisa, Charles Wallrich as Matt, Grant Cowan as Bellamy, Jack Van Evera as Hucklebee, and Charles Palmer as the old actor, Henry. No one I know who saw it can forget the sad clown face of Kenneth Wickes as Henry's sidekick, Mortimer.

With growing confidence the two producers decided that for the 1962 summer they would operate not only at the Red Barn but also at the venerable Opera House in Orillia. Built in 1895 in the French Château style with pointed turrets, this structure was originally intended, as with so many similar buildings in small Ontario towns, to house either the civic offices or a fire hall on the ground floor and a moderate-sized theatre on the floors above. Despite the name, operas as we know them were seldom performed in these theatres. In recent years the Orillia Opera House has been completely refurbished but in 1962 it was a somewhat gloomy venue for escapist summer stock. However, by exchanging productions between the Barn and the Opera House, both companies had the luxury of rehearsing their shows for two weeks and performing them for two.

Marigold and Jean joined with William Frederic and Keith Green for that summer. Mr. Green, who had been a stage manager at the Stratford Festival, had just returned from Britain where he worked for the Royal Shakespeare Company in their newly acquired London headquarters. For the Red Barn he would also direct some of the plays. The season got off to an auspicious start with *Breath of Spring*, which Ron Evans referred to as "a jewel of a show," with lavish praise for its actors, particularly Joyce Gordon, Paddy Croft, James Edmond, and Louise Nicol. He was also enthusiastic about *All for Mary*. But the reviews for *The Glass Menagerie* reveal more about theatre reviewing than about the shows ostensibly their subject. So, I would like to take this opportunity to leave my history of the Red Barn to focus briefly on the criticism it received.

Ron Evans was once again fulsome in his praise writing a commendation to the Red Barn for putting on *The Glass Menagerie* amid a season of "silly British and American farces." He wrote, "It is possible to quarrel with director Marigold Charlesworth's pacing . . . but never with her taste and expert touch. She has captured the wistful mood of the piece perfectly."[29] He called Timothy Findley's performance as Tom, "Outstanding. . . . He is earnest, intense, and compelling. The stage sizzles when he steps on it."[30] Evans considered the set by John Scott "to be far above the standard usually set for summer theatre."[31] Ralph Thomas writing in the *Toronto Star* and Ralph Hicklin in the *Globe and Mail* did not agree. Mr. Thomas began his review with "Last night it seemed that Tennesee Williams just wasn't suited to the approach and style of the Red Barn players, and vice versa."[32] He then proceeded to carve up the cast, the designer, and the director. Hicklin wrote a more perspicacious review stating that, "The production of the play succeeds in some areas, but the glass shatters sadly in others."[33] He then put his finger on what he considered the major pitfall facing the director and actors in the play: "Life in the flat is a constant battle. Amanda is a terrifying combination. She exasperates her son, and us, to distraction by living in her past as a real or imagined southern belle, by hounding Tom for fear that, like her husband, he will cut and run. But at the same time Amanda must excite the audience's pity and even sympathy, for she is on her own terms struggling valiantly with life. Unless the actress — in this production Denise Ferguson — is able to combine the infuriating and the endearing — the glass shatters."[34] In his view this was not achieved until Amanda had her scene with the Gentleman Caller played by Herbert Foster, "the most completely right performer of the production."[35] He castigated director Charlesworth for making Laura wear a leg brace "despite numerous indications in the text that she does no such thing," and for dressing her "tattily" to receive her gentleman caller. The resultant clumsiness of movement and the ugly cut of the dress he wrote "would defy any actress to overcome."[36] Edna Usher, writing in the *Toronto Star* about *Maria Martin, or Murder at the Red Barn*, said that it "has been a rotting corpse for years and should have been left in the ground it never got off."[37] On the other hand, Ralph Hicklin wrote, "I never had so much fun since Genevieve broke her leg."[38] Admittedly, that can be taken two ways, but who should one believe? About Alan Nunn, who played the evil villain, Squire Corder, he wrote, "Always an actor of fine style, he falls superbly into the spirit of the lecherous Regency buck." And about Joseph Maher he said, "He brings a touch of Cyril Ritchard to his gloriously posturized portrayal of Ishmael, the vengeful gypsy."[39] Over my many years in the theatre I have often noted gaps between not only my own responses to shows and those of reviewers but between reviewers themselves. The gaps are often enormous and lead one to ask whether the reports are on the same shows. Given the conditions reviewers are forced to work under — the few hours' lead time, the dreadfully low priority given by the media to theatre reviewing, an attitude that sends a sports reporter to cover the theatre beat — I am not surprised at what we get to read. But these conflicting reviews provide examples to theatregoers that they would be much wiser to see the production and decide for themselves than trust reviewers.

We'll get back to the Red Barn where in 1962 accommodation still proved to be a problem. Louise Nicol recalls most of the company were billeted in an establishment that supplied bed and breakfast, but where her husband had to pay an additional $2 for the privilege of spending the night with her. But she considers that was a real bargain for him because not only did he get her, but breakfast as well. The real bargain might well have been for the Red Barn producers who that year were privileged in having their posters designed by that same husband, the eminent Canadian artist, Angus Macdonald, whose paintings and stained glass windows are in private collections, galleries, churches, banks, and public libraries throughout North America and Europe.[40]

Although there was less pressure on the performers, the fortnightly scheduling meant that two full companies of actors, stage management, and crew were on the payroll simultaneously, vastly increasing the costs. Charles Gerein in an article in the *Toronto Star* wrote that in the first two years at the Red Barn, Marigold and Jean had cleared $3,000 but by the fall of 1962, what with the costs of the Toronto season and the additional expense of two companies that summer, they found themselves in the red by $12,000.[41] They had given it the best shot yet, but the economic curse on the Red Barn Theatre had found two more victims. They decided against a 1963 season.

■

Fortunately for Ontario theatre, a roof collapsed in Quebec, and as a result the Red Barn found a new set of adventurers. The heavy snows of that winter had crushed the curling arena of the North Hatley Inn, in which a summer theatre had been operating for several years, the last of which produced by a trio of theatrical enthusiasts, Roger Dauphin, Patricia Carroll Brown, and Rae Wickins. Roger and Rae had met while students at the London School of Dramatic Art. Patricia Brown was born in Toronto and at St. Clement's School developed an interest in acting and even directing; she took on the challenge of *The Taming of the Shrew*, which she had to edit, being careful to leave in all the suggestive bits, to fit it into the limited attention span of pre-adolescent girls. She attended Columbia University in New York where her enthusiasm for the theatre developed further. In 1955 she went to England on the advice of the first Crest director, John Blatchley, where she studied acting at L.A.M.D.A. When the three had gotten together to produce a season in 1962 in North Hatley, Patricia had christened them the Harlequin Players, which she considered an ideal title for a theatre in Quebec.

The bulk of the funding for this venture came from Roger Dauphin, although Ms. Brown also contributed cash. Mr. Dauphin, an American whose real name was Reginald Winthrop, was the wealthiest of the three. He claimed forebears who came to North America on the Mayflower and an ancestor who had been governor of Massachusetts. The family waxed wealthy over the centuries, but his immediate ancestors had abandoned "the colonies" for a more leisurely existence in the south of France. Reginald was born in Berne, Switzerland, but was raised on the Riviera in Juan Les Pins, a town made famous by Somerset Maugham. Despite their

French residency, the Winthrops kept their American citizenship, and because during World War II that part of France was under the rule of the Vichy Government and not the Germans, they were allowed to remain. After the war the completely bilingual Reginald, now Roger pronounced in the French manner, was drafted into the American army and assigned the macabre task of arranging for thousands of American dead to be transported home. When he was demobilized he enrolled in the London School of Dramatic Art where he became close friends with Rae Wickens. When they graduated, Roger Dauphin returned to the United States. Rae Wickens was hired as an actor for James Balfour at the Arena Theatre in North Hatley, and when Balfour stopped producing there, Rae and Patricia joined forces with Roger to present the 1962 summer season.

When nature disrupted their plans for a 1963 season in the Arena, they sought permission to perform in the local town hall, but found the fire regulations too restrictive. On hearing that Marigold and Jean were not returning to the Red Barn, they decided to put in a bid for it. Although the property by that time was owned by a Mr. Gold, Roberts and Charlesworth had approval of their successors. A counter-bid was made by a Toronto actor, William Kemp, but they decided to turn over their lease to the three more experienced producers while retaining the name "The Red Barn Players" at the Central Library. Thus the Harlequin Players came to Jackson's Point, although the actual producing company was called "Winthrop-Dauphin."

Upon arrival the trio found the Red Barn basement crammed with a mountain of scenery: flats, fireplaces, doors, staircases, props, and furniture left over from previous regimes. Many of these solidly built stage pieces, according to Ms. Brown, were originally for CBC-TV.[42] This windfall, purchased from Marigold and Jean, accounted for the new producers' ability to mount shows comparable in appearance and construction quality to their immediate predecessors. The new management decided to return to a policy of weekly stock and abandoned production at Orillia. They operated under the Equity agreement governing summer stock, which allowed the use of a few non-Equity apprentices. One was Charles Dennis whom Patty

Brown says she found in a Robert Simpson Company Secondary School Drama Festival, and who went on to become a successful scriptwriter in Hollywood. Later Eric Steiner, who became one of our most successful directors, was an apprentice. Even though the trio had proved themselves at North Hatley, no grants were available to them from the funding bodies for their first season at the Red Barn.

While aware that their program should consist of proven popular fare, they decided to wow the public with a first production that would demonstrate that the Harlequin Players were not theatrical yahoos. They chose Shaw's *Misalliance* for which they recruited actors able to perform the style this play requires. John Tarleton was played by John Futerman; Bentley Summerhays by Leslie Mulholland; a recent University of Toronto graduate, Patricia Brown, took on the role of Hypatia Tarleton; Nancy Kerr was Mrs. Tarleton; Eric Donkin, not yet a fixture at Stratford, played John Tarleton Sr.; and William Osler was a sonorous Lord Summerhays. Peter Brockington had the choice role of Gunner. Joey Percival was played by a young English émigré, David Baron Wilson (a triple-barrelled name on a program always inspires confidence), who was on display in subway and television ads at the time as the Buckingham cigarette man. Andis Celms, eventually artistic director of English theatre at the National Arts Centre in Ottawa, was the technical director and the stage manager was John Wood, for some time now one of Canada's most in-demand directors.

Misalliance was a happy choice and won the critics to the company's support. Ralph Hicklin in the *Globe and Mail* led the praise with, "It was a lucky day for Ontario theatregoers when the roof of the North Hatley, Quebec, summer theatre fell in."[43] He singled out the director John Brockington and the principals for kudos and said that "some of the performances were excessive," but, "it was a kind of excess that was welcome. . . . *Misalliance* could have been merely outrageous. Instead it was winningly, occasionally brilliantly outrageous."[44] Wally Wood in the *Toronto Star* echoed Hicklin's enthusiasm.[45] Rose Macdonald came out of retirement and joined her colleagues with only slightly diminished praise in the *Telegram*.[46]

The second production, *Arsenic and Old Lace*, continued to garner critical encomiums. "This looks like a good company at the Red Barn this summer, coming comfortably close to the high standards set in other years by Marigold Charlesworth and Jean Roberts," said Ron Evans.[47] But his enthusiasm waned with the third show, *Not in the Book*, which he described as "so much theatrical mud, sloppy, impossible to mould and not particularly attractive."[48] Then followed *See How They Run*, which prompted Hicklin to urge that "Every 10 years or so some theatrical Savonarola should arise to perform a burning of the play books that summer theatres insist in lifting off the page, however small their merit. One of the first to go up in flames would certainly be Phillip King's *See How They Run* which the excellent Red Barn Theatre Company unfortunately revived last night."[49] But Ralph was enthusiastic over Nancy Kerr's performance as Miss Skillen: "Nancy Kerr does wonders with the tweedy maiden who is not only tweedy, but drunk for two thirds of the play."[50] Ron Evans compared the productions of *Arsenic and Old Lace* and *See How They Run* as "like sitting Sophia Loren alongside Charlotte Whitten"[51] (Ottawa's butch and feisty ex-mayor). Wally Wood in the *Toronto Star* summed up his reaction: "There is an appropriate line in the play: 'Sergeant, arrest most of these people'."[52] The balance of the season received mixed reviews, which was to be expected from critics with such diversity of background and experience as those in Toronto.

What is different about the Harlequin Players is that, although Patricia Brown had the title of artistic director, they divided up the directorial chores among the company and spread the assignments throughout the season. John Brockington guest directed the first show. His brother Peter, Joel Kenyon, and Patricia Brown all directed at least two shows; John Meredith directed one. Incidentally, John Meredith is John Wood, and Patricia reversed the order of her names to Carroll Patricia Brown when she directed, as though she had a split personality, neither portions of which wanted responsibility for what the other did. Thus actors in the company who wanted to try their hand at directing got the opportunity to do so. This had the advantage of presenting the company with a fresh directorial approach for each show, but had the disadvantage of a potential inconsistency of standard of production, depending on the abilities of the directors, which could vary considerably.

Patty Brown remembers how pleased they were with audience response. Whereas the North Hatley audience had been a wealthier, more sophisticated crowd who arrived at the theatre well dined and wined, she claims the Jackson's Point audiences were not primarily from the cocktail set and consequently were not so "loggy" in the theatre. They gave their reactions generously, particularly their laughter, vital to performers in comedy. At the season's end the three producers concluded that they had been sufficiently successful to warrant a second summer. Over the winter, they lined up an impressive list of patrons to give at least moral support to their endeavours and even created a small board of directors whose president was Carmen B. Guild, who also served in a business capacity with the National Ballet. The secretary was Charlotte Holmes, an actress who later was able to assist the theatre arts from a position with the Ontario Arts Council. Hugh Cartwright was the treasurer. Mrs. Helen Brown and a further representative of the acting community, Claude Bede, were also board members.

Jean Anouilh's *Waltz of the Toreadors* is a comedy of quality, and was a prestigious opener for the season, but its first night performance did not live up to the play itself. Paul Swayze, the designer, also directed and had cast Jack Medhurst as General St. Pé and Nancy Kerr as the bed-ridden, self-pitying, nagging wife. Mr. Medhurst had become a clever make-up artist and prided himself on his skill. He has always looked much younger than his years, so in order to make himself appear more like the older General, he hid his youthful physiognomy under a fulsome beard applied with spirit gum. The temperature that day had nudged 100 degrees Fahrenheit and by curtain time had cooled off only slightly. The beard was no problem until the confrontational scene in Act Two between the General and his wife in her bedroom. Jack's perspiration had weakened the spirit gum and the beard began to peel off. In desperation he kept trying to stick it back on. Alas, the fireworks between the distracted General and his wife never got ignited at that performance, the spark smothered by a rebellious beard. Fortunately, in subsequent performances the beard behaved and the scene had the necessary vehemence.

But a wayward beard was not all that served to diminish the impact of Mr. Anouilh's comedy on opening night. Earlier in the evening two bats had entered the barn to take in the show. When confronted with flying bats, actors are prone to press on regardless while ducking the swooping annoyances. But audiences can get quite agitated. A similar bat invasion occurred at the Red Barn in 1958 when I directed there, and a pregnant woman had to be rushed out of the theatre in hysterics. On opening night in 1963 no such event occurred, but the bats added a level of disturbance to that of the recalcitrant whiskers, and both were complemented by matches mysteriously catching fire on a desk forcing the General frantically to blow out the flame. In spite of all these hazards, Ron Evans was able to sum up his review: "Mr. Medhurst, Miss Kerr, Patricia Carroll Brown, Peter Brockington, and Roger Dauphin faced up to all these calamities admirably and gave a most creditable performance under the circumstances."[53]

The opening night of *Charley's Aunt* passed more smoothly but there had been a crisis during rehearsals. On the Saturday before opening, Jack Medhurst, who was to play Fancourt Babberly, a role he had done for the Village Players decades before, took ill and David Hughes, who had played Babberly the previous March in Vancouver, replaced him. Writing in the *Globe and Mail*, Ralph Hicklin expressed awe at such a polished performance with so little rehearsal: "Hughes, whose aunt impersonation resembles a dissolute Edith Evans, has some inspired moments of clowning. . . . His unique interpretation of *Swan Lake* during a lull in the frenzy was unforgettable; so was his assumption of the pose of the Piccadilly Circus Eros on learning that he is loved. As Lord Fancourt he managed to get through lines like 'Won't they be jolly waxy' with a straight face."[54] Hicklin, while recognizing that Brandon Thomas was no Oscar Wilde, suggested that next year they should tackle *The Importance of Being Earnest*.

David Hughes was kept on for *Boy Meets Girl*, a production Ron Evans in a rhapsody of alliteration called, "witless, weightless, worthless." His over-produced vitriol included, "I could find nothing in this production worthy of commendation, neither acting, directing, nor design."[55] This is a good example of a critic undermining himself by excess, viciously dismissing out of hand the efforts of a group of talented artists. Surely a responsibility of a critic is to point out where the artist in this case has gone wrong, assuming, of course, that the critic knows. Mr. Evans devoted half his review to yet another bat that entered the barn, and which he declared, "gave the best performance." Such destructive flippancy is an insult to all involved. When he reviewed the following production, Peter Ustinov's satire on American-Soviet relations, *Romanov and Juliet*, he continued to review the bat, which he christened "Barrymore," describing the twists, turns, and barrel rolls of its flight. He then grudgingly gave a lukewarm critique of the production.[56] But, I have to admit the article makes for amusing reading, albeit at the expense of the actors. Mr. Evans, possibly to redeem himself, reviewed *Gigi* favourably and absolutely cooed over the sets: "I guess even miracles can get to be mundane, and that's why audiences at the Red Barn allow wonders to pass in silence. The wonders I mean are those wrought in design. . . . Week in, week out during the two-month summer season, the Red Barn offers settings and costumes that are outstanding. It has become something of a tradition."[57] Here is an example of a forgetful critic who could find nothing redeeming about the production of *Boy Meets Girl* including the design.

Herbert Whittaker too decried *Boy Meets Girl*, but raised the calibre of criticism of the Harlequin Players with his review of *Romanov and Juliet*. He deplored the fact that there was no bus service to take loads of people to see the production at the Red Barn, and also deplored the desultory support given by the surrounding community. He generally applauded all the cast, the director, Peter Brockington, and the designer, Paul Swayze, and ends his column, "Thus a play designed to show off one man's (Ustinov, the actor) unusual gifts becomes a stronger company show with every member thriving on the opportunities presented. The Harlequin Players show here that they deserve their subsidy from the Ontario Arts Council."[58]

The final show, *Kiss Mama Goodbye*, was the triumph of the '64 season. It was written by an expatriate Canadian, Paul Wayne, who had been an actor with the Hart-Slade Garden Centre Theatre Company when I directed there in 1954. He had then become an announcer for a radio station in Ottawa. Discovering he had an aptitude for writing scripts, he moved to Hollywood about the same time as his friend Bernard Slade, where he found his niche writing for TV and films. When I visited Hollywood in 1966 he was ensconced in a cottage on the Universal Studio lot busily writing screenplays for such adventure epics as *King's Pirate. Kiss Mama Goodbye* had been staged by the Ottawa Little Theatre and a TV version had appeared on CBC-TV. In 1964, during a holiday in Canada, Paul was persuaded by the producers at the Red Barn to let them stage his play, which deals with the rebellion of a young Jewish man whose domineering "Yiddisher" mama has coerced him to enrol in medical school against his wishes.

When the producers asked him about his royalty, he requested $500 or 10 per cent of the box-office receipts. The management opted for 10 per cent and very soon regretted that decision. When tickets went on sale, queues stretched from the box office down the long driveway to the street. Every performance was sold out, and Mr. Wayne did better financially from the show than he had ever dreamed. The Jewish community of Jackson's Point came out in droves. Naturally the management was ecstatic over the public response, and adding to their euphoria was the fact that the Ontario Arts Council had given them their first grant, $3,000, to stage this play by a Canadian.

Herbert Whittaker called the production an "audience pleaser" and stated, "The Red Barn was smart and lucky to have Sylvia Lennick to play its Mama. Miss Lennick divides her considerable acting talent — half to polishing off the jokes, half to exploring the emotional possibilities of the role."[59] He singled out Paul Soles as "the one who strikes the exact note, making a little less of the jokes, pushing the situation only as far as it will go. He is thus very real as Uncle Izzie, funny and even a little moving."[60] He praised the co-directors, Carroll Brown and Danny McFaul, and Paul Swayze for his design, but urged the cast to put more "pace and variation" into it than had been shown on opening night. Lennick and Soles were only two of a cast chosen for their experience, which would bring an understanding of the characters and the cultural background. Stephen Levy, who later changed his name to

Stephen Younger, played Ralphie Edelman, Laurence Cherniak played Herbie, and Nancy Kerr, the only actor from previous productions, was Mrs. Goldberg. Paul Wayne brought the opera singer Irene Balzer from Hollywood because they needed a large lady to play the role of Mrs. Himmelfarb. Hilary Kilbourn, the daughter of Toronto councillor and writer, William Kilbourn, played the daughter Rifka, and Peggy Reagan, who had been an apprentice all summer, was cast as the girlfriend Elsie.

Another achievement of the production was that it brought Nathan Cohen down from Mt. Olympus to the Red Barn. His lengthy and astute review represents for me how a critic can be helpful to the artists and informative to the public without flippancy, sarcasm, or insult. He praised the author because "the mother is no embodiment of all those mammas trying to smother their sons under pillows of Freudian affection. She is simply a hard working, widowed dressmaker who all her life has dreamed of having a son, a doctor. The boy does not stand for all those young men groaning under the tyranny of parental love, while wishing to fulfil themselves as painters, jazz players, or poets."[61] Cohen was critical because he could not believe that a young man who threw up at a discussion of the digestive process could make it through three years of medical school. The play's construction failed to get Cohen's approval but he too complimented the performers, the directors, and set designer, and concluded, "Mr. Wayne's play suffers from two defects. It covers territory which already has been explored to excess across the border. . . . The other is inexperienced craftsmanship and skimpiness of character content. Yet there is enough of interest in the text to make one hopeful that here is something more than a one-shot, that Mr. Wayne has in him the makings of a good playwright."[62]

When the Canada Council cancelled its grant to the Crest Theatre in 1964, there was a chain reaction that benefitted the Harlequin Players. The Crest had been invited to take their proposed production of *Brecht on Brecht* to celebrate the opening of the refurbished Academy Theatre in Lindsay, Ontario. The cancellation of the Crest's autumn season sent the Academy Theatre organizers searching frantically for a replacement show. Realizing that the Red Barn had a box-office hit on its hands, they approached the producers of *Kiss Mama Goodbye* and on September 10, 1964, with the lieutenant-governor present, the story of Mama Edelman, her family, and friends gave the 71-year-old Academy Theatre a worthy rebirth.

Between the summers of 1964 and 1965 the triumvirate of Roger Dauphin, Patricia Brown, and Rae Wickens dissolved. Roger returned to Quebec where he eventually opened a television station, and Rae Wickens, who had proven himself to be a gifted public relations manager, was snatched up to handle publicity for the two-year-old, burgeoning Shaw Festival. Patricia decided to gamble on another season at the Red Barn, despite her decidedly limited financial resources. She followed the advice of Ralph Hicklin that the Harlequin Players would do well to stage *The Importance of Being Earnest* and used it as a prestige opener for an eight-play 1965 season. The talented young John Horton was recruited to play Algernon Moncrieff, Bonita Rose played Gwendolyn, and Mary Benning, Cecily. Elizabeth Jackson was Miss Prism and Ron Chudleigh was Canon Chasuble, with Alan Stebbings as Lane. The set by Douglas Higgins from the University of British Columbia and costumes by Ron Gilmore were apparently the most successful parts of the production, although Charles Dennis, ex-Red Barn apprentice, writing in the *Toronto Telegram*, compared Miss Brown's performance as Lady Bracknell favourably with that of Edna May Oliver as Lady Catherine de Burgh in the Hollywood film version of *Pride and Prejudice*.[63] He implied that the ladies in the company fared better than the men. Peter Brockington as director had himself as Jack Worthing pour tea over Algernon's head at the end of the second act. Brandon Thomas, author of *Charley's Aunt*, might have approved but it seems a very un-Wildean bit of business.

One can only marvel at the courage and versatility of this company in switching from the mannered artificiality of *The Importance* to Tennessee Williams's slice of southern life, soap opera-ish *Summer and Smoke*. But, Ron Evans was so impressed by the show, he discarded flippancy for a change and wrote an astute review in which he denigrated the play but extolled the production. He singled out Patricia Brown who played Alma: "Despite Williams's often trite dialogue, she manages an often moving, always sincere performance."[64] John Horton as the young doctor also received his share of kudos, as did the supporting cast. Evans referred to the set as extremely imaginative, and concluded, "Peter Brockington should be commended for his sure, sympathetic direction."[65] This high standard of performance continued through the third show, *Come Blow Your Horn*, with Ben and Sylvia Lennick receiving a rave notice from Charles Dennis in the *Telegram*: "Make no mistake about it. The Lennicks are absolutely brilliant. They are the Lunts of Jewish comedy. . . . Paul Soles maintained the excellence established by the Lennicks."[66] To Mr. Dennis, Sylvia Shore "was pure jelly — 'cause jam don't shake that way," which I presume he meant as praise. He gave considerable credit for the success to Peter Brockington for "his energetic and skilful direction."[67] Box-office receipts for that show were the second biggest in the Harlequin Players' three-year tenure.

Then the season hit a bump. Ms. Brown and her company thought it an important challenge to stage a successful French-Canadian revue, *Le P'tit Bonheur* by Félix Leclerc, to enlighten an Ontario audience about the subjects considered worthy of satirizing in Quebec. So did the Ontario Arts Council who provided another grant. The occasion was considered sufficiently important to lure all three front-line critics from Toronto. Herbert Whittaker spoke resonantly, "If ever the theatre can serve a country it is now. Separation is not a dirty word but a national condition. From sea to sea there is the need for playwrights and actors to interpret Canada to itself. But the case of Quebec must be given precedence for the language barrier accentuates the difference of thought and feeling. Hence the value of the Red Barn's contribution is paramount."[68] But while finding the idea commendable, they were unenthusiastic about the end result. Ron Evans referred to "the brave souls that have essayed this laudable, lamentable experiment."[69] Nathan Cohen pointed out the difficulties in translating a revue in such a way to make it work in another language.[70] The trouble was that a revue originally delivered with Gallic flair lost that quality when translated into more prosaic English. The songs were delivered in French and the skits were oriented to a Roman Catholic culture, so that most of the aptness of the wit was lost on the Red Barn audience. *Le P'tit Bonheur* was a financial and critical disaster.

Fortunately, Edward Albee's abrasive *Who's Afraid of Virginia Woolf?* — a challenge under the best of theatrical conditions, but verging on the foolhardy for weekly stock in the dog days of summer — was a success. Praise from the Toronto critics was loaded on the director, Brian O'Leary, who had won a Best Director award at the Dominion Drama Festival for *Epitaph for George Dillon* and who became the TV producer of *This Hour Has Seven Days*. The critics also expressed their amazement for so creditable a production with only a week's rehearsal. Actually the cast had almost two weeks to prepare because they rehearsed an extra week in a local hotel room so that they arrived at the first rehearsal in the theatre with the lines learned. It was nonetheless a tremendous achievement and was considered sufficiently successful that, with the same cast — Patricia Brown as Martha, Peter Brockington as a waspish George, and Sylvia Shore and Bruce Gray as the younger couple — it was presented by Aries Productions that autumn at the Poor Alex Theatre in Toronto. Later Jeanine Beaubien, producer of La Poudrière Theatre, took it to Montreal with one of her local actors, Len Watt replacing Peter Brockington who had other commitments. A year later this same production was revived by Jack Merigold at the Garden Centre Theatre in Vineland, Ontario. While the actors benefitted financially from these subsequent showings, the Harlequin company of the Red Barn received no fee whatever from the GCT or La Poudrière for having created such a stage-worthy production in the first place.

Herb Gardner's *A Thousand Clowns* concluded the season, with Paul Soles in the lead and Michael Lennick, Sylvia and Ben's son, as the boy Nick. The Harlequin Players had given themselves some ambitious challenges that summer and had won admiration for their efforts. Patricia Brown had weathered her first season as a solo producer and was sufficiently encouraged to plan for the next. Gate receipts had gone up as a result of increases in ticket prices, although the actual attendance averaged only 40 per cent and private donations had not reached expectations. This resulted in a small but manageable deficit. As in 1965, she budgeted $16,000 with about $10,000 for performers' salaries, including herself. But on a seven-play season she needed 50 per cent capacity to break even. She continued the policy of evenings-only Tuesday through Saturday and offered all seven plays to subscribers Tuesday through Friday for $14 or four plays for $8. The seven-play series on Saturday evenings went for $17.50 and the four-play series for $10. Ms. Brown tried to make things as flexible as possible for the public by allowing all seven tickets to be used up in one evening if the patron preferred. Single tickets Tuesday to Friday sold for $2.25 (in 1965 a two-price system set them at $1.75 and $2.25); on Saturday the price rose to $2.75.

Following the pattern established in the past three years, she thickened the light summer gravy with the flour of what she referred to as "stature plays" but her opening program got a mixed reaction. Edward Albee's *The American Dream*, directed by William Davis and starring Ben and Sylvia Lennick, Sylvia Shore, Patricia Brown, and Bruce Gray as the "dream boy" came out relatively unscathed by the critics, but they were unanimous in their condemnation of the other one-act on that bill, *The Fur Trade*, a new play by John Irvine of Richmond Hill. Ron Evans sympathized with the Lennicks for having to perform in it. However, because it was written by a Canadian, it put a $4,000 grant from the Ontario Arts Council into the Harlequin coffers. Anouilh's *Ardele*, with some of the same characters as *Waltz of the Toreadors*, was mid-point in the season. Ron Evans's review, titled "Down in Glorious Defeat," paid homage to the enterprise of the Harlequin Players, then proceeded to denigrate the play and Anouilh, and was lukewarm about the cast except for Claude Bede as the Count. He finished with, "I am afraid Anouilh has made asses of the Harlequin Players, but God bless them for trying."[71] Whittaker was less brutal: "The endless ironies of Anouilh's style make *Ardele* extraordinarily delicate stuff for any summer theatre . . . but it is another mark in favour of the Harlequin Players that they make so much of the play live for us and none of it is ridiculous."[72] He commended Brian O'Leary for his direction, and the actors Patricia Carroll Brown, Claude Bede, Ron Braden, and in particular Sylvia Shore. For him the rest of the cast were not up to the challenge, but "they are satisfactory enough to enable that excellent quartet to make Anouilh clear and compelling."[73]

Billy Liar, a British Walter Mitty with more profound social tones, and

Invitation to a March were two other worthy contributions the Harlequin Players made to the Ontario theatre scene that season. Ron Evans, who seemed to visit the Red Barn more frequently than the other critics, referred to *Billy Liar* as "well cast, reasonably performed, and, for the most part, deftly directed [by Brian O'Leary]."[74] When he wrote about John Wood's production of *Invitation to a March*, Evans was, for him, quite enthusiastic. He commended Tom Doherty's full stage beach set, with slip stages for two different interiors, and praised actors Sylvia Shore and Don Sutherland. He singled out Lynn Gorman's performance as Camilla Jablonski as "about the best I have seen in the summer circuit this season."[75] That she was onstage at all that night was the result of her strong commitment. On the way to the theatre she was involved in an accident that caused her car to careen into a ditch. She emerged with cuts and bruises and badly shaken up. Nevertheless, in the best show-biz tradition she went on with the performance, and a spectacular one at that.

I have quoted extensively from the extant reviews to substantiate my view that the Harlequin Players' standard was above average for most summer stock companies and comparable with the productions of the Roberts-Charlesworth years, which, with the passage of time, seem by many to be considered the Red Barn's "golden years." But in 1966, despite the variety and quality of the shows, attendance decreased from an average of 40 per cent in 1965 to 32 per cent. Discouraged by the drop in box-office receipts and seeing the debts growing, Patty Brown reluctantly cancelled the last show, *Harvey*, because it had too large a cast for her to meet the payroll. Moreover, the CNE had opened with resultant decrease in the south Lake Simcoe summer population.

For four seasons Patty Brown and her cohorts had been, on the whole, successful artistically, but not financially. At the close of the 1966 summer, Patty was in debt. At first glance the amount did not seem unmanageable and she hoped to return the following year. But upon examining the financial situation more carefully she received several shocks. To help her operate the company that year she had hired a business manager whose attention to business was cavalier at best. For example, she discovered that a stack of posters advertising *Ardele* had not been distributed before opening and were still lying in the manager's car. After the close of the season she had to decipher his haphazard system of bookkeeping. She discovered that she owed about $2,000 to local merchants, and a larger sum to national companies. When the Harlequin Players had first taken over the Red Barn, they faced resistance from local merchants about obtaining credit. That reluctance was based on the merchants' previous experience with some Red Barn producers. But over their four years, the Harlequin Company had always managed to pay off its local creditors. In 1966, in order to maintain that trust that had been built up, Ms. Brown determined to pay these people first. She obtained the money from a friend and wrote cheques to the small creditors. She was just about to mail them when a representative of the federal government informed her that no unemployment insurance had been deducted from the employees that summer and that no payment had been made to the government. In those days, actors and their employers had to pay into the Unemployment Insurance Fund, even though most performers never obtained the requisite 13 weeks of consecutive employment to qualify for benefits. Dismayed, she had to use the creditors' money to pay the government not only the employer's share of the U.I. contributions, but also the employees' share because it was too late to collect from the performers now dispersed to the far corners of the country. The result was that the small merchants did not get paid immediately, although, according to Ms. Brown, they all got paid eventually. However, two larger corporations never did get paid, and she conjectures that since they could not get blood out of a stone, they eventually gave up trying to collect. An utterly honest and honourable person, Patty still regrets that she could not meet all the debts of the Harlequin Players.

Other worrisome events added to her discouragement and her growing pessimism about the chances of survival of summer theatre in Jackson's Point. Vandalism at the Red Barn had become a problem. At the beginning of each new season, the producers would find that the costume and prop rooms had been broken into and left in a mess. After the first season in 1963, the cyclorama had been taken down and stretched over the theatre seats to prevent it from wrinkling. During that winter, vandals broke in and set fire to it. Fortunately the fire was discovered before the whole building went up in flames, but the sky cloth and all the seats beneath it were burned, necessitating the purchase of a new cloth and more seats, this latter obtained from Stanley Mann, who at the time was converting the Bayview Playhouse into a legit theatre.

Fire is always a danger in even the most solidly built theatre, but in the old, dried out Red Barn, with chinks between the wallboards to encourage cooling breezes, it was a special worry. A small flame could turn into a holocaust in minutes. During a rehearsal of *Ardele*, smoke was observed in the vicinity of the electrical panel. At first faulty wiring was thought to be the cause, so the electrical system was shut off. The actors began scurrying around prepared to douse the expected flames with any means at their disposal. The smoke increased and when the firemen arrived they discovered that shutting off the electrical system had also shut off the water pump so that there was no pressure for their hoses. Water had to be obtained from a hydrant a distance away on the main road. Eventually the source of the smoke was discovered below the stage near the electrical panel in spontaneous combustion from the extreme heat of the summer's day on old pieces of wood discarded years before.[76]

Adding to Patty's growing disenchantment was the general deterioration of the barn itself. When Patty and her partners had taken over in 1963, they could not afford to repaint the fading red walls, but they did spruce the barn up by painting the trim and the window boxes white. She says that the landlord of the day claimed that he had spent a lot of money to make the structure safe when Roberts and Charlesworth took over. The parking lot had been enlarged, and an avenue of trees planted along the drive from the road. Jean and Marigold had given the lobby more rustic charm. But since then very little had been spent on the maintenance of the building so that, in a full-page spread on the Red Barn in the *Toronto Star*, Charles Gerein wrote, "The Barn is a little ramshackle. A large hole in the roof needs mending . . . and when the night wind shrieks, so does the Barn; when the hailstones fall, thunder rolls across the tin roof."[77] Added together, these obstacles forced another producer to bite the dust of the Red Barn.

■

After Patricia decided not to pick up her option for 1967, the old barn sat empty until 1968 when Jennifer Phipps and Joyce Gordon took over. They had met at the Manitoba Theatre Centre when they were playing the roles of close friends in *Summer of the Seventeenth Doll.* The onstage friendship blossomed into an offstage one, and they teamed up in 1968 to produce summer stock. Joyce was familiar with the Red Barn from having performed there as Pearl in the 1960 Red Barn production of *Summer of the Seventeenth Doll.* Jenny had attended Al Mulock's actors' workshop in London, which he founded along the lines of the Actors' Studio in New York after he had left the Red Barn in 1949. She had heard about the Red Barn from the founder himself.

Born in London, England, the daughter of a theatrical family, Jenny was building a career there when she met Winnipeger Peter Boretski, who had travelled to England in the Stratford Festival company on their trip abroad with *Oedipus* and *Henry V.* With a recommendation from Tyrone Guthrie, Peter had been accepted into the Central School of Drama in London, and while performing in *A View from the Bridge,* he met Jennifer Phipps. She persuaded him to attend Mulock's studio; Peter, in turn, persuaded her to marry him. When the Manitoba Theatre Centre was started in 1959, Peter was invited by its founders, John Hirsch and Tom Hendry, to become one of the directors in the new company. However, when he arrived with his new bride in Winnipeg, he found that the promised position was no longer available to him. Fortunately for their finances, Jenny was offered the role of Mrs. Manningham in *Gaslight.* In the autumn of 1962, Marigold Charlesworth and Jean Roberts entered into a co-production with the MTC of *Mrs. Warren's Profession,* in which Ms. Phipps played the title role. It opened under the Red Barn banner at the Central Library Theatre in Toronto in late 1962 and moved to the Manitoba Theatre Centre in early January of 1963.

By 1968, Jenny and Peter had moved to Toronto and when Jenny and

Joyce joined forces at the Red Barn, Peter was brought in as artistic director. As their financial contribution toward the launching of the season, the Boretskis borrowed $1,500 from a theatre-oriented neighbour, Harry Weston, a real estate salesman and an active member of Variety Village. The new producers had decided to continue the Barn as weekly stock, opening on Tuesday and running through Sunday at 8:30 in the evenings with no matinees. Everyone got paid $90 a week, including Joyce and Jenny, but Peter Boretski received a little more because of his responsibility as director of most of the plays. When Jack Duffy was asked to play Max Pincus in *The Fifth Season*, he agreed to minimum but was soon greatly shocked to find that the Equity minimum for stock was much lower than his accustomed television rate. Nevertheless, he was consoled somewhat by getting billing, an uncommon practice in Canadian theatre even today.[78]

After Joyce Gordon had struck a favourable deal with Mr. Gold, the Red Barn owner, they planned a season of light fare consistent with the summer stock tradition. Gino Empry, then a novice public relations man, was hired to promote the season, and Larry Stone, my ex-acting student and erstwhile drama critic, was their lawyer. Joyce's husband, Morris (Moishe) Simon, a building contractor, performed some much-needed repairs and cosmetic refurbishing of the old barn, and Peter Boretski tackled the job of re-upholstering the worn seats. They also enlarged the lobby to accommodate the opening night reception they planned in aid of Variety Village — an event that gained the company considerable publicity. They found that the sets stored in the basement were badly in need of repair as a result of vandalism and the winter weather during the year the Red Barn was closed. They even found human excrement on some of the flats, which meant scrapping most of the scenery and building anew.

The opening was *The Fantasticks* with Jack Duffy as El Gallo. As Matt they hired the handsome singer, Doug Crosley. Ken James, who had first appeared at the Red Barn in 1960, tackled the role of the Old Actor. As his sidekick, Mortimer, they drafted Gino Empry, who used the stage name of Gino Emperatori. According to witnesses he also used his large sad eyes to full effect, which rendered his performance doubly funny. As the Mute, they brought in the pint-sized actor/dancer, Durward McGimsie, who had cut his theatrical teeth with the Garden Centre Theatre in 1966. One of the assistant stage managers for this production was a young Guy Sprung, who had been on a walking trip through Canada and took the job at the Red Barn to help pay expenses. As is common knowledge among theatre folk, Mr. Sprung stopped walking, remained in Canada, and became a power in our theatre world.

The Fantasticks was followed by *The Fifth Season*, *The Mousetrap* directed by Jenny, and then *Gaslight* (a.k.a. *Angel Street*) with Jenny as Mrs. Manningham, Ken James as her conniving husband, and Peter Boretski as the detective. In a change of plans Joyce Gordon directed this one. Boretski staged the next play, Murray Schisgall's *Luv*, whose three characters were played by Jack Duffy, Ken James, and Barbara Chilcott. Then came the comedic two-hander, *A Girl Could Get Lucky* with Joyce Gordon and Ken James, also directed by Boretski. The season concluded with yet another staging of *Maria Martin, or Murder in the Red Barn*. For this the cast size jumped to 13 plus a pianist. Having played several small parts during the summer, Mr. Sprung graduated to a more prominent role as the villain, William Corder, the son of the Squire of Polestead. The story of this melodrama is based on fact. In 1827 in England, William Corder murdered Maria Martin. He was arrested, tried, found guilty, publicly hanged, and his naked body was put on view at the Court House of Bury St. Edmunds for an estimated 10,000 spectators to see. Unfortunately far fewer came to witness the story re-enacted in 1968. Perhaps if Mr. Sprung had appeared naked the box office might have been stimulated.

That season was not without its unusual incidents. The company rehearsed in the lobby because there was ample space and double doors on either side, which, when opened, allowed a breeze to blow through, welcome on swelteringly hot days. During one rehearsal for *Luv*, Ken James drove a motorcycle in one door, could not stop, roared straight through and out the other door where after a considerable drop, he and the motorbike ended up against a tree. Fortunately he was not injured but the rest of the cast were in a state of shock. After that James walked the bike in. One night the resident bat, instead of contenting itself with its usual few unnerving swoops over actors and audience, persisted in its acrobatics the whole evening, rendering rapport between actors and audience well-nigh impossible. Three days later the management learned that on the night of the bat's prolonged, erratic flight, Al Mulock had died tragically in Spain where, as the story goes, he had been performing as a stunt man for a film in which he had to leap from a window high in a building, but something went wrong with the cushioning to break his fall and he crashed to the ground with fatal results.

But the producers at the Red Barn did everything within their power to prevent their season from crashing. The residents of Jackson's Point and Sutton were assailed weekly by a sales pitch bellowed through a megaphone by one of the company as he was driven around the area. Joyce Gordon sold enough ads that extra pages had to be added to the program and a small profit resulted from her efforts. Cognizant that while waiting for the play audiences actually read the program, the producers printed bits of information about the theatre, the performers, or anything else they thought might interest and amuse. For example one program had the following: "The Red Barn Theatre dressing rooms were originally the cow stalls. No comment. Maggi Payne lives in the trailer behind the barn. The apprentices live in the chicken coops. The bats live in the belfry." Another gave this bit of Red Barn history: "1948 — The first benefit performance at the Red Barn given by Harry Belafonte. Accompanying Al Mulock and Harry Kohl, the architect, on the first visit to plan the change from barn to theatre, he sang a capella from the rafters." A non-theatrical gem of information: "To keep peanut butter on bread from sticking to the roof of your mouth turn the bread upside down." In an effort to enlighten their audience about the derivation of theatrical terminology, they explained the word "drama": "It is customary to have a dram shop in the vicinity of a theatre (as is the case in this city) where the audience, exhausted by attention to the performers, may recruit their spirits by taking a glass of gin, or something equally stimulating between the acts; and as it often happens upon drinking a dram, the person emits a sound similar to the letters "ah," the dram and the sound have been united, and thus dram-ah, or drama is found." The Oxford Dictionary, obviously erroneously, states that the word derives through Latin from the Greek "drao do." So much for the Oxford Dictionary.

Despite their efforts to keep costs down, every time Jenny and Joyce had to sign the cheques to meet the weekly payroll, they did so fearing that there might not be enough money in the bank to cover them. The box-office receipts for that season were $14,692.10. Their total revenue from all sources including loans and donations was $20,808.11. Their total disbursement before salaries to the producers, but including repayment of loans was $17,489.15. Joyce Gordon and Jennifer Phipps received $720 each for the whole summer, and Peter Boretski the staggering figure of $1,500 for directing 6 of the 8 plays ($250 per play). Talk about minimum! This was before Canadian Actors' Equity took directors under its wing. After these fees were paid there was a net profit of $378.98 that was divided equally among Joyce, Jenny, and Peter. Clearly, being a producer at the Red Barn would never lead to riches. Yet it was a credit to their artistic and management skill that they turned a profit at all on 47 per cent attendance in a theatre with a capacity of 290. Realizing that it takes time to develop a theatre-going habit in a community and apparently ignoring the fact that producers had been trying to develop such a habit in Jackson's Point for 20 years, Peter Boretski had the idea of leasing the Red Barn on a long-term basis and establishing a theatre festival that would occur annually and, he hoped, permanently. With this proposal he approached Mr. Gold who was not interested. As a result neither Boretski, Phipps, nor Gordon tackled producing at the Red Barn for another season.

▪

In a conversation with two young actors, Joyce Gordon said that the Red Barn was going to be available for the following year, and that it might be torn down if it sat empty for a season. Allan Royal and Richard Ayres, full of the enthusiasm of youth, decided to save the Red Barn and try their wings as producers. They interested Zdzislaw (Zaz) Bajon in joining them and enlisted Janet Amos, then closely associated with Mr. Royal, to be in charge of the box office. Allan became business manager and Zaz production stage manager. Richard Ayres was a 28-year-old actor originally from Hamilton, and Allan Royal was a 25-year-old from Montreal who had become stage-struck as a result of acting with his secondary school drama club, and had studied with the Canadian Drama Studio in Montreal and the Actors' Studio in New York. When he returned to Canada he worked for George Luscombe at Toronto Workshop Productions and for Theatre Toronto where he met his partners.

Richard and Zaz put up $5,000 each and Allan and Janet $5,000 between them, giving the new producers a respectable starter of $15,000. To direct four of the shows they hired Ray Lawlor, a director and producer of considerable experience at Toronto's Theatre-in-the-Dell, the Crest, the Straw Hat Players, and Theatre Toronto. He had also studied mime with Marcel Marceau. Tim Bond was hired to direct one of their shows and William Glassco was rejected as a director because of lack of experience. They felt so badly about turning him down that they advised him on how to collect unemployment insurance, unaware that Mr. Glassco never wanted for a buck. Gino Empry returned to the Red Barn as their publicity manager.

They continued the previous management's performance schedule, but they tried a different approach to ticket pricing. They divided the small house into three sections with different prices. Single tickets were $2, $2.50, and $3 Tuesday through Thursday and Sunday matinee, but on Friday and Saturday the price increased by 50 cents across the board. They offered season subscriptions for 8 shows at $14, $17.50, and $21 Tuesday through Thursday and on Sundays, but on Fridays and Saturdays the subscription price was $17.50, $21, and $24.50. Very modest prices for an evening's entertainment even in 1969. The plays they decided to stage were with one exception still in the vein of light summer fare.

But before opening date there were several ominous events. During the pre-season preparations the producers were driving to Jackson's Point in a pick-up truck carrying equipment and supplies. Among the cargo were an electrical dimmer board and several large containers of paint. One of the tins overturned, the lid popped off and brown paint poured over the dimmer board and out of the truck, leaving a trail on the highway and roads of Jackson's Point. The more serious result was it took many hours of labour to restore the dimmer to working condition.

Later, on a fine June day, some of the company, including Zaz, Janet, Allan Royal, and several of the nubile female apprentices were sunning themselves on a dock at Lake Simcoe. Allan, with an eye to impressing the young ladies, suddenly got up, walked to the edge of the dock, and, glancing over his shoulder to see if they were watching, executed a beautiful swan dive to a chorus of "Allan! No!" from the horrified spectators into two feet of water. His head struck the bottom and was momentarily buried in the sand, gravel, and sludge while his legs flailed the air awkwardly. He managed to right himself and standing in water that did not reach his knees tried to re-assure his concerned companions that he was all right until he noticed blood streaming down his face. He had certainly impressed the young ladies and all present. He was hustled off to a doctor for stitches and his aquatic display became a joke for the rest of the summer.[79]

An even more serious accident occurred only two days before the season opening. Allan, Richard, and Zaz were driving to Toronto in Richard's tiny MG for a publicity interview. Zaz and Allan had a friendly shoving match to see who would sit in the one passenger seat. Zaz lost and had to settle for the small shelf seat in the rear, where he curled up beneath the canvas tarp covering it so he was protected from sun and wind. As they were driving down highway 48 at the speed limit, a truck pulled out of a concealed lane directly in front of them. Richard swung the MG so that it hit the rear wheel of the truck or they would have gone directly under its side and probably both would have been decapitated. This being the pre-seat belt era, Allan's head went through the windshield and the steering wheel jammed into Richard's chest pinning him in the car. Zaz unzipped the canvas and was horrified to see Allan's blood all over the dashboard and the shattered windshield. Allan's scalp had been peeled back by the broken glass. He was rushed to the Newmarket hospital where a doctor, upon learning that Allan was an actor, told him that instead of about 25 stitches, in this case he would put in 60 so that there would be no scar. And miraculously, there was no scar to disfigure this handsome young actor. Also fortunately, Richard Ayres had suffered no serious injury. Two days later they opened *The Odd Couple*. Allan had only a small part in the play, but he worried that his accident could have affected his memory and that he would not remember his lines. Fortunately that did not prove to be the case.

The season began propitiously otherwise on a solid base of subscribers and good individual ticket sales. For the first two shows they operated in the black. Allan was sufficiently encouraged that he gave the actors a bonus, much to Zaz's dismay, who, as production stage manager, was pinching pennies to get the shows mounted. It was the third play that dealt them a blow from which they never fully recovered. Although John Sibbald no longer owned the Red Barn, he considered he had the right to read all the plays because of the package deal between the producers and himself on behalf of his hotel guests at the Briars. He read *You Know I Can't Hear You When the Water's Running* and advised the young producers not to present it. But, because it had been a rave success in New York, and because they felt that it contained subject matter that ought to be presented to the public, and because they were young and inexperienced and protective of their "art," they ignored his advice.

The play consists of four one-acts by Robert Anderson, a playwright with several hits to his credit, the most celebrated being *Tea and Sympathy*. The first of this quartet is a debate between a talent agent and a playwright that includes much reference to the male genitalia and their functions, and to the taboo of displaying them onstage. There is an almost complete male striptease performed in an embarrassed fashion by an actor seeking work through the agent. The producers decided to drop this one-act from their production. The second play takes place in a furniture store where a married couple are about to buy twin beds to replace the double bed they have shared for 25 years. The husband wants to retain the double bed because he is worried that with separate beds their now-tepid sex life will diminish even more. This leads to a discussion of sex in general and their own sex life in particular with much recrimination by both parties. At the end he switches his support to twin beds because, we are led to believe, he is planning an adulterous affair with a young woman he has just met in the store. In the third play a middle-class married couple argue heatedly about parental responsibility. The bitchy duo accuse each other of failure in dealing with their daughter's growing involvement with boys and their younger son's increasing fondness for masturbation. In the end they receive a letter from their elder son who renounces college and denounces his parents' lifestyle and attitudes. The fourth play, the only up-beat one, is a very amusing duo-logue between an elderly couple, both of whom suffer from Alzheimer's. They cannot remember each other's names and get their reminiscences all mixed up, but they are fond of each other. Anderson held a serious belief that these subjects were too long taboo and should now be accepted for discussion by the public. Well, perhaps the New York public but not the Red Barn's public. Even with the first play omitted, the second and third proved an anathema to their audience. On opening night incensed customers walked out and demanded their money back. During that week subscribers cancelled their subscriptions. One man came to the box office with requests for cancellation from 80 subscribers.[80] From being in the black for the first two shows, the operation now plummeted into the red for most of the remainder of the season. The producers watched their $15,000 nest egg dwindle away. Only with the last two shows did business pick up again, but not enough to recoup the losses.

But all was not disagreeable that summer. Allan Royal remembers the night during the run of *Goodbye Charley* that the Apollo space astronauts landed on the moon. During the intermission, cast, crew, and audience began watching this momentous event on a television in the lobby. The coverage lasted for several hours and the audience could not be persuaded to return to the auditorium until it was over. Nor did management mind because the concession stand in the lobby was doing a humming business. When the telecast concluded, the audience happily returned to the show. That night the final curtain came down after 1 a.m.

The young producers' idealism, their misplaced faith in the wisdom and tolerance of their public, and their own lack of theatrical savvy combined to do them in. At the end of the season a further $10,000 had to be found. During the next year they worked until every creditor was paid.[81] But they had learned a lot. One of the things they learned was not to return to produce at the Red Barn. Ray Lawlor eventually left the professional theatre and lives a rural existence in Loretto, Ontario. Richard Ayres also left show business for the greater security of photography at which he has excelled. Janet Amos has had an outstanding career as a performer and artistic director. Zaz Bajon and Allan Royal also stuck with the theatre. Zaz became one of the most successful and sought-after general managers in Canadian theatre with a long tenure at the Manitoba Theatre Centre, and Allan pursued an acting career that took him to Hollywood where he appeared on TV and in films. He returned to Canada to perform in the television series *Night Heat* and now he divides his time between Hollywood and Toronto, and professes to have fond memories of that 1969 summer at the Red Barn in spite of the fact that he lost his savings, almost drowned, and was nearly scalped.

When the young director who had been turned down by the producers in the 1969 season heard that they would not be returning to the Red Barn for 1970, he jumped at the chance to take it over. The son of a wealthy business family, William Glassco was born in Quebec and raised in the elegant Forest Hill area of Toronto. He received degrees at Princeton and Oxford and became a lecturer in English at the University of Toronto, but he grew dissatisfied with the prospect of a lifetime of teaching. So in 1968 he enrolled in a theatre arts course at New York University. His first employment as a director was in 1969 at the St. Lawrence Summer Playhouse, a part amateur and part professional company. He then directed *The Odd Couple* in Cobourg. When the Red Barn became free, he decided to produce a season there for experience and to give himself a higher profile in the profession. He invested his own money plus some from family members, and with an eye to the future, formed a limited company in case he wanted to produce in some other location where he could not use the name Red Barn Theatre. His banking advisor told him to choose a name that would not likely have duplicates. He liked salads so he thought of using the name of a seasoning. "Parsley Productions" is one name he came up with, but because he was partial to tarragon he sent that name off to his banker. A year later when he and his wife Jane decided to open a theatre on Bridgeman Street in Toronto, he wanted to avoid names similar to "Factory Theatre Lab" and "Toronto Workshop Productions." He toyed with "Bridgeman Place of Dreams," "The Sidecar Theatre," and "Magic Theatre," but settled on "Tarragon Theatre" much against Brian Doherty's advice. To Glassco the name suggested something more than a place of brick and concrete where people laboured to churn out stage productions. To me it suggests a mildly zestful theatre with good taste.

But for summer 1970, "Tarragon" was not used publicly. Mr. Glassco operated under the banner of the Red Barn Theatre. He retained Zaz Bajon as his production manager, and unfamiliar with Canadian designers at that time, he imported a student friend from Buffalo, Steven Feldman, as designer. As business manager he employed Stephen Nathanson, a University of Toronto law student. William's wife, Jane, handled public relations but also proved herself to be a careful administrator. They formed an impressive production and managerial team.

The program contained some plays that were not the usual summer fare, among them *Black Comedy* by the English Peter Shaffer, Molière's *The Hypochondriac* adapted by Graham Jackson, *Lovers* by the Irish playwright Brian Friel, Noel Coward's *Fallen Angels*, Patrick Hamilton's *Gaslight* adapted to a Toronto setting by Graham Jackson, and *The Owl and the Pussy Cat* by another American, Bill Manhoff. Glassco directed five of the plays himself, but, for the first show, *Black Comedy*, he brought in Brian Meeson with whom he had worked in the summer of 1968 when they presented three plays at 11 Trinity Square using university students. Larry Ewashen directed the third and sixth shows, *Barefoot in the Park* and *Fallen Angels*. Glassco was able to obtain a nucleus of quality performers with other equally stage-worthy actors jobbed in as required. Those appearing most frequently that summer were David Hemblen, his wife, Lynne, and Robin Craig, then known as Robin Cameron. Brought in to play salient roles were Jimmy Douglas, Betty Leighton, Geoffrey Saville-Read, Jackie Burroughs, Mia Anderson, Joyce Gordon, and Walter Massey — a covey of highly skilled performers.

Glassco retained the policy of performing Tuesday through Sunday, but returned to a two-tier subscription of $17 and $21, except for Saturday when prices increased. Business was very encouraging for the first three shows, but as in the previous summer, attendance dropped after that. *Lovers* was not popular but unlike the previous year, the audience returned for the last part of the season. The result was only a small financial loss. Although far from disappointed both artistically and financially, Bill and Jane Glassco decided not to return to the Red Barn. They had enjoyed their first excursion into production and had learned a lot, but felt that they could not learn much more from another season of summer stock. Bill had established his credentials as a producer and director and at the end of the 1970 summer season had become known in the Toronto theatre world. He was now ready to launch himself in that city. That happened in 1971 when the space on Bridgeman Street became available. The Glasscos took it and established "Tarragon Theatre" and, to use a much over-worked phrase, but an apt one, the rest is history.

▪

Because I have ended my history at approximately 1970, the continuing saga of the Red Barn Theatre will have to wait for some future chronicle. But, briefly, in 1973 it was threatened with demolition by a new owner who wanted to build houses on the site. It was rescued by the establishment of the Lake Simcoe Arts Foundation through which John Sibbald has exercised an increased influence. Since 1970, the artistic standard has fluctuated widely with a blend of amateurs and professionals. But the Red Barn still provides entertainment for the summer residents of Jackson's Point and for the patrons of the Briars in particular. When one considers the remarkable talent that has been there, the old Red Barn Theatre should be declared an historic site and preserved for posterity.

PRUDHOMME'S GARDEN CENTRE THEATRE

presents

EDWARD EVERETT HORTON

in

"SPRINGTIME FOR HENRY"

BY BENN W. LEVY

with

MOYA	VERNON	TERRY
FENWICK	CHAPMAN	CLEMES

Settings by JACK McADAM   Lighting by VERNON JEFFREY

DIRECTED BY ROBERT HERRMAN

*   *   *   *   *

THE CAST
(in order of appearance)

A Secretary .... Milo Ringhame

Mr. Dewlip .... EDWARD EVERETT HORTON

Mr. Jelliwell .... Vernon Chapman

Mrs. Jelliwell .... Moya Fenwick

Miss Smith .... Terry Clemes

*   *   *   *   *

THE SCENE
The action of the play takes place in the sitting room of Mr. Dewlip's flat.

ACT 1
Morning

ACT 2
Evening, three months later

ACT 3
Eleven o'clock the next morning

★   ★   ★

SMOKING PERMITTED ONLY IN THE LOBBY

CHAPTER 18

Return to the Fruits

In early spring 1959, an American phoned me explaining that he was about to produce summer theatre in my old stomping ground, the Prudhommes' Garden Centre. He had learned from Larry McCance that I had been there in 1954, so he invited me to the Lord Simcoe Hotel to tell him about the Vineland area and the people's attitude to legitimate theatre. I had heard that the Prudhommes had greatly expanded their complex since the year before, doubtless using the insurance money in the new construction, which included a new theatre. While not exactly thrilled that this theatre had fallen into the hands of an American rather than a Canadian producer, I thought it courteous and expedient to meet him. It turned out to be one of the most beneficial meetings of my career. Robert Herrman was among the most open-hearted men I have ever met, and something of a phenomenon in this world of ostentatious theatre folk — a modest actor. He had no affectation whatever, and he possessed a disarming sense of humour, especially about himself. He recognized and appreciated talent in others and never showed any sign of jealousy or envy toward people who were more gifted than he. Extremely gregarious, slim, and handsome, he loved people, especially women, and enjoyed a good party.

I was astonished to learn how much he knew about me, about roles performed and shows directed, much of it no doubt gleaned from Larry McCance. In turn I learned that Herrman was born and raised in New York

City, yet had no hint of a New Yorkese dialect. I also learned that he had served in the American army during the war, and had subsequently toured with a play that he loved very much, *Mr. Roberts*, often playing the title role. He had a young son, Brad, who had appeared on TV in the U.S., a younger daughter, Susie, and a wife, Terry Clemes, who was also an actor. In 1958 he had directed for the pre-fire producer of the Garden Centre Theatre, Nat Godwin, and had saved enough money to launch himself as a producer. He saw the creation of the new theatre at Prudhommes' as a golden opportunity. To my amazement, without asking me for any audition pieces or even to read anything, he offered me several roles during the summer season that would keep me in bread for three months, an offer I accepted with alacrity. I left his hotel room on cloud nine.

But that afternoon I was brought down to earth. I had been asked by Murray Davis to audition for *The Doctor's Dilemma*. Unreasonable though it may seem, I somewhat resented this because I had twice performed for the Crest. I figured that they knew the calibre of my work and that I ought not be obliged to audition. However, because it was for a director unfamiliar with my work, I swallowed my pride and went along to read. But, following my red carpet treatment by an American, I was in a resentful mood when I entered the Crest. I was greeted by the young director who asked me to go up onto the stage and instructed me to read a speech of one of the doctors. I did so. Then he requested that I read a speech of another doctor, and after that, still another. I tried vocally to differentiate the characters of Sir Colenso Ridgeon, Sir Patrick Cullen, and Cutler Walpole, who was the closest to my own age. As I kept reading more speeches, I grew even more resentful, and when he suggested that I read a speech in a different way, I bristled and blurted out, "Well I'll read it that way if you like. But it will be wrong." No sooner had these words popped out than I realized that it was a tactless and insulting thing to say. The audition was abruptly concluded. Leon Major eventually became a television director, the artistic director of Neptune Theatre and Theatre Toronto, and has directed many productions in theatres across Canada. Needless to say, he never asked me to perform in any of his shows. I wonder why?

The new Garden Centre Theatre was the lakeside appendage of the recently built T-shaped, two-storey motel on the north of the Queen Elizabeth Highway just east of the Vineland sideroad. Since I had worked there, the Prudhomme empire had indeed expanded. There were three times as many rooms in the main building plus another group of rooms in separate buildings behind it. In addition to a coffee shop, the complex now had a large dining room, a cocktail lounge, an enlarged kitchen, a ballroom, both indoor and outdoor swimming pools, a bowling alley, a garden store, a gift shop, even a small zoo, and last but not least, the new ugly 916-seat theatre that could be converted into a curling rink during the winter. The Prudhomme Construction Company had been prominently involved in the creation of this rambling assemblage of unimaginatively functional structures. The unattractive wooden beams in the theatre/curling rink were made of sections of two-by-four bolted together, which were in turn attached together with more bolts and steel plates. The auditorium's raked floor consisted of plywood on trestles with carpeted aisles. These were removed in the winter and the permanent floor below flooded and frozen to create a curling rink. This monotonously grey structure had little of the atmosphere of a bona fide theatre, but it had some advantages. The sight lines were good, the acoustics adequate, and despite a woefully small air conditioning system, it was cool on hot summer nights. But this luxury was not available backstage. The dressing rooms, under the flat tar-paper roof, could become insufferably hot. Electric fans were much in use.

There was no control booth at the back of the elongated auditorium, so the stage manager had to function in the old fashioned way from the wings. The dressing rooms were strategically placed on either side of the stage and, except for a small one to house the visiting celebrity, were communal. Above one of the dressing rooms stage left was a small room that held the light and sound boards. Above the stage right dressing rooms was a storage area for costumes and props. The workshops were in the damp basement below the stage. All this was far from luxurious, but workable and more comfortable than the previous Garden Centre Theatre or that offered by the Red Barn or the La Salle Ballroom and Memorial Hall in Kingston.

Under Robert Herrman the Garden Centre Theatre was tied to the American summer theatre circuit, which functioned for the most part on the "star" system. International celebrities appeared in plays or musicals designed to display their particular talents. A few of these were real theatre stars but mostly they were merely meteors, flashes from the world of television and film whose light soon faded and who operated on the principle of making hay while still holding some box-office drawing power. At the Garden Centre, I was to meet some of the former, charming performers who were delighted to be acting onstage, but also some monsters on ego trips who were chagrined at having to demean themselves to make a buck on the summer touring circuit.

Most summer theatres, then as now, depend on the apprentice system to obtain willing workers for the many joe-jobs and to fill in the smaller roles for next to no pay. In exchange they receive experience, in some cases formal training, credits for their résumé, and credits toward their membership in Equity, who allows these theatres a percentage of non-Equity personnel. Some of the summer theatres in the United States extract a fee from these eager neophytes in exchange for training, but others charge a fee with no formal training offered. Robert Herrman gave free room and board to the apprentices, and organized acting classes for them, until the pressures of mounting a new show every week rendered that impractical.

The "apprenti" were billeted in two large dormitories, one for males and one for females, in the Prudhommes' large, colonial style, erstwhile family homestead with its view of Lake Ontario from the front porch. They ate their free meals at a special table set up in the large kitchen of the motel, and, from the reports I received, ate rather well. The huge frame house also accommodated the paid acting and technical members of the company. Whenever I was engaged at the Garden Centre Theatre I delighted in being "in residence." The rooms were private and cosy, with a shared bathroom for every two rooms. On the main floor was a comfortable lounge, ideal for parties. The salaried employees had to eat in the motel's coffee shop or in the dining room where the food was far from *haute cuisine*, but it was adequate. The prices were reasonable, and, because Bob Herrman paid me a respectable salary, I did not find this a hardship. In fact I discovered that I was paid a higher fee than most of the supporting actors at the Stratford Festival. The residence became a focal point for much of the extra-curricular social activity, especially open-air barbecues, weiner and corn roasts on the beach late at night, and other pleasurable activities of a non-theatrical nature that have no rightful place in this narrative.

In an effort to lure locals and persuade tourists staying at the motel to take in the show, Herrman worked an arrangement with John Prudhomme for a package of $5 per person for a smorgasbord dinner and show Mondays through Thursdays and $5.50 on Fridays and Saturdays. Theatre tickets were a reasonable $1.50, $2, and $2.50 Monday through Thursday and $2, $2.50, and $3 Friday and the second show Saturday night. There was an early 6 p.m. show on Saturday with all seats rush at $1.50. Because it was to be a season stretching almost four months, the producer offered a subscription of five plays for $12.50 for the best seats, which entitled purchasers to see a sixth play of their choice for free.

The whole operation was set up on a thoroughly professional basis and had all the earmarks of being successful. Tickets were sold at the theatre and at agencies in Niagara Falls, Ontario, St. Catharines, Hamilton, Toronto, Welland, Buffalo, and Niagara Falls, New York. Herrman brought in an experienced business manager from a theatre in Michigan. His production stage manager was Henry Velez from New York, with whom I had worked in the International Players years before. The designer Robert DeMora was also American with Canadian Paul Swayze as his assistant. There was a complete backstage staff of qualified technicians plus assistants, some of whom were apprentices. I was very optimistic about that first season under Bob's guidance. Because the previous theatre had burned while *Cat on a Hot Tin Roof* was playing, Bob decided to open on June 15, 1959 with the same play. But it fell far short of the standard I had expected. When E.H. (Betty) Lampard from the *St. Catharines Standard*, who had become an astute critic, referred to it as "turgid," my optimism faltered.

I had been hired for the second show, *Happy Birthday*, starring Ann B. Davis, famous as the loveable comic maid "Schultzie" on the Bob Cummings television show, for which she had won an Emmy. Miss Davis proved to be a pleasure to work with. She had fun performing and that communicated to her fellow performers and to the audience. She had begun her career as a child performer in a puppet show and learned her craft at the Erie Playhouse in Erie, Pennsylvania and on tour in a variety of roles before she found TV stardom. She was a very unselfish performer and did not mind when other actors carried off the comedy laurels, as was the case with Helene Winston, whom I had persuaded Bob to hire, and Betty Riley as the two inebriate regulars of the Jersey Mecca Cocktail Bar in Newark. Because of my familiarity with the Toronto performers pool, for the first year Bob relied on me to help him cast. His desire was to use as many Canadian performers as possible. Another actor I introduced to the Garden Centre Theatre was Ed Holmes after his involvement with Stratford during the Guthrie regime. Also in the cast of *Happy Birthday* was Sylvia Shawn as the tough proprietress of the bar. She was just beginning her career, after studying at the Neighbourhood Playhouse and performing in summer stock companies in the United States. Sylvia was to make a distinct contribution to the Toronto theatre scene as a producer, particularly of revues at the Dell Tavern in Toronto.

I played the male lead, a bank clerk, the first of many stiff and stuffy roles I performed at the GCT. Much of the success of light comedies, which became the bulk of the fare at Vineland, depends on the supporting characters, among whom there is invariably a pompous, overly confident prude or a Mr. Milquetoast who either carries much of the humour himself or serves as the straight man for the leading character. Although in real life these people for the most part are monumentally dull, in the theatre the trick is to make them interesting and entertaining. In the movies, Franklin Pangborn and Edward Everett Horton were past masters at meeting that challenge. I proved to be quite proficient too, so much so that I became, in Bob's phrase, "his resident stuffed shirt." But in *Happy Birthday* perhaps I was too "stuffed." The critics for both the *Hamilton Spectator*[1] and the *St. Catharines Standard*[2] thought that I was too proper to be found in such a crummy joint — a point well taken, but you never know what sort of people go slumming. In spite of mixed reviews, *Happy Birthday* succeeded where *Cat on a Hot Tin Roof* had failed: gaining audience enthusiasm. Ann B. Davis's name and word-of-mouth publicity drew large numbers of local residents and tourists to the Garden Centre.

It looked like a successful season would ensue after all. When a touring show cancelled, Bob decided to produce a musical locally with an all-Canadian cast and chose *Say Darling*, which had enjoyed a moderately successful Broadway run in 1958 largely due to the presence of Robert Morse. Toronto-born Jack Duffy played our lead role. Sharing the limelight were the incomparable Sammy Sales, the supremely talented, leggy musical comedy performer Sandra O'Neill, and the pert singer-dancer, Marylyn Stuart. I played a character with the unlikely name of Morty Krebs.

Jack Duffy had begun his career singing radio commercials. He formed his own vocal group and, while performing at Toronto's Club Norman, was noticed by another Toronto singer of international repute, Ruth Lowe, the composer of the hit song "I'll Never Smile Again." She recommended Duffy's group to Tommy Dorsey in whose band Duffy became a favourite because many people heard a similarity in his vocal style with that of Frank Sinatra. He returned to Canada to appear on the Billy O'Connor television show with Juliet, and eventually had his own variety show on TV. When Bob offered him the lead in *Say Darling*, he jumped at the chance to gain acting experience, even though it meant plunging into the frenetic madness of preparing a musical in six days. Because of other commitments he had to drive between Toronto and Prudhommes' every day. By opening night he was exhausted and he felt that he was performing like a puppet. But with opening night over, he relaxed successfully into the role. Mr. Duffy subsequently played at the Red Barn and in several *Spring Thaws*. A happy result for him from *Say Darling* was that he met Marylyn Stuart who eventually became Mrs. Duffy.[3]

In contrast to *Say Darling* with its seven different scenes and 27 performers, *Champagne Complex* had only three actors and a dog, all of whom received critical and public acclaim — particularly the dog. The stars were Peggy King and John Emery. I was the stuffy suitor who does not get the girl. Miss King excelled as a pop singer. She had made her mark on the George Gobel TV show where "lonesome George" constantly referred to her as "pretty, perky Peggy King," which she hated. She was pretty and petite, which suited the role, but with an equally petite acting ability, her performance consisted of much hair tossing and swishing of skirts. The smooth, urbane John Emery, in the role of her psychiatrist/lover, was a veteran of stage, screen, and Tallulah Bankhead's boudoir, but by then he was divorced from that volcanic personality. A thorough professional, he was a joy to play comedy with, and, along with Bob Herrman, we worked out a fight scene that was a slapstick parody of all movie fisticuffs. I suspect Miss King felt a bit left out, particularly since most of the comedy was given to the two males who sparred over her. But all three of us had to tolerate the scene-stealing of the poodle, Champagne Charlie.

The next show, Ben Hecht and Charles MacArthur's brilliant comedy *Twentieth Century*, gave me one of the most unnerving experiences of my career. The play is set in a pullman coach on the Twentieth Century train travelling between New York and Chicago sometime in the 1920s and 1930s. A great theatrical impresario, Oscar Jaffe, modelled on a combination of the high priest of Broadway, David Belasco, and the Napoleon of Broadway, Jed Harris, is travelling with an entourage of minions. Now down on his luck, Jaffe must find a new vehicle to restore his fortunes. He hears that an ex-protégé, Lily Garland, whom he had rescued from burlesque and who had gone on to Broadway stardom, is also travelling on the train. The plot consists of his efforts to persuade her to return to work for him, and her efforts to resist his inducements. Ann Corio was aptly cast as the ex-burlesque queen. Ms. Corio had raised striptease to a high art and had been one of the biggest box-office attractions in burlesque. From there she had moved on to appear in films and became known as the "Queen of the Quickies" because of the rapidity with which these films were ground out. She said, "They didn't want them good — they wanted them Tuesday." She also branched out to legitimate theatre and discovered that she had a considerable talent as an actress in roles such as Anna Lucasta, Sadie Thompson in *Rain*, and Maggie in *Cat on a Hot Tin Roof.* In 1959 she was touring the summer circuit with Allen Jenkins in *Twentieth Century*.

Jenkins was a familiar face to movie-goers of the '30s, '40s, and '50s with an "also ran" to his credit in 150 films. Something of a sourpuss, he played gruff, sardonic characters mostly in comedies, and had developed a technique of talking out of the corner of his mouth. In this production he played the major supporting role of Owen O'Malley. I was cast as Oliver Webb, and modelled my performance on the unsmiling, cigar-butt-chomping, snarlingly flat-voiced Hollywood character actor, Ned Sparks, born Edward Sparkman in St. Thomas, Ontario. Cast as Jaffe, the male lead, was a rail-thin, ascetic, vegetarian, transplanted-to-Toronto English actor, Carey Nairnes, sometimes known as Richmond Nairnes, depending on his mood. This appeared to be perfect casting because he had a rich voice and a grand manner ideal for the role.

Rehearsals began smoothly enough even though other commitments prevented Allen Jenkins from joining us until the Sunday before our Monday opening. Actually, this did not pose much of a problem because all of the action took place in the pullman compartments and movements were minimal, although the rest of us knew we would have to adjust rapidly to his interpretation and delivery. Ann Corio was friendly, had a healthy sense of humour, especially about herself, and even though she had played the role before, was willing to take direction. All the cast took an instant liking to her. But weekly stock can be a nightmare for those without the technique of learning lines quickly. I was playing in *Champagne Complex* at night as well as rehearsing eight hours during the day. After the performance, we invariably repaired to the bar for an unwinding drink, or two, or three. Then it was home to bed where I would spend an hour with the script, which was also beside me at breakfast, lunch, and dinner, until I had control of the lines. Early in my days with the International Players I had learned not only to commit the words to memory, but also the idea behind the line, so that if the exact word escaped me, I could put the idea into my own words and, hopefully, come up with the cue for the other actors. Sometimes when working from "sides" the cue was the only part of your lines the other actor had in his or her script. Unfortunately Carey Nairnes did not learn quickly. He had been eking out a living as an acting teacher in Toronto and had not performed onstage for some time. His parsimonious vegetarian diet had left him without much stamina. By the Wednesday rehearsal it was clear that he was having difficulty memorizing a part that talks incessantly and dominates the proceedings. We were all supportive of him, especially Ann Corio who even rehearsed with him evenings in her spare time in her motel room. When we learned this, some of us hoped that if we went up on our lines, we too might be asked to spend an evening with the gorgeous Ms. Corio. But no such luck.

By Saturday before opening, Carey seemed to have the task in hand, but Allen Jenkins's arrival on Sunday had an unnerving effect. Apparently Carey misread in Jenkins's dour attitude a silent scorn for himself. Sunday night's dress was a discouraging affair, but by the Monday afternoon rehearsal Carey appeared to have control of his memory, and our hopes rose again. The action of *Twentieth Century* moves from one compartment of the sleeping car to another, and to a section of the observation car, the luxurious atmosphere of which was captured by Robert DeMora's realistic set. Oscar's compartment was at one end and Lily Garland's at the opposite. The members of Oscar's entourage occupied compartments between.

During the first act Oscar had a scene with me in my compartment. Everything was going smoothly when I saw panic on his face and he jumped into the dialogue of a scene I had with him in the second act. By switching my speeches around and by saying some of his lines for him I managed to get him back on track and he weathered the rest of the scene. There are two characters in the play listed as First and Second Beard who are visiting actors from *The Passion Play* staged at Oberammergau in Germany. Tom Kneebone, who played Second Beard, recalls that on opening night Carey skipped the cue for their entrance in the first scene and they did not appear until a short scene they had in the third act when the audience hadn't the faintest idea who they were.[4] Toward the end of the second act, which Carey ploughed through with the aid of his fellow actors, Oscar confronts Lily in her compartment to persuade her, despite a falling out they had had some years before, to star in his next show. Oscar barges in, and after a few sparring preliminaries, he launches into a long speech detailing his plans for the show in which he wants her to appear. He tells her he plans to do *The Passion Play* with her as Mary Magdalene. He will have 100 camels and sand brought over from the Holy Land. There will be a Babylonian banquet that Mary will give her lover, Pontius Pilate, during which she will be covered in emeralds from head to foot. When the Emperor Nero offers her half his empire, she will reply with a "speech that is probably the greatest piece of literature ever written." And he goes on telling her more of the wondrous plans he has for the production.

But on that fateful opening night, when Carey entered Lily's compartment, the sight of a defiantly cool Ann Corio sitting there overwhelmed him, and after stumbling through a few of the lines he stopped cold. The pause seemed interminable and then Ann spoke: "I suppose you have come here to persuade me to appear in your next show, have you, Oscar?" Carey summoned up a "Yes, Lily." There was another pause. Miss Corio ended it with, "I know Oscar. You are going to do *The Passion Play*, aren't you Oscar?" "Yes, Lily," he replied. Another pause. Hoping to lead him back onto the track, Corio picked up again: "And you want me to play Mary Magdalene, don't you Oscar?" "Yes, Lily." Shorter pause. "You are going to have a desert scene with a hundred camels and real sand brought over from the Holy Land, aren't you Oscar?" "Yes, Lily." "There is going to be a Babylonian banquet scene, isn't there, Oscar?" "Yes, Lily." By this time the audience had caught on to what was happening and began to snigger. "And I'm going to be covered in emeralds from head to foot, aren't I Oscar?" "Yes, Lily." In this way Ms. Corio managed to list most of the ideas Oscar had for his extravaganza. At the end of it she sighed a great sigh and stopped. Then, in a panic to break the louring silence Carey remembered the one line he should not have. He rampaged, "I made you. I taught you everything you know: your voice, your walk, your cheap little talent — they're mine. I gave them to you! I gave up everything to breathe them into you! Even your name — Lily Garland — I gave you that. Well, as there is a God in Heaven, Mildred Platka, you'll end up where you belong — in the burlesque houses!" Whereupon Ann Corio turned to the audience and said, "And I wish to God

I was back there now." The audience collapsed in gales of laughter.

I was waiting outside the door to knock and enter. I realized that my cue might not be forthcoming, so I decided to rescue Oscar. I knocked, entered, and pulled Carey out into the corridor, cutting the remainder of the scene he had with Ms. Corio. Haltingly we staggered through the final moments of the act. I was never so glad to see a curtain close. We led Carey off to the wings where the stage manager put him on a chair. He was dazed. He was given coffee. I told the stage manager that this man could not go on. But after a 10-minute rest, Carey, in the best "show must go on" tradition, insisted on tackling the third act. His most taxing speech was over. The curtain opened on the third act with Oscar and Owen O'Malley (Jenkins) in O'Malley's compartment, and I, once again waiting unseen in the corridor outside the compartment door. Oscar began a speech to O'Malley but as it slowly petered out, I heard Jenkins say, "Oscar's going . . . he's going." Then a thud. "He's gone." Jenkins then turned to the audience and said, "Ladies and gentlemen, this man is exhausted after the strain of learning this heavy part in five days. We will ring down the curtain and let you know in a few minutes what will happen. Stage manager, the curtain."

The curtain closed quickly and Allen and I carried Carey to a couch in the wings where he lay eyes wide open. I waved my hand before them. He did not blink. He was in a cataleptic trance. No one could get through to him. Nathan Cohen was in the opening night audience and upon Carey's collapse had rushed to the box office and urged them to call a doctor. He then came backstage and on seeing me asked me a question that revealed how out of touch critics can be with the realities of life in the theatre: "Don't you have an understudy?" "Nat," I replied, "This is summer stock. You're just not supposed to get sick." He stood over the prone, dazed actor and kept muttering incredulously, "The poor bastard. The poor bastard."

After quick consultation, Bob Herrman and the cast decided to continue with the stage manager reading Oscar's lines. Allen was deputized to announce that to the audience and to offer anyone who wished to leave either a refund or a ticket for another performance. Nobody left. People were too intrigued to see how we would cope and were excited to have been part of the unexpected drama of the evening. Now the whole cast was on edge and when the curtain opened on the third act we were so shaken and insecure that in the first scene in Oscar's compartment we were all clustered around the stage manager reading our lines over his shoulder. Somehow we managed to get through the act during which the doctor arrived and administered a sedative to Carey who was then taken to his room where he slept for 12 hours. When the full impact hit me of the actor's nightmare that Carey had been through, I became so upset that I got in my car to unwind and drove and drove, finding myself hours later miles away at Port Dover on Lake Erie.

We discovered that Carey had scarcely slept during the week of rehearsal. He rehearsed for eight hours during the day, then again in the evening with Ann Corio, after which he would stay up to all hours of the morning trying desperately to get control of his lines. Panic took hold of him on opening night and as the play progressed he became more and more insecure until the combination of mental and physical exhaustion, plus a desire to escape from a deteriorating situation, brought on his collapse. I had dinner with him on the day of the second performance. He felt badly "about letting the rest of us down" as he put it. I assured him that we all understood the pressure he had been under. I did my best to encourage him by trying to convince him how right he was for the role, that Allen Jenkins was really a nice guy, and that he, Carey, could act the rest of us off the stage. I like to think that my words had a beneficial effect, but I expect it was because Carey approached the Tuesday night performance refreshed and more relaxed that he got through it successfully. As the week progressed he became more and more in control, and by the final performance his portrayal walked off with the acting laurels. Unfortunately the critics saw only his opening night performance, and Nat Cohen, although meaning well, wrote a sob-sister story in the *Star* that destroyed Carey's career in Toronto. Having read that he had difficulty memorizing, no producer would hire him. Shortly after that Carey departed for the United States. A few years later I accidentally met him in the El Greco gallery of the Metropolitan Museum in New York. He had resumed his career as a teacher and loved living in the Big Apple. A year or so later he returned to Toronto in triumph in the touring company of the

Noel Coward musical *The Girl Who Came to Supper* at the O'Keefe Centre in which, as the valet of a Carpathian prince, he stole every scene he was in. The story has a happy ending, but I still get chills when I remember Carey Nairnes suffering through the actualization of the "Actor's Nightmare."

My next assignment, directing "the mouth" Joe E. Brown in *Father of the Bride* was an almost equally trying job. Certainly it was not a pleasant experience. Mr. Brown's reputation as an irritable, selfish egotist had preceded him. Before he arrived I gathered the cast and crew together and told them that although Mr. Brown had a reputation for being difficult, we must treat him with respect because he had been a famous Hollywood movie star and had entertained millions of people. I wanted to add that, although I had seen him in several films, he had never entertained me, but restrained myself. I had always found his movies hugely unfunny until I saw him as the eccentric millionaire in *Some Like it Hot*. But that was a few years later.

I knew I was going to have trouble when he challenged the very first position I blocked him into. The play opens with the bride's father reading a newspaper at the breakfast table. Because of the sightlines in our house, I decided to seat him at the right end of the table stage right to get him a hearty round of applause when he lowered the newspaper that had been concealing his face. This would have been tantamount to "making an entrance" and the whole audience would have seen him simultaneously. But his long stage career before he began making movies had left him with the old stager's notion that the most important position is centre stage. He refused to accept my direction. I explained my reasoning but he remained adamant, and because he was accustomed to opening the show from centre stage, I agreed. The result was as I expected. At every performance when the curtain opened the part of the audience who could see him applauded, while the rest wondered what they were applauding. His "entrance" made, only desultory applause came when he lowered the newspaper.

On the first rehearsal day I decided to have lunch with him, partly because no one else would, and partly because I wanted to discover the real person under the defensive exterior. I lunched with him every day during the rehearsal week, and concluded that there was no other person to be found.

What you saw was all there was — a hollow man totally concerned about himself. He talked only about himself, and, when I tried to switch the topic of conversation, he would always bring it back to himself and his past career. Admittedly, during the first lunch break, I found the story of his life, from acrobat to film performer, quite interesting. But as lunch followed lunch his anecdotes became repetitive and tedious. During these periods I hinted that a less sullen, and at times belligerent, attitude toward his fellow actors would make for an easier life all round and for a better production. But his ego was such that he could not conceive of anybody disliking him. He seemed convinced that he was the greatest comic in the history of show business. I think I eventually won a smidgen of his respect because I managed to work into the play his trade mark. In every movie he made he would open his cavernous mouth wide and emit a sound between a whine and a snarl that sounded a bit like "Eeeeeeoooooow." I found a spot in the play when he could utter this nerve-grating noise, much to the audience's delight. He was grateful because I was the first director who had found a way to incorporate his gimmick into the play. Perhaps the previous directors had been more discriminating than I. After the opening night performance, to show his appreciation, he presented me with a small photo of himself with "Bestest" printed on it. I kept it as a reminder that if I could direct Joe E. Brown and remain on reasonably amicable terms, I could direct anyone. Actually I cannot really claim to have directed *Father of the Bride.* I refereed it.

Because he knew his lines at the first rehearsal, he could afford the sadistic pleasure of throwing the other actors off. He developed a dislike for an actor whom I found to be most capable and co-operative. The actor had an entrance that had to be dead on cue so that Brown could give a comedic reaction. At every rehearsal when this actor entered, Brown would step out of the play and tell the actor, "You're late." At the opening performance the actor entered right on cue and Brown said in a voice the whole audience could hear, "You're early."

Colin Fox, who was an apprentice at the time working under his real name, Geoffrey Smith, was playing the one-scene part of "Tim's Man," who had to enter carrying a potted plant tall enough to conceal his face.

After a couple of performances in which the audience saw only a large plant supported by a pair of long, trousered legs, Colin decided to poke his head through the foliage. Mr. Brown noticed and onstage abruptly ordered Colin to "put your head back." For the rest of the week Colin remained unidentifiable.[5] He recalls that Joe E. Brown kept a hawk-like eye on everything that went on around him onstage. Brown's mouth was sufficiently large and rubbery that he could keep the downstage side of it closed while he opened the upstage side of it like a flap out of which he would comment to the other actors while the audience was laughing at a previous line. Some of the directions that came out of this cave were: "You're blocking my light," "You cut into my laugh," or "Wait for it." He so threw the younger, less experienced actors off that they dreaded to go onstage with him.

I was not involved in any rehearsals during the week's run of *Father of the Bride* so I returned to Toronto. When I got back to Vineland to begin rehearsals the Monday after *Bride* closed, I was told of the events from the previous week. Mr. Brown had further succeeded in alienating cast and crew by complaining to the audience about the other actors, and in spite of Bob Herrman's threats to report him to Equity, he persisted. But the cast and crew got a kind of revenge. Every Saturday there were two shows, one at 6 p.m. and one at 9 p.m. If there was insufficient time for the actors to go out for dinner between the shows, Equity regulations dictated that food be brought in, which at the GCT usually consisted of soup and a sandwich from the coffee shop. The apprentices and crew so loathed Brown that on the Saturday evening when his inter-show food was about to be taken to his dressing room, they dissolved a large dose of Ex-Lax into his "Equity" soup. All during the second performance that night they watched with breathless anticipation. When nothing happened, they concluded that he must have the digestive system of a goat. But the eruptions did occur the next day when he was on the way to the Buffalo airport. Upon arrival he made a bee-line for the nearest washroom. When I heard what they had done I told the apprentices that Brown's ego was such that he would not connect his bowel trouble with the company's dislike of him. It would have been preferable for all to have gathered in his dressing room after the last performance and told him what they thought of him. That way there might have been the faint hope that he would modify his behaviour for the next company along the summer circuit — which would not be ours. Robert Herrman determined not to invite Brown to the Garden Centre again.

As soon as Mr. Brown had carried his ego away, Joy Harmon moved in for *Susan Slept Here*. Happily I was not involved in that feeble opus, but went into rehearsal immediately for *Born Yesterday* in which I played the corrupt lawyer Ed Devery. Television has had many meteors cross the TV heavens never to be seen again. Dodie Goodman was one such meteor. She had gained prominence as a kooky guest on Jack Paar's *Tonight Show*. Although Bob Herrman had assembled a splendid supporting cast — a handsome young Philip Cusack as the reporter Paul Verrall, the powerful Louis Zorich as Harry Brock, and Ed Holmes as the Senator — the production had a weak centre because Ms. Goodman had about as much sex appeal as an oyster. And if Billie Dawn is not sexy then she can have no appeal for Harry Brock or Paul Verrall, in which case the basic situation does not make sense. But this obviously made no difference to the Garden Centre audience because Ms. Goodman played her comedy so superbly that they loved her. Ed Hocura, writing in the *Hamilton Spectator*, reported, "She tackles the dumb blonde character with enthusiasm, tosses off her wisecracks with aplomb, goes into romantic clinches with ease, and to top it off wears a steady succession of striking costumes with the grace of a professional model."[6] Yes, she went into "romantic clinches with ease," but what she gave us was a rather half-hearted simulation of sexiness. Hocura also wrote that Philip Cusack was "a mite too young for the role of Paul Verrall." What he should have written was that Ms. Goodman was a mite too old for Billie Dawn. However, I found her off-beat sense of humour refreshing and I greatly admired her comedic ability. She was a delight to work with, a very unselfish performer with no affectation, and I suspect, a very clever lady under her "spaced out" persona.

Louis Zorich was also a pleasure to work with. He was so solid onstage that he gave the other actors a sense of security in their scenes with him. His Harry Brock was gross, somewhat stupid, yet wily and venomous — a potential Al Capone. I cannot leave this production without mentioning the Washington hotel room set by Paul Swayze, which was suitably ostentatious and vulgar. It was his best of the season and much superior to the one I had to work with in the International Players' production. On the whole, *Born Yesterday* was for me one of the most enjoyable and rewarding experiences of that summer. Having suffered through the trauma of trying to direct Joe E. Brown, to work with a pleasant cast restored my faith in the profession. Moreover, it gave me the opportunity to plumb more deeply into Ed Devery's character.

Summer stock can lead to some strange casting, and at first glance Ann B. Davis as Julia Sorrell in *Fallen Angels* should raise some eyebrows. Her approach to comedy tends to the obvious, hard-hitting type rather than Coward's high style. But as Betty Lampard of the *St. Catharines Standard* said, "Ann Davis applies more her own brand of forthright humour in a farcical manner. It is just as successful."[7] And this must have been so, for who but an astute critic would have written about my performance as Julia's husband Fred, "Vernon Chapman is priceless as Fred, slightly dense and stuffy." She added that Ed Holmes as Willy was my equal onstage, and wondered about both of us, "Why is it that too-long Bermuda shorts on a man always cause laughter?"[8]

Thus ended Robert Herrman's first summer as a producer at the Garden Centre. Audiences had built steadily during the season and the box office encouraged his return. The standard of production, though varied, had been high if measured against other summer theatres. The stage shows had stimulated booking at the motel and patronage of the dining room, bars, and shops. Of course this was not lost on the Prudhomme brothers who not only liked the jingle of coin in their cash registers, but also the prestige of celebrities on their premises. The season had also been successful for me. I had justified Bob's faith in me, had got along with the visiting "stars" without being sycophantic, and had the satisfaction of playing a variety of stuffed shirts. I had been able to control myself sufficiently to direct an egomaniac without losing my temper and walking out, and last, but not least, I was earning more money than I had ever received from the theatre.

▪

Bob opened his 1960 season in mid-June. My first appearance was in the third show, *The Time of the Cuckoo*, starring June Havoc who had built a career as a singer, dancer, and actress on stage, screen, and television which surpassed in its variety that of her sister, Gypsy Rose Lee. The life story of these two and their mother, Rose, was to be immortalized in that forceful musical *Gypsy*, but in 1960 I knew of June Havoc only from her film appearances, which included *Gentleman's Agreement, A Lady Possessed,* and *When My Baby Smiles at Me. The Time of the Cuckoo* is a charming comedy by Arthur Laurents that was made into an unforgettable film starring Katharine Hepburn and Rossano Brazzi. It is the story of an American sec-retary, well past her youth, who goes to Venice for a vacation. She is an affectionate, uncomplicated, but reserved spinster who does not exude sex appeal. June Havoc had sex appeal to spare. She radiated it naturally. Despite the considerable acting ability she brought to the role, I could not accept this pretty, sexy lady as a woman who had remained an unattached virgin into her middle years. I thought it a poor choice as a vehicle for Ms. Havoc, and a waste of her charms. But Ms. Havoc not only played the leading role, she also directed a cast assembled from New York with me the only Torontonian. I played a boorish American tourist and Terry Clemes my much put-upon wife. Our characters appeared only in the first act and many of my best lines were cut, which did not endear me to Ms. Havoc, whose directing approach I found somewhat schoolmarmish, treating us all like children. However, in this production I met the talented young Nicolas Coster, originally from England, the son of the British journalist, Ian Coster. Nicolas had studied at the Royal Academy of Dramatic Art, the Neighbourhood Playhouse, and with Lee Strasberg. Fortunately he had not allowed any of these influences to suppress his natural talent. At this point in his career, Mr. Coster, as Eddie Yaeger, a young American artist, was struggling to acquire an American dialect. Later in films and soap operas he mastered that problem and sounded like he had been born under the Stars and Stripes instead of the Union Jack.

I was not involved with *Here Today*, a complete package from Hollywood with Vivian Vance (Ethel Mertz in TV's *I Love Lucy*) and John Emery, but was in the fifth show, *The Golden Fleecing*, starring Guy Madison. An agent discovered the handsome, young Mr. Madison in the American navy in World War II, and persuaded David O. Selznick to cast him as the lonely sailor in the film *Since You Went Away*. He became an immediate heartthrob and rapidly rose to stardom, but he is the perfect example of a person catapulted into the light without sufficient experience and training to sustain a career after youthful good looks have faded away. Madison's luck held long enough for a meteoric career in films and in the early days of television as the cowboy hero, Wild Bill Hickock. After that petered out, nothing much newsworthy happened to him until he underwent lung surgery in January of 1991. I suspect that his fade from glory did not bother him unduly because he was one of the most modest, unassuming, easy going, amiable celebrities I have ever met. He seemed aware of his inadequacies as an actor, but he tried hard and I felt sorry for him when the critics were severe with him. In this show I played Benjamin Dane, another pompous ass. A brilliant comedic actor from New York, Ron Liebman, really carried the show, but the actor who stole it was Canadian, John Paris, as a drunken navy signal man. John was brought in from Toronto on only a few days' notice, and completely won the meagre audiences who came to see the production. Unfortunately Wild Bill had but small appeal to the Garden Centre's public.

While performing in *The Golden Fleecing* at night, I was rehearsing *The Desk Set* during the day. The thoroughly affable comedienne, Ilka Chase, played the role originated on Broadway by Shirley Booth, and she was more than adequate to the task. Ms. Chase was one of the most versatile performers to arrive at the Garden Centre Theatre. She had various careers all going at the same time: as a performer in many films, as a guest on TV talk and quiz shows, and as an author with eight best-sellers by 1960. She was fun to be with and intellectually stimulating. Moreover, she was a generous performer without a "star" complex, which made it a pleasure to perform the many scenes I had with her. In this production I played Richard Sumner, another stuffed shirt, but not quite so stuffed as Benjamin Dane in the previous play. In the end Sumner turns out to be a "regular guy."

The Desk Set has a large cast so Bob hired a number of jobbers from Toronto and used most of the apprentices, two of whom, the Mutt and Jeff of the company, were destined to make names for themselves in Canadian theatre and television. In his second year as an apprentice, the tall one had taken the name of Colin Fox, and the short one still performed as James Langcaster, but would eventually become Heath Lamberts. Also in the cast was Larry Reynolds with whom I had not been onstage for several years. Ilka Chase was so convivial that everyone had a great time and I have most pleasant memories of *The Desk Set*. But the next show was to be the highlight of my season as an actor and an avid movie fan.

When I was a tad in regular attendance on Saturday afternoons at the Kenwood or Kitchener (later the Paradise) movie emporiums on Bloor Street in Toronto, I had a favourite group of supporting players who appeared primarily in comedies: Franklyn Pangborn, Billy Gilbert, Edna May Oliver, Sig Ruman, Cora Witherspoon, Eric Blore, Helen Broderick, S. Z. (Cuddles) Sakall, Herman Bing, and Edward Everett Horton. I particularly liked Horton, whom I had seen in almost all of his talkies including the comedies he made for Ernst Lubitsch and particularly his appearances in *Top Hat* and *The Gay Divorcee*. Outstanding in my memory was his portrayal of the hyper, nervous anthropologist in *Lost Horizon*. Naturally I was thrilled at the prospect of working with him in *The Reluctant Debutante*.

Who's Who in the Theatre states that Edward Everett Horton was born in Brooklyn on March 18, 1887,[9] but Joe Franklyn in his *Encyclopedia of Comedians* gives the year as 1886.[10] Whatever his birth date, he was quite an old man by the time I worked with him in 1960. However, he was not old in spirit or energy. In his early theatre days he had been a leading man on Broadway and in North American tours. In the 1920s he produced and directed his own shows in Los Angeles, and broke into silent films and then into the talkies. During the '30s his career flourished in frothy comedies, but when that type of film fell out of favour during the war years he was no longer in demand at the Hollywood studios. He began touring summer theatres with a repertoire of roles, the most frequently performed that of

Henry Dewlip in *Springtime for Henry*. Although in his early days he was a versatile actor, he now injected into his stage roles a lot of the film persona he had constantly portrayed, and which had endeared him to the movie public, that of a fussy, slightly prissy, nervous ditherer, which mostly in real life he was not. He was a master of the "triple take." He could convey more with a simple, self-satisfied smirk or a dubiously raised eyebrow than most actors could with lines of dialogue, and he had the ability to project his thoughts far beyond the footlights with his body language. He was a professional to his finger tips and appreciated skilled performers around him. He had a great understanding for young actors, but could be scathing and irascible to more mature performers who did not live up to his standards. He was a gentleman, a capital "R" Republican, who I am sure would have deplored the petty meanness of the "new right" of the 1990s. He had made several films in England, was pro-British, and greatly admired British actors, British institutions, and the Royal Family. He was a tennis enthusiast, was socially gregarious, and loved parties, food, and drink — the last in moderation. He also liked the challenge of rehearsing with different actors, which made him eschew any "package" shows emanating from Hollywood. Because he invariably knew the play, the rehearsal week was a relaxing time for him, and gave him a chance to get to know the performers, and they him, and they invariably adored him. It also gave him a chance to indulge his hedonistic pleasure of cocktails and gourmet dinners in the best local restaurants for a whole week before having to face an audience. What a difference from Joe E. Brown.

Not only was Horton to perform Jimmy Broadbent in *The Reluctant Debutante*, he was also to direct it, with Robert Herrman keeping an eye on the scenes in which Horton appeared, which was most of them. Bob had arranged for a splendid cast from Toronto and from among the apprentices. The aristocratic Moya Fenwick played the debutante's mother, and the ebullient Helene Winston was her friend, Mabel Crosswaithe. Of course I played the Guards Officer who does not get the girl but in this case gets a lot of the comedy. Whenever Horton toured the summer circuit he liked to drive from location to location in his Thunderbird convertible. But because of his age, he was nervous about long distances on his own. He would always insist that the producers accept into the cast in a major role a young actor travelling with him as his chauffeur. For *Debutante* this was Leonard Raynor, a swarthy young man who looked facially like Louise Rainer and who, in fact, did imitations of her as Poldi in the film *The Great Waltz* at parties. Mr. Raynor played the male romantic lead, David Hoylake-Johnston, the Duke of Positano. For the debutante Bob cast from among the apprentices a very pretty, demur Patricia Farmer. Pat, though blonde, was far from dumb and was one of the most talented of the "apprenti." Horton liked her instantly and he was delighted that she responded so quickly to his direction. The cast was completed by another apprentice, Durell Gardiner, in the role of Clarissa, Mrs. Crosswaithe's mousy daughter.

One thing Edward was adamant about was the set, which had to accommodate the "business" he had worked into the show. He asked that Broadbent's Mayfair drawing room have a long unbroken back wall stretching across the stage to a door up left, beyond which was a floor-to-ceiling bay window that curved down stage left to a short wall on which was an electric wall sconce. There were wall lights along the back wall and one by the door down right that led to the rest of the flat. It was just too plain for a luxurious London apartment, and if Jack McAdam, our designer, had had his way, he would have created something different. Jack designed and built sets for CBC-TV in Toronto, and was too good to design what Horton insisted on. But Horton did not care much about the appropriateness or the attractiveness of the set so long as it worked for the actors and for the "schtick" he had incorporated, particularly at the end of the second act. As written, the two young lovers are kissing on a sofa when they hear Mrs. Broadbent offstage telling her husband, Jimmy, to see if any lights have been left on. Not wanting to be found smooching in the dark the lovers run upstage to hide behind the door. Jimmy enters, sees that the lights are out, shouts that information down the corridor to his wife and closes the door revealing the lovers who kiss as the curtain falls. Horton, claiming that "playwrights don't know how to write plays," altered this ending. He had moonlight streaming in the huge window, one wall sconce left on downstage below the window, another by the down right exit, and a third light in the room off stage right. In his version the lovers are on the sofa when Mrs. Broadbent is heard urging Jimmy to check the lights, whereupon we hear him shouting back to her as he walks the length of the corridor toward the up left door, "Of course they won't be on. After the expense of that coming-out party our daughter would not be so inconsiderate as to leave the lights on." The lovers flee to behind the door. Jimmy then appears wearing his pyjamas, dressing gown, and fluffy slippers, in the doorway whose door opened onstage toward the window. He peers around the room. Seeing the lighted wall sconce down left he mutters, "There now, just look at that. No consideration," and he shuffles down left to turn it off. Then he turns and spies the lighted wall lamp down right. Shuffling over in his floppy slippers, he mutters, "Five thousand pounds for a coming-out party and she hasn't even the consideration to turn off the lights. They think I'm made of money. No consideration. Just no consideration." He turns off that light and exits to turn the light off in the room off right. At that point the young people poke their heads from behind the door and are just about to creep out when Jimmy returns, and crosses to the up left door still grumbling about the cost of everything. He takes a look around the room now only lit by the moonlight from the window and slowly starts to close the door until it is almost shut. Then he quickly opens it again, and stands with the door half open, the only part of him lit by the moonlight is his huge proboscis. He holds that position for a few seconds as he listens intently, the young couple frozen behind the door but now in full view of the audience. Then Jimmy says, "Mice!" and abruptly closes the door leaving the lovers sighing with relief and the audience roaring with laughter as the curtain closes.

Edward was generous in concocting comic business for his fellow actors as well as for himself. He gave me a very effective bit during a scene in which Mrs. Broadbent and Mrs. Crosswaithe chatted about the forthcoming debutante party. While as the Guardsman I stood stiffly and aimlessly to one side of the room, Mrs. Broadbent mixed Manhattan cocktails for us. Horton had instructed me not to drink my cocktail but merely to suck on the cherry that was in it. This I did when Mrs. Broadbent's back was too me. Needless to say, the audience found it very funny that this silly ass officer, all bristling moustache, scarlet, and brass would stand there inanely sucking on a cherry. Because Horton had given me the direction, neither Moya nor Helene could protest that I was scene-stealing from them. During the third performance, as I lifted the cherry out of the Manhattan for the third or fourth time, it came off the stem and fell to the floor. This got a laugh. I assumed a disappointed expression, glanced down at the cherry, then out to the audience, then toward Moya whose back was still to me. I next looked out to the audience again, then down at the cherry and flicked it under a chair with my boot. The audience roared. For the remainder of the run I did not get a cherry in my Manhattan. Moya maintains that the prop department ran out of them. Had I not had such profound respect for her, I might have complained that I had lost my cherry. For the remaining performances the important plot dialogue between Mrs. Broadbent and Mrs. Crosswaithe was heard without distraction from me, except that the audience still found the guardsman funny as he stood there rigidly, ignored by the two women for minutes on end, sipping a Manhattan with his right pinkie extended.

In those days we were still part of American Equity, and the stock company agreement allowed a lower minimum salary for the rehearsal week than for the performance week. Because Edward liked the relaxation of the rehearsal days, particularly if he had played the role before, he accepted the minimum salary for that week, but negotiated a much larger fee of $1,500 for the performances. Although Horton never quite sold out our 916-seat theatre, he had a large number of regular fans, and the show costs were sufficiently low that the producer made a profit. This practice accounts for Horton's longevity in the summer theatre circuit. Because he developed a respect for Moya and myself as performers, he insisted that Bob Herrman hire us to appear in future shows he did at the Garden Centre. I was to work with him in four more plays over the next five years and I looked forward with pleasure to each one of them.

In a summer of stars, the ageing but never-out-of-date Tallulah

Bankhead in a dated play, *Craig's Wife*, followed Edward Horton. She was touring the summer circuit semi-packaged, that is, the leading actors travelled with her but the smaller roles were filled locally, and in the case of the Garden Centre, with apprentices. Because Bankhead and company would not appear until the opening on Monday, the apprentices were blocked in by a director who worked a week in advance of the opening. He gave them their moves and positions, which could not be altered because changes would confuse the late-arriving actors. The apprentices also had the disadvantage of working from "sides," which left them with only a vague idea of what the play was about before their first performance. Colin Fox, who was playing the second detective, Harry, recalls that owing to the way the set was constructed, he could not see onto the stage, so the first sight he had of the fabulous Ms. Bankhead, and she of him, was as he stepped onto the stage on opening night.[11] Colin is over six feet tall, and La Bankhead was momentarily startled to see this towering figure enter.

Although the leading actors did not arrive until opening day, an advance party of Ms. Bankhead's minions arrived a week earlier and plagued the management with their demands on her behalf. They showed their disapproval of the motel, the theatre and its facilities, especially the "star" dressing room. They insisted, among other things, that it be painted Ms. Bankhead's favourite colour, pink, and that a thick, pink runner be laid between her dressing room and the entrance to the set, which was built from a design brought by the advance man. Although footlights had gone out of fashion some years before, a set of them had to be found and installed to please La Bankhead, presumably because, properly jelled, they give off a softer light that helps wipe out facial lines and eye socket shadows. Such was Tallulah's reputation for temperamental explosions that Bob Herrman complied with all the demands. He was considerably shocked when Bankhead arrived only to recoil in horror when she saw her pulsatingly pink dressing room and exclaimed, "My God! I hate pink!" Bob never discovered whether Tallulah was joking, or whether the joke was on her. However, he did discover that she was not so difficult as her reputation had led him to believe.

I had always been fascinated by her sultry voice and her performances in films and on radio. She was unique and had an air of hauteur and grandeur. She played the role of Craig's wife superbly even on an insufferably hot night in that inadequately air-conditioned theatre. When I was introduced to her after the performance, I could not help feeling sorry that this great lady of the New York and London stages, who had rivetted audiences with her performances as the ruthless Regina Giddens in *The Little Foxes* and as that sexy maid-of-all-trades, Sabina, in *The Skin of Our Teeth*, should now be reduced to sweating out a performance, albeit a brilliant one, in a converted curling rink. I had heard about the controversy that surrounded her, her acid tongue and her temper tantrums, and admired her courage in speaking out on issues that bothered her. Colin Fox remembers this as his first encounter "with true charisma — hard to define, but you know it when you see it, and Tallulah had it in spades."[12] But let Ms. Bankhead explain it herself: "Personality has something to do with inner fire, competitive spirit, defiance of the norm, solo effort, showmanship, in the ability to transform a liability into an asset. . . . Personality? Even the hostiles concede I have it."[13] As usual, wherever Tallulah appeared in those days, rumours about her conduct abounded. One was that she shocked Prudhommes' patrons by running naked down the corridor when she was tanked. If true, I wish I had been there. Another was that all the breakable objects had to be removed from her hotel room, because when she got angry she smashed everything in sight. What a pity she was deprived of that satisfaction because the furnishings in Prudhommes' rooms were so pretentiously tasteless that they deserved to be trashed. One of my regrets is that I never got to perform with this fabulous legend.

While *Craig's Wife* was occupying the stage, a group of us were busy rehearsing another frothy comedy, *Make a Million*. It was loosely directed by Bob Herrman — "loosely" because all Bob really did was block the show according to the directions in the stage manager's script that had been sent on a week in advance. The lead roles were filled with Hollywood actors who could not arrive to rehearse until the Sunday night before Monday opening. Once again there could be no deviation from the blocking established weeks before for the first performance by a director whom we never saw. Heading this group was Jack Carson, originally from Carmen, Manitoba, but raised in the United States. An amiable giant, 6′ 2″ and 200 pounds, he usually played the romantic hero's sidekick who invariably shrugged off his disappointment at not getting the girl. In addition to myself, among the other local performers were Colin Fox, Heath Lamberts, Brian Swayze, and Terry Clemes. At the first rehearsal with the Hollywood contingent, when I was introduced as the actor to be playing Harold Fairbanks, an uptight individual devoted to his analyst, Carson said to me, "Oh that's a great part. You'll enjoy playing that part. The guy in Chicago was terrific." "Thanks heaps," I thought, "for those words of discouragement," but I only muttered something innocuous like "I hope so."

I enjoyed playing my scenes with Carson. He was unselfish and we interplayed well. Fairbanks was primarily a straight man, but I managed to squeeze out a considerable amount of comedy. I gave him a slightly whiny voice. At the Friday performance, during our last scene together, Carson said a line in the same voice I used. It sounded very funny coming from this great masculine hulk, and I cracked up. This caused the audience to break up too. He continued for several lines, which made me laugh all the more and, consequently, so did the audience. I determined to try an experiment in audience control. Saturday at the 6 o'clock show when he did the same thing, I ploughed ahead with the scene. The audience did not laugh. Carson persisted with the whiny delivery but did not get a titter. Afterward he did not comment on it. For the second show that night when he imitated me, I pretended to break up and the audience followed suit. The more he spoke, the more I pretended to suppress laughter and the audience rolled about. We kept it up for several minutes and provided me with a great lesson in the power an actor can have over his fellow actors as well as over the audience.

If during a show I had enjoyed performing with the visiting actors, on the Sunday morning I would try to have breakfast with them in the coffee shop to say goodbye before they left for Buffalo airport. I did so with the affable group from *Make a Million*. As they were leaving the coffee shop, Carson turned and shouted back, "Oh by the way, you were better than the guy in Chicago." I felt pleased but a bit sorry for the actor playing Harold

Fairbanks at their next stop who would be told, "The guy in Vineland was terrific." An historical footnote about this production — the local critic singled out Heath Lamberts for favourable comment: "Excellent performer with a small part is Heath Lamberts, who makes Bernie Leeds, an insignificant introvert, seem significant in the play."[14] This was the first use by James Langcaster of the stage name Heath Lamberts.

Bob invited Ann B. Davis, one of our consistent box-office draws, to star in *Mrs. McThing,* a Broadway hit for Helen Hayes. Despite a solid performance by Ms. Davis, the show never lived up to its potential, although the audiences loved it. I had huge fun clowning with Heath Lamberts and Ben Lennick as a trio of zany gangsters, and temporarily free from a "stuffed shirt" role, I wished *Mrs. McThing* could have run for weeks. That would have been preferable for other reasons as well because *The Gazebo,* starring Robert Q. Lewis, was an unmitigated disaster. Mr. Lewis's claim to fame arose primarily from his substituting for Arthur Godfrey on his radio show. He then branched out into TV as a talk show host and MC for a series of quiz shows. He also made guest appearances on *I've Got a Secret, What's My Line?,* and *The Price Is Right.* He even had a brief career in films. He brought with him from New York his co-star, a charming lady named Kaye Lyder. The other major roles in the show were played by Helene Winston, who was becoming a favourite with Vineland audiences, Ben Lennick, Betty Riley, and myself as Harlow Edison, a conservative, but not stuffy, lawyer. Briefly, the plot of Alec Coppel's comedy deals with a successful television writer who, because he is being blackmailed, plans to murder the blackmailer. He does so only to discover that the man he has buried under the gazebo in the back garden is the wrong person. The bulk of the play involves his efforts to discover whom he has buried there.

Lewis was what I call a "personality performer." The role had to be suited to his personality. There is a difference between that and the approach of Edward Everett Horton, who had created an artificial persona that he adapted to each role. It was not his own personality, although there were elements of him in it. Unfortunately, Lewis's personality was not a pleasant one. He brought no charm to the role, just a lot of antics, cavorting about and playing to the audience. He also had the insecure actor's defensiveness, which led to selfishness. He would ad lib onstage, disconcerting his fellow performers. He seemed to be a paranoid man who was always looking for approval. Because I sensed that he was basically very insecure, especially around experienced actors, I felt somewhat sorry for him, which he must have detected. He latched onto me as though I was the only friend he had in the cast, which was probably true.

Lewis had an aversion to firing a revolver, which had to happen several times during the play. The gun, with its safety catch, became a *bête noire* for him. Three guns were concealed onstage. If one failed, Lewis could quickly find the second, and if that failed, a third was at hand. On opening night things seemed to go smoothly, but on the second night, when the *Hamilton Spectator* critic, Ed Hocura, visited us, everything fell part. When the first gun did not fire, Lewis ad libbed instructions to his visitor while he found the second gun. It did not fire. He continued to ad lib while frantically searching for the third. It too went "click." Lewis then pointed to his visitor with his index finger and said "Bang!" The visitor dropped to the floor trying desperately not to laugh, while the audience fell about. When the act was over, Jack McAdam, the designer and production manager, took all three guns out to the back of the theatre and fired them. Lewis had forgotten to flick off the safety on all three. Or had he forgotten deliberately? When at another performance the first gun failed, Lewis did not bother to search for the other two. He simply pointed his finger and said "Bang!" He seemed to prefer the audience's reaction to that rather than playing the scene as written. In the ensuing performances he managed to fire the first gun successfully. But in the final performance, the first gun did not fire and he again shot the victim with his index finger while shouting "Bang!" He then committed one of the worst offenses in the theatrical book. He turned to the audience and said, "You see what I have to put up with. I have never met such an incompetent crew." When the curtain came down on that act he stormed to his dressing room. Shortly I heard a shot and a scream, and rushed in to see what had happened. Seated at his dressing table was a shocked Mr. Lewis, with Jack McAdam standing over him pointing the pistol at him at close range. "You see. If you remove the safety catch, it does work," McAdam said and stalked out. Lewis was so unnerved that he was on the verge of tears. He insisted that the gun had jammed, which was a blatant lie. But I saw then that he was determined to believe that he was the victim of a conspiracy. I tried to calm him by reminding him that he had the rest of the play to perform but I left his dressing room when Robert Herrman charged in to tell Lewis that he considered his comment to the audience totally unacceptable, that he would never ask him back to his theatre, and that he would report him to Equity for unprofessional conduct. By the end of the show that Saturday night, I was the only member of the company still talking to him. But I did not have a farewell breakfast with him on the Sunday.

Ed Hocura had been taken in by Lewis, as had the audience. The result was a review lacing the show. He blamed the director and the actors with the exception of Lewis, Kaye Lyder, and myself. Of Lewis he wrote, "Robert Q. Lewis is a likeable personality who at least deserves an 'E' for effort in sustaining what enjoyment emerged from a play that almost fell apart when three guns failed to go off in a crucial scene." About me he wrote, "Vernon Chapman rose admirably to the occasion. . . . The busiest actor at Vineland this summer, he maintained a surprisingly straight face considering the shamble that was going on around him all evening."[15] This review was bad for business for a production that had been destroyed by the star himself. I sympathized with Kaye Lyder who played Lewis's wife. During their scenes he was continually ad libbing. It was a mark of her stage worthiness that she coped with him. Strangely enough, with me he did not try any tricks, so that our scenes together worked the best in the play, which accounts in part for Mr. Hocura praising my calmness. In a trip to New York the following autumn, I visited Robert Q. Lewis in his apartment where, over drinks, he complained about the incompetent people at the Garden Centre. He remained a paranoid man.

The week following *The Gazebo* an energetic group of students from McGill University burned up the stage with their exuberance in the revue *Got It Made*, staged by the inventive young choreographer, Brian

MacDonald. Two years earlier at McGill, MacDonald had created a Canadian satirical revue with the title *My Fur Lady*, which toured Canada with tremendous success and which Bob Herrman had brought to Vineland in the summer of 1959. *Got It Made* was a delightful successor. It was a complete package in which I was not involved but my days were occupied with one of the most satisfying directing experiences of my career.

When I was playing in *Mrs. McThing*, Bob Herrman had asked if I would direct the 13th show of the season, *Tobacco Road*, with that sterling character actor John Carradine as Jeeter Lester. The play had caused a sensation in 1933 when it began a nine-year run on Broadway. Even in 1953 it led to prosecution for members of a Vancouver stage production, but I suspect that today it would not so much as raise an eyebrow. I had seen a touring company with James Barton as Jeeter where the emphasis was on comedy and crudity, such as Jeeter's turning upstage and peeing, which I suppose is preferable to turning downstage and peeing. They had turned Erskine Caldwell's Georgians into vulgar, clownish yokels. However, in the film version with Charles Grapewin as Jeeter, the crassness was toned down and the film emerged as a social indictment of the appalling condition during the Depression era of many of the backwoods people of America. John Carradine had been playing Jeeter all that summer, and I was reluctant to direct it if he played it for laughs and audience titillation. I told Bob that I would only decide after I had had a talk with Mr. Carradine. This talk could take place only on the Monday morning at breakfast before the first rehearsal, which was scheduled for 10 a.m. Until that time Bob did not know if he would have to direct it himself.

We met as he breakfasted in the coffee shop where I explained that I believed *Tobacco Road* was intended as a play of social comment and that, although there was a lot of humour in it, I did not want the comedy to be over-emphasized in a way that would destroy the humanity of these people. I also told him that if he did not agree with my approach, another director was readily available. I had no idea how he would react to this strong statement. A Joe E. Brown or a Robert Q. Lewis would have misinterpreted it as a challenge to his dominance as the leading actor. When he replied in that deep, sonorous voice of his, "Oh my dear fellow, I could not agree with you more," I relaxed and enjoyed breakfast with an actor whose movies had left an indelible impression on me that lasts to this day. I knew that he had enjoyed a notable career as a stage actor, particularly in Shakespeare, but that haunting voice, those gaunt features, and his unwillingness to play "little" for the camera provide vivid film memories of him: as the preacher in *The Grapes of Wrath*, as the "dirty coward" who shot Jesse James in the back, and of his fulminating as John Knox against Mary of Scotland. Nor can I ever forget his rag picker in the stage version of *The Madwoman of Chaillot*. After our breakfast chat, we worked together most compatibly.

In fact it was a very co-operative and enthusiastic cast Bob Herrman and I had assembled. Carradine brought with him Georgia Simmons, a real "Georgia cracker," to play his wife. She had been playing the role with him off and on for the previous decade and although she was over 70, she seemed 20 years younger onstage. She was a delight to talk to because she had a fund of stories about her life in Georgia and her stage career. Helene Winston revelled in getting her teeth into the role of the ribald, nympho-maniacal, revivalist preacher, Sister Bessie. As Dude Lester, a young William Compton was summoned from the U.S. because he too had played the part with John Carradine before. Dude is somewhat slow-witted, but Mr. Compton certainly was not. He gave the role a belligerent, unpredictable quality that was frightening. The pretty Patricia Farmer was Pearl, the daughter sold into marriage to the loutish Lov Bensey, played by Toronto's John Paris. Among the others in the cast, Heath Lamberts played the small role of George Payne and suppressed any inclination to make more of it than was there.

Accustomed to drawing up detailed blueprints for CBC-TV sets in their large studios, designer Jack McAdam showed his floor plan to Mr. Carra-dine and myself. Carradine looked at it and said, "That's very fine, just so long as the porch is over here, and the well is over there." For an old stager like Carradine, complicated floor plans meant very little. But the squalid set worked ideally, even to the parched earth that covered the stage. For me rehearsals became a great pleasure because I was able to leave my imprint on the production and even to some extent on the performances of Carradine and Georgia Simmons. In an interview in the *Hamilton Spectator*, Ed Hocura quoted Carradine as saying of Helene Winston and myself, "I've been doing *Tobacco Road* for 10 years now in summer stock. Working with these two in this play makes me think that we will have a few surprises for people who have either seen the play before, or the movie."[16] For the ending I wanted to take the light down until there was only a small spot on Jeeter's face as he sat alone on the edge of the porch, sifting the dirt through his fingers. Despite our inadequate lighting equipment, McAdam solved the problem by training three spotlights on the same area, with the second spot covering half the area of the first and the third light's pool just large enough to frame Jeeter's face. By gradually fading out one spot after the other he could get the effect of irising down, which greatly enhanced the final, poignant moment of this disturbing play. Our production was received enthusiastically by both the St. Catharines and Hamilton reviewers. "I went to it last night expecting, frankly, the worst," said Betty Lampard. "The last production of it I had seen was a filthy, slimy affair, done with every leer possible and leaving little to the imagination. The local production was a far cry from that. It goes to show that it is all in the way it is done."[17] I don't want to give the impression that I "tidied up" the play. I just let it play itself without over-emphasizing the cruder aspects of the action and language.

During the week of rehearsals I learned a lot more about John Carradine. His was a fascinating life of a man whose acting talent was enormous and who came close to being a top-ranking star in both cinema and the legitimate theatre. Raised in New York City, he studied to be a painter and sculptor. His early interest in the theatre was stimulated by his being hired by the New York Public Library to catalogue its vast collection of theatrical clippings. He began his acting career at the St. Charles Theatre in New Orleans. In 1927 he went to Hollywood and became a set designer for Cecil B. DeMille, and during the next decade he acted onstage in Los Angeles and in films. He turned in some memorable performances and became catalogued as a supporting player (his friend John Barrymore was the star) but in 1941 he had a golden opportunity handed to him. This is the story as he told it to me.

A friend of his purchased for a very low price some crates, trunks, and scenery that had been stored in a Los Angeles warehouse about to be torn down. The warehouse owners considered that they owned the items because no storage had been paid for years. Carradine's friend asked him to examine what he had purchased. John did so and noticed on the label of one of the costumes the name of an actress who had played in John Barrymore's production of *Hamlet* about two decades before in New York. His friend agreed to sell the whole works for $500. Carradine then spent $5,000 to rent a theatre and a union crew to hang the sets to find out what he had acquired. When the massive, interlocking set had been assembled and the drop curtain hung revealing the huge figures of three knights couchant, Carradine knew that indeed he had purchased the complete set, props, and costumes designed by Robert Edmond Jones for Barrymore's 1922 *Hamlet*. With this theatrical treasure, he decided to fulfil a long-standing dream to establish an American Shakespeare company. Drawing on his savings he put his plan into action in the summer of 1941. He planned to stage in repertory *Hamlet*, *The Merchant of Venice*, and a third play that I cannot recall. (My memory seems to tell me that it was *Macbeth*, but I could be wrong.) He recruited a cast, rehearsed in Los Angeles, and opened there in late summer of 1941. They then moved to San Francisco where they played to great success. He had planned an engagement in Chicago before moving on to New York, but after the Pearl Harbor attack, all unessential shipping and travelling in the United States were suspended. Under such circumstances the authorities are mistakenly inclined to look on theatrical activities as frivolous, and therefore unnecessary. Carradine could not get his company out of San Francisco and was forced to sell valuable property, including his yacht, to avoid bankruptcy. In the panic atmosphere that gripped much of the United States that winter of 1941–42, there was nothing he could do. Patriotism took precedence over theatricalism. But if he had succeeded in establishing his Shakespeare Repertory Company permanently, it would have had a profound influence on theatre in America, and his career would have taken a different direction. He probably would not have turned up in Vineland to give me the pleasure of directing him in *Tobacco Road*. Except for a brief meeting in New York the following autumn, I did not see John Carradine again until decades later when he turned up playing the visiting uncle in *George Washington Slept Here* at the Huron Country Playhouse in Grand Bend, Ontario. After the performance I went backstage and to my amazement he remembered me from 1960 at the Garden Centre. Although he had tried to conceal it during the show, his hands were cruelly twisted with arthritis. Despite this handicap, he dominated every scene in which he appeared.

I got to direct another celebrity in my next assignment. I became a fan of Zasu Pitts when she appeared with Thelma Todd in a series of short film comedies in the 1930s. Her fluttering hands and whiny voice had captivated millions through the more than 400 films she had made since her first screen appearance with Mary Pickford in *The Little American* in 1917. In the 1950s she had found new fame as the spaced-out "Nugey" on the Gail Storm television show. I looked forward with pleasure to directing her in a play that I had previously staged for the International Players, *The Curious Savage*. Zasu (a name derived from combining the last syllable of Eliza and the first of Susan) arrived with her travelling companion whom I dubbed her "duenna." Rehearsals began in an amiable atmosphere, but, as I expected, the blocking had to be arranged to suit what Ms. Pitts had done in previous productions of the play that summer. The atmosphere became slightly charged when the cast and I grew tired of hearing her say, "In Chicago we did it this way." At one point, after following her instructions, we had three people standing behind the sofa, three people seated on the sofa, and three people standing directly in front of the sofa. I said that it wouldn't do. "But," she replied, "that's the way we did it in Chicago." "Well, you may have done it that way in Chicago," I said impatiently, "but we're not doing it that way here." "Oh, well," she said, and with a few flips of the hands she flounced to the far side of the rehearsal room to be consoled by her companion who was present at all rehearsals. I continued with the rehearsal and ignored her. Soon she drifted back. On another occasion she started to move Jimmy Edmonds physically, but, resenting this, he shrugged her hands off his arms. "Well," she whined, "if that's how you feel," and again went to be comforted by her duenna. Once again I ignored her and went on with the staging. As before, seeing that no one was going to make a fuss over her, she got over her sulk and rejoined the rehearsal.

When the blocking was concluded, rehearsals became more pleasant for everyone. However, Ms. Pitts was somewhat anti-social, preferring the company of her travelling companion to mingling with the cast, which was her loss because they were a very convivial bunch. The production went down well with critics and audience. The vagueness Ms. Pitts had developed for characters in the movies was perfect for the role of the eccentric Mrs. Savage. Among the supporting cast, Ben Lennick as the greedy Senator and Billi Tyas as the equally unscrupulous divorcee daughter were sufficiently mean without losing the comedy. In his review, Ed Hocura remarked on the stunning gowns Ms. Tyas wore for each scene, all of which were from her own wardrobe. Those were before the days when Equity regulations required managements to supply all clothing worn onstage, or else pay the actor compensation for supplying his or her own. In my summer stock days I was required to have a wardrobe that consisted of a suit, a sports coat, a tuxedo, with accessories to match, plus black and brown shoes. That tuxedo, with wide satin lapels, had been my father's and was two decades out of fashion by the 1950s, but it had to do until I was eventually able to purchase a second-hand one in the latest style from Syd Silver.

Although the performances of *The Curious Savage* went smoothly enough, Zasu blotted her copy book so far as the producer was concerned. Some years earlier in an interview in Vancouver she got on one of her hobby-horses, Canadian-American relations. She had expressed an opinion that, since our peoples were so much alike, Canada should be part of the United States. This had caused quite a furore and Bob Herrman was anxious that she not return to that theme when in Vineland. To prevent this he made sure that the publicity manager was present at all interviews. However, a reporter from the *Toronto Star* got to her privately and gave her an opportunity to sound off. When this interview appeared, irate calls came into the office of the GCT, some patrons cancelled reservations, and some even demanded refunds. I was surprised at the reaction because I had not thought we Canadians could get so upset by what a spaced-out actress from Hollywood had to say. Bob, an American who appreciated the differences between the two countries, was furious and vowed Zasu would never be invited back. The show made money, but not as much as it might have.

The 16th and final show of that long season was Richard Nash's beautifully written play *The Rainmaker*. It starred Lee Marvin as Starbuck, a seemingly inspired piece of casting. Bob wanted me to play Noah, the sour, down-to-earth brother of the spinster Lizzie and the ebullient Jimmy. But I was tired of roles in which I did not get the girl and I persuaded Bob to let me play File, the Sheriff's deputy who eventually does win the heroine. File is a taciturn, shy cowboy, lacking any confidence in himself where women are concerned. I was fortunate in his choice of Terry Clemes as Lizzie. Although as a type, File was a stretch for me, I believe I carried it off, and showed the Garden Centre public that I was capable of playing more than your average, buttoned down, conservative executive or lawyer.

Lee Marvin had by 1960 become widely known for his films, particularly *Raintree Country*, which pushed him into stardom, and also for his television appearances in the series *M Squad*. But he was not yet as famous as he was to become after his remarkable performance in *Cat Ballou*. He had a magnificent stage presence, with a powerful voice and a solidly masculine quality that radiated sex appeal. On the Friday afternoon run-through before we opened the next Monday, he gave an electrifying performance. We were all in awe of the power of his presence, and we looked forward to the performance week with this dynamic actor. But he never achieved this level again. His performances varied drastically from evening to evening. He did not know how to duplicate and retain the mood that had allowed him to be so vital on that Friday afternoon. A great pity, but often typical of film actors who can muster the right forces for one shot before a camera, though never do the scene the same way again.

■

The Rainmaker marked the closing of the 1960 Garden Centre season. Although I was to continue acting and directing for Bob Herrman over the next four years, I was not to be so regularly involved again. In fact, the 1961 season consisted mainly of packages from the U.S., and I was not involved until the 11th production, *The Little Hut*, which you will remember I had directed at the Red Barn in 1958. But my second staging was not without its problems. Bob had cast all of the roles except for the Stranger and the Monkey. The French actress of movie fame, Denise Darcel, was to play Susan, married to Philip (me) but having a secret fling with Henry (Don Ewer) before the three become shipwrecked on a desert island. When it is revealed to Philip that Susan and Henry have been having an affair, in typical British stiff upper-lip fashion and sense of fair play, Philip agrees to share her. The play requires a lot of physical activity, much of it involving Susan. Because the role of Philip was right up my alley, and because I had played it before, Bob wanted me to play in *The Little Hut* as well as direct it. I would have preferred not to do both, but that summer I could not afford to turn down the double fee. Another incentive for me to direct was Bob's offer to fly me to New York and pay my accommodation to see Ms. Darcel perform the role in an off-Broadway production of the play. However, when I arrived at the small basement theatre, the box office was closed and inside I found a crew tearing apart the set. When I inquired what had happened I learned that the show had closed the day before because of poor business, and then I was told the stunner that Denise Darcel was eight months' pregnant. The prospect of having an obviously pregnant woman rolling about with two men was too gross for me. I immediately phoned Bob, urged him to get out of the contract and hire someone else. I returned to Toronto the next day to be told that Bob had tried but that Ms. Darcel's agent had threatened a lawsuit. I tried to persuade Bob to thumb his nose at the agent on the grounds that the contract was void because Bob had not been apprised of her pregnancy when he contracted her. I felt that the agent's threat was a hollow bluff. But Bob did not want to risk it. He could not afford to fight a lawsuit. I was stuck with Ms. Darcel.

With deep misgivings I approached the first rehearsal consoling myself that I had a strong comedic actor in Don Ewer. Ms. Darcel chose to arrive only two days before our opening. While an apprentice stood in for her, we rehearsed for almost a week using the blocking from the stage manager's script from the New York staging. During that week I was building up a profound antipathy toward Denise Darcel, but my feeling rapidly dissipated when we began to rehearse because she proved to be a sweetheart to work with. We had intense rehearsals on Sunday and Monday and opened Monday night. Of necessity I had eliminated some of the business that was called for in the script. It was ludicrous to chase her around the stage because it was too easy to catch her, and putting her over my lap to spank her was not only disgusting but impossible. Despite her loose diaphenous costumes, her size could not be completely hidden and the audience twigged that here was a very pregnant lady supposedly having sexual intercourse with two men. All during the week of performance I worried that what little rough and tumble was left in the play would affect the baby. As a result, much of the fun of *The Little Hut* was diminished, and the tolerance and credulity of the audience were sorely tested.

However, I enjoyed playing the scenes with Don Ewer, whom you met briefly in connection with the Princess Theatre in Niagara Falls. He is a wonderful character actor who had come to Canada from England in 1954 and had built a very successful career in Canadian television. By 1961 he was already making inroads in the New York theatre where eventually he won an Obie. Since then he has worked in a variety of theatres throughout North America. But in this version of *The Little Hut*, the great scene-stealer was the young man who played the Stranger, actually the Danish cook from the wrecked ship. He has very few lines, but he must be a superior physical specimen to the two actors playing Philip and Henry. In the case of Don and myself, such an actor would not have been hard to find. But I went beyond the average and cast a young body builder with whom I had worked on the Wayne and Shuster shows. Vaughn Wright had been a Junior Mister Ontario, and when he appeared onstage clad only in a loin coth and feathered headdress, the audience visibly perked up. After the opening night the fan mail began to pour in, not for Denise Darcel, Don Ewer, or me, but for

Mr. Wright. Moreover, as the week wore on the ticket sales picked up not to see La Darcel but to stare at this muscular Adonis. I resolved that if I ever directed *The Little Hut* again, the Danish cook would be physically puny.

The production was received by the critics with mild tolerance. Ralph Hicklin, writing in the *Globe and Mail* said he found it "a bit of a bore," but praised Ms. Darcel for her vivacity and me for my "comic resource."[18] But he faulted me for the show's slow pace. He could not have known how few rehearsals we had with Ms. Darcel to get accustomed to her thick French accent and her style of delivery. But then one should never expect a critic or the audience to be sympathetic toward the reasons for a faulty production. They are only concerned about the end product as it unfolds before them.

While performing *The Little Hut* at night I was renewing my acquaintance with Edward Everett Horton during the day. Horton had chosen for his return engagement at the GCT a play he had appeared in more than 2,600 times over the years, *Springtime for Henry*, in which he played the name part, Henry Dewlip. I was cast in the role I had played for the International Players, Johnny Jelliwell. To add to the strength of the cast, Edward had insisted on including Moya Fenwick because he had such admiration for her performance in *The Reluctant Debutante* the previous summer. Terry Clemes played Miss Smith, and Milo Ringham, then an apprentice with loads of talent, played a secretary. A young Ron Francis also got his start that season as a production assistant, and Mary Webb was the P.R. lady. Francis would eventually become one of the country's top-notch stage managers and involve himself in production, until his untimely death in Singapore in 1995 while the production manager for the South East Asia tour of *The Phantom of the Opera*. Mary Webb went on to replace Mary Joliffe as the public relations officer for the Stratford Festival.

I doubt if Mr. Levy would have recognized many of his lines after Edward had "improved" the play. For example, Jelliwell has a long soliloquy while trying to impress Miss Smith, in which he relates his version of the classic tale of Perseus and Andromeda. Horton had altered and added to this speech so that it became infinitely funnier. He did this even though it was always another actor who delivered it. In the last act, when one should be "rolling for curtain," Levy had given Dewlip a long speech. Horton kept only that portion necessary to forward the plot, such as it was. He never wanted his audience to get bored. At one point a whole page of dialogue between Dewlip and Jelliwell was altered so that the former could give the latter a misguided lesson on the use of the pronoun, which revealed that Horton was a master of the non sequitur. It was an education to work on this meagre comedy with a man who knew how to shape it into a hilarious evening for the audience. Ralph Hicklin's review in the *Globe and Mail* was headed "Horton Makes Gems of Paste," and he began by saying that, "A few weeks ago to atone for some of my more serious sins, I read a dismal little comedy called *Springtime for Henry*, concocted some decades ago by Benn W. Levy. Tonight at the Garden Centre Theatre, Edward Everett Horton appeared in a play of the same name by the same author; but by some alchemy known only to this great and everlasting comedian, the play has become hilarious."[19] As well as admiration for Horton, Hicklin had kudos for the rest of the cast, especially for Ms. Fenwick, who, he wrote, "looked superb as the wife-mistress, as sinuous and cold as a Mayfair Nerfertiti, and played with a high-snooted manner that I found delightful."[20]

Rehearsals were a lot of fun and during one of them Horton, who also directed, took a chair and, as Dewlip, turned it so that he straddled it with his back to the audience. "There," he said to me, "It's your stage." "Don't be silly, Edward," I replied. "I can't take stage. You can do more acting with your back than most of us can with our front." He laughed and appreciated that I was aware of his stage trickery. In a proscenium theatre, any actor who sits with his back to the audience automatically draws focus because it is so rarely done.

Following the rousing success of *Springtime for Henry*, the final play of the 1961 season came close to being a disaster. Despite the loss he took at the box office with his previous presentation of a Canadian play, *Generation of Strangers*, Robert Herrman decided to try again with a first effort by an Ottawa civil servant, George Blackburn. It was an attempt at comedy entitled *A Button Missing* and was yet another version in modern terms of Pygmalion and Galatea. In order to attract an audience to this new play, Herrman had hired Edward Mulhare who had catapulted to fame in North America when, in 1957, he had replaced Rex Harrison as Henry Higgins in *My Fair Lady* on Broadway. Mulhare had begun his career in Cork, Ireland, and developed it in English repertory companies. He had Harrison's clipped style of delivery that was just right for Henry Higgins, and which Bob thought would also be right for Mr. Blackburn's Pygmalion, a character named Norman Drinkwater, a misogynist inventor who has created a life-sized, battery-powered female doll, which upon pressing certain strategic buttons will respond with affection and related reactions. Unfortunately *A Button Missing* had more missing than just a button. It lacked an essential ingredient of comedy — wit. It also lacked a strong performance from its star, who gave up on the play before it even opened. He simply ambled through it, tossing off the lines when he could remember them.

Fortunately for me I had only two scenes as an attorney. Two of the three critics who reviewed it waxed exceedingly unenthusiastic about the whole affair although Sheila Billing, who gave a clever performance as the puppet, won Ed Hocura's admiration for her sheer beauty. But Betty Lampard seemed to have seen a different play because she found it a "barrel of laughs."[21] Actually the play had potential but it needed a clever play doctor. Although Mulhare might have been a Broadway star, he had not played enough film or television roles to make him a household name for the GCT audiences. Attendance had dwindled and Bob Herrman's third season at the Garden Centre Theatre ended not with a bang, but a whimper.

■

Although I had hoped to play Charles Condomine in *Blithe Spirit*, the opening show of the 1963 GCT season, I was again cast as Dr. Bradman and consoled myself with the pleasant prospect of acting with Joyce Gordon as Mrs. Bradman. Tom Harvey was brought in to play Charles and Marjorie Lord, the television wife of Danny Thomas, was the box-office inducement in the role of Elvira. As we approached opening night I began to thank my lucky stars and Bob Herrman that he had not cast me as Condomine. The closer opening night came, the more nervous and insecure Marjorie Lord became. By opening night, either as a result of an actual virus, or through psychosomatic auto-suggestion, her voice began to show signs of strain. By Wednesday a full-blown case of laryngitis had developed, and she could barely be heard above a whisper. Since the GCT could not afford under-studies, the only solution was to place one of the apprentices, Milo Ringham, on the floor behind the sofa to read the lines while Ms. Lord mouthed them. This meant that when Elvira was onstage she clung close to the sofa and everyone else had to adjust to her like satellites circling a planet. Nor did the situation improve much during the week, although Milo was moved off stage left, which led the "star" to play all her scenes stage left. I could not see the show from out front, so I have no idea how successful this lip-syncing was, but I suspect the audience was not fooled. By the first intermission on the Wednesday performance, Ms. Lord pleaded with Milo to slow down. Milo's nervous enthusiasm had her racing like Man-O-War, but Marjorie Lord's jaws could not keep up the pace. Robert Johnston, the publicity manager for the GCT that year, remembered that it was a very sheepish Ms. Lord whom he drove to the airport on the Sunday after the week's run. We never got to know whether or not she would have been a fascinating Elvira but Herbert Whittaker, who had seen the show on Monday before her laryngitis completely took over, found Ms. Lord's performance "amusing, light hearted, petulant as a child, and altogether easy on the eyes."[22] But he was not so kind to Bob Herrman's overall direction of the play. He commented in words that should be studied by anyone essaying a Noel Coward play: "There was also a tendency to act through or despite the lines to give naturalistic inflections to his dialogue. There is nothing naturalistic about Mr. Coward — he is as stylized as Oscar Wilde or a Restoration playwright. The lines contain their own wit and do not have to be made funny. In fact they resist comedy improvements quite strenuously."[23]

After the stuffy Dr. Bradman, yet another stuffy role followed, Albert Kummer in Norman Krasna's comedy, *Dear Ruth*. By now I had developed a facility for playing these up-tight roles, and my challenge was to make each of them different. The twin stars of this show were Pat O'Brien and his wife, Eloise Taylor, who were pleasant both on and offstage and with whom I greatly enjoyed playing. The O'Briens gave the impression of being the ideal married couple. They took pride in their 32-year marriage, not a small achievement in the promiscuous atmosphere of Hollywood, and in their four children and grandchildren. In fact they traded on the wholesome, Irish-Catholic image to a slightly nauseous degree. Movie buffs of the '30s and '40s will remember Pat O'Brien in countless films, the most famous of which was his portrayal of the famous Notre Dame football coach, Knute Rockne. His other screen triumphs were in *The Fighting 69th*, *Fighting Father Dunne*, *Some Like It Hot*, and *The Last Hurrah*. He had quite a following among the elderly and middle-aged patrons of the GCT, and gave a sentimental curtain speech at the end of each performance, which the audience loved. So, business was good that week. *Dear Ruth* received two out of three favourable reviews and I received three out of three. The *St. Catharines Standard* and the *Toronto Telegram* both gave thumbs up, but Wally Wood in the *Toronto Star* turned thumbs down: "*Dear Ruth* was like flat pop."[24] Although I am inclined to agree with him, I must say that it was a pleasant week altogether, except for a couple of minor contretemps between Mr. O'Brien and the publicity manager, Robert Johnston. Bob had joined the Garden Centre that spring after seven years as general manager of the Royal Winnipeg Ballet during its expansionist years. He had arranged an autograph signing for Mr. O'Brien at a St. Catharines school. At first things went smoothly and the students surrounded the celebrity. But after getting O'Brien's autograph they turned to Bob Johnston for his autograph as well. Flattered, Bob gleefully obliged. Soon everyone was clustered around Johnston and O'Brien was left abandoned. This stopped when O'Brien broke through the crowd and glowered at Bob. What O'Brien had probably sensed was that the students really did not have a clue who he was, but simply jumped at a chance to get out of the classroom. Getting Bob's autograph simply added to their moment of freedom. Bob had one other amusing encounter with Mr. O'Brien. On opening night, a few minutes before curtain, he entered O'Brien's dressing room to wish him good luck, and fell flat on his face over the legs of a kneeling priest. He was unaware that O'Brien always received a priest's blessing before the opening of a show. Mr. O'Brien was not pleased by this sprawling intrusion.

E. E. Horton returned for the sixth production of the '63 season in *Miss Pell Is Missing*, an unpretentious little play he was trying out for his repertoire. Pat Moffatt was brought in from Toronto to play Louise Pell, and the role of Oscar Ritter was played by an elderly character actor, Robin Flynn, who had pioneered silent films, had a career in radio and TV in New York, and who had appeared in the previous GCT show, *The World of Suzy Wong* (known to many as "The World of Woozy Song"). Flynn brought out a side of Edward's character that I had not seen before. Horton had no patience with performers he considered to be incompetent no matter how experienced. I thought Mr. Flynn was giving a satisfactory, if somewhat unimaginative, performance, but Horton thought otherwise, and, as rehearsals wore on, he became more and more irascible toward Mr. Flynn. It was an embarrassment for the cast when Horton would snap at him, but Edward had nothing but sweetness and light for the rest of us. *Miss Pell Is Missing* did not have much of a stage life after Horton toured with it. Without his ability to turn lead into, if not gold, at least shining brass, it could not survive.

My friendship with Edward deepened during those two weeks of 1963. Myron Natwick, the nephew of Mildred Natwick, was Edward's designated chauffeur and actor this time. The handsome young man had perfectly arrayed gleaming teeth that had been an asset for toothpaste commercials in the United States. He hoped to achieve similar results with his choppers while in Canada, so I set up a meeting for him with an agent, and Horton let him take the Thunderbird to Toronto. That morning I agreed to drive Edward, an avid tennis player all his life, in my car to his workout on the court. At the appointed time I picked him up at the Casablanca Motel where I found him clad in his boxer shorts adding pads to shins, knees, and elbows. Over these he put on the traditional costume for tennis worn by his generation — white trousers, white shirt, and white running shoes. As he dressed he said, "These days young men take most of their clothes off to play tennis. I have to put all this padding on to keep me from falling apart." At the tennis club he paid a tennis pro to play with him, but they had to play by Edward's rules. He played at the back of the court. Any ball that landed in the forecourt was a point for him. I was full of admiration and amusement to see this 77-year-old dashing back and forth, viciously hitting the ball with obvious enthusiasm and enjoyment. Essentially averse to any kind of strenuous exercise, I marvelled at his energy and zeal.

Edward had a great liking for Chinese food. In fact he had a liking for any kind of food. Next to acting, I think eating was his chief delight. His consumption leaned slightly more toward the gourmand than the gourmet. In addition to the after-show party he gave at the Casablanca at least once during the week's run, he would treat some of us to a repast at a late-night Chinese restaurant in St. Catharines. I had discovered one in a small house that would stay open until the last customer decided to leave. Although not a heavy drinker, he would enjoy the occasional relaxing drink after a show to unwind. He hated the public rooms of the Prudhommes' motel, but he appreciated the quiet homey atmosphere of this Chinese restaurant where the proprietor's small children ran about even at 1:30 in the morning. Through Eddy Horton, not only did I learn a lot about comedy timing, but I also learned to like egg drop soup and jasmine tea.

Mercifully I was spared involvement in the show following *Miss Pell Is Missing*, but I am glad I saw it because it was a perfect example of how a "star personality" can almost single-handedly destroy a play and yet give an audience an evening of riotous entertainment. The show was *The Tunnel of Love* and the one-man wrecking crew was Mickey Rooney. This was a complete package show that the ageing gamin was touring that summer, aided and abetted by television personality, Bobby Van. Robert Johnston was assigned to pick up the cast at the Buffalo airport in his new Chevrolet convertible. Because of the size of the cast a second vehicle was required, but the only one available was a slightly dilapidated pick-up truck. When the cast emerged from the airport, Rooney and another actor willingly got into the Chevrolet, but Bobby Van balked, maintaining that they were always picked up by a limousine. Johnston informed him that a larger vehicle would be along shortly. Mr. Van found himself obliged to ride from Buffalo to Vineland in a bouncy, non-luxurious truck — and was not at all pleased.[25]

The playwright would never have recognized his play, which became a hilarious romp for Rooney. At one point he deliberately interrupted the action by kicking his running shoe into the audience so that he could climb down off the stage to reclaim it. This gave him the opportunity for some kibitzing with the audience. The result was a show not presented according to theatrical Hoyle, but, nonetheless, a lively entertainment that the audience adored. However, I was glad I was not one of his unfortunate supporting cast, who were straight men or women for Mr. Rooney most of the time. One of the actresses had a speech at the end of the first act that on opening night, according to Bob Johnston, got a laugh. She never got it again because on the second night, Rooney stole it from her. Just as she concluded her speech, he pretended to get his finger caught in the door when he slammed it.[26]

For ticket sales, it was important that visiting stars appear on *Meet the Millers*, a talk show on Buffalo television. Some of the *Tunnel* cast members were co-operative, but Bobby Van and Rooney — despite his high fee of $6,000 per week — refused to make any personal appearances. The Millers were incensed and the GCT was deprived of valuable publicity, which contributed to Bob Herrman's losing money on this expensive show despite happy houses.

My next assignment for the GCT was in the season's 11th show, which starred another of the silver screen's almost-leading men, Donald Woods, who was born in Brandon, Manitoba, but who moved to California when he was seven. He had performed major roles in such great films as *A Tale of Two Cities*, *Anthony Adverse*, *Watch on the Rhine*, and *Never Say Goodbye*. He had also appeared in several American drama series that crowded the television networks in the 1950s and 1960s. I had seen most of his films and I had always thought of him as a rather unexciting actor. However, he turned out to be a very likeable person. Two weeks earlier that summer he had played in *The Moon Is Blue* for the GCT. He now appeared as the father of the co-ed heroine in *Take Her, She's Mine*. Joanna Pettet, who had made her professional debut at the Garden Centre in 1960 with the McGill student revue *Got It Made*, was hired by Robert to play the co-ed daughter. Following that tour, Ms. Pettet hied herself off to the Neighbourhood Playhouse in New York. She was chosen by Elia Kazan to be part of the Lincoln Centre Repertory Company. After that she played a major role in the Broadway production of *Take Her, She's Mine* and graduated to the female lead when that show went on the road. In only three years this talented young lady made the transition from amateur to a leading role in a Broadway show and was now returning to play that role at the theatre where she had her first professional engagement.

But an otherwise pleasurable rehearsal week was marred by a tragedy in Joanna's life when her two roommates were murdered in their New York apartment. The rehearsal was cancelled the afternoon we heard the news, and Ms. Pettet, naturally in shock, retired to her room. She preferred to live in the residence with the other members of the company rather than in the motel. The whole company were highly supportive. We were all aware that had she been in New York rather than Vineland, she too would likely have been a victim. Her room was just across the hall from mine. I collected Robert Johnston and Andrew Johnson, the juvenile in the show, and at cocktail hour we decided that she should not be left alone. We went to her room and by dint of funny anecdotes, theatre chat, and my lethal martinis managed to ease her grief if only momentarily. The best distraction for her was rehearsal so the next day she escaped into her role with renewed zeal. Eventually a man was arrested, confessed to the crimes, and spent 11 years in prison before another man confessed to the murders. The first man, somewhat slow-witted, had sought the notoriety of being charged with a double murder. Joanna Pettet went on to have a brilliant, if brief, career in the United States both on the stage and in films during the '60s and '70s.

Take Her, She's Mine has 18 characters, most of them university students for whom all the "apprenti" were drafted, including a young Larry Goldhar, who later became one of Toronto's most successful talent agents. His brother, Marvin, also made an appearance in this show. Like several of the actors, I doubled in the play: early I made a brief appearance as a stereotypical, dry-as-dust high school principal, and later turned up as a stereotypical, dry-as-dust, bumbling professor of English. Andrew Johnson, who had played in *Dear Ruth* earlier that summer, returned to play in this show. Milo Ringham re-appeared, as did a young actress who had also made her mark in *Dear Ruth*, Sue Kiss — a name ideally suited for an actress playing effervescent teenage roles.

That I was able to create two distinct characters in *Take Her, She's Mine*, one of which was a scene-stealing vignette, gave a happy ending for me to Bob Herrman's fourth season among the grapevines of the Niagara Peninsula. He concluded the 1963 season with *No Bed of Roses*, a musical adaptation of Jan de Hartog's *The Fourposter*, which was being tried out in the summer circuit. It was a failure that left the door open to an extremely successful later adaptation called *I Do, I Do*. That season had not proved to be a profitable one for the Herrman family. Several expensive packages from Hollywood with their high-priced stars ate up the profit made on the other shows with local actors and less expensive names. Raymond Burr, for instance, received $5,000 a week plus a percentage of the gross over $15,000. In addition there were the salaries of the rest of the cast in American money, and the cost of flying the whole company directly from Hollywood. Bob threw in an extra matinee performance on the Wednesday and had another row of seats added to give the theatre an enlarged capacity. Because Burr was at the height of his TV popularity and because it was a well-acted, no-nonsense production, every performance sold out. In spite of that, the producer lost money on the show because the ticket prices had to remain relatively low. Herrman looked on these shows as "loss leaders" because they enticed people to the theatre who had never been there before and who hopefully would return.

In 1963, a subscription series for $15 gave the purchaser the choice of any six plays. The regular top price was $3 per ticket, which seems ridiculously low when compared with today's inflated prices, but everything is relative. A haircut could be obtained for $2.50 and $3 could still buy a meal in a lower-priced restaurant. Bob kept prices deliberately reasonable to match the local audience's pocket book. I was never convinced that Bob was a very shrewd businessman. He was so easy going and loved the theatre so much that I fear he was often taken advantage of, particularly by the unscrupulous Hollywood agents with whom he had to deal. Because it was a summer stock operation with an American producer and mostly American stars, even though it employed a lot of Canadian performers, the Garden Centre Theatre did not qualify for any grants from the arts councils. The sole source of revenue was the unpredictable box-office receipts. By the end of 1963 the optimism the Herrmans had four years before was beginning to wear thin. But Bob and his wife Terry determined to return for a fifth season, which they opened on June 15 of 1964.

▪

I was brought in for the second show, a new play unimaginatively titled *Mr. and Mrs.* by a man with the alliterative name of Sherwood Schwarz. Originally an hour-long television comedy written for Bob Hope and Lucille Ball, it had become a full-length play padded with more bawdy humour than television of the day would allow. The box-office draw consisted of Jackie Coogan, Ruta Lee, and Steve Dunne. Mr. Coogan was famous for his endearing performance at the age of four in Charlie Chaplin's 1921 silent film, *The Kid*, and was about to reach renewed fame in *The Addams Family*, which was scheduled to begin that summer on television. Ruta Lee originally hailed from Montreal and with Frank Sinatra's assistance built a notable career in film and TV, while Steve Dunne came into the tinsel world of movies and TV via radio. He also had a considerable background as a leading man onstage. Of the three, Coogan was the one I most wanted to meet because he had been a child star when I was a child just beginning to go to the movies. But my relationship with this threesome did not get off to an auspicious start.

At the outset of the 1964 season when Bob's decision to use the impressively named "Niagara Public Relations Bureau Press" did not work out, he brought in Shirley Stonehouse as the publicity manager. In the interim, there was no P.R. person to meet the visiting celebrities of the second show when they arrived. Bob pleaded with me to take his car and claim the three stars at Buffalo airport. His was a large car, and because I had only driven small vehicles all my life, I was nervous. However I drove off to the airport to meet my charges after their long flight from L.A. They were a friendly trio and the drive to Vineland started out pleasantly enough. But, because I was unused to the size of the car, at one point I almost bounced Steve Dunne and Ruta Lee off the back seat and when I drove over a curb Coogan in the front seat almost hit the roof. Then I missed the turn to the Peace Bridge to Canada and found myself trapped going west to Erie, Pennsylvania. It was miles before I was able to find a cloverleaf that permitted me to turn around. By the time we reached the Prudhommes' motel my weary, anxious passengers were a not-too-amiable group, although they breathed a sigh of relief to be out of the clutches of this unreliable driver.

Rehearsals proved to be a more rewarding experience, especially for me. I had a large role, that of a banker who, instead of being rejected by the girl, eventually rejects her. Despite my driving, I found the three stars very supportive. And I was part of a very co-operative cast that included Terry Clemes and that fine character actor, Joel Kenyon, who joined the company that year. Also there were colleagues from the Maple Leaf Theatre days: Eric Donkin in the role of a TV producer, and as a TV director, Martin Lager. Tim Henry was an apprentice that season and soon proved himself to be a real asset to the company. Ron Weston had been in several previous shows at the GCT and now his grown-up son, Steve Weston, joined him.

Mr. and Mrs. received favourable reviews on the whole. Betty Lampard in the *St. Catharines Standard* wrote that, "It took Vernon Chapman of Toronto, a veteran of many Garden Centre plays, to virtually walk away with the show as the stuffy Walter. Chapman is so smooth in his timing, so perfectly in character all the time, that he steadied the pace of the production several times."[27] There! Did I not say she was a perspicacious critic? Ms. Lampard, Stewart Brown of the *Hamilton Spectator*, and Ralph Hicklin in the *Globe and Mail* were all enthusiastic about Ruta Lee both for her performance and her glamorous appearance, but Jackie Coogan was criticized by all three for playing every scene at top volume, which made for a stagey performance out of sync with the rest of the cast.

I had enjoyed myself immensely during *Mr. and Mrs.*, and because I liked the visiting trio I made a point of having the Sunday departure breakfast with them in the motel coffee shop. As they were going out the door to be driven by someone else to the airport, Jackie Coogan turned and shouted to me across the restaurant, "We wouldn't want to drive with you again, but we would be willing to act with you anytime." At that moment I became a fan of *The Addams Family* before the first episode was ever shown.

I directed the season's fourth show, *A Thousand Clowns*, which had been a considerable success on Broadway but was to be a frustrating experience for me. This funny, often sentimental comedy is about a bachelor scriptwriter whose precocious 12-year-old nephew was left in the writer's charge six years earlier when his sister stepped out to buy a package of cigarettes and never returned. The plot deals with the investigation by a female psychologist and a male social worker into the unorthodox lifestyle the boy is leading with his off-beat uncle — a serious theme treated in a light-hearted way. To play the leading male role of Murray Burns, the producer had hired a young stand-up comedian who had been catapulted from second-stream night clubs to international television fame because of his brilliant imitation of and facial resemblance to President Kennedy. Clever though Vaughn Meader was as a solo comic, he was an inexperienced stage actor, so I surrounded him with a cast of extremely skilled performers, including Marvin Goldhar and Shirley Knight (the Canadian one) as well as Ben Lennick as the brother Arnold, and Allen Doremus as the social worker. With this cast I had high hopes for the show.

Mr. Meader was a delightful fellow with a cheerful outlook on life, but he was another who had not developed the necessary facility for learning lines and he seemed to look upon these stage appearances as a vacation from the more serious business of being a stand-up comic. He did not know how to get inside Burns's character, so he was simply Vaughn Meader saying the words when he could remember them. As the rehearsal week wore on and he seemed to make little progress, I blew my cool. Shirley Knight says that it was the only time she ever saw me lose my temper.[28] Friendliness, patience, and cajoling had not pressured Meader into learning his words. I thought bullying might. I cancelled the afternoon's rehearsal and sent him out into a nearby field with an apprentice to help him memorize the lines. Unfortunately I made the mistake of assigning an attractive female apprentice that had the effect of diminishing Vaughn's ability to concentrate on the script. Not many lines were learned that afternoon. There was another weak link in the cast. Brad Herrman, Bob's son who had been a clever child actor, now at 13 was passing very quickly into the self-conscious teens. As a result he lacked the vivacity and unreserved enthusiasm of the boy, Nick.

The opening night dragged horribly. Meader was slow at picking up his cues, and the rest of the cast assumed his lethargic pace. Perhaps I too was at fault for not pressuring him earlier in rehearsals. I didn't need the reviewers to tell me what was wrong with the production, but I was frustratingly powerless to correct it. Meader just was not an actor. What was good about the production were the performances by some of the supporting actors, particularly Marvin Goldhar, who revelled in portraying the insensitive and insecure Leo, and Shirley Knight, an actress with deep sensitivity as well as a flare for comedy, as the uptight psychiatrist in need of a psychiatrist. The reviewers had high praise for her. Since, I have often wondered what became of Vaughn Meader. The assassination of President Kennedy brought an abrupt halt to his specialty act. But was that the only string to Meader's bow? I hope his experience at the Garden Centre Theatre discouraged any ambition he might have had to become an actor. If it didn't, it should have.

As the 1960s wore on, television was claiming more of my time, and my appearances at the GCT became less frequent. Besides, there were other actors capable of playing the roles in which I was most often cast. So I did not appear again that season until the eighth show, which was *Petticoat Fever*, that dated turkey I had directed for the International Players and which you may remember gave me a lesson about theatre critics. Bob Herrman directed this second time around for me, and brought in the handsome and amiable Jack Kelly, brother of Nancy Kelly of the dozens of short film comedies. Jack Kelly had started as a child model and became a child performer for the Schuberts in New York, appearing with many of the Broadway stars of the day. After serving in the United States Air Force during the war, he began his film career. But it was on TV that he achieved his greatest and most financially rewarding success as James Garner's brother, Bart Maverick, in the long running *Maverick* series. He was a charming person with no affectation about him, and he and his wife, Peggy, who did not act in the show, fit right in with the rest of the company.

As in Kingston, I again played the fat-headed Englishman whose plane crashes near the Arctic research station occupied solely by a scientist with the unlikely name of Dascom Dinsmore. Accompanying the pilot is his fiancée, who becomes the object of a plot by the sex-starved Dinsmore to satisfy his desires. The situation is further complicated by the arrival in the third act of an old flame of Dinsmore's. The third act is the best, but it takes a glacial age for the author, Mark Reed, to get you there.

The cast uniformly received enthusiastic notices. Tim Henry made the most of his moments as Kino, Dinsmore's grinning Eskimo valet, and Moya Fenwick and Lawrence Beattie lifted the third act with their skill as comedy performers. I had a ball playing the British booby. But Ralph Hicklin summed up the problem in presenting this 1935 play in 1964: "In the years between we have been conditioned by playwrights of awesome sophistication, technical ability, and occasionally wit to expect a great deal on the comic stage. Reed's play, serving this week as a vehicle for Jack Kelly, seems a bit naïve and terribly slow."[29] Nevertheless, it made money. Jack Kelly was both a disarmingly affable performer and a stimulus at the box office.

Another engagement followed by Edward Everett Horton who had grown to like Vineland and the actors Bob hired to appear with him. Horton pulled another play out of his theatrical bag, *The White Sheep of the Family*, a zany English farce that had premiered in London in 1951. I got the opportunity to wander through several scenes as an absent-minded Anglican Vicar. The family in the play, except for the white sheep, are engaged in criminal activity, and at one point the Vicar jokingly gives a toast "to crime." Horton as the father of the crooked family, was standing beside me and was to react suspiciously to my remark. At one performance after I gave the toast, he decided to thrust his face toward me. I then thrust my face toward his in bewildered response. He in turn thrust his face even closer. I responded the same way. After several more forward thrusts our beaks were touching. He had the next line, but he did not say it. Instead he turned his head away and gave me one of his famous triple takes. I also turned my head away and was able to reciprocate with a triple take of my own. A grin of appreciation spread over his face and he said his next line, which was simply a repeat of the words "To crime?" Edward and I had indulged in an interplay enjoyable to us, but it was a mark of Horton's generosity as a performer that he did not resent my extracting as much comedy out of the character of the Vicar as possible, even during the scenes in which he appeared. In fact he encouraged it, and he admired actors who could hold their own with him. He loved Moya Fenwick and Myron Natwick for that reason and delighted in playing scenes with them. Edward had been touring in *A Funny Thing Happened on the Way to the Forum*, but he took a leave of absence from that show to honour his commitment to Bob. Fortunately he did because once again he brought out the fans and made us a profit on the show. The critics correctly diagnosed *The White Sheep of the Family* to be one prolonged joke, but they praised Horton and the cast for making it into a hilarious romp.

While performing *White Sheep* I was once more rehearsing a major role during the day. Bob had decided to stage *Champagne Complex* again. As you'll remember, the previous production had John Emery playing the male lead and I played the amiable prude. This time I pleaded with Bob and he agreed to let me play the leading role of the psychiatrist, Carter Bowen. I was thrilled that the female role was going to be filled with the luscious Miss Denmark of 1958, Greta Thyssen. The dog T. S. Eliot was played by another scene-stealer, Cantata, a poodle.

I arrived a few minutes late for the first rehearsal, and, slightly flustered, I did not fully appreciate Ms. Thyssen's stunning beauty when I was introduced to her. Later in the rehearsal she rose and walked over to stand beside my chair. I looked up from my script to find myself staring into a shapely expanse of bare midriff. I was then able to absorb the total effect of this splendid body. She was perfectly proportioned and I was soon to learn that she was perfectly charming as well. She had no delusions about herself as a great actress, but she was intelligent and talented enough to bring a sparkling, bubbly personality to the role. That day I took her to lunch at the Beacon restaurant just along the Queen Elizabeth Highway at Jordan Harbour. The Beacon had a dining room that was built right over the Lake Ontario shoreline. We were shown to a table across the dance floor by the windows. As we crossed the floor, her spiked heels clicked so loudly that the sound drew the attention of a bus load of senior citizens having their lunch. Old men and women stared at this beautiful, sexy creature and I basked in the aura of her presence. Our table was on the route to the men's washroom, and every old boy in the room eventually contrived to have a weak bladder so that he could pass our table for a closer look.

A very level-headed young lady, Ms. Thyssen was not vain about her extraordinary prettiness. She was pert, bright, and a thorough delight to be with. We spent a lot of time together that week, and I regretted that I was also involved in the following show, which forced me to rehearse when I could have been squiring her around the Niagara Peninsula. She saw no reason to refrain from showing as much of her exceptional body as decency would allow. The producer quite naturally endorsed this attitude because he was also susceptible to her charms, and because it sold tickets. So, for much of the play, she wore only a halter top and low slung, tight slim jims revealing acres of midriff and testing my powers of concentration.

I greatly enjoyed playing Carter Bowen, although I realized that few were looking at me while Greta was onstage. There is nothing very dashing about the psychiatrist, but I received satisfaction in carrying off a romantic role, and I was pleased that I had not let Bob down. Ralph Hicklin in the *Globe and Mail* paid me a large compliment: "Vernon Chapman, a regular at Vineland this season, plays the psychiatrist. He makes a great deal out of a pretty flat character, and offers his best work of the season. It is no easy job to play straight man to Venus de Milo, but he manages to be present at all times."[30] However, it was fortunate he was not present on Friday night. At the beginning of the third act, Allyn Macy, the role Greta played, fakes a suicide to make her psychiatrist, with whom she has fallen in love, drop his professional reserve and demonstrate how he feels about her. Just as he arrives at the door, she turns on the gas oven and fakes a collapse on the kitchen floor. The psychiatrist bursts in, discovers her, picks her up, carries her to the sofa in the living room, and proceeds to bring her around uttering words of consolation and endearment for half a page before he realizes she is faking. Greta was far from a heavy woman, but since I am no Hercules, it required all the strength I could muster to pick her up in a dead lift from the kitchen floor and carry her to the sofa. I managed it success-fully Monday through Thursday, but, on Friday night, just as I lifted her off the floor into my arms, my left leg twisted under me and I toppled back pulling her on top of me. I rolled her off, picked her up and started to carry her to the sofa. She was laughing so hard that the rise and fall of her beau-tiful breasts was obvious even to the last row. All the dialogue of concern became redundant, so I dumped her down on the sofa and skipped to the line where I accuse her of fakery. But neither she nor I nor the audience could help laughing at my clumsiness. Actually I consider it to be one of my most glorious theatrical moments. Not every actor gets a chance to roll on the kitchen floor with Miss Denmark.

Leprechauns are supposed to be found only in Ireland, but in 1959 a particularly gifted one with the anatomical name of Tom Kneebone arrived from Auckland, New Zealand, via the Old Vic Company. After the Old Vic concluded its North American tour in New York that year, Tom was offered a job with the Australian Elizabethan Trust. He was about to leave when he was cabled that the job had been cancelled. He found himself stranded in Manhattan with very little money and no work permit. He had made some friends in Toronto when the Old Vic had played there and contacted Bar-bara Hamilton, who helped him get established. In short order he had engagements at the Crest Theatre as Diggory in *She Stoops to Conquer*, in Mavor Moore's *The Ottawa Man*, with Barbara Hamilton in *That Hamilton Woman*, and in the musical delight, *Salad Days*, which took him back to New York. In 1964 he won the *Toronto Telegram Award* for the best variety performer of the year. He had previously appeared at the GCT in *Three Men on a Horse* and in that lamentable production of *Twentieth Century*. Bob Herrman brought him back in a highly improbable vaudeville known as *Good Night, Ladies* or *Ladies' Night in a Turkish Bath*. To put this hectic farce across, Bob recruited a high powered cast of farceurs from Toronto, including Lynne Gorman, Barbara Cummings, Maureen Fitzgerald, and Lawrence Beattie. He also used many of the talented apprentices from that season: June Keevil, Cheryl Thurston, Carroll Gair, Beverley Aston, and Sandra Smyth. He even drafted Shirley Stonehouse from publicity to play Mrs. Tarleton.

Kneebone played a misogynistic arachnologist who had been alienated from the opposite sex by his knowledge of what certain female spiders do to their male mates. His cronies, played by Larry Beattie and myself, try to cure him of his aversion to the sight of female flesh by taking him to an Artists' Ball. When this affair is raided by the police, the three men take refuge in a steam bath on ladies night. You can write the plot of Cyrus Wood's mad caper from there on. Of course the men get dressed up in drag and masquerade as women. Wearing fright wigs (I was a bleached blonde for the occasion), the men conceal themselves in steam cabinets. While they are trapped in these apparati, Maureen Fitzgerald, affectionately known as "Big Mo" to her friends, in the role of Miss LaBouche, does a semi-striptease. This show-stopping event is indelibly imprinted on my memory. A large lady, even in 1964, Maureen performed with all the seductive guile of an over-sized Sally Rand. In those days Toronto had a burlesque house known as the Victory, at the corner of Spadina and Dundas Streets. So impressed was Ralph Hicklin with Maureen's undulations that he wrote "She might have stepped right out of the Victory, Toronto's or Nelson's."[31] In that same review he extolled Mr. Kneebone's virtuosity, noting that the plot turned out happily and innocuously, "but not before we have seen Mr. Kneebone give a tremendous display of his comic resources. . . . I commend to you one moment in particular wherein the Spanish lady [Kneebone], encased up to her neck in a steam cabinet, watches a blood curdling display of the art of striptease presented by another denizen of the Turkish bath. With only his huge eyes and tiny face, Mr. Kneebone shows a horror, frustration, and lust that Maurice Schwarz might envy."[32] (Maurice Schwarz was one of the great actors of both drama and comedy of the American and Yiddish theatre of the first half of the 20th century.) Although the whole cast entered into the spirit of this romp, I am sure it would have been a very vapid affair without someone of Kneebone's clowning ability to sustain it.

Good Night, Ladies was the closing play of that season. The Herrmans were beginning to show the strain of six years of struggle with no appreciable profit at the end of each year. They shortened the 1964 season to 12 weeks and closed on September 5. Television was having an impact on theatre attendance, and the shows, especially the imported ones, were becoming more expensive. In my opinion, because he was nervous about losing his audience, Bob kept the ticket prices too low, particularly when the company received no subsidies. The Herrmans — Bob, Terry, and family — had to live during the winter on the salaries they paid themselves during the summer, unless they were lucky enough to get some work when they returned to New York. I think the worry over the finances of the Garden Centre contributed to the increase in the volume of alcohol both Bob and Terry consumed. By the end of the 1964 season I noticed a deterioration in Bob's health and a discouragement that was reflected in the stoop of his shoulders. Yet, although 1964 had not shown a profit, they determined to soldier on for another year.

▪

The 1965 season began early in June with *Absence of a Cello*, starring Hans Conreid, the Uncle Tanoose of the Danny Thomas TV show, but I was not involved until the second show. Bob had hired me to direct Norman Krasna's little bit of fluff, *Sunday in New York*. The box-office draw for this was to be another one-day wonder of the American television world. By now experienced enough with Hollywood celebrities to know that the "star" might only be a fragment of a meteorite so far as stage ability was concerned, I cast the show with the strongest actors I could find: Irena

Mayeska in the female lead, and Robert Koons, Tudi Wiggins, Ray Bellew, and Tony Moffat-Lynch in supporting roles. Irena had been building a career at Stratford, on tour with the Canadian Players, at the Crest Theatre, and on TV. Tony Moffat-Lynch began in pantomime and children's theatre and became noticed by Toronto audiences through George Luscombe's Toronto Workshop Productions. The handsome Raymond Bellew was becoming a popular TV actor in Toronto. A few years later with his fill of the rat race, he accepted the position of a radio announcer in Newfoundland where his looks were no asset, but his voice was. Tudi Wiggins had built a reputation as a clever actress in the Eve Arden comedy vein. I wanted her and Tony for the variety of roles that the script indicated should be played by the same actors, and which I knew from seeing them perform that they were capable of handling. They proved to be wise choices.

Monday morning rehearsal time arrived and the cast assembled except for the star whose name escapes me — which is probably just as well. He was supposed to fly in from Britain that morning, but the person sent to Toronto to meet him reported that he was not on the flight. Bob immediately phoned the star's agent in Hollywood, who blandly informed him that the star had another commitment that he would be accepting even though he had signed an Equity contract with the GCT. The actor in question had flown from Britain to New York to Hollywood. Bob was fuming and threatened to bring him up on a breach of contract charge with Equity in the United States. To no avail. That actor refused to honour Bob's contract.

The immediate problem was replacing him on such short notice. On hand was a cast waiting to rehearse, but no leading man. Bob racked his brains for an eligible Hollywood name who might conceivably be able to act and might be a box-office draw. While Bob was frantically searching, I decided to start blocking the play using an apprentice as a stand-in. After a frustrating day of calling various American agents, on the Tuesday Bob came up with the name of John Saxon, once a teenage heartthrob whose career had hit the doldrums now that he had become an old man in his mid-20s. Bob phoned Saxon's agent who said that Mr. Saxon would not be interested in stage work. Undaunted, Bob phoned Saxon directly, who eagerly jumped at the chance because he wanted to get more stage experience. When Bob relayed this to me my heart sank. Was this another Guy Madison, a name but little acting ability? Bob instructed Saxon to go to the Los Angeles office of Samuel French and purchase a copy of *Sunday in New York*. Bob would book him a flight from L.A. to Buffalo for that day. A fee was arranged with Saxon's agent and Saxon would arrive to rehearse the following day, Wednesday. This left only five rehearsal days for Saxon to learn a major role before opening on the Monday night, June 27. Mindful of Vaughn Meader's inability to memorize his lines in a week, I looked with trepidation to the next five days.

On Wednesday morning the awaited star arrived, and a more disarmingly charming young man I have rarely met. The cast warmed to him instantly. He made it quite clear immediately that he had taken the engagement because he wanted more stage experience and that he would need all the help he could get. We all realized that here was a man who was serious about acting and about his career. Born in the Bronx of Italian-American parents, he had no interest in acting but his handsomeness led to his becoming a model for magazine illustrations. He used the name Coby Bennet because it placed him near the top of photographers' lists, but when eventually he did succumb to the blandishments of Tinsel Town he took the name of John Saxon. At 17 he was given a contract at Universal-International Studio and rapidly became a favourite with the younger audience. As he grew out of his teens his popularity waned and he appeared in a series of pot-boilers, including some science fiction films made in Italy and England. Just before coming to Vineland he had been studying acting with Stella Adler and in an interview with Ralph Hicklin he confessed, "I've come to love acting — in just the last few years. I never used to."[33]

As soon as the introductions were over, we got to work. Irena Mayeska sat down beside Mr. Saxon, glanced at his script and said, "I don't know what play you're doing, but we're doing *Sunday in New York*." The script he had purchased at Samuel French's in Hollywood and had been frantically studying during the long flight to Buffalo was *Barefoot in the Park*. Now he was even further behind the other cast members who had already learned at least the first act, and the challenge for him to be ready for the following Monday was even more daunting. Fortunately he was a quick study, and, although on opening night he was a little shaky, the other cast members were secure enough to cover for any line changes or miscues he gave them, which were not many. Unlike Vaughn Meader, Mr. Saxon knew how to learn lines and he possessed a natural acting talent. Moreover he was so right for the role and radiated such charm and sex appeal that he could have read a shopping list and the audience would have loved it. During the brief rehearsal period my task was to fit his vitality into a frothy sex-comedy without destroying his naturalness. On opening night, Saxon ploughed nervously through all his laughs, but after I explained to him the technique of waiting and cutting into the laugh half way into its downward curve, he began to use it and by the closing performance he was in control of the character, its comedy, and the audience. He had entered into the spirit of light comedy without sacrificing any of his charm, sensitivity, drive, and vitality. When he finished at Vineland he accepted another role in a play in San Francisco, and from that city sent a letter generously thanking me for my help and stating that the Vineland experience had built his confidence about stage acting. Soon after that his film career got a boost when he was cast as the Mexican bandit in *The Appaloosa* starring Marlon Brando, and he more than held his own opposite that powerful actor. Since then he has made many films and in recent years has appeared in soap operas on television. Not bad for a young man who in the beginning did not like acting.

I turned up next as director for *Love and Kisses*, a comedy about teenage romance, which marked a return engagement for Jack Kelly. As the two lovesick adolescents I cast two apprentices, Marylu Moyer and Tedd Reed, who walked away with the show. Marylu hailed from Winnipeg where she had performed at the University of Manitoba and the Manitoba Theatre Centre. Her duties at Vineland ran the gamut from dresser, scene painter, and property obtainer to stage sweeper. These duties she shared with the other apprentices including Mr. Reed. Tedd had just joined the company as a replacement apprentice and his signing on was a stroke of good fortune for the company. Both Tedd and Marylu were short in stature but large in talent. They were good-looking, wholesome young people with intelligence, abundant enthusiasm, and energy. They radiated the innocence necessary to portray the idealized, junior members of North American middle-class families fashionable in those days on television and in films. They took direction easily, responded to suggestions quickly, and were willing to work hard. I was fortunate to have two such young people in the show.

I was also lucky to have persuaded Bob Herrman to hire Eleanor Beecroft to play a Nanny. Eleanor had been a vital part of the Toronto amateur theatre during the '30s and '40s, and became a professional as soon as work could be obtained in summer stock and on television. When Bob saw her perform he asked me where I had been hiding her. As the father, Jack Kelly played Jack Kelly, which was ideal. Herbert Whittaker wrote, "Kelly is reasonable and Kelly is easy. He isn't even fazed when he mixes up the names of his stage family." He went on to say that Kelly's performance was "topped by that of an 18-year-old York University student named Tedd Reed. Reed, although making his first professional appearance here as the teenaged Benedict, takes over with his highly credible study of a perplexed but confident youth. . . . Reed is well balanced by Marylu Moyer, 19, as his child bride. . . . Miss Moyer is both sincere and appealing, and in her big scene, entirely convincing."[34] I was delighted that these two bright young actors had received not only critical kudos, but the admiration of Jack Kelly and the whole company as well as the audience.

While *Love and Kisses* was performing I was rehearsing the role of Granville Prescott in *Wake Up, Darling*. This was a play starring and directed by Michael Rennie who had discovered two years earlier that it was an ideal vehicle for him and had been touring the summer circuit with it since then. A graduate of Cambridge University, the York Repertory company, the RAF, and 50 movies including such costume epics as *Desiree, Rains of Ranchipur, Demetrius and the Gladiators, Les Misérables,* and *The Robe,* Michael Rennie proved to be a very encouraging, sensitive, and understanding director. Everyone liked him and it was a happy two weeks for us all. Also in this production were Eleanor Beecroft playing another maid, Tudi Wiggins as a secretary, and Jackie Burroughs as Polly Emerson, the wife of the leading male character. Rennie was so impressed with Tudi Wiggins that he encouraged her to try her luck in Hollywood, which she did later that year with the result that she spent many years appearing in TV soap operas. For me one of the great rewards of this production was being able to work with that remarkably intelligent and sensitive actress, Jackie Burroughs, famous in recent years for her performances in *Road to Avonlea* on CBC-TV. She was a delight both on and offstage. Some of the members of the cast, including Michael Rennie and myself, spent several late nights after the show drinking up the atmosphere and the liquor of the Oban Inn in Niagara-on-the-Lake, run by that gracious lady, Ms. Burroughs, Jackie's mom. There we compared notes with some of the cast members of the infant Shaw Festival, which had been founded three years before by Brian Doherty.

In order to fill a broadcasting day, television demands a vast number of varied programs, many of them quite dreary. Quiz shows were always present and one of the progenitors of this genre was *Queen for a Day*, whose Master of Ceremonies for over 20 years was Jack Bailey. By 1965 he was a household name, and Bob hoped he would be a big box-office draw at the GCT in yet another formula family comedy, *Time Out for Ginger*. In this one I was another school principal. Also in the cast was Terry Clemes who, despite a versatile talent, became the most over-exposed actress at the GCT. I ran the same risk and by the 1965 season was quite content not to appear in every show. One reviewer referred to me as Vineland's "comic fixture." The play was entirely forgettable but Jack Bailey was not. Originally a stage actor, he brought much more to the role than the ersatz charm of a Quiz Master, and he was a convivial fellow to work with. He won the audience not only because of his performance, but also because at his curtain speech he summoned onstage and introduced individually all the apprentices. Then he would bring out his trombone and play a chorus of "Who's Sorry Now?" and as the critic for the *Toronto Telegram* wrote, "By that time nobody was."[35]

But our next audiences were. Following Mr. Bailey's popular appearance was an egregious package of *The Student Prince*, which revealed the dangers of the package system: the theatre had no control over what it was getting. Elaine Malbin was completely unknown to Canadian audiences of the day, but received top billing over Robert Rounceville, who had spent much of his career performing in that treacly operetta. This package was tacky, and, except for Rounceville, had inept performers. They were also accident prone. One of the male singers broke his leg and spent the week sitting around the actors' residence, and a female singer broke her wrist after falling down the backstage stairs in what appeared to be an inebriated state.

Fortunately packages were not all the same, because my final appearance with the GCT that season was in a semi-package. Tom Ewell and Joan Bennett arrived with a group of American actors to perform *Never Too Late*, about a husband and wife who, in their middle years, find out that they are going to be parents again. Every movie fan will be familiar with Joan Bennett who appeared in over 70 films. For a star of her fame and beauty she was remarkably self-effacing, and believed that only a few of her films had merit. I had seen her in *Disraeli, Little Women, Father of the Bride*, and *The Woman in the Window*, among others, and I had always found her performances convincing, truthful, but somewhat statuesque, and lacking the vivacity of those of her sister, Constance. I had become an admirer of Tom Ewell when I saw him opposite Marylyn Monroe in the film version of *The Seven Year Itch* in a part he had created on Broadway, and again when I saw him in *Adam's Rib*. By 1965 he and his wife had a Mister and Missus morning talk show on NBC radio that had become very popular. Only two local actors were used in this show, an apprentice named Robert J. Browning, and myself as a character called Mr. Foley about whom I remember absolutely nothing.

I have reported in my narrative that the visiting celebrities were occasionally egocentric monsters, but most of them were very pleasant to all involved, even though some may have felt wanting when confronted with actors more experienced than they. At the end of the 1965 season the apprentices took a vote on who was the most likeable of the visitors that summer. All eight agreed that Jack Kelly had been the most friendly, largely because he had treated all of them to dinner. Jack Bailey also rated because he had introduced them all to the audience during his curtain speech. Jayne Mansfield was tops because she had been a lot of fun and so were her children who accompanied her on tour in *Nature's Way*. I regret I did not perform in or see this production because I had admired her since seeing *Will Success Spoil Rock Hunter?* and because she was a very unaffected, out-going, fun-loving person. And John Saxon received approval because, after he had relaxed into the role he played, he drove some of them on an excursion to Ball's Falls (yes, there is such a place) and proved he was only human by running out of gas. To be rated high in popularity among the "apprenti" was a status not easily achieved.

Financially, 1965 was an encouraging improvement over the previous season despite the fiasco of *The Student Prince*. The first show, *Pajama Tops*, had done sufficiently well to start the GCT in the black for the first time in several years. The biggest moneymaker had been *Never Too Late*, which brought in $13,900 out of a potential gross of $20,000. Profit was also made on the Jayne Mansfield package because she had agreed to a contract that gave her only 20 per cent of the first $9,000 of receipts and 33.3 per cent of the rest with no guaranteed basic fee. Even though that show grossed only $10,000, the producers made money on it. I suspect that the reason Ms. Mansfield did not pack them in was because her fame then rested more on her reputation as a Broadway sex goddess and not a Hollywood or television one. Considering the greater expenses and the low ticket prices of the Garden Centre when compared with the other summer stock ventures in the province, it was not doing too badly. The Red Barn was in financial trouble, the Straw Hat Players were optimistic that they might end up with a small profit on the summer, and the Kawartha Summer Theatre finished its first season in the red, although encouraged by the increasing attendance as the summer wore on. The Shakespeare Festival was flourishing and the Shaw Festival was just beginning to toddle toward success.

■

Encouraged by the profit, however tiny, in 1965, and the fact that they had acquired a co-producer in Rad Weaver (the only source of cash outside the box office), the Herrmans decided to chance another season. The first two shows of 1966 were *Mary, Mary* starring Kathryn Crosby, and *Dear Me, the*

Sky Is Falling with Gertrude Berg. I rejoined the company for my eighth summer to direct the charming comedy *Rattle of a Simple Man*, whose designer was to be my Red Barn colleague, Wilf Pegg. John Astin was to play the male lead and he brought with him Maria Lennard as his leading lady. I obtained Donald Hemmings to play the girl's brother. A graduate of Johns Hopkins University and the American Academy of Dramatic Arts, Astin first appeared on Broadway in Charles Laughton's production of *Major Barbara*. He eventually became known in millions of homes for his role in the series *I'm Dickens . . . He's Fenster* and as Gomez Addams in *The Addams Family*. His performance as Gomez, though competent, did not cause me to jump for joy at the prospect of directing him.

My attitude changed during the first rehearsal when I realized that before me was an actor whose potential had not been realized in film or television. A dedicated performer with great comedic skill, he surprised me with a reasonable facsimile of a Lancashire football fan's dialect. Maria Lennard was equally gifted. She was a genuine "Lancashire Lass" born in that English county and she had studied at the Royal Academy of Dramatic Art, performed in London's West End, at the Old Vic, and at Britain's National Theatre. Movie buffs would know her as one of the terrifying females in *Pure Hell of St. Trinians*. She had arrived in California only the previous year, and was immediately involved in theatrical productions there, which led John Astin to make her his co-star for his tour of the summer circuit. David Hemmings had arrived in Toronto in 1965, after 10 years of stage, television, and films in Capetown, South Africa. I had seen him as the boxer, Sandy, in the Crest Theatre production of *Hay Fever* and recommended him for the role of Ricard in *Rattle of a Simple Man*. It was an excellent cast and we got along famously. In addition, Wilf Pegg's set caught the right atmosphere for the girl's somewhat depressing London flat. The result was one of the best shows of the season and one of my most satisfying directing efforts. Contrary to his frequently denigrating approach, Ron Evans in the *Toronto Telegram* absolutely cooed about the show, and even praised my directing.[36]

When *Rattle* closed I immediately was involved for the second time in

All for Mary with Edward Everett Horton. This time I played the French proprietor of the Alpine Hotel where the action occurs. I also directed *All for Mary* with considerable advice from Mr. Horton. As Ralph Hicklin perceptively noted, "Vernon Chapman . . . had the good sense not to get in Horton's way."[37] Myron Natwick once again travelled with Edward and played the second major male role. The rest of the cast were strong farceurs, particularly Nancy Kerr as Horton's wife and Eleanor Beecroft as his Nanny. This required a vast willingness to suspend disbelief on the part of the audience because Horton was several decades Eleanor's senior. Filling out the cast in the role of Alphonse, the bell-boy, was a talented, 19-year-old, French Canadian apprentice actor from Ottawa named Ron Tanguay. Horton treated this inexperienced actor with patience and understanding. He again demonstrated his mastery at taking thin material and embroidering on it, which in this play included fractured French and triple (sometimes quadruple) takes. He even turned to his advantage a line that commented on the energy of his 80-year-old Nanny, which he punctuated with a knowing look to the audience that said, "We know better, don't we?" They all knew that Horton was 80 and Eleanor Beecroft much younger. The audience loved watching him make bricks out of straw. I did not realize it at the time, but *All for Mary* would be the last play I would act in with Eddie Horton.

During the week we were rehearsing *All for Mary*, onstage at night was a complete package of *The Glass Menagerie* with an all-black cast in which Claudia McNeill gave a superb performance as Amanda. Some plays do not transfer easily from one ethnic milieu to another. For example, *A Raisin in the Sun* with an all-white cast just would not make sense. But my favourite Tennessee Williams play is ideally suited to black actors. No adaptation was necessary because the situation and dialogue apply just as poignantly to a black family as to a white one.

For the next show I was in, *Stalag 17*, Ed Byrnes of *Route 66* had agreed to come to Vineland to play the lead role of Sefton, but he cancelled. Bob did some cast shuffling and sent an SOS to Robert Crawford, a friend of his in the U.S., who had already played Sefton. Because of the large male cast, all the male apprentices plus a group of stalwarts from Toronto became prisoners. Marvin Goldhar, Nicholas Simons, Franz Russell, Allen Doremus, and Larry Alford came from Toronto, and another friend of Bob's, a fine character actor, Mason Wright, came from the States. I was moved to the role of Price, the informer. He was not my usual type but I derived great satisfaction out of playing the apparently amiable, ordinary G.I. who betrays his fellow prisoners. The challenge in such a role is similar to playing the villain in a murder mystery. Nothing specific must be shown about his activity in advance of its first revelation, but clues must be planted so that the audience can say in retrospect, "Ah yes. It adds up."

Robert Crawford could not arrive until the Sunday before opening, so we rehearsed for a week without him. But on the close of his current engagement, he drove all night to be on time for a rehearsal on Sunday morning. Fortunately he knew his lines when he arrived, and even though we had rehearsed without him, everybody's heart was in the show and the cast became as close to an ensemble company as weekly stock will allow. It showed in the finished product, whose realism was believable and compelling. Solid performances were given by the male apprentices Hans Monvik, Ron Tanguay, and Durward (Cody) McGimsie, who that week decided to list himself as Derry McGimsie. Franz Russell and Marvin Goldhar very capably handled the comic relief, and in the scene when the youngest prisoner has to take a bath in a washtub, Tedd Reed's innocence was a perfect foil for the amiable teasing of those two. Bob had directed three previous productions of this play, and he loved it. As a result it was one of the smoothest, most effective summer stock shows in which I had ever performed.

Everybody fell in love with Zena Bethune, a fortunate choice to replace Yvette Mimieux who cancelled her scheduled appearance as the title role in *Sabrina Fair*. Allen Doremus, who played Lynus Larabee Jr., was smitten with her, and being a musician as well as an actor, composed a song for her. Tedd Reed wrote a mash note to her and as a reward got a kiss on the cheek, which, he claims, he did not wash for a week, and I, as Tom Fairchild, her father in the play, got to hold her on my lap every performance. I did not press my trousers for the whole run. Born in New York City, Zena was trained as a dancer and an actress, and by 1966, although still very young, had a long list of plays and musicals to her credit. She had been seen in prominent roles in TV soap operas and in prime time dramas and comedies, including *Naked City, Route 66, The Jackie Gleason Show,* and *The Hit Parade.* Bob also imported Ann Driscoll, a very dignified lady with an extensive background in American regional theatre. Mason Wright transformed himself from a Nazi Stalag Commandant to the head of a wealthy Long Island family for *Sabrina Fair.* Cast as David Larrabee was Nicholas Simons, born in Surrey, England. He had worked in English repertory companies and at the Old Vic before settling in Canada in 1962 where he appeared with the Canadian Players, at the Stratford Festival, and at the Manitoba Theatre Centre, and in *Oh What a Lovely War* at the Crest. Joining the GCT for the first time was Linda Livingston, a young actress from Britain who played Gretchen.

Sabrina Fair is a gentle comedy about high society on Long Island. Part of the appeal of such plays and films to the average theatregoer is that it reveals a lifestyle that is codified, refined, mannered, and probably envied by many in the audience. Alas, I fear we failed in capturing this complex and subtle world. The director, Bob Herrman, did not really understand these people. Our production at the Grand Theatre in London, under Joan White's direction, was much more successful.

While cavorting with the Nabobs of Newport at night, I was communing with nuns in the day. I was directing a new play by a Monsignor John O'Donnell of Chicago, which starred that perennial favourite, Spring Byington. *Haloes and Spotlights* was an unpretentious but clever script that dealt with the events that follow when a pretty young nun wins a patriotic essay contest and, as a result, is expected to become the scantily clad model in an advertising campaign for a brand of shampoo. The idea was gleaned from the Miss Rheinegold billboards that dotted the highways and byways of the United States in the '60s. When the advertising agency discovers that the contest winner is a nun, they and the sponsor want to renege on the arrangement, depriving the nun and the nunnery of the $5,000 in prize money. In order to protect their interests, a phalanx of nuns, led by the Mother Superior (Spring Byington), descends upon the offices of the advertising agency and chaos ensues. Not the greatest of plots, but novel and worthy of being presented more frequently than the few showings it got during that summer of 1966. The size of the cast — 20 females and five males — mitigated against its being staged very often. But it did give the female apprentices their turn to shine. As the nun who won the contest I cast a very pretty apprentice, Cheryl Thurston, who even managed to look sexy in a nun's habit. Added to the cast were such stalwarts as Nancy Kerr, Terry Clemes, myself as Professor Curd, Nick Simons as Professor Shay (Curds and Shay?), and Mason Wright as a character with the multi-syllabic name of Professor Nikolosantopopolov. We were a sort of pedagogical three stooges. The other major male role was played by a very experienced actor from New York, Edgar E. Meyer, who had many scenes with Miss Byington.

Those of us who grew up with the talkies are familiar with the face of Spring Byington. She usually played sweet, soft, extremely feminine types. She was everybody's mother. My first memories of her were as Marmee in the 1933 film version of *Little Women*, in *Ah, Wilderness!* in 1935, and *You Can't Take It with You*. By 1966 she had appeared in 75 motion pictures and many television shows. Unlike some actors, Miss Byington was in real life just as warm and bubbly, yet dignified withal, as the roles she portrayed on the screen. She exuded a great love of life that led to everyone in the company developing an immediate affection for her. She was an avid reader and cultivated a talent for communicating with other people. When asked if she ever contemplated any other occupation than acting, she replied, "No. I haven't done the best I can in this one yet." Even though she had played the role of the Mother Superior in Chicago, unlike Zasu Pitts, Miss Byington told me at the first rehearsal that she wanted direction and that if I wanted to change anything she would go along with it. The result was a happy rehearsal period for all involved and a joyous production in which I did my best to flesh out a thin script with comedy shtick. For one scene I added television cameras and an inept cameraman. The cameras of those days were large bulky boxes that had to be pushed on mobile stands with great lengths of cable behind them over which people had to step. The comic possibilities were endless. It was all very corny, but things were kept humming and the audience was given very little time to feel that the one joke plot was wearing thin. But what really made this bit of froth acceptable were the performances of the whole cast who frolicked through its three acts. Because the script we used was devoid of stage directions, the cast and I had to be more inventive than usual. The whole venture became a challenge for us and I believe Miss Byington was sincere when she told me at the end of the week's run that we had given the Monsignor's comedic romp a better production than had been the case in Chicago. I regret that this bright lady could only spread her sunshine among us for two weeks and departed never to be seen by me again except as a remote figure on the movie screen.

Tom Kneebone had been such a success in *Good Night, Ladies* that Bob decided to bring him back in a role that might have been written for him when Brandon Thomas penned that vintage favourite, *Charley's Aunt*. This was by far the best of the three productions of that overplayed opus with which I had been involved. Every actor in the show understood the style with which this hoary chestnut must be played. I had matured enough (synonym for growing older) to play Sir Francis Chesney, and Joel Kenyon returned to the GCT to give a brilliant performance as Spettigue. Nicholas Simons stayed on to play Jack Chesney, and Edwin Stephenson as Charles Wickham made his first appearance in Vineland. The three young females were Mary Barton as Kitty Verdun, Linda Livingston as Amy Spettigue, and Sylvia Shore as Ela Delahay. The senior and most imposing female member of the cast was Christine Bennett as Donna Lucia D'Alvadorez "from Brazil where the nuts come from." In the role of Bassett, Herrman cast Larry Beattie, who stole every scene he was in simply by underplaying it. But fine acting and proper style by the cast would go for nothing were there not a nimble comedian with a fine sense of the absurd playing Lord Fancourt Babberley who masquerades as Charley's Aunt. This is not a female impersonation role. The challenge to the actor is to play a man trying ineptly to pass himself off as a middle-aged Victorian lady. Tom's comic sense, energy, and inventiveness really carried the show. Although the

rest of us were well-suited to our roles, and were giving polished performances, we were satellites circling around Kneebone's sun. But that is the
nature of the play. The reviews were enthusiastic, the audiences raucously
responsive, and the cast jovially friendly. *Charley's Aunt* was held for two
weeks and made a fitting conclusion to the 1966 season. Although we did
not know it at the time, it also concluded Robert Herrman's tenure as producer at what he termed the Garden Centre's "Palace of Laughs."

By the end of the previous season, 1965, the Herrmans had no money
left to put into the GCT. The family had moved from Brooklyn to Ventura,
California, and had purchased a modest house with an immodest mortgage. When I first met Bob in 1959 he was a man of boundless good
humour and optimism. By 1966 his optimism had waned, his humour was
increasingly forced, and he was worried about the accumulated debts of the
Garden Centre Theatre, his mortgage on his house, the education of his
maturing children, and his own future career as a middle-aged actor. Over
the years, as the worries increased, so did the consumption of alcohol by
both Bob and Terry. They held their liquor well and I never saw them
uncontrollably drunk. Nor did Terry allow alcohol to interfere with her
performances onstage. But it did take its toll, and by the end of the 1966
season Bob was well on the way to becoming an alcoholic, if he had not
already arrived. Therefore, I was not surprised when he told me that they
would not be returning to the Garden Centre in 1967.

▪

Bob was not a spendthrift manager. He hired competent staff on the business side of the operation as well as on the artistic side. His approach was
business-like without being mean. There was ample publicity for each
show. So, why did that theatre not make a profit over the eight years of his
stewardship? You already know some of the reasons. I told him several times
over the years that his prices were too low, but he was afraid to increase
them. In 1966 the cost of a single ticket ranged from $2.75 to $3.30 and $3.85
top, which included provincial entertainment tax. For $19.95, the purchaser
of a subscription had the choice of any six shows of the 12. But even with

these low prices, the public did not respond in sufficient number to meet the high cost of many of the productions. Athough big names increased attendance, if they were in package shows the producer lost money because they were so expensive. On the other hand Bob made a profit every time Horton played at the GCT because he did not demand a huge fee. Edward had concern for the health of a particular theatre, the theatre in general, and the low salary his fellow actors received in order to meet the "star's" exorbitant one. Horton's attitude was to keep theatres solvent so that they would be there for him to return to year after year. But he was unusual. Despite the lure of the star system, attendance over the years averaged only 42 per cent or 384 people per performance in a 916-seat theatre. According to Rad Weaver, quoted in the *Globe and Mail* (10 September 1966), the 12 shows staged that summer had cost $50,000, not including other permanent expenses such as box-office staff, rental on the residence for actors and staff, food subsidy for the apprentices, and amortization and replacement costs on equipment.

But the Garden Centre Theatre had another problem that existed through no fault of Bob's, the staff, or any of the artists who performed there. It was the fundamental unpopularity of the Prudhomme family in the area. Local resentment of the Prudhommes, whether deserved or not, was carried over by many to the Garden Centre Theatre. Robert Johnston told me that when he was the publicity manager for the GCT, it was very difficult to persuade merchants in the nearby towns to display posters of the shows in their store windows, the rancour against the Prudhommes was so great.

The summer of 1967, the Prudhommes tried to run the theatre as a cabaret. Tables were placed in the auditorium and drinks were served during the show. The calibre of production sank and the season was a monumental flop. Then one night when no one was in the theatre, it mysteriously caught fire. However, this time, because the theatre was attached to the centre wing of the motel, and because it had been constructed with wooden beams and a tar roof, the blaze spread like a holocaust. It took 20 minutes for the Beamsville fire department to arrive, but by that time the flames, aided by an off-shore breeze, had spread through the auditorium, the theatre lobby, the kitchens, the main dining room, the ballroom, the bar, and roared through the spacious lobby of the motel. Only some of the rooms to the west of the lobby were saved. Tragically, one of the night security guards died from asphyxiation when he checked the kitchen to see if anyone was trapped inside.

Naturally there was speculation that the fire had been deliberately set, particularly when people remembered the burning of the previous theatre under similar circumstances a decade before. Surmise was that the arsonist had counted on the fire department arriving in time to isolate the blaze in the theatre wing before it could spread to the main section of the motel. At the inquest into the death of the security guard, the Coroner's jury found no evidence against the Prudhommes for staging the fire, but, the Coroner, breaking with precedent, stated that he believed arson was involved. Whatever the cause of the fire, it had a disastrous affect on the fortunes of the Prudhommes. The very heart of their empire had been destroyed, and, because of the suspicions attached to both fires, they were unable to get insurance to cover any rebuilding. Very soon after that the whole complex — zoo, swimming pool, bowling alley, coffee shop, and the remains of the motel — was sold. The Garden Store continued to operate and the motel was partially rebuilt under the banner of the Best Western chain. But, sadly, the theatre was never rebuilt, which was a loss to the performers of Ontario and to the loyal patrons of that area. Except for the burgeoning Shaw Festival there were now no summer theatres operating in the Niagara Peninsula, when at one time there had been three.

Although he gave up as producer at the Garden Centre, Bob Herrman did not give up trying to establish a theatre company elsewhere in Canada or the United States. One scheme he developed along with George Blackburn, the author of *A Button Missing*, was to operate a summer theatre at Upper Canada Pioneer Village at Morrisburg, Ontario. But after a year of planning and several costly trips from California, that scheme fell through. On one of those trips I got a clear picture of the financial bind in which Bob and Terry were trapped. He had flown up to Toronto on a one-way ticket because he could not afford the two-way fare. He had hoped to collect some money for his work in planning the project for Morrisburg, but that money was not available at that time. I drove him to the airport where he bought a return flight home, which he paid for on his credit card. After he had passed through American customs into the departure lounge, and as I was walking back from the gate, I was accosted by the panicky ticket clerk, who had discovered that Bob did not have enough credit left on his card to cover the ticket. The clerk wanted to get a guard to stop Bob in the waiting room. Rather than see him humiliated, and mindful not only of the employment he had given me and of our deep friendship, I told the clerk not to worry, that I would cover the cost. I never told Bob about this, but he became curious when he received a statement from American Express without the flight charge listed. He surmised that I had picked up the cost and phoned me to ask me about it. When I told him what had happened, being a proud man, he repaid me the amount as soon as he was financially able.

One Sunday in the early 1970s, when I was entertaining my childhood friend Bill Freeman to dinner, I received a phone call from California. It was Bob calling from a hospital where he was suffering from cirrhosis of the liver. He was again in trouble financially because of his large medical bills and could not meet an $800 mortgage payment on his house. He had tapped the American Actors' Fund so much that they were reluctant to help him further. He was desperate and I could hear that he was choking back tears at the other end of the line. He hesitantly asked me if I could lend him the money to cover the mortgage payment. Being a freelance performer who spent many weeks in the year without any income, and no Uemployment Insurance because like most actors I did not have long enough engagements to collect, I hesitated at parting with $800 from my emergency reserve fund. I told Bob that I would think about it and call him back. I returned to the dinner table and told Bill about the dilemma. Bill had a steady position as a secondary school teacher and, over the years, had amassed a small fortune from playing the stock market. The situation was now the reverse from the days of our childhood when he did not even have 10 cents a week spending money. He was now much wealthier than I. "Well," he said."It's obvious. You must lend him the money, and if you find yourself strapped I will let you have the $800." With this insurance, I phoned Bob in his hospital room and told him I would wire him the money the next morning. His relief was palpable even over several thousand miles of telephone wire. I never expected to see that money repaid.

However, I mentioned this matter to Bernard Chadwick, who was then the executive secretary of the Canadian Branch of American Actor's Equity and on the board of the Actors' Fund of Canada. Knowing that I was not too secure financially myself, he offered to ask the Canadian Actors' Fund to re-imburse me the $800, and notify Bob that the money would be owed to the Fund and not to me. After all, Bob had been a producer in Canada, and had given employment to a large number of Canadian actors and stage technicians over the eight years he had operated the Garden Centre Theatre. The Actors' Fund Board agreed and I received $800 from them. The Actors' Fund is a charitable organization whose sole purpose is to assist actors, singers, dancers, mime artists, musicians, and stage technicians in financial distress. Whom they assist is normally kept confidential, but in this case I have revealed their generosity to show that the performing community has a great giving heart, that Canadians appreciated this American who had come to Canada, who had given so much employment to Canadians and so much pleasure to the audiences who patronized the GCT, and who had been destroyed in the process. Within a year after I received that phone call, Bob died, still only in his middle years, burned out with worry and alcohol. Within another year his devoted wife, Terry, followed him.

I shall be forever grateful to Bob Herrman for giving me the golden opportunity to expand my technique and talent through the many and varied roles I played. As actor/director I worked for the GCT more frequently than any other performer, Canadian or American. My salary was not humungus but it was as good as the Stratford Festival was paying its rank-and-file performers at that time. I had the opportunity to act with and direct a lot of different performers, and in so doing I discovered certain things about myself. After the pressure-cooker of the Garden Centre Theatre I felt that I could cut it under any circumstances that an actor or director would be likely to meet. Thanks to an American I was given this expanding experience that few Canadian actors are privileged to enjoy.

Another legacy of my summers at the GCT was my friendship with Edward Everett Horton. During his visits to Vineland he and I had developed a mutual respect for each other that gradually grew into friendship. A similar relationship had developed between Moya Fenwick and Edward, who was so impressed with her that he invited her to appear with him in *Nina* in California. While there she stayed in his home in Encino, which, always a bachelor, he shared with his sister, Hannah Belle, and his mother. I remember on one of his visits to the Garden Centre, he described for us the gigantic party he gave to celebrate his mother's 100th birthday. Longevity seemed to be a family trait. On a Thursday during the run, a telegram came to the theatre office expressing deepest sympathy for Edward on the death of his mother. She had died on the Monday, and Edward had not revealed this to the company. When I went to give him my condolences, he explained that it was his own private grief and he had not wished to distress the company and dampen our enthusiasm for the show.

In the spring of 1966 I took a holiday that began with a leisurely drive to California. I had written Horton telling him the day I planned to arrive, and that I would look him up. He had given me his home phone number, which I had written incorrectly. When I arrived in California I spent three days phoning the wrong number with no reply, and after that I decided to drive north on the Ventura Freeway to Encino where he lived. I had been told that his house could be easily recognized from the highway because it was a classical revival style perched on a hill right above the freeway. I had also been told that if Edward was home, the Stars and Stripes would be flying from the flagpole. Sure enough, it was — on a classical revival anachronism surrounded by Spanish-style haciendas and villas. I drove off the freeway along a side road until I came to a short street called Edward Everett Horton Drive. The house sat back from the road with a long, semi-circular drive up to it. Built in a "U" shape, it had two wings jutting out toward the drive, one of which had classical pillars and a huge portico over the main entrance. The other wing had a large picture window overlooking the drive to the road. I decided to park on the street in case this was not the right house, and walk up the drive. There were two smaller houses on the right side of the driveway. When I approached the picture window, I looked into a very large room with a huge fireplace, many sofas and chairs, and in the middle, all alone on a sofa, clad in a white dinner jacket and black bow tie, sat Edward Everett. When he opened the door the first thing he said was, "Where the hell have you been? I've been waiting for you for three days." It was flattering to think that this celebrated man had been sitting there, all dressed up, for three days patiently waiting my arrival, but he was actually expecting a couple of representatives of the Encino Historical Society who wanted to see through the house, hoping that he would bequeath this unique home to the Society when he died.

The room I entered was easily a hundred feet long and half as wide. It was sumptuously furnished with a variety of over-stuffed chairs and sofas. Just inside the picture window was a long Tudor refectory table that revealed the scars of the dirks and poignards that had been stuck in it when generations of forkless people ate at it. The opposite end wall supported a balcony on which was a grouping of what appeared to be Victorian chairs and table, and a chaise longue resting in the corner of which was a china doll in a long white dress. I wondered if I might discover in some corner a child's sleigh with "Rosebud" written on it, as in *Citizen Kane*.

When the Encino visitors arrived I joined them in a tour of the house. Underneath the balcony was a door concealed from view by a protective screen beyond which was the "small," private dining room where Edward and his sister ate their regular meals. Further beyond that was an extremely large modern kitchen with a screened door to the outside, where, only a few feet away, was a small cottage that Edward had built for Hannah Belle. She had told him that if the house was to be kept in order consistent with Edward's meticulous standards she could not live in it. So he built her a house where she could live how she liked. Off the dining room was a spacious, walk-in pantry in which Edward kept his collection of glass — shelf after shelf of tumblers, wine glasses, and goblets, mostly pressed glass from the Victorian and Edwardian periods. The spacious central hallway was adorned with a wide staircase and a landing, above which was an enormous, beautiful stained glass window. The hall's sombreness was relieved by a life-size, cut-out photograph of Horton looking impish as Elwood P. Dowd in *Harvey*, standing at the foot of the stairs. The formal dining room was graced with a long table that could seat dozens, but the room's most striking feature was a candle chandelier that seemed to be made of spun glass shaped like the branches of a tree, the stem and smaller branches of which were flecked inside with gold, and where the leaves would be were candle holders of ruby glass. Even in the European palaces I have visited, I have never seen a chandelier so original or so beautiful.

To balance the American Colonial wing, Edward had another built in which was the music room housing two rare Bozendorfer concert grand pianos he had purchased in the mid-'30s in Germany. He required Herman Goering's permission to bring them to the U.S. Edward told me with pride and a little sadness that the furniture in that corner was just as it had been on the day a few years earlier when his mother, reclining on a chaise longue, had received well-wishers on her 100th birthday. In fact, so was her bedroom. Nothing had been disturbed. One expected her to return any moment. There was a slightly haunted atmosphere about the whole house. Without servants about, Edward rattled around all alone, his sister cosily ensconced in her wee cottage beyond the kitchen door.

Edward's own apartment was on the second floor just behind the portico over the main entrance. In his sitting room were glass cases full of memorabilia including awards and citations he had been given: honorary mayor of some towns and honorary fire chief of others. In the middle of this room was a highly polished table on which rested various of his prized gifts including Queen Alexandra's Birthday Book given to him by Cicely Courtneidge. His bedroom boasted a large four-poster bed with an olive green and gold spread on it on which was embossed the intertwined initials of his name, EEH, in gold thread. The whole effect of this house was tasteful but eclectic and a decided anomaly in California. Unfortunately the State of California had expropriated his tennis courts to make way for the Ventura Freeway, which cut through a hundred feet or so below his sun room where he often had a siesta lulled to sleep by the traffic noise that sounded like the distant roar of the surf. However, he dared not open a window in that room because of the carbon monoxide rising up from the steady stream of vehicles below.

One of my regrets about the closing of the Garden Centre Theatre was that I did not get another opportunity to perform with Edward Everett Horton. However, I did see him twice after that. He turned up in Toronto in a touring company of *Once Upon a Mattress*. During the visit he sent my mother a huge bouquet of flowers, even though he had met the lady only once at Vineland. Knowing his weakness for Chinese food, I took him to what at the time was considered by connoisseurs to be the best Chinese restaurant in Toronto, the Sai Woo on Dundas Street, and he was ecstatic about it. His next appearance in Toronto was in *A Funny Thing Happened on the Way to the Forum*. Also in the show were the two comedians, Jerry Lester and Paul Hartman. I had enjoyed Mr. Hartman immensely in the revue *Tickets, Please*, which I had seen in New York in 1950. Edward rented a large car and asked me if I would be good enough to drive the trio around Toronto and the surrounding countryside. I considered it a privilege and I drove them on a sunny afternoon as far north as Jackson's Point, showed them the Red Barn Theatre, the veree olde Englishe St. George's Church, and the grave of Stephen Leacock. During the trip the three of them kept me rocking with laughter as they told hilarious stories from their careers, laced with jokes and spicy gossip about show-business celebrities. For me it was a day of joy.

In the summer of 1970, I heard that Edward had developed pneumonia while staying at his summer house on Lake George in upper New York State. I tried to find time to drive there, but it was a particularly busy summer for me and I was unable to get away. I have always regretted that because, although he recovered sufficiently to return to California, the journey proved too much for him. He had a relapse and unexpectedly died. The newspapers claimed he was 84. For Edward Everett Horton, 84 was too young to die. He enjoyed living so thoroughly.

CHAPTER 19

In the Big Apple

My connection with the Garden Centre Theatre gave me an opportunity to direct for the Community Players of Westfield, New Jersey. My experience will give you a picture of what it was like for a young, emerging Canadian director to live and seek work in the New York area at the time. In 1962 the restrictions on Canadians working in the United States were not so stringent as they eventually became under Lyndon Johnson's regime. Bob Herrman had been their respected director for several years, but, in 1962 other commitments prevented him from staging their spring production. He recommended me to them, and they agreed. I was delighted because I could live in New York, investigate its theatre scene, and commute to Westfield three nights each week for the nine weeks of rehearsal. The Community Players had chosen George F. Kaufman and Edna Ferber's *The Royal Family*, a very workmanlike and romanticized comedy about American theatrical life in the early years of the 20th century and the temperamental types who lived it. Because the Community Players would cover travel expenses only from New York City, I had to pay for my transportation to Manhattan, but that was no hardship because we negotiated the largest fee I had ever had for directing. That spring I had another stroke of good fortune. A friend of mine from the Village Players and college days, Jack Anderson, had become a stage manager in New York and suggested that I sublet his flat for two weeks while he was home in Toronto. Rents were still controlled in New

York and his rent was only $40 a month. I agreed with alacrity to pay him the full $40 for the two weeks, leaving him a monstrous profit of $20.

In the '50s and early '60s I sought roles on television as executive types: bankers, capitalist tycoons, professors, ministers, and even undertakers. To impress producers that I was right for the roles I dressed very conservatively. I acquired a navy blue trench coat (which might also be worn by a detective), a navy blue homburg, a black briefcase, and if rain threatened, I carried a black, furled umbrella — a sort of poor man's Anthony Eden, but without the moustache. It seemed to work because I played a goodly number of those roles. However, these were the only street clothes that I had to take to New York. Jack's apartment turned out to be in one of Gotham's ancient brown stones, and as I struggled up the stairs with my bags, my heart sank. My nostrils were assailed by 100 years of garlic and corned beef and cabbage. The walls of the corridor were covered in graffiti. I wondered what I had got myself into. I could not visualize Jack, who was such a fastidious person, living in these slum conditions, but I had not reckoned on the exigencies of existing in New York. I laboured up five flights to the top floor and knocked on Jack's door. The one opposite opened and a stranger said, "You must be Vern. Come on in. The party's in here." Jack came out, I deposited my bags in his apartment and joined the party where I was introduced to his friends, all of whom were in the theatre. I immediately felt part of the New York theatre world. I was ecstatic.

Jack's flat had been what used to be called a "cold water walk-up," but had become a "cold and hot water walk-up" when the city, belatedly in the middle of the 20th century, had forced the slum landlords to make hot water a requisite. It had one bedroom so I slept on the sofa my first night there. Jack departed for Toronto the next day and for two weeks I had the place all to myself. It had been decorated very tastefully if inexpensively, and proved to be reasonably comfortable. The main room, overlooking 73rd Street, consisted of a cosy living room area at the opposite end of which was a combined dining room and kitchen off which was a small room containing the toilet. The bedroom was another small room beyond the kitchen area. The latter consisted of a few cupboards, a stove, a refrigerator, a sink, and a

five-foot long, oil-cloth covered drain board that rested on top of a long, gal-
vanized metal tub angled in toward the wall at the bottom. This served as
both laundry and bathtub but the first time I bathed I got wedged in it and
had a struggle to free myself. After that I only squatted in it.

The apartment opposite, where the party had been, was occupied by
another stage manager, Marvin Poons, a real New Yorker, and a very intelligent, well-educated young man, with a delicious sense of humour and a
philosophical approach to life. We became very good friends. Marvin eventually became the executive secretary of the Association of American
Dinner Theatres, which he administered from his beautifully appointed
house in Sarasota, Florida. In 1962 his flat was sparsely furnished. But we
were not the only denizens of our respective apartments, which we shared
with an army of cockroaches. Fortunately they remained around the sinks
and bathtubs. I knew when Marvin was working because he did not have
time to wash his dishes and the cockroaches would vacate my premises for
better pickings in his. Conversely, I knew when he had washed up because
they would all return.

The neighbourhood was a polyglot one. There was an Italian family on
the first floor of Jack's building, and the liquor store on the corner opposite
was run by an emigrant Polish Jew. The shops in the area were operated by
a cross section of the American melting pot. The basement of the brown
stone was occupied by a Chinese laundry. The first day I emerged onto the
street, the Chinese lady sitting outside stared in amazement. I must have
appeared very odd indeed in my navy blue trench coat, homburg hat,
furled umbrella, and black briefcase. After a few days we greeted each other
warmly, as happened with all the other people I met each day when I made
my dignified way up to the Third Avenue Subway line. Nodding graciously
to my neighbours as I went, I must have appeared yet another New York
kook. However, I felt at home from the outset. I found the neighbours and
the shopkeepers more friendly than in Toronto, and I enjoyed walking
about the area.

When Jack returned he persuaded me to stay on in the apartment rather
than move to a hotel. I slept on the sofa, which was quite comfortable, and

because I had already paid him $40, he did not charge me for the next two weeks. We got along splendidly. The arrangement worked out well for both — I got cheap accommodation in an expensive city, and he got his rent paid for two months during which he was out of work.

I had been visiting New York at least every two or three years and my stays of a week or two had always been crammed with the latest hit plays and musicals. Over the years I had seen shows that not only gave me a clearer idea of what our own theatre was like but I invariably returned with my enthusiasm for theatre rejuvenated. During my 1956 sojourn I experienced one of the most moving and emotionally draining evenings I have ever had in the theatre. My old acquaintance from *Spring Thaw*, Lou Jacobi, was playing Mr. Van Daan in the *Diary of Anne Frank*. Before I could go backstage after the performance, I had to walk around the block to collect myself emotionally. That night Lou treated me to late supper at the Russian Tea Room, my first encounter with that unique restaurant. In 1957, I saw Basil Rathbone in *Hide and Seek* with one of my favourite film actresses, Geraldine Fitzgerald, who, in my opinion, never got the roles in films that she deserved. Barry Morse, whom I did not know at the time, also appeared in this production. For me the high point of that year's visit was *Separate Tables*, starring Eric Portman with Phyllis Neilson-Terry as the odious Mrs. Railton-Bell. Playing the romantic role of Charles Stratton was Donald Harron, who had graduated from the Stratford company to Broadway. My 1960 trip was worthwhile if only to see Tyrone Guthrie's production of Paddy Chayefsky's *The Tenth Man*, which, because it takes place in a synagogue, had a largely Jewish cast, including Lou Jacobi, except for that nice goyish boy, Donald Harron. Don was extremely effective as a drunken young Jew who wanders into a synagogue just as an exorcism of a dybbuk from a young girl is about to occur. But my real reason for the 1960 trip was the Broadway opening of *Love and Libel* by Robertson Davies, when that superb novelist was still trying to be a playwright. As staged by Tyrone Guthrie it had many actors I knew in a cast that was a Who's Who of the Canadian theatre. It was presented under the auspices of the Theatre Guild and Laurence Langner. As I recall, although it was brilliantly staged and acted, the opening night audience was not enthusiastic, except for a Canadian contingent who had travelled to encourage the cast, and the play did not run as long as was hoped. *Love and Libel* had some powerful competition that season with Brendan Behan's *The Hostage*, which bowled me over, and *Becket*, which boasted two of the most impressive performers on Broadway, Laurence Olivier and Anthony Quinn. It also had Harry Brock from Vineland's *Born Yesterday*, Louis Zorich in a variety of roles, and, as the Pope, Edward Atienza, who has since become deservedly celebrated in Canada.

In 1962, with a nine-week stay, I indulged myself in an orgy of theatre viewing. I saw a splendid off-Broadway production of *The Hostage* at the Sheridan Square Theatre, with ex-Irish-via-Toronto Paddy Croft as Meg Dillon, and Norman Roland, an alumnus of the New Play Society, as Monsewer. Another Paddy Chayefsky play, *Gideon*, also directed by Tyrone Guthrie, starred Frederick March and Douglas Campbell, and launched George Segal's career. Edward K. Holmes, who had become a fixture in almost all of Guthrie's productions in New York, played the role of Shethulah. A show in which I would eventually perform in Sudbury, Ontario, was *A Man for All Seasons*, which I saw in 1962 at the ANTA Theatre with Paul Schofield giving a sensitive performance that is still indelibly etched on my memory. What a master of underplaying that man is! Also in that production were Albert Dekker as the Duke of Norfolk, proving himself once again to be a strong stage actor, George Rose as the Common Man, and Olga Bellin (Blanche in my production of *Streetcar Named Desire* in 1954). Olga had become a much sought-after actress. In 1956 she had more than held her own in a production at the Phoenix Theatre of Turgenev's *A Month in the Country* directed by Michael Redgrave and starring Olga's teacher and mentor, Uta Hagen.

My prolonged stay allowed me to renew acquaintances with old, expatriate friends from Toronto such as Olga, and with newer ones I had made during their visits to the Garden Centre Theatre. One of the people I always contacted was my friend from the New Play Society and my Oakville adventure, Christine Thomas, who had won small parts in a variety of New York shows. Each visit in those days, Christine and I would make at least one pilgrimage to Sardi's restaurant to hobnob with the aspiring and sometimes successful creatures of Manhattan's "show-biz." This went on until eventually Christine became disillusioned with New York theatre and retreated to a more sedate existence in London, Ontario. Joan White was another friend I normally contacted on my jaunts to the Big Apple. By 1962 she had established herself as an American resident and for a while she lived with Robert Grose in the Hell's Kitchen area west of central Manhattan, which was the setting for *West Side Story*. Robert's house and its expensive furnishings belied the sordid neighbourhood surrounding it, but on the several occasions that I visited Joan, I never felt any fear wandering through that district.

Back in 1962 Broadway was dominated by British imports. One of them was *A Passage to India* starring that most beauteous and dignified of English actresses, Gladys Cooper. Joan White had a supporting role, and when I went backstage after a performance to see her she introduced me to Ms. Cooper. She was a most gracious lady and I was privileged to escort her to a taxi when she left the theatre. Yet another import from across the Atlantic was *Ross*, Terence Rattigan's play with John Mills in the title role. In that cast was Nicholas Coster with whom I had performed in *The Time of the Cuckoo* at the Garden Centre Theatre in 1960. When I went backstage to see him, we agreed to meet the following night for a drink after my return from a rehearsal in Westfield. We chose the Theatre Bar, where after a sufficient number of drinks, I gladly accepted his offer to drive me home, but, when we emerged from the bar, to my horror I discovered that his transportation was a monstrous motorcycle. He assured me that I would love it. Reluctant to appear too much of a coward, but with butterflies in my stomach, I tucked the skirts of my trench coat into the belt around my middle, jammed my homburg down on my head, clutched my umbrella and briefcase in my left hand, and wrapped my right arm tightly around Nick's waist. This must have been an extraordinary sight even to jaded New Yorkers. We set off with a roar. "My God!," I thought, "he is going to go through Central Park with all those curves." When we approached the first curve, Nick did not slow down one bit, but I remembered to lean with him.

When we had negotiated the first curve without disaster, the next one seemed less frightening, and my fears diminished as we rounded each subsequent curve. By the time we arrived at 2nd Avenue and 73rd Street, I was loving it and wanted the ride to continue all night. It was exhilarating. My dormant adrenalin had been awakened. I could understand the thrill a biker must get from roaring along with umpteen horsepower and the gale-force wind rushing past. But I determined that if ever I rode a motorcycle again I would be dressed appropriately. The next time I saw Nick Coster was on my TV screen in the soap opera *Santa Barbara* in which he had a major continuing role.

I also used the opportunity provided by my long stay to investigate breaking into the theatre there. I easily obtained an agent, Georgia Gilley, a most friendly and helpful person who saw some possibilities in me, and arranged an audition for a Broadway production entitled *Lorenzo*. It was a play about a group of itinerant performers in Renaissance Italy who run afoul of the local absolute ruler of an Italian City-state, a role modelled on Lorenzo de Medici. The lead was to be played by Alfred Drake and the director Arthur Penn. I auditioned for the part of a cowardly actor who, in the end, finds courage and sacrifices his life to save the others in the company. It was a great role, perfect for a Broadway debut and one for which I was ideally suited. I was allowed to have the script a day in advance and I learned a large part of it. The audition was not a cattle call. There were only a select group of auditionees. The auditioners were Messrs Penn, Lasko, and Richards. My audition went beautifully and I knew they were impressed because Mr. Penn, whom I could not see in the darkened theatre, came down to the stage afterwards, and chatted with me inquiring about my background. That night I received a phone call from Georgia Gilley full of enthusiasm. "I think you've got it," she bubbled, "They were very impressed." "No," I replied, "I doubt it. It is the sort of role they will offer to a name who is sliding down the ladder, or to a semi-name who is half-way up." I was correct. It was given to Hurd Hatfield who left the show during its pre-Broadway tour and then Fritz Weaver took over for a Broadway run of only a few days.

Even after I returned to Toronto, Georgia arranged auditions for me and I flew down to New York on two occasions. One was for C.P. Snow's *The Affair*, which was to be directed on Broadway by the American-born English director, John Fernald. Once again it was a good audition. Later I read in a newspaper that my biker friend, Nick Coster, had been cast in the role, which I found a bit strange because we are quite different types. There was another play I flew to Manhattan to audition for, but the title of it escapes me. It had been a success in London and was to be directed on Broadway by another English director. When I arrived for the audition, the backstage area of the theatre was swarming with expatriate British actors of which New York had a plentiful supply. But I knew from the disinterested way the director was interviewing each of us that this exercise was only window dressing to please American Equity. He really wanted to bring over his London cast. He subsequently made representation with Equity that he could not find suitable actors in New York. Equity accepted his argument and the English company was imported. This, in addition to the fact that Broadway was dominated by British productions that year, caused a furore among the American Equity membership.

Georgia Gilley tried to arrange another audition for a New York show for me, but I was busy televising in Toronto and could not get away. I found the flights to Gotham were taking a healthy chunk out of my meagre savings. In order to cut it in that city one really had to be there. I had become established at home in Canada, working regularly on TV and acting and directing for the stage. Although my earnings were nothing tremendous, I was surviving. Any enthusiasm I once nurtured for a career in the Big Apple waned as time went by.

I greatly enjoyed my directing in Westfield. I had a pleasant bus ride three times a week from Manhattan to Westfield, which, for the most part, was a well-to-do residential community. I was extremely pleased with the talent available among the Community Players and I was able to obtain a well-balanced cast for all 16 characters in *The Royal Family*. Although the play deals specifically with the foremost theatrical families in the United States, the Drews and the Barrymores, it is also about a period when the

American theatre came of age and Americans realized that they could match anything European theatre had to offer. Therefore I kept the play in the period in which it was written, the 1920s, which allowed for highly effective art deco sets and furnishings, and costumes from the flapper era that were supplied by the Manhattan Costume Company.

This was the Community Players' 55th production, so they were extremely well organized and had a lot of theatrical savvy. There was a producer who very obligingly fulfilled all my requests. The designer knew what he was about and was able to obtain suitable props and furniture from the co-operative merchants and households of the community. The cast were willing to take direction and included no prima donnas that one often finds in amateur theatre. The local high school auditorium had a decent size stage and was sufficiently well equipped to handle the production. For the final week, when I rehearsed every evening, I was able to stay in Westfield each night because of the generous hospitality of the Newcomb family. All this contributed to a successful production that surpassed in quality some of the professional shows I had seen or in which I had been involved. The pleasure of working with these dedicated theatre buffs of Westfield added to the invigorating experience of living in Manhattan among convivial friends and made those 10 weeks in the spring of 1962 some of the happiest of my life.

Cast:

Carter . . . . Cliff McDonald
Greta . . . . Jean Archdeacon
Sir Wilfrid Robarts, Q.C. . . . . . . Franchot Tone
Mr. Mayhew . . . . Vernon Chapman
Leonard Vole . . . . Francis Bethencourt
Inspector Hearne . . . . Robert Coates
Romaine . . . . Donna Pearson
Clerk of Court . . . . Geofrey Bennett
Mr. Myers, K.C. . . . . Michael McAloney
Mr. Justice Wainwright . . . . . . Richard Aherne
Judge's Clerk . . . . Reg Phillips
Dr. Wyatt . . . . Douglas Lawrence
Janet Mackenzie . . . . Joan Panton
Mr. Clegg . . . . Harvey Harding
The Other Woman . . . . Lynn Lapointe

Synopsis of Scenes:

ACT ONE

The chambers of Sir Wilfrid Robarts, Q.C.,
in London.
Late afternoon.

❧

ACT TWO

The Central Criminal Court (The Old Bailey)
in London.
Morning, six weeks later.

❧

ACT THREE

Scene I:
The chambers of Sir Wilfrid Robarts, Q.C.,
in London.
The same evening.

Scene II:
The Old Bailey. The next morning.
(The lights will be lowered during this scene to
denote the passing of one hour)
Time: The present.

Rainbow Stage Presents . . .

FRANCHOT TONE

in

AGATHA CHRISTIE'S

"WITNESS FOR THE PROSECUTION"

with

FRANCIS BETHENCOURT
Michael McAloney, Richard Aherne,
Vern Chapman, Joan Panton

ALSO STARRING

DONNA PEARSON

❧

PRODUCED & DIRECTED BY
Mr. McAloney

❧

ASSOCIATE PRODUCER
Joyce J. Sloane

❧

Stage Manager
and
Technical Director
VERNON JEFFREY

❧

FOR THE THEATRE

Executive Producer & Director . . . . Michael McAloney
Associate Producer . . . . Joyce J. Sloane
Press, Advertising, Promotion . . . . R.B.M.
Executive Secretary . . . . Dorothy Anderson
Production Manager . . . . Vernon Jeffrey
Scenic Lighting Designer . . . . Jack McAdam
Assistant Stage Manager . . . . Mary Nelson

❧

SPECIAL THANKS . . .

Royal Alexandra . . . *Furniture*
Manitoba Theatre Centre and Junior League
Thrift Shop . . . Props
Mallabar Ltd. . . . *Costumes*
Stern Trucks . . . *Transportation*
Wig Shoppe . . . *For Hair Stylings and Wigs*
Vic Pinchen and Safeway Stores . . . *Facilities*
for Technical Staff

CHAPTER 20

Anne Frank,
a Mad Irishman,
and Honest Ed

In October 1964 I received a frantic phone call from a friend from Victoria College days, Charles Brown, who was by then an eminent lawyer in London, Ontario. He was also a member of the London Little Theatre and had been a staunch supporter of both the Trans-Canada Theatre Company and the Maple Leaf Theatre Company. He was slated to direct *The Diary of Anne Frank* for the LLT but had lost the actor he had cast as Otto Frank. Charles asked me to take over the role on an Equity Guest Artist contract. I had been so moved by the play in New York, and so impressed by Joseph Schildkraut as Otto Frank, that I jumped at the chance even though the fee was so small that I would probably be out of pocket in the end. To prevent this I negotiated with Peter Dearing, the new, paid executive director of the London Little Theatre, a $20 transportation allowance and my accommodation costs during the weeks of rehearsal and performance. As it turned out, by accepting this eight-week engagement away from Toronto, I lost out on a television drama and a Wayne and Shuster show that was broadcast not only on CBC-TV but also on British television. By accepting the role of Otto Frank, I figure I lost upwards of $2,000, not a vast sum but important to a struggling Canadian actor in the 1960s. However, the satisfaction of being in one of the most influential plays of the latter half of the 20th century far outweighed any financial loss I suffered. *The Diary of Anne Frank* is the greatest plea for understanding and tolerance of any play I know. The emotion I displayed in the final scene, when Otto finds a scarf Anne left in the loft where they had been cooped up for two years before being carted off to the extermination camps by the Nazis, was not acting. I could not stop my tears. I know actors are not supposed to lose control of their emotions, but if I had played the role for a year I would have felt the same way every performance.

The strength of the company that Charles Brown had assembled is reflected by J. Burke Martin in his *London Free Press* review: "In fact there was not a single casting weakness in this entire drama."[1] Several cast members were Jewish, for whom this play had a special significance, but the gentiles in the cast were equally affected by the emotions it generated. The young lady who played Anne was outstanding. Although 17, Caroline Dolny looked younger and imbued the role with deep warmth, sweetness, humour, and sincerity, and subtly revealed Anne's first stirring of womanhood. Miss Dolny could have had a brilliant career in the theatre had she chosen to follow it up.

A member of the cast who has had a spectacular theatrical career was the young man who played Peter Van Daan. Both he and Miss Dolny acted their shy, tentative love scene with such sensitivity that it became a high point in the play. This teenage actor had spent the previous summer in a theatre course at Hart House Theatre under Robert Gill's tutelage. Soon after *Anne Frank* he moved to Toronto where he studied with Eli Rill, a disciple of Lee Strasberg. In 1965 he played a small role at the Bayview Playhouse in *She Loves Me*, which starred Barbara Hamilton and Bill Cole. He then joined the Lunch Bunch and appeared in a revue, *The Best of the Bunch*. During those exciting years of the so-called "flower children," he sang and played at a variety of Yorkville coffee houses, and helped form "The Sugar Shoppe," a group that gained international fame. He soon found himself in various American regional theatres and eventually arrived on Broadway as the young sailor, Anthony, in the musical *Sweeney Todd* and as the young man in *Deathtrap* for which he received a Tony nomination. He gained international recognition in the role of Jesus in the film version of *Godspell* and performed on American and Canadian TV. In 1993 he played Lord Louis

Mountbatten with suitable arrogance in the CBC docudrama *Dieppe*. If you haven't already guessed, his name is Victor Garber.

The London Little Theatre had always had high standards and this production continued that tradition. This beautiful play, the cast, the direction, the set, the cooperation of the LLT staff, and the lovely city itself, where I had many friends, made *Anne Frank* one of my most pleasant and satisfying experiences. But not so my next theatrical excursion away from Toronto.

Winnipeg has seen several catastrophes — the first Riel Rebellion, a general strike, floods — but I never dreamed that I would be involved in even a minor one there. By the mid-1960s the Canadian branch of American Equity was well on the way to organizing the English theatre across the country. I was elected to the Canadian Executive Committee of Equity in 1963 and ultimately became its chairman. Even though we had almost complete freedom from the American office, the business of the association (it is not a union) often required the Canadian representative, Larry McCance, and myself to attend meetings in New York. In the evening after one such conference, Larry asked me if I wanted to meet a "mad Irishman." Since I have a weak spot for the Irish, I thought that might be fun. We walked a few blocks up the Avenue of the Americas to an ancient building (since replaced by the Americana Hotel) where Larry buzzed an apartment and we were invited up. It was about 10 o'clock when we entered but we found a whole roomful of people about to sit down to dinner. A jovial man with a great sweeping cavalry moustache greeted us. I was introduced to Michael McAloney and his wife, the marvellous pop singer, Julie Wilson. There were several children of various ages including a baby. Larry and I were invited to join them for dinner, but, as we had just eaten, we declined. However we sat at the table with the assembled diners. The scene was somewhat chaotic. There were not enough spaces at the table for all so I held the baby on my lap and messily fed it dinner, while Julie Wilson busied herself serving the guests. I felt as though I had intruded on the Mad Hatter's tea party. I knew that Michael McAloney had been the artistic director of Rainbow Stage in Winnipeg for the 1964 summer season and I had learned from Larry that the season had not been a howling success financially. I gleaned from the table conversation that McAloney was returning for a second season and that a production of Agatha Christie's *Witness for the Prosecution* was planned for the spring of 1965. When I heard this I piped up that I had played Myers in *Witness*. McAloney stated bluntly, "You can't play Myers. I'm playing Myers. You can play Mayhew." Mayhew was the less exciting of the two roles but he had several decent scenes, nonetheless. Larry knew McAloney quite well and seemed to like him. I soon concluded that he was an Irishman who had kissed the Blarney Stone a bit too often. Although he claimed to have been a steeplechase jockey in Ireland and an alumnus of the famed Abbey Players, his dialect seemed more New Yorkese than Dublinesque. An hour or so later as we departed from this bedlam, I asked McAloney if he was serious about my playing Mayhew. He replied that he was, and I left thinking how fortuitous that I had been in New York because as a result I would be playing a role in Winnipeg.

However, weeks went by and I heard nothing from McAloney. I had written off my being involved particularly when I heard that *Witness* was about to begin rehearsals. About noon on a Monday in early spring of 1965 I received a telephone call from George Bourne, who was then Larry McCance's assistant in the Toronto Equity office. To my surprise George asked, "Aren't you supposed to be in Winnipeg this morning?" "Am I?" I replied, "This is the first I've heard about it." "I've just received a phone call from Michael McAloney in Winnipeg," George explained, "and he thought you were going to play Mayhew and he wondered why you are not at their first rehearsal." I explained to George that I had heard nothing from McAloney since that mad dinner in New York weeks before. I obtained McAloney's phone number in Winnipeg and contacted him immediately. He explained that there had been some sort of foul up but re-affirmed that he wanted me to play Mayhew. We dickered about terms and he said that Rainbow Stage could not afford to pay me what I was asking but that "he would make it up to me at some other time." I had nothing to do for the next few weeks, and the star of the production was to be Franchot Tone whom I had admired in many films, so I agreed upon the condition that McAloney wire me and Equity the terms of the agreement and arrange a prepaid return plane ticket. That night I found myself on a flight to Winnipeg with no inkling that I was on the verge of one of the saddest experiences of my life.

Of the several Canadian cities I have played in, Winnipeg has the feeling of being the most isolated. Psychologically it feels cut off from eastern Canada by the wilderness of the Canadian Shield. To the west and south stretch the great expanse of the North American prairie and to the north more flatland leads to the sub-Arctic tundra. Heat waves roll up from the American mid-west to bake the city in summer and cold Arctic blasts sweep down across a thousand miles of space to congeal the city into a vast ice cube in winter. On one occasion when I was in Winnipeg, with the temperature 20 degrees below zero Fahrenheit, I heard a radio announcer state that Winnipeg had on average the coldest temperature of any city in the world except one, and that was Yakutsk in Siberia. Yet these extreme conditions and the sense of isolation have made Winnipegers possibly the most self-reliant citizens in Canada. They are an extremely energetic, enterprising people. This is well exemplified in the arts: after World War II that city became home to the Royal Winnipeg Ballet, the Winnipeg Symphony, and the Manitoba Theatre Centre, the nation's first regional theatre. In addition, Winnipeg is the site of a long-lived outdoor musical theatre, which is still in existence at the time of writing.

Rainbow Stage was originally the name given to a stage erected during 1951 and 1952 in Winnipeg's Kildonan Municipal Park to replace a bandstand that had been washed away in the disastrous floods the previous year. It was framed with a curved arch, which, when lit, reminded some people of a rainbow, hence the name. Benches to accommodate 3,000 people were added in a natural amphitheatre surrounded by a fence, and it was officially opened in 1954 with the first of 19 performances of a special concert organized by one of Winnipeg's eminent musicians, James Duncan. Artists donated their services and the proceeds went towards expansion of the facilities. Expectation was that open-air theatre would have a better chance of survival in Winnipeg's much drier summers than in Vancouver where "Theatre Under the Stars" had been established in 1940 but eventually drowned after several rainy seasons.

In 1955 a variety of entertainment took to the Rainbow Stage including The Inkspots and a production of *Brigadoon,* in which a young Winnipeg singer, Evelyn Anderson, appeared in the role of Meg Brockie. She went to England that year to study at the Bristol Old Vic School, but returned to grace musical theatres in Canada including the Beaverbrook Playhouse in Fredericton where several years later she and I worked together in *The King and I.* A total audience of 40,000 in 1955 encouraged those behind the Rainbow to form the Winnipeg Summer Theatre Association whose purpose was the administration and artistic development of the Rainbow Stage and a regular season of musicals each summer. The 1956 budget was a meagre $15,000 but they ambitiously scheduled *Annie Get Your Gun, The Wizard of Oz, Our Town,* and *Kiss Me Kate,* plus a pop concert by the Winnipeg Symphony with Don Garrard as soloist, and another by the Winnipeg Concert Orchestra with Roland Garnier as the soloist. Syd Perlmutter, John Hirsch — one of the directors of Theatre 77, a precursor of the Manitoba Theatre Centre — and Peggy Green were the directors. Nenad Lhotka and Arnold Spohr of the Royal Winnipeg Ballet were the choreographers. The Royal Winnipeg Ballet supplied the dancers and the James Duncan Singers the chorus. Among the performers were Evelyn Anderson, Pat Armstrong, Joan Karasevich, Tom Hendry, Grant Cowan, and Robert Jeffrey. Attendance swelled to 80,000 and Rainbow Stage established itself as a permanent and important part of the Winnipeg theatre scene.

Rainbow subsequently fluctuated between years of financial profit and loss. Gradually more grants were received, although the Canada Council held off for years on the grounds that Rainbow was presenting American musicals and was not contributing to Canadian content, regardless that all of the talent was Canadian and the money spent, except for royalties, remained in Canada. In 1960 total revenue was $89,470, but expenses reached $106,054 resulting in a shortfall of $16,584. The Province of Manitoba began helping in 1963 to the tune of $4,000. Nevertheless, the total deficit continued in the region of $21,000, daunting to fund raisers in the 1960s. As the standards of Rainbow's productions improved, the cost for the talent increased. Actors' Equity had gradually been upping the number of Equity artists Rainbow had to hire to work with the non-Equity performers. Most of the singers and actors were members either of Equity or the Association of Canadian Television and Radio Artists, and, because of a reciprocal understanding between the two associations, an ACTRA member appearing onstage with Equity members was expected to join Equity. By 1964 most of the major roles and many in the chorus were Equity members. As well, the dancers of the Royal Winnipeg Ballet were all Equity members. A series of managers, including Tom Hendry and David Robertson, struggled to keep expenses under control and the prices within the reach of the average Winnipeger, and it is to their credit that by 1964 the accumulated deficit was only $33,914.[2] When Robertson left, the board of directors decided to advertise for a director-manager to match the combined dynamism of Hirsch and Hendry. They received an application from Michael McAloney and after an interview in Winnipeg, they made their fateful decision. McAloney was their man.

I understand why they were impressed. I was similarly impressed that night I met him in New York. A smooth talker with great panache, he was theatrically flamboyant and could be very persuasive. He gave the impression that his brand of theatre would be exciting theatre. The board admitted that they were looking for someone who "could represent Rainbow Stage to the community in high style and high profile."[3] That, Mike McAloney was very adept at doing. He took over in 1964 and proceeded to put Rainbow Stage on the map internationally by bringing in a lot of American and a few Canadian stars. For the first season he presented Carmel Quinn and Jan Rubes in *The Sound of Music, Anything Goes* with Eddie Foy Jr. and Winnipeg's Lillian Lewis (the dancer I had met back in 1948 at Barbara Chilcott's flat in London), *Finian's Rainbow* with the long forgotten Bert Wheeler of the 1930s movie comedy team of Wheeler and Wolsey, and *Gypsy* starring Julie Wilson. Malcolm Black, who was then the artistic director of the Vancouver Playhouse, was the director of these productions. The musical director, Phillip Fradkin, was imported from Broadway and the stage manager from the Louisville Theatre Association.

McAloney also brought in an associate producer, Joyce Sloane, who had been a guiding spirit behind Chicago's Second City Comedy Theatre. Sergei Sawchyn became general manager, which was fortunate because he acted as a restraint on the producer's tendency to spend as though he were Flo Ziegfeld. Although Sawchyn managed to increase grants and box-office revenue by revamping the seat prices, and even though attendance fell off and the deficit increased, it grew only to $47,770. The following year McAloney brought a new general manager with him, William Conn. The production of *Witness for the Prosecution*, scheduled to open in May 1965, was intended to raise money to reduce the deficit and fund an even more ambitious summer season.

The day after my telephone conversation with Michael, I found myself in Winnipeg, living in a huge room at the charming old Canadian Pacific Royal Alexandra Hotel, which, I am sorry to say, has since vanished. This was McAloney's headquarters, rehearsals were held in its ballroom and many of the imported cast, including Franchot Tone, also stayed there. McAloney had assembled a fairly strong cast. Tone, who was a much more skilled actor than his early movies revealed, was cast as Sir Wilfrid Robarts, defence lawyer for the accused murderer, Leonard Vole, who was played by a very handsome Francis Bethencourt. Mr. Bethencourt, who gave the impression that he knew he was handsome, hailed originally from London via New York and Hollywood where he had impressive credits. I thought he was ideally cast because he captured a certain smug, male vanity that is the core of the role. From the outset I found Franchot Tone a most ami-able gentleman who did not act the "star" in any way. He was a modest man with a keen sense of humour who respected his fellow actors. He had enjoyed a long career onstage and in films, many of which I had seen in my childhood. I particularly admired him in *Richelieu, Mutiny on the Bounty, Lives of a Bengal Lancer*, and later, as the President in *Advise and Consent*. He had undergone an operation for cancer and was quite frail, but was scheduled to appear soon in the Ben Casey television series. Donna Pearson, an ex-wife of Michael's, also came from New York, and carried off the difficult role of Romaine Vole with as much competence as the limitations of this production would allow. Also in the cast were two Winnipeg actors with whom I became friends, Joan Panton and Harvey Harding. On the technical side, I was delighted to see two cronies from the Garden Centre Theatre, Vernon Jeffrey as both stage and production manager, and Jack McAdam as set and lighting designer. McAloney himself directed and played Myers, the Crown Attorney.

Although I was a day late in joining the rehearsals, I was not far behind because nothing much seemed to have been accomplished the first day. I was to discover that this was true most days over the inadequate two weeks of rehearsal. From my first rehearsal I had reason to become apprehensive. We began at 10 a.m. and at 20-minute intervals a bell hop would bring Mr. Tone a vodka and coke. At one o'clock we broke for lunch and McAloney, Franchot Tone, and I repaired to the bar where Franchot introduced me to Bloody Marys. I found these lunches, which were repeated every day, quite entertaining because both Tone and McAloney had a plethora of anecdotes about show business personalities, but as the week wore on I grew more worried about the production. The lunches lasted up to two hours. While I limited my drinks to two Bloody Marys, Franchot and Michael would knock back several more and perhaps a sandwich. The drinks did not seem to phase McAloney, but, after we returned to rehearse, Franchot would fold up in about half an hour and retire to his room for the rest of the afternoon. We would rehearse without him, but since his role was so pivotal to every scene, it became difficult and often impossible. During the second week even McAloney became concerned, but nothing was done to curtail Mr. Tone's vodka and cokes and Bloody Marys.

I suspect that he knew he had not won his battle against cancer. Quite possibly he was in continuous pain and needed the alcohol to deaden it or to give him the illusion of energy. But Tone was not winning control of his lines. During the play Sir Wilfrid Robarts asks the same questions in different words three times. In the courtroom scene he must cross-examine witnesses and sometimes badger them by rapidly firing the questions at them. During rehearsals he would get hopelessly lost in the trial scene and would lose patience with himself. It was pitiful and unnerving for the rest of the cast. In order to protect myself and help him out if needed, I learned Robarts' lines as well. When we got into the theatre and I saw the courtroom set, I realized that a theatrical idiosyncrasy allowed another way I could help him.

The courtroom arrangement defied all tradition. McAdam had been forced to design it not with the hierarchy of the British judiciary in mind, but in accord with the pecking order of our theatre company. The crown prosecutor and the defence attorney were seated on risers higher in the courtroom than the judge. McAloney, as the Crown Prosecutor, was dead centre and Tone just left of centre. The judge sat profile to the audience in the weaker position down stage right, and the jury box was down left. The witness box was right of centre. I was hoping Tone would object to this arrangement but he didn't. I was placed most conspicuously at a small table just below Sir Wilfrid's seat, as though I were a clerk of the court instead of the solicitor for the defendant. However, this position gave me a further opportunity to help Franchot. After our dress rehearsal, which was a shambles, I decided to write Sir Wilfrid's trial dialogue on foolscap paper, which took me most of the next day. In the theatre that opening night I explained to Franchot that I would hand the appropriate sheets as though they were notes from me, which he would peruse and then ask his questions. Unfortunately, even this did not always work because he would lose his place despite the clarity with which I had printed the lines.

The first act had not gone too badly, but the second dragged at a sloth's pace, especially when Sir Wilfrid was speaking. McAloney and Bethencourt managed to make the second act closing reasonably exciting but it had taken so long to get there that the audience could not be aroused from their somnolent state. The third act seemed interminable. Tickets for this opening night fund raiser had been $25 a pair, quite steep for Winnipeg in the '60s, although the gala included a post-show reception in the ballroom of the Royal Alexandra Hotel. At about 11:30 we began hearing the audience departing. When the curtain finally came down at 12:15 a.m., less than half the audience remained. By the time we had got out of costume and make-up and arrived at the reception, the huge buffet looked as though it had been devastated by swarms of locusts. All that was left was a few bits of sardine on soggy toast. The audience, quite justifiably, determined to get something for their $25, and I don't blame them.

Franchot knew where the problem lay, and felt so badly about it that he donated back half of his $4,000 per week salary. The situation was very disturbing: this once fine actor was a dying man. What with his age, his weak physical condition, his medication, and his alcohol consumption, he could no longer really function as an actor, at least not onstage. After he left Winnipeg he appeared in some of the Ben Casey TV series, but died soon after that. This experience caused me to resolve that if I ever become too weak or senile to act, I will give it up gracefully and not try to stagger on, an embarrassment not only to myself but to all around me.

The local critic quite naturally lambasted the show even though it had some very good performances. Word of mouth got around and the audiences fell off for the rest of the run. Instead of raising money, the production lost $6,396. As a result McAloney began his second season with Rainbow even further in debt. But that did not stop him and his grand designs. He made an agreement with Ed Mirvish to take four of the Rainbow Stage's musicals – *Flower Drum Song, Can Can, Guys and Dolls,* and *Annie Get Your Gun* — to the Royal Alexandra in Toronto. But with no regard for the logistics involved in transferring sets from a 12-foot-high proscenium to the 30-foot-high and much wider opening of the Royal Alex stage, the plan became a nightmare for the new designer, Peter Wingate. At the conclusion of that summer, McAloney returned to New York, and the Rainbow Stage deficit had swollen to an unmanageable $93,488.[4]

One cannot blame McAloney alone for this. The board of directors had wanted someone who would give Rainbow Stage a high profile. He accomplished that and in so doing changed it from a local, summer musical theatre to one of national, and even international note. He could not have been aware of the parochial attitude of the Winnipeg public that resented so many Americans being brought into their "little musical theatre." After all, McAloney was an American, a New Yorker with the traditional attitude of the Broadway theatre. In his world stars put bums on seats. But attendance decreased only in part because too few locals were being used. The re-arrangement of seat prices had eliminated many of the cheaper seats, a decision that was not McAloney's. Nor was it his fault that public and private funding for the 1964 and 1965 seasons fell short of the expected figure. At the time, too few Canadians had the know-how to raise money for the arts. Overall, the main reason for the deficit increase was that he was extravagant in establishing a fully professional musical theatre company in Winnipeg, a development which Equity had been encouraging. Unfortunately, after the party came the hangover.

Bankruptcy stared the Rainbow Board in the face. Amid recriminations and resignations, they persuaded creditors and the banks to hold off. A group of Winnipeg businessmen formed a new company, Rainbow Stage Inc., as a non-profit, charitable corporation with Sidney J. Spivak, a Conservative member of the Manitoba Legislature, as president. A member of the previous board, Jack Shapira, who had been critical of McAloney's productions, was given the job of both managing and producing at Rainbow Stage. A musician and owner of a Winnipeg radio station, Shapira was also a performer and producer for CBC radio and television. He brought in a consultant, William Wylie, the clever general manager of the Manitoba Theatre Centre. Gerry Eldred became production manager and Robert Sherrin and Ray McConnell became two of the directors. Muriel Sherrin also moved from the MTC to be Rainbow's business manager. The new musical directors were Glen Harrison and Bob McMullen. Taras Korol and Peter Kaczmarek designed sets and costumes, and Ted Patterson and Connie Campbell choreographed the shows. In the 1966 season, Shapira and his teammates returned Rainbow to a community-oriented showplace using local performers such as Evelyne Anderson, Bill Walker, Vi Cowdy, Ed Evanko, Cliff Gardner, and Vic Pinchin.

I was on the Canadian Executive Committee of Equity at the time and I remember Jack Shapira pleading with us to allow the company to run with fewer Equity members, and those members who did appear with Rainbow to sign Guest Artist Contracts, which had a lower fee than the Production Contract used in the previous years. Realizing Rainbow's desperate situation, Equity figured that a smaller cake was better than no cake at all, and reluctantly agreed — a perfect example of performers sacrificing to save a theatre company that was in dire straits because of mismanagement by the board and its administrators. I met Shapira on those occasions and realized that he was a shrewd operator indeed who would try to sweeten me with a promise of my playing in one of the shows. I never took him seriously and he never followed through. But he was just what Rainbow needed at the time. Under his guidance the 1966 season saw increased attendance and the deficit reduced by $22,000. The following year was even more successful.

Because bad weather could have catastrophic effects on the revenue, both the provincial and municipal governments chipped in to help install a much-needed roof. When their contributions were insufficient to pay for it, the Winnipeg Rotary clubs came to the rescue with a generous donation, as did several corporations and private citizens. Further funds were raised to improve the backstage facilities. By opening night of the 1970 season, when Catherine McKinnon sang "Somewhere Over the Rainbow" in *The Wizard of Oz*, the audience was being sheltered by the new triodetic dome. Travelling with Ms. McKinnon to the Land of Oz were Dean Regan, Jack Duffy, and Heath Lamberts.

In 1972 Malcolm Black directed the musical version of *Peter Pan*, which Walter Burgess choreographed, with Tom Kneebone as Peter and Murray Matheson in the dual roles of Mr. Darling and Captain Hook. How could Peter, Wendy, John, and Michael be flown on a stage with a height of only 12 feet? The same man who had flown Peter for the New Play Society 20 years earlier was contacted. Peter Foy had spent most of the intervening years in the United States where he had established his own company, "The Flying Foys." He adapted his equipment to meet the limitations and Tom successfully flew across Rainbow's small stage. But at one performance Peter nearly came a cropper. In preparation for the flight, Tom had to climb a 30-foot ladder in one wing of the stage. When the time came to fly, one stage-hand removed the ladder and another, working the apparatus, sent Tom soaring across the stage. One night an overly eager, substitute stage-hand removed the ladder too soon and Tom, with no stage-hand on the wire as a counterweight, started to crash to the floor. Fortunately his fall was stopped by a third stage-hand who caught him just in time and Tom was sent flying off to the Land of the Lost Boys. Had he not been caught, Tom might have been a "lost boy" forever.[5] At another performance the hundreds of children in the audience were a bit restless when Tom was coming to the end of the song "Never, Never Land" and paused to get their attention before the pick up that would conclude the song. The young actress playing Wendy, thinking Tom had dried, and wishing to be helpful, whispered the line "You'll never, never grow old" into Tom's ear and his body mike. Her whisper boomed out over the audience. According to Tom, that actress never knew how close she came to being fed to the crocodile.[6]

Attendance escalated now that the audience could sit snug and dry during the heaviest of downpours. Well, possibly not entirely so. The sides of the auditorium were still open and Winnipeg can get quite cool at night in late summer. But in 1975, 20 years after Rainbow Stage was founded, it received belated support from the Canada Council. Then a second phase of re-construction was begun to give the auditorium a steeper rake. Immediately after the floor had been torn up, a construction workers' strike began that was not settled in time for the 1975 season and forced the cancellation of *Gypsy*. With the help of the Manitoba Theatre Centre, which gave Rainbow space to rehearse and build its scenery, *My Fair Lady* was staged indoors at the Centennial Concert Hall with enthusiastic public response.

The total reconstruction cost a million dollars, but as a result Winnipeg gained one of the most pleasant and functional environments for open-air theatre in North America. The list of Canadian performers who have played there reads like a Who's Who of Canadian theatre. In the '50s and '60s it was one of the few outlets for the increasing musical talent in this country. Thanks to a staunch group of supporters, Rainbow Stage continues to this day, although, in recent years it has undergone some stormy weather. Because my chronicle about the theatres for which I have worked covers only the years from the '30s through the '60s, Rainbow's later history must be dealt with by someone else. But I can assure you that it is a fascinating story of success and failure, both artistic and financial, of scandal, of a general manager being jailed for misuse of funds, of rumours of an attempt to put a "contract" out on his successor, and of the dedication of concerned citizens of Winnipeg to maintain Rainbow Stage, despite its troubles, as a much-needed musical theatre in an artistically progressive city.

Here I must return my narrative to 1965. In the late summer of that year I had a drink at the Lord Simcoe Hotel in Toronto with Joyce Sloane. The four musicals produced in Winnipeg to financial loss fared little better in Toronto. Joyce told me that Ed Mirvish had dropped a quarter of a million on the summer's misadventure. She also told me that she was amazed when Mirvish had asked her and McAloney to produce a winter season for him. This was the first indication I had of Ed Mirvish's loyalty to people he liked. *What Makes Sammy Run?* starring Sal Mineo opened the season and ran the week of January 2, 1966. The major roles were filled by imported actors, but the show had a strong Canadian contingent including Sean Mulcahy, Larry Reynolds, and Vincent Berns. This was followed by Darren McGavin in *The King and I*, a remarkably fine production, despite a brief rehearsal period. McGavin was virile and domineering as the king, and his two American co-stars, Barbara Williams as Anna Leonowens and Patricia Newy as Lady Thiang, kept him in good company. The Canadians in the cast included Allen Bateman, a promising show-biz singer, Garbut Roberts, an expert on Oriental and Asiatic Indian dancing, and Edward Evanko, brought in from Winnipeg to be a handsome Lun Tha. Then came the show in which I was involved, *Teahouse of the August Moon.*

I had received a phone call from Michael, this time asking me to play Captain McLean, the American army psychiatrist who would rather be an agronomist and who is sent into ecstacy by the smell of manure. Tom Harvey was cast as Colonel Wainwright Purdy the Third, a role played on Broadway by Paul Ford. Ted Follows was perfectly cast as the Okinawan, Sakini, but Douglas Crosley who looked right as Captain Frisby, lacked the acting experience to carry a leading role. A great pop singer, exceedingly handsome, with a warm outgoing personality, Doug had become a star on cbc-tv. Originally from Winnipeg, whence so many of our entertainers have sprung, he had cut his theatrical teeth as Curly in *Oklahoma* and Conrad Birdie in *Bye Bye Birdie* for Rainbow Stage. Since then he had appeared on many important TV shows in Canada and the United States. As a singer he was supremely confident, but as an actor without a song, he was not. Because Doug was — and still is — such a charming man, and because we had scenes with him, in order to protect ourselves, Ted and I offered to help him. He accepted eagerly. We coached him on line delivery and tried to make him relax so that he would not be so stiff onstage. By dint of his own determination and our efforts, we partially succeeded, but not enough within the limited rehearsal period to protect him from the critics.

Ted Follows was marvellous as Sakini. Since the day he had departed from the New Play Society he had built a thriving career via the Stratford Festival, tours of the Canadian Players, the Manitoba Theatre Centre, and television drama. He had just spent three years as one of the pioneering members of the Neptune Theatre in Halifax. Nat Cohen, in his review of *Teahouse* referred to him as "a deft and dimensional actor." He pointed out that Sakini could be portrayed with "fake, unspoiled, native quaintness and self-indulgent whimsy. Mr. Follows never succumbs. He surrounds Sakini's charm and good nature with a wall of innocent but definite opportunism."[7] Herbert Whittaker wrote that, "It was hard to steal scenes from the Americanized Sakini of Follows for the star of Halifax's Neptune Theatre is just the right kind of comedian for this popular role: impudent, communicative, and friendly with excellent timing. It was impossible to steal them from Chapman, bland, suspicious, fanatical."[8] I am unsure whether Cohen liked my performance. He simply said that, "Vernon Chapman's psychiatrist . . . has an entertaining centre."[9] Did he find my extremities wanting?

Brilliant as many in the cast were, we could not compete against Lady Astor, an unpredictable goat brought on in the village scene. Almost every night it left evidence onstage of its critical disapproval of the proceedings. Even though the show missed the mark, I received immense satisfaction playing Captain McLean, enjoyed working with the friendly cast, and with the director, Charles Tate, from the U.S. Tate knew what he wanted in the production, but some miscasting and only one week of rehearsal robbed him of his complete goal. I was also rewarded by getting to know Ed Mirvish who presented many of the cast members, including myself, with an autographed copy of his brother's book, *Business Is People*. Every performer who played the Royal Alex in those days was asked to give Ed an autographed photograph of him or herself to be hung in one of his newly opened restaurants in the block west of the theatre. I once saw my photo hanging in one of them, but I do not know if it is still there today.

Notable among the shows that followed *Teahouse* that winter of 1966 was *Oklahoma*, which included among the Canadians in the cast Sylvia Lennick, Stan Francis, and Paul Elsom, a jovial dancer from the Wayne and Shuster shows. *Oklahoma* was followed by the appearance of a really big star — and I do mean "big" — in the person of Jane Russell in *Pal Joey*. With only a week, or slightly more, to rehearse these productions, it is amazing that they were as sleek as they were. For that the credit must go to the musical director, Philip Fradkin, the choreographers, Don Gillies and Vivian Ainslie, the technical director, Harold Courchene (an alumnus of the Garden Centre Theatre), and particularly to the director of all of them, Charles Tate, whom I admired for putting these complex shows together so quickly.

By the end of the winter season, Ed Mirvish had seen several hundred thousand more dollars slide down the theatrical drain. Many of us in the entertainment field worried that, having ventured into production and lost so much money, he would abandon producing and simply run the Royal Alex as a touring house, as it had been for much of its existence. But we underestimated him. A few years later he backed a Canadian production of the rock musical *Hair*, ran it for months, and made back all the money he had lost and more. In his book *How to Build an Empire on an Orange Crate*, he has a chapter where he tells anecdotes about experiences he has had as a storekeeper and a theatre owner. At the end of each story he draws a conclusion that leads invariably to an astute maxim. All of these are valuable, but, for theatre folk, some are more useful than others. One of these reads, "As long as you keep a theatre locked, you *know* how much it costs every week. Once you open the doors and put on a show it can drive you into bankruptcy." Another applies to every performer trying to build a career: "No amount of hard work and brains can beat plain dumb luck." And here is another that explains why so many of us, including Ed Mirvish, got hooked on the theatre: "Theatre is like a love affair. Utterly frustrating when it fails, but sheer magic when it flourishes."[10]

While Honest Ed was trying out his theatrical wings, I became the occasional drinking buddy of Michael McAloney. I found him a convivial, entertaining fellow with a weakness for self-delusion and pretension. Although the amount of the sauce he consumed in an evening would have had me under the table in short order, I never saw him drunk. For this he won my reluctant admiration. Despite his capacity to shoot the bull and, seemingly, believe what he was saying, and despite his cavalier approach to the theatre and to life, I liked him, and I was grateful to him for paying me a good salary for *Teahouse* to compensate for the small fee for *Witness*. He had told me that he would make it up to me, and he did, albeit at Ed Mirvish's expense. I am also grateful to him for introducing me to such likeable people as Franchot Tone, Julie Wilson, and Ed Mirvish, and for the opportunity to perform with Ted Follows, whose work I have always admired. I am also in McAloney's debt for giving me a chance to show my home town audiences that, when it came to comedy, I had learned my craft.

At the end of that winter, McAloney returned to Manhattan, and, for the time being, dropped out of my life, which gave me the opportunity to dry out. I did not hear from him for several years. Then one evening, during one of my trips to New York, as I was walking up Eighth Avenue on my way to the theatre, I passed the Haymarket Bar, in those days a hangout for theatre folk. I glanced at the entrance way, and there, peering at me over the swinging doors, was Michael's moustached face. I was genuinely pleased to see him. He beckoned me to come in and have a drink with him. I declined because it would have made me late for the show. "There is a bar next to that theatre," he said, "I'll meet you there during the first interval." I agreed and met him at our appointed time. During our brief conversation, he told me that he was desperate. He had broken up with Julie Wilson, had not been able to get work, and had "had it with this town."

He then asked me if I could do anything for him in Canada. I told him that I was not producing any plays at the time, and that I had very little influence over those who were. But I promised that I would do what I could.

When I returned to Toronto I contacted Ed Mirvish and said I wanted to talk to him about Michael McAloney. He invited me to lunch at Ed's Warehouse. When I arrived he apologized and said that he had to go to a meeting but his brother Bob would have lunch with me instead. I explained to Bob how desperately depressed and frustrated Michael was, and suggested that they would be throwing him a life preserver if they could hire him for any show they might be producing for the Royal Alex. Having done what I could for Michael, I thought no more about it until soon after I read that he had been hired to direct Brendan Behan's *The Hostage*. In the meantime in Manhattan, he had scored a considerable triumph in staging Behan's *Borstal Boy* and won a Tony Award for it. Quite probably this success induced Ed Mirvish to bring Michael to Toronto but I like to think that I might have pushed him slightly in that direction.

I did not see Michael during the rehearsal period for *The Hostage*, which was a very creditable production. However, some years later, I received a phone call that began, "This is Michael McAloney's stage manager. He wants to know about your availability." "For acting or for drinking?" I asked. "Both, I suppose," the stage manager replied. Reluctant to become involved in another disaster like *Witness*, I said, "If it's for drinking I am available. If it's for acting, I am not." McAloney was staying at the Waldorf-Astoria on Charles Street, in those days a favourite hotel for visiting performers. We met at the Pompeii Court cocktail lounge, and over several drinks Michael told me of his latest project once again with Ed Mirvish. The Charles Manson slayings had occurred a few years before in Hollywood and a play, *Sugar and Spice*, had been written about that grisly event. Mirvish was going to produce it as part of the Royal Alexandra's subscription series and it was to star Sal Mineo as the slayer. McAloney told me that John Ireland had been scheduled to play a major role as one of the victims, but had been taken ill. Michael was now in a quandary as to a replacement with box-office appeal. I suggested Jack Kelly, whom you will remember from the Garden Centre

Theatre. The *Maverick* series was over and I understood that Kelly had retired to his ranch in Texas. Michael thought it a splendid suggestion. He then asked me if I would play the role of a lawyer who has two telephone conversations, one in the first act, and one later in the play. I asked him to let me read the script first. That night I did so and was horrified at the ineptness of the writing. It struck me as nothing more than a tasteless, morbid attempt to cash in on those ghastly slayings in California. I turned down the role even though I could have used the money.

On opening night I was in the audience as the play wound its dreary way toward the climactic chopping up. At least, I thought, that scene will be Grand Guignol and the audience could be shocked at its callous brutality. But no. McAloney staged it in slow motion under strobe lights, which always upset my stomach and keep me from watching such scenes. As strobe-lit ballet, even the sadistic passions of the killers were diluted. With no horror and no attempt at analysis of the murderers, the play was just dull. In addition to the play's tediousness, there was disappointment for Sal Mineo fans because he did not appear until the last act and then in an unsympathetic role. When the final curtain fell, there was at first stunned silence, then the audience erupted with such vehemence that I thought my companion, Daphne Gibson, and I were going to be involved in a theatre riot. Some man down front yelled, "Boy! Mirvish must be hard up to bring us this crap!" There was a chorus of agreements. The man beside me cried out, "This was awful! Just awful!" Three teenage girls immediately behind him, obviously Sal Mineo fans, stood up and one screamed, "We think it's great." "More fool you," replied the man. I thought one of the girls was going to hit him. The curtain rose for the single curtain call and the boos and catcalls drowned out the applause of a few polite patrons. The house lights were quickly brought up and a grumbling audience departed. I had to go backstage to see Jack Kelly, although neither I nor Daphne wanted to do so. I took a positive attitude and, because I thought he had done what he could with a lousy script, I congratulated him on his performance. As I was talking to him in his dressing room, McAloney's face appeared at the door. He beckoned to me and I stepped out into the corridor. "Vern," he asked, "What have I got here? Have I got something or have I got a pile of shit?" "Michael," I replied, "You've got a pile of shit," and I sadly marvelled that he did not recognize it himself.

The next day the radio news programs were full of the story of the disaster at the Royal Alex. Subscribers began to cancel their tickets for the show. But Ed Mirvish came to the rescue. He went on radio and talked about this controversial play. He suggested to the public that they should come and see for themselves what all the fuss was about. A campaign was hurriedly launched to sell the show as something shockingly different. The regular, more critical audience, was replaced by newcomers to the Royal Alex. To everyone's astonishment and admiration, Mirvish and his publicity staff turned an artistic disaster into a financial success. McAloney returned to New York licking his wounds. I have not seen him since. In spite of his faults, I liked him and found him fascinating because of his panache, his grand style, his brazen braggadocio, and his capacity for alcohol — in short, a man theatrically theatrical who was never dull.

BELMONT THEATRE PRODUCTIONS

presents

THE COLLECTION

by

Harold Pinter

— and —

THE AMERICAN DREAM

by

Edward Albee

starring

BEN and SYLVIA LENNICK

CARROLL PATRICIA BROWN   VERNON CHAPMAN

BRUCE GRAY   NANCY KERR

directed by

JACK MERIGOLD

CHAPTER 21

In Steel City, Greenwich Village, and the Hydro

After my stint at the Garden Centre Theatre in summer 1965 and before my *Teahouse* engagement in winter 1966, I was invited to direct *A Thousand Clowns* for the Hamilton Players Guild, one of Ontario's best amateur troupes. I welcomed the opportunity to tackle this play again after what I considered a far from successful production with Vaughn Meader in 1964. To my satisfaction the Players Guild amateur staging was far superior. This was largely due to a longer rehearsal period, more money for set design, a larger and better equipped stage at the Westdale Collegiate Auditorium than at Vineland, and the fact that Steve Weston, who played the lead, was an infinitely better actor than Mr. Meader. The rest of the cast were on a par with Steve, especially David Mallis, a very funny actor with whom I was to work professionally years later. The show proved that the only certain difference between professionals and amateurs is not in talent nor quality of the work, but that the former get paid.

As a corollary to my directing in Hamilton, I was approached by the Burlington Little Theatre to be a paid consultant for *Sunday in New York*, their entry into the Ontario Drama League Festival in the 1965–66 season. I told some members of the Hamilton group of the invitation and one of them responded, "You won't want to work with them. They aren't very good." That remark was all I needed to accept the Burlington offer, which entailed driving from Toronto to the Nelson Community Hall on the

Dundas Highway near the Guelph Line several nights a week for seven weeks during the dead of winter. But they were a happy group and I enjoyed great satisfaction working with them. They were determined not to miss the Festival that year as happened previously. James Costley was the nominal director, and I was on the program as associate director, but in actual fact I directed the show via suggestions to Mr. Costley. The lead male role was taken by Russel Korenowski, better known to drinkers of the Yonge-Bloor area of Toronto as the proprietor for many years of the Chez Moi Tavern on Hayden Street. *Sunday in New York* was a play well within the capabilities and technical resources of the group. The result, which pleased me immensely, was that they were accepted into the Ontario Festival, and the Hamilton Players Guild was not. Even though Burlington's efforts were not given an award by the adjudicator, Barry Morse, they were not bothered very much. They had at last got into the Festival. For many years I had held Mr. Morse in high regard, which went up several notches when he announced at the Festival that he did not approve of competitive drama festivals, an opinion I had held since winning the Inter-College Festival at the University of Toronto. But the 1960s brought such ideas into the amateur theatre. In 1971, the first non-competitive "showcase" of amateur companies replaced the annual Dominion Drama Festivals.

The 1960s also witnessed a phenomenal growth in the performer population of Toronto, drawn there from across the country and elsewhere, particularly from Great Britain, by the lure of television and the growing theatrical activity at last aided by an increase in public funding. Some of these new arrivals, finding that Toronto was not yet the land of theatrical milk and honey — too many performers and too few opportunities — decided to move on to the United States or into some other field of endeavour. Others decided to create their own theatre opportunities, which laid foundations for the post-centennial blossoming of theatre and Canadian playwriting. I want to take you back to a couple of these 1960s' ground-breaking ventures in which I participated as artist and audience member.

The first is the Village Playhouse, so-called because it was on the fringe of Toronto's Greenwich Village, a Bohemian section by then being eroded by the expansion of the hospitals that dominate this area today. It was started by one such émigré, Elspeth Gaylor, a bright young lady of 24, who with Donald Meyers, Alan Maclean, and Louise Clayton took over a tiny basement theatre at 49 LaPlant Street in fall 1961. The space had originally been converted into the York Community Theatre by Donald Ford, Louise Clayton, Don Meyers, and Alan Maclean as a venue for their amateur productions. They had staged several plays there that had been successes in London and New York, including *Home at Seven* and Noel Coward's *Nude with Violin*, with Elspeth Gaylor in her first Toronto stage appearance and an aspiring young Kenneth Pogue in leading roles.

In 1949, Elspeth had won an open audition for the London Academy of Music and Dramatic Arts, but was persuaded by her parents and one of her school teachers not to accept the offer. Instead she attended the University of Nottingham where she received an Honours Degree in Geography and Languages, and upon obtaining a Diploma in Education, taught Geography in the British equivalent of our high schools. Between 1949 and 1958 she became more and more involved in amateur theatre. In 1958 she emigrated to Canada, picked up her career as a teacher, and immediately continued her interest in amateur theatre by joining the York Community Theatre. Her first professional engagement also came in 1958 when she and Don Meyers worked as apprentices at the Garden Centre, which taught them that they needed more training. She returned to England and Don accompanied her. They saw as many plays as they could, and immersed themselves in the British repertory world. Eventually she worked at Lincoln's Theatre Royal not only as an actress, but also as a lighting technician, assistant stage manager, stage manager, and production manager. Mr. Meyers had come to the acting profession by the circuitous route of lab technician, business machine repairman, salesman, and, for the York Community Theatre, a lighting technician and an actor. In Britain he worked with Elspeth in a variety of theatres and soaked up as much knowledge and experience as he could. In 1961 they returned to the Garden Centre as apprentices, but this time as knowledgeable ones.

That October they joined Louise Clayton and Alan Maclean to establish the Village Playhouse. Louise and Alan soon withdrew, leaving Don and Elspeth to carry on in a Lilliputian theatre of only 82 seats, an advantage in gaining concessions from Actors' Equity and keeping overhead costs down, but, so small that with the necessity of keeping ticket prices low, they faced a daunting task to make the operation viable. They gave themselves an objective: to present new plays and plays new to Toronto (shades of the original goal of the New Play Society). Their operating capital came from their own pockets and in order to meet expenses, Elspeth returned to supply teaching. At one point she could not afford room rent, so she lived in the backstage area of the theatre until her earnings became more stable.

Although the Village Playhouse lasted only two years, the number and variety of plays they offered were astounding. Their 1961 season opened with the North American premiere of John Arden's *Sergeant Musgrave's Dance*, followed by another North American first, Ionesco's absurdist *Amadée*. Then they staged *One More River* by Beverley Cross, J.P. Donleavy's *Fairy Tales of New York*, O'Casey's *The Drums of Father Ned* (another introduction to North America), and they ended that season with the "Don Juan in Hell" section from *Man and Superman*. Because they could not afford to have a dark summer during which they would have to pay rent with no revenue, they continued to produce shows through July and August of 1962. John Van Druten's *The Voice of the Turtle*, James Bridie's *Doctor Angelus*, Gore Vidal's *Visit to a Small Planet*, and Emlyn Williams's *Trespass* made up that summer. With nary a breathing space they opened the fall season with another North American first, *The Red Eye of Love* by Arnold Weinstein, followed by Arthur Miller's *A View from the Bridge*, *Celebration* by Keith Waterhouse and Willis Hall (which was yet another premiere for North America), Lorca's *House of Bernarda Alba*, another O'Casey, *The Purple Dust* (which also had never been staged in North America), followed by two more premieres, *Live Like Pigs* by John Arden, and *Naked Island* by Russell Braddon. No other theatre companies in the city at that time, including the Crest, were so daring.

Nor had we ever enjoyed such a varied theatrical feast in so short a time. They were bringing world theatre to Toronto, broadening the experience of the city's theatre artists, and creating great excitement among theatre buffs, which included many university students. The scene was enlivened during the long winter months of 1962–63 with another North American premiere of a second Waterhouse/Hall collaboration, *Billy Liar*, followed by a premiere anywhere of two one-act plays by Martin Lager that I was brought in to direct: *The Master Mind* and *Who Is on My Side, Who?* Then Toronto audiences saw for the first time *The Making of Moo* by Nigel Dennis, followed by a throw-back in theme and approach, *There's Always Juliet* by Van Druten. To perform this kaleidoscope, they managed to persuade many of Toronto's best actors to participate, such as Barbara Chilcott, Donald Ewer, Ken James, Joyce Campion, and Bruce Gray. Experienced Canadian directors also got on their bandwagon: George Bloomfield, Sean Mulcahy (for the Shaw and O'Casey plays), Robert Christie, John Douglas, Fred Euringer, Jean Roberts, Marigold Charlesworth, Peter Boretski, and myself. Elspeth and Don wound up their two-year marathon of intensive theatre with *The Hidden Room* and then collapsed from exhaustion, both physical and financial.

I had met Elspeth and Donald during their second Vineland apprenticeship, and I followed their courageous adventure with keen interest and hopes for their success. I admired many of their productions. When they asked me to direct Martin Lager's plays I jumped at the chance. With one or two exceptions, all the plays I had hitherto directed had seen previous productions and came with the original director's guidelines included. But with Martin's plays I could discover whether or not I was a sufficiently resourceful director to bring these scripts to life. I was helped by Lager's sheer theatricality and by the inventive co-operation of both casts. *The Master Mind* had only four characters portrayed by Joel Kenyon, Bruce Dellar, Rena Jackson, and Milo Ringham. The scene was a storeroom over a garage, which was designed by Tony Van Tulleken. The second play was a C.B. DeMille-like epic with 33 characters played by 17 performers. Elspeth and Don designed its circus venue; Don designed the lighting and Elspeth the sound. Martin had found the title for this script in a passage from 2 Kings 9:32: "And he lifted up his face to the window and he said 'Who is on my side? Who?' and there looked out to him two or three eunuchs." I never thought the script lived up to the potential in that quote. In fact it had nothing to do with the Jezebel story as told in 2 Kings. Mr. Lager used the biblical quote merely to indicate the bewilderment of an Everyman character as he pursued his embattled way through life.

Because these were the first Canadian plays the Village Playhouse had staged, the producers attempted to persuade the Canada Council to contribute, but the Council refused. When Ron Evans heard this, he wrote a scathing attack in the *Toronto Telegram* that began, "Now will someone please explain to me again what the Canada Council is all about?" He quoted from the Council's 1961–62 report, "We still cannot see in any number those essential figures on the theatre landscape — the playwrights of great talent. We are only hoping that they are lurking around the corner." Then he outlined the Village situation: "Because the producers had scheduled Martin Lager's plays into their season at short notice, there was not sufficient time for the appropriate panel of the Canada Council to meet, but individual Council members have the power to make emergency grants. They [the producers] quickly prepared the necessary documents requesting a meagre $1,000 . . . only to be rejected because the Council could not underwrite a 'young and untried' writer." Evans conjectured that the Council's "playwrights of great talent" meant playwrights of proven commercially-profitable talent and mentioned two established playwrights who had received grants. He concluded, "I suppose the Canada Council knows what it is after. But the Village Playhouse producers don't, and neither do I."[1] After reading that my opinion of Mr. Evans as a critic improved immensely, but not for long.

Who Is on My Side? Who? was a blend of two writing styles. The protagonist was a mute played by mime artist Joseph Liberatore. The plot followed the progress of Mr. Average Man, whom we first saw as a babe in arms, then in nursery school where regimentation began to take hold, through grade school where his creative impulse was crushed, then in the army where the regimentation was completed, from which he emerged into a dreary career in commerce. But then, through the love of a beautiful girl, he found his path back to his real identity and his personal integrity, which presumably led him to fulfilment and content. Shades of *Peer Gynt, Candide,* and *Schweik.* But Don and Elspeth thought it worth showing, and I found it a challenge to make it theatrically engaging. I was greatly aided by a cast that included Denise Ferguson, Joel Kenyon, Bruce Armstrong, Marvin Goldhar, Milo Ringham, and Len Doncheff, all of whom rose to the challenge. The preceding production, *Billy Liar,* sold out and was held over giving us a welcome additional week to rehearse.

No one pretended that these plays were *chefs-d'oeuvre,* least of all Mr. Lager. But they were intriguing early efforts and demonstrated creative imagination and theatrical sensitivity. Ralph Hicklin wrote in the *Globe and Mail* that, "Martin Lager . . . showed that he is already a writer of workable plays."[2] He thought *The Master Mind* more successful than the longer *Who Is on My Side? Who?,* which is ironic because Martin whipped the former up quickly to give a full evening of entertainment. Hicklin went on to praise Joel Kenyon's performance in *The Master Mind* and my direction for its tightness, but faulted me for not achieving the same tightness in the second play. He was probably correct. Mr. Lager has gone on from this humble beginning to greater achievements. He has written scripts for radio, revues, films, and for a variety of television programs including *World Religion, Profiles of Nature, Political Biographies,* and for the series *Top Cops.* At CTV, he has been a story editor and advisor, and executive producer for drama. He has achieved all this while retaining his love of writing for the stage as exemplified by *The Magnificent Slowpoke, The Magic Mountain,* a mime for children called *The Vagabonds, A Time to Reap,* and a dozen more plays that have been produced at theatres across the country. In recognition of his talent even the Canada Council came around and awarded him not just one, but two grants.

At the Village Playhouse three more productions followed in that spring of 1963 before Elspeth and Don threw in the towel. After two seasons of low budget but high standard shows, Don was quoted in Gordon Froggatt's column: "Of course we feel sad about closing, but despite the fact that many people thought we were wrong to battle against what seemed on occasion like overwhelming odds, we feel that we have accomplished what we set out to do — prove that the new and untried will be accepted in Toronto." Ron Evans quoted Elspeth in his column: "We're stopping now because we can't go any further under these conditions. With our present standards of production, we just can't make it pay in an 80-seat house. And rather than reduce our standards, we're stopping here."³ Praise came from all corners. Nat Cohen summed up their achievement: "For two seasons Miss Gaylor and Mr. Meyers confounded the business experts, gave several talented people a showcase, and made their chamber theatre the one place in town where one could get some idea what was happening in modern English drama. And their presentation of *Live Like Pigs* was the most completely successful show any local company presented this season."⁴ Incidentally, *Live Like Pigs* was directed by Jean Roberts. Among the *Toronto Telegram Awards* for 1963, the best production went to the Village Playhouse presentation of *Naked Island*, directed by Peter Boretski, the award for the best newcomer to Toronto theatre went to Heath Lamberts for his performance in the Village Playhouse's *Red Eye of Love*, and the best actress award to Barbara Chilcott for *The Making of Moo*, also directed by Peter Boretski. For two brief seasons the Village Playhouse had flashed like a comet across the Toronto theatrical sky and burned itself out. In 21 months from October 1961 to June 1963 the Village Playhouse presented 22 productions. Naturally not every show was top drawer, but they managed with meagre resources to present some of the most exciting, enlightening, and controversial theatre Toronto had yet seen.

The careers of Donald Meyers and Elspeth Gaylor, which had been intertwined for several years, now separated. Donald began working for theatres across the country. He and I were to be together again at Theatre New Brunswick six years later. Elspeth, after a brief return to acting with the Straw Hat Players, became the production manager for the Canadian Players during their season at the Central Library in Toronto. She then became a design assistant to Mark Negin at the Stratford Festival, and quickly moved from assistant stage manager to stage manager and to production manager at the Festival's Avon Theatre. A lady of great integrity, she resigned from the Festival when she became disillusioned with the leadership of that theatrical behemoth. Meanwhile, she became the wife of a Stratford physician and happily manages his office for him — the physician's gain but the theatre's loss. Sadly Donald Meyers, one of the most affable actors it has been my pleasure to work with, left this world far too soon, still in his prime — another loss for the Canadian theatre.

■

I watched a lot of history behind the Belmont Theatre before I worked there in 1966. It began for me one day in 1942 when, travelling to the University of Toronto on the College streetcar, I noticed a new sign on an abandoned movie house near College and Dufferin Streets. The old sign "Belmont" still hung there, but below it had been added "Group Theatre." Naturally I was curious and learned that here was a new theatre founded by Sylvia Paige and Benjamin Lennick. Sylvia had started singing and dancing as a child, and directing children's plays at the Synagogue on University Avenue. In her teens she began acting with adult amateur groups and eventually enrolled in the school run by the Theatre of Action under the tutelage of the embryonic teacher and director from New York, David Pressman. Ben Lennick was not a child actor. He graduated from Toronto's Central Technical School with a Commercial Art diploma only to find that during the depths of the Depression no one was hiring commercial artists. His sister, Sally, was involved with the Theatre of Action and persuaded him to see their presentation of Irwin Shaw's *Bury the Dead* with a curtain raiser of Molière's *The Affected Young Ladies*. Ben was captivated by the Shaw play. At the end of it the audience rose to its feet and cheered. A spark was lit and Ben decided that he had to become a member of this group of dedicated, somewhat-socialist theatre activists. (For the story of the "Theatre of Action" I recommend Toby Gordon Ryan's comprehensive book, *Stage Left*.) Ben had no money, but the Theatre of Action needed actors so he was given a scholarship to study with Pressman, and he appeared in several of Theatre of Action's productions including *Waiting for Lefty* and *The Inspector General*. And Ben met Sylvia Paige there.

When World War II broke out, the Theatre of Action, as a social commentary theatre, faded out. Many of the other amateur groups turned to staging shows for armed forces at their bases and in military hospitals. But this endeavour did not meet the needs of the more dedicated performers who were hoping to establish a professional theatre in Canada. Four of them, Sylvia Paige, Ben Lennick, Leo Orenstein, and Lucille Kallen as the catalyst, decided to form a "peoples" theatre modelled on the Group Theatre in New York. They found the abandoned movie house at 1114 College Street, and because the electric sign above the marquee read "Belmont" they decided to call their organization the "Belmont Group Theatre" for two reasons — they liked the sound of it and they could not afford to have the sign removed.

The rent for this 150-seat theatre was a whopping $50 a month, the total of Sylvia's savings from working as a cashier for Adams Furniture. She paid the first month's rent. They operated the Belmont Group Theatre as a sort of club. Dues for the "members" (actors, directors, and technicians but not the general public) were $2 per person per month, which gave them enough to pay the rent. Because the company was "amateur" in the sense that nobody got paid, all the people actively involved had to have daytime jobs. The old movie house was a long shoe-box and needed considerable surgery to convert it to a workable, legitimate theatre. The screen and speakers had to be removed and a stage built forward. The stage wings beside the fire exits became dressing rooms. Conditions were primitive and the drawbacks were tolerated when not overcome. During the ensuing years, Ben and Sylvia often enlisted members of the Royal Alexandra's crew where they performed professionally in summer stock. The prop man loaned them stage properties and short flats from the Alex to help them keep costs down.

Their premiere program consisted of three one-act plays from three different countries: a Mexican comedy, *Sunday Costs Five Pesos* by Josephine Niggli, *Hello Out There* by the Armenian-American William Saroyan, and *The Marriage Proposal* by the Russian, Anton Chekhov. Lucille Kallen had the temerity to write Mr. Saroyan for the rights to *Hello Out There* and received a supportive letter in return granting them the permission to stage it royalty free, much to the annoyance of Samuel French Publishing Company, which held the royalty rights. The two lovers were played by Leo Orenstein and Lucille Kallen, who got so involved in the relationship onstage that they got married in real life soon after in 1943. There must have been a cupid hovering over the theatre because one week later Ben Lennick and Sylvia Paige tied the knot. Now there were two husband and wife teams running the Belmont Theatre.

I did not see any of their earliest work, such as *Let's Be Offensive*, a revue in support of a second front in Europe, but I did catch a 1946 production of *The Taming of the Shrew*, which had Sylvia Paige as Katherine, Charles McBride as Petruchio, Hugh Watson as Vincentio, Henry Karpus as Grumio, and John (Sean) Sullivan as Lucentio. Also in the cast as the Pedant was the late George Hislop, who was to become a mover and shaker in Toronto's Gay Liberation movement, and Araby Lockhart, doubling as the stage manager and playing the role of Curtis, usually performed by a male actor. Most of the cast had duties in addition to acting. Araby was the property mistress and on the publicity committee with John Sullivan and Ralph Messinger who played Baptista while functioning as business manager. Sylvia Paige designed the costumes, which were made and assembled by a committee consisting of Sylvia, Pearl Glass, and Mary Hoffman. Ben Lennick directed and designed the set, which he helped Ken Drummond and Syd Pearl construct. They must have been an exceedingly busy group of ardent people.

For *The Shrew* program, Ben wrote an article expressing the mood of the artistic communities all across Canada: "There is a rising wave in Canada today. A feeling that this country is entering into an era of cultural maturity. From coast to coast we have reports of Canadian writers, painters, musicians, dancers, and actors who are successfully contributing to the common cultural heritage." He continued with an exhortation to the public to support this country's cultural emergence and concluded with "Perhaps we shall witness the emergence of a true 'People's Theatre,' a theatre to which the actors, artists, and technicians can turn as a worthy profession, and of which every Canadian can proudly paraphrase 'This is my own, my native theatre'."⁵ Those were sentiments many of us shared in 1946.

That same year, another Belmont production of *Hello Out There*, featuring Sylvia and Ben, won a drama festival sponsored by the newly founded Toronto Civic Theatre. When the building at 1114 College Street was sold and the Belmont Group Theatre found themselves without a home, they went ahead with the 1946–47 program and rented, as needed, the Temple Auditorium on the west side of Bathurst Street just south of Dundas. They staged *My Sister Eileen* in November 1946, *A Sound of Hunting* by Sergeant Harry Brown in January 1947, *Macbeth* in February, and *Awake and Sing* in mid-April. Ticket prices were $1 each, but one could get two tickets for all four productions for $5, thereby saving $3 — hardly a prohibitive price. They also rented the small auditorium of the YMCA on College Street to present another evening of one-act plays: Chekhov's *The Bear*, which Ben directed, *The Key*, an original play by Lucille Kallen that she directed, and Norman Corwin's *The Untitled*. Leo Orenstein performed in the latter two plays as did an actress making an early appearance, Dallas Damer, whom you may recognize as Mary Damer. I admired both this evening of plays and the Belmont's production of *The Shrew* and I thought at the time that it would be rewarding to work with them. But that was not to be for another 20 years.

The Belmont Group Theatre continued for several more years after 1946. In the summer of 1952 they performed in the open air at Mart Kenney's Ranch. Their schedule that summer was *The Voice of the Turtle*, which was held over for two weeks, *Private Lives*, *The Second Man*, and *Hay Fever* in which Sylvia played the scatter-brained Judith Bliss. Her director, Ben, decided that she should sing a sultry French song when trying to seduce the very reserved diplomat, Richard Greatham. On opening night, as soon as Sylvia hit her sultry low notes, she was joined by a bovine chorister from the nearby corral. Every night, as soon as she began her sexy number, she elicited the same bellowing response. Sylvia wondered if it was a bull aroused by her seductive tones. Wisely, she decided not to find out.

In the early '50s, the Belmont began losing its players. Sean Sullivan was growing popular on television and in the newly founded theatres around the province, Mary Damer was a professional summer stock actress, and Araby Lockhart, a unique comedienne, also found herself in demand. Leo Orenstein was becoming one of the CBC-TV's busiest producers, and Lucille Kallen went to New York where she became a novelist and wrote comic material for TV's *Show of Shows*. Sylvia and Ben had developed *Mama's Family*, a radio show in which they used a number of the Belmont actors. That was followed by a quarter-hour program, *Linger with the Lennicks*, which metamorphosed into the half-hour *At Home with the Lennicks*, which Sylvia wrote and which continued for seven years. The result was that they too were beginning to make a living as professional performers and could not devote the time to the Belmont's amateur productions. So in 1952 the Belmont Group Theatre folded.

Thirteen years later, Ben and Sylvia read two one-act plays by Murray Schisgall, *The Typists* and *The Tiger*, which had been successes Off-Broadway. Two-handers with a pair of equally challenging roles, they were perfect vehicles for the Lennicks, who determined to appear in them. But where? In 1965 Toronto had a dearth of affordable performance spaces. Ontario Hydro had recently taken over the Royal Conservatory buildings at College and University where there were two auditoriums named the Recital Hall and the Concert Hall. Hydro was willing to rent out the latter for $100 a month. When Marcia Bossin, sister-in-law to Hye Bossin who edited the *Canadian Film News*, informed them of this, the Lennicks grabbed it. They considered calling it the "Hye Bossin Theatre" — Hye had recently died — but decided on the "Hydro Theatre" because the name and the location would be more familiar to the public. They reactivated the Belmont name for the producing company, but dropped the word "Group" because such nomenclature was out of date, and because it was stretching the term to apply it to an opening show that used only two actors. Because they would be playing in both plays, and because *The Typists* is the longer of the two during which they would be required to age, they decided to reverse the order with *The Tiger* as the first play on the bill. They entered into a partnership with Jack Merigold, who joined them as co-producer and director. Ever since he emerged from that goose costume in *Spring*

Thaw, Jack had enjoyed a very busy career as a stage manager as well as an actor. By 1965 he had spent nine seasons at the Stratford Festival, and had become the assistant to the artistic director, Jean Gascon. He had stage managed Tyrone Guthrie's *Tamburlaine* when it went to New York, and continued to work with Guthrie there for 10 years. The new Belmont trio hired Joanne and Robert Hall as their designers, whose sets for *The Tiger* and *The Typists* cost $400 including their fee — which Ben and Sylvia paid out of their own pockets. They planned to run the plays every evening, Tuesday through Sunday, with tickets moderately priced at $2.50 and $3, and special rates for theatre parties and students. When on February 9, 1965 at the beginning of *The Tiger*, Ben carried Sylvia onstage over his shoulder, the audience applauded. She and Ben found it heartening to have an audience indicate, as Sylvia puts it, "Welcome. We are glad you are here."[6]

The critics were, on the whole, enthusiastic and encouraging. Nat Cohen wrote somewhat grudgingly, "Ben and Sylvia Lennick are a warm and comfortable couple, and in the sum of their efforts, they are responsible for a fairly pleasurable evening. . . . The occasion is dramatically acceptable, and gives the Hydro Theatre a good start as another outlet for worthwhile professional theatre in Toronto."[7] Herbert Whittaker concluded that the plays were "an admirable choice for beginning Ben and Sylvia Lennick's plan to revive the Belmont Group Theatre."[8] But Ron Evans waxed most eloquent in his praise, dubbing the Lennicks "the Luntnicks" after the famed acting couple, the Lunts, and saying that the plays were "a long overdue demonstration of their remarkable acting ability. . . . Ben Lennick makes of this letter-toting loony a delightful, gruff, moody, capering fraud, all bluff and no bully. . . . Sylvia Lennick paints the Long Island predator perfectly. . . . As terror ebbs, and sympathy steals in, she becomes a sly, simpering seductress."[9] *The Typists* and *The Tiger* were so successful that they were able to run them for 14 weeks — unprecedented for a Toronto production to that time.

Cindy, Stephen H. Stein's unpretentious little musical, also proved to be a hit with audiences and reviewers in November 1965. Stein, a New York producer, had been looking for a Toronto venue and hooked up with the

Lennicks, whose Hydro Theatre provided an apt intimacy for his charming show. Jack Merigold directed, and recruited Ben McPeek as the musical director and Glenn Gibson, a dancer from the Wayne and Shuster TV show, as choreographer. Jack also directed *The Country Girl* in January 1966, with Martin Lager as Bernie Dodd, and the Lennicks as Frank and Georgie Elgin. That spring Ben directed Neil Simon's *Come Blow Your Horn* in whose cast was a young actor who performed his role adequately, but only worked the one Belmont show. He persisted, despite protests from Sylvia and the stage manager, Robert Spearin, in banging down a bottle from which he was pouring a drink during one of Sylvia's punchlines, thereby killing the laugh.[10]

Having seen Belmont Theatre productions over 20 years, most often with favour and always with admiration for their courage in play selection, I was delighted when asked to perform with them in October 1966. In a double bill of *The American Dream* and Harold Pinter's *The Collection*, the cast of the former was the same, with one exception, as the Harlequin Red Barn production that summer. It included Ben and Sylvia as Daddy and Mommy, Carroll Patricia Brown as Grandma, Nancy Kerr instead of Sylvia Shore as the visiting Mrs. Barker, and the handsome young man played by the handsome young Bruce Gray. In the four-character Pinter play, Ben and Sylvia played a heterosexual married couple, and I played a middle-aged man living with a young man (Gray) in presumably a homosexual relationship. *The Collection* raises questions about a possible liaison between the young man and the wife. There are questions, answers, and then different answers. In the end, the audience and the two jealous lovers, the husband and the middle-aged homosexual, are left wondering if the affair between the wife and the young man ever really happened. I derived immense satisfaction out of the role.

Three of the Toronto newspaper reviewers came and their reactions once again reveal that to put one's faith in the judgement of critics is a very uncertain basis on which an artist can judge his or her work. The art of the theatre is a collaboration among many creators onstage and off, including an audience who bring their own experience to their appreciation of this ensemble achievement. All have limitations, and critics are no different. Their contrasting reactions to the double bill demonstrate how diverse backgrounds and attitudes toward the theatre affect what different critics say about the same show.

Herbert Whittaker wrote of *The Collection*, "What he [Pinter] does concern himself with is suspense, a commodity his cryptic rhythms of speech can build to electrifying heights. Last night those heights weren't sparked steadily enough, for in their anxiety to explore the Pinter style, the actors played with far too great deliberation. Each performance was heavily faithful and thus the delicacy of the play was destroyed."[11] Nat Cohen wrote, "Mr. Merigold paces his cast of four smartly and negotiates the lighting and sound effects with adroit skill. Watching the play is like watching a quickly moving, montage-composed revue anecdote."[12] Ron Evans profoundly disliked *The Collection*: "Mr. Merigold directed this one as though he were laying bricks — bricks the size and weight of coffins."[13] Were he and Cohen at the same play? Evans preferred the presentation of *The American Dream* to that of *The Collection* but Cohen was the exact opposite, and Whittaker seemed to slightly favour the *Dream*. And what did they say about my performance? "Special marks go to Mr. Chapman for his witty interpretation of a suave sadist nagged by growing bewilderment," wrote Cohen. Whittaker agreed, with a reservation: "In the Pinter, Vernon Chapman scored most points as the older homosexual, though even he pushed too hard." Vitriolic Evans could find nothing positive in any of us, or Pinter, which put us in good company, at least. Calling *The Collection* Pinter's exercise in terror and tedium (a contradiction in terms?), he wrote, "Given brilliant playing this four-finger exercise might well be briefly absorbing. Given the juiceless routine performance of Mr. and Mrs. Lennick, Mr. Gray, and Vernon Chapman, the best reaction I could muster was: So?" A failure of critical imagination?

Jack Merigold had worked with George Tabori and Gene Frankel in New York when they compiled *Brecht on Brecht*, a revue derived from Brecht's works that Jack next directed at the Belmont. To complement a very strong cast of the Lennicks, Pamela Fernie, and Lawrence Beattie, Jack wanted Bruno Gerussi, who, by 1967 had established himself as one of the few Canadian actors whom the theatre-going public recognized as a "star." Because the Belmont fee was limited to about $65 a week, the producers felt they had little hope that Bruno would accept their invitation, but he agreed, saying, "There comes a time when you get tired of doing garbage."[14] Not that "garbage" had figured prominently in Mr. Gerussi's career. He had distinguished himself at the Stratford Festival as Romeo, Feste in *Twelfth Night*, and Yasha in *The Cherry Orchard*. On Broadway he had played Ishmael in *Moby Dick*, and in Toronto El Gallo in *The Fantasticks*. On television the nation had seen him as Louis Riel and as Peer Gynt. Hardly a career built on garbage. But he was enthused about *Brecht on Brecht*, which became one of the most rewarding shows for the Belmont, mostly because Bruno brought his dynamic talent to it, and his reputation brought his fans to the box office. In the week of performance, Sylvia learned that during the rehearsal period Tyrone Guthrie had offered him an engagement at the Guthrie Theatre in Minneapolis at several times the Belmont salary, but he had turned it down. When she asked about the Guthrie offer, he replied, "Do you think I would walk out on you in the middle of a show? What would happen to the show?"[15] Here was an actor who put his responsibilities before opportunism. It should happen more frequently.

After *The Days and Nights of Beebee Fenstermaker*, which did terrible business, the Belmont shifted to *Uncle Vanya*, which I was asked to direct. In high school I read *The Cherry Orchard, The Three Sisters, The Seagull*, and several of the one-acts in a beautiful blue, grey, and gold edition of Chekhov's plays that I had purchased for 79 cents, and despite the stilted translation, for which no credit was given, I became, if not an outright devotee, at least a respecter of his profound ability to create characters who functioned on many levels of thought and emotion. I realized that a proper production of the great Russian master's play in merely two weeks was nigh to impossible. But I had never had the chance to direct Chekhov, and I welcomed the opportunity.

In plays with such complex characters and as subtle as *Uncle Vanya*, each actor and director can find something different to emphasize, but the director must blend these discoveries into a consistent whole. As I saw it, *Uncle Vanya* was not quite so despairing as some of Chekhov's plays, but a wry comment, at times farcical and at other times pathetic, on the dreariness and lack of purpose of rural life in late 19th-century Russia. I felt it was imperative that as interpreters we must not become judgemental about the characters but must present them with sympathetic understanding, even though we recognize them as often silly, foolish, stupid, or bored, as did Chekhov. As interpreters we must convey how bound these people are to their situation and how powerless to escape, either through lack of will or through circumstances beyond their control. Any production of a Chekhov play that does not evoke this empathy in the audience has failed.

Although restricted by the Belmont's salary limitations, I felt it essential to hire a cast with an ability for fast analysis of characters, who had a rapport with each other, and could quickly absorb the atmosphere of the play. In the title role I cast Nicholas Simons because I knew his work and because I believed he would be able to capture Vanya's gentle ineffectiveness. As Vanya's niece, Sonia, I was lucky to have the extremely intelligent and sensitive Daveena Turvey and as her counterpart, Yelena, the beautiful, statuesque American, Jess Walton, who was at the time performing with me in *The Right Honourable Gentleman* at the Central Library Theatre for Aries Productions. A year or two later, Jess returned to the United States where she became a star in TV soap opera. As Doctor Astrov, the frustrated environmentalist and naturalist, I was fortunate to have cast a handsomely grave actor of Dutch origin, Henry Hovenkamp. Marina, the old nurse, was Nan Stewart, and as Maria Vasilievna Voinitskaya, I cast Dora Dainton, both fine character actresses originally from Britain. Gino Marrocco, who came to Canada from Italy at the age of 12, was the guitar-playing Ilyitch Telegin. As the irascible, self-pitying Professor Serebriakoff, I cast William Osler with his booming voice. We brought in Peter Wilde, who had studied Russian, to advise us on pronunciation, and who helped revise the stilted sections of the Stark Young translation in the Samuel French edition into more natural, actable speech. I stressed with the cast that they must always be aware of the subtext, essential for the interpretation of Chekhov, indeed, for most modern plays. Pauses in his plays cannot simply be empty spaces, but must be filled by the actor with thought consistent to the character in the situation. Even though we were not able to mount the *Uncle Vanya* we would have liked, it was still a well-acted production and the cast and I were in harmony with our approach. With such a cast and with sufficient time to immerse ourselves in the play, I believe we could have achieved my idea of how this play should be presented. We did not, but we had a good shot at it.

Capturing the atmosphere of this comedy-drama on the Hydro Theatre's small stage was more than a challenge. *Uncle Vanya* requires three realistic sets if one follows Stanislavski's approach to Chekhov's plays, although it was an approach the playwright did not wholly endorse. Designer Joanne Hall and I decided against elaborate set changes. Modern audiences are not conditioned for such delays. We also decided to combine the dining and living rooms into one area that occupied most of the stage, with a corner of Vanya's room elevated upstage. The terrace occupied downstage right with a brick wall covered in vines to indicate that it was outdoors. Although bricks were not unknown in 19th-century rural Russia, this wall might have looked more Russian if made of wood. In the living-dining area, Joanne tried to capture the pretension to grandeur of this farmhouse by painting classical pilasters on the back wall. Vanya's office wall was filled with book shelves and the requisite map of Africa belonging to Dr. Astrov. It was a crowded stage. The furniture was suitably period but nothing that said this is particularly Russian except the samovar. I divided the play into two acts and simply dimmed the stage lights to indicate scene breaks. I tried to create the warm glow of candlelight and coal oil lamps by amber and yellow jelling, and bringing the stage lights down slightly, except for the opening garden scene, which was brightly lit. Alas, we only partially succeeded in our efforts to catch the atmosphere and also keep a fluid staging.

Although ostensibly a comedy in the sense that the human condition is revealed in its absurdity, *Uncle Vanya* has farcical moments. So that he can live in comfort in St. Petersburgh, the selfish Professor Serebriakoff announces he plans to sell the estate without consulting Vanya, who has been struggling to keep it going. Enraged, Vanya charges offstage after the

Professor. A shot is heard and Serebriakoff rushes back onstage pursued by Vanya who has shot at him but missed. In his temporary derangement, Vanya shoots at the Professor a second time and misses again. My problem as a director was how could he miss in the small confines of our set. I had the Professor duck down behind a chair, but then it dawned on me that the normally peaceful, placid, even timid Vanya would be afraid of guns so that when he fired he turned his head away. It worked and added to the farcical elements in the scene.

Both Whittaker and Cohen recognized the problems we faced, and on the whole, their reviews were not unkind. Whittaker called my direction "level headed" and Cohen wrote that my "adult approach was intelligent and sympathetic. He does not treat *Uncle Vanya* either as a gloomy drama about sad people wandering in a crypt of boredom, the way Checkov used to be done in English, or as today's conventional broad farce edged in occidental pathos."[16] Then he balanced those compliments with a comment on the fundamental weakness in the production: "Even if it achieved an ensemble manner, the production would still have a certain thinness. It would lack a continuing lyricism and a full-bodied humanity."[17]

Since my Belmont attempt, I have seen two other stagings of *Uncle Vanya* and performed in yet another. In 1970 I saw Paul Schofield as Vanya in a production by the English Stage Company, which revealed to me just how far short of the mark we had been. I also saw the production staged at the Royal Alex starring Peter O'Toole and taken on tour to the U.S. Two decades later I was delighted to play Professor Serebriakoff for Persephone Theatre in Saskatoon. Both these productions made me feel considerably better about our version at Belmont. There was yet another production of *Uncle Vanya* by Theatre Plus some years after ours for which the advance publicity presumptuously claimed that *Uncle Vanya* had never been staged in Toronto before.

The grant that the Belmont Theatre had received from the Canada Council was not renewed for the 1967–68 season. That summer Ben and Sylvia had been busy in summer stock and Jack Merigold had been at the Stratford Festival, commitments which left them with very little time to plan a fall season. That, coupled with the disappointing news from the Council, made them defer opening until January 1968. In the meantime, Ontario Hydro offered the theatre to other organizations, and Dennis Sweeting of the Kawartha Summer Theatre Festival in Lindsay leased it for a production of *Charley's Aunt* as light Christmas fare. Apparently things got too light because on Christmas Eve the Lennicks were shocked by a phone call informing them that the theatre and a portion of the old Conservatory had burned down. A cigarette left on a dressing room table after the show was believed to be the cause of the fire. The Kawartha Festival lost their sets, their furniture, and their costumes for the play, and the Belmont Theatre lost all the props they had stored plus a refrigerator backstage. A small fire insurance policy did not adequately cover the material loss. The Lennicks' plans for the new year went up in smoke with the theatre.

Something else disappeared with the Hydro Theatre — its ghost. From the day the Lennicks moved in they often heard a violin being played in the distance. Except for those employed for the Belmont's musical shows, musicians had not been seen or heard in the building since the Royal Conservatory vacated the premises. After the organ pipes had been removed from below the stage and that space converted into a green room, the faint violin sound would often drift up from there while the actors were onstage. Someone always went down to the green room to investigate, but no one was ever found there. Old buildings can have unexplainable noises, but Sylvia Lennick had a theory about the ghost. When she was eight years old she had to accompany on the piano a young violinist during a recital on that very stage. At one point she had to turn the page of the music, but it got stuck. She had to stop playing, but the violinist continued all the time hissing at her, "Keep going," while she hissed back, "I can't, I can't." Eventually he too had to stop and glowered at her until she could get the page unstuck, after which they continued. Sylvia maintains that the "ghost" they heard years later was that boy having his revenge on her.[18]

In spite of the loss of the Council funding during one of its periodical purges, and the loss of the Hydro Theatre, Merigold and the Lennicks made plans for the autumn of 1968. Their problem was to find an affordable theatre that would be audience accessible. Because the payment rates established by Equity were pegged to potential box-office revenue at 100 per cent capacity, and because ticket prices had to be reasonable to encourage the public to support local productions, it behoved producers of small budget companies to find theatres small enough to keep the performers' fees within their financial range but large enough to offer at least the potential to meet expenses. Marigold Charlesworth and Jean Roberts had enticed audiences to the tiny but charming Central Library Theatre, and after they departed, Aries Productions had been using it. With the loss of the Hydro Theatre, the Central Library became more in demand, with the result that it had to be booked months in advance. Shortly after the Hydro fire, the Belmont producers booked the Central Library Theatre for four productions during the 1968–69 season.

They planned plays not previously staged in Toronto, and which audiences would not otherwise have an opportunity to see: *Eh?*, a satire on man and his relationship to machines, which had been a success in London and New York; *The Victim*, a psychological thriller by Mario Fratti; *Filumena Marturano (Marriage, Italian Style)* by Eduardo de Filippo, a comedy that had been made into a hit movie; and *Take a Litter*, a farce about life in Canada by Gordon Diver. They hired three guest directors, Brian Meeson for *Eh?*, Leslie Yeo for *The Victim*, and myself for *Filumena Marturano*. Sylvia Lennick directed the season's last show, *Take a Litter*. They also made plans for the Monday nights when no performances would occur. For one Monday they proposed a panel discussion of plays and productions. For another they planned play readings, and for another they hoped to arrange for actors to meet critics. I had profound misgivings about the wisdom of that last proposal.

Eh? opened in October to two generally favourable reviews and one damning one. Whittaker praised David Hemblen as Valentine Brose and Lyn Wright who "is as lissome as required and is entirely delicious as the bride in the boiler room." He also singled out Kenneth Dight who "bubbles beautifully as the Vicar, rising to a super-sermon in the second act."[19] Ralph Hicklin, who had replaced Ron Evans at the *Toronto Telegram*, was even more enthusiastic. He wrote, "Despite its loose irrationality, *Eh?* at the Central Library Theatre has a kind of wild, night-marish logic, thanks largely to the intelligent resourceful playing of David Hemblen as Valentine. . . . He induces a momentary suspension of disbelief, a credulity in the spectator toward what is evidently a certifiable nut. He is beautifully supported by Lyn Wright as Betty Dorrick."[20] Nathan Cohen's was a dissenting opinion: "So, although *Eh?* is a farce of limited and fluctuating quality, it is contemporary in tone, with the constituents of an entertaining theatre piece. For that to be shown it must be staged with unswerving attention to its slapstick and fantastical situations. No such appreciation distinguishes the Belmont performance. The only actor that makes his role at all visible is Kenneth Dight as the Clergyman."[21] Cohen's brief review of *The Victim* continued his sniping at Belmont productions: "To put it conservatively, the play plumbs the depths of banality that would make the writers of TV junk thrillers turn in their membership cards rather than admit authorship."[22] In the *Telegram*, Hicklin shared Cohen's opinion of the script referring to it as "hasty pudding," but he did give credit to the actors and director.[23] Whittaker was kinder: "*The Victim* is a good choice for Belmont productions, for Ben and Sylvia Lennick are by now fearless in the face of strong drama."[24] He continued by praising the cast, especially Sylvia, and Peter McConnell as the psycho who "offers a handy package of neurotic virility."[25] These reviews leave me wondering why was Cohen so unable to see anything theatrically valuable in the productions when two of the three most widely-read critics in the country found elements to praise? He continued his assault on the Belmont Theatre in his next review, which dealt with my production of *Filumena Marturano*.

There are 13 characters in this play, and I added one more. Such a large cast was an ambitious financial gamble. The play was also an ambitious gamble for another reason. It depended on a Neapolitan atmosphere and actors who would be able to understand and perform the volatility of its southern Italian temperament. And it required a director who understood that. Sylvia and Ben had cast themselves as Filumena Marturano and Domenico Soriano before I was hired to direct. But I did have complete say in the casting of the other roles. As Filumena's three grown sons I cast Peter J. McConnell, Dan MacDonald, and Martin Blackwell. When Dan was offered a more lucrative engagement, I brought in Alan Bleviss to replace him. I was ecstatic when Jane Mallett was persuaded to take on the role of Rosalie, the old servant and confidante of Filumena. Lawrence Elion was Alfredo Amoroso, the long-time crony of Domenico, and Françoise Vallée (a.k.a. Felix Francis or Frances Walsh) was Lucia, the maid. Max Hammer played a lawyer, Nocella.

The plot is quite simple. Filumena has been living as the mistress of Domenico Soriano for 25 years. Now, in their middle years, he has decided to marry a sexy young bimbo and jettison Filumena. By conspiring with Rosalie and feigning death, she tricks Domenico into making her respectable for heaven by marrying her on her supposed deathbed. Having trapped him into marriage, she keeps him trapped by another ruse when he threatens a divorce. She explains that one of her three grown-up sons is his. Domenico endeavours to discover which is his heir, but she refuses to tell him. The end of the play leaves the answer unresolved and Domenico resigned to living with Filumena for the rest of his life. An uncomplicated storyline but one that presents opportunities for eruptions of temper, floods of tears, and wild, farcical situations.

The play as written begins with the scene of recriminations after the deathbed trick. I thought it a pity that the deathbed scene did not begin the play as it did in the film version. I decided we needed that opening fillip, so I took the liberty of creating a prologue that was mostly in mime, staged in front of the curtain with the bed downstage centre. The priest, present to give the last rights, instead read the marriage ceremony after Domenico was persuaded by Rosalie and the priest to marry Filumena. When Filumena sprang out of bed to triumph over Domenico, the bed slid off behind the curtain, and as the quarrel gathered steam, the curtain opened revealing Joanne Hall's set for the dining-living room of a Neapolitan family of some wealth but dubious taste. Unlike the *Vanya* set, this one helped create the required atmosphere. The opening prologue surprised and delighted the audience.

During rehearsals I realized that unbridled passion at full volume in an intimate theatre could be very annoying for our audience. The vehemence of the emotions could lead the major performers into the trap of over-playing, so I watched this carefully and occasionally put a check on it. At one point Sylvia began crying during a long speech of Filumena's in which she related her sorry, sordid past. I stopped her, and, according to Sylvia's memory of the moment, said, "If you cry during that scene I will person-ally come onto the stage and hit you. They [the audience] are the ones who must cry, not you."[26] Of course, I would not have done such a thing because Sylvia would most certainly have hit me back. However, she refrained from crying, and every night, after that speech, to use an old theatrical cliché, there wasn't a dry eye in the house.

On the whole, I was quite pleased with what we had accomplished so I was shocked to read Cohen's brief, but dyspeptic, review. Hicklin criti-cized Eric Bentley's clichéd translation (which Cohen liked) but was generally favourable to the production and the actors. Cohen headed his review "Smog Over Naples." His opening statement belied what actually happened on the stage opening night: "The paramount handicap of *Filu-mena Marturano (Marriage, Italian Style)* now at the Central Library Theatre, is that its two leading and, in fact, only important roles, are enacted without a shred of feeling for their comic bustle, emotional effer-vescence, and volatility and maturity."[27] He devoted much of the review to further attacks on Sylvia and Ben, which, in my view, became personal. He concluded, "Save for Jane Mallett as Filumena's aged companion and Françoise Vallée as the maid, the rest of the acting does not dispel the smog that fills the library theatre stage. Vernon Chapman's direction is hon-ourably intended but helpless against the labyrinthine obstacle course set up by misguided casting."[28]

This completely negative and bad tempered review is for me an example of irresponsible criticism. It is not constructive in any way and completely ignores the reaction of the critic's fellow theatregoers. Nat Cohen claimed to set a high standard for the Canadian theatre, and I believe that to be so, and admired him for it. But this type of review shows an arrogant lack of respect for the artists and even for the audience. Fortunately, the public chose to ignore Cohen's vitriolic outburst and continued to buy tickets on the basis of word-of-mouth publicity from happy customers. As well, perhaps Ralph Hicklin's enthusiastic review counter-balanced Cohen's influence with beneficial results at the box office.

Why Cohen was so vehement in his attacks on the Belmont Theatre productions that '68–69 season when he had been a supporter three years before on its opening is a mystery. Possibly he felt that the productions did not live up to his standards, whatever those were. But it is also possible that his changed attitude was a result of the following incident. Sometime before *Filumena* opened, Ben and Sylvia were guests on the Don Sims late night talk show on CBC radio. Sims asked them what they thought of the critics, and Sylvia expressed an opinion shared by many performers: "Critics are often influenced by what they had for dinner or if they've had a fight with the wife."[29] The next day Cohen attacked them in his column, and did not give them a favourable review after that. I find it difficult to believe that he could be that petty, but something motivated him to write derogatory comments about the Lennicks in *Filumena Marturano* that were manifestly not shared by anyone else.

For the final offering that season the producers bowed to a commendably growing trend in Canadian theatre — to stage more Canadian plays even though they were still a risky undertaking at the box office. Jack Merigold and the Lennicks took a chance with Gordon Diver's *Take a Litter*, which treated a theme becoming prominent in the news of the day. A married woman who had been on birth control pills, one day forgot and found herself pregnant. The doctor advised her that she could have multiple births. Diver, an ex-actor from Montreal, teaching at the time at Forest Hill Village Junior High School, wrote a comedy around this situation. In leading roles were David Hemming, Rod Coneybeare, Ben Lennick, Françoise Vallée, Diana Barrington, and Graham Teear, who apparently stole the show as a theologian helping deliver the multiple babies. In the role of Dr. McMonigle, Paddy (Browne) Robertson, erstwhile of the Globe Theatre in Chatham, made what must have been her only

Toronto stage appearance. According to Sylvia Lennick, Nat Cohen attended opening night with his wife, sat in the front row, roared with laughter, and the next day wrote a devastating review, which probably had a detrimental effect on the box office because the public response to this production was only moderate. The results of the inclusion of a Canadian play in the season did not encourage the producers to repeat the experience and marked the demise once more of the Belmont Theatre.

▪

My Belmont story would be incomplete without some reference to the special programs the producers organized for Mondays. I became involved in one of them as a performer in a musical concert. Actor Alan Doremus was a splendid musician, not only a composer and a fine pianist, but an aspiring orchestra conductor. Toward that end he became the conductor for the Harmony Symphony Orchestra, an amateur group based mostly in Scarborough whom the Lennicks invited for one of these Monday soirées. The first half of the program was pieces by Mozart and Handel; the second half was Prokofiev's *Peter and the Wolf* with yours truly as narrator. While I am not enamoured of this children's story told in words and music, the ham in me welcomed it and, as a result of my youthful assault upon the piano, I was able to read the score. Several rehearsals were required during which I admired Alan Doremus's patience. The nucleus of this small orchestra included some very qualified musicians, but there were a couple who seemed to be novices and frequently played off-key. At one rehearsal the orchestra sounded more like the "Disharmony Symphony." Since no one was paid, the conductor had no control over how many members would turn up to practice. On the final rehearsal before the Monday performance, the percussionist was up north enjoying winter sports. *Peter and the Wolf* minus the timpani is insipid — and worrying. Fortunately, all the musicians were there for the concert, everybody played with surprising harmony, and I had a lot of fun. Actually, for the audience it was a very rewarding evening, considering the admission price was only $1.50.

Another money-raising activity the enterprising Lennicks entered into was organizing the occasional "Industrial Show" for some company or other. One they organized, which required me to act, sing, and (horrors) dance, was *Conversion Piece*, presented at the Inn-on-the-Park for Ontario Hydro employees. It was a one-hour show in which we cavorted about extolling the virtues of converting Ontario Hydro to 60 cycle. Hardly *My Fair Lady*, but it was fun and lucrative.

By the end of the run of *Take a Litter* the producers felt the need to take stock of their finances. Belmont received financial assistance from the Ontario Arts Council, the Metropolitan Arts Council of Toronto, the Atkinson Foundation, and private donors, as well as items donated for stage use, and time and service given gratis by many individuals. All of this, even with box-office receipts, proved to be insufficient. Despite the low fees required by Actors' Equity and despite the fact that some of the shows did good business, too frequently the producers had to meet expenses out of their own pockets. By the spring of 1969, they realized that they could no longer stand the drain on their own financial resources. With great regret they decided to call a halt. They had given Toronto almost four years of exciting, eclectic theatre, and if one includes the 10 years of the amateur Belmont Group Theatre, Ben and Sylvia Lennick contributed immeasurably to the development of the theatre in Canada and in Toronto in particular.

There is a postscript to the Belmont story. In 1995 Ben and Sylvia, who had kept active over the years, read a script that turned them on. A hit in New York, *Three Viewings* consisted of three monologues in a funeral parlour. They planned to present it with their daughter Julie under the Belmont banner in the winter of 1996. But in January of that year, Ben had a fatal heart attack. As a tribute to Ben, Sylvia decided to go ahead with the production. They had rented the Studio Theatre of the new North York Centre. She invited me to direct and Paul Soles to take over the role Ben would have played. It is one of the most beautifully written scripts I have ever read, well laced with humour, and it was a pleasure to work with these three fine actors to bring it to life. I think Ben would have appreciated the result.

CHAPTER 22

The Firebugs
and the British
Upper Crust

On January 2, 1968 I began an assignment with high hopes that turned into deep frustration. I had been hired to direct *The Fire Raisers*, sometimes known as *The Firebugs*, by the Swiss playwright Max Frisch, for the Kitchener-Waterloo Little Theatre. Among amateur groups this organization had a commendable reputation and they hoped this production would be their entry into the Western Ontario Drama Festival. Although, as you know, I have an aversion to competitive drama festivals, I was mindful of the enjoyment I had directing the amateurs of Westfield, New Jersey, and, because the play intrigued me so much, I decided to accept their offer. The rehearsals necessitated my driving from Toronto to Kitchener three nights a week for five weeks, with a final full week of evening rehearsals before opening a three-night run on February 8. The advance adjudicator was to arrive on February 9th to assess the production's worthiness for the Regional Festival that spring in Sarnia. It was fortunate he came on the second night, because the first night was a disaster.

Frisch describes his play as "A morality without a moral with an after piece." It is an allegory about how a ruthless, bullying group, such as the Nazis, can take over a society in the face of public complacency. It is also a metaphor for a world terrorized by the threat of an atomic holocaust, and a very theatrical piece requiring artificiality and exaggeration in playing. Frisch was strongly influenced by the so-called Absurdist works in which modern problems are treated as parody and tragi-comedy. The original version, on which the first British performance was based, contained the "after piece" omitted from Mordecai Gorelik's translation for the American production. I decided to stage the version with the after piece, believing that it helped illuminate the main play while ending it on an upbeat note of redemption. Moreover, it gave additional opportunities for effective staging.

There are only three women in the play, but there are six male roles plus five or six men as firemen who act as a chorus. Usually in amateur groups women outnumber the men, but I was fortunate in finding some very good male actors for the major roles. On the whole, the acting was of a fairly high calibre, with a couple of outstanding performances by Bill Koski and Leo Burns as the two firebugs. The chorus too proved to be very effective. Had the production depended solely on the acting, it would have been quite successful. But there were many lighting and sound effects. All during rehearsals I kept checking with the volunteer technicians about the progress being made in solving their problems. I was repeatedly assured that things were well in hand.

The play was to be presented in the Eastwood Collegiate auditorium. I had planned on two technical rehearsals, a rough dress, and a final dress with invited guests. For the first technical rehearsal the set was not ready and the additional lights required had not been installed. A technical rehearsal was impossible. The next night the conditions had barely improved. With the exception of the sound effects, nothing was ready for a technical rehearsal before the full dress. Had it not been for the effort of some zealous high school boys in preparing the set and the lighting, I would not have been able to have even a dress rehearsal. However, by opening night at last the set was ready and the lights installed. The first performance seemed to be going smoothly when suddenly several of the over-loaded dimmers blew. Nobody had checked whether the stage lighting equipment could take the extra load. The rest of that evening's performance had to be played in murk and we lost essential lighting effects.

By the second night, when the adjudicator, Leslie Yeo, was present, the problems in the electrical system had been solved and the show went comparatively smoothly. At one point in the after piece, Frisch's instruction reads, "A gorgeous figure dressed somewhat, but only somewhat, like a bishop appears with splendid and solemn bearing." I had decided that he would make an impressive entrance by descending on a cloud from high up in the stage's fly gallery. I had the figure, Leo Burns, arrayed in clerical robes surmounted by a mitre and lowered to the ominous opening chords of Poulenc's organ concerto. The problem was that, because there was no way of mounting his "cloud-throne" from the flies, Leo had to be hoisted up before the epilogue and remain there surrounded by hot lights sweltering in his heavy robes for about 15 minutes. I was unsure whether or not Leo would pass out before his descent to reveal a rather limp deity. However, he had the required stamina and it was one of the most effective and surprising moments in the play.

The adjudicator quite justifiably criticized us for choosing a play that was technically too difficult for the group and for the collegiate stage's limited facilities. He awarded Leo Burns the award for best actor in the play for his portrayal of Eisenring and gave me the dubious accolade of "best director who did not get into the Festival."

Unfortunately, the Kitchener-Waterloo Little Theatre had bitten off more than they could chew technically, and, although the actors strove valiantly to give all that I asked of them, the experience soured me on directing for amateur theatre. Someday I would like to direct *The Firebugs* in a theatre with proper equipment and skilled technicians.

You may remember in a previous chapter my briefly mentioning that while I was directing the Belmont *Uncle Vanya* in 1967 I was performing in *The Right Honourable Gentleman* for Aries Productions. This company is almost forgotten now, but it originally sprang from David Baron Wilson's desire to produce a show as a vehicle in which he could be seen. Wilson was a recent immigrant from Britain who had been working with amateur groups since his arrival in Canada and had performed professionally at the Red Barn Theatre. He and his Toronto apartment mate, Bruce Gray, determined to stage plays that were "feasible," that is, plays not done in Toronto previously and that had suitable parts for the producers.[1] They became co-actor/managers and decided to lease the Poor Alex Theatre on Brunswick Avenue just south of Bloor Street. This toy theatre of III seats had been created by Ed Mirvish in a section of his former plastics factory with some of the leftovers from his refurbishing of the Royal Alexandra, but it was ideal for their limited objectives.

For their first offering they decided on *Yours Faithfully*, a frothy comedy adapted by Robert Rietly from an Italian play by Sergio Pugliese. Through his connection with the amateur theatre, Mr. Wilson recruited actresses Morna Wales and Norma Clark. Paisley Maxwell, who had been working professionally, was also induced to join the company. Charles Sivell was brought in to direct, and Larry Helzog to design, although for economy, the set was borrowed. Publicity consisted mostly of a few posters in store windows. On April 30, 1964, *Yours Faithfully* opened before an audience mostly of friends and two critics who also turned out to be friendly. The show ran for 10 days and broke even. It was all very encouraging, and, as a result, Morna Wales and Norma Clark joined Wilson and Gray as producers, forming Aries Productions, so-called because Morna, Norma, and David were born under the sign of Aries. Bruce Gray was the lone Virgo of this quartet.

Bruce was born in Puerto Rico and was brought to Canada at the age of six. He graduated from the University of Toronto in 1960 with an M.A. in psychology, but, instead of using it to analyse real people, he decided to apply it to fictitious characters in plays. Because of the lack of opportunity in Canada, like so many aspiring performers, he went to England where he established himself as an attractive juvenile, working for the Mermaid Theatre in London, the Theatre Royal in Bath, and the Colchester Repertory Theatre. He also performed in London's West End at the Adelphi. On returning to Canada, his former frustration from lack of performance opportunities returned and urged him to team with David. Together they could make their own opportunities. Not only did Bruce act and handle the finances, he also had a flare for design, so he designed, helped build, and painted many of Aries' sets.

Morna Wales had trained at the Gina Mawr School of Mime and

Drama in London, England, and broke into the professional theatre at the Dundee Rep. in Scotland as both an actress and assistant stage manager. When the war came along, Morna joined the British army where she was recruited to put on shows for the soldiers. Like Paddy Robertson, she met a doctor in the Canadian army, married him, and after the war moved to Etobicoke where she had several babies, but found time to act and to learn to design and make costumes with amateur groups in Etobicoke and Weston. When David Wilson approached her in 1964 to resume her professional career, her children were grown enough to look after themselves, and she welcomed the chance. On the other side of Toronto, Norma Clark was gaining experience with the Scarborough Little Theatre. Her training in school had been in music and drama and she had won several public speaking awards. She met David Wilson in the Scarborough group and was lured into Aries as one of the producers, as an actress, and as publicity manager for which she had considerable aptitude.

Although she performed with Aries in the first two shows, Paisley Maxwell did not become a producer until the third production. She had studied drama at Alma College and the London Little Theatre School. She attended McMaster University and in 1951 graduated from Lorne Greene's Academy of Radio Arts with the Drama Award. She also took a degree in Speech Arts at the Toronto Conservatory of Music, and immediately found work with the Straw Hat Players and CBC-TV in the series *Mr. Member of Parliament*, which starred Gordon Pinsent.

Yours Faithfully did not set the Toronto theatre world on fire but it achieved its purpose. The Aries group was noticed. Audience response and the relative friendliness of the critics, plus a solid 72 per cent attendance, encouraged them to continue. But they realized that they had broken even only because they had not paid themselves any salary. Screwing their courage to the petite marquee of the Poor Alex, they decided to plunge into more powerful work. David Wilson was a Tennessee Williams enthusiast, and with Morna had been involved in an Etobicoke Little Theatre production of *Garden District*, the collective title for the double bill of *Suddenly Last Summer* and *Something Unspoken*. There were good roles for the producers, and because the Poor Alex was available for another 10 days that May, they decided to produce these potent pieces. The experienced Robert Christie was brought in to direct *Suddenly Last Summer* and Mr. Wilson directed *Something Unspoken*.

The plays marked an extreme switch from the light comedy of *Yours Faithfully* to Williams' dark and fascinating studies in human aberration, where the degree of staging difficulty is infinitely greater. *Something Unspoken* is a *tour de force* for two actresses with the ability to act "in depth," a requisite for all of Williams' characters. For the actress playing Cornelia, especially, the many long speeches will greatly tax her technical ability. With seven in the cast of *Suddenly Last Summer*, the burden on each individual is more evenly distributed, but it requires intense ensemble playing. When I saw the plays, although I felt they didn't succeed completely in living up to Williams's challenge, they came close. I greatly admired the group for tackling these demanding works, and I was very impressed with the sets on this pocket stage, particularly the lush foliage for *Suddenly Last Summer*. The designer, Bruce Gray, had co-opted florists into lending dozens of plants on which green and blue light played as the mood of the play changed. Herbert Whittaker positively gushed over the show: "It makes for a compelling program, marked by excellent staging, sound casting, and good acting. . . . Also, a quite splendid garden setting for the second play [*Suddenly Last Summer*] gave the whole evening the stamp of professionalism."[2] He continued, "Paisley Maxwell took top honours for her graphic, beautifully controlled monologue. . . . Morna Wales brought the disclosures of the mother great clarity. . . . Emmie Fuller, Doris Petrie, Norma Clark, Bruce Gray, and David Baron [Wilson] were an almost flawless supporting cast. . . . The Christie direction is sensitive, uncluttered, and intelligently orchestrated."[3] Ron Evans's opinion is best summed up in his opening remark: "Courage and sensitivity are much in evidence, the skill somewhat more difficult to trace."[4]

With *Garden District*, the Aries company proved that it was possible to stage shows at the Poor Alex provided costs were kept to a maximum of $1,000 per week. For their first weeks of operation their approach had been somewhat heuristic, but now they decided to plan a season in advance for 1964–65. Aries founder, David Wilson, returned to England but Paisley Maxwell joined the production team. The members each contributed $75 to cover the cost of renting the theatre and royalty payments, and drew up a set of guidelines balancing idealism and practicality. They would present plays of "intellectual appeal and dramatic impact," but capable of being staged in the Poor Alex space and within their budget, which had to include money for posters, mail, and advertising costs. In order to economize, all four producers agreed to share production and promotion responsibilities. They would hire the best directors available for what they could afford and train a reliable technical crew to be called upon when required. They abjured "deficit budgeting" and any profit would remain in the Aries account for future use. Any loss would be sustained by the producers — not such a financial hardship for the three female producers who had husbands with reliable incomes, but a potential burden for Bruce Gray who lived on his earnings as a performer and model.

They were encouraged by Yale Simpson and an enthusiastic Ed Mirvish. Simpson had been a boyhood friend of Mirvish and had become, more or less, Ed's right-hand man. When the Poor Alex opened, Yale became its manager and was most co-operative with the Aries company. Ed Mirvish himself, who admits to knowing nothing about the theatre before buying the Royal Alex, had by 1964 been severely bitten by the theatre bug and was suffering from theatrical fever. He was so supportive of their efforts that he had a large sign made for them that graced the top of the marquee on Brunswick Avenue. He would often come to watch their shows from the lighting booth. According to Morna Wales he wanted to start a repertory theatre and urged Aries in that direction.[5] But the three lady producers found that prospect too staggering because, while they had very supportive husbands, among them they had 10 children to raise.

Since they had been so successful in Williams country, they followed Herbert Whittaker's advice to travel further into that murky landscape. *The Milk Train Doesn't Stop Here Anymore* was a product of Williams's decline. His great plays were from that extraordinarily prolific period between 1945, when *The Glass Menagerie* first appeared, and 1961 when *Night of the Iguana* made its debut. *The Milk Train* had two New York productions, the first a flop with Hermione Baddely as the eccentric Cissie Goforth, and the second even the formidable theatricality of Tallulah Bankhead could not save. One wonders why Aries Productions would try such a challenge. The answer probably lies in the mandate they had given themselves: it could be mounted on the Poor Alex stage, it had great roles for the producers, and it was a Williams play that had not been seen in Toronto. Moreover, give an actor/manager the chance to tear into a meaty role, and the temptation usually cannot be resisted. I cannot report firsthand, but my impression is that although they could not make the play work, their efforts won admiration.

The Aries producers next swung to another extreme, the mannered comedy of Viennese sex and infidelity, *La Ronde* by Arthur Schnitzler. First produced in Vienna in 1900 under the German title *Reigen*, it had been made into two films in 1950 and 1964 under the French title *La Ronde*. The play is a series of 10 scenes dealing with sexual affairs between interchangeable couples. Schnitzler looks on them with a clinical realism and refined detachment, neither condemning nor condoning the couplings. The actors and the director must take a similar approach, an objective the Aries company achieved admirably.

Directed by Robert Christie, with sets by Rudi Dorn and costumes by Morna Wales, *La Ronde* became a genuine *succès d'estime*. Mr. Dorn, a designer for CBC-TV, realized that he could only accommodate the many sets on the Poor Alex stage by means of a revolving stage, a costly addition but necessary for the smooth flow of the action. Ed Mirvish came to the rescue, had it built and installed. He also paid for radio advertising. Under Bob Christie's guidance, the cast — Paisley Maxwell, Sylvia Shore, Emmie Fuller, Norma Clark, Dennis Thatcher, Ron Braden, Morna Wales, William Osler, Robert Koons, and Bruce Gray — found the right style for this play. I was so delighted with the production that, having purchased a ticket at a reduced price on the strength of my ACTRA membership card, I sent them a cheque to make up the balance to the full price ($2.50) with a covering letter raving about the show. Since I am an inveterate bargain hunter, I must have been deeply impressed to squeeze out extra cash when it was not necessary. My letter was ultimately combined with others from members of the profession in a package to the Canada Council when Aries producers were eventually compelled to seek assistance.

Their first four productions had made the Toronto theatre community take notice. As I have recorded in the Red Barn chapter, the Harlequin production of *Who's Afraid of Virginia Woolf?* with several Aries actors in it was such a success that the Aries producers decided to make it their opening show in September 1965. This too received favourable reviews and did 88 per cent capacity business. The profit of $1,500 from the three-week run allowed each of the actors and director an additional 10 per cent share, and the balance was divided between Aries Productions and Harlequin Players. The financial success of their last two shows gave the producers enough money to pay not only the actors they hired, but also themselves a small fee for the 1965–66 season. In 1965 the rates for employment under the Actors' Equity Small Scale Theatre or Studio Theatre Agreement were $15 a week during the rehearsal period and $35 for each week of performance. This scale was designed to accommodate small theatres with small revenues, and yet give the performer enough money to cover expenses. Of course the fee was ridiculously low even in 1965 because the performer's time, effort, skill, knowledge, experience, and talent have to be applied as much in a small theatre as in a large theatre where the performer might possibly get a living wage. In effect, not only has the taxpayer been subsidizing the theatre through grants from government agencies, but the theatre artists have been heavily subsidizing the theatre by too frequently being obliged to work for a wage far below the poverty level — a condition which is still too painfully prevalent and which should be kept in mind by those who are critical of government support for the arts.

By the end of 1965, with only their own money for backing, the four producers considered themselves lucky that their first five presentations had kept them debt free. Thus encouraged they went ahead with plans for spring 1966. Their artistic success led some of our more prominent actors and directors to want to work for them. That is why they managed to get

Andrew Allan to direct and Sean Mulcahy to appear in Jean Anouilh's *The Rehearsal*. This was quite a coup because the duo had just spent the previous years putting the Shaw Festival on the map after its inauspicious beginning in 1962. Bruce Gray even had the temerity to offer a major role to Paul Massie, who had recently made an international name for himself in film, and who was in Toronto rehearsing for a CBC-TV show. At first Massie agreed, but just before rehearsals began he bowed out because of a more rewarding offer. Bruce stepped into the breach in the role of Hero.

Mulcahy had been cast as the Count, but after the first reading when he was driving Andrew Allan home, Sean suggested that he would be better as the two-faced, devious producer Hero, and that Bruce Gray, an actor with an open, honest face would do better as the Count. Allan agreed and at the next rehearsal, at his insistence, switched the roles.[6] For Gray, it was the beginning of an unhappy rehearsal period during which he and Allan had a cool, formal relationship.

Allan was a stickler about pronunciation. Sean had to use the word "banal," which he pronounced as most of us do with the accent on the last syllable, "ba*nal*." Allan insisted that it be "*ba*nal" with emphasis on the first syllable. "It rhymes with flannel," he said. Sean protested that the majority of the public would think he was mispronouncing the word. But Allan was adamant and Sean bowed to his authority on language.[7] Besides, Allan was the director — and Allan was right, of course. It is a French word with the accent on the first syllable, as the Oxford English Dictionary confirms.

A more serious contretemps developed between Bruce Gray and Allan over the word "emerald," which is used frequently during the play. Allan wanted it pronounced with a slightly trilled "r." Gray had difficulty doing this, first because he thought that pronunciation pretentious and affected, secondly because his lifelong habit had been to pronounce "emerald" without the trill, and thirdly because he claimed only a Scot would say it that way, and the character he was playing was not a Scot. It was a seemingly picayune matter over which to disagree but at the preview, with an invited audience mostly of fellow actors including many of Bruce's friends, when Bruce did not pronounce the word as Allan desired, Andrew walked down to the stage, interrupted the action and repeated the word "emerald" several times with the trilled "r" — a most serious breach of theatrical etiquette.[8] When the curtain descended on the final act, Bruce, in a fury over this public humiliation, called the cast together — his right as one of the producers — told them that he did not have to take that kind of abuse, announced that he was quitting the show, that the show was cancelled, and that everybody would be paid out of his own pocket. All hell broke loose. After a lot of discussion, cast members calmed Bruce down and persuaded him to continue in the play — a very unhappy actor in a role in which he was dissatisfied with his own work.[9] His opinion of Allan as a stage director confirmed my own. He was a marvellous radio director, a master at extracting great vocal performances from his casts, but directing actors in physical performances was not his *métier*. In fairness, I need to add that Allan was suffering from acute alcoholism at the time. Although several of the cast found rehearsals a traumatic experience due to Allan's imbibing, he would not have been so tactless if he had not been in his cups.

While Bruce was not happy about his performance in *The Rehearsal*, his set was something of a triumph. Anouilh set his play in a French château, which gave Bruce a chance to design a portion of a stunning 17th-century drawing room. The period of the play is 1950 (or contemporary) but the characters are rehearsing a play by Marivaux. This calls for 18th-century costumes, which Morna created for the women from material she scrounged hither and yon and from cloth she purchased on the cheap at Honest Ed's. She stiffened them with some of her friends' discarded bed sheets.[10] The men's costumes were borrowed from the University Alumnae Dramatic Society. The result was a visually sumptuous production on a shoestring budget. When asked by a patron how much the impressive set had cost, Bruce replied, "One fifty." "Only a hundred and fifty!" exclaimed the man. "No. A dollar fifty," Bruce explained. "The cost of the paint."[11]

The Rehearsal found favour with the reviewers. Ralph Hicklin even wrote that the Poor Alex and the Royal Alex, then showing a tacky production of *Pal Joey* starring Jane Russell, should exchange shows because *The Rehearsal* was worthy of the larger stage. He added, "*The Rehearsal* is as good as we are likely to see this year."[12] Ron Evans, after gently chastising Andrew Allan as director, rather grudgingly admitted that, "It's an absorbing play, earnestly performed by the Aries Players." He particularly admired the set and costumes: "Bruce Gray's tasteful, surprisingly spacious setting is one of the best to grace the Poor Alex stage, and Morna Wales' gowns are most becoming."[13]

The Aspern Papers, which opened on June 1, 1966, was the last production Aries staged at the Poor Alex. The Michael Redgrave adaptation of Henry James's novel had been described by the critic for the *New York Daily News* as, "Bewitching, tantalizing, exciting. . . . A work of uncommon suspense and exceptional literary merit."[14] Herbert Whittaker gave it his stamp of approval: "Aries Productions' plays are distinguished by delicacy and taste and a sensitive use of the facilities of the Poor Alex. *The Aspern Papers* fully lives up to that reputation."[15] Marilyn Beker's column in the *Toronto Star* was headed "Poor Alex production overcomes difficulties of a delicate play" and she went on to give it a favourable notice.[16] On June 15, Nat Cohen felt the need to give it his good housekeeping award: "[Director] Sean Mulcahy's production strikes a disciplined balance between the main characters' formality of speech and conduct, and their deep internal confusions. Bruce Gray's set makes the tiny stage look large and authentic. . . . Paisley Maxwell's portrait of H. J.'s friend, a woman of breeding and quietly astute discernment, is unpretentiously and handsomely accurate"[17] — high praise coming from Mr. Cohen. I suspect he wrote his review, four days before the *The Aspern Papers* was to close, to counter the harsh and disparaging comments by Ron Evans in the *Telegram* on June 3, 1966, one day after Whittaker's and Beker's articles appeared. Evans's column, headed with unfathomable perversity *Aries Goes Out with a Thud*, belittled the plot while revealing it, and then complained, "All these vital events creak along at the merry pace of a glacier." He then stabbed Sean Mulcahy with his vitriolic pen: "Director Mulcahy, mesmerized by novelist James's appallingly convoluted mandarin dialogue, and determined to have mood at any price . . . has each and every line delivered as though lifted from the gospels."[18] His comments about most of the performances were cruel and personally insulting, but he did admit that "Carroll Patricia Brown brings a certain amount of wistful burnt-out charm to the ugly niece and Guy Sanvido is responsible for some fleeting delight as the conniving valet, but they cannot rescue this olde Englishe clinker."[19] I am left unable to understand where Evans was coming from. Surely it was not as simple as his disliking Henry James or wanting to show how clever and witty he could be. He was often a dyspeptic distance from other reviewers' opinions. Certainly his comments reveal once again just how unreliable a touchstone critical opinion can be, but why did he have to be so vicious about the performers involved? Fortunately, in this case the public did not let Mr. Evans influence them because *The Aspern Papers* was rewarding to the producers at the box office. In fact their three productions in the 1965–66 season had brought in sufficient revenue to allow the producers to pay at least a small fee to the actors, all outstanding bills, and even a small stipend to themselves. It also gave them a nest egg of $2,000 to start the 1967 season.

But they were suffering from growing pains and other ailments. In spring 1966, Actors' Equity decided that performers should make less of a financial sacrifice to support the small theatres in Canada. Accordingly, the new studio contract increased the weekly salary to $50 for both rehearsing and performing weeks. Aries usually rehearsed for three weeks and performed at first for 10 days and eventually for three weeks. The producers, while recognizing that the fees they could afford were absurdly low, complained that the Equity increase would cause their rehearsal salaries for a six-character play to jump from $90 a week to $300 and for a performance week from $210 to $300. For a five-week engagement that would mean an $810 increase for six performers — not a large sum, but given the small capacity of the Poor Alex and low ticket prices, it was sufficient to put them out of business unless the four of them contributed more from their own pockets, which meant that they would once again be working for nothing. Their very success threatened to strangle them. On May 26 in a column surprisingly different from his subsequent *Aspern* review, Ron Evans had made their plight public: "If we lose this tiny but superior theatre group which has fought so earnestly and so triumphantly to raise its own standards and the standard of Toronto drama generally, it will be a tragic loss to this city. One theatre has just gone under, we cannot afford to lose another."[20]

Aries management resolved to continue but realized that economically they could no longer reside at the Poor Alex. They leased the Central Library Theatre from January 1, 1967 and sought outside funding to add to the $2,000 they had in the kitty. Their Canada Council application presented a budget, now grown to $57,789, for four productions including *This Glittering Dust* by John Coulter, scheduled because it seemed the best of the many Canadian plays they had read, and because its being Canadian might induce the Canada Council to cough up some money for its production. Antony Ferry reported in the *Toronto Star* that with the closing of both the Crest and the Canadian Players the previous year, the only companies in Toronto besides Aries using professional actors in January 1967 were the Belmont Theatre, George Luscombe's Toronto Workshop Productions doing experimental work in a warehouse basement on Fraser Avenue, and Eli Rill's shows for children at the Colonnade Theatre. In this environment, the Aries company assumed new importance, and their move to the Central Library Theatre, where many fine productions had been mounted in the immediately preceding years, brought them more public recognition and prestige. In short order they raised $17,000 — $8,500 from the Canada Council, $4,000 from the Ontario Arts Council, $3,000 from the Laidlaw Foundation, $1,000 from a donor who had seen all their shows but wished to remain anonymous, and the balance in small donations from enthusiastic patrons.

They opened their four-month season with *Tchin-Tchin*, adapted from French by Sidney Michaels. A strong cast was headed by the lovely Hilary Vernon. George Sperdakos, who had got his start in Toronto Workshop's co-operatively created play about the circus, *Hey Rube*, took the male lead. Robert Marsh played the third of the three major roles and Jeannie Coulthard and Graham McCannell played "a multitude of people." The producers devoted all of their energies to launching the new season but unfortunately things did not work out quite as they had hoped.

Tchin-Tchin moves through 10 different locations. A difference of opinion developed between the director and the designer, Bruce Gray, about the most effective way of staging it. The director's decision, whether wise or not, must prevail and he opted for box sets. But the Central Library stage did not have the facilities, nor could Aries afford enough crew to make the set changes smoothly and quickly. The consensus of opinion, based on the acting, was that it was a reasonably successful show. Hilary Vernon was splendid as Pamela Pew-Picket and George Sperdakos gave a clever study of the Italian, Caesario Grimaldi. But Bruce Gray's sets did not live up to the standards he had established at the Poor Alex and the delays in the set changes, in his own view, "ruined" the play.[21]

However, by the next production, *The Right Honourable Gentleman*, Mr. Gray had found a way of presenting multiple set shows on the small Library stage. *The Right Honourable Gentleman* calls for only three different sets but the action passes back and forth among them. The problem was solved by limiting the play to two locations, Sir Charles Dilke's study and Mrs. Rossiter's sitting room, and creating a unit set with the desk of the study on a riser upstage beyond the sitting room. A slight re-arranging of furniture and the removal of a throw cover from a chaise longue changed Dilke's study into the Rossiter living room. The action flowed with minimal interruption for set changes.

The locale was Victorian London in 1885 and the story was drawn from real life: the undoing through a sex scandal of Sir Charles Dilke, a prominent, progressive politician who had been groomed to be the successor to Prime Minister Gladstone. Partially due to its timeliness just after the Profumo affair in Britain, the play had been quite a hit in London and a moderate success in New York with Charles Gray and the feisty Coral Browne in the leading roles. It was a good choice for Aries because it could be staged on the small Library stage, had not been done in Toronto, had publicity value, and had good roles for three of the female producers. Bruce Gray assumed the minor role of a butler. But it had a cast of 14, which, even at the Equity Studio Theatre salary, put a heavy strain on the Aries budget.

Sir Charles Dilke was played by John Gardiner, who looked perfect for the role of a handsome, well-spoken gentleman in his early '40s with style, intelligence, and sex appeal. Morna Wales played Lady Dilke and Jess Walton played Nia Crawford, one of Sir Charles' mistresses. I was cast as the shrewd politician Joseph Chamberlain, a friend of Dilke's, who was a sort of *éminence grise* behind the whole affair, and was suspected, but never proven to have connived at Dilke's downfall. It was a very solid cast who knew how to play the attitudes and manners of the period and who could carry the upper crust English dialect. As well, it was a very affable company from which some lasting friendships developed for me during the show. Claude Bede, often referred to as "the venerable Bede" after his Medieval namesake, and John Gardiner and I have worked happily together many times since. I regret that this book did not appear before their unexpected deaths, Claude in August 1996 and John in January 1997. I was so impressed with the acting of Paisley Maxwell and Jess Walton that I recommended the former to Walter Learning when he became the producer for the Beaverbrook Playhouse and I cast the latter in my production of *Uncle Vanya* at the Belmont. Both Christine Bennett and the outspoken Sheila Haney gave rivetting performances and were a pleasure to work with. My friendship with Nancy Kerr deepened during this show and lasted until her death after a lengthy bout with cancer while she was a long-standing member of the Shaw Festival.

This was my first involvement with Sean Mulcahy as a director. I had met him in the mid-'50s at a party at the Tyas's house just after he had arrived in Canada. At first I did not take to him, but as the evening wore on I realized that, unlike most people with a compulsive urge to talk, when Mulcahy spoke, something worth listening to came out. He has the gift of oratory into which is mixed a healthy dollop of Irish blarney, and he has a very retentive memory in which he has stored a wealth of knowledge on a variety of subjects, particularly the theatre. But after that party our paths seldom crossed until *The Right Honourable Gentleman*, by which time he had established himself as a stage director and a fine stage, television, and radio actor. As co-director with Andrew Allan of the Shaw Festival in its formative years, he used his ability to promote a cause in which he believed to make the country aware of that company. But his outspokenness irritated some of the influential people behind the Festival so he had been eased out.

If this production had been a skating contest, its scores would read something like 5.9 out of 6 from Herbert Whittaker, 5.2 from Peter Gzowski, who had inexplicably emerged as a critic for the *Toronto Daily Star*, and at tops about 4 from Ron Evans. Once again from the reviews one would wonder if those three had seen the same show. Whittaker's review was alliteratively headed, "Dyne's Dilke Drama Is Fine, Old Fashioned." Gzowski's header read, "It's a Juicy Play Juicelessly Done," and Evans's article had at the top, "Sex Bites the Dust." Whittaker was, in my view, excessive in his praise, and Evans excessive in his denunciation. Both Gzowski and Evans misconstrued John's control over Dilke's emotions as not caring. Evans wrote, "John Gardiner, in a 1950s left bank beard, carries the role of Sir Charles as though it were a handsome but fragile walking stick."[22] But Whittaker caught what his performance was about: "Aries has found an ideal actor to fill out that central portrait of Dilke. Gardiner has the dignity, good looks, and presence to merit Gladstone's approval; he also creates a saturnine figure who might well be guilty of horrifying excesses. A voice that can command and a gift of stillness carry the performance to complete success."[23] I like to think he was accurate about my performance as well: "Two especially emphatic contributions are made by Christine Bennett, impure joy as the madam, and Vernon Chapman, who plays Joseph Chamberlain with a great sense of history and how it is made."[24] I assume that was meant as a compliment. Evans wrote of me, "Vernon Chapman can't seem to get that reference to Chamberlain 'as the handsomest man in Europe' out of his head, and postures constantly."[25] Chamberlain is in several scenes, but, until the final scene, tends to stand around listening. What Evans seemed not to realize is the way costume reflects the style, manners, and social stratum of the person and the period. Victorian gentlemen in striped trousers, frock coats, and stiff collars, with enough affectation to wear a monocle, did not slouch. Costume influences how the actor stands, sits, and moves. Too often I see modern actors in period costumes moving as though they are wearing contemporary clothes, with no indication of how restricting of movement certain period dress can be. But, in all fairness to Mr. Evans, he could not have been expected to understand such actors' matters.

Attendance was high but so were the costs. The money the producers had begun the season with two months before was evaporating like steam from a boiling kettle. The next show had to be a big box-office draw or financial disaster would follow. *This Glittering Dust* is John Coulter's study of the life of the 19th-century English actor, Edmund Kean. When asked to play Kean, Sean Mulcahy objected to the title and suggested that it be called *Darling Edmund.* But that did not sit well with the author, who came up with *A Capful of Pennies* because in his early days Kean used to do tumbling acts in public places and in pubs and collect the pennies thrown to him in his cap.

The play, wisely, does not try to reproduce any of Kean's great performances but deals with the man's private life. In a clever *coup de théâtre*, an early scene shows Kean in make-up as Othello having a quarrel with his wife in his dressing room during which he hurls her to the sofa and, in a rage, begins to strangle her, just as a knock is heard at the door and the call-boy warns him of his next scene. Kean releases his wife and storms on stage to perform a role in which he strangles his stage wife, Desdemona. In another scene he leaves the dressing room to begin that fateful performance of Richard III at Drury Lane, and returns in an identical costume covered in the garbage that the audience had hurled at him.[26] In short, it is a *tour de force* for the actor playing Kean requiring many costume and make-up changes. Character changes might be a different thing.

It bears repeating that when an actor is rehearsing or performing a role, he or she often, to varying degrees, takes on attributes of that role. Both Kean and Mulcahy had a volcanic temperament. In *A Capful of Pennies*, the make-up table in Kean's onstage dressing room holds an array of wigs from Kean's various roles: Hamlet, Lear, Shylock, Richard III. During the action the actor handles each as he talks about the respective character. According to Mr. Mulcahy, during rehearsals they were never in the right order on their stands. Eventually, despite his many complaints, at the first dress rehearsal when they were still not in the right order, Mulcahy blew his top and proceeded to trash the set. A young friend of an assistant stage manager standing in the wings saw this display and said, "He's really very good, isn't he?" "Yes," replied the ASM, "and that's not even in the script."[27]

Although *A Capful of Pennies* appealed to members of the theatre profession, it was caviar to the general public. Most of the Toronto public had not heard of Edmund Kean, nor had they got over their aversion to new works not endorsed by London or New York audiences. Moreover the play had the stigma of being Canadian. By the end of *A Capful of Pennies* all the pennies in Aries's treasury were gone and the producers faced the prospect of dipping into their own pockets much more deeply than before if they were to complete the season. When Odetta, the drawing card they had counted on for their final show, *In White America*, decided not to appear, the producers called it quits. Several other factors also influenced that decision. Their Poor Alex seasons had been more or less co-operative ventures among friends with volunteers helping in various departments, such as the box office, to keep costs down. But the Central Library box-office staff had to be paid. As the producer who dealt most frequently with the performers, Bruce Gray found that he was increasingly in a confrontational situation as an employer with employees, and often looked upon with suspicion by actors whom he considered his friends. He was not happy wearing that mantle, nor did he wish to continue dealing with actors who were prone to temperamental outbursts.[28] As well, the four were beginning to receive offers from other companies that they had to turn down to work with Aries.[29] But the major factor was simply burn-out. They had carried on their various capacities as well as performing during the 1967 season and they were exhausted. As a parting contribution, they gave a benefit showing of *A Capful of Pennies* to raise money for the city's belated centennial project, the construction of the St. Lawrence Centre. Ironically it was to be a home for some yet-to-be-created theatrical company in a city that had seen the demise of three hopeful theatrical endeavours in the previous two years. To make Toronto the cultural centre of English Canada was going to take a lot more effort by a lot more dedicated people. In 1967, when filling out a questionnaire for the Ontario Arts Council, Bruce Gray answered the question, "How do you see the future of theatre in general?" succinctly but aptly with "Cloudy."

The foursome paid off all the debts and donated their scenery to the Central Library Theatre. Shortly thereafter Bruce Gray used his dual citizenship to work in the United States. He spent 10 years in New York, modelling and acting for regional theatres and in soap operas. He was Kim Hunter's husband in *Edge of Night* for a year and also appeared in the Toronto-made soap, *High Hopes*. He toured in *Who's Afraid of Virginia Woolf?* and went to Hollywood in 1980 where he has appeared in films and more soap operas. In 1996 he captivated Canadian TV audiences as the boss of the brokerage firm in *Traders* for which he won a best actor Gemini in 1997. Currently he spends his time between his comfortable home in the Hollywood Hills and Toronto. Morna Wales continued for a few years to perform professionally, but, because of the increasing illness of her husband, gradually phased out her professional career. However, she continued to perform for the University Alumnae Players until her death. Norma Clark had a brief professional career after Aries folded, but she too reverted to amateur status and performed mostly with the University Alumnae, while continuing as a wife, mother, and school teacher. Paisley Maxwell, of whom I shall say more when writing about Theatre New Brunswick, continued as a professional actress. Although their original motive in establishing Aries Productions was as a showcase for themselves, the result was that for three brief years they too gave Toronto exciting productions of plays that otherwise might never have been seen in that city.

CHAPTER 23

In United
Empire Loyalist
Country

In her autobiography *That Beaverbrook Girl,* Janet Aitken Kidd, the daughter of Lord Beaverbrook, wrote about her father's efforts to lift an embargo in Britain against cattle imports from Canada: "I think he felt he owed a debt to Canada. Perhaps it was because he had taken so much out, that now he wanted to put something back."[1] For that same reason, the beautiful capital of New Brunswick, Fredericton, on the St. John River in the heart of United Empire Loyalist country, has one of the finest small art galleries in the nation and a playhouse that is one of the best in the land. In 1954, the expatriate Canadian, Max Aitken, Lord Beaverbrook, set up the Beaverbrook Foundation and in 1959 opened his public art gallery on the banks of the river. The combined collections of Beaverbrook and Sir James Dunn, including a large representation of Krieghoffs and three Dalis, gave it one of the finest holdings of any small gallery in the country. Shortly, half a block up the street opposite the Lord Beaverbrook Hotel and across a side street from the New Brunswick Legislature, the Beaverbrook Playhouse opened. The architect's original design had included a fly gallery, but that was struck from the plan because, as the story goes, Lady Beaverbrook thought it spoiled the look of the building and that it would dwarf the one-storey Beaverbrook Art Gallery down the road. Another story, probably apocryphal, was that Lady Beaverbrook objected to the term "fly gallery" as being too vulgar. Whatever the reasons, the result was that when it opened in 1964, Fredericton had been bequeathed a large concert hall rather than a theatre.

From outside this one-storey building was very handsome. Built of light grey brick, with a row of Windsor windows on the south side, it had a classical Greek front and a semi-mansard roof. It was a million-dollar edifice intended by Beaverbrook as a memorial to his friend, the steel baron Sir James Dunn. Seating 750 on the main floor and 250 in the balcony, it had a 9-foot by 30-foot-wide forestage that could be lowered to form an orchestra pit large enough for 60 musicians. The proscenium was a respectable 40 feet wide by 20 feet high with a 35-foot stage depth, but its flexibility was decidedly limited without the "fly."[2] Although its size was suitable for concerts, musicals, ballet, or even opera, the fact that the curtain line was 30 feet from the front row of seats did not allow for much intimacy between actor and audience. Beaverbrook had indicated that the theatre was to be a rental house, not meant to produce shows on its own. So, behind the stage was a grossly inadequate workshop lacking in storage space. Two large communal dressing rooms flanked the "workshop" along with a Green Room where the performers could relax. But the room was so small that a large choir or orchestra would have had to relax on each other's laps. On the south side was a very pleasant long gallery for the audience during intermissions, and an entrance foyer boasting a 40-foot-wide mural, "The Masque Ball," by the Irish artist, Sidney Smith.[3] Over 50 mostly masqued figures in 18th-century costume are depicted mildly enjoying themselves looking down from a balcony presumably at dancers below. Some are dressed as characters from plays, from commedia dell'arte, and from opera. It is very colourful and very innocuous. No hanky-panky at that ball. Unfortunately the foyer of the theatre is not deep enough to give the viewers a proper perspective on this vast canvas that was shipped from England in three sections and took three weeks to mount.

Because Lord Beaverbrook had died that summer, the opening ceremonies on September 26 and 27, 1964 were somewhat curtailed. Nevertheless, Roberta Peters from the Metropolitan Opera, the Carl Tapscott Singers, Anna Maria and David Holmes of Les Grands Ballets

Canadiens in Montreal, the New Brunswick Symphony, Gloria Richard, a favourite singer from New Brunswick, the Band of the Royal Canadian Dragoons, politicians, provincial and civic officials, and Lady Beaverbrook were all assembled for this great occasion. Alexander Gray, recently appointed general manager of the Playhouse, had been a victim of polio, walked with a brace on one leg, and supported himself with two caliper crutches. Nervous about the opening ceremony, he instructed Doreen Grinstead, secretary-treasurer of the Playhouse, not to leave his side: "Carry a bottle of whisky in one hand and a bottle of aspirin in the other. If I should fall down, give me the whisky, and you swallow the aspirin."[4] He did not fall and the opening ceremony went smoothly.

To make this new building an integral part of the culture of New Brunswick in particular and Canada in general, Alex Gray faced a tremendous challenge. But he did not lack experience or resourcefulness because he arrived in Canada after many years operating repertory theatres in Great Britain. At one in Carlisle he had hired Edwin Stephenson in 1955 just as Ed was finishing his training at R.A.D.A. Ed had acquired a sufficiently English-sounding dialect to be employed as the second juvenile and assistant stage manager. Near the end of his contract, Ed discovered that Alex had been born in Ottawa, and Alex found out that Ed had been born in Winnipeg.[5] Gray, who had travelled to Britain in an RCAF show called *All Clear*, had picked up his English dialect when he stayed on in Britain after the war, acted in the West End, and directed at a variety of repertory theatres. He also had the challenging experience of working with Joan Littlewood in preparing the famous *Oh What a Lovely War*. In 1955, he was dealt an almost fatal blow by polio only a few months before Dr. Salk perfected his miraculous vaccine.[6] After a long struggle back to health, Gray accepted the offer to take charge of the Beaverbrook Playhouse.

The Playhouse was intended to be at the disposal of the whole community, and it very quickly began to fulfil that purpose. It was used by the New Brunswick Symphony, the New Brunswick Film Society, the Kiwanis Club for travelogues, the University of New Brunswick Drama Society, the Creative Arts Committee, the Knights of Columbus for a St. Patrick's Day concert, and by an amateur theatre company that Alexander Gray and his wife, Elizabeth (Val) Orion, started to circumvent the Beaverbrook ukase that the Playhouse should not produce anything on its own. The Beaverbrook Foundation had granted $100,000 for the operation and maintenance of the building covering a three-year period and this money was not to be used for any other purpose.

But Alex and Elizabeth were determined to establish a professional company in the Playhouse. "The Company of Ten" was a first step toward their goal. Among the founders were Alex, Elizabeth, Doreen Grinstead, and Alvin Shaw, a professor at the University of New Brunswick, mentor of the University Drama Society, and a power in the Dominion Drama Festival. Soon to join this group, in charge of the box office, was Sharon Pollock, now one of Canada's most celebrated playwrights. Even before the Playhouse opened in September they had begun rehearsals for *Little Lambs Eat Ivy* in which Shaw, Pollock, and Orion, directed by Alex, appeared on October 2nd, 3rd, and 5th, only six days after the Playhouse officially opened. Alex wrote in the program of *Little Lambs Eat Ivy*, "We consider ourselves a team working together towards a common objective — a professional theatre."

Another clever ploy to circumvent Beaverbrook's restriction and the watchful eyes of both the Beaverbrook Foundation and Lady Beaverbrook, was the establishment of the Playhouse Memorial Fund as part of an organization known as "Patrons of the Playhouse." A tax-deductible donation of $5 ($7.50 for couples) made one a "Patron." In this way Gray hoped to raise backing without the Beaverbrook operating money. The first result of this plan was a Christmas pantomime, *Cinderella*, complete with a *corps de ballet* of students from the Academy of Ballet, 13 extras as villagers and courtiers, Elaine Fowler in the Principal Boy role of Prince Charming, Sharon Pollock as Dandini, Elizabeth Orion as the Fairy Godmother, and the Maritimes' sweetheart, Catherine McKinnon, as Cinderella. Equity members Joseph R. Sicari and David Renton, on loan from Neptune Theatre, played the ugly sisters, Lovey and Dovey. The show also featured Bill Stone and His Dogs — an animal act not a rock group — and an orchestra of 10 plus a conductor and musical director. Virginia Dailley, a Texas graduate of the American School of Ballet who was teaching in Fredericton, was the choreographer, Elizabeth Orion designed the scenery and costumes, and Alex pulled it all together as director.

Encouraged by the success of the first two locally produced shows, Gray and the Company of Ten next staged Vanbrugh's Restoration comedy *The Provok'd Wife*, which must have been a first for Fredericton. Sharon Pollock appeared as Lady Brute and Elizabeth Orion as Lady Fancyfull. Terence Rattigan's *Separate Tables* followed in April and *Mary, Mary* in May. The public response to *Cinderella* led to another of those peculiarly British curiosities the following Christmas, *Aladdin and His Wonderful Lamp*. Alex renewed his association with Ed Stephenson by bringing him from Toronto to play the Widow Twankey. Tudi Wiggins as Aladdin and James Van Evera as Abanazar, "a villain to be reckoned with," were also brought from Toronto. Michael Ball, in the early stages of his career, played the Emperor of China, while Elizabeth Orion turned up as the Genie of the Ring "who only does good" and Sharon Pollock as Prince Pekoe "who is up to no good."

From the Playhouse opening in September 1964 to Christmas 1965, by using The Company of Ten and the Patrons of the Playhouse, Gray had produced three plays and two large-cast Christmas pantomimes. With the invaluable assistance of Doreen Grinstead and Sharon Pollock, he had also managed the day-to-day running of the Playhouse. By 1965 the Stratford Festival, the Canadian Opera Company, and the National Ballet had become aware of the Beaverbrook Playhouse and began to bring their touring productions on a regular basis. The Playhouse had given the culture of New Brunswick a hefty shot-in-the-arm, and Alex Gray had begun the process of making it into a home for a professional theatre company.

However, all was not sweetness and light. A contretemps developed between Gray and the board of directors that resulted in his being given six-months' notice without the board spelling out the reasons. Some people believed the underlying reason was accusations by rival amateur organizations that he gave priority to booking his group over theirs. Some believed that Lady Beaverbrook had expressed disapproval of the Company of Ten and the Patrons of the Playhouse as ways to evade Beaverbrook's instructions about the Playhouse. Amid acrimony and rumours, Gray denounced the board publicly, but they still refused to reveal the reasons for their decision. Mr. Gray did not wait out his six-months' notice in Fredericton but departed after *Aladdin* and headed for Ontario's Straw Hat country. In response to an inquiry I made of him in 1995, Mr. Gray wrote, "The Brigadier became out of favour with those people handling Lord Beaverbrook's affairs and as I had been hired as the manager for the new theatre by the Brigadier, I was asked to leave. I certainly had no desire to continue where I was not wanted."[7] Whatever caused his dismissal, in his brief tenure at the Playhouse, Gray and his team had whetted the appetite of Frederictonians for more theatre.

The aforementioned Brigadier Wardell was the editor of the *Fredericton Gleaner* and had been a close friend of Lord Beaverbrook. It fell on his shoulders to find Mr. Gray's replacement. By happenstance, he was found very quickly. The story, as it was told to me, goes as follows: In late autumn 1965, a reporter from the *Toronto Star Weekly*, on assignment to write about theatre across the country, wandered into the *Gleaner* office. In conversation with a local reporter he happened to mention that he had had some theatrical experience. The reporter took him to see his boss, the Brigadier, who asked the *Star* writer if he could recommend anyone as general manager of the Playhouse. "Certainly," he said, "Me!" Without much further discussion the reporter was hired on the spot.

Whether Brian Swarbrick's appointment as the new manager of the Playhouse happened that quickly is doubtful. But it seems that the board member responsible for approving his appointment rubber-stamped the Brigadier's recommendation. Certainly not much time, if any, was spent checking Mr. Swarbrick's credentials or all concerned might have had second thoughts. Swarbrick arrived to take up his post before *Aladdin* closed on New Year's Day of 1966. Up to that date his was a very limited theatre life. A native of Toronto, he began his career as a copy boy for the *Globe and Mail*, worked for Canadian Press as a reporter and editor, and later became an editor for CBC Radio News.[8] During the Korean war he served as an interpreter in the Canadian Intelligence Corps. He became a writer of radio plays and comedy sketches, but his theatre experience was derived primarily from his writing and producing *Return to the Mountain* at the Royal Alex in which John Vernon, Dawn Greenhalgh, and Hugh Webster had major roles. This venture was not an overwhelming success either artistically or financially, but apparently it was sufficient to convince those responsible for the Beaverbrook Playhouse that a Flo Ziegfeld had come among them.

Swarbrick decided to carry on Gray's policy of gradually working toward a professional company housed in the Playhouse. He retained the Patrons of the Playhouse to sponsor the first show he produced, *King of Hearts*, which opened on March 31, 1966. Nonnie Griffin, Larry Reynolds, and Hugh Webster were brought from Toronto for the lead roles, and the other players were recruited from the strong amateur contingent in Fredericton, which included Pegi Chalmers and Alvin Shaw. As an appetizer for the summer fare Swarbrick brought in *The Loving Couch*, a package from the United States that displayed the minor acting talents of Hollywood personality Virginia Mayo and an English sex-goddess named Sabrina. The American packager must have been happy because before moving on to Halifax, it sold out the two Fredericton performances, which gave the lie to a widely held belief that Fredericton was a "blue-nosed" community.[9]

For the main summer season Brian established the nucleus of a permanent company. The first show was *Bell, Book and Candle* with Anna Cameron and Sean Mulcahy in the leads and the considerable talents of Larry Beattie, Jodi Pape, and Howard Ryshpan in support. Peter Shaffer's *The Private Ear and the Public Eye* followed with Ed Stephenson, Jodi Pape, Sean Mulcahy, Anna Cameron, and Howard Ryshpan. The last play of that season was *The Knack*, also with Pape, Beattie, Stephenson, and Mulcahy. These shows operated on a repertory schedule with ticket prices at a reasonable $1.75 to $2.75. Subscribers received a $1.50 discount. The play selection proved appropriate for supposedly conservative Fredericton, and the roles suited the group of actors Swarbrick had hired. His planning showed good sense but his directing left something to be desired.

Mulcahy, who liked Swarbrick personally, deplored him as a director: "Brian Swarbrick's idea of directing was to read the play, block it, about which he was quite good, and tell you 'I'll see you on opening night'."[10] Rehearsals would last only a few hours each afternoon and then Swarbrick would leave the actors on their own. After the first part of *The Knack* was blocked during the first day of rehearsal, Swarbrick left the theatre without blocking the scene in which Ed Stephenson appeared. The same thing happened the second day. Stephenson went to Doreen Grinstead and asked where Brian was. "Oh," she replied, "He's gone to play golf." Stephenson was furious and decided that he did not wish to be in a production that would be a shambles because of a lack of rehearsal. He started to pack his bags for Toronto. Alarmed, Larry Beattie phoned Brian who drove, in great consternation, the five miles out of Fredericton to where Beattie and Stephenson shared digs. He persuaded Ed to remain and after that sacrificed his daily golf to rehearse a full three hours every afternoon.[11] However, Larry had to quit half way through rehearsals on the verge of a nervous breakdown caused largely by the frustration and tension in the company. Gerard Parkes was brought in on short notice, and according to Sean Mulcahy, Mr. Parkes, appalled at the lack of rehearsal time, obtained a key to the stage door and had a duplicate key made. The scheduled rehearsals were held from 2:00 to 5:00 each afternoon, but at 7 p.m., by use of the duplicate, the cast would let themselves into the theatre and rehearse another three hours until 10 p.m., unbeknownst to Swarbrick. At the end of a week of these clandestine rehearsals, a surprised Swarbrick was so impressed he exclaimed, "Hey! You guys are getting good."

Despite Swarbrick's cavalier attitude about rehearsals, the shows that summer were generally successful. The Fredericton public was becoming educated into the theatre habit and the local newspaper reporter, "J.A.C.," who had been drafted into reviewing, began to develop a critical sense. Like so many novice reviewers, J.A.C. filled the review of *The Private Ear and the Public Eye* with plot summaries, but did realize how skilled Sean Mulcahy was in *The Private Ear* and Ed Stephenson in *The Public Eye*. Ironically, J.A.C. also reported that "Brian Swarbrick has created a fine pair of hits. . . . Fredericton has waited a long time for such first-rate entertainment."[12] An obvious example of how a competent cast can make an incompetent director look good.

Because the Christmas pantomimes had been so popular, Brian decided to continue the policy. After rejecting *Peter Pan* when he discovered how difficult and how costly it would be to stage with Peter Foy's flying equipment, he found a short, gentle children's play written by actor Christopher Wiggins. *Sinbad and the Mermaid* had been presented in the tiny Museum Theatre in Toronto, but for the vast Beaverbrook stage, Swarbrick decided that it needed to be greatly expanded with singers and dancers, and because he had made a commitment to Peter Foy, the mermaid would appear to swim across the stage. He hired a cast of Toronto performers and local supporting actors, choristers, and the Virginia Dailley Dancers. A musical director, Edna Knock, was brought in. Director Desmond Scott, who had established a reputation with work he had been doing at the Manitoba Theatre Centre, found himself in charmingly staid Fredericton trying to make an evening-long entertainment that would appeal to adults out of a once-short script for children. He was dismayed by Swarbrick's new, blown-up version, appalled at the expense for Peter Foy to teach the stage-hands how to use the complicated ropes and harness, and frustrated at the time it took to rehearse flying in the evil magician, Ting Tang Tong, and make the mermaid "swim." He deplored Swarbrick's nonchalant disregard for costs, as though Swarbrick really did visualize himself as the Ziegfeld of Fredericton. However, it was Scott's responsibility to create an impressive production and, on the whole, along with his cast, he did that and enjoyed himself in the city where mermaids fly.[13]

The following summer's opener was *The Owl and the Pussycat,* a package from the U.S. with Pat Suzuki of *Flower Drum Song* fame and Richard Voth. But for *A Thousand Clowns* Swarbrick lined up an all-Canadian cast to support Bruno Gerussi as the lead. Bruce Gray and Norma Clark were the two social workers. On Sean Mulcahy's advice, Swarbrick wisely cast Guy Sanvido as the egocentric comic, Chuckles the Chipmunk. Warren Van Evera, another of the Van Evera clan, was cast as Arnold Burns, and yet another

Canadian show-biz family, the Barringers, were represented in the company. Leslie Barringer, who had played Ali Shebam in *Sinbad* the previous Christmas, returned to play Nick, although at 14 he was a tad too old for this precocious 12-year-old. Leslie had credits as long as your arm from TV appearances in the United States and the Canadian series *Quentin Durgens, M.P.*, as well as the Hitchcock film *The Birds*.

The first rehearsal got off to an inauspicious start for Bruce Gray. He rushed into the rehearsal hall in a panic, announced that he could not stay, and that he had to drive back up the Trans-Canada Highway. On the way to Fredericton he had removed his suitcases from the trunk of the car in order to get the spare tire to replace a flat. After changing the tire he was so worried about being late that he drove off leaving his luggage on the side of the highway. Upon arrival at the Playhouse he realized what he had done. When he drove back up the highway, the luggage was gone. His first hours of rehearsal were spent lamenting the loss of many of his personal belongings. However, his spirits lifted when later in the day the police turned up with his lost bags, which an officer had found by the roadside.

A Thousand Clowns proved to be very popular fare, with Gerussi ideally suited to the leading role. "J.A.C." filled half her (J.A.C. was a woman) review with the story but added that she had enjoyed an outstanding performance from Mr. Gerussi. He also took on the role of the inept rapist in the first part of *The Typists and the Tiger*, with Norma Clark as the garrulous victim who eventually turns the tables on him. In *The Tiger* the two parts were played by Gerard Parkes and Patricia Carroll Brown, now listed as Patty Brown. Once again J.A.C. found Gerussi fascinating, but had reserved praise for the other performers. She found the set for *The Typists* did not make sense and the one for *The Tiger* flimsy. J.A.C.'s criticism would seem to indicate that the technical side of the Playhouse's operation was not up to the standard of the acting. This was the case also in the succeeding show, *Never Too Late*. On the positive side, J.A.C. reported that Patricia Carroll Brown, who had reverted to her three-barrelled name, and Syd Brown (no relation), handled the show's comedy brilliantly.[14] But she also pointed out that the set was too modern and bright. By this time, half way through the season, J.A.C. was allowed to identify herself with a byline. J.A.C. stood for Jo Anne Claus. She still revealed the novice critic's tendency to find minor flaws and exaggerate them, but she showed an increasing ability to apply clear judgement.

The final show of that season, *Billy Liar*, which was carried by Gerry Parkes, Paul Craig, and Joyce Campion with Swarbrick directing, marked Swarbrick's swansong at the Playhouse. From all reports, theatre was a lark to him. In a letter to me on March 14, 1968, Walter Learning wrote that Swarbrick's "first season . . . lost a fair sum" and "the second season . . . lost an incredible sum."[15] The board of directors decided to change managers. Mr. Swarbrick's tenure had lasted less than two years, after which in soldier-of-fortune fashion he moved on to further diverse adventures, such as writing political speeches for people like Peter Lougheed and kicking the drinking habit so rampant in Fredericton. Despite his faults, Swarbrick had made a profound influence on the Playhouse and Fredericton. During his brief sojourn he had built on his predecessor's achievements. He had staged productions using paid professional actors, had increased attendance by 300 per cent, had created a healthy nucleus of theatregoers in that city, and had demonstrated to the board of directors that it would have to be more circumspect in the future when it selected a general manager.

▪

On the board's committee to find a new manager was at least one theatre-lover with a practical knowledge of the Canadian theatre world. Alvin Shaw was a graduate of the University of Toronto where he had performed at Hart House under Robert Gill's direction. While teaching at the University of New Brunswick, he became active with the Dominion Drama Festival where he worked with a young philosophy graduate who had also developed an enthusiasm for the theatre. In 1960–61, Walter Learning was the DDF's national vice-president and shouldered much of the volunteer load when Saint John, New Brunswick hosted the National Festival. During the summer of 1967, he directed a course in drama at U.N.B. and was the production manager at the Beaverbrook Playhouse. When the general manager's position became vacant, Shaw persuaded Learning to submit his name to the Search Committee. It wasn't a shoo-in. There were other candidates, but Walter Learning got the nod and became the third person to undertake the daunting task of making the Playhouse a viable, integral part of the cultural life of New Brunswick. He was to succeed beyond anyone's wildest expectations.

Walter was born in Quidi Vidi, one of the oldest sections of St. John's, Newfoundland. He describes it as a place so tough, "they had to tie up the kids so they wouldn't eat the dogs."[16] His father, who operated a hotel, was imbued with that tongue-in-cheek sense of humour common to many Newfoundlanders, which Walter inherited and has carried him through many difficulties. On graduating from the University of New Brunswick, where he had acted in the Drama Guild, Learning decided to try a career as an actor. This decision led him to Toronto and the Grenville Street Playhouse following in the wake of a man calling himself Leslie Charles. No one seemed to know where Charles originally came from, but Learning first met him when Charles worked for a Fredericton radio station. Charles, who was eventually discovered to have several aliases, talked the U.N.B. Drama Guild into presenting a play he had written, *The Midnight Hour*, dealing with pimps and hookers. But the university authorities found it unsavoury and banned it. Charles decided to try his luck in Toronto where he produced his play in the Grenville Street Playhouse, the cosy theatre recently set up in the converted north portion of the Ward Price Antique Furniture and Art Gallery on College Street just west of Yonge. There Charles started "The Actors' Company," which consisted mostly of amateurs, some of whom received a fee for their services. In the summer of 1961 he enticed Walter to Toronto to try his wings as a professional actor for the sum of $55 per week. Walter recalls that he was paid for only a couple of weeks in a much longer engagement.[17] The production of *The Midnight Hour* did not establish Charles as Canada's gift to dramaturgy. He staged another show at Grenville Street, Moss Hart's *Light Up the Sky*, then abruptly decamped leaving rumours of bad debts and defaulting in payments to the actors. Chastened by his experience in the wilds of Toronto, Walter returned to the calmer atmosphere of Fredericton to lick his wounds and pursue his studies away from theatre.

In 1963, studying for his doctorate on a Commonwealth Scholarship in Australia, he augmented his income by working at the Canberra Repertory Theatre. There he gained valuable experience building and painting flats and performing American male roles, for which he had to suppress his strong Newfoundland dialect. He returned to New Brunswick in 1966, taught a drama summer course at U.N.B., then took a full-time position as a professor of philosophy at Memorial University in St. John's. In summer 1967 he assumed the double duties of a course at U.N.B. and production manager at the Beaverbrook Playhouse. When he was offered the position of general manager of the Playhouse in spring 1968, he left the relative security of a university post for the rough-and-tumble of the theatre.

I discovered through Margot Christie, secretary of the Canadian Theatre Centre in Toronto, that Mr. Learning was setting up appointments to interview actors in March 1968. She reserved a time for me, but I decided to send him a photo and résumé so that he would know something about me in advance. Fortunately I did because it led to a deep friendship and a collaboration that would create one of Canada's most important regional theatres. But it did not appear fortunate at the time. I received a terse two-sentence reply from which I discovered that I had mis-spelled his name, omitting the "a" in Learning. I concluded that there was little likelihood of my working in Fredericton. To my surprise, a day or so later, I received a telegram from Walter asking if I would be interested in directing some of the plays that coming summer. Because I knew that Ted Follows had been offered that assignment, I felt clarification was necessary. I contacted Ted and learned that he had indeed bowed out because of other commitments. I then telephoned Walter in Newfoundland and said something like, "Mr. Learning, neither you nor I know each other. Before either of us commits himself, we must meet and have a talk." He agreed and we made an appointment.

In a letter, Walter explained the financial situation and the scheduling of the plays already selected. He indicated that he expected an audience increase that would give him a potential box office of $23,000 on the season. This would be his operating budget with actors' salaries totalling $7,500 or an average of $125 per actor per week. Because of the limited financial resources, he was planning on small cast shows. He further outlined the very peculiar performance schedule that had been in effect the previous years. A "performance week" at the Playhouse was only from Monday through Thursday. Friday and Saturday nights were dark. Show A would open on July 8 and run for four nights. Show B would open on July 15 for four nights. In the third week, show A would run Monday and Tuesday and show B on Wednesday and Thursday. In the fourth, fifth, and sixth weeks, shows C and D would repeat the pattern. This insane scheduling seemed an attempt to blend weekly stock with the repertory approach. He also indicated in the letter that he wished me to direct the second and fourth shows for which I would be paid $1,350. I considered it a fair sum. Since I was now going to direct two shows I insisted in my letter of reply on being involved in the interviews with actors that Walter had scheduled for March 28, 29, and 30 at the Canadian Theatre Centre studio.

As a result of an announcement in Nat Cohen's column that I would be directing at Fredericton, my phone rang for several weeks with actors wanting to play there. An extra day of interviews was added and I suggested to Walter that he arrive a day early so that we could have our get-acquainted meeting, after which I would decide whether or not to accept the offer. We had dinner in the quiet, tiny roof dining room of the Park Plaza Hotel. According to Walter, I refused to let him pay for my drinks until I decided to work for him. Within five minutes I was swept up in his euphoria about the potential of the Playhouse and professional theatre in New Brunswick. I loved his sense of humour, which indicated to me that he would not be prone to let the heavy responsibilities he was assuming get him down. I also saw very quickly that he knew little about the problems entailed in producing a professional company, and that he was indirectly asking for help. I thought here was a man I could work with to establish another theatre on a solid basis in an area of the country until recently devoid of any professional theatre. His *joie de vivre* and enthusiasm were infectious. He was a person with a dynamism that would complement my knowledge and experience. In hindsight I can see that, with the exception of my season at Oakville and the Vineland hurricane disaster in 1954, I have linked my talents to people with the sustained energy and drive that I seem to possess only spasmodically — Dora Mavor Moore, Joan White, Robert Herrman, and in 1968, Walter Learning. As a result of our conversation over dinner that evening, I decided to contribute what I could to help Walter realize his dreams for the Playhouse — and I let him pay for the drinks.

During the interviews, when an actor arrived with whom I had worked, I left the room because I wanted Walter to form his own judgement, and I wanted the actors to feel free to promote themselves with Walter unhampered by the presence of someone who had worked with them before. Afterwards Walter asked me my opinion of each actor. It was not easy to find performers flexible enough to play the very British, somewhat mannered comedy of *Springtime for Henry* and *The Little Hut*, and also able to carry the more breezy, less mannered, American style of *Any Wednesday* and *Barefoot in the Park*. Moreover, we had to find actors who would be willing to come to Fredericton for the fees Walter was able to offer. But find them we did, and they all proved to be happy choices.

In my early letter, I had questioned the wisdom of performing only Monday through Thursday, pointing out that the cast would be paid for a full week of eight performances. Despite my going to bat for Walter with Equity, he had been unsuccessful in obtaining a contract designed for this unique schedule. It seemed wasteful not to have the cast perform for whatever size audience could be enticed into the theatre on Friday and Saturday — peak nights almost everywhere else in the world. But Walter was not sufficiently confident about the public's response to altering an established routine, fortunately, because I later discovered that after the four shows had opened, the schedule gave lovely long weekends off to enjoy the beauty of the Maritimes.

When Walter had been interviewed for the position of general manager, he had told the board that he wanted to establish a theatre company, not just manage a building. Their reply was that he could go ahead as "long as it did not cost them anything," so he decided to fund his company out of the Playhouse operating budget plus box-office receipts and any donations that might come from enthusiasts.[18] He apprised me of the parlous state of the finances, but since I had always been involved in penurious theatrical adventures, I was not discouraged. Here was a new challenge and Walter's ardour rubbed off on me and on everyone else.

We assembled a small company of versatile actors: Paisley Maxwell, fresh from the turbulence of Aries Productions, and Milo Ringham, who had recently been with the Neptune Theatre. Milo gave youthful feminine sex-appeal to the shows. Don Sutherland (the one who did not go to Hollywood) was a splendid singer as well as an actor and had worked in theatres from Neptune to the Citadel in Edmonton. He added youthful male sex-appeal. The fourth core member was Walter Massey, the nephew of Vincent and Raymond Massey. He had trained at the Neighborhood Playhouse in New York, and had established a thriving career in Canada in radio, TV, film, and onstage. Michael Egan was hired as designer. While a student at U.N.B., he had been encouraged by Alvin Shaw to study stage design, which he did at the National Theatre School. He returned to Fredericton to design for Swarbrick's productions, and Walter sensibly hired him. They were a hard-working, quick-study group who very rapidly developed an ensemble spirit with tolerance for each other's foibles. One of the personality glitches we had to rise above was Walter Massey's incessant, but often very clever punning for which he has an awesome facility only surpassed, in my experience, by Don Harron.

In the opening show, *The Little Hut*, I again played Philip, with Paisley Maxwell a very beautiful and dignified Susan, Walter Massey as the frustrated Henry, and Don Sutherland in a loin cloth and feathered headdress as the Danish cook masquerading as a savage. His was less a strong-arm savage than a gentlemanly one who enticed rather than forced Susan into the little hut with him. Michael Egan's set was a romanticized display of lush, tropical foliage in vivid colours that created just the right mood for this highly artificial comedy. The production was a great success and the audience received it with enthusiasm — an auspicious beginning to Walter

Learning's tenure at the Playhouse, despite criticism of his directing from the Saint John *Telegraph Journal* reviewer, Maude Maheal Day.

I directed the second show, *Any Wednesday*, and played John Cleves, with Paisley Maxwell as my wife, Milo Ringham as the sweet, sexy Ellen Gordon, and Don Sutherland revealing his matinee idol charm and comic flair as the romantic Cass. Walter Massey had the week off. The third show gave me a needed rest. *Barefoot in the Park*, directed by Alvin Shaw, brought Alvin as the Delivery Man and Walter Learning as a Television Repair Man back to the Playhouse stage to join Milo, Paisley, Don, and Walter Massey in the major roles. Our production of *Springtime for Henry* was my third go-round with Benn Levy's bit of froth. I had to suppress my memory of E. E. Horton's interpretation of Jelliwell and let Walter Massey develop his own, although I retained much of the dialogue Horton had incorporated to make the characters, particularly the two males, more zany and inept than in Levy's original script. JoAnn Claus, who had telescoped her two first names into one, and who by 1968 was a confident critic, aptly summed up the play: "You sit there not believing that any play could be so impossible. The characters and situations are beyond farce. Then you give up and just laugh."[19] On the whole this production was moderately successful, although I regretted agreeing to stage it as contemporary with 1968 to save the cost of renting costumes. JoAnn Claus was sharp enough to pick this up: "Both women wore contemporary clothes, which made such remarks as 'I play the gramophone rather well, I think' sound stupid instead of funny."[20] The actual line is "I was playing the gramophone. I play it rather well," and it is said by a male character. However she did have a point.

Overall, our shows had been well received by both public and press. With the exception of her criticism of Learning's direction of *The Little Hut*, Maude Maheal Day had waxed enthusiastic in the *Saint John Telegraph Journal*. But Walter decided that she should cease to function as a critic. She had only become a reviewer that summer because the young reporter from the *Telegraph Journal* who had been assigned the task was not enthusiastic about theatre and asked Walter if he could find someone locally who would see the opening night shows and phone the reviews to Saint John. Walter discovered Maude Maheal Day who reluctantly shouldered the chore. So that she could socialize with the cast after the show, she would phone in her opening night review at 10 p.m. before the show was over. But Walter became tired of this and his antagonism to her finished her as a critic at the end of the summer. Rarely has an artistic director been able to exorcise a critic. But in this case it was not difficult because Maude Maheal Day was none other than Walter himself using his mother's maiden name.

At the end of the season, Walter took a long hard look at the reality of the operation. After the extravagance of his predecessor, Walter knew that to build a permanent company at the Playhouse he would have to budget to the bone. He had financed the 1968 operation solely from box-office revenue and his ability to rob Peter to pay Paul. For example, by having a stage manager who was also the Playhouse janitor, Walter paid one salary of the producing company from the Beaverbrook funds set up to operate and maintain the building. Our stage manager-cum-janitor subsequently obtained employment with the African Safari near Brampton, Ontario where he found dealing with lions less stressful than dealing with theatre folk.

Walter concluded that Fredericton alone was insufficient to sustain a theatre company. He remembered from his DDF days that there were facilities in the various towns throughout New Brunswick where plays could be presented, and that there was a nucleus of enthusiasts in each town who would support productions. With the Playhouse in Fredericton as his base, he would organize tours of the province. He contacted people he knew around the province and received a favourable response. That was hardly surprising to me, because I had seen indications that summer of Walter's talent as a promoter. He has the great gift of being able to talk to people on their own level. This, added to his sense of humour, his education, and his command of the language, made him a much sought-after speaker at service organizations, lodges, and banquets. In his person he revealed to those who held that the arts were something esoteric for an "effete elite," that a "regular guy" could be an enthusiast for theatre. He gave the impression that he knew what he was doing, and was delighted doing it.

Walter calculated that the average cost for a tour would be $1,200 per night. He estimated that ticket sales and local sponsorship could bring in a minimum of $600 per night. The balance he would try to get from the Beaverbrook Foundation. He exaggerated somewhat when he told them that he had discovered a demand from the public for such a tour, and persuaded the Foundation to put up $20,000 for the venture. Armed with this backing he decided to launch the tour in the dead of winter of 1969. During one of our discussions in summer 1968, I had made several suggestions about developing theatre in Fredericton. I advised him to establish a producing company separate from the administration of the Beaverbrook Playhouse, with a separate board, a separate budget, and independent funding. So long as there was any suspicion that the Beaverbrook Foundation, which funded the Playhouse, was also funding the producing company, there would be little chance of obtaining support from the arts councils. Walter did so, creating a new production company that he called Theatre New Brunswick, the logo for which is the same in French as in English, TNB, Théâtre Nouveau Brunswick.

The productions were to rehearse in Fredericton, play there for a week, including Fridays and Saturdays (another change for the better), and then tour the major towns for two weeks doing one or two-night stands. This schedule would give cast and crew a five-week engagement making employment in New Brunswick more financially attractive. *The Marriage Go Round* starring Walter Massey and his wife Anne Butler inaugurated the touring on January 16, 1969 with James Swan as stage manager. He had recently emigrated from England where he had worked as production manager for the National Theatre of Great Britain and as a stage manager at the Old Vic. The scenery and some of the crew travelled by truck, but the actors toured in relative comfort in a rented car. *The Marriage Go Round* was well received, although the person reviewing for the Saint John paper, now that Maude Maheal Day had mysteriously vanished, found the cast "made more of the play than the play deserved. . . . Indeed the actors were much better than the play."[21]

The second production was John Osborne's *Inadmissable Evidence*, which involved Walter Learning as an actor, Alvin Shaw as the director, and students from the University of New Brunswick. This unique co-operative venture was primarily an amateur production that later competed in the Dominion Drama Festival where Walter received the best actor award for his performance as Bill Maitland.[22] The other two shows that season had professional casts: *Boeing, Boeing,* directed by Peter Boretski, featured Melanie Morse and Belinda Montgomery; *The Glass Menagerie* had Nancy Kerr as Amanda and Dan Macdonald as the Gentleman Caller, and was directed by the TV producer Herbert Roland. In a report to the Beaverbrook Foundation for the period ending March 31, 1969, Learning hailed the first season as a success both artistically and financially. He estimated that the shows had played to 20,000 people with 2,200 season tickets sold in an area of the country that is not densely populated.[23] It proved there really was a demand for legitimate theatre in the towns of New Brunswick.

Walter proposed to the board an eight rather than six-week summer season for 1969 and that they get out of their compromise stock-repertory situation into a full repertory system to take advantage of the transient tourist population. He estimated the gate receipts would leave an operating deficit of $18,000, which he argued could be met from a municipal grant of $2,000, provincial and federal grants of $5,000 each, private citizen donations of $2,000, and the use of the $4,000 still in the coffers of the now-defunct Patrons of the Playhouse. He also indicated that he planned to increase the salaries of the hitherto underpaid staff. Persuaded by Learning's record of the past year, his boundless energy, and the vision in these proposals, the Foundation coughed up $20,000 to produce the season. This was in addition to their funding of the Playhouse building. The creation of Theatre New Brunswick as a separate corporation had made it possible for the Canadian Beaverbrook Foundation to support the theatre company and still operate the Playhouse on a rental basis, thus appeasing Lord Beaverbrook's ghost.

In my second Fredericton summer, 1969, I tackled a murderer sandwiched between two holy men — Canon Chasuble in *The Importance of Being Earnest,* Mr. Manningham in *Gaslight,* and the Bishop of Lax in *See How They Run.* First, in addition to directing *The Importance,* I pontificated humorously as its Canon Chasuble. Of my three productions of Mr. Wilde's artful gem, this was the most satisfying so far as the visual effect was concerned. Michael Egan created stunning sets and costumes. But we had trouble finding a suitable wig for Lady Bracknell. Even though Her Lady-ship need not be played by an ageing gorgon, Anne Butler was not much older than Milo Ringham as Gwendolyn and Jacquie Bradley as Cecily. I decided that we needed her in a grey wig. However, salons with real hair wigs were non-existent in Fredericton, and our budget did not allow importing one from Toronto. Finally we found a synthetic wig of enormous proportion, which, alas, we could not trim because it was borrowed. Thanks to the ingenuity of the costume department, it eventually resem-bled an Edwardian hairstyle, somewhat excessive but impressive, although the only way it would fit onto Anne's head was backwards.

All the actors turned in fine individual performances, but the produc-tion as a whole did not jell. Possibly it was because this was the first show of the season and the company was not yet accustomed to working together; possibly I was too unfocused in my direction. At any rate, I was not satisfied with it. Kent Thompson in the *Saint John Telegraph Journal* commented that we found the play difficult.[24] He was right. Comedy of manners is always difficult. However, he mistakenly referred to *The Impor-tance of Being Earnest* as Wilde illustrating "what theatre of the absurd is all about."[25] Absurd it may seem, but "theatre of the absurd" it is not. How-ever, he did point out one of the problems of performing in that huge concert hall. With the vast space for the orchestra pit between the stage and the front row, the actors had a tendency to lose subtlety in order to belt out the lines to the last row of seats. Thompson justifiably praised individual performers, but chastised the cast as a whole for failing "to attack the play with the vitality necessary for farce."[26] The application of the word "farce" to what Wilde called a "trivial comedy for serious people" is indicative of what performers often have to tolerate when reporters who are inexperi-enced and ignorant about theatre are drafted into becoming "critics."

We had more success with *Gaslight* because it had the advantage of mystery and suspense. When first presented on Broadway in 1938 as *Angel*

Street, it made stars of Vincent Price and Canadian Judith Evelyn. I undertook the role of the urbane, calculating, fortune-hunting Jack Manningham — a role I relished because of the challenge of displaying the patient tolerance of a seemingly concerned husband whose wife seems on the verge of insanity, while underneath his surface lurks a ruthless schemer plotting to drive her crazy. Anne Butler showed her versatility in switching from the domineering Lady Bracknell to the subdued and cowed Mrs. Manningham. As the amiable housekeeper, Eleanor Beecroft, in her first season of many at TNB, was ideally cast, as was Jacquie Bradley as the pert teenaged maid, Nancy. Herbert Roland directed with great understanding of the characters and a feeling for the mood and atmosphere of this essentially Victorian melodrama. But there was one bit of action he staged toward the end of the play with which I did not agree. The author's instructions are that when Inspector Rough, a difficult role played by Walter Learning, reveals to Manningham that the jig is up, Manningham lunges toward the door to escape but is blocked by two policemen. After a minor struggle they tie him to a chair. Roland decided to expand the struggle by having Manningham break away a second time, vault the settee and once again head for the door where Rough subdued him. Only then was he tied to the chair. The enlarged struggle seemed to me at odds with the suave, always-in-control Manningham. It also caused problems at least for me because the action seldom played as Herbert had intended. There had not been enough rehearsal time for us to get the timing of the moves exactly right. I would vault the borrowed Victorian settee, careful not to damage it, but Walter rarely arrived at the right spot at the right time. One night he grabbed my left leg as I was hurdling the settee which brought me down crotch first on its wooden back. When I managed to get my leg free, he rushed around and grabbed me in a headlock. Walter is a fairly husky man, but somehow my head managed to slip out of his grasp. When I was in England in 1948, the use, or misuse, of a hair shampoo lost most of my hair at the crown, leaving me with a tonsure that I subsequently concealed, when a role required it, with a splendid crown piece made for me by Bob Rybka, who created many wigs and hairpieces for CBC performers. As my head slipped from Walter's headlock, my hairpiece came unglued and fell upside down in the centre of the stage just inside the entrance to the room. Fearful that the audience would think I had suddenly been scalped, I played the rest of the scene tied to the chair with my head tilted back. When Anne Butler re-entered the room she spied this oval thing with its hairy fringe in her path and adroitly swept past it to avoid it being caught under her skirt. When the curtain calls were over, we all gathered round this forlorn, obscene looking object. "Well," said Walter, "Shall we kill it now or let it live?" "Please," I pleaded, "Let it live. It is my crowning glory." Thereafter Walter never again tried a headlock, and I was able to keep my scalp where it belonged.

Don Meyers, Algernon in *Earnest*, had spent several seasons at Neptune Theatre since the demise of the Village Playhouse. Geoffrey Saville-Read, originally from England, had appeared at the Stratford Festival and worked extensively at Toronto Workshop Productions before playing John Worthing in our *Earnest*. Both were given an opportunity to show their range in types of comedy in *Star Spangled Girl* and as the wayward clergymen in *See How They Run*. This latter play also gave Eleanor Beecroft as the drunken Miss Skillen, and Milo Ringham as the ungainly maid, a chance to display their comic gifts. Walter Learning turned up in this one as a Russian spy. Once again I had great fun as the spaced-out Bishop of Lax. A good time was had by all, except for Joanne Claus, who that summer seemed to think that anything more than 10 years old was out of date. In *Gaslight*, Anne Butler had deservedly won her praise, as had Jacquie Bradley and I. She had given credit to Herb Roland for making an antique melodrama tolerable "by rapid pace and constant flow of action. One rarely had time to notice how silly some of the lines were."[27] This time she again found our play old fashioned: "*See How They Run* is an old comedy that shows its age in every speech. What may have seemed funny immediately after the Second World War, now sounds cliché or silly."[28] Apparently the audience did not agree. Kent Thompson in the *Telegraph Journal* pointed out that "there were times last night when you could not hear the lines for the laughter."[29]

By mid-season all four plays were playing in repertory. Since none of us was in all of the shows, we each had at least one night off a week in addition to the required day off according to Equity rules. During my two seasons, I had come to love Fredericton. I appreciated its quiet, laid-back quality, and, although we worked hard, I found these summers quite relaxing. Part of this was due to the fact that Walter ran a happy company. Although he was quite serious and dedicated to his jobs as artistic director of TNB and general manager of the Playhouse, his sense of humour and of the ridiculous prevented his becoming morose if things did not work out as expected. His attitude was infectious and made for a contented group of performers. Moreover, the accommodation was comfortable and inexpensive. For my first summer, I had a small, self-contained apartment in the house of the local rabbi, which was cosy and clean with a charming landlord and landlady. In 1969 all the theatre could arrange for me was a rather bleak pad in a large, somewhat dilapidated Victorian house. "Munster Mansion" as the actors dubbed it, was owned by a wealthy local playboy, Boyd Ritchie, who may have been reluctant to spend much on its maintenance but whom I grew to like because his attitude was more cosmopolitan than most Frederictonians and he loved giving lavish parties for the performers. My apartment was clean and spacious, the bare essentials of furniture made it comfortable enough, and it had a bedroom that previous tenants had painted a shocking pink so that in the morning, when the sun shone in the uncurtained window, the room positively pulsated.

If the increase in audience attendance was any criteria, the 1969 summer season had been a success. After two seasons, Learning had proven to the Playhouse Board, the Beaverbrook Foundation, the public, and even the government of New Brunswick, which had representation on the board, that he was a level-headed administrator determined to create a permanent theatre company for the whole province to enjoy. James Swan, both stage manager and production manager, had kept costs under control. With the title of assistant to the director, Doreen Grinstead continued as a general factotum whose main function was as bookkeeper and financial comptroller. A local lady, Iris Young, ably handled publicity and public relations. Walter was building up a team of experienced, capable employees.

I was not to appear again with Theatre New Brunswick for two years, during which time the opening of the touring season was changed from January to September, which allowed the final show of the summer to become the first of the touring season. The summer program reverted from repertory to a stock company basis. Additional funding was beginning to come in from granting agencies who recognized the growing importance of TNB to the cultural and economic life of Fredericton and New Brunswick. In the autumn of 1969 the City of Fredericton gave a grant of $16,000 to TNB.[30] The Canada Council agreed to pay Learning's salary with a grant of $12,500, which, because it was a grant, in those fiscally carefree days of the '60s, was tax exempt. By the standards of CEOs of large corporations, $12,500 was weekend spending money, but it was a reasonable salary in the context of fees paid to other artistic directors in the penurious theatre arts. This grant continued for two years. When his salary reverted to the payroll of TNB and the Beaverbrook Playhouse, it was taxable and he had a take-home pay of not much more than the $7,500 he had earned at Memorial University. But the Montreal Trust, which administered the Beaverbrook Foundation, agreed to help him buy a house in Fredericton for his family, which now consisted of his wife Leah and his son Warwick. The Montreal Trust gave him a low mortgage rate of four per cent so long as he remained the artistic director of Theatre New Brunswick and general manager of the Playhouse.

Walter also managed to persuade the Foundation to rebuild the Playhouse. In our discussions during my first summer I had advised him to renovate the building from its concert hall state to a more intimate and flexible theatre. I expected it would take him at least 10 years to overcome opposition and accomplish this. But he needed only four. One day in 1970 he took Jack Main, vice president and general manager of the Montreal Trust, hence head of the Beaverbrook Foundation in Canada, onto the Playhouse stage where he pointed out how the lack of a fly gallery restricted the kind of productions that could be mounted. He also pointed out that the ropes holding up light and teaser batons were wearing out and that they were tied off with 20-pound stage weights. "How would you feel as an actor knowing that a 20-pound weight could fall on your head?" he asked Mr. Main. He in turn asked Walter, "What is our insurance situation?" "We don't have any," Walter answered.[31]

That settled it. Mr. Main decided that the fly gallery, eliminated from the original design, had to be restored and the stage properly equipped. Walter drew up a list of backstage changes he thought were necessary and the Foundation's Board of Governors contacted Arcop and Associates who had designed the National Arts Centre, the Confederation Centre in Charlottetown, the Newfoundland Arts and Culture Centre, and Place Bonaventure in Montreal. Arcop's Fred Lebensold and Art Nichol suggested even greater changes than Walter had envisioned, much to his delight. They recommended that the auditorium be reduced in size, that the stage be built forward over the orchestra pit, that the old stage be used for increased workshop space, that more dressing rooms and storage space be created, and that there should be above the old stage a rehearsal space equal in size to the new stage area. The lobby was also to be enlarged. It was a conversion that would create one of the most attractive, most workable theatre structures in the country. Reconstruction was scheduled to begin in May of 1971.

The winter tour of 1970–71 was expanded and more adventuresome fare was presented: *Who's Afraid of Virginia Woolf?*, *A Man for All Seasons*, *The Playboy of the Western World* leavened by comedies such as N.F. Simpson's *A Resounding Tinkle*. Among the directors used during this period when the rest of the country was beginning to hear about Theatre New Brunswick and Walter Learning were Ed Stephenson, James Swan, John Wood, Bill Glassco, and Herbert Roland. Jacquie Bradley, a lady of many talents who had remained in Fredericton after the 1969 season to marry Robert Muller, an assistant stage manager at the Playhouse, alternated with James Swan as designer of many of the shows. About this time the publicity and promotion department got a shot in the arm when Walter's charming and bright wife, Leah, became the public relations manager. Over the next years she was to design some of the most striking theatre posters ever seen in Canada.

In the spring of 1972 I received a telephone call from Walter during which he told me that the rebuilt Beaverbrook Playhouse was scheduled to open on May 16 with *The King and I*, and, because of my contribution to the early years of TNB, he wanted me to be in it as Sir Edward Ramsay, the British Ambassador to the Court of the King of Siam. I was honoured that Walter wanted me to be part of this gala affair. That winter in Toronto I had played in *The Heart's a Wonder*, a musical version of *The Playboy of the Western World*, which made me want to learn more about the logistics of staging a major musical. So, with nothing better to do for the next few weeks, I agreed with pleasure. As a learning experience *The King and I* was to prove to be a very salutary lesson indeed.

On previous trips to Fredericton I had driven my own car but this time I flew, and being without transportation in that city, I decided to hole up in the Colonial Inn just a block from the theatre. The narrow corridors, the sloped floors, and the tilted walls reminded me of the set for the silent film *The Cabinet of Dr. Caligari*. It was a pyromaniac's dream of a fire trap. But it had atmosphere, was clean and cosy, and was run by two amiable middle-aged gentlemen friends. The place was casual, suited my mood at the time, and was within my budget. I obtained a room on the second floor over-looking the street.

Walter had selected *The King and I* for several reasons. He wanted to open the refurbished theatre with a musical on a sufficiently large scale to demonstrate why the theatre was rebuilt at a cost of almost $1.5 million, and why the 69-foot fly gallery had grown out of the roof dominating every edifice around it. He also wanted a production that would involve the community and to that end local youngsters were cast as the king's many children, and local matrons, most of whom had never been onstage before, became his many wives. Walter's third reason was that it was a show he was already familiar with after an amateur production in St. John's, Newfoundland. It seemed like an ideal choice. He brought the musical director from Newfoundland, and selected an orchestra conductor who was a bright, young musician. The orchestra consisted of 24 professionals recruited from the Atlantic Symphony and a military band at Camp Gagetown. Dances were to be staged by Maria Owen-Fekete who had studied dance at the University of Michigan and in London, England. When the cast met for the first rehearsal, we were shown Michael Egan's brilliant scarlet and gold set designs and the colourful costumes. It all augured well for a top-notch production.

The orchestra was not due to arrive until a few days before the opening, so the musical numbers were rehearsed with the musical director at the piano. At the first rehearsal I was surprised to find out that for economy reasons the Uncle Tom Ballet was to be omitted. That number is a high point of the show. We had been told that for the opening Sir Max Aitken and his wife were to fly over from London with a plane load of critics and dignitaries. The chairman of the Arts Council of Great Britain, Lord Goodman, was to officially open the rebuilt theatre. The premier of New Brunswick and representatives from the Canada Council were also to be present. "Surely," I thought, "for such a prestigious occasion, the extra money to hire dancers for this celebrated number could be found." But mine was not to reason why. For days I was not called to rehearse, but I was kept posted about the progress by some of the cast members who would repair to my cell at the Colonial Inn for martinis after an exhausting day. After the first week I began to hear that all was not well at the Court of the King of Siam.

The role of Anna Leonowens might have been tailor-made for Evie Anderson. Far from being a prima donna, she is nonetheless a perfectionist who knew from past experience how the show should work. Michael Fletcher brought to the role of the young lover, Lun Tha, a wealth of experience as an actor and singer, particularly in opera. He has solid musical training from the Toronto Conservatory and the College of Music at the University of Western Ontario, and he too had a strong sense of how *The King and I* should work. As the King, Jack Medley had years of acting experience behind him, and although not a singer, was no different from Yul Brynner in that respect. Barbara Kyle was a graduate of the National Theatre School, and had sung in a variety of musicals, including, like Mike Fletcher, *The Heart's a Wonder*. These are all strong performers who, being thoroughly professional, make the good of the show their paramount concern.

As the rehearsals progressed, the visits to my bar increased. There was growing dissatisfaction with the musical direction. I could help these increasingly frustrated performers unwind with a cocktail or two and lend a sympathetic ear, but not being sufficiently experienced in musicals myself, I had no helpful advice. A few days before the orchestra was to arrive, Jack Medley came to my room in deep despair. The musical director had insisted that he sing the one good number the King has, *It's a Puzzlement*, a patter song that should not be sung. The technique is known as sing-speak, or, "Rex Harrisoning it" after Rex Harrison's approach to singing in *My Fair Lady*. Medley became so uptight about the prospect of singing that he lost his voice and the number was cut. Another high point gone.

The orchestra arrived on Friday before the Tuesday opening. When I watched the first orchestra rehearsal, I realized that the young conductor was nervous when confronted by this array of professional union musicians almost challenging him to take charge. When he conducted he never took his eyes off the score. A good musician in his own right, he was accustomed to working with a trio or quartet of buddies, and lacked the authority to control seasoned musicians. Because the old orchestra pit was gone, Walter had planned to have the orchestra behind the cyclorama that surrounded the set. A monitor there would allow the conductor and orchestra to watch the performers on stage televised from a camera attached to the balcony. This might have worked for the musicians, but Walter failed to realize the panic that grips singers when they cannot see the conductor. Chaos reigned at the first rehearsal with cast and orchestra. After I had rehearsed my two scenes I fled the theatre to avoid the growing tension.

The following morning, Saturday before opening, when I arrived for rehearsal, Walter came to me wearing his depression like a cloak. He asked me to his office where the leads in the cast had requested a meeting. When we had all assembled, one of the leads stated that they had no faith in the musical direction of the show. These performers knew that if matters were allowed to continue the show would be a disaster, and they would be out there on the stage with egg on their faces, in front of people from Britain and across Canada. Their reputations were at stake. Angry words were exchanged. The musical director burst into tears, and the young conductor sat staring at the floor and saying nothing. After about half an hour of recrimination, which Walter tried to arbitrate, things seemed at an impasse.

Although wishing I were anywhere but there, I spoke up: "What I am hearing is the nervousness of singers who have not had sufficient rehearsal with the orchestra. There is a union orchestra sitting out there at great expense waiting to be used. I suggest you all go out there and go through your numbers several times with them, and you will probably feel more confident about things after that."

There seemed to be no alternative, so they left Walter's office. As soon as they had gone, I suggested that he contact Rainbow Stage in Winnipeg to see if the orchestra leader who had conducted it there was available. I also suggested that he phone the Atlantic Symphony's office in Halifax to find out if they knew of an experienced conductor who might be free. While he was phoning, Michael Fletcher returned to tell us he had just discovered that our concertmaster was a conductor. We went out to the stage where the orchestra waited. The middle-aged concertmaster agreed to pick up the baton and see what he could do. When he raised it, the orchestra, hitherto lackadaisical, suddenly came alive. Within two minutes we could see that the musicians respected him. Visibly the singing actors brightened and they began to rehearse with renewed confidence.

I then asked Walter to come with me. A few days earlier Alvin Shaw, who was playing Captain Orton, and I had descended to below the new stage into what had been the old orchestra pit. I took Walter down there and said that this is where the orchestra must go and where the TV monitor must be. "Three separate grids must be constructed across the downstage width of the stage through which the orchestra sound can rise, and in the middle of the apron a place for the conductor to stand must be cut so that he can conduct the singers with one hand above the stage floor and the orchestra with the other hand below the stage floor." Realizing that drastic action was needed, Walter agreed. That night construction workers were brought in with a jackhammer. To their dismay they found that the stage apron was unnecessarily supported by a thick concrete wall. It took hours and $1,000 to cut what I dubbed "the conductor's hole." Although not the ideal arrangement, particularly for the conductor, at the dress rehearsal it was clear that disaster had been averted. The singers could see the conductor and hear the orchestra, and the orchestra could see the conductor, hear the singers, and see them on a TV screen in their basement bower. The new conductor had taken charge of orchestra and singers. Leadership had been found at almost the 11th hour.

The dress rehearsals went relatively smoothly, but during the March of the Siamese Children I was appalled to see one little girl hobble out on crutches with a huge white cast on her leg on which her school chums had scribbled their names. I asked Walter why he had left this child in the show. He replied that he did not have the heart to kick her out, she had been so upset at the prospect of not being involved. Something of a theatrical purist myself, I suspect I would have given the show primacy over the child's desires. But Walter was not only softer hearted, he was also more shrewdly community conscious. The Playhouse and TNB belonged to the people of Fredericton and the province. The opening of *The King and I* and the revamped Playhouse made one of the most important events in Fredericton in decades. He knew that his audience would appreciate his understanding at leaving the child in the show, and that the guests from abroad would appreciate that this particular show was a community effort. At that point I realized that this was not just another production of *The King and I*. It was a manifestation of Fredericton's awareness of and pride in the fact that in eight short years, the town had changed from a quiet cultural backwater to an important point in the increasing cross-country grid of Canadian theatres. Like Stratford, Ontario, after the advent of the Festival, Fredericton would never be the same again.

During the after-show reception at the Lord Beaverbrook Hotel, David Gardner, who was then head of the English theatre section of the Canada Council, remarked to me that, although the overture seemed muffled, after the curtain went up the orchestra sound seemed to come from the same place as the singers. Rather than being drowned out, as is often the case when the orchestra is in a pit between the stage and the audience, the singers were backed by the orchestra sound. A lesson to be learned from all this is that out of adversity emerged possibly the most flexible theatre building in the country. Placing the orchestra below stage even worked for the visits of the National Ballet and the Canadian Opera Company, although those larger orchestras must have found the space cramped. Some years later, however, more stringent fire regulations forced the Playhouse to discontinue using this space for orchestras, which diminished the theatre's flexibility.

■

Although this book is meant to cover the years up to approximately 1970, in some cases I have felt compelled to move beyond that date. I have done so with TNB in order to chronicle Walter Learning's remarkable achievement. In four short years he developed an organization that brought professional theatre to communities, which up to that time saw only amateur productions, built an audience to support that organization, and created as a base for TNB a theatre plant that is one of the most adaptable, comfortable, up-to-date theatres in North America. He had lots of help from professional theatre people, enthusiastic support from some citizens of Fredericton and other towns of New Brunswick, and a sympathetic Beaverbrook Foundation, but he was the engine driving it all.

His tenure at TNB was to last 10 years. That story is not germane to this present book. But there is one incident that Walter tells about himself that I cannot resist including. In 1975 Walter had to hurriedly submit an application to the Canada Council for a grant for the next season. By the deadline he was short one play. He saw a copy of *Sleuth* by Anthony Shaffer, quickly glanced at the cast list, saw that there were five characters, and, without reading the script, budgeted accordingly. When David Gardner at the Canada Council saw this, he called Walter and pointed out that there were only two characters in *Sleuth* requiring only two actors to play them. Still ignorant of the play's plot, Walter insisted that there were five. David very tactfully explained the gimmick in the plot that required fooling the audience into thinking that there were three additional characters in the play. For once Walter was speechless. Gardner altered the budget for *Sleuth* accordingly and the Canada Council allowed the revised grant. As Walter remarked, "David could have clobbered me. It looked as if I was trying to get money from the Council under false pretences. But he didn't."[32] A theatre person himself, David was aware of the pressures theatrical producers face and consequently was sympathetic.

I was to make several appearances with TNB in the next 10 years, a story that must wait until later. But the early years of my involvement with Walter Learning, the Beaverbrook Playhouse, and Theatre New Brunswick were, on the whole, challenging, satisfying, stimulating, and heaps of fun.

CHAPTER 24

Thespis Telectronicus

I was present in the control booth in September 1952 when the first play was sent out live on CBC-TV. It was Mavor Moore's version of Dodie Smith's English comedy *Call It a Day*. In his autobiography, Mavor writes about the incident during the televising when a cameraman fainted, was replaced by a substitute cameraman unfamiliar with the show, and was guided through the program by the director, Peter McDonald.[1] But another incident occurred that Mavor does not mention. One of the scenes took place in a second floor bedroom. At one point Harry Geldart, playing a leading role, had to turn his back to the camera and walk toward a large window. Just as he did so, a stage-hand with one end of a ladder resting on his shoulder walked past outside this second-storey window. Harry froze in his tracks. So did everyone in the control booth. The ladder seemed interminable. I was reminded of the Olsen and Johnson vaudeville routine when Johnson entered stage right with one end of a long ladder on his shoulder, walked across the stage, exited stage left, and almost immediately re-appeared stage right carrying the other end of the ladder. I thoroughly expected to see the same stage-hand on the other end of that CBC ladder. But in that I was disappointed; a different stage-hand carried the other end. When everyone had recovered from the shock, the show continued without further incident. But I have often wondered what happened to those two stage-hands afterwards. They probably became CBC executives.

The advent of television and the growth of a native film industry led by the National Film Board and Crawley Films were a godsend to Canadian actors whose meagre earnings from theatre work could be augmented by TV and film. In the very second week of TV programming, I appeared on a quiz show directed by Drew Crossan where actors had to act out a scripted situation and the panel had to figure out what the subject was. I performed in several of these sketches, which served as an invaluable training ground in technique for acting before a camera. The extent to which TV and film roles increased our livelihood might well be indicated by my own career. Although at first I did not keep a record of my contracts, between 1957 and the end of December 1970, I appeared in 31 CBC-TV programs, six films for the National Film Board, 16 films produced for CTV by Baton Broadcasting, and I worked for 16 independent film and TV producers. The income supported my theatre habit.

When private-enterprise television was introduced, commercials provided another source of revenue. But, like many stage actors in England and America, many of us in Canada at first did not deign to become involved in the crassness of commercials. As more and more actors weakened under the blandishments of the almighty dollar, I too jumped off my high horse. For my first commercial audition I did not see the script before I went in to be interviewed by the advertising agency representatives. When I started to read, the script struck me as so inane that I blurted out, "You must be kidding." Needless to say I did not get that commercial. But in 1963 I went to an audition for a Glidden paint commercial seeking a Franklyn Pangborn type to play a department store floorwalker who becomes entranced with the smoothness with which a demonstrator applies Glidden paint to the wall. I did my best prissy act and won the role. It was fun to make and brought me over $5,000 because it was seen on Johnny Carson's *Tonight Show* in the U.S. as well as in Canada. After that I decided I could ill afford to be so proud as to ignore commercials. Two of my most lucrative ones were for Heinz Ketchup and Cadbury Caramilk Chocolate, both of which brought revenue in the five-figure category. For Heinz I played a *Maitre d'Hôtel* who summons for a dining couple a "bottle of the best," which turns out to be a bottle of ketchup. It had such an extensive showing that clerks in stores and children at family reunions would come up to me and say "a bottle of the best." I would have liked to have poured a "bottle of the best" over the heads of all of them. Ah, the curse of celebrity!

Sometimes an actor knows that the commercial is not going to run. I made one for Cook's Travellers Cheques in which I was a middle-aged sugar-daddy buying a diamond necklace for his luscious young doxy. At the end of the commercial the director asked me to laugh lasciviously as I put the necklace around her neck. I protested, but the director insisted. I knew that Thomas Cook would not want this image of people who used their travellers cheques shown across the land. This commercial never even got to a 13-week cycle. A scene where a father is buying a toy for his son was shown instead — a much more wholesome association for Thomas Cook.

Some commercials can be so cute (particularly with children or animals), amusing, or artistic, that the viewer is distracted from the message. One such was an Eno commercial I was in called "The Tuba Player" in which a tuba player in a symphony orchestra is discovered eating his lunch, and when he blows his tuba only a squawk comes out. The annoyed conductor, me, reaches over and hands the tuba player a package of Eno anti-acid pills. Simple enough. Apparently the budget could not bear the cost of a full symphony orchestra, so the director and designer contrived that both the tuba player and the conductor would be visible through a mass of gleaming brass instruments. The studio lights were artfully arranged so that portions of the instruments would be highlighted. Some of these lights were so close and intense that while I was conducting a portion of Vaughn Williams's "Concerto for Bass Tuba and Orchestra," the back of my tail coat began to smoke. I saw the commercial only once and I thought the director and designer had created something visually beautiful but it ran for only one cycle. It was probably too artistic.

I have made three commercials during which I was in bed. The first I spent in bed with Barbara Anne Scott, the second with Mrs. John Bassett, and the third with a shaggy English sheep dog. The two ladies were no problem, but the English sheep dog was recalcitrant. It was supposed to leap onto the bed and lick my face to awaken me. Probably because it was a very fastidious dog it refused to lick something that did not appeal to it. Nothing the trainer or director could do would persuade it. Eventually, resentful at being spurned by a dog, I told the property man to get some bits of cheese from the snack trolley and put a piece in my left ear. It worked. The dog stopped being so snooty and slurped the cheddar out of my ear. From such inventiveness great commercials are made.

■

Most of the programs in the 1950s emanated from Toronto, attracting actors from across the country, the United States, Great Britain, and even as far afield as Australia and New Zealand. The acting community quadrupled and Toronto became the third largest pool of performers in North America after Hollywood and New York. They were heady days. There was nothing like a live telecast to get the adrenalin flowing. If an actor made a mistake or "dried," millions saw it. In order to avoid such embarrassment and to give a polish to the show, weeks were spent rehearsing it in the CBC studios before the actor ever saw a TV camera. But inevitably bloopers occurred. One memorable incident was the result of altered timing. One of our most brilliant and reliable actresses had to lie in a coffin while a scene was played in front of it. When the scene was over, the actress was to lie there for a specified count until the camera had been shut off and the action picked up by another camera in another set. This had worked perfectly during the camera rehearsals. But in the live telecast, the next camera was not yet in position when the producer wanted to switch, so he held the first camera on the actress in the coffin a few seconds longer than hitherto. Not realizing this, her eyes being closed in death, the actress gave the specified count to herself and proceeded to get up. To her horror she saw the red light indicating that the camera was still on. Viewers across the country were treated to the sight of the corpse, Lazarus-like, rising from the coffin. The actress was overcome with chagrin, but it was not her fault. Nor could the producer be blamed, nor the cameraman who might have had an unforeseen problem in getting into position. That is what made the early days of live television so exciting. The best laid plans went "aft a-gley."

Before the News and Public Affairs Departments gained hegemony at the CBC, drama, comedy, and variety dominated its broadcasting. Most producers and directors categorized me as a "type," hence leading roles rarely came my way. But my "character" turned up in a broad range of shows. I appeared in a variety of CBC-TV series: *Case for the Court, Wojek, The Time of Your Life, Quentin Durgens,* and *McQueen.* I performed in many of the CBC dramas, such as *Laburnum Grove, The Doctor's Dilemma, Le Misanthrope, Diary of a Confessed Sinner,* and *Mr. Member of Parliament.* For the National Film Board I was in *Tribune of Nova Scotia, Return from Night, A Matter of Identity, War of 1812* (not the whole war), *Shattered Silence,* and *Flight Safety.* When independent television began about 1958, another opportunity opened up for me. I turned up in an episode of a soap opera, *The Trouble with Tracey,* and in 16 episodes of *Famous Jury Trials* for Baton Broadcasting. Hollywood discovered Toronto in the '50s and independent producers came to the city to make series to sell in the international market. The Lakeshore Studios became home to *The Last of the Mohicans* and *Tugboat Annie,* starring Minerva Urecal, one of those familiar faces in Hollywood films, but known particularly for her portrayal of Grace Pool in *Jane Eyre.* Profit, not art, was behind these series and the episodes were ground out like sausages from a machine. The director for *Tugboat Annie* had a very casual manner, spoke with a New York dialect and always wore an engineer's cap. One of his instructions became a common quote among the Toronto acting community of the day. When a young enthusiast asked what his character motivation was, the director simply replied, "Just say de woids. We'll put de actin' in latuh."

I also appeared in a couple of the *Forest Ranger* series, designed for younger audiences but using some of Canada's top talent such as Rex Hagen and Ralph Endersby (both child actors at that time), Gordon Pinsent, and on occasion a very svelte Barbara Hamilton. The location was an especially constructed rustic village at the studios in Kleinberg. In one episode, director Peter Carter asked me to drive a Volkswagen Beetle at high speed past the camera positioned on the surface of a dirt road. I was reluctant for fear of hitting the cameraman who was lying flat on his stomach behind the camera. I made several runs at it but never came closer than a foot from the camera. Peter wanted it closer and urged me not to be nervous. I determined to give him what he wanted. On the next run I roared past within three inches of the camera. When I got out of the car I found a delighted director and an ashen cameraman. In another episode directed by Eric Till, I played a villain who got his come-uppance and was seen at the end standing on a dock as it and he slowly sank ignominiously into the river. *Forest Rangers* was a lot of fun and became a very popular series that sold widely throughout the world — which made it moderately lucrative. For many years thereafter small residual payments would surprisingly arrive in the mail.

I was cast as Charles Darwin in a science series by Normandie Films in Montreal. Because dubbing was not yet common in Canada, there were two casts, one French and the other English. I believe I was cast in the lead role because I was the same size as the French-Canadian actor, thus saving the producer the cost of renting another costume. Whether director Guy Hoffman could speak any English I do not know but he did not to me. A product of the Ontario secondary school system of the '30s, I learned how to read French but not to converse in it. Also in the film was Michael Kane, that brilliant Montreal actor who had made such a mark on American television in Edgar Allan Poe stories adapted for Studio One in New York. He spoke French fluently and obligingly helped me out when I got into difficulties, as did other members of the cast and crew. Hoffman gave me no direction whatever, almost as though he resented my presence. However, he was very explicit in his directions to the French Darwin. I simply copied that actor's movements when it was my turn as the English Darwin. Although Hoffman was aloof, I enjoyed working with the Quebec actors and crew. They had such a *joie de vivre* that it was infectious, and they were very friendly toward me. They appreciated my feeble efforts to speak to them in French and did not sneer at my *faux pas*.

A less satisfying experience, which I stupidly allowed myself to get sucked into, was a film version of Guy de Maupassant's *The Madman*, produced by Ferma Commonwealth Pictures, which seemed to be backed by a consortium of Toronto lawyers, one of whom was my ex-pupil from the New Play Society School, Lawrence Stone. The director, Lindsey Shonteff, had made at least one previous movie, a western in black and white that I saw but mercifully I can remember nothing about except a shot of Hagen Beggs, his eyes rolling upward and chocolate sauce trickling down his face from a bullet hole in his forehead. Ferma needed an experienced but inexpensive actor to play the demented French judge who has sentenced so many murderers to death that he decides to discover for himself what it is like to be a murderer. To achieve this he clobbers a man in the Bois de Boulogne. Larry Stone urged me to tackle the role and I agreed for ACTRA scale plus a percentage of the gross receipts, should the film get distributed. The role was a heavy dramatic challenge that the ham in me could not resist. Moreover, at the time I wanted more work in front of a film camera. I looked upon it as a learning experience. It became that all right — how to make a film in all the wrong ways.

The well-equipped studios at Kleinberg were rented. The cameraman and technicians were all union professionals, as was the cast drawn from the ACTRA membership. The adaptation was adequate from an actor's viewpoint, but there was no shooting script. As a filmmaker, Shonteff was an amateur and seemed to be improvising as he went along. After he decided to shoot in the sequence of the story, the most costly way, I spent the first five days being paid for lying in a coffin. When my turn came the camera seemed to me to be too static. Shonteff was shooting the scene as though he had placed a camera in the auditorium of a theatre to photograph a stage play. When I realized this I began discussing each scene I was in with Shonteff and the cameraman. I even persuaded Lindsey to stand in for me while I looked through the lens and worked out more interesting shots with the cameraman. This was enlightening for me and, between us we managed to shoot my scenes in a more dramatically effective way. Lindsey seemed willing to go along with this, and I began to enjoy directing my own scenes. However, I soon realized that I was involved in an enterprise that was going nowhere. Shonteff's lack of a thought-out plan lost him the confidence of cast and crew. His improvisational method gave the film the look of home movies, inadequately lit and haphazardly filmed.

The final scene to be shot was the murder in the woods. We were filming in the depths of winter with three feet of snow on the ground and a temperature that was five degrees Fahrenheit. Without having looked for a location even remotely resembling the Bois de Boulogne, Lindsey thought he could film the scene in the fields around the studio at Kleinberg. But he concluded that the area did not look much like a park, so we all climbed into cars and headed for High Park in Toronto. I was clad in a light cape, rented from Malabar, meant to be worn on a cool evening, hardly suitable for the frigid temperature that January day. We did not get around to shooting until mid-afternoon when the sun began to descend behind the trees. Lindsey had found a location near Bloor and Keele Streets that had a hill but no one had obtained permission to film in High Park so naturally there were no police on hand to control the children who came to ski down the slope after school. As soon as they found out we were filming it became great fun to ski between the camera and the actors, ruining shot after shot. After each skier the tracks in the snow had to have fresh snow brushed over them, skiers not being a common sight in the Bois de Boulogne in the middle of the 19th century. As the afternoon wore on I became more and more glaciated, frustrated, and irritable. Before I caught pneumonia or froze my various appendages, I decided to call a halt to this whole fruitless process. I organized a shot where I crept up behind a man, played by Alan Rose, who was trudging for no good reason through the knee deep snow, struck him on the back of the head with my heavy handled cane, and turned to the camera to reveal the orgiastic fervour on my face. When that last scene was shot, I told Lindsey that I was going home before I turned into a block of ice, got into my car wearing my costume, and drove away. I never saw or heard from Lindsey Shonteff again. Later I learned that he had tried to peddle the film in New York and one of the distributing agents Lindsey had approached remarked that he was glad to have eaten breakfast before watching the movie because he could not face food after it.

■

In the early days of television, Harvey Hart directed and produced a short-lived CBC series on comedy in which narration by Bruce Belfrage linked selected scenes from great plays over the ages. I was engaged to play John Worthing in the garden scene from *The Importance of Being Earnest*. The scene worked beautifully, but with Corinne Conley as Gwendolyn, Diane Van der Vlis as Cecily, and William Shatner as Algernon, that might be expected. For a TV drama Henry Kaplan asked me to perform the role of a banker, even though it was a small part that appeared at the end. You may remember Henry as my competition in the first post-war Inter-college Drama Festival at the University of Toronto. After graduating he directed a highly polished performance of *Another Part of the Forest* with a cast of brilliant young actors including Anna Cameron, William Hutt, Eric House, Ted Follows, and Kate Reid at the Royal Alexandra in the 1949 Dominion Drama Festival. He managed to get in on the ground floor of CBC television as a producer and he cast many of the people in his TV productions with whom he had associated at college and in summer stock. At our first rehearsal Henry had the cast sit in a semi-circle and each actor was to have worked out a biography for the character and even the character's ancestors, a very commendable approach for plays that require "in depth" character analysis. Most of the actors present had worked with Kaplan before, and had prepared lengthy analyses often going back, unnecessarily in my opinion, for generations. Unaware of Henry's requirements, I had not prepared a background for my character, a banker who conducted himself in a business-like, no-nonsense manner, who issued orders and got things done. Authority, toughness, and crispness were required. I was seated at the end of the semi-circle and was the last to speak. After listening to an hour or so of pseudo-psychiatric analysis, the mischief in me could not resist. "This character is simply the deus ex machina brought in at the last minute to tie up the loose ends of the plot," I said. There was a silence that was tomb-like. Kaplan gave me a baleful glance that seemed to say "that man is hopeless." Although some of the cast later expressed their amusement at what I had said, I never worked for Henry again.

The TV drama directors for whom I did work most frequently were Melwyn Breen, Leo Orenstein, and Eric Till. Mel and Leo had been actors. Eric became a director after gaining experience as a floor director, receiving and transmitting to the crew and actors orders from the boss director in the booth. All three had a sensitive understanding of actors, and helped find the best way of interpreting the role. Eric seemed almost unflappable, an essential strength for a television director, particularly before kinescope recording or videotape when the programs were sent out live. Another director and producer I greatly admired, and still do, is the now famous Norman Campbell. I was directed by him when he briefly took over *The Wayne and Shuster Variety Show*. That show also had other highly talented directors with whom I worked.

I became part of their television stock company in the mid-1950s, and appeared on many of their shows until 1966. Johnny Wayne, Frank Shuster, and their international television success are common knowledge. But because they influenced the lives of so many entertainers, including mine, I must write about their shows from my point of view.

When I entered Harbord Collegiate, Frank and John were in their graduating year, so I never got to know them there. I had enjoyed Frank's performance as Koko in *The Mikado* at Harbord, and admired them in *The Army Show*, but I never became a radio fan because I had difficulty telling them apart vocally. However, when they turned to television I became an avid viewer and hoped that someday I would have the pleasure of working with them. Their comedy was generally satirical sketches — human situations parodied to their most ridiculous, often insane, extreme — that required skilful, inventive acting. Unlike comedians on the American networks, they were not forced to limit their sketches to five or six minutes. Their satirical playlets could run as long as 15 minutes and occasionally longer.

My chance to perform with them came when Drew Crossan was producing their shows in Studio 4, the converted automobile showroom and garage on Yonge Street by the C.P.R. tracks. I do not recall which of the numerous comedy roles was my first with them, but many over the years are etched in my mind: the head of Scotland Yard in a Sherlock Holmes parody, the wicked Sheriff of Nottingham to Frank's Robin Hood and Johnny's Friar Tuck, the Emperor Tiberius (Or was it Nero? Anyway, one of those old Romans) in a take-off on *Ben Hur*, an Indian Chief in a *Bonanza* sketch, and an assortment of scientists, pompous members of the English upper crust, gentlemen's gentlemen, butlers, and even a Trojan warrior.

The half-hour shows were presented fortnightly during the autumn, winter, and spring and usually consisted of an introduction by Johnny and Frank, then the first sketch, followed by a musical number, frequently one that used the talents of the brilliant dancer and choreographer, Don Gillies. A second comedy sketch followed, which led to the closing by the two comedians. Studio 4 was grossly inadequate for staging variety shows before an audience, who were forced to sit uncomfortably on bleachers at one end of the narrow space. A curtain would come in to mask the scene changes, which had to be done in a brief, tightly proscribed few minutes and as quietly as possible so as not to distract from the announcer, singer, or Wayne and Shuster performing in front of the curtain. Behind the curtain seeming chaos prevailed, and God help any actor who got in the way of the crew frantically changing the set.

One of the most difficult playlets to stage in that limited space was their parody on the story of Helen of Troy. *You Are There* was an American TV series that re-enacted moments in history, and which Johnny and Frank parodied in *There You Are*. An unseen announcer would establish the historical background for the opening scene, and at intervals between the acted scenes would deliver further narration as the story progressed. Quite often I would be one of those announcers, but would also be an actor in the scenes. In the Trojan War satire I was extremely active. In the costume of a Trojan warrior I would read the narration over an off-set microphone, draw my short sword, rush onto the set to do battle with a Greek, dash out breathless, read some more narration and then dash back to do battle. It was frantic, but great fun. The final scene revealed the Greeks, including Johnny, climbing out of the Trojan horse, which almost filled the end of the studio. During the ensuing fracas all were killed except Johnny, who, wounded, climbed back up the ladder, peered into the hollow horse and delivered the one line that he told me was the reason he had always wanted to write a skit about the Trojan War. Painfully and gasping for breath he shouted "Is there a doctor in the horse?"

The most celebrated line from all their sketches became a familiar quote in show-biz circles, and elsewhere, for several years. During a take-off on Shakespeare's *Julius Caesar*, when Caesar's wife, Portia, played by Sylvia Lennick, heard that Caesar had been assassinated, she cried, "I told him. I told him. Julie don't go." It wasn't the line itself that tickled the viewers' funny bones. It was the absurdity of calling Caesar "Julie" and the slightly Yiddish lilt that Sylvia gave the line that sold it. Johnny and Frank were the most literate comedians of their day in North America. Both had good educations and were extremely well-read. But they were not cultural snobs. They lampooned pomposity and the highbrow. The finest example of their literacy, which revealed an appreciation of Shakespeare's style and idiom, was their Shakespearian baseball game. The setting was a baseball diamond and the players were all in Elizabethan costume. Except for the baseball references, Shakespeare himself might have written the dialogue. At one point Johnny accosted the Umpire, played by Paul Kligman:

> Johnny: "You, sirrah, that ball was fair."
> Umpire: "That ball was foul."
> Johnny: "So fair a foul I have not seen."

There were many such lines. Another of my favourites was Johnny's command to MacDuff: "Lay on MacDuff, and watch out for that breaking stuff!" Shakespeare would have applauded.

In the 1950s they had become noticed by television executives in the United States and were invited to do a sketch on the Rosemary Clooney Show. They presented their 11-minute English baseball sketch. It was a hit with the public and they soon were invited to meet with Ed Sullivan. He offered them a contract to do 26 shows. Eventually, with repeats, they were to appear on the *Ed Sullivan Variety Show* 67 times.[2] Because they employed a lot of actors in their parodies, they were very popular with the American Federation of Television and Radio Artists so AFTRA did not object to their importing from Toronto some of their Canadian colleagues. I was invited to appear on that show in their version of a British western. Those Sunday night broadcasts emanated live from the CBS studio in a converted theatre on Broadway. The sketch began with a street scene in a wild west town. Two Colonel Blimp types, played by Glenn Morris and myself, are discovered seated on a porch concealed from the audience and cameras by two newspapers. While extras milled about on the street, we had the opening dialogue, which consisted of several lines delivered by me in a frightfully, frightfully English accent as I read items from the newspaper to each of which Glenn replied "Good Show" until the last item when he said "Bad Show." These were not boffo laugh lines but were Johnny's and Frank's way of setting the scene and easing the audience into the sketch. The audience for the dress rehearsal did not seem too receptive so a hurried conference occurred between Ed Sullivan, the director, and Johnny and Frank. They decided to shorten the introduction and get on with the comedy. My second and fourth lines were cut and I had to make a blend of my first, third, and fifth lines. This without a further rehearsal before the broadcast. During the dress rehearsal it was arranged that all the extras would exit stage left "in one" — that is, between the proscenium and the first tab upstage above which the stage manager was positioned in order to give me a hand signal when to lower the newspaper. But on the broadcast the extras, sheep-like, followed a leader who decided to exit upstage of the first tab, sweeping the stage manager into the wings. All I could see of him was an index finger above a sea of Stetsons frantically flexing my cue.

One did not need to be the greatest actor in the world to play the type of comedy that Johnny and Frank created, often slapstick with sight gags and verbal humour. But there was no greater test of an actor's versatility than to perform on their comedy program. One needed a keen sense of timing, a talent for characterization, and an ability as a straight man to set up the gags for the comedians. With the exception of Sammy Sales and Doug Romaine, both of whom occasionally appeared on the show, the rest of us were not comedians. Actors are interpreters and there are wonderful comic actors, but they do not necessarily think funny as do comedians who are creative people with a keen sense of the absurdity of the human condition. Johnny and Frank certainly were that.

When CBC-TV opened its big Studio 7 on Mutual Street, just behind "The Kremlin" (the nickname given to the ancient buildings of Havergal Girls School that had been the centre of CBC Radio since the mid-'40s), *The Wayne and Shuster Show* moved there and was stretched to one hour. Don Hudson had taken over as the director several years before. Johnny and Frank had a long association with him going back to *The Army Show*, and because he was usually on the same wavelength with them, they relied on him. So, it was a great loss when the plane he was on flying from Montreal to Toronto crashed in 1962. Various producers were tried after that: Norman Jewison, Norman Campbell, who had become a brilliant TV producer of ballet, and Stanley Jacobson. All were tops in their field, but a certain type of person was needed to deal with Johnny, who was mercurial and could be outspoken. He knew how their kind of comedy should be presented, and how it should be photographed, but he was often impatient and would flare up at actors, even those who were close friends, if he thought they were not giving their best. Yet he was not vindictive. If he was irate one minute he would be joking the next. Don Hudson had had the facility to listen, and if he felt he was right, to quietly dig in and let Johnny blow off steam. Even Frank did not escape Johnny's outbursts. It was Frank's patience, his imperturbability, plus his appreciation and affection for Johnny that held the partnership together. Almost all the regular members of the stock company felt Johnny's annoyance at one time or another, except me. I have never been able to understand why I was the exception. If Johnny did not like something I was doing or disapproved of a line reading, he would tell me so quietly and politely. In the 10 years I worked that show he never raised his voice or spoke deprecatingly to me. Both Johnny and Frank always treated me with respect.

When videotape was introduced, some of the production pressure was eased because part of the program could be pre-taped and incorporated into the show as it was being telecast. But I felt that a lot of spontaneity was lost and by 1966 the fun had gone out of it for me. After Stan Jacobson became the producer I did a couple of their shows, but I did not seek further work with them. In the era of the flower children, popular comedy on television changed. The rapid fire delivery of the American show *Laugh In*, starring Rowan and Martin, made satirical sketch comedy seem slow and old hat. Wayne and Shuster continued with a new producer, Peter Scott, an ex-actor who had been their long-time floor director. During the late '60s and early '70s, their popularity waned but parody always has a following and they continued their show, although less frequently. Eventually their type of comedy began to have a resurgence. In 1996–97, the CBC revived many of the black and white episodes from the '50s and '60s, and in recent years I have seen re-showings of their programs from the '70s and '80s in colour on the Comedy Channel, which made me appreciate even more the cleverness of the sketches, the brilliance of the satire, the talent of the supporting cast, and how well they have stood the test of time.

In the early days of *The Wayne and Shuster Show* I found working with them, Don Hudson, and the versatile collection of performers in their stock company a garden of delights. I received great satisfaction that, in a small way, I was helping them make people laugh all across the nation. They offered family entertainment with nothing vulgar or scatological. It was not highbrow, nor did it cater to the moron as have so many stand-up comics of the '80s and '90s. They considered their public to be reasonably intelligent and informed. They never indulged in humour at the expense of any particular group or minority, and they proved that Canadians have a sense of humour and can laugh at themselves. It was great joy in great times with great people.

CHAPTER 25

Tangents: Teaching

In spring 1968, Eleanor Beecroft had been told by John Dodd, from the board of directors of the Crest Hour Company, that they were looking for a new artistic director. She gave him my name and told me that she had done so. In due course I had a telephone call from him inviting me to have lunch at the University of Toronto Faculty Club. Professor John Dodd was also head of the English Department of the Ontario College of Education that university graduates were obliged to attend to obtain a teacher's certificate on the assumption that such a document qualified them to teach in Ontario's secondary schools. At lunch he did not ask me to become director of the Hour Company, but astounded me by offering the position of lecturer in Theatre Arts at the College of Education. He told me that Esme Crampton, who had taught the course for many years, would not be returning. I would be required to teach for two to three hours three afternoons a week from September until May for a salary of $9,000 a year. I realized that in addition to the teaching, there would be many hours of preparation. The course covered every aspect of theatre, from acting to make-up, speech training, directing, theatre history, and even lectures on the technology involved in modern staging. In theatre schools, these subjects are taught by several experts, but I was to be a one-man faculty. It had been 18 years since I helped establish the New Play Society School and, although I had done some coaching of actors in the interim, I had not taught so comprehensive a program before. I needed time to think it over.

To one who since 1949 had never known economic security, a year's guaranteed salary payable monthly was most enticing. Professor Dodd was a genuine theatre buff, a member of the Toronto Shakespeare Society, and possessed a wicked sense of humour. I felt that he was someone with whom I could get along. Although this would be a tangent from the main thrust of my career, I would still have two days a week plus the weekends to devote to any acting or directing jobs that might come along. Although I knew by May of 1968 that I would be spending that summer in Fredericton, I believed there would be ample time that spring and in early September to prepare the courses. I decided to accept the offer on the understanding that I teach the subjects for one year only or until the College found a permanent replacement for Ms. Crampton. Little did I realize the hassles that would follow.

Professor Dodd gave me several curricula to study. I visited Ms. Crampton whose advice was most helpful. I decided to utilize a more up-to-date approach to Speechcraft than Elsie Fogerty's on which Dora Mavor Moore had based her training of me. I purchased Ms. Crampton's very useful book, *A Handbook of the Theatre*. I found Virgil Anderson's *Training the Speaking Voice* the best approach for North American students. I refreshed my memory about Stanislavski's method of training actors in *An Actor Prepares* and read Marguerite Dow's recently published book, *The Magic Mask*. I also boned up on the history of the theatre from Aeschylus to Osborne. By the beginning of September I felt better armed to meet the students.

Classes were held in a large double classroom with a small stage at one end in the west wing of the building on Bloor Street at Spadina Avenue that houses both the College of Education and the University of Toronto Schools. I had been told by Professor Dodd that because Theatre Arts came under the English Department in secondary schools, I was obliged to accept into the course any students who would be teaching English and who wanted an extra credit. I could also accept any students whose major subject was other than English if I thought they were sufficiently interested.

For all, some acting talent and stage experience would be desirable but not necessary. I decided to reject any student who was not an English major and had no theatrical experience. There were 55 English majors who wanted the course, an unwieldy size to which I added 10 more who were keen and had experience but were not going to be teaching English. I thought that if I had to accept students who had no experience or real interest in Theatre Arts, I might as well help those 10 enthusiasts get a credit to teach the subject. I never had such stage fright as the first day I faced that class of 65 university graduates. There were at least 10 people in the class who were quite qualified to teach the subject in secondary schools without taking the course from me. Three of them were graduates of American universities where they had undergone extensive theatre training. One 54-year-old man had produced and directed plays at the Westminster Theatre in London, England for "Moral Re-armament," a post-war offshoot of "The Oxford Group." Others had been actively involved in amateur theatre. Some from the University of Toronto had benefitted from working with Robert Gill, and one was a disillusioned professional actor who was seeking the security of the teaching profession.

Ironically, never having attended the College of Education to get my teacher's certificate, I could not qualify to teach the subject in Ontario's secondary schools, but I was considered qualified to teach the aspiring teachers. Theatre Arts was relatively new in the schools in 1968 and there were too few trained teachers available. Dodd had chosen me because he knew I had active experience in the theatre, had taken some training, and had helped set up the NPS School. Qualified although he thought I was, and even though I had done some homework, I felt most unqualified when I first faced that regiment of students, several of whom wore the challenging expression of young know-it-alls. I had no problem teaching techniques of acting, speech, make-up, or an approach to directing. But when it came to the history of the theatre I took the wrong tack. I lectured on the subject. I had been given a schedule, inherited from my predecessor, governing when during the week each subject should be taught. At first I saw no reason to question this scheduling. History of the theatre, a subject that I enjoyed, was Friday afternoon. After several lectures, I realized that I was losing their interest.

This was the era of the "Flower Children," Haight-Ashbury, Jack Kerouac, Lenny Bruce, Woodstock, Rochdale, and student protest. Disillusioned with the world bequeathed to them by previous generations, students from Berkeley to Paris were becoming militant. "Student Power" had moved through the University of Toronto, and that year hit the College of Education. Early in my term I attended a meeting of the governing body of the College that was also attended by the leader of the students, a Maoist. To my amazement angry words were exchanged between this student and several faculty members, and one teacher threatened to punch him out. The ensuing pandemonium shocked my sense of decorum. It was worse than anything I had encountered at the many meetings of ACTRA and Equity. Since I was only a temporary member of the faculty, I decided not to take sides, although much of my sympathy went with the students who were chafing under a tradition that assumed that teachers knew best and students should listen, learn, and not rock the boat.

Because many in my class had no theatre experience whatever, I was appalled when after only three weeks of classroom work they were obliged to go for a week of "practice teaching." For the experienced students this was a piece of cake, but for many this prospect was extremely frightening. I hurriedly gave them a series of improvisations they could use to keep their high school students occupied. During the week I travelled to as many schools as I could fit in to watch my students teach, and to talk to the permanent Theatre Arts teachers in the different schools. In the early autumn most of them were giving their classes improvisation exercises, essential in helping their students overcome the inhibitions and self-consciousness that overwhelm teenagers. That also helped the teacher ascertain who in the class might have some ability as an actor, although the purpose was not to develop actors for the professional theatre. My untrained students managed to get through relying heavily on the improvs I had given them.

During a mid-morning break at one of the schools when I was talking to some of my class, I imprudently mentioned that I had not been inside a secondary school since I graduated decades before. That autumn the student newspaper, *The Varsity*, had turned its analytical searchlight on the College of Education to appraise the calibre of teaching there. An article appeared in that paper written by one of my students in which she used my admission to support her argument that the teaching staff at the College left a lot to be desired, and that one teacher had taught them nothing of the "methodology" of teaching the subject.[1] She did not name me but all the faculty would know to whom she was referring because I was new and was the only faculty member who had not formally trained as a teacher. "Methodology" was an educator's term that was new to me. I had thought that "the method" I was teaching was based on Stanislavski's "method." Then it dawned on me that these students could not be expected to have the same interest or enthusiasm for acting technique as students in a theatre school because they did not intend to become actors. They would become teachers and they needed to have a "method" of teaching the subject. Even though the books I had referred them to gave an approach to teaching the subject, they expected this wisdom would come from me. It also dawned on me that 64 of my 65 students (I exclude the 54-year-old) had come through grade school, secondary school, and university where for at least 15 years of their early lives they had been obliged to sit through dreary lectures. No wonder they found my Friday afternoon classes in theatre history sleep inducing. I concluded that drastic measures were required.

Just before the Christmas break I solicited written comments from my class on my methodology and any suggestions they might have to improve the course. The majority did not respond, partly because of disinterest, partly because they too had no idea how to teach the subject, and partly because I had given the theatrically uninitiated students a basis for surviving practice teaching. It was the experienced students who responded and in no uncertain terms. I spent that Christmas break studying their comments and working out a new plan of attack in which I combined acting with directing and both with theatre history. When the college re-opened in January of 1969, I divided this monstrous class into groups of five. I selected scenes from plays covering the evolution of western theatre from the Greeks to the moderns. At random I selected a director for each scene and cast five students in each, but not necessarily to type. There were more women in the class so some of them played men's roles. Another group of five were given the task of preparing a presentation for the class on the period — not just about the author and the play itself, but the socio-political environment. They could adopt any method they wanted to get the history across to the audience: a quiz show with the panel of five asking questions of the audience, a brains trust during which the audience would ask questions of the panel, each member of the panel could give short talks, or they could be characters from the period meeting to discuss the play in relation to its environment. One group even wrote a short play about the play and the society in which it was written.

Professor Dodd had informed me that my whole budget for the year was $375. I decided to blow this munificent sum on these Friday afternoon events. At the back of the classroom was a huge wardrobe full of costumes. When required I would augment these with costumes from Malabar where, because I had done business with them on many occasions, I could get a slight reduction. Make-up was supplied and I made the classroom available for rehearsals whenever the students could find the time. I sat in on most of them guiding the young director when necessary. On Friday afternoons from January until the end of the school year the period from 2 p.m. until 5 p.m. was divided into three segments. The first hour was given to the group charged with instructing the class about the history of the play, the second hour was devoted to the performance, and the third to an appraisal of the performance and a discussion of the historical era in which the play was written. I arranged for the television department to televise the first two hours, the recording of which would be studied at a later date. The television instructor was delighted because he did not have enough to do to occupy his time. My role would be to sit with the class, prepare questions to ask those charged with the responsibility of teaching about the play and its background, and control the appraisal of the performances during the discussion period so that any criticism was tactfully constructive rather than destructive.

When in the first week of January I announced this innovative approach to the class the room visibly brightened. I divided the class into the groups of five, cast the plays for the rest of the semester and appointed the teaching panels. I selected a director from among the experienced class members for the first presentation, which was to be a scene from Sophocles' *Antigone*. Then I dismissed all of the class except those assigned to the first program, one group of which had to read the play in one corner of the room while the other group decided how they would approach their teaching assignment. I hovered between the two prepared to answer questions or make suggestions if asked.

The following Friday the teaching group conducted their part of the program as a quiz show modelled on *What's My Line?* with four panelists and a quiz master. They were allowed notes and reference books. They had a pre-arranged group of questions, but allowed questions from the audience, including some from me. It was a great success as was the performance that followed. The informal discussion about Greek classical theatre, Sophocles, and the Theban plays was most stimulating. Many had done a lot of research and I learned as much from the discussion as my fellow students did. I next had the class delve into the Medieval Mystery plays. Then, because I suspected that they had had a surfeit of Shakespeare, I used Ben Jonson's *Volpone*. For this the tutoring group wrote a one-act play in which they were characters from the early Jacobean years on their way to see a performance of *Volpone* at the Globe Theatre. Their clearly delineated characters cleverly prattled on with the latest gossip, chatted about the merit of "Will" as compared with "Ben," reminisced about the days of the late Queen Bess, and in general gave a clear picture of the events of a day in the early years of the reign of James I. By the third week of these Friday afternoon performances, the class had increased by at least 50 per cent. Students crammed in from other courses and even stood at the back of the classroom-theatre. One of those was our Maoist friend.

Halfway through the winter term the student body organized a day when they would conduct an appraisal of the college and the effectiveness of its teaching staff. Most of the professors decided that they would boycott the school for that day, so that all the classes closed except for mine. I had conducted my own appraisal of my "methodology" the previous December, and the theatre students did not want to give up precious rehearsal time to bother with such a survey. At the end of the year the class had a big party where I found myself the guest of honour. The dissident group of the previous autumn had become very supportive and I concluded my year as a teacher with the satisfaction that somehow I had managed to survive. A year later I received a letter from the lady who had written the article in *The Varsity*. It is a letter that I cherish because it shows great courage and sensitivity on her part, and because it reminds me that by being flexible and willing to take criticism I had managed to turn a deteriorating situation into a positive one. In that letter she wrote, "Your unflinching ability to roll with the punches . . . taught me a lot about the need for strong and pure, old-fashioned guts in education."

The college found a permanent replacement for Ms. Crampton, so it was "Goodbye, Mr. Chips" after one year. I took it upon myself to write a report on what I thought was wrong with the way Theatre Arts was taught in the schools. Because the course was relatively new, English teachers with little or no experience were often drafted to teach the subject in the days before qualified teachers could be graduated from OCE. I was disturbed to find that some teachers who began the autumn semester with improvisations were still giving improvisations to their bored students when I revisited them in the spring. That would be enough to turn a student against theatre for life. Of course there were a few excellent teachers in Toronto who had previous experience as amateur actors, or, in one case, as a professional. As the years went by more qualified teachers raised the standard of instruction in Theatre Arts, and I am confident that some of my students contributed to that improvement. My successor, John Saxton, told me that he had used my report to extract $65,000 out of the college to expand the course. He converted it largely into one in filmmaking, which, according to the ex-apprentice from the Garden Centre Theatre, Tedd Reed, who took the course in 1969, the students found most enlightening. Though, how it was going to help him teach Theatre Arts baffled him.

The following year I was retained by the college to teach new Canadian students how to pronounce the English language. Anyone who attempts this must realize that trying to explain the inconsistencies in the language brings one to the conclusion that it is an absurdity. There are rules that are regularly broken. The fact that it derives from Latin, French, Teutonic, and Celtic roots has led to a mishmash of pronunciation. How does one explain why the vowel sound in "though" is pronounced like the one in "dough," while "through" is pronounced like "threw" and not like "throw," and "thou" is not pronounced like either of them but like "bough," which has the same pronunciation as "brow," but "bow" is pronounced like "dough" if you are going to shoot an arrow from it, but like "brow" if you are going to make an obeisance from the "waist," which is pronounced exactly the same as "waste" but different from "wasp"? The rule that the vowel is short before two consonants is applied to the latter word but not to the former because the two consonants are followed by a vowel. But in the word "happen" that formula is ignored and the "a" is short. The rule that in a word of three or more syllables, the accent goes on the anti-penultimate holds for words like "harassment" and "embarrassment," but is ignored for such words as "fundamental" and "detrimental." There are no certain guidelines for the unfortunate person learning English.

During my classes I began to wish that those linguistic experts who championed the phonetic writing of English had succeeded. Most of my students, although they spoke English with an accent, spoke it more grammatically than most Canadians. They were overly precise but that would ease with fluency. I had them all reading aloud prose, poetry, and scenes from plays, teaching the use of articulation, inflection, and diction to utilize the voice to interpret meaning. I tried to teach them an actor's approach to vocalization to indicate subtleties of meaning, mood changes, and rhythms. My charges seemed to enjoy the classes but it had been a greater challenge than I had originally anticipated.

The spring of 1970 marked the end of my two-year tangent at the College of Education. It had been a rewarding and satisfying experience and I realized that nothing that I would ever face in the theatre would be as daunting as those first weeks of teaching at OCE.

CHAPTER 26

Tangents:
Equity and ACTRA

In 1951, Donald and Murray Davis of the Straw Hat Players arranged a meeting with Jack Blacklock of the Allenburg Barn Theatre, Michael Sadlier of the Peterborough Summer Theatre, and myself representing the New Play Society and the International Players for both of whom I was working. Its purpose was to discuss the feasibility of inviting American Actors' Equity to organize the performers in Canada. I was opposed because I feared that too many controls and regulations would smother the newly born indigenous theatre. Dora Mavor Moore, Drew Thompson, and Arthur Sutherland were also opposed and instructed me to vote "no." The Davis brothers and Sadlier were in favour. With my two votes added to Blacklock's, the proposal was defeated. Ironically, I was eventually to serve almost 16 years on the Canadian Executive Committee of Actors' Equity and was chairperson of that committee for five terms. The fascinating history of the entertainment unions (strictly speaking they are not "unions" but "associations" of self-employed professional performers) in Canada deserves volumes on its own. But my involvement with both ACTRA and Actors' Equity was another tangent that devoured much of my time and energy. Through Equity I was able to have some influence on the development of the theatre nationally.

After the first season of the Stratford Shakespeare Festival, which had already become a million-dollar enterprise, a group of actors from that company approached ACTRA for protection. The Canadian Council of Authors and Artists (CCAA), the national umbrella organization of all the ACTRA locals, considered their request but discovered that there was already an association in the field, American Actors' Equity, chartered in 1919 by the American Federation of Labor to represent actors throughout North America, and endorsed by the Canadian government of the time. This jurisdiction had been exercised in Canada primarily over touring companies originating in the United States. In 1953 ACTRA was busy organizing for television and did not want to get into a dispute with another association. Under the CCAA's auspices, American Actors' Equity was invited to send representatives to meet with actors in Toronto to discuss the organizing of Canadian theatrical performers. Despite some understandable nationalistic opposition, the performers agreed to have the experienced American association represent them. It proved to be a fortunate decision for two reasons: the willingness of the Americans to allow considerable autonomy to the Canadian branch while bearing the costs of organizing, and the choice of the first two Canadian representatives of American Equity, Dennis Sweeting followed by Larry McCance. Dennis Sweeting was the executive secretary of ACTRA and served simultaneously as the Canadian representative of American Equity, his salary and office space shared by both associations. His was the difficult task of bringing producers on side and persuading actors to join. For several years ACTRA members were allowed to join Equity for no initiation fee when offered an Equity contract. In that way a nucleus membership was formed. After four years of groundwork, he left this position and McCance replaced him, presiding over the phenomenal growth of the Association and the Canadian theatre through the years from 1959 to his death in January 1970.

Of Irish stock, Larry McCance came from Vancouver where he grew up with an interest in theatre. In his early years he helped found Theatre Under the Stars (TUTS), which performed in Stanley Park, the first Canadian outdoor musical theatre company since the movies and the Depression killed the legitimate theatre. He served in the Royal Canadian Air Force and after the war followed the migration of actors to Toronto where he became part of Andrew Allan's radio stock company. He was one of the organizers of Radio Artists Toronto Society (RATS) that evolved into ACRA and then ACTRA. He stage-managed various shows around Toronto, including some for the NPS, was one of the earliest members of the Canadian Advisory Committee of Actors' Equity, and from 1956 to 1958 was the executive secretary of the British Columbia Centennial Committee. When that celebration was over, he returned to Toronto just in time to be offered the position with Equity. It was fortunate for Canadian theatre that he accepted.

A member of ACTRA for several years, I joined Equity in 1956 and was elected to the Canadian Advisory Committee in the autumn of 1962. Thus began an association with Larry, who taught me about tact, diplomacy, how to chair meetings, when to be adamant and when to compromise, and not to take debate in negotiations personally. Short in stature, with a dapper moustache and a tendency to be chubby, he could not bear having the collar of his shirt tight around his neck. Invariably it was undone, with his necktie knotted loosely. This helped create the impression of a hard-nosed union boss, which could have an intimidating psychological effect on negotiators who did not know him. When they did get to know him they found that he had a wry sense of humour but could not tolerate humbug or pretentiousness. He was a reasonable but tough negotiator, willing to compromise on some issues but hard on exploiters of talent. Larry loved theatre and theatre people, and he was dedicated to the development of the theatre arts in this country. He knew that if Equity became too rigid, too authoritarian, too by the book, the growth of the theatre could be stifled, and there would be increased resistance to the association. Many performers were quite willing to work without an association's protection and many producers feared that hiring Equity artists would bankrupt them. Aided by the Canadian Advisory Committee (later the Canadian Executive Committee), he set about to convince performers of the benefits of membership and to calm the apprehensions of producers and directors. Through the years I learned first to respect, then to admire, and eventually to love that man.

Inevitably I took a more active role in the Association. I served on various committees, particularly the Canadian branch of the Constitution

Review Committee, a sub-committee of the Equity Council in New York. I was involved in negotiations with the Stratford Festival, the National Ballet, and assorted other companies. I attended International Conferences of Equity in New York and was part of delegations to several government officials in Ottawa. During the years between 1964 and 1967 when Paul Kligman was chairperson, Equity came into conflict with the recently formed Union des Artistes in Montreal over jurisdiction in the Quebec theatre. It was a long, drawn-out, and sometimes bitter dispute, which sucked into its vortex the Canadian Labour Congress, ACTRA, the American entertainment unions, the American Federation of Labor, Mayor Drapeau, René Lévesque, Pierre Laporte, international booking agencies, and the Canadian government. Eventually a compromise was reached that protected Equity's interests and gave the Union des Artistes jurisdiction in the French language theatre and over opera and dance in Quebec. While that dispute was going on, Equity was also trying to settle a contretemps with the International Inn in Winnipeg, which split the professional community in that city into two camps.

I was vice-chairperson of the CEC when Tony Van Bridge was chairperson. I eventually became chairperson, a position I held during the last half of the 1960s and again for two terms in the early 1970s. During that time, Leslie Yeo and I wrote the Reciprocal Agreement between ACTRA and Equity that was formally adopted in 1972, and when Equity in Canada separated from American Equity I was determined that, because of the tremendous support, understanding, and relative freedom of action American Equity had given us, the separation should be amicable with a binding agreement between the two associations. Accordingly, in consultation with Theo Bikel, who was then president of Equity, I wrote the Reciprocal Agreement to formalize the relationship between Canadian and American Actors' Equity. Then I compiled the first constitution and by-laws for the newly independent association.

In addition to the normal duties of an elected officer and a member of various committees, on two occasions I had to assume temporarily the function of the Canadian representative. Larry had a history of heart disease but his doctor had assured Equity that he was physically capable of the responsibility. However, the pressure of countless meetings, negotiating with producers, other associations and even governments, and dealing with dissident members added to his exhaustion from constantly flying back and forth across the country. In 1968 he had a heart attack in New York and for eight weeks was either in hospital there or recuperating at home. Alas, there was no one who had been groomed to substitute for Larry, so for eight weeks I, as chairperson of the Canadian Executive Committee, tried my best to oversee the business of the Association and keep it running smoothly. On one occasion during those weeks I had to wield Equity power in circumstances that did not win friends for me.

In 1968 the Grandstand Show at the Canadian National Exhibition was an extravaganza starring a host of Canadian performers including Robert Christie, Catherine McKinnon, Don Harron, and dancers of the National Ballet. They performed on a vast, open stage. The weather turned inclement and one morning in the Equity office I received a complaint that during a heavy electrical storm the night before, the dancers had been asked to perform on a wet, slippery stage and that singers had been asked to sing clutching metal microphones. According to Martha Harron in *A Parent Contradiction*, that night when the dancers refused, Don strode out with a microphone to fill the gap with his Charlie Farquharson routine.[1] After I received that call I attended performances when rain was predicted. One night there was a fierce downpour with lightning flashing all around. For the safety of the performers I felt obliged to order them not to perform while the storm lasted, which was the rest of the evening. The result was the last half of the show was cancelled. I was not very popular with the management. Since I was an unpaid officer of Equity, and was dependent on my earnings as a performer, I realized I was antagonizing potential employers, but someone had to protect the performers involved.

When Larry returned, Equity decided to hire Burnard Chadwick as his assistant to be trained to replace him should such a crisis arise again. Larry died unexpectedly on January 5, 1970 before Mr. Chadwick's preparation was completed. When Burnard was obliged to spend several weeks in the

New York Equity offices for further training, I was once again deputized. Shortly, I was called upon to make a decision of world-shattering importance about stage nudity, both female and (horrors!) MALE. The revue *Spring Thaw* had new producers. After Bob Johnston gave it up following his financially disastrous 1968 production, Mavor Moore leased the title to a tandem of producers who decided to stage the 1970 edition at the Bayview Playhouse. One day I received a phone call from one of them asking me to give him my opinion of the nudity in the show. One of the numbers was a *pas de deux* between a naked male and a naked female. The male dancer was of average physique, but the female was tall and statuesque with impressively outsized breasts. At one point when the male dancer had to lift her by the waist, while these appendages were brushing against his nose, I worried that I would see a hernia develop. The producer asked for my opinion when the number was over. Because the routine was meant to be profoundly serious and "artistic," and because the participants were actors first, dancers second, and were making a valiant show of it, I dare not tell him that I thought it was the funniest ballet I had ever seen. Instead I informed him that I personally did not find the nudity offensive, but that I was no arbiter of public standards, and that I would have to warn the performers that if they were charged by the police for giving a lewd performance, Equity could not stand behind them. However, I added, according to the reciprocal agreement Equity had with the Musicians' Union, the guitarist who spoke lines in another sketch would have to join Equity. The producer went into shock and screamed that I would be putting him out of business. But I insisted and the guitarist joined Equity. In the end, no charges for lewdness were laid against the dancers or producers, which was a sign that Toronto was growing up.

Four days after Larry's death I was offered the job of Canadian representative but turned it down for several reasons. We had been grooming Burnard as Larry's successor. As well, I had just received a Canada Council grant to visit theatres in Europe. I felt the job would put an end to my career as an actor and director, but primarily I felt I lacked the necessary toughness, patience, persistence, and diplomacy for the job. During the years I was chairperson of the CEC, Larry and I made a good team because we complemented each other and had the same objectives for the association and for Canadian theatre. But his was a hard act to follow. Larry's legacy was that he had contributed more than anyone toward the building of a strong association of performing artists that could protect its members from coast to coast, that could eventually function without his firm control, in a theatre world that he had given his heart and soul, and probably his life, to help nurture into maturity.

Although this book is devoted to the years up to 1970, there is an incident in 1976 I would like to include because it reveals a further area of potential impact of Equity's responsibilities. In fact, it shows how an obscure actor from Toronto might have had some influence on an international event on the other side of the world. After our independence from American Equity, Canadian Equity shared the Canadian seat on the Executive Committee of the International Federation of Actors ("FIA" from Fédération International des Acteurs) with ACTRA and the Union des Artistes. In 1976 Burnard Chadwick and I, substituting for the chairperson of Canadian Equity, attended a meeting of that committee in Dublin during the course of which a resolution was passed unanimously condemning the Pinochet regime of Chile for its mistreatment of performing artists. While the discussion on that resolution was going on, I looked across at the delegates from the Soviet Union, Hungary, and East Germany. At the time the Panovs, a husband and wife pair of ballet dancers, had been trying for some months to emigrate to Israel but the Soviet government refused permission. I thought it was hypocritical of us to condemn an oppressive Fascist regime in Chile and not an equally oppressive Communist regime in the Soviet Union. On an impulse, I rose and made a motion that FIA should urge the Soviet government to grant the Panovs freedom to emigrate. Consternation ensued. The presiding officer of FIA was greatly alarmed because he did not wish to offend the east block delegates who were completely taken by surprise. There had never before been a resolution critical of their governments' policies at FIA. But enthusiastic support came from the representatives of American Equity, the Screen Actors'

Guild, the American Federation of Television and Radio Artists, Irish Equity, the Norwegian performers' union, and half-heartedly from my Canadian colleagues. Although each country has only one vote there were enough in favour to outvote the east block countries, and the resolution passed. Shortly after that the Panovs were granted permission to emigrate. I expect that a petition drawn up by Sir Laurence Olivier in support of the Panovs had more influence, but my resolution endorsed by FIA, which embarrassed the Soviet delegates, might have helped win their release.

While on the CEC, I was also active on the ACTRA Toronto Branch Council, on ACTRA's National Board of Directors, and on various of its subcommittees. As a member of the ACTRA Constitutional Review Committee I was instrumental in bringing some semblance of order out of the early chaos of the talent agency business. Concurrent with the growth of work in TV, film, and commercials, talent agencies and casting houses developed at first primarily in Toronto and Vancouver. As the agencies grew in number, a competitive free-for-all ensued to make money from the performers. There was no control over how much commission could be charged. On the other hand, artists were free to accept auditions from whatever agency got to them first. ACTRA decided that something had to be done to protect its members, but it could not force rules and regulations on the agencies until it could control its own members. This it did through an amendment I wrote to its by-laws, in effect telling members that they could deal only with talent agencies and personal managers approved by ACTRA. ACTRA then negotiated with the talent agents and established regulations to protect its members while obliging them to deal exclusively with one agent on a contractual basis. Thus the performers were rescued from excessive exploitation and order was established among the talent agencies although, predictably, some agents looked on ACTRA's intervention as meddling in their private affairs. I met one such agent in the lobby of a theatre who grabbed me by the lapels and shouted, "You! You! You're the one who is putting me out of business." I regretted that he blamed me because I liked the guy, but I knew then that ACTRA's new by-law was having a beneficial effect.

ACTRA is made up of many disciplines with locals across the country, a condition which has sometimes led to internal turbulence. After one such eruption during which an ACTRA president had to be eased out because he was trying to corral too much power into his own hands, Leslie Yeo and I were charged with amending the constitution to prevent such an incident recurring. We spent weeks and drafted a whole new constitution that served well for several years. But, unlike Equity, ACTRA periodically turns on itself. Now there is very little of that constitution left and ACTRA, responding to the parochialism that threatens to pull this country apart, has reverted to giving more power back to the locals, contrary to the aims of earlier boards of directors to have a strong national organization.

Where I found time to be so deeply involved with both ACTRA and Equity and still earn a living has become a mystery to me, but I have not been the only one. Many performers, announcers, and writers have spent countless hours working voluntarily for these organizations, most without the recognition that I have received. In the early 1980s Equity created the Larry McCance Award to be given "in appreciation for outstanding service to the Association and its members." In 1984 I was the third person to receive that award. In 1997 I was presented with ACTRA's prestigious Bernard Cowan Award, named after a man who for decades had a profound influence on the development of that association with immeasurable benefits to its members. I cherish both these awards because, although my contribution has been minuscule compared with the achievements of Larry McCance and Bernard Cowan, to have my name linked with theirs is for me a signal honour indeed.

■

Although it was mostly involved with theatre and had considerable influence on my future approach to that art form, I suppose one could call my three-month sojourn in Europe in 1970 a "tangent." My visit to several European companies at Expo '67 had whetted my curiosity about theatre abroad. Except for the occasional visit by the Old Vic or the Comédie Française, the only recent touchstone I had to measure our Canadian theatre achievement against was New York. On the basis of what I had seen there in the 1960s and the immense improvement in theatrical conditions in Canada between 1950 and 1970, I concluded that we compared quite favourably. But I now wanted to make comparisons with British and European theatres, and hopefully learn something from them that would help me as an actor and director. Accordingly I applied to the Canada Council for a grant to travel for three months visiting theatres from Dublin to Athens.

I collected the required references, outlined my objectives, my itinerary, and estimation of cost, mailed my application, and waited for a reply. An employee of the Council phoned the new Canadian representative of Actors' Equity, Burnard Chadwick, and asked him why I wanted to visit Athens. Somewhat amazed Chadwick replied, "Probably because that is where our theatre began." Despite that, the Council decided it was unnecessary for me to see any modern or even classical Greek theatre in its home country. It awarded me airfare only as far as Rome. The Council, or its panel of consultants, also decided that three months to see the theatres of Ireland, Britain, France, Austria, Greece, Italy, Germany, Denmark, and Sweden was too long. I could do it in two months. It also decided to give me a senior artist's grant of $450 a month for two months, and instead of the airfare of $1,005.60 I requested, allowed me a travel allowance of $642. If this sum seems low when compared with travel costs now, consider that the Canadian dollar was high relative to most European currencies (a good seat at the Paris Opera for *Rigoletto* cost me only the equivalent of $7.20 Canadian), and it was possible to have stop-overs at no extra charge in those happier travelling days. I had requested what I considered a modest and reasonable sum of $2355.64 for my three-month expedition and planned to add to that some of my own savings. I was given a total of $1,542 as a "non-competitive" grant that was, according to the form, the maximum available. I found that a bit surprising because I knew that the Council had granted tens of thousands of dollars for artists in various fields to study in Europe. However, because I could not afford to drain my savings to the extent that I would have no reserves to fall back on should no work be available after my return, I was grateful for that amount of assistance. But

I decided to delete the German and Scandinavian portion of the tour and to take a more leisurely approach to the remaining countries, and, since I would be spending more of my own money than the Council had granted, I decided to broaden the scope to include opera and concerts as well. Ultimately I spent $3,500 of my own money in addition to the Council grant.

But before I flew to Dublin in late March of 1970, I had a sad parting. My long-time friend, Ralph Hicklin, was in hospital suffering from the final stages of throat cancer. I have referred to him many times in this book quoting many of his reviews, and you will remember that I stayed in his apartment while directing for the Globe Theatre in Chatham. Soon after that Ralph went to work for the *Windsor Star*, but in 1960 he left that paper and turned up in Toronto almost penniless. Ralph had always been careless with money and spent it as quickly as he earned it. When a student at Victoria College, Ralph rarely drank alcohol, but when I visited him in Chatham he had become a heavy drinker and by the time he reached Toronto he was an alcoholic. Despite that he soon obtained work as an instructor in English at Ryerson Institute of Technology and through an old friend, the editor of the *Globe and Mail*, was taken on as a freelance reviewer for that paper. He soon advanced to second-string drama critic to Herbert Whittaker, and first-string ballet and film critic. He began writing reviews for CBC radio and was heard regularly on several of their talk shows. He also proved to be an adept interviewer of celebrities. In 1967 he left the *Globe and Mail* to become drama and dance critic for the *Toronto Telegram*, a position he held, sad to say, for only three years.

Just after he got on his feet in Toronto he had himself "detoxed," and for most of the 1960s he remained on the wagon. During those years our friendship deepened even further, and for both of us, and for many of his friends, the high point of his career was a Canada Council grant in 1966 to enable him to travel to the Soviet Union to report on the schools and performing companies of the Bolshoi and Kirov Ballets on their home turf, as well as the Royal Danish Ballet in Copenhagen, and the Royal Ballet in London. He and I regarded this as a reward for the self-discipline required for years of abstinence. His journey was a great success. He wrote many articles about those companies, and, because he was a skilled photographer, he took many action photos of the dancers of extremely high quality and composition.

Ralph certainly was the wittiest person I knew, and at times seemed to be the happiest, but he was inclined to have bouts of deep depression. He was also a homosexual, and because of his social conditioning, in his depressed moments, castigated himself for it. When he confessed his homosexuality to me, I tried to persuade him to accept it and make the best of it. Although I loved the man, our relationship was not of a sexual nature. In 1968 during one of his depressed moments, brought on, in my opinion, by a frustratingly unrequited love for a young dancer, he returned to alcohol and was in and out of the detox clinic several times during the next two years. In 1969 he developed cancer of the throat, which the doctors tried to burn out with the cobalt bomb, an attempted cure that seemed to me to be worse than the disease. In March of 1970 he entered hospital for the last time where I visited him every day. On the day before my departure for Europe his sense of humour had not left him, and, even though it was painful for him to speak, we joked and laughed. It was forced gaiety because we both knew that we would never see each other again. Other friends had rallied around him in those last days and while I was in London I received a telegram from David King that Ralph had died on March 30. He was 48.

The years 1960 to 1970 had held intense activity and achievement for him, as though he felt the pressure of lack of time. Before I left for Europe he asked me to rescue his ballet photographs from his apartment because he suspected that his relatives would not appreciate them and might throw them out. I did so, and after his death I donated them, including the photos of the Bolshoi and Kirov companies, to the National Ballet of Canada, which, during its next season, put them on display in the lobby of the O'Keefe (Hummingbird) Centre in his memory. He had been a great friend of the ballet and when he died, Celia Franca, founder of the National Ballet, expressed the feeling of loss felt by many, particularly in the ballet world, when she asked simply, "What will we do without him?" When I returned after three months of distractions in Europe, I found that I acutely missed Ralph, so I plunged immediately into writing a report about my expedition abroad.

The Council required only a brief report but mine consisted of six closely-typed pages plus a two-page list of the performances I had witnessed: 16 plays, eight operas, one ballet, two musicals, a revue, and four concerts from Dublin through England, France, Switzerland, Austria, Greece, and Italy. Where there was a language barrier, I had tried to choose plays whose plots I knew, but even when I had been unfamiliar with the play, I was still able to glean a lot from studying the acting and staging, much of which was impressive, but much of which was not. It was a journey of discovery that proved extremely valuable to me as both an actor and director. Most importantly I returned home with a renewed zeal for the theatre and a new confidence that what we were achieving in Canada compared favourably with, and frequently surpassed, what I had seen elsewhere. I mentioned this in the concluding paragraph of my Council report and pleaded for funding for our theatres that would equal the level of financial support given to many European companies by their governments so that we could improve our standard of production and encourage even further the phenomenal growth in the Canadian theatre.

▪

My European jaunt not only gave me new faith in the Canadian theatre but a new pride in my country. My visits to New York and Hollywood had taught me that far away pastures are not necessarily greener. Now my travels overseas made me appreciate more fully that Canada is a mighty good place to live even for a low-income artist. I concluded that if I were going to be a poor, struggling actor in those communities, I might just as well be one in my own country and contribute something to the performing arts at home. From 1970 on I gave up all thoughts of building a career abroad. That year marked a turning point in my life. After that I began actively to seek work in the newly formed regional theatres across the country. The late '60s and early '70s witnessed a further expansion of the Canadian theatre with the emergence of the so-called "alternate theatres" across the country. This development was an indication that after 25 years of pioneer growth, professional theatre in Canada had come of age. There was now a sufficient number of people in the larger centres who had developed the theatre-going habit and who would support experimental theatre where new Canadian plays could be showcased. The funding bodies, both public and private, had at last begun to realize the cultural value to the nation in supporting theatres that would encourage Canadian playwriting. We had come a long way since the founding of Les Compagnons de Saint-Laurent in Montreal, Theatre Under the Stars in Vancouver, and since Dora Mavor Moore persuaded a handful of amateur actors in Toronto to help her start a professional theatre company in the home of dinosaur skeletons and Egyptian mummies.

Epilogue

By the 1990s there was a growing awareness that our theatrical history had been lamentably ignored. I hope that in this volume covering my own career to the beginning of the 1970s, I have been able to assist in the rescue from obscurity the story of some of those remarkable people who touched my life and who were so dedicated that they struggled through discouragement, criticism, and adversity to establish and consolidate the theatre arts in this country. I have tried to tell their story honestly and accurately, with hope that this book will serve through revelation of their achievements to encourage future generations of actors, singers, dancers, directors, designers, and other theatre artists to realize their dreams. I hope it will also serve to enlighten those who would jeopardize what the post-war generations have built, and discourage them from sacrificing the whole cultural fabric of this uniquely wonderful nation on the altar of the false god of Fiscal Righteousness, or barter it away in the name of Free Trade to please the multi-national corporations who for the almighty buck will sell out this country's hard-won cultural achievements which at long last are beginning to give Canada an identity of its own.

Notes

Chapter 1

[1] Constantin Stanislavski, *An Actor Prepares*, trans. Elizabeth Hapgood (New York: Theatre Arts, 1946), 51.

Chapter 2

[1] *Toronto Telegram*, 1 December 1939.
[2] Ibid. 30 March 1940.

Chapter 3

[1] Dennis Wrong, *The Varsity*, 4 December 1943.
[2] Rose Macdonald, *Toronto Telegram*, 31 January 1944.
[3] Ibid.
[4] Mavor Moore, *Reinventing Myself*, (Toronto: Stoddart Publishing, 1994), 71.
[5] See Mavor Moore, *Reinventing Myself*, (Toronto: Stoddart Publishing, 1994) and Paula Sperdakos, *Dora Mavor Moore*, (Toronto: ECW Press, 1995), 115–117.
[6] Paula Sperdakos, *Dora Mavor Moore*, (Toronto: ECW Press, 1995), 115-117.
[7] Martha Harron, *A Parent Contradiction*, (Toronto: Collins Press, 1988), 64.
[8] *The Varsity*, 12 February 1946.
[9] Rose Macdonald, *Toronto Telegram*, 11 July 1944.
[10] *University of Toronto Monthly*, April 1946.
[11] Roly Young, *Globe and Mail*, 27 June 1945.
[12] Mavor Moore, *Reinventing Myself*, (Toronto: Stoddart Publishing, 1994), 111.
[13] Ibid.
[14] Paula Sperdakos, *Dora Mavor Moore*, (Toronto: ECW Press, 1995), 139.
[15] Roly Young, "Toward a Civic Theatre," 17 July 1945.
[16] Ibid.

Chapter 4

1 Paula Sperdakos, *Dora Mavor Moore*, (Toronto: ECW Press, 1995), 155.
2 Colin Sabiston, *Globe and Mail*, 12 October 1946.
3 Augustus Bridle, *Toronto Star*, 12 October 1946.
4 Rose Macdonald, *Toronto Telegram*, 12 October 1946.
5 Ibid. 26 October 1946.
6 Paula Sperdakos, *Dora Mavor Moore*, (Toronto: ECW Press, 1995), 150 & 154.
7 Andrew Allan, *Andrew Allan, a Self-Portrait*, (Toronto: MacMillan of Canada, 1974), 131.
8 Frank Chamberlain, *Radio World*, 15 March 1947.
9 Nathan Cohen, *Canadian Jewish Weekly*, 27 February 1947.
10 Rose Macdonald, *Toronto Telegram*, 21 February 1947.
11 New Play Society Papers, Thomas Fisher Rare Books Library, University of Toronto.
12 For more detailed information about the New Play Society spring 1947 season see Paula Sperdakos, *Dora Mavor Moore*, (Toronto: ECW Press, 1995), 164–170.

Chapter 5

Chapter 6

1 Letter to Mavor Moore from Amelia Hall, 26 December 1947. New Play Society Papers, Thomas Fisher Rare Books Library, University of Toronto.
2 Paula Sperdakos, *Dora Mavor Moore*, (Toronto: ECW Press, 1995), 173 & 174.
3 Nathan Cohen, *Canadian Jewish Weekly*, 8 October 1949.
4 Ibid.
5 New Play Society Papers, Thomas Fisher Rare Books Library, University of Toronto.
6 Ibid.
7 Ibid. Financial Report from period 16 April 1949 to 30 June 1950.
8 Andrew Allan, *Andrew Allan, a Self-Portrait*, (Toronto: MacMillan of Canada, 1974), 119.
9 Herbert Whittaker, *Globe and Mail*, 4 February 1950.
10 Ibid.
11 Mavor Moore, *Reinventing Myself*, (Toronto: Stoddart Publishing, 1994), 178.
12 Program for *King Lear*, 10 March 1950.
13 Martha Harron, *A Parent Contradiction*, (Toronto: Collins Press, 1988), 118.
14 New Play Society Papers, audited statement from Price Waterhouse, Thomas Fisher Rare Books Library, University of Toronto.
15 Bronwyn Drainie, *Living the Part*, (Toronto: MacMillan of Canada, 1988), 150.
16 New play Society Papers, Thomas Fisher Rare Books Library, University of Toronto.
17 Ibid. Press release to Jack Karr, 10 October 1950.

[18] Martha Harron, *A Parent Contradiction*, (Toronto: Collins Press, 1988), 158.

[19] Jack Merigold, interview by author, tape recording.

[20] Tom Patterson, *First Stage*, (Toronto: McClelland and Stewart, 1987), 54 & 55.

[21] Gary Montgomery, interview by author, tape recording, 22 December 1994, and letter from Isabelle Dunlop (Gale), 1 April 1992.

[22] Gary Montgomery, interview by author, tape recording, 22 December 1994.

[23] Ibid.

[24] Paula Sperdakos, *Dora Mavor Moore*, (Toronto: ECW Press, 1995), 207.

[25] Mavor Moore, *Reinventing Myself* (Toronto: Stoddart Press, 1994), 227.

[26] Letter from Gary Montgomery, 22 December 1994.

[27] Mavor Moore, *Reinventing Myself* (Toronto: Stoddart Press, 1994), 281.

Chapter 7

[1] Program for *Twelfth Night*, Earle Grey Players, 4 & 5 June 1946.

[2] Rose Macdonald, *Toronto Telegram*, 28 June 1949.

[3] E. G. Wanger, *Globe and Mail*, 13 July 1952.

[4] Nancy Erb Kee, "The Earle Grey Shakespeare Festival," *Early Canadian Life*, August 1947.

[5] Ibid.

[6] Herbert Whittaker, *Globe and Mail*, 16 April 1960.

Chapter 8

[1] Rose Macdonald, *Toronto Telegram*, 28 February 1950.

[2] Florence Fraser McHugh, "Arthur Sutherland and the International Players," thesis.

[3] Ibid.

[4] Grant Macdonald, *Kingston Whig-Standard*, 9 October 1951.

[5] Helen Milton, *Kingston Whig-Standard*, 20 November 1951.

[6] Norma Renault, interview by author, tape recording, 22 July 1993.

[7] Ben Travers, *A-sitting on a Gate*, (London: W.H. Allen, 1978), 21.

[8] Rose Macdonald, *Toronto Telegram*, 16 July 1951.

[9] Florence Fraser McHugh, "Arthur Sutherland and the International Players," thesis.

[10] Helen Milton, *Kingston Whig-Standard*, 13 November 1951.

[11] Ibid. 4 March 1952.

[12] Ibid. 18 March 1952.

[13] Ibid. 25 March 1952.

[14] Val Lewis, *Kingston Whig-Standard*, 22 April 1952.

[15] *Globe and Mail*, 17 July 1952.

[16] Ibid.

[17] Ibid.

[18] Ibid.

19 E.G. Wanger, *Globe and Mail*, 27 January 1953.
20 Ibid. 17 February 1953.
21 Gary Montgomery, interview by author, tape recording, 22 December 1994.
22 Ibid.
23 Letter to the editor in *Kingston Whig-Standard* by Douglas Duff.

Chapter 9
1 *Hamilton Spectator*, 24 June 1953.
2 *Oakville Trafalgar-Journal*, 7 July 1953.
3 *Globe and Mail*, 10 July 1953.
4 Ibid.
5 Hugh Thomson, *Toronto Star*, 15 July 1953.

Chapter 10
1 Jack Blacklock, interview by author, tape recording.
2 Bernard Slade, interview by author, tape recording.
3 E.H. Lampard, *St. Catharines Standard*, 6 April 1954.
4 Ibid. 17 August 1954.
5 Herbert Whittaker, *Globe and Mail*, 15 June 1954.
6 Ibid.

Chapter 11
1 E.H Lampard, *St. Catharines Standard*, 19 October 1954.

Chapter 12
1 Mavor Moore, *Reinventing Myself*, (Toronto: Stoddart Publishing, 1994), 236.
2 Ardis Smith, Buffalo Evening news, 27 July 1955.
3 Mary Damer Risk, interview by author, tape recording.
4 Ibid.
5 Timothy Findley, interview by author, tape recording, 16 June 1991.
6 Ibid.
7 Ernst Wanger, *Globe and Mail*, January 1956.
8 Nathan Cohen, CBC Reviews the Shows, January 1956.
9 Ibid.
10 Letter to the author from Ivor Jackson.
11 Timothy Findley, interview by author, tape recording, 16 June 1991.

Chapter 13
1 Herbert Whittaker, *Globe and Mail*, 6 March 1956.
2 Jack Karr, *Toronto Star*, 6 March 1956.
3 Paddy Browne Robertson, interview by author, tape recording.
4 Ibid.

5   Letter from Mavor Moore to the author, 17 September 1994.
6   Paddy Browne Robertson, interview by author, tape recording.
7   Nathan Cohen
8   Herbert Whittaker, *Globe and Mail*, 22 November 1955.
9   Ibid.
10   Ralph Hicklin, *Chatham Daily News*, 26 April 1956.
11   Ibid.
12   Ibid.
13   Christopher Wiggins, interview by author, tape recording.
14   Ann Saddlemeyer and Richard Plant, eds. *Later Stages*, (Toronto: University of Toronto Press, 1997), 83.

Chapter 14
1   *London Free Press*, 1 August 1956.
2   Ibid.
3   J. Burke Martin, *London Free Press*, 17 July 1956.
4   Ted Wilson, *London Free Press*, 28 August 1956.
5   J. Burke Martin, *London Free Press*, 25 June 1957.
6   Herbert Whittaker, *Globe and Mail*, 5 July 1957.
7   J. Burke Martin, *London Free Press*, 9 July 1957.
8   Ibid. 20 July 1957.

Chapter 15
1   Letter from William Whitehead, 14 November 1991.

Chapter 16
1   Donald Davis, interview by author, tape recording.
2   Ibid.
3   Jack Karr, *Toronto Star*, 24 October 1953.
4   Ibid.
5   Herbert Whittaker, *Globe and Mail*, 6 January 1954.
6   Ibid.
7   Ibid. 21 March 1955.
8   Pearl McCarthy, *Toronto Star*, 7 September 1957.
9   Antony Ferry, *Globe and Mail*, 24 July 1958.
10   Nathan Cohen, *Toronto Star*, 8 May, 1959.
11   Ron Evans, *Toronto Telegram*, 20 April 1960.
12   Morris Duff, *Toronto Star*, 26 April 1960.
13   *Toronto Star*, 27 April 1960.
14   *Globe and Mail*, 21 May 1960.
15   *Toronto Star*, 27 April 1960.
16   Herbert Whittaker, *Globe and Mail*, 30 April 1960.

[17] Ibid.

[18] Mavor Moore, *Toronto Telegram*, 23 April 1960.

[19] Maurice Hecht, "Theatre with a Marketing Problem," *Executive Magazine,* October 1960.

[20] Norma Renault, interview by author, tape recording, 22 July 1993.

[21] Maurice Hecht, "Theatre with a Marketing Problem," *Executive Magazine,* October 1960.

[22] Ron Evans, *Toronto Telegram*, 31 December 1960.

[23] Herbert Whittaker, *Globe and Mail,* 25 February 1961.

[24] Sydney Katz, "How (and Why) We Run the Crest," *Mayfair*, 1955.

[25] Herbert Whittaker, *Globe and Mail,* 24 November 1962.

[26] *Toronto Star*, 2 November 1963.

[27] Herbert Whittaker, *Globe and Mail,* 4 September 1964.

[28] *Toronto Telegram*, 31 August 1964.

[29] Ibid.

[30] *Toronto Star*, 3 September 1964. Letter from Dr. Trueman of the Canada Council.

[31] Ibid.

[32] *Toronto Star*, 3 September 1964.

[33] Nathan Cohen, *Toronto Star*, September 1964.

[34] Ibid.

[35] Herbert Whittaker, *Globe and Mail,* September 1964.

[36] *Toronto Telegram*, September 1964.

[37] Ibid.

[38] Ron Evans, *Toronto Telegram*, November 1964.

[39] Ibid.

[40] Ibid.

[41] Ibid. 27 March 1965.

[42] Jeremy Brown, *Toronto Telegram*, 24 April 1965.

[43] Murray Davis, in an article announcing the Crest's 1965-66 season.

[44] Nathan Cohen, *Toronto Star*, 3 April 1965.

[45] Ibid. 17 February 1966.

[46] Ibid.

[47] Ibid.

[48] Ibid. 23 July 1966.

[49] Ibid. 7 November 1970.

[50] Donald Davis, interview by author, tape recording.

[51] Ibid.

[52] *New York Times*, 28 January 1998.

Chapter 17

[1] Herbert Whittaker, *Globe and Mail,* 31 May 1949.

2   Ibid.

3   Ibid.

4   E.M. Margolese, interview by author, tape recording.

5   Ibid.

6   Jack Karr, *Toronto Star*, 26 July 1949.

7   Jack Northmore, interview by author, tape recording.

8   David Gardner, *The History of the Red Barn Theatre*, 1998.

9   Hugh Thomson, *Toronto Star*, 18 July 1950.

10 Jack Northmore, interview by author, tape recording.

11 Amelia Hall, *Life Before Stratford*, (Toronto: Dundurn Press, 1989), 174.

12 Ibid.

13 Ibid.

14 Harold Burke, interview by author, tape recording.

15 Herbert Whittaker, *Globe and Mail*, 19 July 1955.

16 Ibid.

17 Jack Karr, *Toronto Star*, 3 August 1955.

18 Ibid.

19 Herbert Whittaker, *Globe and Mail*, 3 August 1955.

20 Harold Burke, interview by author, tape recording.

21 Herbert Whittaker, *Globe and Mail*, 19 July 1955.

22 Ibid. 2 July 1958.

23 Ibid. 15 July 1958.

24 Ibid.

25 Kenneth Johnson, *Globe and Mail*, 2 August 1960.

26 E. Lawrence Stone, *Globe and Mail*, 15 August 1961.

27 Ibid.

28 Ibid. 22 August 1961.

29 Ron Evans, *Toronto Telegram*, 9 August 1962.

30 Ibid.

31 Ibid.

32 Ralph Thomas, *Toronto Star*, 8 August 1962.

33 Ralph Hicklin, *Globe and Mail*, 8 August 1962.

34 Ibid.

35 Ibid.

36 Ibid.

37 Edna Usher, *Toronto Star*, 22 August 1962.

38 Ralph Hicklin, *Globe and Mail*, 22 August 1962.

39 Ibid.

40 Louise Nicol, interview by author, tape recording.

41 Charles Gerein, *Toronto Star*, July 1966.

42 Patricia Carroll Brown, interview by author, tape recording.

43 Ralph Hicklin, *Globe and Mail*, 29 June 1963.

44 Ibid.
45 Wally Wood, *Toronto Star*, 29 June 1963.
46 Rose Macdonald, *Toronto Telegram*, 29 June 1963.
47 Ron Evans, *Toronto Telegram*, 10 July 1963.
48 Ibid. 17 July 1963.
49 Ralph Hicklin, *Globe and Mail*, 24 July 1963.
50 Ibid.
51 Ron Evans, *Toronto Telegram*, 24 July 1963.
52 Wally Wood, *Toronto Star*, 24 July 1963.
53 Ron Evans, *Toronto Telegram*, 2 July 1964.
54 Ralph Hicklin, *Globe and Mail*, 9 July 1964.
55 Ron Evans, *Toronto Telegram*, 15 July 1964.
56 Ibid. 23 July 1964.
57 Ibid. 13 August 1964.
58 Herbert Whittaker, *Globe and Mail*, 23 July 1964.
59 Ibid. 19 August 1964.
60 Ibid.
61 Nathan Cohen, *Toronto Star*, 19 August 1964.
62 Ibid.
63 Charles Dennis, *Toronto Telegram*, 29 June 1965.
64 Ron Evans, *Toronto Telegram*, 8 July 1965.
65 Ibid.
66 Charles Dennis, *Toronto Telegram*, 14 July 1965.
67 Ibid.
68 Herbert Whittaker, *Globe and Mail*, 21 July 1965.
69 Ron Evans, *Toronto Telegram*, 21 July 1965.
70 Nathan Cohen, *Toronto Star*, 21 July 1965.
71 Ron Evans, *Toronto Telegram*, 4 August 1965.
72 Herbert Whittaker, *Globe and Mail*, 18 August 1965.
73 Ibid.
74 Ron Evans, *Toronto Telegram*, 20 July 1966.
75 Ibid.
76 Patricia Carroll Brown, interview by author, tape recording.
77 Charles Gerein, *Toronto Star*, 9 July 1966.
78 Jack Duffy, interview by author, tape recording.
79 Allan Royal, interview by author, tape recording.
80 Ibid.
81 Ibid.

Chapter 18
1 Joyce Goodman, *Hamilton Spectator*, 24 June 1959.
2 E.H. Lampard, *St. Catharines Standard*, 23 June 1959.

3   Jack Duffy, interview by author, tape recording.

4   Tom Kneebone, interview by author, tape recording.

5   Colin Fox, interview by author, tape recording.

6   Ed Hocura, *Hamilton Spectator*, 23 September 1959.

7   E.H. Lampard, *St.Catharines Standard*, 29 September 1959.

8   Ibid.

9   John Parker, ed., *Who's Who in the Theatre*, (London: Pitman & Sons, 1947).

10 Joe Franklyn, *Encyclopedia of Comedians*, (New York: Bell Publishing, 1985).

11 Colin Fox, interview by author, tape recording.

12 Ibid.

13 Tallulah Bankhead, *Tallulah*, (New York: Harper & Brothers, 1952), 306–307.

14 Larry Perks, *St. Catharines Standard*, 9 August 1960.

15 Ed Hocura, *Hamilton Spectator*, 24 August 1960.

16 Ibid. 3 September 1960.

17 E. H. Lampard, *St. Catharines Standard*, 6 September 1960.

18 Ralph Hicklin, *Globe and Mail*, 22 August 1961.

19 Ibid. 29 August 1961.

20 Ibid.

21 E.H. Lampard, *St. Catharines Standard*, 5 September 1961.

22 Herbert Whittaker, *Globe and Mail*, 11 June 1963.

23 Ibid.

24 Wally Wood, *Toronto Star*, 18 June 1963.

25 Robert Johnston, interview by author, tape recording.

26 Ibid.

27 E. H. Lampard, *St. Catharines Standard*, 23 June 1964.

28 Shirley Knight, interview by author, tape recording.

29 Ralph Hicklin, *Globe and Mail*, 7 August 1964.

30 Ibid. 18 August 1964.

31 Ibid. 1 September 1964.

32 Ibid.

33 Ibid. 24 June 1965.

34 Herbert Whittaker, *Globe and Mail*, 1 September 1965.

35 *Toronto Telegram*, 6 July 1965.

36 Ron Evans, *Toronto Telegram*, 4 July 1966.

37 Ralph Hicklin, *Globe and Mail*, 15 August 1966.

Chapter 19

Chapter 20

1   J. Burke Martin, *London Free Press*, 14 November 1964.

2   "Rainbow Stage — 25th Anniversary" booklet, July 1979, 12.

3   Ibid.

4   Ibid. 13.

5   Tom Kneebone, interview by author, tape recording.

6   Ibid.

7   Nathan Cohen, *Toronto Star*, 1 February 1966.

8   Herbert Whittaker, *Globe and Mail*, 1 February 1966.

9   Nathan Cohen, *Toronto Star*, 1 February 1966.

10   Ed Mirvish, *How to Build an Empire on an Orange Crate*, (Toronto: Key Porter Books, 1993), 211.

Chapter 21

1   Ron Evans, *Toronto Telegram*, 21 March 1963.

2   Ralph Hicklin, *Globe and Mail*, 6 April 1963.

3   Ron Evans, *Toronto Telegram*, 25 May 1963.

4   Nathan Cohen, *Toronto Star*, 27 May 1963.

5   Article by Ben Lennick in *Taming of the Shrew* program, June 1946.

6   Ben and Sylvia Lennick, interview by author, tape recording.

7   Nathan Cohen, *Toronto Star*, 10 February 1965.

8   Herbert Whittaker, *Globe and Mail*, 10 February 1965.

9   Ron Evans, *Toronto Telegram*, 10 February 1965.

10   Ben and Sylvia Lennick, interview by author, tape recording.

11   Herbert Whittaker, *Globe and Mail*, 24 October 1966.

12   Nathan Cohen, *Toronto Star*, 24 October 1966.

13   Ron Evans, *Toronto Telegram*, 24 October 1966.

14   Ben and Sylvia Lennick, interview by author, tape recording.

15   Ibid.

16   Nathan Cohen, *Toronto Star*, 1 April 1967.

17   Ibid.

18   Ben and Sylvia Lennick, interview by author, tape recording.

19   Herbert Whittaker, *Globe and Mail*, 11 October 1968.

20   Ralph Hicklin, *Toronto Telegram*, 11 October 1968.

21   Nathan Cohen, *Toronto Star*, 11 October 1968.

22   Ibid. 28 November 1968.

23   Ralph Hicklin, *Toronto Telegram*, 28 November 1968.

24   Herbert Whittaker, *Globe and Mail*, 28 November 1968.

25   Ibid.

26   Ben and Sylvia Lennick, interview by author, tape recording.

27   Nathan Cohen, *Toronto Star*, 7 February 1969.

28   Ibid.

29   Ben and Sylvia Lennick, interview by author, tape recording.

Chapter 22

1   Bruce Gray, interview by author, tape recording.

2   Herbert Whittaker, *Globe and Mail,* 4 June 1964.
3   Ibid.
4   Ron Evans, *Toronto Telegram,* 4 June 1964.
5   Morna Wales, interview by author, tape recording.
6   Sean Mulcahy, interview by author, tape recording.
7   Ibid.
8   Bruce Gray, interview by author, tape recording.
9   Ibid.
10 Morna Wales, interview by author, tape recording.
11 Bruce Gray, interview by author, tape recording.
12 Ralph Hicklin, *Globe and Mail,* 10 March 1966.
13 Ron Evans, *Toronto Telegram,* 10 March 1966.
14 Samuel French catalogue 1988, 44.
15 Herbert Whittaker, *Globe and Mail,* 2 June 1966.
16 Marilyn Beker, *Toronto Star,* 2 June 1966.
17 Nathan Cohen, *Toronto Star,* 15 June 1966.
18 Ron Evans, *Toronto Telegram,* 3 June 1966.
19 Ibid.
20 Ibid. 26 May 1966.
21 Bruce Gray, interview by author, tape recording.
22 Ron Evans, *Toronto Telegram,* 9 February 1967.
23 Herbert Whittaker, *Globe and Mail,* 9 February 1967.
24 Ibid.
25 Ron Evans, *Toronto Telegram,* 9 February 1967.
26 Sean Mulcahy, interview by author, tape recording.
27 Ibid.
28 Bruce Gray, interview by author, tape recording.
29 Morna Wales, interview by author, tape recording.

Chapter 23
1   Janet Aitken Kidd, *That Beaverbrook Girl,* (London: Wm. Collins & Sons, 1987), 37.
2   *The Atlantic Advocate,* September 1964, 67.
3   Ibid. and the *Montreal Star,* 18 July 1964.
4   Letter from Doreen Grinstead, 19 April 1994.
5   Edwin Stephenson, interview by author, tape recording.
6   *Montreal Star,* 18 July 1964.
7   Letter from Alexander Gray, 26 August 1995.
8   *Fredericton Daily Gleaner,* 4 January 1966.
9   Ibid.
10 Sean Mulcahy, interview by author, tape recording.
11 Edwin Stephenson, interview by author, tape recording.

[12] *Fredericton Gleaner*, 13 July 1966.
[13] Desmond Scott, interview by author, tape recording.
[14] Jo Anne Claus, *Fredericton Gleaner*, 1 August 1967.
[15] Letter from Walter Learning, 14 March 1968.
[16] Walter Learning, interview by author, tape recording.
[17] Ibid.
[18] Ibid.
[19] JoAnn Claus, *Fredericton Gleaner*, 30 July 1968.
[20] Ibid.
[21] Kent Thompson, *St. John Telegraph Journal*, 17 January 1969.
[22] Walter Learning, interview by author, tape recording.
[23] Report from Walter Learning to the Governors, Custodians of the Playhouse, and to the Canadian Beaverbrook Foundation, 31 March 1969.
[24] Kent Thompson, *St. John Telegraph Journal*, 8 July 1969.
[25] Ibid.
[26] Ibid.
[27] Joanne Claus, *Fredericton Gleaner*, 11 July 1969.
[28] Ibid. 30 July 1969.
[29] Kent Thompson, *St. John Telegraph Journal*, 30 July 1969.
[30] *The Stage in Canada*, vol. v, #8, December 1969.
[31] Walter Learning, interview by author, tape recording.
[32] Ibid.

Chapter 24
[1] Mavor Moore, *Reinventing Myself,* (Toronto: Stoddart Publishing, 1994), 48–49.
[2] Interview with Frank Shuster on June Callwood's *National Treasure* television series.

Chapter 25
[1] *The Varsity*, University of Toronto, 18 December 1968.

Chapter 26
[1] Martha Harron, *A Parent Contradiction,* (Toronto: Collins Press, 1988), 294–296.

Index